CADILLAC
STANDARD OF THE WORLD
THE COMPLETE HISTORY

An Automobile Quarterly Library Series Book

THE

Cadillac

STANDARD OF THE WORLD

COMPLETE HISTORY

by Maurice D. Hendry

WITH THE EDITORS OF AUTOMOBILE QUARTERLY

Bonanza Books
New York

Author's Dedication

for Marion

AUTOMOBILE QUARTERLY PUBLICATIONS

Staff for this book

Publisher and President: L. Scott Bailey

Editorial Director: Beverly Rae Kimes

Book Editor: Richard M. Langworth

Art Director: Theodore R.F. Hall

Production Editor: Mary B. Williams

Editorial Assistants:
Roberta Schottland, Judy Faulkner,
Kathy Smith

Contributors:
David R. Holls, Jeffrey I. Godshall, Harry Pulfer,
Joe Trainer, William R. Tite

Copyright © MCMLXXIII, MCMLXXVII, MCMLXXIX by Princeton Publishing Inc.
All rights reserved.

This 1983 edition is published by Bonanza Books, distributed by
Crown Publishers, Inc. by arrangement with Princeton Publishing, Inc.

Manufactured in Hong Kong

Library of Congress Cataloging in Publication Data

Hendry, Maurice D.
   Cadillac, standard of the world.
   Includes index.
   1. Cadillac automobile—History.   2. La Salle
automobile—History.   I. Automobile quarterly.
II. Title.
TL215.C27H45   1983   629.2'222   83-11743

ISBN: 0-517-422816

h g f e d c b a

CONTENTS

PUBLISHER'S PREFACE

AUTOMOBILE Quarterly's *Library Series is a collection of books devoted to the history of the automobile. We launched the series with* The American Car Since 1775, *a book surveying the overall spectrum of the automobile in America—from Oliver Evans' pre-Revolutionary War diary entries pertaining to a "steam waggon" to the modern day production race, wherein the survivors of America's automobile heritage strive to remain alive and healthy in one of this country's most demanding and exciting industries. It was, we believed, a particularly appropriate book with which to begin the Library Series. It was the leader of our automotive parade.*

The choice of the second book for our Library Series was carefully considered. We wanted, we knew, to focus next on one particular marque, and an American one—but which one? This country's automotive parade has been long and distinguished, and the candidates were numerous. But as discussions progressed, one marque began to stand apart: Cadillac. And one fact suddenly made itself forcefully clear: There never had been a definitive history of this preeminent American car. The discussion was closed. Cadillac would be our second Library Series book.

Cadillac is a splendid American success story, of course. Indeed, to the vast majority of Americans the car itself is the personification of success. Research polls have verified that among car owners the

Cadillac is more than a motorcar, it is a tangible symbol of attainment. To own a Cadillac is to have arrived. This enviable regard for the marque did not simply spring forth one glorious day, catching the automotive world unaware. How it happened is what the Cadillac story is all about—and that story is more than seven decades old.

Our choice for an author for the Cadillac story was readily made. AUTOMOBILE Quarterly *contributing editor Maurice D. Hendry shared with us an abiding interest in the marque Cadillac—and his scholarship in the field of American automotive history has long been highly regarded. To him the assignment was given. Several years ago we brought Mr. Hendry to the United States on a research visit to automotive plants, museums and libraries—and also to interview scores of those engineers, designers and managers who made automobile history happen. The results of that visit—combined with Mr. Hendry's decades-long research into Cadillac lore—will be found herein.*

To Mr. Hendry's narrative has been added a chapter on the LaSalle, authored by Jeffrey I. Godshall; a study of Cadillac heraldry researched by Harry Pulfer and illustrated by Joe Trainor; a production table by William R. Tite; and comments on classic Cadillac styling by David R. Holls.

To the aforementioned historians, we wish to express our gratitude. Save for their contributions, this book would have been impossible. Still, the narrative is but part of the Cadillac history; without the documentation in photographs the story would have been but half told. The search for illustrations for the book has been an arduous one to which many hands have contributed. Indeed, it all began almost ten years ago when AUTOMOBILE Quarterly was researching a short history of Cadillac for a subsequent issue of the magazine. We met with Cadillac's Cliff Merriott, who showed us the company archives, quite disorganized at the time and housed in an old warehouse. But what treasures it held—awaiting only the concerted effort of Mr. Merriott and others to sift through the conglomeration, a project begun after a move to new quarters.

Our appreciation is extended in full measure to the men of Cadillac public relations—Mr. Merriott, Bill Knight, Norm Bartos, Guy Roberts, and their able assistants—who gave us access to those files and themselves directed a massive search for illustrative material on our behalf. Their help in providing data when requested and in checking over our statistical references should also be noted—and mention made of Ansel Sackett's, Bill Gillies' and Roy Schneider's guidance throughout. For research into the history of Cadillac advertising, we thank Wendel D. Moore of D'Arcy MacManus Advertising.

The late Warren Fitzgerald, an advisor and contributor to AUTOMOBILE Quarterly over many years and whose gracious counsel and friendship we shall always sorely miss, contributed valuably to the overall project. A special note of appreciation for their efforts goes to our chief of research Henry Austin Clark, Jr., and our research associate James J. Bradley, curator of the National Automotive History Collection of the Detroit Public Library. Finally, sincere thanks to the many owners of Cadillacs of all ages whose kind cooperation made possible the photography of so many splendid motorcars for our color portfolio.

For decades the Cadillac motorcar has been deserving of a full-scale presentation of its history. It was that goal which prompted all our efforts in producing this book. The response to the First Edition of this history was overwhelming—and this, together with the fact that so much new history has been made by Cadillac since our original publication, prompted in turn a Second Edition, and now this expanded Third Edition. The Cadillac saga is fascinating to contemplate, the seventy years to 1972, the seven exciting years to 1979—and the promise of the years to come. What lies ahead? We can't answer that question precisely, neither indeed can the people at Cadillac. But for our part, so long as Cadillac continues to make history, we shall be recording it.

—L. Scott Bailey

AUTHOR'S NOTES

In 1902 Cadillac built three cars. In 1972, on its seventieth anniversary, the company produced more than a quarter million. So it seemed a good time to publish something on the subject. The timing, however, was almost fortuitous. Ernest Seaholm told me that the V-16 was "a dream of the Roaring Twenties." This book began, for me, as a dream of the 1950's, but I cannot recall now for certain whether I seriously put anything on paper at that time. I did draft out something in the following decade. But work began in earnest about two years ago, and the decision was not mine, it was L. Scott Bailey's. A Cadillac history was among the books he and his editors envisioned for the AUTOMOBILE *Quarterly* Library Series. I was wholeheartedly for the project — and delighted to receive the assignment.

The result you now see. I provided the text of the narrative and the background for the specifications of Cadillac motorcars. The gathering together of correlative contributions to the book as well as its presentation from cover to cover has been the work of the staff of AUTOMOBILE *Quarterly* — to all members of which I am very grateful. As a publishing-editorial-art team, so far as sheer quality of presentation is concerned, I think they are the "standard of the world" and better fitted than anyone else to do justice to this subject.

I have had help from a great many people in compiling material for this history. Some contributed a great deal, others a little here and there. All of it has been of value. Not all the assistance was in the shape of actual material usable in the text, some of it was in the form of leads and introductions, or just plain old-fashioned hospitality.

First and foremost come two people: Mrs. Ottilie Leland,

widow of Wilfred C. Leland, and Mr. Ernest W. Seaholm, its chief engineer for twenty-two years. Mrs. Leland made available to me a bulky bundle of Henry Leland's personal papers, including many items in his own handwriting, to peruse, analyze and comment upon as I wished. To describe Ottilie's help adequately would take many pages. Mention also must be made of two other members of the Leland family who contributed to this effort: Miss Miriam Leland Woodbridge and Mrs. Gertrude Woodbridge Hope, granddaughters of Henry Leland.

To walk and talk, drive and dine with Ernest Seaholm has been one of the high points of my automotive writing career. He is exactly the "quiet, friendly giant" of Olley's description, and it will be a lasting pleasure to me to have put his great achievements on record.

It was also an honor to talk to Benjamin H. Anibal, who for years worked directly under Henry Leland, saw the introduction of the self-starter and the V-8 engine, and knew so many important figures at Cadillac during this period. He also worked under Colonel Vincent in the room of the Willard Hotel in Washington, D.C., where the Liberty engine took shape on paper, and gave me an interesting appreciation of the personality of the famous Packard chief who was — as Seaholm aptly put it — "Cadillac's bogeyman for years."

Colonel Vincent died many years ago, but I felt that for balance in the narrative, it was essential to have a top-level assessment from the Packard point of view. The ideal man was Clyde R. Paton, for years Seaholm's opposite number. Clyde was another memorable personality—courteous, affable, and constantly helpful.

Edward N. Cole gave me both anecdote and evaluation, Thomas A. Boyd told me about Kettering. If any serious omissions have been made in the following list of others to whom I am indebted, I apologize in advance: the late Maurice Olley, Ronald Barker, Anthony Bird, Griff Borgeson, John Bond, the late W. F. Bradley, K. E. Brooker, Charles L. Betts, Donald Berkebile, O. J. Barratt, Bellm's Museum, the late Carl Breer, Ken Caldwell, Briggs and Laura Cunningham, M. L. "Bud" Cohn, John A. Conde, Russell B. Day, Francis W. Davis, Bill Deutsch, the late Herbert M. Dawley, Ray Dietrich, Barbara Forton, Alfred H. Feldmann, Jan Norbye, Jerry Sloniger, Karl Ludvigsen, the late William R. Gibson, James K. Gaylord, Louis J. M. Gravel, Roland V. Hutchinson, Lawrence F. Hope, Mark Howell, Dick Hempel, John T. Horstmeier, Leonard D. Hayes, Bill Hamlin, Les Henry, Oliver K. Kelley, Robert B. Meyer, Jr., Otto Klausmeyer, Bert Lobberegt, J. B. Nethercutt, Maurice Platt, the late Laurence Pomeroy, Jr., George F. Qua, Theodore W. Reed, Edmund L. Robinson, Gaylord R. Jim Pearson, Barney Pollard, Jack Passey, Marcus Lothrop, Wally Rank, Alfred N. Rodway, Steve Sharp, Dennis Shattuck, F. W. Slack, Sid Strong, Dick Teague, Lyle C. Thompson, C. W. Van Ranst, Pete Warvel, Ray Wolff, John A. C. Warner, James C. Leake, James C. Zeder, Michael Sedgwick.

Thanks go, too, to my good friend and fellow Pierce-Arrow Society member Bernie Weis, who allowed me unlimited use of the personal papers of the late David Fergusson, former chief engineer of Pierce-Arrow and Cunningham; and to Norm Uhlir and Paul Schinnerer, fellow Cadillac-LaSalle Club members, whose club monthly, *The Self-Starter*, was a mine of information; to the ever-helpful and friendly Jim Bradley of the Detroit Public Library, and my good friend Walter F. (Frank) Robinson, Jr., who are the answers to an auto historian's prayer.

At Harrah's Automobile Collection in Reno, the red carpet was rolled out, and my gratitude is extended to Mr. William F. Harrah, Ray Jesch, Chris Cagle, Jim Edwards, Gene Trefetheren and those others who made my stay there such a pleasure.

At Cadillac the public relations team was help personified, and my thanks go to Bill Knight and his staff. Bill Knight "gave me the key" to the fabulous GM Proving Grounds at Milford, which is to me what Disneyland would be to my six-year-old son. There at the Proving Grounds, I was capably hosted by engineer Dick Levenick.

Mention of appreciation should be made, too, to Lord Montagu of Beaulieu, who more than a decade ago gave me my start as an automobile writer; to W. A. Robotham and C. W. Morton, veterans of the old Rolls-Royce firm and to Rudolf Uhlenhaut of Daimler-Benz.

In my own country the number of pioneers and enthusiasts who have broadened my knowledge of motoring, history and engineering is so great that I cannot possibly name them all, but Gerald Nairn, Jack Newman, Arthur Gregory, the late Frank Shuter, Eric Burmeister, Geoff Hockley, Andrew and Mollie Anderson, Ted Fairburn, Bob Alexander, P. Martin Smith, Noel Sprosen, Rob Shand, A. B. Lake, Barrie Grant, John McLauchlan, Alf Seccombe and Maurie and Charlie Stanton stand out. A special place belongs to Hubert and the late Tyrrell Turtill (and their magnificent 61 phaeton). Tyrrell greatly looked forward to the completion of this book, and his untimely death is regretted by many automobile enthusiasts, none more so than me. From them I have learned a great deal.

I want to make it quite clear that not everyone mentioned above was necessarily aware that such a book would be written, and the various associations in some cases go back many years. But such background is essential to produce a work of this kind, and in some cases even a single sentence gave valuable insight into some aspect or other. All the opinions herein are, however, my responsibility as author, unless otherwise specifically stated.

Finally appreciation to my wife Marion, who not only typed the entire narrative and shared with me the toil and trouble, but who at so many points discussed the narrative and presentation and made many suggestions that have been incorporated. When Marion returned to a busy professional career, the onerous task of typing out the specifications from my longhand was taken up by Mrs. Lucille Cooper, who has done excellent work quickly and reliably.

Maybe the motivation for this book was best expressed by my friend Ken Moss, president of the Cadillac/LaSalle Club of Australia. "When I was a boy," joked Ken, "I scorned my dad for not owning a Cadillac." I had never looked at it quite that way, but I was well aware of the part the Cadillac played in the development of my own country, and the story of the marque and its founder has fascinated me for many years. I thought it ironic that there should have been a Book-Cadillac (hotel), but no Cadillac Book. So here it is. I hope you enjoy it.

Maurice D. Hendry

Auckland, New Zealand
January, 1979

PROLOGUE

The setting is French North America — then known as New France. The time: the waning years of the seventeenth century. Using a little known river as their waterway, a small party of men have made their way upstream from the vast inland sea of Lake Erie. They have stepped ashore on the west bank some seven or eight miles downstream from Lake Saint Clair. Some of the group are dressed in the prevailing French fashion; others wear the fringed hide jackets and leggings of the North American Indian.

The officer commanding the detachment is a tall, handsome figure in thighboots, dark blue frock coat and red sash, white lace jabot and cuffs — his blue cocked hat and sword at his side, symbols of leadership and authority. Behind him walks a standard-bearer carrying a flag with a white cross and multiple fleur-de-lis on a dark blue field.

Surveying the area with a long-practiced eye, the leader holds a conference with his officers and Indian advisers. After some discussion a decision is reached. They will build a stockade and establish a trading post and a permanent settlement here. It will be named Ville d'Etroit, or "village of the straits."

Such is the mission. Who is this leader and what is his authority? He is a forty-three-year-old Gascon of noble family. A *capitaine de marine*, he has served as military commander in two important posts in other parts of the continent before coming here. The assignment is his own idea, but has the backing of Count Pontchartrain, minister of Louis XIV, and the authority and approval of the French King himself.

He is Le Sieur Antoine de la Mothe Cadillac. And he has just established the site of what will ultimately become Detroit.

On July 24, 1701, Cadillac returned and landed near the present site of the Veterans' Memorial Building. This time he had fifty soldiers, fifty voyageurs and settlers, and about a hundred friendly Indians. A stockade about two-hundred-feet square was built and named Fort Pontchartrain. Cadillac's carefully thought-out scheme for a strategically located strongpoint was to safeguard the French fur trade in the area against British encroachment. It was successful and he headed a company enjoying a trade monopoly. His experience as commander previously in Acadia and later at Mackinac stood him in good stead during Detroit's early years. But, as might be expected of a man who was "daring, sharp-tongued, energetic, and ambitious," his career had its conflicts. He antagonized the Jesuits, and in 1704 was arrested and tried at Quebec. Acquitted, he returned to Detroit, where he presided until 1711. He was then appointed Governor of Louisiana, where he remained until 1716. He had opponents there also, and was recalled to France in 1717, where he was tried and imprisoned. However, his name seems to have been cleared at some time during this period, for after his release he was made Chevalier of the Military Order of St. Louis, Colonial Commissioner to the Crown, and Governor of Castle Sarazin until his death in 1730.

Cadillac was a great Frenchman. But he was also an "early American." He spent some thirty years in the New World, and at the end of his career, his name had become part of the story of Maine, Michigan, Alabama, and Louisiana. For more than a century thereafter, however, he was — save for the history books — largely forgotten.

CHAPTER ONE

THE YANKEE MECHANIC

The Leland practice of precision from Colt in New England to Olds in Detroit

That the name of Le Sieur Antoine de la Mothe Cadillac would someday emerge from the historic obscurity into which it plunged in the mid-eighteenth century, and become a legend in the annals of Detroit, was assuredly the last thing in the minds of men for well over a century after his death. Yet this was to be the case. And the beginnings of rebirth of the name of Cadillac, from whence it ascended to heights that even that stalwart explorer of La Belle France could have never anticipated, began a thousand miles away from Michigan in a simple farmhouse near Barton, Vermont, on February 16, 1843, when Zilpha, the wife of a farmer named Leander B. Leland, presented her husband with their sixth son. In the case of the Lelands, though, there was no question of mixed national ties: The founder of the family in America, Henry Leland, had arrived in New England years before the colorful servant of Louis XIV was born.

The boy was named Henry Martyn, not after his paternal ancestor, but for an English missionary whose work and courage the Lelands had read of and admired. This moral emphasis was significant in the boy's upbringing, as was the background of the farm in general. His Quaker parents taught young Henry Leland Christian ethics and a set of moral standards to guide him throughout life. The emphasis was on practical Christianity — square dealing, kindness, and assistance to others. From the same source he received patient instruction in everyday duties on the farm — the necessity for doing every job properly, no matter how small. Not just because it was the right thing to do, but because it was the most economical way, and in that hard country, with a heavily mortgaged farm, there was no other way. Frugality and the will to survive were nurtured in Henry Leland from the start. His toughness and moral fiber were inherent, and typical of American pioneer stock. Hard work and the healthy country atmosphere made him physically fit and powerful. He was tall and well-built, and developed a well-balanced philosophy of life. Henry Leland always took great interest in the history of his country. His own home background had a romantic aura in that the farm had previously been owned by an American Revolutionary War hero who was associated with General Lafayette.

Yet the early years were a bitter struggle. His father had to sell the farm, and the two older boys had to find work. Henry later had these recollections about his parents in those trying times: "My father, Leander B. Leland, was born March 2, 1803. . . . He began driving a team with a covered wagon in 1824, except that he had eight horses instead of (the usual) six. Father drove this team from Boston, Massachusetts, to Montreal, Canada, going through northern Vermont, the home of his family.

"In 1827 he married my mother, whose maiden name was Zilpha Tifft. She was seventeen years old when they were married. I was . . . the youngest of eight children. My father continued driving his team until 1848. There were many such teams on the roads of New England in those days, this being the only mode of transporting freight then. For this hard work and strenuous life my father received the wages of fifteen dollars per month. During this period my parents were raising their family of eight children.

"The highways then were plain dirt roads. When the frost was coming out of the ground in the spring it was very difficult and trying for teamsters as the wheels often were in mud to the hubs. Due to alternate areas of snow covered and bare ground, they were obliged frequently to change from wheels to sleds and back again. My father's load going north was usually what was then

At left, the Leland farm home in Vermont. Below, the Worcester, Massachusetts, home to which the Lelands moved in 1857.

called West India goods and dry goods. Going south it was hemlock bark and pearlash or saleratus. This load was usually about five tons.

"Due to the bad roads the teams at times could go but a short distance each day. Therefore, the hotels, which were usually small frame houses, were not more than five to eight miles apart. At times, in bad weather, there were many teams at one hotel over night. This required very large barns or sheds for the horses. I think my father said he had seen as many as 150 horses at one stopping place at night. Each driver had to care for his own horses. It was a real job to feed, clean, and harness eight horses before starting each morning.

"We children used to love to gather around my father and listen to the interesting stories he had heard when night after night these groups of teamsters, after the day's work was over

Henry Martyn Leland.

and supper had been served, gathered in the sitting room before retiring for the much needed rest."

When Henry himself went to work at the age of eleven, he soon showed his aptitude for improving methods. He developed a way to peg soles that enabled him, as a schoolboy, to earn money comparable to adult pay levels. Three years later, in 1857, the Lelands moved to Worcester, Massachusetts. There was work there, for the Cromptons of England had helped set up a textile industry. This had prospered and local industry grew to supply its needs. Henry's father got a job in the Crompton-Knowles Loom Works and his sons worked in local factories. Edson and Henry worked in a wheel factory which supplied the loom works, while their brother Frank ran a planer in a machine shop. Later Henry joined the loom works as an apprentice mechanic at the age of fourteen, working a sixty-hour week for what was then considered good pay — three dollars weekly.

Four years later, as Henry was in the finishing stages of his apprenticeship, the American Civil War broke loose. Lincoln was young Leland's idol, and he tried to enlist in the Union Army, but was rejected as under age. But at Cromptons he had won the regard of Gordon, the factory superintendent, and when Leland finished his apprenticeship he was given a war priority job. The Springfield Armory asked the factory to supply a Blanchard lathe for gunstock manufacture. Most of the men had gone to war so Leland, as Crompton's most outstanding apprentice, was selected to do the job. As was his custom, he did it well, and won the approval of the armory inspectors. They told him that the armory was short of expert mechanics, and offered him a job at Springfield. He went there and remained for the rest of the war.

The association with gunmaking was decisive in Leland's career, and, ultimately, in a much wider context — that of the Republic herself. Industrially, although America was beginning to "feel her oats," the nineteenth century was primarily Great Britain's era — the age in which, benefiting from her lead in the Industrial Revolution, England became known as the "Workshop of the World." British machines and British methods were the envy and the model for other nations, and halfway through the nineteenth century, the British lead seemed unassailable.

In fact, the British engineer believed his tools were incapable of improvement. Leland himself had experienced the smugness and complacency of the English mechanics at Cromptons, and once described them as "viewing the world from a self-created summit of superiority. There were no great men but Englishmen. They said it was simply impossible for an American to achieve real competence in mechanics."

One had ridiculed Leland rhetorically by asking, "What can one expect of a Yankee? Thou'lt never be a mechanic, lad."

The man's inability to recognize a potentially great mechanic when he saw one typified the British national outlook toward America. This complacency was soon to be shattered. Over the previous fifty-odd years a historic American development had been taking place. The following fifty years end with industrial leadership passing to the United States.

The first hint of change came right in the heart of an event staged to demonstrate British industrial prowess. At the Great Exhibition of 1851 in Hyde Park, London, an American arms firm — Robbins and Lawrence of Vermont — had been awarded a medal for their exhibit. It was a set of rifles built on the novel principle of interchangeable parts. Two years later, a group of British engineers, headed by James Nasmyth and Joseph Whitworth visited the Robbins and Lawrence factory and other American arms works. They returned much impressed with the new system of manufacture, and shortly afterward the British government established a rifles factory at Enfield equipped with 157 American machine tools.

The interchangeable part was America's "secret weapon." Actually the concept had begun at the end of the previous century, when the earliest of the great American inventors, Eli Whitney, had followed up his invention of the cotton gin by going into the manufacture of muskets for the U.S. government. Whitney and the federal authorities had decided that all the parts on all muskets must be made so accurately as to be interchangeable. The early American settler, scout, or soldier had to have good firearms; he was otherwise at the mercy of the Indian. But he might also be at the mercy of his own weapon, for a lost or broken part, or any malfunction requiring replacement of a component, required a skilled gunsmith who might be hundreds of miles away. Interchangeability meant that stocks of spares or the cannibalizing of damaged weapons would make possible quick repairs on the spot, and adequate stands of arms in the frontier farms, settlements, forts, and compounds of the West could be maintained.

Whitney began his work in 1798, and by 1806 he had delivered 12,000 muskets with interchangeable parts, and some years later got a contract for a further 30,000. He was assisted by the government engineer, Capt. John Hall, and from 1815 onward the U.S. government laid down that all hand and shoulder weapons must be made on the interchangeable principle. Other famous names followed Whitney and Hall — Simeon North, Smith of Smith and Wesson, Robbins and Lawrence and, of course,

Samuel Colt of Hartford, Connecticut.

Colt had produced the first successful revolver as early as 1835 but it did not come into its own until the war with Mexico. After that, the demand for Colt's revolver became worldwide and Colt had to plan an entirely new armory. In 1848 he hired a forty-year-old toolmaker named Elisha K. Root. The son of a Massachusetts farmer, Root was known as "the finest mechanic in New England" and received the highest salary in Connecticut. He was worth every cent of it. As Colt's superintendent he was responsible for conceiving, planning, and equipping the new factory. Impressed by the Whitney armory, where their revolver had been made previously, Colt had decided to advance the state of the art as far as possible. They equipped the plant with no less than 1,400 machine tools, many of them designed by Root. In addition to many special metal-cutting tools Root introduced die-stamping

Ellen Hull Leland

From left: Wilfred Leland (manning hidden camera); his sister Gertrude; the venerable H. M.; Blanche Leland, first wife of Wilfred.

machines for making accurate small forgings in quantity. Even the burrs on machined parts — formerly removed by hand — were eliminated by Root's special machinery.

The most comprehensive array of jigs, fixtures, and gauges ever assembled under one roof ensured the accurate manufacture of all parts to a rigid standard and made them completely interchangeable. In fact, when a biography of Root was written in 1934 — eighty years later — it was found that many of Root's tools were still in use, and their accuracy and production economy still stood comparison with modern practice. Such equipment involved a very high initial cost and had never been attempted on such a scale before. Other arms makers who closely watched the Colt project thought Root and Colt were mad and predicted failure. Instead the plant doubled itself by 1864.

Leland came to Colt at the end of the Civil War, when the Springfield Armory work force was reduced; like many others, he had been laid off. Already familiar with interchangeable manufacture, he now experienced it at Hartford in its most ad-

The Brown and Sharpe Universal Grinder, 1876.

vanced form. He spent two years at Colt, enhanced his reputation as a mechanic, and made precision his passion.

There was another passion, too. Her name was Ellen Hull, and she lived in Worcester, Massachusetts. In the year they married, 1867, Leland left Colt and worked at several tool and arms works in Worcester. His next step, in July, 1872, took him to another firm as famous as Colt: Brown and Sharpe of Providence, Rhode Island, prosperous manufacturers of precision machinery established in 1833 by the father and son team, D. and J. R. Brown. (Lucian Sharpe had joined them in 1853.)

Here Leland found precision standards that surpassed even Colt's. Tolerances were in hundred-thousandths, or even on occasion, millionths of an inch. Joseph Brown was a master technician with a fresh eye and a mind schooled in the exacting disciplines of the instrument maker. Up to 1850 the firm repaired watches, clocks, and scientific instruments. In that year, however, Joseph Brown invented an automatic linear dividing engine for graduating rules, and began making steel rules and other precision tools.

"This proved the stepping stone to fortune," comments the distinguished British engineer-historian L. T. C. Rolt. "From it stemmed the vernier calipers, the hand micrometers, and the precision gauges and measuring instruments which made the name Brown and Sharpe familiar in the workshops and toolrooms of the world."

In 1867 Brown and Sharpe developed the first practical, quantity-produced hand micrometers with compensation for wear and accurate to one-thousandth of an inch in measurement. The commercial demand was so great that in the year Leland joined them, they opened a large new building and had a payroll of three hundred. Starting in London in 1862 the list of prizes won both at home and abroad for "The Excellence and High Quality of Brown and Sharpe Products" lengthened year by year. Grand Prix awards came in Paris, Brussels, Liège, Milan, and Turin.

The company modestly explained, "All Brown and Sharpe products are made with the intention that they shall be the best in their respective classes. Careful attention is constantly given to ensure workmanship of the Best Quality." With considerable justification they advertised their superb instruments and tools as "The World's Standard of Accuracy."

For these reasons Leland decided to join them. Here, he felt, he would get the best possible training in a field where, ultimately, he hoped, he would be able to start his own business. Actually benefits were mutual, for many improvements at Brown and Sharpe arose from Leland's budding genius. An order for horse clippers came in, and after Leland made a close study of the device, he developed an improved version suitable for human hair. Leland's passion for perfection is shown by his hair clipper test. He found that calfskin had the finest hair of any animal he knew of, so he got calfskins and mounted them on boards. To test the clippers, the blades were thrown to one end of their travel, the clippers thrust into the hair and released to make one stroke. The clippers were then drawn out and all loose hairs blown off. If a single hair was caught between the blades, that pair of clippers went back to be refitted. Soon the firm was making three hundred pairs a day.

One of the greatest factors in the early expansion of the Brown and Sharpe plant was the manufacture of the then-famous Wilcox and Gibbs sewing machine. The contract to make this had been secured from Wilcox and Gibbs by Lucian Sharpe in 1858, and its success can be gauged from the fact that eighty years later Brown and Sharpe were still featuring this sewing machine in their catalogues.

Working in the sewing machine department, Leland encountered problems in grinding processes. Lathes were being used to grind the shafts for the sewing machines, and the grinding grit affected the accuracy of the lathes. To produce consistently accurate work called for the greatest skill and care — so much so that Thomas Goodrum, the firm's first grinding operator, "commanded a wage of seven dollars a day in 1867, and was the only man in the place, other than the two managing partners, who assumed as of right the dignity of a tall silk hat."

Leland saw that the situation caused a serious bottleneck in manufacture. Studying the problem, he concluded that an entirely new and specialized grinding tool was necessary. Approaching Brown and Viall with his suggestion, he found that Brown had had such a machine in mind as early as 1868, but had put it aside for lack of suitable grinding wheels. In 1873, however, a potter named Pulson, working in the machine shop of Franklin B. Norton in Worcester, Massachusetts, had developed a suitable wheel using a mixture of emery, clay, and glazing clay. The way was now clear, and in 1874, Joseph Brown, Henry Leland, and Richmond Viall set about the design of a machine that was to influence profoundly all kinds of precision manufacture — none more so than the as yet unborn automobile industry.

The Brown and Sharpe Universal Grinder, announced in 1876, was the parent of all precision grinding machines and is recognizably the same tool today. It first ran in prototype form in July, 1876, a few days after the untimely death of Joseph Brown. Leland was well aware of its significance, and years later stated that he considered the machine "Mr. Brown's greatest achievement. . . . He stepped out on entirely new ground, and enabled us to harden our work first and then grind it with the utmost accuracy . . . . none deserves a higher place or has done so much for the modern high standards of American manufacture of interchangeable parts."

The Universal Grinder reversed lathe principles in that work traveled past the wheel on a traversing table, a principle used earlier in the classic Brown and Sharpe milling machine. The length of travel was automatically controlled, an easy adjustment converted it to taper grinding, there was provision for internal grinding (parallel and taper), and the machine was protected against abrasive dust.

Now at last the production engineer could order a standard machine that could produce hardened work, round, true, and accurate in every detail and to the closest limits. Precision grinding became widespread in American production — although for years European manufacturers distrusted it in the mistaken belief that it left abrasive particles in the ground surface. Eventually the Brown and Sharpe grinder (designed in Brown's watch and instrument tradition) proved too light for its work, and Leland and Charles H. Norton redesigned it in 1886, strengthening it, stepping up its speed and power, and improving the coolant supply.

In February, 1878, Richmond Viall became factory superintendent, and Leland was appointed head of the sewing machine

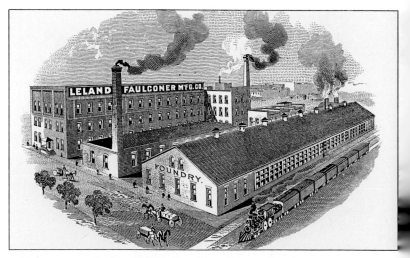

The company, sited at 480-500 Trombley Avenue, Detroit, as illustrated in Leland and Faulconer promotional material in 1896.

section. Given a free hand by Sharpe and Viall, Leland improved efficiency and halved manufacturing costs in the space of a single year. He even wrote a paper on the subject, entitled "The Art of Manufacturing."

"He knew how to increase production," ran one report, "not by oppressive but by progressive methods. He did two more things, which to those who do not know him and his methods, may seem anomalous or impossible — yet he did them. . . . Besides increasing volume, he actually reduced production costs and, at the same time bettered infinitely the quality of the things produced . . . He has made it a life principle always to do things better than they have been done before."

Another dream of Leland's took shape at this time, but only in his mind. When he saw the profits that came to the firm from his improvements, and received himself no more than half a dollar a day increase in pay, he decided he would go into business for himself. But the burden of supporting his parents, now ailing, and the birth of Henry's third child, put the idea on the shelf for years to come.

In 1883 he suffered illness himself. After a typhoid attack, he was compelled temporarily to give up his responsibilities and, on medical advice, seek a change. He worked for about a year making roller casters at Jordon and Meehan of Columbus, Ohio. While there, he stayed at Neal House, near the state capitol, and a favorite gathering place for senators, politicians, socialists,

Leland and Faulconer workmen posing for a company photograph inside the Trombley Avenue foundry around the turn of the century.

radicals, and economists. Always interested in politics and social problems, he found the atmosphere stimulating, particularly when vigorously defending from attack his own conservative New England views.

In 1885 he returned to Brown and Sharpe. Now forty-two and an accomplished engineer, designer, production man, efficiency expert, technical adviser — and social philosopher — he was recognized by Sharpe and Viall as a unique asset. "He had compelled recognition as an artisan of an uncommon kind," says one account. "Manufacturers sought his counsel. They engaged him to reorganize their equipment and men."

Sharpe and Viall asked him to become a sales representative for the firm. Impressed by the vigor and enterprise he had met in Columbus and the Midwest, Leland specified the whole area "from Pittsburgh to the Pacific." He got it. From 1885 to 1890 he traveled the West as Brown and Sharpe's super-technologist, bringing Yankee mechanical know-how to the expanding "cowboy culture." The names associated with him breathe the combined atmosphere of American industrial and frontier history: Colt, and Brown and Sharpe, as we have already seen, and others like Westinghouse and Pratt and Whitney. He advised on the operation and installation of the latter's machine tools as well as that of his own firm, and in the case of the former, he contributed substantially to its early success.

The picturesque American locomotives that raced across the prairies a century ago actually had "more go than whoa." In 1869 George Westinghouse provided the answer with his celebrated air brake, but its early manufacture fell short of the brilliant conception. After Leland introduced the works to the most up-to-date precision-grinding processes for pistons and cylinders, the Westinghouse company abandoned its hand scraping and installed Brown and Sharpe grinders.

By the late 1880's Leland could think seriously about his own business. He had been a regular visitor to Detroit, where his friend Charles Strelinger sold hardware and machine tools, establishing a business still existing today. The city attracted him because of its liberal labor policy, its pleasant tree-lined streets and river location, but the real reason he chose it for business was money. Leland left Brown and Sharpe on August 9, 1890. Strelinger introduced him to Robert C. Faulconer, a wealthy lumber man from Alpena, Michigan. Detroit was vigorous, expanding, and strategically sited. It had a variety of industry, but there was a crying need for machine shops, for in this town of over 200,000 there were only six such concerns listed in 1887 and nine by 1890. Faulconer was easily convinced such a business would do well, and the firm of Leland, Faulconer, and Norton was organized in Detroit on September 19, 1890. The capital was $50,000, of which Faulconer supplied $40,000, Leland $1,600 plus a further $2,000 loaned to him by Brown and Sharpe. Faulconer was president, Leland vice-president and general manager at $2,000 a year, and Strelinger was secretary. As machine tool designer, Leland hired his old Brown and Sharpe associate, Charles H. Norton, later to become a famous manufacturer of crankshaft grinders in his own right. The firm's main work was gear grinding and the design and building of special tools. Although they looked forward to making a profitable quantity product, they gained plenty of business from the beginning, and within three months the labor force rose from the initial twelve to sixty.

Henry Leland's son Wilfred had been studying medicine at Brown University, but his father was keen to have him in the business, and Wilfred joined them on November 7, 1890, his twenty-first birthday. Proving to have his father's mechanical skill, Wilfred agreed to go to Brown and Sharpe for special training. In a single year there he covered most of the normal apprentice course taking three years. At the finish he personally made a master set of plug and ring gauges to tolerances of one-hundred thousandth of an inch. Joining Leland, Faulconer, and Norton, Wilfred took charge of the gear cutting section.

Master machinists both, the father and son made precision a religion in the factory. They strove to instill in the workmen their standards of accuracy and efficient planned production. "This is simplified," runs a contemporary account, "when the executive and his chief assistants can go into the shops, and with their own hands perform practically every task and operation, from the ground work to the finished product."

The name of Brown and Sharpe was invoked so much it became a standing joke that the boss would inadvertently end prayers with "Brown and Sharpe" instead of "Amen."

The firm produced tool and lathe grinders, milling machines and gear cutters, a riveting machine and various other tools of their own design. They also acted as engineering consultants to inventors and local industry. In 1893 a new factory was built on Trombley Avenue near Dequindre and Widman on Detroit's east side. The following year Norton left, and the firm was reorganized as Leland and Faulconer, known locally as "L and F."

By 1896 L and F's capital stood at $100,000. They had difficulty in obtaining satisfactory castings from local foundries, so that year they set up their own foundry next to the machine shop on Trombley Avenue. The most up-to-date methods were used, comparable with the best in the East, and a scientific study of various mixtures for different grades of casting was instituted. The quality of Leland castings was soon recognized, and although the prices were high, the foundry never lacked customers. The quality and the close tolerances requiring minimum machining made them an economical proposition in the long run.

However, in no field was Leland prowess held in higher esteem than in their precision gear making. When the bicycle boom swept the country in the nineties, many manufacturers advertised the advantages of gear drive — no maintenance, no oily chains to dirty clothing and collect abrasive dust. But the cycle firms at first struck trouble with these "trouble-free" gears. They were noisy and wore out quickly. Leading makers — Pope of Connecticut, Pierce of New York — approached Leland. Their hardening process was faulty, he said, and distorted the teeth profiles. Leland and one of his engineers, Frank E. Ferris, developed a hardening and profile grinding process using a

The offices of Leland and Faulconer, around the turn of the century.

From the left, Messrs. Johnson, Phipps, Sweet; Wilfred and H.M.

special gear generator they designed for the job, and soon L and F was building thousands of gears for Pope, Pierce, and other chainless bicycle firms. The gears were accurate to a half-thousandth of an inch and fully interchangeable. Leland gear cutters were supplied to Pope and Pierce, both of whom found this experience of precision manufacture invaluable when they later entered the automobile field.

During 1896 L and F went into motive power, both steam and internal combustion. The steam engines were for Detroit tram cars, hundreds being ordered by John Healey. The gasoline engines were for marine use in river and lake boats built for Frank J. Dimmer's boat shop at Wayne and Woodbridge streets. Later, at the request of Charles Strelinger, L and F built a range of marine motors from five to twenty horsepower. The experience gained with this application, added to Leland's early experience with gasoline engines in New England, was shortly to prove invaluable.

In the same year that Leland, Faulconer, and Norton was founded in Detroit, the Olds Gasoline Engine Works was incorporated in Lansing, Michigan, some seventy-five miles northwest. The capitalization was of a similar order, at $30,000, and the founder, Ransom Eli Olds, had already amassed some experience with gasoline engines and self-propelled vehicles. He and his father had built the gasoline engines for farm use, while early Olds vehicles were steam powered, and included the first American self-propelled vehicle sold abroad, this being a steamer Olds sold to the Francis Times Company around 1893 for use in India.

By this time, of course, the gasoline vehicle idea was making headway, following the pioneering — and independent — work of Daimler and Benz in Germany in the mid-1880's. By the early nineties a number of American inventors — among them John William Lambert in Pennsylvania, the Duryea brothers in Massachusetts, Elwood P. Haynes with the brothers Apperson in Indiana — set themselves to the proposition. Soon thereafter Ransom Olds joined them. His first effort, completed in 1896, was one of the pioneer gasoline automobiles in Michigan — a state which subsequently would build more than the rest of the world put together. In 1897 the Olds Motor Vehicle Company was established with a capital of $50,000, and the directors asked Olds to build one car "in as nearly perfect a manner as possible and complete it at the earliest possible moment." This was duly done. A local capitalist named E. W. Sparrow was among the Olds "angels," as was Samuel L. Smith, an industrialist from Detroit. Lansing's population was only 12,000 and it had no paved streets, so headquarters were moved to Detroit. The Olds Motor Works was incorporated in 1899 with a paid-in capital of $350,000 and total capital of $500,000. It absorbed the Olds Motor Vehicle Company and the Olds Gasoline Engine Works, and thirty-five-year-old Ransom Olds was president and general manager. Its factory on Jefferson Avenue near Belle Isle Bridge, built in 1899–1900, was reputedly the first American factory specially designed for automobile production, and the largest of its day. Here Olds put his famous curved dash model on the market.

Olds was a brilliant, daring, farsighted man who, possibly more than anyone else, was responsible for starting Detroit on its course to becoming "Motor City." But he was still, in manufacturing methods, essentially a "farm mechanic." We have it on the authority of Roy Chapin that one of his first tasks on joining the factory was the hand filing of transmission gears to make them mesh. This was costly, laborious, and time consuming; in addition, the transmission as installed in the car was intolerably noisy.

H.M. with his partner, Robert Faulconer; Wilfred and a stenographer.

Wilfred Leland and his secretary during a morning's dictation.

Olds went to the temple of precision on Trombley Avenue and laid his problems before the high priest. Leland soon supplied him with a quiet-running transmission in which all the gears were precision ground and interchangeable car to car without any hand fitting.

Following this, in June, 1901, L and F was given a contract to make two thousand engines for Olds. Here again the man of precision demonstrated the superiority of his methods. The only other suppliers of engines to Olds were the Dodge brothers, John and Horace. Born in 1864 and 1868 respectively, their first experience was gained in their father's small foundry and machine shop at Port Huron, Michigan. Later they worked for several concerns, including the Murphy Motor Company, before setting up their own machine shop, first at Beaubein Street, Detroit, then at Hastings Street and Monroe Avenue. Despite their experience their engines were low powered compared with those Leland supplied to Olds. Tests showed that a Dodge-built engine produced about 3.0 horsepower, whereas the Leland-built version developed 3.7 bhp.

The first inkling of the difference came to the Lelands when they were standing in the old Armory Building on Larned Street in 1901. The occasion was the first automobile show held in Detroit, and a prominent exhibit was the Olds stand with an L and F and Dodge engine running side by side, dials indicating identical speeds for each. Wilfred recalled: "Father and I stood looking at the dials, and a stranger said 'Look behind that dial.' We saw a cheat brake load holding our own engine down to the same speed as the unbraked Dodge-built engine. It amused us. The man left. Some years later, when Henry Ford called to ask H.M.'s advice on grinding pistons, we recognized him as the man we had met at the stand."

With the brake load removed the Leland-built engine ran at higher speeds than the Dodge counterpart. It had lower friction losses because of closer machining. As mentioned earlier, it developed some twenty-three percent more horsepower. The engines were otherwise identical — the superiority, Wilfred commented, "was solely due to the higher craftsmanship embodied in our motor."

Intrigued by the comparison, Henry Leland realized his experience could be of great value to the swaddling automobile industry. He set about improving the Olds engine, putting all his engineers to work on it: Ernest E. Sweet, Frank Johnson, Walter Schwartz, Lyle Snell, Walter H. Phipps, Fred Hawes, and Clair Owen. Charles Martens acted as liaison man between Olds and L and F. He was in charge of the engine testing department at Leland and Faulconer, and Leland sent him to the Oldsmobile plant to study their methods.

A study of the engine itself showed room for improvement. Olds was a fortunate combination of commercial sense and general mechanical ability, but his views on research were "rough and ready." To make his engine reliable he had simply throttled it down. It was grossly inefficient, and normal speed was only 500 rpm. It did have a mechanical inlet valve, but Olds took no advantage of this power potential.

Already well-experienced, the Leland design team were past masters at bettering gas engine performance. They designed an improved version of the Olds engine, enlarging the intake and exhaust passages and ports, increasing the valve diameter, regrinding the cam and increasing the duration. In other words the venerable Henry Leland and his "boys"—as he called them—performed what was probably the first thoroughly engineered "hot-rodding" in U.S. automobile history. The "breathed-on" engine ran at 900 rpm and developed 10.25 bhp by actual dynamometer test — nearly three times that of the standard model built at L and F and more than three times the power which Olds himself considered satisfactory.

However, the Lelands' pride in this accomplishment was soon replaced by dismay. They took the engine over to the Olds plant, expecting to be greeted with open arms. And at first Frederick L. Smith, the business manager, did consider installing the new engine in the Olds. But after looking into the cost of retooling for stronger chassis components to go with the greatly increased power, he rejected the idea. It would be too expensive and would delay production. Already, the Olds company was behind with deliveries because of the plant fire of March, 1901, and orders for 1902 — at 4,000 cars — were many units ahead of realized production figures. Undoubtedly Smith made the correct business decision. Olds built 4,000 cars in 1903, 5,508 in 1904, and 6,500 in 1905. "No other automobile production record of the period approached this one," comments Arthur Pound. The company had no need for a new engine right then, and would have been unwise to jeopardize their run of success.

For the Lelands, of course, Smith's decision was a disappointment. They had a first-class product but no use for it. The actual engine went into Henry's personal Oldsmobile and the Lelands turned back to their business. However, one warm August day in 1902 Wilfred Leland, whose office was next to his father's, heard unfamiliar voices in H.M.'s office. (They worked wall to wall with a common, always open doorway.) Soon his father's secretary called Wilfred in.

Wilfred Leland and his sister Gertrude in their first car, a curved dash Oldsmobile.

CHAPTER TWO

WHOSE NAME
BUT CADILLAC'S?

The courage and enterprise of the man reflected in the company that remembered him

When Henry Leland's secretary had beckoned Wilfred into his office that August day in 1902, Wilfred had found it occupied by two visitors. He was introduced to William Murphy and Lemuel W. Bowen, both men previously unknown to either Wilfred or his father.

Murphy explained that H.M.'s reputation in machine tools had brought him to Leland. He and his associates were liquidating a motorcar firm that they had originally organized three years previously and named the Detroit Automobile Company. Their chief engineer, as it happened, had been the mechanic who had spoken to the Lelands at the Detroit Automobile Show in 1901 — Henry Ford.

Ford, then in his late thirties, already had some engineering background with James Flowers' machine shop and the Detroit Edison Company. Starting in 1896 he had built two cars, selling the first one, and joining forces with Murphy's group while building the second. The Detroit Automobile Company's career was undistinguished and ranged from dormant to moribund, but it had built a small number of cars. Authorities differ on this point — some say two only, others put it as high as a dozen. The company had failed in November, 1900, but had been revived and reorganized a year later, again with Ford in charge of construction. This company was named the Henry Ford Company, but its life was even shorter than its predecessor. Ford left within three months. The Murphy group alleged that he was interested mainly in building cars to race; Ford claimed that the company was in too much of a hurry to make a profit and had no long-term plans. When Ford resigned, Oliver Barthel, who had earlier assisted Charles B. King's automobile projects as well as Ford's, succeeded him. Barthel, however, soon left the company, and

its situation was so unsatisfactory that by August, 1902, the directors decided to liquidate.

Murphy and Bowen had come to ask Henry Leland to appraise their automobile plant and equipment for a sale. He agreed and later went down to the factory and looked it over. Back in his office, working on the appraisal sheets, he had an idea. Maybe this was the opportunity to apply the new engine.

H.M. had some of his workmen remove the engine from his Oldsmobile and replace it with a standard motor. With the high-powered engine tied onto the rear deck of their Olds, he and Wilfred drove down and parked on Amsterdam Avenue. Carrying the engine with them, they walked in at the Cass Avenue entrance of Murphy's company, while Murphy, Bowen, and the other directors, Clarence A. Black and A. E. F. White, waited.

Placing both appraisal sheet and engine on the table before them, Leland told them that he had made his appraisal as requested, and the figures were ready. "But, gentlemen," he said, "I believe you are making a great mistake in going out of business. The automobile has a great future. I have brought you a motor which we worked out at Leland and Faulconer. It has three times the power of the Olds motor. Its parts are interchangeable, and I can make these motors for you at less cost than the others for the Olds works."

Leland stated that his engine had one further advantage: "It's not temperamental." This brought laughter from the group. No doubt the claim was hard to believe, since most motors known to the directors were of the other kind. Nevertheless, impressed by the man before them, they voted to continue the business, accept Leland's engine, and give him what proved to be a leading role in the company.

Alanson Brush (at the wheel) and Wilfred Leland in the first Cadillac, late summer of 1902.

On August 22, 1902, Murphy, Bowen, Black, and White held a special meeting to reorganize the firm. Among other things, it had to be renamed. The name selected that day could not have been bettered. The directors hoped that theirs would be Detroit's first successful automobile company. What more appropriate title than the one the great French adventurer had first brought to this very spot some two hundred years before?

Cadillac!

"In [the Marquis'] high courage, enterprise, and ability, the founders saw the very qualities which they hoped to bring to their fledgling company," wrote Arthur Pound. As John Bentley commented, the name "conveyed the proper impression of dignity; it was historical, and it was attractive." As Detroit had just celebrated the two hundredth anniversary of its founding, the name selection was perfectly appropriate both in locality and timing. It was first-class advertising and excellent public relations — qualities which would distinguish the company ever after.

Cadillac's crest was also adopted shortly afterward. A design was prepared using the celebrated many-quartered shield surmounted by a seven-piked coronet and garlanded with a laurel wreath. The application was filed by Cadillac attorney Newell S. Wright on August 18, 1905, and a registered trademark —

number 54,931 — granted on August 7, 1906.

The capital of the new company stood at $300,000. Lemuel W. Bowen became the first president, and William E. Metzger the first sales manager. Metzger had earlier experience in a similar position at Oldsmobile. Henry Leland was given a seat on the board of directors, and took a small block of stock.

The initial arrangement between the companies was for Leland and Faulconer to produce engines, transmissions, and steering gears, while the Cadillac company would build chassis and bodies, and install the components supplied by Leland. Work on the first Cadillac car began in September, 1902, and a complete car was ready by October 17. In contrast to production plans, this prototype was built at the L and F factory, as were two others finished that year and turned over to William Metzger for display at the New York Automobile Show in January, 1903.

Who actually designed this first Model A Cadillac has been the subject of conjecture. Both in overall layout and in many details it was remarkably similar to the first car built by the new Ford company, marketed in 1903, and also known as the Model A. There were also similarities with the prototype Ford had built for the Detroit Automobile Company, although whether Ford left this behind or took it with him when he departed in 1902 is uncertain.

That the first Cadillac should have been designed by the soon-

Left, workmen in the Cadillac foundry; right, engines being assembled—then essentially a one-man operation—in the factory in 1902.

THE ONE-LUNGER:
CADILLAC'S FAMOUS ONE-CYLINDER ENGINE

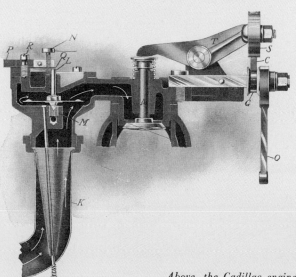

Above, the Cadillac engine as produced for 1906. Below, a sectional drawing of the carburetor and inlet valve mechanism as used on all single-cylinder models.

to-be-great Henry Ford, and its manufacture taken up by the already-great Henry Leland adds a romantic flavor to the story of the marque, and historians and enthusiasts are understandably attracted by the drama of the association. However, as usual, careful research shows that the story is not quite so clear-cut and simple; furthermore, the similarities have a logical, historical inevitability about them.

Taking the last point first, automobile designers — the successful ones, that is — never create in a vacuum. If they have any idea of making money at all, they design first for a local need. The market which early Detroit or midwestern auto builders aimed at naturally centered on "frontier" requirements — a mechanical replacement for the horse and buggy. It must have comfort, yet "go-anywhere" capability, for roads were either unknown or a stock joke. It had to be reliable, because of the vast distances and thinly spread population. It had to be easily and cheaply repaired, because skilled labor was scarce and expensive.

These demands were characteristic of not only North America, but many overseas markets as well. For these areas the early American designers evolved the "buggy-runabout" concept with flexible suspension and high frame with ample ground clearance, overall light weight, and a simple single- or twin-cylinder engine with two-speed planetary transmission and chain drive. Admittedly crude compared to the sophisticated designs France and Germany were producing — designs that would remold the automobile — the American mechanical buggy still holds a substantial place in automobile history. It brought personal transportation into areas of the world that had never seen a European automobile, and it was designed with that purpose expressly in mind.

Viewed in this light, many of the common features of early Ford and Cadillac designs are easily explained. Their common ancestor was the curved dash Oldsmobile, whose designer had himself been influenced by Duryea. Duryea in turn followed the earlier work of American pioneer constructors who had been developing a distinctive American style of horseless vehicle over the preceding century, as outlined in *The American Car Since 1775*. Duryea had carried their concept a stage further, adding a power unit based on the German Benz. From these diverse origins evolved a vehicle of admittedly limited performance, but withal, light, simple, and reliable, well-suited to its tasks.

Both Ford and Cadillac followed Olds with horizontal engines having the cylinder head to the rear and two-speed planetary transmission, but where Olds had used tiller steering and full-length springs running from front axle to rear axle, both Ford and Cadillac used wheel steering and individual springs at the four corners. Some major differences in the Ford and Cadillac were:

	Ford	Cadillac
Engine:	Parallel twin	Single cylinder
Frame:	Channel section	L section
Springs:	Full-elliptic	Semi-elliptic
Spring attachment:	To frame directly over axle	Bolted-on gooseneck spring hangers

Underlining these differences are the testing and production dates. The first Cadillac, as mentioned earlier, was completed and run in October, 1902. Alanson Brush drove it, accompanied by Wilfred Leland. Cars were on display in New York by January, 1903, and production began in March.

On the other hand, assembly of Ford's prototype model did not begin until the end of November, and while it may have been completed by Christmas, whether it ever ran in 1902 at all is doubtful. The Ford Motor Company was not even formally organized until June, 1903, and it was July before production began.

The production of the Model A Ford, therefore, cannot have influenced the design of the Model A Cadillac. In fact, the reverse would be more likely. For instance, the prototype Ford,

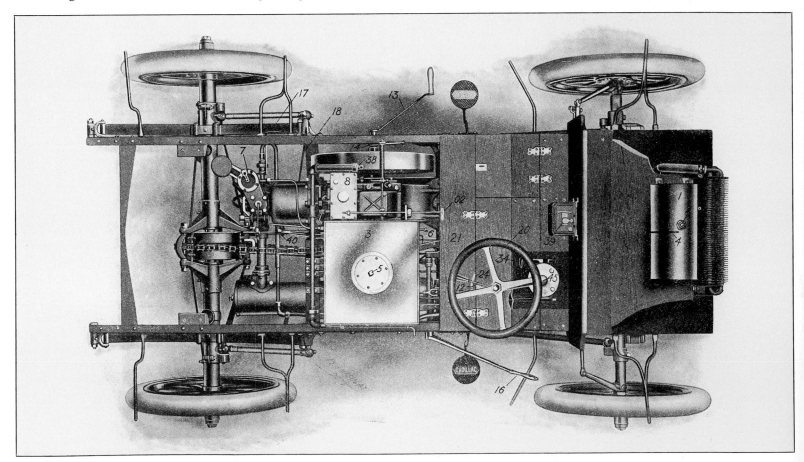

Plan view of the single-cylinder Cadillac circa 1904.

built at the Detroit Automobile Company in 1902, had left-hand steering. From the start Cadillac used right-hand control, and Ford adopted this for 1903.

Since Ford had been the Detroit company's chief engineer and had left before the Lelands became involved, since the Leland engine and not the Ford was used, and since the first Cadillacs were built at Leland and Faulconer, the probability is that the design of the first Cadillac, or its modification at least, was carried out by Leland and Faulconer engineers and draftsmen under Leland supervision.

There was ample talent available at Leland and Faulconer for the job: burly, brown-haired Ernest Sweet, H.M.'s engineering consultant and right-hand man; Frank Johnson, thirty-one-year-

old design draftsman who looked like a typical clean-cut bank clerk of the period; Walter H. Phipps, factory superintendent; Clair Owen, a graduate electrical engineer; and engineers Fred Hawes, Walter Schwartz, and Lyle Snell. Present, too, was Alanson P. Brush, a brilliant young man, later to leave Cadillac and put his mark on the products of many famous companies. Brush was only nineteen, but is believed to have been second only to Frank Johnson in contribution to the design. The actual designing, according to a friend of Charles Martens, who was in charge of engine testing, was carried out in a converted streetcar barn on Amsterdam and Woodward avenues.

The engineering conferences were held in H.M.'s office, where the patriarch daily scrutinized new designs and suggestions, pass-

Sectional view of the single-cylinder Cadillac circa 1904.

ing or rejecting every feature and every change. From the very first model, the manufacture of Cadillac engines, transmission, and steering gear was to be as perfect as human beings could make it.

"Yes, boys, that's good, but it isn't quite good enough," he would say, or, "We must sweat blood for a superior product." And: "We must make every piston so exact, and every cylinder so exact, that every piston will fit perfectly into every cylinder. Then, if anything happens to either, it can be replaced by another and the car owner will not be obliged to buy both cylinder and piston if only one should be injured."

"This wrist pin must be made accurate to the half-thousandth of an inch," he would admonish. "Its bearings must be made with the same precision. Then there will be a perfect fit, and practically no wear-out to it. Otherwise the slightest 'play' means early wear and destruction."

Covering design, specifications, materials, manufacturing tolerances, and methods, the conferences went on for hours at a time, day after day, until, says one report, "the last nut and bolt had passed scrutiny."

The latter was no mere figure of speech, for a striking feature was the specially-designed and patented locknuts used throughout. Incorporating a split-core which secured the nut effectively on the thread, these one-piece locknuts were self-sufficient, required no lock washers, and were the forerunners of modern self-locking devices.

Manufacturing tolerances were specified that would not be surpassed in the automobile world for decades. The general limit was set at a thousandth of an inch and, in some cases, reduced to half this figure, as already mentioned.

A complete set of limit gauges was made for all finished parts, using the "go–not go" principle. These gauges were constantly

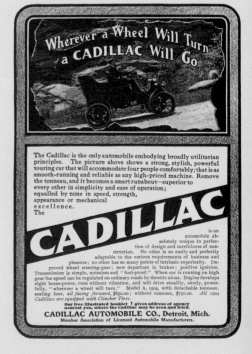

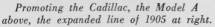

Promoting the Cadillac, the Model A above, the expanded line of 1905 at right.

Utility, not luxury, the keynote in the advertisement above from 1904.

checked by other gauges, which in turn were subject to check from super-accurate master gauges correct to one-hundred-thousandth of an inch. Their limits in turn were established by optical comparators.

All machined components built at Leland and Faulconer had to submit to the limit gauge principle. Even humble grease cups had to pass thread gauge tests laid down by the inexorable "old man." "No special fitting of any kind is permitted," said one factory instruction: "Craftsmanship a Creed, Accuracy a Law."

To avoid any holdup in production, the gauges were designed to permit rapid checks by the workmen rather than actual measurement. The gauges used for measuring bores, for instance, were "plug" type in two sizes. One was marked "5.000 GO," the other "5.002 NOT GO." The cylinder had to be large enough to pass the "GO" gauge, but not the "NOT GO" gauge. If it failed to pass the "GO" gauge, it was returned to the grinding shop to be correctly sized. If the bore admitted the "NOT GO" gauge, the cylinder was scrapped. Pistons were similarly gauged, using a reversal of the cylinder test. Oversized pistons were reground to the correct diameter, undersized were melted down for reuse in the foundry.

The wholesale scrapping of pistons and cylinders (and other parts) only a few thousandths "out" must have struck many observers as wasteful, since with a little selection, many could have been "paired" and used. Furthermore, the gauges were expensive, and were themselves ruthlessly scrapped the moment a regular check showed any inaccuracy.

Leland's reply to this was: "While this method and the refinements that it secures is expensive for us, it is the only correct method. The advantages will be best appreciated by the motorist who on being obliged to replace parts of his car has usually — or always — found it necessary to call upon an expert to fit them."

A Cadillac part, on the other hand, could be readily installed by the owner provided he had a little mechanical knowledge, and parts were very reasonably priced. A new cylinder, for instance, cost no more than $4.50 and a piston only $3.50.

Apart from interchangeability, there was the refinement factor. Precision tolerance manufacture allowed the designer to specify closer fits, thus increasing efficiency. Closer fits meant less "blow-by" of combustion gases between cylinder piston and piston rings, therefore improved power and lower fuel and oil consumption, better durability and quieter operation.

"In finishing the cylinders and pistons," continued Leland, "we do not stop at simply machining. Every one of them is ground to a polished surface with the result that practically perfect compression and maximum power is obtained. Even the piston rings are finished with the same precision. They are made to our own special formula, not easily affected by the heat of the motor. They retain their efficiency long after the ordinary ring has been rendered practically worthless."

Valve gear could be more accurately timed, accurately made bearings had lower friction, and so the improvement went throughout the vehicle.

Actually, Leland methods were not so expensive as they appeared. The testing of parts was quick, since the inspector did not have to carefully "mike" every piston, bore, or shaft. Instead, with the infallible limit gauges, he carried out a simple fail-safe operation.

Another aspect will be obvious to anyone associated with engineering work and production, and it made for economy. Every workman at Leland and Faulconer knew that one hundred percent inspection was placed on his work. Every job had to pass the tests. Naturally the men held a high standard, willingly imposing it on themselves. Once established, production of any unit was not accompanied by high rejection rates. Employees who consistently turned out an excessive amount of inaccurate work were assigned to less skilled jobs or discharged. Actually, men were so carefully selected that this seldom occurred. It has even been claimed that Leland himself personally selected machine operators, and one of his checks was to run his fingers through the prospect's hair. If fine-textured, all was well, but if coarse, the old man would reject the applicant. His experience had been that coarse-haired men were not naturally precise with their hands and lacked the sense of touch and delicacy for fine work.

Workmen were taught to examine stock carefully for flaws before working on it, to check their work as it progressed, and to be as careful at the finish as at the start. "If an operation is to be performed on a piece worked on by someone else, check it too before starting," runs one instruction. "These precautions will prevent the possibility of wasting time on a piece that may be eventually thrown into the scrap."

And in Leland's own words: "It is the foreman's place to know that every piece of work turned out by his department is RIGHT, and it is his work to teach his men how to make them RIGHT. It doesn't cost as much to have the work done RIGHT the first time as it does to have it done poorly and then hire a number of men to make it right afterward."

That the latter alternative may have been fairly commonplace in what passed for an auto industry in that day can be seen from the earlier references to Olds' methods, as well as from the comments of Henry Ford's biographer, Professor Allan Nevins. Many of the defects of the first Ford cars, Nevins writes, "were the fault of the Dodge Brothers' hasty, botched work"— all of which had to be returned to the Dodges to be put right, or else had to be corrected by the Ford factory or Ford dealers. This situation continued for some time, in fact; Nevins instances Ford's difficulties in making accurate camshafts as late as 1906.

The early Cadillacs, too, soon developed flaws, but not in the parts constructed by Leland. The engines, transmission, and steering gear stood up well, but the chassis, originally intended for a less powerful unit, showed numerous weaknesses. The superior Leland engine, far in advance of the power originally envisaged for the car, hurled it over rough country roads at speeds hitherto unknown for gas buggies. The car was about ten miles an hour faster than the curved dash Olds — and while this sounds unimpressive, it actually represented a fifty percent increase in speed.

Weaknesses also showed up in the organization of the Cadillac factory. The demand for the new car was widespread and heavy. The first Cadillac had been sold to a man in Buffalo, the second unit went to Chicago. The company exhibited at the New York Automobile Show in January, 1903, and Cadillac's brilliant sales manager, William Metzger, had conducted an astonishingly successful sales drive. Accepting the very low deposit of ten dollars, he took orders for 2,286 cars by midweek, and then announced that Cadillac had been "sold out" and must refuse further orders. Having achieved one of the greatest sales coups in automobile history, he then turned to "getting out the goods." At first, results were encouraging.

A total of 1,895 cars were built from March, 1903 to March, 1904. This was an exceptional achievement in the first year production, more so in view of a fire on April 13, 1904, that gutted the Cadillac plant and temporarily put the firm out of business. Yet despite all efforts, production kept falling behind sales. The bottleneck in assembly lay in the chassis and body departments;

The Cadillac factory, as shown in a 1902 catalogue.

neither could keep up with the methodical regularity of engine deliveries from Trombley Avenue. The troubles with the car itself further complicated the manufacturing situation — vehicles returned for repairs began to hinder production.

The solution was obvious to the Cadillac management: Leland must take over the whole operation. Murphy and Bowen called on Leland on Christmas Eve, 1904. Their man had not initially shown great enthusiasm, and commented later: "I never intended to get into the automobile business; there was too much trouble in it." But Murphy and Bowen had retorted, "Either you come and run our factory, or we go out of business."

Faced with the loss of their valuable contracts, the Lelands agreed to direct Cadillac operations as well as their own. The following day, December 25, had seen them pounding through the snow and into the Cadillac plant. At first they thought two or three hours daily would suffice, but from the beginning they had to devote increasing time to Cadillac and less to their own well-equipped, harmonious organization.

Not only did Cadillac production have to be reorganized, but also the car itself required redesign. This meant transferring Leland and Faulconer's top engineers to Cadillac. It was becoming apparent, too, that a successful automobile business must not be at the mercy of its suppliers, whose failure to deliver could shut down the operation. If Leland and Faulconer dropped their other lines and converted fully to automobile work, they could make other parts which were now being bought from outside suppliers.

The Lelands and Cadillac directors worked out a consolidation plan. Cadillac stockholders bought up Leland and Faulconer stock except for the Leland holdings, and by October, 1905, the merger was completed. Faulconer liquidated his investment, and the name Leland and Faulconer disappeared from company registers. Leland became the first general manager of the new Cadillac Motor Car Company at $750 per month. Wilfred drew a similar salary and was assistant treasurer under William H. Murphy. Of the 15,000 company shares, H.M. held 1,583 and

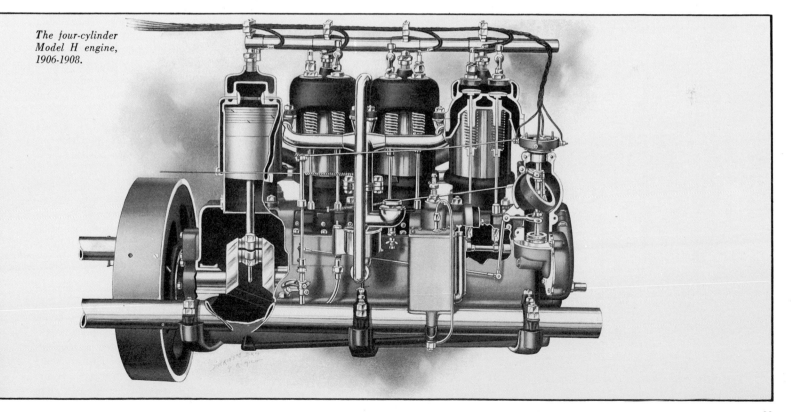

The four-cylinder Model H engine, 1906-1908.

Wilfred 1,250. They shared five percent of the annual profits, and directed the work of a thousand men — six hundred at Cadillac and four hundred at the former Leland and Faulconer plant. The combined floor space of the two plants totaled 500,000 square feet. At Trombley Avenue was the pattern shop, with the railroad on one side, and on the other the foundry, sheet metal department, and machine shops. At Cass and Amsterdam, again with its own railhead, stood the engine and automobile assembly plant and general offices. The uniting of the two establishments into one company under one management, claimed a Cadillac brochure, "brings into existence the largest and most complete organization in the world for the production of high-grade motorcars." Its assets stood at one-and-a-half million dollars. The

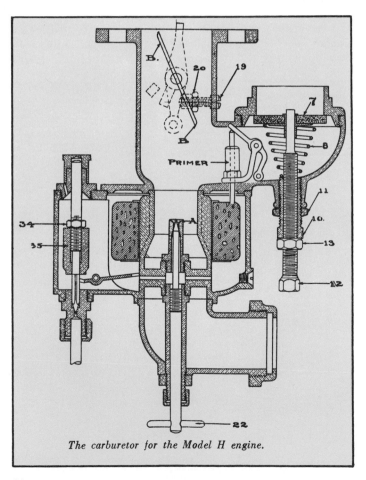

The carburetor for the Model H engine.

capital stock was divided into 15,000 shares of one hundred dollars, Black, Bowen, and Leland nominally holding 5,000 each, though portions of their allotments being held as trustees.

The net assets of Cadillac were as follows: business and good will, $200,000; buildings and land at Amsterdam and Cass, $418,000; cash, $39,416; merchandise (finished products and raw materials), $358,733; machinery, tools, patterns, models, fixtures, supplies, etc., making up the remainder of the $1,000,000. Leland and Faulconer contributed: cash, $123,249; machinery and foundry equipment, $104,059; all merchandise and supplies, $93,866; business and good will, $75,000.

At the time of the merger the officials of Cadillac were President C. A. Black, Vice-President A. E. F. White, Secretary Lemuel C. Bowen, Treasurer William H. Murphy, Assistant Treasurer Wilfred Leland, and General Manager Henry Leland. For Leland and Faulconer the officers consisted of President Lemuel W. Bowen, Vice-President A. E. F. White, Secretary William H. Murphy, Treasurer Wilfred Leland, and General Manager Henry Leland.

"The business of both companies has shown remarkable growth," said Henry Leland. "While the original companies were organized with a capital stock of $300,000 and $175,000 respectively, I can say that every dollar of the present capitalization is represented by something tangible. The Cadillac Automobile Company [was] a larger business last year than any other automobile company in the world, its output being 4,000 machines. We do not believe in declaring dividends before they are made or counting our chickens before they are hatched, but we think we are safe in expecting a still larger business next year."

The design staff had been very busy too. The Model A had been redesigned into the Model B. A new pressed-steel channel section frame and an entirely different front suspension and axle were used, probably because of failures in the bolted-on gooseneck spring hangers. Henry Ford had avoided this weakness in his design by using full-elliptic springs, but the Leland answer was a transverse semi-elliptic spring, shackled and pinned, clamped to a tapered section I-beam axle. The axle was located by tubular radius rods anchored amidships in beautiful little ball-and-socket joints. A new vertical radiator and dummy hood, which provided a convenient luggage compartment, were adopted. At the rear end, apart from improved spring attachments, there was little change. These improvements eliminated major faults in the car, and the "one-lunger" became renowned as an amazingly tough little vehicle, better made than anything else in its class and justifying the significant claim, "When you buy it, you buy a round trip."

Even those critical of its design today award it left-handed compliments, saying, "The only thing that saved it was the workmanship," although others, closer to the truth, comment, "while the car on first glance appears to offend many accepted principles of automobile engineering, it does on closer inspection emerge as an extremely well-thought-out and practical vehicle for its purpose."

While the car's main forte *was* its impeccable construction, and low running and maintenance costs, it *did* have some unusual or "advanced" features in design. From the start it used mechanical operation of both inlet and exhaust valves. This was not common practice until about 1904, whereas Leland had almost certainly used it before 1900, because he spoke of controlling inlet valve operation on his marine engines of the period, and this would not have been possible with the commonly used "flutter" valve. He knew a great deal about engine breathing. Very early he used "independent" valve timing with overlap. The inlet valve timing was deliberately calculated for maximum intake of the mixture, and the exhaust valve opened early to expel the burnt gases. Speed was controlled by varying the lift of the inlet valve, an unusual but effective arrangement that permitted a very simple, trouble-free carburetor design having neither jets, throttle, air valve, or float. Its only fault seems to have been a tendency to leak gasoline at the feed valve spring when idling. With the engine running at its normal full load and speed, the quantity of the mixture and the suction inducing its flow to the cylinder were at a maximum. When the driver reduced the engine power, the period but not the fierceness of suction was altered, giving a series of sucks at the carburetor of about the same intensity, but getting shorter and shorter in duration with reduction in the load on the engine. "Compared with the constant period of suction with varying intensity obtained with the throttle type," wrote the English expert Worby Beaumont, "the Cadillac method should result in a more uniformly carburetted supply, and is cheaply and ingeniously obtained."

This principle later gave way to the throttled, jet-type, float-feed carburetor pioneered by Maybach in the 1901 Mercedes, but the method developed by Leland was probably equal in actual practice to any contemporary system except Maybach's. It was in keeping with the car's general simplicity of design, and understandably Cadillac used it exclusively until 1904, when their four-cylinder model was designed for a throttled, jet-type carburetor. The Leland-type valve motion and carburetion con-

tinued on the single-cylinders until withdrawn in 1908.

To appreciate its value, we should briefly examine the performance characteristics of cars of this period. Carburetion was a problem because liquids and gases behave differently, and settings of air-fuel mixtures were correct for one speed only. The "automatic" carburetor, i.e. one that automatically gave the right mixture at all speeds, was almost unknown, and the few that existed were accused of automatically giving the wrong mixture unless a hand adjustment was provided and constantly used.

As a speed control, some makers used spark advance and retard, others a governor, with overriding manual control, while De Dion used a variable-lift *exhaust* valve. Although the primitive surface carburetors had throttles, they were almost useless except for stopping the engine.

Consequently, most engines were "inflexible," or limited in their speed range, a reliable tickover was something to marvel at, and the best drivers were good jugglers with a spot of tap dancing thrown in.

In America designs overcame (or sought to overcome) these deficiencies by using some ingenious carburetors and accepting a relatively low engine output for the piston displacement. From the start the Cadillac used a high-efficiency engine. Yet it had a smooth, even tickover, coupled with the ability to run up to 1,200 or even 1,600 rpm. It pulled well at all speeds and could climb an eight and a half percent grade on high gear. Such a performance greatly offset having only two forward gears. In "low," its ad-

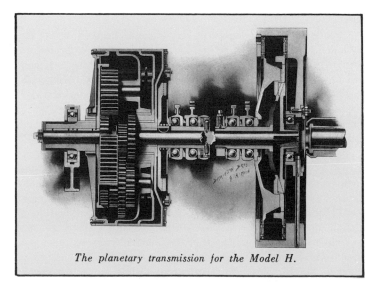

The planetary transmission for the Model H.

vertisements claimed, the car could take a forty-five percent gradient, and ad copy punned, "The Car of the Highest Grade."

It is a common fallacy among certain writers to lump the Cadillac in with other early American engines as "inefficient" in terms of specific output. Actually the Cadillac's output was specifically quite high — 6.3 bhp/liter — and remarkable for a refined, high-torque touring engine of such simple design. In contrast is the contemporary Lanchester, darling of English historians. This had an extraordinarily complicated engine design, yet produced only 2.7 bhp/liter. It might be more than coincidence that when Lanchester designed a new engine about 1905 he adopted the same opposed-valves-across-the-bore principle of the single-cylinder Cadillac! Generally speaking, touring engine output at this time equaled the year of introduction, 4 bhp/liter in 1904, 6 bhp/liter in 1906, and so on. The Cadillac, therefore, was well ahead of the average when introduced and remained competitive for most of its production run. With some justification company literature claimed "the Cadillac marked the beginning of a new era in the principles of gasoline engine construction, and the introduction of entirely new methods of valve timing." The valve gear and variable inlet control was patented, and was quite different from that in the Olds.

The engine had "square" bore/stroke as compared with the long-stroke Olds, and its "desaxe" or offset crankshaft was one of the earliest such applications on a production automobile. This feature had been pioneered by Duryea on his three-cylinder about 1899, but did not come into general use until about ten years later.

The spun-copper water jacket allowed inspection of the cylinder after casting, and gave a measure of frost protection because of the expansion qualities of soft copper. It was lighter than a cast-iron water jacket, and if damaged could be cheaply replaced. For ease of manufacture, the copper water jackets were "spun" from sheet copper rather than electrolytically deposited on a wax mold. This probably insured more uniform section and a lighter product.

Because gaskets were then unreliable, the patented construction of valves housed in an antechamber screwed into the cylinder head, combining the leak-proof advantages of a non-detachable cylinder head with the accessibility of a detachable head. Ignition was by dry-cell, trembler coil connected to a unique double-core spark plug which "permitted the secondary current to be kept separate from the other mechanism" and was free from fouling. The spark advance lever had an ingenious linkage which, when advanced, moved a slide across the crank-

The 1905 Model D side entrance tonneau.

hole, thus ensuring that the car could be started only on retarded spark.

Both cooling and oiling were by pump and the car was free from the common problems of overheating and lubrication failures. Unlike most contemporaries, the efficiency of the cooling system was such that the car used no more water than a modern automobile.

The planetary transmission made shifting quite simple as there were only two controls (gear and throttle) to coordinate, instead of three (gear, throttle, and clutch). An instance of Leland's engineering approach in this area was his use of a balancing linkage instead of an anchor for the transmission band brake, so that there was no side pull on the transmission drum or strain on the crankshaft.

Perhaps in keeping with the "sporty" power-to-weight ratio, the steering gear was rack and pinion — a principle popular many years later with the sports car set, and actually used in highly refined form on power-steered Cadillacs of recent years!

The body could be taken off the chassis after removal of only six bolts, and without disturbing a lever or wire on the chassis. The engine bearings could be replaced without removing the crankshaft, the engine remaining in place in the chassis, although itself easily removed.

Initially only one body style was provided, but a model offering a detachable rear entrance tonneau soon appeared, followed by an enclosed coupé. Weights varied from 1,100 to 1,470 pounds, and the factory provided four sprocket combinations to suit.

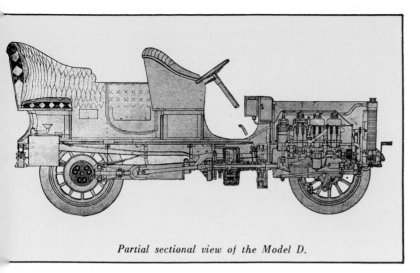

Partial sectional view of the Model D.

These gave a top speed ranging from 25 to 35 mph. As a Fargo, North Dakota, Cadillac dealer commented to a prospect in April, 1905, "the Cadillac runabout is the highest powered for its weight in the market."

There have been many stages in the evolution of automobile bodies, but briefly it can be divided into the coachbuilt and the pressed-steel eras. In the horseless carriage age, the automobile was a new assembly of components adapted from existing practice. In the case of bodies, their manufacture was based on the crafts of the wagonmaker and the coachbuilder. Like all automobiles with a long history, the Cadillac has passed through all the styles and developments from that period to the present operations of "twentieth-century tinsmiths."

As is obvious from illustrations, the earliest Cadillac bodies were the simplest possible. Many parts considered essential just a few years later were conspicuous by their absence — windscreen, doors, windows, and roof, to name only a few. What little style existed came mainly from the horse-drawn surrey, coach, or phaeton. Even so, we can detect a certain "art" and "style," distinctive to these early bodies.

Styling of the single-cylinder Cadillacs falls into two distinct approaches — with dummy hood and without. The latter style came first, and its general layout was predicted by the prototype cars built in 1902. The body was wood framed and paneled, with a curved dash treatment quite different from the sleigh-front type made famous by Olds. On the Cadillac the horizontal tube radiator was mounted at the front, angled to conform with the

general dash line and flanked on either side by continuations of the dash extending almost to the frame. This treatment was an early example of "styling," as was the flowing curve of the entrance cutout, seat sides, and the decorative scroll-type molding on the sides of the dash structure. In the four-seater the seat-line treatment was similar and equally pleasing, but the lower half, in the two-seater runabout form, showed less imagination. This straight-lined rear deck, however, facilitated the ready addition and removal of a two-seat tonneau, and if lacking aesthetically, was certainly practical. Similar in style to the Model A Ford — the original Model A, that is — this body design was much superior to the Pierce Stanhope type, or the Vis-à-Vis, both of which placed additional passengers at the front of the car, in an "occasional seat" ahead of the driver, who had to steer by peering around them.

Entry to the front seat was from either side via round, pendant step plates similar to those in the family surrey, and similar access was provided via the central door in the rear of the tonneau compartment. The usual wicker hampers were carried at the sides if required; they were useful for picnics, among other purposes.

Three brass kerosene lamps were carried, two at the front and one at the rear, and a brass bulb horn was clamped to the steering column. Upholstery was in quilted and buttoned leather, chosen for its long-wearing qualities and ability to stand exposure to weather, rather than for richness of grain or texture.

The earliest fenders were apparently of patent leather, but soon a change to iron was made. These fenders were supplied by the Wilson and Hayes Manufacturing Company, who had built an automobile body paneled entirely in metal before the turn of the century. Moving from Cleveland to Detroit in 1903, they had set up a shop with ten employees to supply Cadillac.

The influence of Panhard had made hoods fashionable, and as Anthony Bird has written, the publicity from racing successes of Panhard-type cars convinced the public that this was the proper design for a car — and the longer the bonnet, the better the car. "The manufacturer ignored fashion at his peril," Bird comments. "Customers simply were not interested in the technical niceties of the mid-engined Lanchesters or the space-saving virtues of the horizontal, under-floor engines used by so many American manufacturers. Such excellent single-cylinder cars as the Oldsmobile and Cadillac had to be adorned with dummy bonnets, which contained nothing but a tool box and several cubic feet of air — or the chauffeur's supply of bottled beer."

Of course, the dummy hood was a very practical storage compartment, but although the radiator was moved forward on these models, the wheelbase was also increased. This occurred on the Model B in 1904, and the chassis changes on these models are detailed elsewhere. The chief improvement in convenience in these models, of course, was the side-entrance tonneau, which allowed entry and exit at either side of the car, by two people simultaneously. This also allowed passengers to climb out onto the sidewalk — if there was one — instead of stepping back into the quagmire of the roadway. Other passenger comforts began to appear about this time also — windscreens and tops. There was even a styling foretaste of the twenties. In 1905, the Cadillac runabout could be had with a definite boattail! Like the dummy hood, this styling feature had its pragmatic side and also a storage compartment.

Upholstery was handbuffed leather over seats stuffed with genuine curled hair and deep coil springs. Finish of the lower part of the bodies was black, with upper parts, including seat panels and doors, in purple lake (a deep wine color), striped in light carmine. Frame, axles, and wheels were finished in a dark shade of carmine and striped in a lighter shade of carmine and black.

"The purple lake gives a finish of the very latest style and taste," said the company, "which for quiet richness and beauty will not be excelled." They were right. Certainly the quality of finish matched that of the construction. As Arthur Pound has written — and others concurred —"It was a beautiful little car, definitely built up to a standard and not down to a price. It was then the last word in superior workmanship."

The improved Model B was so successful and popular that the touring car continued with little change for the 1905 model year. It was joined, however, by a side entrance tonneau version, the Model F, and the B runabout was superseded by the Model E runabout, which was two inches shorter in the wheelbase. Models E and F had a new radiator and vented hood, and the arch-truss tubular front axle. They were substantially lighter than the B series, the F weighing 1,350 pounds against the B touring's 1,460, and the E only 1,100 pounds against the previous 1,300, thereby justifying its catalogue title of "Light Runabout."

The company worked through 1904 on a six-day, five-night weekly shift, built 3,863 cars between May, 1904 and May, 1905, and by August, 1905, had completed its eight-thousandth automobile. It would soon be able to claim, for a brief period, to be the largest automobile manufacturer in the world.

In December, 1904 Cadillac announced a new four-cylinder car, the Model D. Four-cylinder engines were nothing new, the first having been built by Daimler in 1896. By the early 1900's there were many fours on the market, including a number of American makes, so there is nothing in the claim by the company's publicity writers that the Cadillac four "pioneered" multicylinders. It was, however, as might be expected, one of the best designed and built. It had been designed after Cadillac's engineers had experimented with two-, three-, and four-cylinder engines, and at first the company was reluctant to say much about it until they could get it into production.

Motor World for December 22, 1904, said: "While the veil of secrecy regarding the details of the new four-cylinder Cadillac still screens it from view, some of the principal specifications have come to light. The engine is rated at 28–30 horsepower, has planetary gearing, and will list at $2,800. A flywheel clutch is employed in connection with the gearing, and the three speeds forward and reverse are operated by a single lever."

When more details were released, it was seen that while some of the well-proven features of the single were continued, the new automobile was a completely different concept in most respects. It was, in fact, a European-type car built to American standards of manufacture for American conditions.

Gone were the horizontal engine and chain drive, gone was the buggy idea with wheelbase "shorter than a frog's chassis." The vertical inline engine was under the hood behind the radiator, and the transmission elements — flywheel, clutch transmission, and drive shafts — were in line with the chassis. The wheelbase at a hundred inches was nearly fifty percent greater. The weight had doubled and the price had trebled.

The engine was an L-head of $4\frac{3}{8}$ by 5 bore/stroke. The forged steel crankshaft ran in five bearings in the aluminum crankcase, with gear drive to the camshaft and water and oil pumps at the front. A single camshaft on the right operated the side-by-side valves via roller-ended tappets. Although the opposed-valves across the bore axis were abandoned, the separately cast cylinders with spun-copper water jackets and detachable cylinder heads were retained. A few makers were starting to cast their cylinders together, with integral cast-iron jackets, but Leland maintained that his method guaranteed uniform cylinder sections and unobstructed water passages, thereby providing equal cooling, and making repairs cheaper in case of cylinder damage. The latter was the main reason for the detachable heads; these were not for valve access, since the valves had to be removed first. Screwed caps permitted valve grinding with cylinders in place.

In adopting the L-head, Cadillac engineers showed clearer foresight than many contemporaries who used T-heads — Mercedes, Hispano-Suiza, Locomobile, Pierce, Peerless, and

Thomas to name a few. The T-head was expensive, having duplicated camshafts and primary drive, and its combustion chamber was the worst of all the major types. Despite some plausible arguments in its favor, it soon proved hopelessly inefficient, whereas the L-head became standard American practice over the next four decades.

Intake manifolds in the L-head were on the right with a float-feed, single jet-type carburetor having butterfly throttle control and spring-loaded air valve. This carburetor, in general design, was the basis for Cadillac carburetor development over the next thirty years, and operated on the Krebs principle. The exhaust manifolding was carried through to the left of the engine and the center of its three branches carried a hot-spot tube connected to the carburetor.

The automatic engine governor was standard, centrifugally operated and concentric with the commutator shaft. The governor was controlled by a lever on the steering wheel, and could be set for any speed desired within the capabilities of the car. This speed would then be maintained, stated the handbook, "with but little variation, the action and efficiency of the governor being uniform at all speeds and under all road conditions." It could be instantly overridden by the acceleration pedal. It was, in fact, an early form of "Cruise Control!"

Another advanced feature was the transmission. It retained the planetary principle of the singles, but a third speed had been introduced. A cone clutch in the engine flywheel enabled the engine to be run separately from the transmission, but normally all shifting on the road, including reverse, was done with the gear lever alone. It lacked a fluid-coupling and the all-important brain-box, but mechanically it had the essentials of a three-speed Hydra-Matic, and some of its convenience of operation.

So, Cadillac had "Cruise Control" and three-speed clutchless shift in 1905!

Cadillac booklets stated: "The fact that there are over ten thousand Cadillacs in use throughout the world, every one of which is equipped with our planetary transmission, and every one of them proving serviceable and satisfactory in the highest sense of the word, is ample evidence of the merit of our type of construction. . . . The three forward speeds and reverse are all controlled by one lever at the side of the car. It requires but a single movement to change from one speed to another, and as no skill is required, this can be accomplished by a mere novice as well as by an expert. It is impossible to 'strip' the gears in changing."

It was also impossible, they remarked pointedly, for the transmission to try to run on two different gears at the same time

CADILLAC MODEL "H"

To the motorist whose ideals are realized only in a car which affords the highest degree of comfort and luxury with ample power for all reasonable requirements, we unhesitatingly recommend the "Model H."

The true worth and merit of this car cannot be gauged by its price. Our factory is the largest of its kind in the world. Our facilities and equipment are unequalled. Our enormous plant is one of the most modern in existence and is replete with the latest, most improved and best machinery possible to obtain.

It is largely because of this situation, that in Cadillacs we can offer values which cannot be excelled in cars selling at from twenty-five to fifty or even one hundred per cent. higher but which are necessarily produced under less favorable and less economical manufacturing conditions.

In the purchase of a motor car there are several points of prime importance which the experienced and practical motorist considers — General Efficiency, Accessibility, Simplicity, Durability, Interchangeability, Economy and "Value Received."

With these requisites in mind, we believe that in the "Model H" Cadillac we have obtained the most evenly balanced combination of the several virtues which human genius has yet been able to accomplish.

While the "Model H" possesses an abundance of "talking points" there is not one of them whose value is being simply a "talking point," but they are features of genuine merit and adopted only because they are such.

The Cadillac "Model H" is not a new and untried experiment, its worth has been practically demonstrated, not only by factory tests but in the hands of many actual users during some months past.

Its luxurious riding qualities, its ease of control and its perfectly balanced action, testify more forcibly than words can express to its skillful design and the consummate care exercised in working out every minute detail.

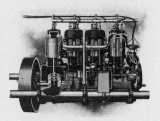

TERMS AND INSTRUCTIONS FOR ORDERING

PRICES on automobiles and parts are positively net F. O. B. Detroit.

DISCOUNTS. We do not allow discounts excepting to bona fide automobile dealers with whom we make annual contracts for a quantity of cars and who are properly equipped to conduct their business successfully and serve the best interests of Cadillac owners.

TERMS. Our terms on parts are strictly cash with order excepting to our regularly appointed dealers with whom we have accounts. We do not open accounts with others.
Orders accompanied by remittances will receive prompt attention, otherwise we will be obliged to hold them and write for the money.

When parts are desired by mail, the remittance must be sufficient to cover postage also. If remittance is more than sufficient, we will refund the amount overpaid.

REMITTANCES should be made by New York or Chicago exchange, Post Office Money Order or Express Money Order. When checks on local banks are sent, we hold the order until we receive returns from the check.

WHEN ORDERING, state definitely what is wanted. Do not leave anything to be inferred. Write and sign your order plainly, on a separate sheet from your letter. When ordering ANY part, always give the number of motor in your car. This is imperative. Also state the model and year's make of your automobile.

WHEN RETURNING GOODS to us for any reason, charges must be prepaid or they will not be accepted from the Railroad or Express Company. They must also be tagged with YOUR name and address (or we cannot identify them), and accompanied by a letter of instructions.

CORRESPONDENCE. Our executive force is large, the Finance, Sales Agency, Order, Repair and Shipping departments being under separate heads. It is therefore important that correspon-

dence bearing on different subjects should be written on separate sheets, dated and signed so that each may be sent immediately to the department to which it belongs, thereby making it unnecessary for one letter to go the rounds of several departments, which causes delay. Address all correspondence to the Company, not to individuals.

SPARK COILS, BATTERIES AND RADIATORS. When repairing is required which necessitates shipping these to the factory, do not send them to us, but forward prepaid to their respective makers or to any of their branches which are established in most large cities.

CRATING. When automobiles are to be shipped long distances, singly, it is sometimes advisable to have them crated. The cost of crating is $10.00 extra for single cylinder cars and $20.00 extra for four cylinder cars, NET.

TIRES. The standard 1907 equipment for Cadillac cars will be Hartford or Morgan & Wright Dunlop type of tires.

We will also furnish without extra charge, when so ordered, either Hartford, Morgan & Wright or G. & J. Clincher tires.

We have adopted as standard equipment the Midgley Universal Rims with which either of the above makes and either of the above types (Dunlop or Clincher) may be used.

NOTE—When make and type of tire desired is not specifically stated in ordering, we will equip cars with the Dunlop type of tire made by either the Hartford Rubber Works Co. or Morgan & Wright at our option.

TIRE GUARANTY. All tires and rims used on Cadillac automobiles are guaranteed by their respective makers and in case of claims should be sent to the factory or to any of the branches of said makers (not to us), transportation charges prepaid.

The Model H Limousine, from a 1907 brochure.

— as in some types — with a good-sized repair bill as a result!

Drive was through universally-jointed shaft to a bevel-geared, fully floating rear axle. Hess-Bright ball bearings throughout the drive line cut friction loss to a minimum. "These bearings," commented Cadillac literature, "are universally recognized as the highest type, and nearest perfection ever devised. They are made of the best grade tool steel and both races and balls are gauged to the one-ten-thousandth of an inch."

The rear axle had an aluminum differential housing to reduce unsprung weight, but the axle tubes were of steel. A tubular torque arm relieved the rear springs of driving and braking loads. The front axle was of tubular steel, and Hess-Bright wheel bearings were used on both axles. Springing at the front was semi-elliptic, and at the rear three-quarter elliptic. Steering was by irreersible worm and nut.

The braking system had the footbrake on the drive shaft and the emergency handbrake on the rear wheels. Its theoretical advantage was that it provided equalized braking throughout the differential, but Cadillac engineers soon saw the disadvantage of applying high stresses to the differential gears, and this arrangement was abandoned after one year in favor of having both

sets of brakes on the wheel drums.

Since the power had trebled, much care went into silencing the new four. The L-head naturally made for mechanical quiet, as did the usual Leland practice of careful cam and valve gear design, precision-ground working surfaces, and fine tolerances and fits throughout. The cams, for instance, were accurate to five-ten-thousandths of an inch. In keeping was an elaborate muffling system on the counter-current principle, using two large tubular silencers, each thirty inches long and six inches in diameter. "Although very effectual, back pressure is reduced to a minimum," said the catalogue. Typical of the time, however, they backed their horse both ways and provided an exhaust cutout with a foot trigger, so that the driver could, at the touch of a toe, change a refined "woffle" into a lusty rumble!

In its first year the four-cylinder model had one body style only, a five-passenger touring model in either wood or — at $250 extra — aluminum. The standard factory colors were Brewster green with primrose running gear. The price of the car was $2,800, with top extra.

Although there were faster and more powerful cars on the road in 1905, the four-cylinder Cadillac was an excellent performer. Its

301-cubic-inch engine gave 30 bhp at 1,000 rpm (about the same specific output as the single-cylinder) and was a refined, quiet running, tractable unit giving the car a high-gear range of 5 to 50 mph, and a comfortable cruising speed exceeding the maximum of the single-cylinder.

For its time and market the performance was quite adequate — in fact, speeds above 50 mph in 1905 were limited to the race track or those few localities with extensive good roads. These localities did not include Detroit — indeed, they were scarcely to be found in the United States at all.

The Model D was a well-designed, carefully considered car, superbly built, free from major faults, offering, in the words of the catalogue, "a high degree of comfort and luxury, with ample power for all reasonable requirements." In London *The Autocar* acclaimed it as "most interesting and original throughout. We may characterize the design as American, for here there has been no slavish following of foreign models."

While the four would ultimately supplant the single entirely, at the time of introduction in 1905 it was very much "second fiddle." The little one-lunger had established an astonishing record. In the second year of manufacture (1904) its production was second largest in the world; at the end of the third year (1905), it was the largest and, in fact, approximately equal to that of the next two makes combined. (Like the British Navy at that time, Cadillac could boast a "Two-Power Standard.")

The following year saw a further spectacular increase in output. "During 1906, the production of singles exceeded that of any three models combined of the other makes," claimed the company. "There are now nearly 14,000 single-cylinder Cadillacs in use throughout the world, the earliest models built still giving service."

All this could not last forever, of course, and 1906 proved the peak year for the singles, although they remained Cadillac's staple product for two more years. Despite the introduction of additional four-cylinder models, Cadillac sales in 1907 dropped by no less than thirty-seven percent and the company turned all its energy toward a successor capable of equaling the single's sales.

There was still another chapter to be written, however, before the single's career finally closed — a crowning achievement that would give it a permanent place in automobile history. Henry Leland's little machine would set a standard for the world.

CHAPTER THREE

SETTING
THE STANDARD
A gentleman in England, a brash challenge,
and the Dewar Trophy for Cadillac

In February, 1903, Frederick Stanley Bennett was two months short of his twenty-ninth birthday. He was an obscure young Englishman working for the Anglo-American Motor Company in London, the Dewar Trophy had not been instituted, Brooklands Track had still to be built, and a Cadillac had not been seen in England.

But that month Bennett, already interested in automobiles — he was at that time building a motorized tricycle — flipped open a copy of the American *Cycle and Automobile Trade Journal.* On page 129 he saw an advertisement for the new Cadillac car. In it, sales manager Metzger listed twenty-one agents who had already been appointed. Bennett liked the look of the car and the cocky sales talk that went with it. He also noted that no agents were outside America.

At Bennett's instigation, Anglo-American bought at retail and imported into Britain a 1903 Cadillac, a rear entrance tonneau, car number 530. It arrived in London, was unpacked from its crate and was immediately entered in a hill climb up Sunrising Hill, organized by the Midland Automobile Club. This was one of the most important of the early club events run for the English sporting motorist, and was described as "actually the hardest and the most trying hill climb that has ever been organized and successfully carried out." But this was no deterrent to the confident, irrepressible Frederick Bennett. He described himself and his entry as dark horses: "A dinky little American car and a tall spare young man," a pair of unknowns, "the character of unknown further accentuated as car and driver resembled nothing so much as an interrogation mark on wheels."

The total distance for the course was 1,000 yards, starting from level ground with an initial gradient of one in fifteen, stiffening to ten and then one in eight, but easing for the first bend (to the left). Immediately afterward the grade again stiffened to one in nine, and at this point the first stop and restart had to be made. On restarting the cars had at once to negotiate, on a very sharp curve to the right, one in nine, in eight and in seven, continuing to the next stopping place, where there was another sharp bend to the right. Here on a grade of one in six and one-half, the cars again had to be stopped and restarted. After a severe pull, the grade "eased" to one in eight at the finish.

The competition was exclusively for touring cars with a full complement of passengers and their ordinary kit of tools on board. Thirty cars entered, but ten dropped out, three failed to finish, and there were protests against two more. The protests clearly showed that the competition rules were strict, for the objection against S. F. Edge's twenty horsepower Napier was that the engine was far above the stated power and was actually an ex-Gordon-Bennett racing engine, while the protest against C. S. Rolls' fifteen horsepower Panhard was that its body was "not a touring body in the generally accepted sense of the definition."

The performance of Bennett and his Cadillac, however, was hailed as "an example of what can be done. . . . The Cadillac made a steady ascent with a full load of four passengers, the total weight being over seventeen hundredweights (nearly 2,000 pounds)." Its average speed was 8.09 mph.

"The performance was so much of a surprise to everyone," later commented one observer, "that even the staid judges, who rarely allow anything like enthusiasm to creep into their official report, pronounced the feat of car and driver as 'best yet.' The award," he continued admiringly, "while never adopted as a trademark of the Cadillac, has remained nonetheless the com-

In September of 1903 Frederick Stanley Bennett contested the Cadillac in England's famous Thousand Miles Trial, an eight-day affair the end of which saw the Cadillac awarded first place in the up to £200 class. Bennett is seen at left on the way to Bexhill, aboard—so The Autocar said—the "one car [that] stood out alone in its class on the outward run."

That prestigious motoring magazine The Car called it "a test of a distinctly unique character." It was the standardization test held under the auspices of the R.A.C. in 1908, and Cadillac alone came forward to accept the challenge. Above right, the three Cadillacs involved are seen in front of the Royal Automobile Club; directly above, in a formal portrait taken at the Brooklands track.

ment of all who have watched the progress of both car and driver."

Later, the car again demonstrated its prowess by ascending Arthur's Seat, near Edinburgh, Bennett thereby stealing the thunder of the great competition driver Charles Jarrott, who had made a well-publicized climb of the hill in a large Crossley of more than double the nominal power of the Cadillac.

Greatest of the car's early feats was the Thousand Miles Trial of September, 1903. This event had begun in 1900 and was run by the Automobile Club of Great Britain (later the Royal Automobile Club). Its aim was to prove to the public that "the automobile was not a freak, but a vehicle to be considered seriously." The 1903 event consisted of a series of daily runs from the Crystal Palace, London (where the early Motor Shows were held), to the following centers: Margate, Eastbourne, Worthing, Folkstone, Southsea, Bexhill, Winchester, and Brighton. Each car carried an observer, one of whom gave a word picture years later in the New Zealand magazine *Beaded Wheels*:

"Each day trip was to be over 100 miles. An arduous undertaking in view of the roads, unreliable high pressure tires, complete lack of weather protection, not to mention the ever present bogey of mechanical breakdown. . . . There was no windscreen, and goggles had not yet become popular. Chief recollection of one day was incessant dust, having drawn a position well back in the convoy. . . . Faces badly burnt from several days of sun, dust and wind, we suffered agonies in the later stages when with a change in the weather, we ran into a bitingly cold Scotch mist."

The observers' duties were to keep a careful time record, see that the rules were followed, help the driver by keeping a watchful eye for police traps, and assist with the ever-present tire repairs. The latter carried no penalty in points — it was sufficient "penalty" to have to make the repeated roadside repairs, involving the difficult job of replacing the numerous security bolts, and the arduous task of inflating tires to sixty or eighty pounds pressure.

Police traps were very much in evidence throughout the trial, but a system of signals was quickly developed by the competitors. The first to spot a Blue Helmet partly concealed in a hedge signaled the fact to the following car by displaying a white handkerchief on the side away from the Limb of the Law. This signal quickly passed back along the line of cars, unless obscured by the dust clouds and, if necessary, brakes were promptly applied.

On one fine morning during the trial all cars were put through a "dust raising" test before leaving Crystal Palace for the day's run. The dust nuisance had become a major problem for the motorist and a cause of much unfavorable comment from the public. For the test, flour was spread evenly over a section of the grounds and each car was driven over it at speed. The judges then attempted to award points according to the magnitude of the "cloud" raised. The results were inconclusive except for the certainty of the powdering administered to drivers and vehicles!

Starting on September 15, the eight-day affair totaled 1,084 miles and attracted 104 entries, of which seventy-four finished. *The Motor* for September 30, 1903, reported that "The 6.5 hp Cadillac has performed best in the way of reliability, making five non-stop runs." In the table of results the car took first place in the up to £200 class. It was awarded 2,976 out of a possible 3,000 marks for reliability, took third place for hill climbing ability, and was awarded full marks for engine power and restarting on hills.

An incident during the contest illustrates Bennett's ingenuity, resourcefulness, and quick thinking. On the Eastbourne run, at the foot of River Hill, Seven Oaks, the Cadillac was rammed by entry number ninety-five, the Chelmsford steamer. Bennett's car had its steering gear and front axle bent and one rear wheel smashed to pieces. It was the only Cadillac in Britain and no spares were available. "Things looked somewhat hopeless," said Bennett. "I think that everybody who saw the wreck shared my first thought that the trial was over as far as the Cadillac was concerned."

Examining steering gear and axle, Bennett and his mechanic found they could possibly be repaired, but the wheel was hopeless. Then Bennett suddenly remembered his friend Billy Wells (later distributor for Indian motorcycles) who worked for the South British Trading Company, agents for Fiske Tires. He had earlier shown his Cadillac to Wells and the latter had commented that he had at the London showrooms a sample wheel mounting Fiske tires, similar to Cadillac's.

Leaving his mechanic to attend to steering gear and axle, Bennett hotfooted for the nearest railway station, several miles off, and caught a London train. Arriving at the Cannon Street station, he had eleven minutes to get to Finsbury Pavement, pick up the wheel, and return to catch the next train to Seven Oaks.

"Thinking I could do it quicker on foot than by cab I ran the distance," said Bennett. "I saw the wheel of the right size on the premises of South British Trading Company, seized it — much to the bewilderment of those in charge — and bolted with the fewest possible words of explanation."

The Cadillac drivers receiving kind words from Frederick Stanley Bennett.

Jumping aboard as the train left, Bennett fell flat on the floor with his wheel. Other passengers helped him to his feet and dusted his clothes. He found that the wheel took the correct tire size, but its two-inch hole was too small for the unusually large Cadillac hub, three and a quarter inches in diameter. However, back at the accident scene, a burning-out using a red-hot poker and other irons heated in the fireplace of a nearby cottage solved the wheel problem. Mutual joy ensued as Bennett, fitting the enlarged wheel, looked up to see his mechanic returning with the repaired axle and steering gear.

The official trial observer had long since given up and gone home, but Bennett obtained permission for a substitute, and the Cadillac completed the day's run within the time limit. The whole incident, of course, dramatized the car's trial success, and orders started to come in. The wheel, incidentally, remained on the car for the rest of its career.

Bennett, a man of limitless energy, resourceful and a good athlete, had a flair for publicity, a ready wit verbally and in

print, including the ability to laugh at himself, excellent business sense, and a well-balanced philosophy, and he lived life with gusto. He admired Leland's moral standards and a lifelong friendship developed between them. Certainly Cadillac could have no better agent in Britain. Equally certain, they needed one of Bennett's caliber.

Of all the major countries, Britain was probably most hostile to the automobile. Considering that she was the nation that had brought about the Industrial Revolution and had produced a long list of great names in science and engineering, this seemed a paradox. But there were good as well as not-so-good reasons for the prevailing British attitude toward the newfangled motorcar.

British power was at its zenith. King Edward VII ruled the largest empire in the world, his navy was equal to those of the next two nations combined. One national catch phrase was "splendid isolation," another was "God bless the squire and his relations, and let us keep our proper stations." The British ruling class was conservative and wedded to its country estates where the horse held sway. The noisy, shaky automobile was a foreign invention and a blot on the fair English countryside; it might upset the social order, and would certainly frighten horses. As for safe, reliable long-distance travel, Britain had the world's most highly developed railway network.

Even among engineers the prevailing attitude was scornful. British engineers were tied by tradition and sentiment to steam power, on which they wholly relied. Certainly no automobile then conceived could approach the steam train for speedy travel. BBC television watchers have seen how Sherlock Holmes and Doctor Watson nonchalantly boarded a train to be taken into the country in drawing room comfort at sixty miles an hour. These traditions had been established in the nineteenth century. How could the automobile compete against them?

The ultimate answer, of course, was that the automobile offered *personal* transportation, at a time and place (one hoped) of one's own choosing. A train journey involves starting at a fixed time —"we leave on time whether you're on board or not"— with sometimes tedious waiting for connections, and the family man had the accompanying worry of tired and peevish children. To many city dwellers the benefits of a weekend in the country and the nervous strain of getting there broke down about fifty-fifty. The professional man also found the automobile to have other advantages. Unlike the horse, it required feeding only when in use. The sportsman auto enthusiast, of course, asked for no economic or convenience justification at all!

Despite all this, as Maurice Olley recalls, "All respectable engineers in Britain in 1906 believed in steam for cars. Fred Lanchester was the outstanding exception. . . . My first motor trip in England was in January of 1906 in a steam car from North Wales to London. I was raised in Britain around the turn of the century, and still recall the scorn of these 'respectable' engineers (Pendred of 'The Engineer' or Col. Crompton) on the subject of the French, German, and American 'petrol cars.'. . . It was incredible to them that so-called 'engineers' could conceive of an engine for a land vehicle which 'lit a fire inside a machined cylinder, got only one working stroke out of four, had *no* starting torque, required a whole electrical system to fire the charge, and in its 'manners' resembled a cross between a grandfather clock and a machine gun!' They were eloquent in their contempt."

Bennett, we can see, although a very clever and determined man, had not picked the easiest row to hoe. Like the representatives for French and German automobiles, he had to combat the Englishman's distrust of foreign products. Admittedly, the cars he imported came from a country which spoke something

Above, a stripped Cadillac chassis; above right, the R.A.C. committee examining and mixing up the parts; below right, the result.

resembling English and which worked (mostly) to good old imperial units of measurement. But American products by and large were regarded with patrician disdain.

Even Bennett admitted there were some grounds for this attitude, because many poor quality American goods had been imported into Britain. The earliest American cars and bicycles were notorious examples — the tubing of cheap "dumped" bicycles failed to stand up even on well-surfaced English roads, and the first American cars imported — the little Stanley-Locomobiles — turned out to be "as troublesome as they were entrancing." Anything American was labeled as poorly finished, lacking artistry, priced to sell — but not built to last. So it was said, rightly or wrongly, whether the product was a bicycle or a Baldwin locomotive.

Bennett delighted in demolishing these claims at every opportunity. He took two main lines of attack, both highly effective. In the press, he used his wit to puncture the more pompous of detractors. A typical example was a pamphlet he authored which lampooned various British makes under thinly-veiled parodies of their own names — for example, "Daimler" as "Damliur." In the field, he exploited to the full the outstanding reliability and comparatively good performance of the Cadillac. In so doing, he consciously or subconsciously played on another characteristic of British temperament — sportsmanship. Though the Cadillac was still a small car, it competed with and often bested the feats of

Putting one of the Cadillacs back together again.

much larger machines. The inborn British sympathy for the "little 'un" who courageously tackles heavy odds, then overcame national prejudice, and the doings of Bennett and his Cadillacs aroused genuine admiration and, finally, affection.

But one valid objection remained. A British car could readily be returned to the "works" for repair. Even the continental makes had their factories just across the Channel. A favorite knock against the Anglo-American Motor Company was: "the cars may be good, but how do you get replacement parts with no factory near you and a dearth of mechanics in the country to do any fitting work on the car?"

Bennett's answer, of course, was that with a Cadillac no "fitting" was required, and the parts always went together without hand fitting or special selection. Factory attention was unnecessary. He had an adequate parts stock, and his English mechanics — or for that matter any Cadillac owner having some mechanical ability — could install Cadillac replacement parts.

Although completely true, this claim often met total disbelief. The American method of interchangeable manufacture was virtually unknown in Europe. It was true that, contemporary with Eli Whitney, early attempts at standardized manufacture had been made both in Britain and on the Continent. Brunel had made interchangeable pulley-blocks for the British Navy in the early 1800's, and even earlier, the Frenchman Bodmer had worked on an interchangeable system for firearms. But neither had initiated any development comparable with Whitney's. Brunel's system was no real demonstration of interchangeability because the pulley-block was a very simple item. Bodmer is believed to have failed because he did not use a proper system of limit gauges. Consequently, the pioneer efforts were not followed up, and the century of nationwide application that stood behind Leland was unmatched in Europe. The nearest approach to success was Lanchester in Britain, whose application was probably inspired by a visit to the United States by F. W. Lanchester himself. However, their production rate of approximately two cars per week showed that they had little or no appreciation of the capital costs involved. They went bankrupt in 1905, and although reorganized, paid no dividends for several more years. Other European makers avoided these difficulties altogether during the 1900–1914 period. As Laurence Pomeroy comments, "With their small outputs, there was little to be gained by installing expensive machinery for automatic operations."

The general view was that interchangeability was neither desirable nor practicable. Bennett had great difficulty in convincing customers, and practical demonstrations were inconvenient and time-consuming. Even then, it could be argued, a workshop job might have been "set up."

In October, 1907, Bennett discussed this point with staff journalists of the English weekly trade paper, *The Motor*, and the idea arose of a public test, supervised by the Royal Automobile Club, as a guarantee of validity. Bennett looked forward to the prospect. He had visited the Cadillac plant earlier that year and had seen for himself the rigorous standardization practices in effect. Sure of his ground, he approached the R.A.C. At first they could see little point in an interchangeability test, because expert opinion held that the necessary tolerances were impractical. Others argued that some wear was inevitable in automobile operation and a new part could never be matched to an existing one. For these reasons, they contended with monotonous repetition, that "interchangeability was not feasible."

But Bennett persisted, and finally the R.A.C., still somewhat skeptical, and probably secretly relishing the prospect of unmasking this rather forward young man, agreed to draw up a set of rules for the demonstration, submit them to manufacturers, and supervise the test. As an inducement, it was even hinted, successful performance of the test — unlikely though it seemed — might even qualify the maker for the Dewar Trophy.

The trophy had been instituted in 1904 to encourage technical progress. Its sponsor was a wealthy member of the British Parliament, Sir Thomas Dewar. The trophy was a handsome sterling silver cup with ebony base, a masterpiece of engraving and repoussé work, standing two feet three inches high. Awarded annually to the company making the most important advancement in the automotive field, it was considered the Nobel Prize of the automobile world. Its high prestige was justified, because the investigation and judgment involved in awarding it was expert, serious, and impartial.

When the R.A.C. announced the terms of its Standardization Test to be performed under the open competition rules of the club, the conditions were seen to be "dramatic and severe." They were no deterrent to Bennett, who immediately accepted what was, in effect, his own challenge. Significantly, however, none of the other manufacturers claiming standardization were prepared to participate in the test.

On February 29, 1908, the Technical Committee of the R.A.C., which included the distinguished engineer Mervyn O'Gorman, visited the depot of Bennett's Anglo-American Motor Company at 19-21 Heddon Street, London W.1. Awaiting them were eight Cadillacs from a shipment just delivered from the docks. They selected three cars, all two-seater runabouts, with engine numbers 23,391, 24,111, and 24,118 and registration numbers A2, EO, A3 EO, and A4 EO respectively.

The cars were driven twenty-three miles across London to the new Brooklands motordrome at Weybridge. To check their as-new performance, each was run around the track for ten laps, twenty-seven more miles, bringing their total mileage to fifty. The cars proved capable of maintaining an average speed of thirty-four miles per hour.

The cars were then driven to a multiple, brick garage at the track and locked up until the following Monday, March 2. The R.A.C. committee and Bennett's mechanics returned on the Monday morning and dismantling began.

Although Brooklands had been opened only the previous June, it was already the last word in testing facilities, but its youthful nature left many amenities lacking, and the work on the Cadillacs was done under "bush mechanic" conditions. The only pit was improvised from planks, bricks, and trestles, resting on a bank beside the lock-up garages. The mechanics had no tools other than wrenches, screwdrivers, hammers, and pliers. Even nails in the garage walls were removed — the R.A.C. took no chances. This was a pointed reply to Bennett's "fix it yourself" claim.

By Wednesday the three cars were completely dismantled to the last nut, bolt, and screw. Pistons were separated from rods, rings were separated from pistons, and all assemblies that could be taken apart were reduced to their components. The frames were stacked in one shed and the other parts, totaling 721 from

Nearing the end of the Cadillac reassembly.

each car, were piled on the floor of the garage. Excepting, of course, body parts identifiable by color, the parts were thoroughly mixed so that identification of any particular part with any particular car was completely impossible.

The R.A.C. officers then had the conglomeration of more than 2,000 parts regrouped into three separate stacks, each having the parts for one complete car. At one stage — and the timing seems to conflict in various accounts — the committee selected eighty-nine parts including such items as oil pump and transmission components, clutch bands and at least one piston, piston pin and rod, and had these placed in a crate and removed, to be held by the R.A.C. under lock and key. They then directed that these parts be replaced from Bennett's stock to represent, in the test itself; spare parts as might be sold over the counter. Bennett readily and happily complied.

On Thursday, March 5, at 11:45 A.M., the mechanics (claimed to be two in number, though some photographs show as many as six men) began rebuilding three new cars from the piles of components. Still under the watchful scrutiny of the R.A.C., they continued with the same simple tool kit used for the dismantling. Under the conditions of the trial, no filing, "fitting," or scraping of bearings or grinding with abrasive cloth was allowed. As Bennett promised, none was required.

The first Cadillac was on its wheels by the end of the first day. That night there was a rainstorm which left three inches of water in the garage and covered many of the parts with a film of rust. One account states that this was the reason the R.A.C. removed nearly one hundred parts — to ensure that they were not furtively "dressed down" to fit. From the timing given in most accounts, however, this seems unlikely, though of course the parts must

The three reassembled Cadillacs pose on Brooklands track before beginning the 500-mile run.

have been wiped down with a rag to remove the thin rust film. All agree, however, that the first car was complete and ready to start by the end of the next day, Friday, March 6.

Now came a dramatic moment. Would the car start and be satisfactory in operation? To many of the onlookers it seemed unbelievable that a car assembled "in this remarkable manner" could possibly be expected to run. Tensely they watched as the mechanic, after oiling and fueling and filling the radiator with water, switched on the ignition and, stepping around the side of the car, took hold of the crankhandle and swung.

At the very first pull the engine caught and settled down to a steady "chuff-chuff," idling easily, smoothly, perfectly. Whether there was a stunned silence or a burst of applause — or both — from the onlookers as they realized the greatness of this achievement, is not recorded. However, it is reported that Cadillac personnel standing by took the incident as calmly as if it happened every day — which, in fact, it did — at the Cadillac plant.

The other two cars were fully assembled and ready for starting by March 10. The steering rack eccentric adjustment on the third car finished was accidentally broken in assembly, and was replaced from stock, making a total of ninety replacements. As with the first car, the second started on the first pull of the crank. The third, reluctant by comparison, took no less than *two* swings of the handle.

At 11:30 A.M. on March 11, the cars were driven out on the concrete, looking a comic trio with their mismatched colors on mudguards, bodywork, and wheels. Press observers, struck by the resemblance to clowns in parti-colored costume, dubbed them "The Harlequins." As a final check on their condition, they set out on the last stage of the trial, a 500-mile run around Brooklands at full throttle. On the great concrete oval they looked like flies crawling around a dinner plate. But all three completed their 500 miles each at an average speed of thirty-four miles per hour, identical with that prior to disassembly.

The average fuel consumption was 29.64 mpg — very satisfactory for cars driven at full throttle — and on official examination after the run, the cars were found to be "in perfect condition." The R.A.C. commented on the achievement in their Certificate of Performance Number 56:

"The cars were assembled without any 'fitting' and without scraping any bearings. The parts were found to be a proper fit, without undue slackness."

The press reported that "the parts slipped together as easily as drawing on a glove." All London papers treated it as a news event of the first magnitude, devoting great space to a description of the entire test in detail and commenting editorially. Cables were sent to the United States and tributes were widespread on the Continent.

The impression created was so profound that even sixteen years later, Bennett himself wrote: "The effect of this test on the public mind makes it stand out as historic and unique, and even this morning as I write this, I received a press clipping with reference to this test. I can truthfully say that during the sixteen years no week has passed in which a clipping from some newspaper in some part of the world has not arrived referring to this test. . . . It had the effect of giving the Cadillac car in particular, and the American-made car in general, a place in the sun in this country. On this side of the ocean it answered completely the adverse criticisms against the American-made car, and opened wide the gate for many American manufacturers to come into this market."

The test alone could have been enough to convince most people, but Fred Bennett never did things by halves. To drive home further a point already well and truly made, Bennett had one of the three cars locked away in the R.A.C. garage directly after the Brooklands test, until the occasion of the R.A.C. 2,000-mile trial in June. The other two cars were repainted and returned to stock.

Bennett's utter confidence in the Cadillac can be gauged from the fact that not only had it undergone a severe test of its standardization, but also it was handicapped against others of its class, since they were able to be fitted with special tanks and undergo special preparation. And there was another requirement of the trial which could have undone in five minutes all the good will arising from the standardization test. As in 1903, said the R.A.C., the event was organized in order to provide an exhaustive test and to demonstrate the capabilities of the modern touring car — the next sentence showed that they meant it. "Should a car be withdrawn or fail to complete the trial, *the car must be dismantled sufficiently to allow the observer to note the exact cause of failure.*" (Italics added.)

The trial was a trade event, restricted to manufacturers and dealers, and divided into eleven horsepower classes by R.A.C. rating. It was run in conjunction with the Scottish Automobile Club trial. The route led from London to Glasgow, then in the S.A.C. section for 772 miles on the Scottish Highland roads, back through the Lake Country, Welsh Border district and Cotswolds to Brooklands, finishing with 200 miles at the motordrome. It included twenty-two miles of hill climbs and eleven timed hills, the total distance being 2,200 miles over a period of fifteen days.

The time-loss principle, rather than the points-loss, was used.

For each road section a time was set, and minutes were deducted for early or late arrival. In hill climbs a car lost a minute for every sixty seconds slower it was than the fastest car in its class. The time taken for any roadside stop, whether for tire changing, oil or water or repairs, was deducted as a penalty, and every additional gallon of fuel cost another minute. Cars had to be certified as genuine touring machines and carry a full passenger load with luggage.

The conditions were severe for crew as well as car. The route was stiff, and as it turned out there were five days of bad weather

— rain, hail, fog, and bitter cold. Most cars, including the Cadillac, had neither windscreen nor top. For this reason, or because they thought that a woman's place was in the kitchen, the R.A.C. stated that "no lady will be allowed to participate in the trial as driver, observer, or passenger." At least this saved women from one chore, for another condition was that each "car must be properly washed as often as is required by the Club."

Bennett and his little car turned in an excellent performance over the entire course, arriving back at Brooklands at the top of their class. Next in marks was a French competitor, rated at either twelve or thirteen R.A.C. horsepower against the Cadillac's ten: the four-cylinder Zedel. Its crew had dubbed the Cadillac *"Compote de troits"* (composed of three). These two were paired in a two-handed runoff for the final section of the trial, a 200-mile speed run on the track. Once again Cadillac number three had to cover a long run at Brooklands under full throttle. This was necessary because although the Cadillac was allowed a handicap, its French rival was much faster — although certainly not the 100-mph car implied in one account.

The cars begin the 500-mile run round Brooklands.

However, the Cadillac, "cheered at every lap as it passed the grandstand, and finally arriving after a most exciting last lap," won the race on handicap and was awarded the R.A.C. Silver Cup for its class.

The award history remembers, however, was not made until eight months later. In February, 1909, resulting from the Standardization Test, the Dewar Trophy was awarded to Cadillac — the first foreign car to win this coveted trophy for "the greatest advancement of the year."

Upon the conclusion of the 500-mile trek, the three Cadillacs return to the Weighing Court for one final official examination.

"However commonplace such a level of Standardization may have been among American manufacturers, it was a tremendous eyeopener for the British motor industry, still living in a cloud-cuckoo land in which cars were individually 'tailored' by skilled workmen earning shamefully low wages," comments one British periodical. "It was, however, to take a world war to force Britain into following the Cadillac policy of standardization."

Fred Bennett had thrown down the gauntlet. Finding no takers, he had gone ahead with a tournament anyway, compelling, in tangible form, recognition of a unique achievement.

It was, of course, the era of gauntlet throwing and spectacular feats. But few had the historical significance of this one. Certainly no Cadillac triumph — and there have been many since — has ever surpassed it.

By 1908 much of the earlier resistance had been overcome. The United Kingdom was probably the largest importer of automobiles anywhere in the world. In 1907, for instance, although 11,700 cars and chassis were built in Britain totaling in value £4,181,000, imports were of a similar order. Thanks to Fred Bennett a sizable proportion were Cadillacs. He was the only importer of the cars in those days, and he was quite a success at it, always retaining a healthy percentage of the total U.S. car sales in England. A measure of his success was the fact that the single-cylinder Cadillac, though not made after 1908, was regarded in England as entirely up-to-date through 1910.

Elsewhere, even without the publicity, prestige, and glamour of the Dewar Trophy, the name of Cadillac was already well-known. Some of this reputation stemmed from the earlier fame of Leland

and Faulconer, whose products were esteemed throughout the United States (where "Leland-built" had become a synonym for quality) and had been exported to several European countries. There was respect for the fine qualities of the new four-cylinder models. But the bulk of the credit undoubtedly belongs to the single-cylinder, which had earned acclaim around the world.

In its native United States, as related earlier, the Cadillac was an outstanding success from the start, even allowing for trouble in the very first model. During the years 1903–1906, the company had built 12,156 cars, compared with 17,608 for Oldsmobile and

Fred Bennett and the Cadillac at the 2,000 Miles Trial.

Victory again, Bennett and the Cadillac, "passing the fork at top speed," enroute to a Class C win in the 2,000 Miles Trial.

ROYAL AUTOMOBILE CLUB

CERTIFICATE OF PERFORMANCE

(Under the Open Competition Rules of the R.A.C.)

No. 56

in a

Standardisation Test

of three 10 h.p. Cadillac Cars

29th February to 13th March 1908.

This is to certify, that three 10 h.p. (By R.A.C. Rating 10 h.p.) single-cylinder, (cylinders 5 in. by 5 in.) Cadillac Cars completed a Standardisation Test, under the following conditions :-

The three cars to undergo the test were chosen from stock at the Anglo - American Motor Car Companies Depôt, 19·21 Heddon Street, w.

The engine numbers of the three cars chosen were:- No.1 car, 23391; No.2 car, 24111; No.3 car, 24118.

The average weight of each car with driver was 14 cwt, 2 lbs.

After they had been selected, they were driven to the Brooklands Track (under observation), where each car ran 10 laps (of 2¾ miles each lap), afterwards being locked up until the following Monday.

On March 2nd, the dismantling of the cars was commenced. By March 4th, the three cars were entirely dismantled, and on March 5th the Expert and Technical Committee inspected the dismantled parts at Brooklands and regrouped them in separate heaps from which the cars were to be re-assembled. The Committee also selected component parts to be replaced from the Entrant's stock, the original parts being retained by the R.A.C. The number of parts selected was 89

Thereupon the cars were assembled, without any "fitting" and without scraping any bearing. The parts were found to be a proper fit, without undue slackness.

One part alone was broken in the re-assembling (viz: steering rack eccentric adjustment on No. 3 car) and this was replaced by one from stock

The engines were found to start up without trouble, and the three cars completed 500 miles each on the track without adjustment of any kind having to be made to any of the three cars, save the replacement of a split pin in the ignition rod of No. 2 car, which was effected without stopping the engine.

The average speed of the three cars during the running of the 10 laps was 26⅔ miles in 47 minutes.

During the 500 miles run, after the completion of the re-building, an average speed was maintained of 34 m.p.h.

The number of parts dismantled, including balls, nuts, bolts and split pins, totalled 721 from each car

The total quantity of petrol used for the three cars was 51 gallons, and the total mileage was 1512, giving 29.64 miles to the gallon

Tires:- During the 500 miles run, No. 3 car had a puncture in the near side driving wheel, the cover and tube were changed, the time taken being 13½ minutes.

J. W. Orde   Secretary.   _Francis of Teck_   Chairman.

21st April 1908   Date   _Mervyn O'Gorman_   Chairman of Technical Committee.

119 Piccadilly, London, W.

13,731 for Ford in the same period. Of these three leading makes the Cadillac was almost certainly the toughest and most reliable in service, and the company frequently took promotional advantage of the motoring prowess of their customers. A typical performance was that of I. L. Atwood, described as "an auto novice," who drove a single-cylinder Cadillac with four passengers up the ninety-three miles from New York to Waterbury, Connecticut, in just over seven hours nonstop, averaging thirteen miles an hour. Considering the load and road conditions, this was sufficiently outstanding to feature in an advertisement. One Cadillac on display at the 1904 Detroit Auto Show was later taken to the railroad for a demonstration by its owner, A. H. Wilson of Canton, Ohio. It drew two truckloads of railroad iron consisting of seven seventy-foot rails, the total of trucks and load over eight tons, up a four percent grade from a standing start. This indicates a tractive effort of 320 pounds for the car measured at the rear wheel! The demonstration was repeated several times. "A two-cylinder opposed engine, rated at 8 bhp tried it and failed to move it forward an inch," crowed Cadillac publicity. "Remodel the Cadillac engine? Certainly not."

In 1902 Alanson Brush had driven one of the prototypes, equipped with chains, up and down the front steps of the Wayne County Building, while the people in Cadillac Square stood and cheered. From photographs, the gradient alone appears to have been on the order of at least twenty-five percent, not to mention the added difficulty of surmounting the steps. Later, in 1904, an enterprising Washington dealer got someone drunk and persuaded him to drive a Cadillac up the steps of the Capitol. Cadillac publicity left much between the lines when they quipped, "He paid for his fun, but it was worth the money to know the power of the Cadillac." In April the same year, the *Detroit Free Press* published a photograph of a Cadillac climbing Shelby Hill, Detroit, with sixteen passengers aboard. The car, perforce, was scarcely visible. But the point was made.

In Florida in 1906, a single-cylinder Cadillac driven by Dr. W. N. Stinson won the 371-mile Jacksonville-Miami endurance run over some of the worst roads in the country. Carrying three passengers and competing against cars up to three times its rated power, it won by seventy-five miles over its closest rival, and was awarded the trophy for the best all-around showing.

Such competitive prowess — whether against other cars or the primitive road conditions of the day or both — was the Cadillac's forte, oft demonstrated in America, Europe, and as far away as New Zealand where the sturdy little car enjoyed considerable

Wilfred Leland, Jr., gracing the Dewar Trophy, 1909.

vogue. But for a performance of undeniable romantic appeal, one must turn again to Fred Bennett. The year: 1953. Mr. Bennett was eighty years old. The occasion was a jubilee reenactment of the entire 1903 thousand-mile trial, following the same schedule over — as far as possible — the same routes. And using the same car.

"His thoughts were for the fun of the thing," wrote Elizabeth Nagle of the Veteran Car Club of Great Britain, ". . . it was going to be the greatest fun he had thought up, and his long life abounds with adventures galore. . . . In 1913 he had repeated the trial, and now, the only survivor from the 1903 event still to be driving the same car, he planned to honor the past and satisfy himself that he and his car were as good as ever. It was a challenge typical of the man, and he tackled it as only he would."

The Veteran Car Club of Great Britain acted as official observers, and virtually the whole nation watched unofficially, what the club secretary dubbed "the great adventure." It began on Friday, September 18, 1953.

"[It] stirred the imagination of thousands at home and overseas," wrote Miss Nagle. "In America, sound broadcasting and television carried daily reports and the Dominion newspapers showed similar enthusiasm. In the United Kingdom no fewer than thirty stories and pictures were published in the national and Sunday papers, over eighty in the provincial weeklies, BBC Newsreel gave a five-minute interview, TV a short film, and the BBC News reported the event twice." Even *The Times* honored Mr. Bennett with an editorial!

The first day's run to Margate and back, 166 miles, was done at an average speed of 20.1 mph. "Nothing for the book except the securing of a loose mudguard," commented the observer, Major H. Browell. "Twenty minutes after dismounting, your exhausted observer was being given a nice whiskey by Mr. Bennett — washed, brushed, and changed into a neat suit — looking as bright and gay as only he can."

With a series of distinguished observers riding in the car — Dennis Field, technical adviser to the Club, E. H. K. Karslake, pioneer of the vintage movement, and W. Boddy, editor of *Motor Sport* among them — one trouble-free run followed another day after day. Eastbourne, Worthing, Folkstone, Southsea, Bexhill, and Winchester. Finally, amidst mounting excitement everywhere, the final journey to Brighton was completed and Fred Bennett and his Cadillac returned to London punctually at the preset arrival time of 2:30 P.M., having covered 1,084 miles without mishap in faster time than they had done fifty years before.

"Punctual to the dot," said Miss Nagle, "the Cadillac swept along the last hundred yards of highway through a cheering crowd to come to a triumphant stop beneath a huge banner which read, 'HATS OFF TO MR. BENNETT.'

"Television Newsreel technicians then took control, and before anyone had really realized that this wonderful man and his wonderful car had together achieved their epic task, the man was talking into a microphone as if he was sitting in his drawing room after an afternoon's stroll!"

The car, number 530, the first Cadillac imported, had not been in Bennett's sole ownership. It was carefully preserved and brought out only for special occasions. Bennett had sold it very early in its career. But in 1913, always ready to impugn the fallacy of "shoddy American products," he had traced the car to a chemist in Slough who used it as a delivery van. It had done some 50,000 miles but retained its original chassis components, having had only replacement drive chains and bearings. With a few adjustments and minor repairs, Bennett submitted it to a repetition of the 1903 test, under R.A.C. observation, which the car readily completed.

During the next forty years Bennett drove it an estimated 200,000 miles, with no more repairs than the replacement of the gas and water tanks and the radiator. So its total mileage at the start of the Golden Jubilee Commemoration Run was some quarter-million — this from a model which Henry Leland considered unsatisfactory in chassis design!

Equally remarkable was its retention of its original performance — 1,094 miles at 21.2 mph. This was actually faster than in 1903 or 1913, but as Bennett pointed out, "In those days we were restricted to 20 mph and roads were nothing like as good as they are now."

Observers were lyrical about the car's performance. Major Browell commented of the Margate run: "Coming back the route was slightly altered to include Wrotham — a VILE hill — up which the Cadillac quietly went." The *Daily Telegraph* reporter wrote: "I went to meet Mr. Bennett at Wrotham, Kent. But he had changed his route slightly and I missed him by about twenty minutes. Following his altered route at speeds up to 55 mph I failed to catch him."

Of the Maidstone run, observer H. J. Budd remarked: "It was an uneventful run without any premeditated stop, chiefly remarkable for Mr. Bennett's amazing stamina, the amazing average speed of 22.5 mph, and the climbing of Pol Hill in top gear at 15–18 mph."

On the Southsea run, the *Portsmouth Evening News* reported that "Today Mr. Bennett touched 42 mph and had many stretches between 35 and 40 mph."

But the twinkling octogenarian and fifty-year-old car had saved the best until last. On the final (Winchester) run, said the V.C.C. secretary, "the fog gave way to brilliant sunshine and Mr. Bennett immediately hotted up the pace. . . . The last fifteen miles to Bolney crossroads was accomplished in the astonishing time of twenty-five minutes. (Average speed, 36 mph.) Stanley Sears [Vice-president of the V.C.C. and a noted Rolls-Royce enthusiast], who lived at Bolney, had planned to welcome Mr. Bennett at the crossroads, but the wholly amazing time of arrival defeated him and the road was deserted — much to the delight of the Cadillac's driver. Fetched by the observer, Mr. Sears would only believe that Mr. Bennett was in fact there when he saw him, and then had to be convinced that the starting time had not been advanced."

For nostalgic appeal, Bennett's car is surpassed by only one other single-cylinder —"Osceola." Named by Henry Leland after the famous chief of the Seminole Indians whom he admired, Osceola was for many years the personal car of the Cadillac chief himself. The car was built in 1905, and featured a two-seater body reminiscent of the old sedan chair, and which bore more than passing resemblance to a closed car designed by Louis Renault several years earlier. It was an economical and handy little runabout for Leland to use between his home and the factory and around Detroit. He drove it for many years, even well after the advent of the V-8. Cadillac engineer Bill Foltz has recalled in *Master of Precision* how Uncle Henry drove Osceola many evenings up the Avenue of Poplars (La Salle Boulevard) not far from his boulevard home. He drove it at high speed and Foltz claims that since the little car was high and somewhat top-heavy, he often tipped it over into a snowbank in the wintertime, or while cornering too fast. Then there would be a telephone call to the company for help to put Osceola on its wheels again.

"Uncle Henry used to tear around at 28 miles an hour when Osceola was new," relates Foltz. "Once he hit a street car on his way to the office. Going home the same night he ran into a coal wagon. And whenever he was out of town, his daughter would call me and ask me to lower Osceola's speed by changing the sprockets. I'd be called on the carpet for doing it as soon as the boss returned. His family worried about his fast driving. He was not a speedster actually, but he forgot himself and drove to keep up with his speeding thoughts." These recollections have been criticized as overdrawn by H.M.'s granddaughter, Mrs. Gertrude W. Hope of Detroit, who remarks, "I'm not at all sure of the validity of these recollections of Far Too [H.M.'s family nickname, from 'Father II'] and Osceola tipping over in assorted snowbanks at odd times! I certainly don't remember hearing about it and I don't think the wooden body would have stood it and most of all I can't believe Far Too would have treated any machinery that way! But possibly I'm exaggerating the importance of this."

As to Osceola itself, Mrs. Hope's sister, Miriam Leland Woodbridge, has said, "My true love is this single-cylinder Cadillac I grew up with, and when I start talking about Osceola I don't know when to stop."

Osceola was built late in 1905, especially for Henry Leland, to satisfy him as to the feasibility of building a closed car. It was painted blue and black, becoming colors for its height and simplicity, and luxuriously upholstered with black leather over horsehair padding. It was eighty-two inches long, fifty-one inches wide, and eighty-seven inches tall, riding on 30 x 3½ inch tires.

The body was built under the supervision of Fred J. Fisher in the Wilson Body Company plant in Detroit.

Osceola was the last car Henry Leland drove: he often had passengers with him with whom he discussed engineering. Then there was a period of about five years when the car was retired to the Leland homestead and brought out only to be shown off or to take the children for a ride. Later it was sent to the family cottage in Kingsville, Ontario, to serve as an errand car, and finally Miriam Woodbridge adopted it. One day she asked her grandfather to whom it actually belonged, and he replied, "As near as I can figure it out, it's yours."

The Lelands referred to Osceola in later years as "Old Plug Hat," and it was a constant attraction to their visitors. It was taken to the 1933 and 1934 Chicago World's Fairs, and used in two industrial movies around the same time.

The movie appearances and resultant fan mail caused the family to decide that Osceola should be made available for display purposes, portraying the first step in closed-car design, and the car was sent back to Chicago — this time to the Museum of Science and Industry — to appear in the "Yesterday's Main Street" exhibit. There it spent twenty years.

A Cadillac climbing the courthouse steps in Columbia City, Indiana, 1907.

In 1953 Osceola was transferred to the Detroit Historical Museum's Hall of Industry, where it remains to this day, making it possible for the people of Detroit and their visitors to share in an important phase of industrial history.

In these and other events recreating the atmosphere of half a century earlier, the single-cylinder Cadillac has relived and renewed its legendary past. From the examples given, its popularity in veteran circles is easily understood. If nothing else, it would be popular for the cynical reason that no one likes to fail in a rally, and in a Cadillac, you are virtually certain of reaching your destination.

For those to whom fate has unkindly refused permission to actually drive a one-lung Cadillac, a few remarks about the experience might be in order.

First of all, some mountaineering is needed to reach the driver's seat. Once there, you look down on people instead of up at them. And you might receive another reminder of your altitude with a crack on the head unless you duck as you drive out of your garage door — you need a lot more clearance than is customary today. So duck!

Why did they build them so high? The quality of rubber dic-

tated large-diameter tires for acceptable durability, the techniques for making dropped axles and frames were not developed until later, and high ground clearance was an advantage anyway.

In the seat, one finds excellent visibility matched only by a motorcycle or a horse — this position being somewhere in between. One can see the ground beneath the front and rear axles, and the only familiar control is the steering wheel. At the right in a slot in the driver's seat is the spark lever. One must retard the spark before inserting the starting crank — a thoughtful precaution on the designer's part. Low gear is engaged by depressing a pedal, high and reverse by moving a lever on the right. Forward for high, back for low, in the center for neutral. In low gear, the driver revs up with the hand throttle lever under the steering wheel, pushes into high at about five miles an hour, and surges away, counting each power stroke.

A good cruising gait on these Cadillacs is somewhere between twenty and thirty miles an hour, depending on the sprockets fitted. Torque, and therefore acceleration, are best between five and twenty-five, and the car will climb most main road hills in high. On steep grades, one will have to hold the car in low gear with his foot firmly on the pedal — just as on the Model T Ford, and

A Cadillac owner prepares for a breezy motoring jaunt in a 1903 model.

The Thousand Miles Trial reenactment in 1953, Fred Bennett in the derby.

emergency stops call for more hands than one has: pull lever to neutral and retard spark, close throttle with the other hand while continuing to steer, stomp the brake pedal with a foot — but don't mistake low gear for the brake, or you could ruin the crankshaft.

There is little or no self-centering action, and with its wide track and short wheelbase, the Cadillac would appear to be an oversteerer. The ride is hard, and the passengers are well aware of machinery working purposefully — which may be one reason why the makers thought no instruments were needed — and weather protection is zero.

What then is so wonderful about the car?

In the context of its contemporaries, the answer is simple. Judged by modern standards none of the cars of the time had an ideal combination of power and refinement. Some were smooth, but complex and gutless. Others were powerful, but hairy, heavy, and expensive to run. The Cadillac was light, efficient, powerful, durable, reliable, cheap to run, and had as refined a single-cylinder engine as it was possible to manufacture. Even today — provided you are patient enough — a single-cylinder Cadillac will cover ten miles, or one hundred, or one thousand as easily as the day it was built.

From the aficionado as well as from those who will never own an antique car, the little vehicle commands admiration and respect. Michael Sedgwick called it "Henry Leland's indestructible little single," and A. C. F. Hillstead of the old Bentley company wrote, "I never remember a bad Cadillac, and the first one I drove was the single-cylinder model similar to that used by F. S. Bennett."

The writer once bought his four-year-old son a children's book on automobiles, printed in England. It included a Cadillac single, and the text was an ideal summary: "This was one of the best cars of the time, beautifully made, very quiet, and much more reliable than the average car of its day."

It was the product of a great artisan, who said, "It is as perfect as we can make it." He imbued every one of its more than seven hundred parts with his own granitic character, integrity, and unyielding standards. This, combined with his unrivaled experience in quality manufacturing, resulted in a product that was outstanding from the beginning and, seemingly, built to last forever.

But it could not go on *selling* forever. By 1908 a successor was ready that would equal its fame and duplicate its achievements. Commercially, it would far surpass its most illustrious predecessor.

Henry Martyn Leland, aged eighty-seven, posing with the Cadillac known as "Osceola" in 1930.

CHAPTER FOUR

THE THIRTY
AND GENERAL MOTORS

Coming of age with a sophisticated new car and a promising corporate partnership

The year 1908 was a momentous one for the American automobile in many ways. From a position behind Germany and France (but well ahead of Britain and Italy), the United States had become the foremost automobile producer in the world. In 1896, the only organized American output was thirteen cars built by Duryea, but by 1900 annual production was 4,192, doubling the following year. By 1904 there were seventy establishments in the United States making and dealing in automobiles, with a capital of $20,000,000. A total of 24,419 cars were built that year, valued at about $45,000,000. Of these, cars valued at $2,695,655 were exported, more than half to British territories. Even this was merely a beginning, for 1908 saw the introduction of the Model T Ford and the incorporation of General Motors.

Imports from Europe had grown from twenty-six cars, valued at $43,126 in 1901 to 423 in 1904, valued at $1,446,303. French primacy among European makes was shown by the breakdown: 368 cars were French, twenty-two German, fifteen British, and thirteen Italian — seven times as many French cars as the rest put together. Imports increased up to 1909, when 1,624 European cars valued at $2,905,000 came into the country, but shortly afterward there was a decline, for by this time the American buyer could get anything he wanted from domestic factories, whether a Model T Ford, a Mercer raceabout, or a $7,000 Pierce-Arrow limousine.

Symbolizing the new stature of the American industry were the New York-to-Paris victory by the Thomas, the Vanderbilt Cup win by Locomobile and, of course, the Dewar Trophy award to Cadillac. Of the three, the third was the most significant, for the round-the-world event had little practical meaning and would never be repeated, while the occasional big motor race win by

American cars hardly reflected the international status of the nation's industry. Nevertheless, all three enhanced the American image, and there was even some reflected glory in the 1909 Dewar Trophy. Although it went to the English Daimler firm for pioneering sleeve valves, everybody knew that the man behind the development was an American — Charles Y. Knight.

Changes and trends at Cadillac both mirrored and influenced the industry. In either 1907 or 1908 Henry Leland imported the first "Jo-block" gauges from Sweden for use in the Cadillac factory. These gauges were the creation of the Swedish-American toolmaker Carl Edward Johansson, who had worked and been partly educated in the United States as a young man. In 1885, at the age of twenty-one, he had returned to Sweden. Working at the government arsenal in Eskilstuna as a toolmaker and foreman, he became dissatisfied with the existing gauges, and about 1897, after years of experiment, produced his own. A decade of development followed, and in 1906 Johansson publicly announced his gauging system in hope of finding a sponsor. At that time, with the exception of Leland, nobody took Johansson's claim seriously. "It was so incredible that it was not accepted for several years," said the *Automobile Trade Journal.*

In 1911 Johansson resigned from government service to start commercial manufacture of his gauges. At the same time he established an American representation, at first for sales, but later actually to make the gauges. America had proved to be his market, so he returned to the United States permanently in 1917 and set up his factory at Poughkeepsie, New York. It was later taken over by Henry Ford. The general acceptance of the gauges was made possible by Maj. William E. Hoke of the United States Bureau of Standards, who developed mechanical methods of pro-

1/1000 OF AN INCH

is the standard of measurement in the

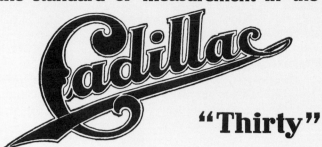

"Thirty"

It may surprise you to know that even the costliest cars fall short of that fineness of measurement in component parts upon which the operation and the life of a motor car are wholly dependent.

What is the peculiar quality in any motor car for which you pay $5,000 or $6,000?

It is not reputation—no matter how fine that reputation may be; because no reputation could be worth $2,000 or $3,000 to each purchaser.

It is not mere external elegance.

It is a definite, concrete excellence; for which the maker is justified, in a sense, in charging.

You pay $5,000 or $6,000 for running qualities—and an element of longevity which no car of lesser price, save the Cadillac, will give.

Those running qualities and that longevity are in turn *directly dependent* upon the accuracy with which more than 100 essential parts are made and the perfect alignment resulting therefrom.

Your $5,000 car (or your Cadillac) runs more smoothly and lasts longer, because of the time, the care, the money and the expert workmanship expended in eliminating friction by producing between those hundred or more vital parts a fineness of fit which *no eye can measure and no words describe.*

And this leads to a disclosure of the utmost concern to every automobile owner.

In the production of more than ten thousand Cadillac "Thirtys" in the past fifteen months it has been demonstrated beyond peradventure that in this element of synchronization, harmony, fit and elimination of friction, the Cadillac standard *has not been attained by any other plant or any other car.*

Thus, the one element which justifies a $5,000 or $6,000 price is present to a higher degree in the Cadillac than in any other car in the world.

In the Cadillac there are 112 parts which are accurate to the one-thousandth of an inch.

Thus—as a single illustration—the Cadillac "Thirty" piston is made to work perfectly within the cylinder bore which is 4¼ inches. To guage the accuracy of the piston diameter, two snap guages are used. These snap guages are shaped similar to the letter "U." The distance across the opening of one snap guage is 4.248 (four inches and 248 one-thousandths of an inch) and is marked "Go." The other is 4.247 (one one-thousandth of an inch less) and is marked "Not Go."

The "4.248 Go" guage must slip over the lower end of the piston, but the "4.247 Not Go" guage must not. If the piston is so large that the "Go" guage will not slip over it, the piston is ground down until it does. If the piston is small enough to permit the "Not Go" guage to slip over, it is discarded as imperfect.

Crank shafts, cylinders, pistons, gears—scores of essential Cadillac "Thirty" parts are rigidly subjected to the scrupulous test of 1-1000 of an inch accuracy.

Not $5,000 or $6,000 can buy the magnificent assurance of smooth, velvety operation and long life obtained in every Cadillac "Thirty" at $1,600.

The great Cadillac factory in Detroit is always open to visitors; and it would be a pleasure to us to offer you verification of the interesting information contained herein by a trip through the plant at any time that you may be in this city.

Four cylinder, 33 horse power. Three speed sliding gear transmission, shaft drive.

$1600 (F. O. B. Detroit)

Including the following equipment:—Magneto, Delco system four unit coil with controlling relay and dry batteries, one pair gas lamps and generator, one pair side oil lamps, one tail lamp, horn, set of tools, pump and tire repair kit, robe rail, tire irons.

Furnished as Touring Car, Demi-Tonneau or Gentlemen's Roadster

Cadillac Motor Car Company - - Detroit, Mich.

Member Association Licensed Automobile Manufacturers.   Licensed under Selden Patent.

Precision a byword: above, a Cadillac workman testing the "Go-Not Go" gauges. At left, the Cadillac advertising department taking appropriate advantage of the company's manufacturing standards in promoting the Thirty. Below, the demi-tonneau as offered in 1909.

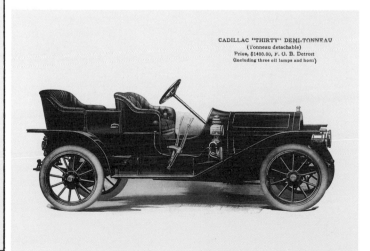

CADILLAC "THIRTY" DEMI-TONNEAU
(Tonneau detachable)
Price, $1400.00, F. O. B. Detroit
(including three oil lamps and horn)

duction that lowered the cost of manufacture. They were then liberally accepted in the automobile and other industries.

The use of these famous gauges, therefore, dates from the introduction of a pilot set in the Cadillac factory years before they were generally available and when expert opinion was openly skeptical. For this bold move, full credit goes to Leland, who appreciated the meaning of his fellow toolmaker's achievement years before anyone else. No record exists of any meeting of the two men, although it would have been a "scoop" for any trade journalist of the day: the bearded, fatherly Leland in his middle sixties, the younger Johansson, in his early forties but already shaggy-browed and sporting a walrus moustache—both names forever after to signify the ultimate in toolroom precision.

The "Jo-block" gauges have been confused by some writers with the "GO-NOT GO" gauges. Further, some think that the Dewar Trophy award would have been impossible without the "Jo-blocks." Neither statement is correct. The "Jo-blocks" were never used as manufacturing checks at all, and may not even have been in use when the Standardization Test was made. To

use them for gauging parts would have been like using a Dresden jug to pour the breakfast milk, for they had to be handled with great care and were used only to check the working gauges.

The "Jo-blocks" were based on the principle developed in the 1830's by the English toolmaker Joseph Whitworth. The gauges consisted of a series of small metal blocks having two opposite surfaces formed into a pair of "Whitworth planes," which were parallel and a given distance apart, accurate to tolerances ranging from two millionths up to four one-hundred-thousandths of an inch. They were so accurately made that several blocks pressed and "wrung together" by hand would adhere and form a component with length exactly equal (within the tolerance) to the sum of the lengths of each unit. Thus a limit gauge of a 2.502-inch gap would be checked by using a 1.000-inch, a 0.500-inch, and a 1.002-inch block assembled together.

The use of these gauges was not initially essential to standardized manufacture. The Cadillac plant had already operated for some years without them. However, they were a decided improvement over previous checking methods, saving time and cost,

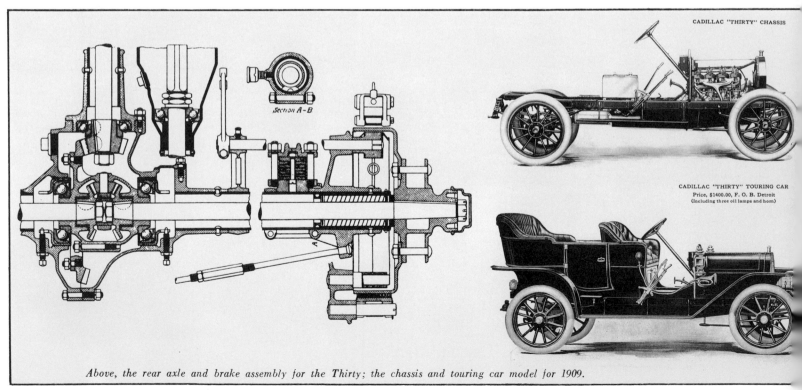

CADILLAC "THIRTY" CHASSIS

CADILLAC "THIRTY" TOURING CAR
Price, $1400.00, F. O. B. Detroit
(including three oil lamps and horn)

Above, the rear axle and brake assembly for the Thirty; the chassis and touring car model for 1909.

and permitting the work to be carried out by any competent mechanic rather than specially trained men. As the increasing complexity of automobile design required more and more precisely machined surfaces, they became indispensable. Manufacturing details of the gauges themselves for many years remained unpublished, although it was known they were finished in laboratory conditions at a constant 68° F. However, by the thirties, because of the considerable demand, similar and equally accurate gauges were being made elsewhere.

The adoption of the Johansson gauges—then unique to Cadillac—the halo of the Dewar Trophy, and the success of standardized manufacture called for something special in advertising: a commercial war cry that would epitomize it all, and fix it readily in the public mind. Lengthy paragraphs, full of qualifying phrases, however well-written, would not do. Something short and pungent was needed. Fortunately someone came up with the ideal answer. In 1908, along with the new Cadillac script, company publicity began promoting the slogan "Standard of the World." Catalogues, advertisements, and even

hubcaps of the cars carried it. It was not new, and did not originate at Cadillac, but it has undeniably been made Cadillac's own. It may have been suggested by Leland's association years before with Brown and Sharpe who advertised the "World's Standard of Accuracy," while De Dion actually used the identical phrase in at least one early advertisement.

It can be criticized as a sweeping generalization, and for arrogance, hauteur, or conceit — call it what you will — it has been equaled only by a few other marque slogans, but it is one that survives today. Some cars of similar class, such as Lincoln and Mercedes-Benz, take the other view and avoid the issue — or imply that they are so good and famous that no slogan is necessary.

However, this is a negative approach. The Cadillac slogan is positive, brief, uncompromising — and catchy. All these make it an ideal "image" tool, and even today, more than sixty years later, no one has been able to come up with a superior replacement.

By contrast, models were constantly superseded. In 1908 the

A plan view of the Thirty chassis, as depicted in a 1909 brochure.

company introduced a new four-cylinder chassis that succeeded both the single and all previous fours, and was the only production car of the 1909 program. The sales of D, G, H, and L models had been normal for their price class — around 150 units in 1905, increasing to about 250 in 1906 and 1907, and 500 in 1908. These were satisfactory figures by the standards of Peerless and Pierce and could have been maintained, or even steadily increased. But the price range — $2,400 to $5,000 — precluded any production figures comparable with those for the single-cylinder. Yet that model was now outmoded and its sales steeply dropping. The country was in a business slump. Cadillac employment was down to 650 men — half its normal work force. The company balance sheets were so discouraging that Lemuel Bowen mournfully predicted bankruptcy. No dividends had been declared for 1905 and 1906 because the increasing demands for the single had dictated constant plant expansion. Since Leland invariably insisted on the best and the most up-to-date machinery, expenditure had been heavy. The company had borrowed on short-term bank credits, paying the loans off within the year from seasonal sales. A new car was necessary if Cadillac was to keep its substantial following and pay its debts. The writing on the wall was clear by June of 1907, and in that month H.M. and his engineers had begun design work on the new model, the Cadillac Thirty.

Designwise, the new car was a consolidation of existing experience rather than a step out onto fresh ground. But its commercial success far outstripped any previous Cadillac. It was deliberately planned to meet the needs of a clientele whose requirements had outgrown the single. Its potential market was gauged by Wilfred Leland, and he drew up a schedule of supplies, production, and sales which carried Cadillac through the lean year of its gestation period and kept loan repayments flowing.

When the Cadillac Thirty was announced in August of 1908 it was a combination of the best selling points of the two main lines which preceded it. It had the luxury and performance of the fours, and the moderate price of the single. Its engine and transmission were substantially that of the previous Model G, which meant that no more Cadillacs were being built with a planetary gearset. Doubtless many followers were disappointed at the complete abandonment of planetary transmission in favor of the selective sliding gear (used first on the Model G introduced for 1907). But it was simpler and more robust than the three-speed planetary, easier to service, and cheaper to make, and was now more widely accepted in America than it had been five years

The Thirty engine: above and below from 1909; at the right from 1913.

earlier. So, despite its driving convenience, the planetary gear had to go. (To emphasize the change, the new Thirty's pedals were clearly marked "clutch" and "brake" on the pedal pads themselves.)

The chassis was freshly designed, with platform rear suspension in place of the earlier full-elliptics, and wheelbase increased to 106 inches — six inches more than the G and greater than any previous Cadillac, with the exception, that is, of the 110-inch limousine of 1906. This had been priced at $5,000 — "without lamps."

In contrast, the Thirty, including full four-passenger body work *and* three oil lamps *and* horn, was only $1,400. Its design had been simplified, but its standard of manufacture was in no way inferior to its predecessors. How then had such a price reduction been achieved?

As opposed to the three "P's"—Packard, Peerless, Pierce-Arrow — and others who ran several models and seldom built more than a few hundred of each, Cadillac had rationalized to one chassis, and on that chassis they offered only three body styles. Every aspect of manufacturing cost had been studied, and the profit margin set at a mere twenty-five dollars per car. This was only possible because the company made an unusually large proportion of the car in its own shops. It operated its own iron and brass foundries, pattern shops, sheet metal shops, machine shops, gear cutting plant, and painting, finishing, and upholstering departments. It made its own motors, transmissions, radiators, hoods, and fenders, and even its own cap screws, bolts, and nuts. Its own toolmaking department designed and made most of the 16,000 special tools, jigs, dies, and fixtures used in the plant. (Standard tools and equipment totaled an additional 74,000 items.)

With a factory largely self-contained and buying its supplies in bulk at much lower rates, it was easier to control costs, maintain quality, and yet offer such exceptional value for the money. The payoff came in instant public acceptance of the Thirty and record sales in the first year. In the first six months sales at 4,500 units surpassed the previous best *year*, and the annual output of 5,900 cars was sold before the end of the season in August of 1909. That year the directors declared a forty-five percent dividend to the stockholders.

Production of the Thirty followed the principles of the earlier Cadillac models, although extra tooling was installed. "Cadillac plant in the matter of fine machinery, fine tools, jigs, and fixtures is not equaled in any other motor car factory in the world," claimed the company. "This equipment includes more than 500 special automatic labor saving machines, some of which are capable of turning out from two to ten times the volume of work produced by the ordinary methods which obtain in most factories — and doing it far better." Methods were constantly improved, and in 1909 alone 10,000 new tools, jigs, and dies were added, of which over 3,000 were designed and built by the company's own toolmaking department. "The expense for tool maintenance alone has exceeded $60,000 in a year," said one booklet.

The system of inspection was so exacting, said the factory, "that it practically precludes the possibility of an imperfect part being incorporated in the car so far as can be detected by the most accurate measuring instruments known to engineering science. . . . From the time the raw materials reach the warehouse until they leave the plant, they are under the careful scrutiny of the corps of experts trained in accordance with the high standards of the Cadillac organization. This inspection extends to the smallest pieces, even nuts, bolts, and screws."

Suppliers found these statements true, sometimes even at their own cost. One manufacturer of grease cups who lost a contract, inquired why, and was told too many of his were substandard. To his amazement he found that every single grease cup he supplied had to pass thread gauge and other tests.

Assembling was divided between several gangs, each assigned to particular work. One group after finishing crankshaft bearings installed the crankshaft in the motor and ran it in with a belt on the flywheel. Another group assembled the camshaft and its drive. Another assembled the cylinder, cylinder head, and copper water jacket. Final assembly was done on stands. Methods were more elaborate than with the single-cylinder model, where whole motors were assembled with only two men per stand, but subdivision of labor had not gone far, and the line was stationary. (Even at Ford, the moving line was still some years away.)

After the completed chassis had been inspected, it was placed on a roller dynamometer where final adjustments and a power check were made. The 1909 models, with four-inch bore, were rated at 25.6 hp, but developed an actual 30, hence the model designation. When the bore was increased to four and a quarter inches for 1910, the rated horsepower was 28.9 and the actual went up to 33, but the original Thirty designation was retained.

Following dyno testing, in which the car had to pass a standard specification sheet, there was a road test. "I can remember the times when four-cylinder Cadillac chassis were tested on Grand Boulevard near Woodward Avenue," recalled one engineer. "That was a mighty long time ago! They were left on the sidewalk before the bodies were installed and the drivers with a box over the chassis drove them on the public roads. The early test drivers

Model Thirty Cadillacs on dynamometer test, 1913.

all used highways, and they had no compunction about doing anything they chose. Of course, this policy had to be changed later because of the increasing traffic and speeds."

To avoid production holdups, the dyno room was made big enough to take many cars at once, and a large staff of test drivers was retained.

For many years engine testing was supervised by Charlie Martens. He had joined Leland and Faulconer in 1899 at the age of twenty-three, and designed the first dynamometer room for Cadillac engines in 1902. One of Leland's closest and most trusted associates, his name could well have been Martinet. "He was one of the most stubborn and fantastic old mechanics I ever knew," a friend recalled. "He was the most virtual dictator I have ever seen in a machine shop, and I still vividly remember one time he dressed me down as the stupidest man he had ever met. I had designed some inter-operation trucks for carrying crankshafts, and made the mistake of supporting the shafts on the end bearings only. The result was that they bowed by several thou. if left over the weekend."

Their own store of experience and standards being equal or superior to specialist vendors, Cadillac preferred to cut and finish all their own gears, both transmission and axle. Their foundry had a similar reputation and for years made cylinder, piston, and piston ring castings "for a number of other automobile manufacturers making the highest priced cars in America." Although they mentioned no names, it is known that one was Pierce-Arrow.

The selection of materials was given as much attention as the actual manufacture of the car. "Where in most cars, particularly in those selling at (the same) price, cast iron is used in many parts, we used steel drop forgings." The cylinders, pistons, and piston rings were cast in Cadillac's own foundry, the grade and formula being "the result of years of experience, experimenting and testing *in our own laboratories*." These statements, made in 1908 and 1909, would have stupified many company executives who thought laboratories were only found in colleges and scientific establishments.

So much for the Thirty's research and manufacture. What was it like in service and on the road? Did it justify the claim that despite its medium price, it was "accorded a position alongside of those few cars which stand at the pinnacle of the world's esteem"? Was it really what Cadillac claimed it to be — a "high-grade motorcar"? The answer to the first question is "highly satisfactory," and to the second and third, a loud yes, but the answers require more detailed explanations.

On the road the Thirty was a pleasant, easy-handling, sweet-running car. It did not equal competitors' sixes for smoothness, but the engine was as tractable, quiet, and generally refined as a four could ever hope to be. Specific output at about 8.3 bhp/liter was average for 1909, and gave very good torque through a limited rev range, the cars pulling well and having a good reputation as hill climbers. Three axle ratios — 3.0, 3.5, and 4.0 to 1 — were available, the 3.5 being standard on the touring, demi-tonneau, and roadster models and giving a high gear range of five to fifty miles an hour. The standard limousine ratio was 4.0 to 1, this also being available on the touring, demi-tonneau, and roadster. The roadster could be ordered with a 3.0 to 1 axle giving 50 mph at only 1,580 rpm.

The clutch and transmission were refined, the cars rode well, and had the characteristic appeal of the big four-cylinder effortlessly tugging a high-gear ratio. On restored examples, the gentle bubble of the exhaust and the high driving position give today's driver the impression he is traveling at 20 to 25 mph when the car is actually cruising at 40 to 45.

What the Thirty could do on the track when stripped was surprising. T. J. Beaudet drove a 1911 Thirty speedster into second place at a Los Angeles board track meeting twenty-four-hour race, covering 1,448 miles at an average speed of 60.33 mph. Although in racing trim, the car had to carry lighting equipment

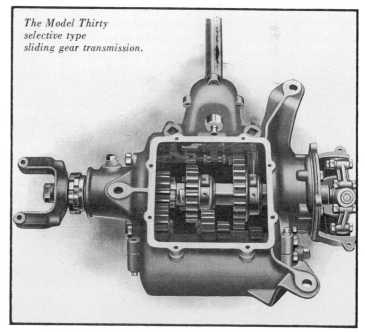

The Model Thirty selective type sliding gear transmission.

and a riding mechanic, and its time was the best ever put up by a car of its horsepower class up to that time.

We have already examined some of the reasons why, after several years of producing cars in the "luxury" price bracket, Cadillac elected to pin all on the "under $2,000" range. But these were factory reasons. Much also was based on the attitudes of the buyers. In the older centers like New York, Boston, Cleveland, and Washington, there was a sufficient core of wealthy buyers to make production of the most expensive cars viable. The title of one O. Henry book, *The Four Million*, shows that New York, as always, was Number One. Detroit's population was barely 300,000. Cars such as the six-cylinder, sixty-horsepower Pierce, Peerless, Thomas, and Stevens-Duryea, to name a few, were well-suited to the social New Yorker or Bostonian. Like the people who bought them, they were smoother, more refined, and more powerful. But they were less practical in the cities of western expansion, where the old frontier virtues of simplicity and lower running costs were better appreciated, and in fact practically mandatory. The prospect in Detroit, or in the Midwest, or on the Pacific Coast, was not particularly interested in the New Yorker's ideal automobile or even, for that matter, the Clevelander's. Conditions were different — more primitive. For this reason six-cylinder cars never had the early success in Detroit that they enjoyed in Cleveland and New York State, and even Packard sold cars in the $4,000 to $5,000 price range with no more than four cylinders right up to 1912.

One major shortcoming of the big sixes (successful medium-sized sixes did not appear until the second decade) was inadequate cooling in severe conditions. Richmond Viall, Leland's old superintendent at Brown and Sharpe, bought one of the first Cadillac Thirty models, and in September, 1909, he reported to Leland that during a seventeen-day tour he had no cooling problems, whereas a neighbor's $5,000 Peerless, traveling in company, boiled frequently. And in a private interoffice memo of July, 1912, the chief engineer of Pierce-Arrow admitted that boiling problems increased with the displacement, being least on their 38 hp and most on their 66, which "almost invariably boiled in hot weather conditions."

Another big six drawback was running costs, including tire bills, which would have startled all but J. P. Morgan. The log of a 1908 Pierce Great Arrow operated by a Boston doctor for the three years 1909–1911, averaging five to six thousand miles a year, shows that the annual tire bill averaged $533! Gas and oil came next, at $326. For comparison at the other end of the scale, a Model T Ford operated by the same man cost $85.20 for tires and $69.15 for gas and oil. The Cadillac Thirty offered a reasonable compromise between these extremes, and combined something of the best attributes of both vehicles.

Then there was the question of sheer size. The lightest six-cylinder Pierce weighed well over 4,000 pounds, the heaviest exceeded 6,000, and their wheelbases ranged from 119 to 135 inches. Although the Pierces in particular were remarkably easy-handling for their size and era, cars of these proportions were generally considered to be a handful for the owner-driver and

A lineup of Cadillacs outside the factory, 1912.

more suited to a chauffeur. And he cost even more than the tires!

Therefore (as Henry Ford had found already), few people in Detroit were in the market for a big six when the Thirty was designed. Cadillac was undoubtedly capable of building such a car, but marketing it would have probably led them straight into bankruptcy.

In answer to the second of our leading questions, then, the Cadillac Thirty was a well-chosen concept, and the car was properly designed and thoroughly tested throughout. Despite its moderate price, it was manufactured according to standards unsurpassed even in factories building cars costing several times the price. Several of them, in fact, had been shown by Leland how to build quality and precision into the product, rather than the other way around. By comparison with those of costly contemporaries, the Cadillac's specifications were modest — but a logical, practical answer to the needs of its environment. And although it conceded points in power, speed, and refinement to the bigger cars, it certainly scored over them in other, equally important respects.

Pierce-Arrow catalogues of the day proclaimed that there were "three classes of car — cheap cars, cars of compromise, and cars of quality." Immediately listing their own in the third class, they remarked that cheap cars were bought because they were cheap, and compromise cars were bought because the purchaser could not afford true quality.

This was a shrewd summary, but not entirely correct. In effect, Cadillac had created a fourth category with their Thirty — a car of true quality but moderate in price and running costs. Both at the price and above, it had few contemporaries of comparable reputation and success. One Studebaker-produced car in the same price range became known as the "Every-Mechanical-Failure." Another manufacturer, Thomas, trading on its reputation, built a car selling for twice the price and virtually ruined itself honoring the warranty on defective cars. A third, Lozier, watched its own fortunes decline for five years, then set out in 1913 to recover them — with a car that used the four-cylinder Cadillac as its model.

During 1908, promoting their new six-cylinder, Pierce-Arrow generously admitted "the great and lasting merits of the four-cylinder." (They were still making some themselves.) "Well made cars of this type," they continued, "have wonderful possibilities of motoring accomplishments, both for city use and country touring; they are most satisfying and have all the possibilities of the six, save in very slight degree." This advertisement was probably drafted by Pierce-Arrow's chief

engineer, David Fergusson. Some years later he was more specific, for he wrote: "Cadillac for years had the reputation of producing the best medium-priced car in the world."

Overseas the four-cylinder was regarded as a worthy successor to earlier models, and the English observer, F. A. Talbot, stated that by 1912 the Thirty was already "an old favorite amongst British motorists . . . all the parts of this car are fashioned with precision and care . . . (it is) a homogeneous and silent whole."

More than fifty years later English historian Anthony Bird echoed this comment, remarking that the cars were "as refined and reliable as money could make them."

The company was therefore justified in saying that the Cadillac Thirty needed no fancy price tag to bolster its claim to be a car of world class, and they harped on it at every op-

The sumptuous interior of the 1913 Model Thirty Limousine.

portunity. They were unperturbed by the European propaganda campaign directed against the rising menace of the American automobile. In fact they met this criticism head on. A typical example is the following little lecture, printed in *The Saturday Evening Post* in 1910:

> We in America are sometimes accused of unduly acclaiming our own achievements. As a matter of fact we are singularly indifferent about our own accomplishments. We make a seven-days wonder of our engineering triumphs and then we forget them.
>
> In England they are still discussing the fact that a moderate-priced American car won the world's trophy for fine manufacturing two years ago. And in reality, that was an achievement worthwhile. That America should invade the Old World and give that Old World an object lesson in standardization was significant. It was significant because standardization means painstaking care, devotion to seemingly trivial details, measurements minute beyond optical perception — means in short the very things in which American manufacturers have been assumed by their Continental critics to be more or less shiftless. These qualities embodied in the Cadillac were a source of surprise abroad because they were scarcely expected in an American product.
>
> The subject has recently been revived by British technical writers and is of interest to every man who owns or contemplates owning an automobile. Any motor car which does not incorporate in greater or lesser degree the precise qualities which won for Cadillac the Dewar Trophy is not in the last analysis good value for the money it costs you.

In service the cars were building up a fine reputation for durability and reliability. During 1910 the factory commented that "we have yet to hear of the first broken crankshaft although a vast number of cars have seen more than a year's service," while later on they reported "recently we had occasion to examine the bearings of a car which had traveled 46,000 miles, yet the wear proved not to exceed the one-one-thousandth of an inch."

Nothing illustrates better the Thirty's longevity than some service records established under the particularly rugged conditions that existed in New Zealand. During 1911 a number of Thirties went into service with Newman Brothers, a renowned South Island coachline. Established in Nelson in 1879, the concern was making the changeover from horses to horsepower. In 1912 a Thirty made the first automobile journey from Nelson to Westport via the Buller Gorge. The same year a regular run was established and the cars made the round trip three times a week. "Motor Mail Coach" conversions were made, the chassis being lengthened and special bodies installed with extra rows of seats. This included a return to the old rear-tonneau-entrance style, but with a total load of ten passengers — not always the stated limit being observed either. Sometimes up to sixteen passengers were carried, with scores of mailbags and luggage. With luggage loaded on first — along running boards, between hood and guards, and even on top of the hood — the driver sometimes had to sit on top of parcels to get a clear view of the road. Passengers above the normal load had to sit on mudguards, on the luggage, and at the back on the folded top.

Rough roads, steep climbs, and frequent river crossings were normal; the cars were specially prepared for these river crossings, as they were sometimes all but submerged. Portable windlasses — known as "pull-me-outs"— were carried for hauling out stranded cars. Reliability, long life, and low running costs were paramount, for the time table was public, and the company private. The thrice-weekly round trip totaled 900 miles, or approximately 46,000 miles per year. In service for twelve years, each car clocked up more than half a million miles.

It is worthwhile at this point to review behind-the-scenes developments within the walls of the Cadillac plant during the era of the Thirty, and particularly to study the two Lelands, father and son, who were the major personalities.

The morale among the work force was high. Leland himself was regarded with admiration and affection by his close associates, with respect by responsible workmen, and with awe by the juniors and apprentices. To the latter he was a legendary figure whose experience seemed to stretch back almost to the beginnings of the machine age, certainly before many of them had been born. Though of an age when most men reserve their energy — or what is left of it — for retirement, hobbies, and grandchildren, he had the mental alertness and physical fitness of men twenty years younger in the prime of their careers. His endurance earned the respect of the toughest men on his payroll, as did his manual skill. Managing the great industrial organization which he had sustained in a new and increasingly competitive field, he could still enter any shop in the factory and produce work at the bench equal or superior to that done by the best employees. Even in his seventies, although his hearing was poor as it always had been, and he constantly had to wear spectacles, "his hands were still drawn to steel and machinery as if by a magnet," his sharp eyes could still read off the graduations on a micrometer barrel and detect the slightest variation. It was said he was "never seen without a micrometer in his hand." This, of course, is a figure of speech, but it is likely he carried one in his pocket and often used it. One celebrated instance was the occasion when he demonstrated to Alfred P. Sloan that Hyatt bearings, which the latter was selling, were inaccurately made. Sloan, then a young graduate engineer of about thirty, had to sit humbly in Leland's office watching the old man's beard wag at him as he emphasized the importance of sticking to tolerance.

In *Adventures of a White Collar Man*, Sloan described the incident: "Under Mr. Leland's brown hand with its broad thumb was a micrometer. He had measured the diameters of several specimen bearings. Then he had drawn lines and written down the variations from the agreed tolerances. . . . We discussed interchangeability of parts. A genuine conception of what mass production should mean really grew in me with that conversation."

Physically H.M. was a big man — over six feet tall, straight and broad shouldered. "In his rugged, masterful strength few men could measure up to him," wrote his secretary, John Bourne. "Only by his silvered hair would one think of the ripening of time. Nothing of age was suggested by his voice or manner. Vigor characterized all that he did. His skin was fresh, his eyes twin-

*On the road
with the Model Thirty.*

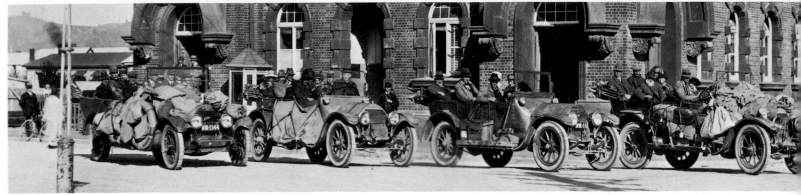

A quartet of Cadillacs in the Newman Service, outside the post office in Nelson, New Zealand, before embarking cross country, circa 1918.

kled. He walked and talked and thought rapidly."

Intensely human, Leland liked to mix with men and be one of them. He played no golf or other popular sports, but was the family champion at dominoes and lawn bowls, and occasionally a ball game appealed to him. He liked hearing and telling good, clean stories, had a nimble wit and a soul-satisfying laugh. Although a teetotaler and nonsmoker, he could sit serene and unannoyed through long meetings in dense tobacco smoke, though needless to say, these meetings were outside his own plant.

But H.M. was also a good hater. He always "carried his backbone around," and knew when and how to be severe. Always intolerant of blundering, carelessness and indifferent workmanship and thinking, he possessed the biblical hatred for some things, and his frown was "bleak as winter."

"When he opened the floodgates of his wrath," wrote John Bourne, "he swept up everything pertaining and poured it out in caustic denunciation," while L. D. Burlingam tut-tutted, "In spite of Leland's strong religious background and high ideals, he is somewhat free in using strong language and telling experiences of his life where such language has been applied."

Yet he was essentially a kind and gentle man, constantly visiting hospitals, giving to charities (sometimes as much as a third or even half his annual salary), paying the mortgage of an employee's widow, holding up businessmen while discussing the hopes and troubles of one of his shopmen. He even bailed an old bum out of jail, saying, "How would you like to spend the night in jail if you were eighty and had no friends?"

Leland worked on the principle that you should make it dif-

ficult for people to do things the wrong way. "He used to say that he would fire any man who had a file at his bench," said Le Roi J. Williams. "The parts had to be made so that they didn't require any file, and H.M. wouldn't tolerate the manufacture of any parts that had any burs or sharp points that a workman could cut his finger on."

"H.M. wasn't impressed by theories," continued Williams. "He was an apostle of direct experiment and in finding out whether or not things worked you must demonstrate their success. H.M. was one of the first to propose putting untried new models on the road for twenty-four hours — grueling road tests with cars loaded with sandbags and subjected to treatment and road conditions far beyond normal."

H.M. could be cryptic, as during the awarding of the Dewar Trophy in London when he was asked how Cadillac was able to manufacture cars with interchangeable parts. Williams recalled he answered that "it was a rather simple process, that you first of all had to know what you were going to do, and second you had to know how you wanted to do it, and thirdly you had to do it that way."

And he could be brutally blunt on the same subject, noting on another occasion, without mentioning names, that "I was in an assembly room once four times as large as the assembly room I had at the Cadillac factory, and they had five times as many people because 'they had fitters.' Fitters everywhere, and so many turned out fifteen engines when I was turning out 100. Five times as many men; four times as much room — and it was all due to poor tolerances. . . . Don't bother with fitters — you should get along without fitters. That is the trouble with the whole of

Europe today; labor is cheap — they make the parts and give them to fitters to fit together."

On "running-in" engines, Leland was equally scathing: "They don't know what their limits are. They said they run it with a belt for ten hours and then run it on its own power for thirty hours. Now I never started an engine on anything but its own power."

H.M. was always interested in the welfare of his workmen, whom he continued to call "his boys" even when they had served with him for several decades. "I still call them boys," he said on one occasion, "because they were not really much more than that when they came to us twenty years ago."

Plant conditions in the early days were primitive. Charlie Martens recalled that "We had no washrooms or lockers, no cafeterias, no canteens, no gum machines. We used to put our clothes on a long pole and hang them way up on a wall or post. We did have a medical department . . . sort of. [It] had a nurse and doctor."

The plain fact was that in the early days the company could not afford "luxuries," nor was it a period of workmen's amenities, smoking rooms, and the like. However, as the company prospered, conditions improved.

Leland was autocratic about some things — particularly liquor and tobacco — to an extent that would bring a plant out on strike today. "His moral concepts tolerated no compromise," recalls Ernest W. Seaholm. "Thus if caught smoking on the premises the penalty was a summary discharge."

In time, however, apparently influenced by the milder-tempered Wilfred, Leland's attitude in these areas became more flexible. Although intolerant of sloppy work, Leland was warm in his praise of a job well done. His reaction to the winning of the Dewar Trophy was typical. When the cup itself, a magnificent piece of silverwork of very high value, was sent over from England complete with engraved baseplate, Leland had it displayed in the factory for all to see. Each workman was given a small leaflet describing the test, with H.M.'s personal congratulations for making its success possible — the handshaking involved about a thousand men — and Leland told them, "The honor belongs equally to every honest, sincere, and conscientious member of this organization, no matter what his position."

"That was a day!" recalled Charlie Martens. "Everybody felt mighty proud when Mr. Leland displayed the trophy in the lobby."

Both Lelands were, according to members of the family, "typical New Englanders, who were practical men literally to their fingertips, yet appreciative of finer culture." Both had

Above, Newman Service Cadillacs; below, a Model Thirty from 1912.

traveled widely and Wilfred had been to Europe as early as 1896. Both kept thoroughbred horses and Henry enjoyed riding even when he was approaching seventy. Both were great readers and lovers of classical literature. The elder Leland remembered few quotations, although he liked to quote Macaulay's *Horatius*. Wilfred, however, had a prodigious memory in this regard, and his widow, Ottilie Leland, told this writer: "Wilfred had a memory that even Henry Ford admired, saying 'Wilfred had the figures at his fingertips.' He never used notes. He had a photographic mind. He could stand at a gift shop window and read a poem on a card, and then turn and repeat it to me. I was always amazed. He could recite 150 poems and was asked to recite at many parties — long, humorous ones, or long epics, or tiny gems about a brook or a flower. He was a charming speaker, like his father, although less forceful. He was a real gentleman of the old New England school in thought and manner, as was his father."

Both Lelands were public spirited men too, and H.M. was as well-known in local politics as he was in the engineering world. Both community interest and Cadillac's interest benefitted from one Leland project: the founding by H.M. in 1907 of the Cadillac School of Applied Mechanics. The growth of the industry was outstripping the supply of machinists, technicians, and toolmakers, and this was his answer. It was the first such school in the automobile industry and was another of the many ways in which he influenced the industrial development of his country. Trainees were given two years' grounding in all phases of machine work, automobile design and assembly, drafting, mathematics and metallurgy. An additional year on an advanced course was available (bringing the total hours of instruction to 9,000) provided the pupil continued with Cadillac for a further two years. Characteristically, Leland laid down as requirement Number One: "Students must be of good moral character."

While most of the graduates continued to work for Cadillac, others went to the Dodge Brothers, Hudson Motors, Studebaker Corporation, Ford and numerous machine shops in the Detroit area. The school's success was followed by the founding, nine years later, of the Ford Trade School, organized by S. E. Wilson, who had been an instructor at the Cadillac school. From then onward other major manufacturers adopted the idea.

Shortly after the Thirty was announced in 1908, a representative of General Motors, Arnold Goss, had called on the stockholders of Cadillac. He had been sent by William Crapo Durant to make an offer for the company.

Durant, born in 1860, was an automotive Napoleon. At the age

*The equestrian
Henry Martyn Leland, 1910.*

of twenty-five he had joined with Dallas Dort to form the Durant-Dort Carriage Company. In 1904 he bought and reorganized the Buick Motor Company. After an unsuccessful attempt to merge Buick, Maxwell-Briscoe, Ford, and Reo in 1908, he organized a new corporation in New York on September 16, 1908. Charles Eaton was the first president, Buick was its initial substance, and the incorporation involved no more than two thousand dollars. The company was known as General Motors.

Durant's aim was to combine into one large industrial organization a variety of makes covering the market from top to bottom, together with the associated suppliers of all components and accessories. Although this in principle, to some extent, had already been put into practice — unsuccessfully — by the Pope organization, it was a remarkably farsighted view for 1908, anticipating much of the corporate development of later decades. Durant, however, had some serious personal weaknesses, summarized by Alfred Sloan as "the ability to create but not administer." These were to bring trouble within a few years. In 1908, however, he was riding high.

Already in control of Buick, Durant next acquired Oldsmobile, then turned his eyes on Cadillac. He wanted Cadillac first because it was a very sound company promising profitable operation and secondly because it produced a car of superior quality.

Provided they could show a profit, the major stockholders at Cadillac were interested in selling out, for their experience in the new automobile business had been hectic, strange, and anxious. Naming Wilfred Leland as negotiator, they set a price of $3,500,000. After consultation with Durant, Goss returned the next day with a bid for $3,000,000. Wilfred stuck to his price and insisted on cash. Since Durant operated on equities and stock issues, he was unable to find the money and the deal fell through.

Six months later, however, Goss returned to reopen negotiations. By now, with the aura of the Dewar Trophy adding to the standing of the company, and sales of the Thirty surpassing all previous figures and bringing substantial profits, the stockholders instructed Wilfred to up the price to $4,125,000, and limit the offer to ten days.

For the second time Durant had to let the option pass. However, Goss again returned — this time Wilfred met him with a figure of $4,500,000. By now delays had already cost Durant a million dollars, and had brought him no nearer control, so he reputedly accepted the Leland quotation: "cash on the line within ten days." It was Buick who had to foot the bill. The full purchase price, actually $5,669,250, was paid for by Buick in return for GM preferred stock to the value of $5,169,200, only the

remaining $500,000 being cash. The transfer went through on July 29, 1909, and it was the largest financial transaction that had occurred on the Detroit stock exchange up to that time.

In the transfer papers the net value of the whole organization was assessed at $2,868,709. The remaining $1,800,000 represented the good will built up by a company that Arthur Pound sums up as "well managed, highly prosperous, financially conservative and of unquestioned eminence in the automobile world." Far from paying too high a price, Durant had a bargain buy. Although the company was capitalized at $1,500,000, well over a million had simply been plowing back of profits. Only $327,000 in cash had gone into the company. The report of August 31, 1909, listed net earnings for the year as $1,969,382. Three dividends totaling $45 had been paid separately in May and June, 1909, and the stockholders received $300 per share on the sale of stock.

"Actually the company was a tremendous bargain which only William Durant appreciated," comment Henry Leland's biographers. "A concern that earned almost two million a year was not over-priced at four and a half million."

Since Cadillac continued to earn at this rate and above for the next ten months, returning to General Motors an additional two million dollars, Durant had every reason to feel pleased with himself. And in addition, he had obtained the continuing services of the men who had made such earnings possible. The latter, however, had not been possible without a further concession by Durant.

Immediately after the transaction had taken place, Durant had called the Lelands to the Russell House in Detroit, where he was staying, and asked them to continue as managers of Cadillac. The Leland reply was that their standards and principles mattered more to them than any other consideration. If they could continue to run the company as they had in the past, all would be well, but if their ideas were going to be compromised they wanted no part of it.

Durant readily nodded his assent, saying, "That is exactly what I want. I want you to continue to run Cadillac exactly as though it were your own. You will receive no directions from anyone."

Thus, having sold Cadillac on their own terms, the Lelands returned to it, again on their own terms. The advantages of membership in General Motors, an assured market position in their chosen field, mutual benefits with associated companies — all were to become obvious to Cadillac in later years. But at the time there were more problems than benefits.

For all his business flair, salesmanship, and confidence, Durant

Wilfred Leland.

moved too far and too fast. He was temperamentally a gambler and acquired too many companies too soon. This required overcapitalization, and Durant and General Motors was soon at the mercy of the bankers. When loans were called, some constituent companies proved worthless and the others could not earn sufficient income to carry their debts. Buick, for instance, in 1910 owed $7,000,000 to the First Bank of Boston, and Durant's bank loans as a whole had been overextended by about $12,000,000. Cadillac's part in this period deserves some comment.

Since Buick had been the cornerstone of GM, the bankers were in favor of rescuing Buick, if possible, and winding up General Motors if necessary. However, they reckoned without Wilfred Leland. He was usually content in his father's shadow, but at this critical time the elder Leland, reassured by Durant that banks would come through with the necessary credit, had gone overseas for a tour of the automobile plants on the Continent. Wilfred decided to take a firm stand on his own.

Twenty-two bankers had assembled in the Chase National Bank in New York in September, 1910, and had agreed that they would neither grant any new loans nor extend any existing loans to General Motors for a single day. They had lost faith in both Durant and his corporation. And they questioned the treasurer of Cadillac closely about his company's affairs. Wilfred remonstrated with them vigorously. "Father was in Europe," he said later, "and I did my best to save his reputation and our company."

A committee was appointed that afternoon by the bankers for the purpose of deciding nothing less than whether or not to dissolve General Motors. It met that evening at eight o'clock in the old Belmont Hotel. Wilfred's spirited performance earlier that day had impressed the bankers, and he was invited to put his case for GM in front of the committee that night.

For several hours the younger Leland argued with the group of hard-headed financiers who had already made up their minds to cut their losses. Quietly he recounted the triumphs of Cadillac, technical and financial, its secure position and reputation — now worldwide — the integrity and genius of his father, and the determination and ability of the Leland organization to imbue the whole of General Motors Corporation with similar success — provided they were given the opportunity. He had no doubt that the bankers' investment would be retrieved and large profits made within a few years.

The committee chairman, a Chicago banker named Ralph van Vechten, was the first to be convinced, and by 2:30 A.M. Wilfred

Leland had won the rest over.

However, because the bankers distrusted Durant, the terms were stiff. General Motors received $12,000,000 in cash, but had to repay $15,000,000 at six percent interest, the bankers took $6,000,000 in General Motors' stock, and Durant was compelled to withdraw from active management. He was to return again dramatically five years later.

James J. Storrow of Boston succeeded Durant as president of General Motors and was followed by Thomas Neal, a Detroit businessman. These men vigorously overhauled the corporation's finance and organization, leaning heavily on Wilfred Leland. Henry M. Leland, on his return from Europe, went through the engineering side of GM, raising efficiency and standards. In H.M.'s office, either the old man or a deputy was always on call, twenty-four hours a day.

In the rebuilding process, the Lelands imparted to the other GM units their methods and techniques, either personally or through their key associates. H.M.'s foundry superintendent, Joe Wilson, sorted out Buick's foundry problems, while his factory superintendent, Walter Phipps, advised Oakland and Buick on production. Ernest Sweet, Leland's most capable engineer, made frequent trips through the other companies, advising, guiding, and reporting back to Henry. Charles Oostdyke, Wilfred's purchasing agent at Cadillac, was appointed purchasing agent over all GM divisions. Henry Leland himself personally taught the key machinists to use precision gauges and instructed them in inspection and testing methods. Charles Nash and Walter Chrysler, then at Buick but later to found their own companies, spent weekends at the Leland country home discussing manufacturing problems. H.M. even visited the Fisher Body Plant, recommended a change to metal-paneled bodies and other improvements, and placed an unheard-of order for 150 units to start off quantity production of closed bodies — a new development in this field. Thus General Motors was carried through its most critical period, on the shoulders of Buick, with Cadillac as the "head."

Since Alfred P. Sloan has stated that Buick and Cadillac were the "substance" of the original General Motors, and since Cadillac was the only solvent member of the corporation, had probably the best management, and certainly the finest engineers, it is clear that Cadillac's role was decisive. This corporate achievement, hard on the technical triumphs of 1908, would have provided sufficient laurels for most companies, but Cadillac engineers were already preparing for other far-reaching mechanical advancements.

CHAPTER FIVE

KETTERING AND THE SELF-STARTER

A new face, a brilliant breakthrough, and another Dewar Trophy is won

In the waning years of the twentieth century's first decade, Cadillac engineers started on two exciting new trails that were to lead them for the second time to the Dewar Trophy. Actually the path they would follow was already well-trod, and even with Cadillac there were two separate approaches, one within the factory and one without. These parallel courses eventually merged, bringing in a man whose influence on Cadillac and General Motors was to rival that of Henry M. Leland himself — Charles Franklin Kettering.

Kettering's association with Cadillac actually had begun before the introduction of the famous self-starter, and in the electrical field at that. Born in Ohio in 1876, Kettering had graduated from the state university with degrees in mechanical and electrical engineering. He first engaged in telephone work, then joined National Cash Register, taking charge of the "Inventions 3" department, where he first developed the OK Charge Phone, a system which combined the cash register with a telephone and a magnetic stamping device. This was used in department stores to authorize charge sales from the central credit department to the various counters, greatly increasing sales of cash registers. Kettering's next step was to electrify the operation of the cash register itself, eliminating the hand crank, which needed two turns to ring up even five cents. The problems were not easily solved, for the motor had to be small, and since it was operating a counting mechanism, had to be stopped at exactly the right point. But Kettering produced, in 1905, a small "overload" motor, with a roller-type overrunning clutch timed to engage and release the cash register mechanism as required. He followed this with a simple spring-operated cash register in which the closing drawer reset the spring.

These and other inventions greatly broadened National Cash Register's sales, but by about 1908 Kettering decided the automobile business was becoming far more interesting. His assistant, W. A. Chryst, noted in his diary on August 10, "CFK full of auto ignition project."

Earl Howard, whom Kettering had met at National Cash Register, had joined Cadillac as assistant sales manager. Visiting Kettering one Sunday, Howard told him of Cadillac's dissatisfaction with existing auto ignitions and suggested that it would be a worthwhile field to explore.

On July 23, 1908, Kettering sketched out a simple coil ignition system, dated it and had it witnessed by B. A. Orrd and P. M. Lincoln. It was a very crude sketch, because it showed only a battery in a primary circuit, with an induction core winding and a holding relay. The secondary circuit showed a condenser and the plug points — nothing more. Actually a timing device was necessary, and for engines of more than one cylinder, a commutator or distributor also. These units were already in use in other ignition systems, while the battery and induction coil principle was even older than the automobile industry. The condenser principle had been tried by the Holley Brothers in 1906. What, then, was so special about Kettering's "new ignition"?

The key feature, it seems, was the ignition relay, which was a sophisticated vibrator. The four induction coils — one per cylinder — were connected in series through a single master vibrator, separate vibrator coil units being eliminated. The coils, in fact, were considered a single unit, being embedded in a heat-resistant insulant compound and unitized in an armored steel box.

The vibrator operated for starting. The holding coil kept the

The electric self-starter, which first appeared
on the 1912 Cadillac, was born in the
humble surroundings of an Ohio workshop,
the Dayton Engineering Laboratories Company,
developed by one Charles F. Kettering.
After the announcement of it as standard equipment
Cadillac lost no time in advertising
as, per the sample at right, "The Car That Has
No Crank." Charles Kettering's device
was destined to set in motion an entirely
new approach among manufacturers, and
by 1916 ninety-eight percent of American cars in
production would feature electric starters.
The acronym for the small Ohio shop, "Delco,"
would soon become a familiar one that would
rival the renown of its progenitor as a world
standard. In France it soon became usual
to call any battery ignition "Le
Delco," whether it had originated at
Cadillac, in the United States, or anywhere else.

The CAR
THAT HAS NO CRANK

contacts open after separation, and only a single spark occurred for each operation of the breaker contacts. The condenser absorbed induced primary current and discharged instantaneously back to the coil. This assisted in collapsing the magnetic field and produced a much higher secondary voltage with a much hotter spark. At the same time it eliminated the undesirable effect of this higher voltage — arcing at the points — by acting as a reservoir for the induced primary current. These characteristics produced better spark intensity and timing, the elimination of the destructive arc at the contacts, and a greatly extended life for the dry-cell batteries, and made necessary only one adjustment at the master vibrator instead of four at the coils.

Much of the developmental work was done in a converted barn at the home of E. A. Deeds, who had brought Kettering into National Cash Register. When the ignition system showed promise, Deeds wrote to Henry Leland about it, and Kettering followed this with visits to the factory. Shortly afterward, Leland telegraphed that he was sending Ernest Sweet to look into Kettering's ignition.

Meeting Sweet at the railroad depot the next morning, Kettering and Deeds took him around the hills south of Dayton with their test car, Kettering's own Cadillac roadster. During an all-day session, Sweet drove the car and put it through every road test he could think of to try the ignition. It performed literally without a miss, and the Cadillac engineer went back to Detroit with a favorable report.

It might have been less favorable had Sweet known what happened just after his train had left the depot. Kettering and Deeds returned to the car and couldn't start it. They found a broken ignition wire — and breathed sighs of relief that it happened no earlier!

Sweet's report to the boss was followed by negotiations between Dayton and Detroit, and in July, 1909, Leland asked Kettering and Deeds to call and discuss a contract to supply Cadillac with enough ignition sets for a full year of production. This meant some 8,000 units, and for a moment the two men felt they had bitten off more than they could chew. They had no manufacturing facilities. They had considered themselves researchers and had named their organization Dayton Engineer-

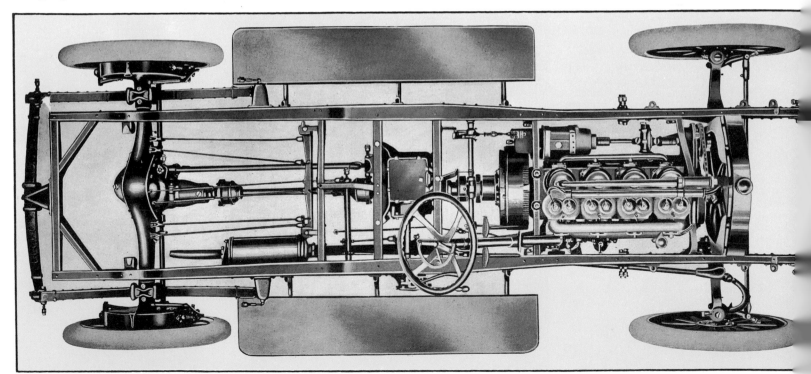

ing Laboratories Company — or DELCO, which was to become its famous acronym. But they knew that Leland's offer was a golden opportunity, so they decided to sign the contract on the spot and worry about how to fill its requirements later.

As they left Cadillac, dazed at what they had let themselves in for, Kettering took the contract out of his pocket and offered it to Deeds, saying, "Here, you take it, I don't want it." Deeds, however, was just as determined to leave it with Kettering.

Uncertain how they were going to manufacture 8,000 ignition sets, they approached J. B. Edwards, president of Kellogg Switchboard and Supply Company of Chicago. Kettering had known Edwards from his telephone and OK Charge Phone days, and Kellogg had assisted him in his ignition research. Edwards put their minds at ease by undertaking to make the requisite number of sets for Cadillac, using the abbreviation to call it the "Delco ignition system."

The Delco acronym had been suggested by Bill Chryst. It was a simple idea, used as well by companies such as Deaco and Aplco, the latter founded by a former Delco employee, Vincent G. Apple, but none were to attain the fame and success of Delco.

The 1914 Cadillac chassis, on the facing page, illustrates the Delco self-starter mounted to the left of the engine block. Note that right-hand drive is still retained. Above, a factory photograph of "a striking test: a four-cylinder Cadillac car, with twelve passengers, being propelled round a room by its self-starter."

In fact, "*Le Delco*" has become a French synonym for all automobile electrics — regardless of make.

Kettering resigned from National Cash Register and devoted all his time to correction of faults that began to show up in Delco ignition when a number of installations made on various Cadillacs were extensively tested by the factory. Despite Sweet's and Leland's enthusiasm, the "not-invented-here" factor colored Cadillac engineers' attitudes at first, and they did their best to fault "the Delco." Leland, although convinced and committed, still insisted on many detail improvements. In addition, malfunctions began to occur. This was a trying period for Kettering, but his ability to track down and eliminate the cause of various problems, his drive and energy — and his wit — soon overcame the problems.

Typical difficulties were misfiring on cold engines and sticky relays. The first was cured by reversing the polarity of the induction coil — connecting the positive high-tension lead to the plugs instead of the negative as had been occurring. "Before that, no one knew that it made any difference which polarity was used," comments Kettering's biographer.

The second trouble was finally traced by accident. Unable to analyze the cause after a day of testing at Cadillac, Kettering took some relays with him on the midnight train to Dayton. Worried and unable to sleep, he felt one of the relays in the dark — and discovered that the core end was slightly rounded. This, he realized, would concentrate the magnetic pull and cause sticking. When the relay poles were machined flat the trouble vanished.

Another "problem" turned out to be trickery, and was traced to magneto interests who were attempting to discredit Delco ignition. A Pittsburgh dealer demonstrated that with the engine running on "magneto" switch, the car would easily climb a test hill. On "coil," the car stalled. Even Leland was disturbed at this demonstration, until Kettering proved that the driver had merely taken advantage of the characteristics of the Cadillac air-valve carburetor. When on magneto he had opened the throttle gradually and the carburetion was satisfactory, but when on coil, he had surreptitiously snapped the throttle open quickly, upset the carburetion, and stalled the engine.

The new Delco was announced as standard on the Cadillac Thirty for the 1910 model year. It did not supplant the magneto, but was used in conjunction with it, giving two complete and independent systems. The car could operate on either, although the company evidently considered Delco the normal system, with the low-tension magneto as a reserve. In their shop and owners' manuals, Delco was treated at length, while the magneto was discussed only briefly. Citing the Delco catalogue, they emphasized the "practicability and reliability" of the unit as "far beyond what has ever been done before in automobile ignition. . . . We have had in mind the man who owns the car, drives for pleasure, and has neither the time nor the inclination to be continually 'fixing' any part of the car. . . . (1) It stops all sparking at the primary contacts. A pair of contacts should last years without attention or renewal. (2) It will run 2,000 miles on six dry cells. No storage batteries are required. (3) It stops all sparking at the commutator and is the only system that does. The usual commutator troubles will not occur. (4) It will not require the constant adjustment necessary with other systems. There is but one moving part and one simple adjustment no more than once a year. Sets have been run 20,000 miles without a single adjustment. (5) It makes but one spark for each explosion, a good spark, at exactly the right time. The timing is equal to any magneto and the spark is the same at all speeds. (6) It removes everything from the dash but the switch, greatly improving appearance. (7) It stops switch troubles and is equipped with a lock to prevent theft."

These claims were quoted from Delco's own catalogue, but after some months of field service, Cadillac themselves wrote, cautiously but optimistically: "Cadillac users have been more than delighted with their experiences and we have yet to discover any reason why we cannot concur in the representations made by the makers as to the advantage of the system."

At that time the majority of makes favored the high-tension magneto, and continued to do so for another five years in the United States alone. However, the first blow against the magneto had been struck. Preparations were now being made for a second blow, which was to prove fatal — the self-starter.

The development of the self-starter at Cadillac "started" with a well-documented incident in the winter of 1910.

The event took place on one of the old wooden bridges on Belle Isle in the Detroit River. A woman (whose name seems lost to history) stalled her Cadillac and had difficulty restarting it. Across the bridge at that moment came an associate of H. M. Leland, a fellow industrialist. He cranked the car for her, but she forgot to retard the spark, the engine backfired, the crank flew off, and the man was seriously injured. Next on the scene, within minutes, appeared another car carrying Cadillac engineers Ernest Sweet and Bill Foltz. They started the woman's car and left with the injured man. Unfortunately his severe injuries developed complications and he died a few weeks later.

The deceased was a friend of H. M. Leland, and the fact that

In September, 1912, Cadillac entered the 2000-mile road phases of the Royal Automobile Club test which would result in their second Dewar Trophy Award the following year. At the R.A.C. garage (below), officials have checked the voltage of the battery and the current consumption of all lamps. The Cadillac is about to begin the first of twelve day-long runs, this one of 170 miles. F. S. Bennett stands proudly at the side of his car. Note glass bonnet panel, allowing a view of the engine.

On the facing page the Cadillac pays a toll on its last day out. Symbolizing its electrical propensity is a miniature Cadillac with battery and starter, holding W. C. Leland, Jr. and his cousin.

the vehicle responsible for his death was a Cadillac added to Leland's grief over the incident. He even told Ernest Sweet that he was "sorry he had ever built an automobile." Recovering his composure, however, Leland called a special conference of engineers: Johnson, Sweet, Lyle Schnell, Fred Hawes, Herman Schwarze, D. T. Randall, Herman Zannoth, and R. T. Wingo. Still visibly affected, H.M. announced that a substitute for the crank handle must be found. The project must take priority over all others. He concluded: "The Cadillac car will kill no more men if we can help it."

Various self-starters had been tried on automobiles in the early years of the century — mechanical, pneumatic, electric — including the Prestolite system which filled the cylinders with combustible gas. None worked well. All were inefficient, complicated, unreliable, and bulky. A light, efficient, reliable starter was required, and a suitable heavy-duty storage battery to operate it. Also needed was a sound arrangement for keeping the battery charged under the variable speeds inherent in automobile use.

When Leland set his engineers to the problem, they investigated all previous attempts. They concluded that an electric

motor was the answer, with a starter motor and generator combined in one unit. However, they began with a flywheel-type motor generator on the Diehl principle, in which the engine flywheel of the car was wound to form the armature of the motor and the drive was direct onto the crankshaft, giving a ratio of one to one. This was bulky and inefficient, and at this point Kettering was invited to take a hand.

There has been some controversy about this phase of Cadillac history in recent years, so it may be illuminating to consider the comments of Benjamin H. Anibal, later chief engineer of Cadillac. Anibal was born in Linden, Michigan, and studied engineering at Michigan State University (then Michigan Agricultural and Technical College). Graduating with an M.E. degree in 1908, he worked at Oldsmobile in 1909-1910 before coming to Cadillac. He recalled:

At the time I started with Cadillac, the engineering organization setup was somewhat as follows: The top man, who had his finger on everything was, of course, Henry M. Leland, a great mechanical engineer. I looked on him as my old schoolmaster. E. E. Sweet was the director of engineering and handled most

engineering assignments between the Lelands and the engineering department. He relayed all the information direct to and from the Lelands and technically . . . the final decisions came from the real big boss, Mr. Leland. . . . Fred Hawes was chief engineer under Sweet. Fred was a very fine gentleman and eminently qualified for the post. Frank Johnson had charge of engineering the engine, transmission, clutch, and control items that went with these units. Lyle K. Schnell had charge of chassis, which included the frame, rear and front axles, spring suspension, steering, etc. The experimental department was directed by Dwight Randall, and under Randall as foreman of the experimental department and dyno testing was F. M. Holden. He had a Michigan B. Sc. degree (1908). There was also an engineer in charge of the body program, Roy Milner.

The electrical engineering came under the factory. The general setup was supervised by Walter McKechnie, and he had two associates, Herman Schwarze, who handled the car engineering end of the program, and Herman Zannoth, who looked after all the factory electrical engineering.

Schwarze was very closely associated with Boss Ket during the early development, both as regards size and manufacturing of the original starter setup for Cadillac. I had some very interesting contacts with Boss Ket during my early years at Cadillac as I handled most of the design work for Frank

Johnson and had a drawing table in Frank's office. Ket, naturally, during his many, many trips to Cadillac, would contact Johnson in connection with engineering problems relating to starting. I remember that he was instrumental in selling Johnson on the idea of developing and building experimental six-cylinder engines, which were built and tested before the V-8 came into being.

I started as a draftsman in the Cadillac engineering department the day after Labor Day, 1911. The 1912 Cadillac, which was equipped with a Dayton Engineering Laboratories starter, was just starting production about the time I started my association with Cadillac engineering.

During the Fall of 1911, I had many contacts with Mr. Kettering due to doing certain layout work in conjunction with some necessary changes in starter controls, etc. My recollection of the first starter of the Cadillac engine . . . was that Cadillac had for test purposes one car equipped with what was known at the time as a flywheel starter. It was a series motor built in to the flywheel and provided a ratio of one-to-one torque in turning over the crankshaft of the engine. It did not prove at all satisfactory, other than [that] it was able to crank over and start the engine under certain temperature conditions. In other temperature conditions the starting motor was inadequate. It did not have enough torque. . . . Kettering had also given some consideration to this starter, but had already discovered its in-

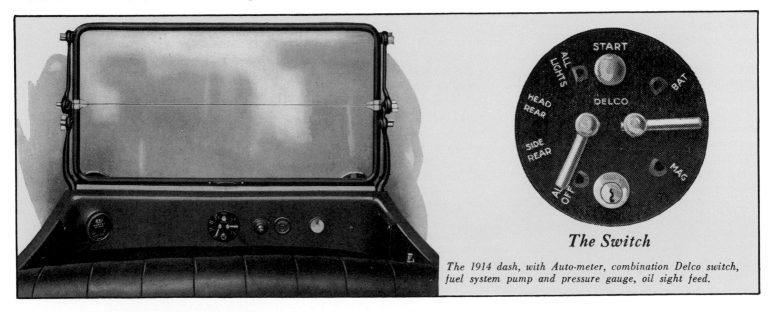

The Switch

The 1914 dash, with Auto-meter, combination Delco switch, fuel system pump and pressure gauge, oil sight feed.

herent lack of torque. It was not given serious consideration by Delco.

However, he did present to Cadillac engineering management his ideas of how a starting motor could be rigged to work and start an engine successfully. That was the layout applied to the 1912 Cadillac, a combination starting motor and generator equipped with the necessary overrunning clutch and reduction gear and teeth on the flywheel to provide a reduction, as I remember, of about 20 or 25 to 1, between the starting motor and the crankshaft. This allowed enough build-up in power to crank the engine successfully and start it successfully at any temperature, probably as low as zero degrees. . . . It is my understanding that Mr. Kettering and his group working in Dayton developed the system in its entirety on the 1912 Cadillac. The system consisted of many, many other details necessary to make [it] work.

Kettering and his Delco group started work in 1910. In a letter to J. B. Hayward, November 15, 1910, Kettering wrote: "After thoroughly investigating the subject, we decided to abandon the flywheel-type generator and to make some other form which would be attached to the motor the same as is customary with magnetos." This was to retain the motor generator principle. Later he wrote: "One thing stumped us at first and that was how to arrange for the two-gear ratio — one to drive the motor for cranking the car at slow speed and the other for charging the battery by the generator, after the engine got running. When once we got that worked out, the rest came pretty easy."

"That" was "worked out" simply by obtaining a license agreement with Clyde J. Coleman, who had been working on starter inventions since 1899. He licensed his two-gear ratio patent to Delco. Who was responsible for "the rest" is the center of the dispute. Kettering's own statements, his biographer T. A. Boyd, and his associates Zerbe C. Bradford and Lewis B. Case, all state that the starter as an operative unit was developed by Kettering's group and supplied to Cadillac, who after tests adopted it as a standard item. As can be seen from earlier quotations, this version is supported by Anibal, who was then in Cadillac employ. Anibal's version is also backed by Ernest Seaholm. Although not employed at Cadillac until two years after the adoption of the self-starter, Seaholm knew Anibal, Johnson, and Kettering, as well as others who were there at the time of the self-starter's introduction. Later, as chief engineer, Seaholm had access to all engineering records. Finally, in published advertisements, Kettering was given credit by Henry Leland himself: in *The Saturday Evening Post* for September 7, 1912, the Cadillac company

advertised "The simple, centralized, Delco system of starting, igniting, and lighting." And in an interview by W. A. P. John in 1921, Leland confirmed this version.

The opposite view has been presented by Mrs. Wilfred Leland, who after many years of patient research produced a first-class biography of H. M. Leland. She quotes her late husband; Frank Johnson, along with Clair Owen; Charles Martens; and Christy Borth, to the effect that the starter was developed at Cadillac via H. M. Leland, who thereupon gave Kettering a contract to manufacture 5,000 starters. Mrs. Leland also states that her husband's version of the story, as stated above, was confirmed by Kettering in a letter dated May 24, 1946.

Mrs. Leland's version not only challenges the generally accepted view, including that of the United States Patent Office, but also raises the whole question of Kettering's participation. If

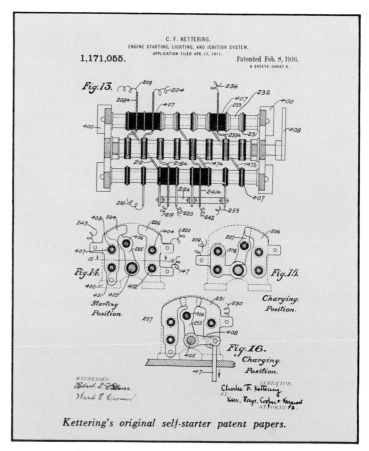

Kettering's original self-starter patent papers.

Cadillac had already produced a satisfactory unit, why was Kettering brought in at all? A number of reasons are given. First, GM refused to allocate funds for the manufacture of the starter. Calling on Kettering's aid was Leland's way around the roadblock. But it is doubtful that Delco had the facilities to carry out this manufacture on their own at this time. We have already seen that only a year earlier, when the Delco ignition contract was awarded, Kettering and Deeds virtually panicked because they had no plant! Even in 1911 much of their work was done by virtue of a subcontract.

A second reason given is that the Cadillac motor was "too big" and Kettering was asked to produce something smaller. This itself tends to confirm the Delco version as stated by B. H. Anibal. And, as we have seen, the all-essential two-ratio geartrain feature was of neither Cadillac nor Delco origin, but had come to Cadillac via Delco. This also tends to confirm the Delco version of the origin of the starter.

Actually the whole episode has polarized around only one major feature — the self-starter. There were really three prime functions of the Delco system, all of them extremely important: starting, ignition, and lighting. It is significant that Mrs. Leland's version freely grants Kettering credit for the second and third of these items. Mrs. Leland writes that "only the lighting and ignition were added to the Cadillac starter."

Even the most careful examination, weighing both sides, must attempt to reconcile contradictory statements made by the best authorities. History tends to favor the Delco story. It seems that the version of Mrs. Leland seeks credit for initial unsuccessful research, whereas the Delco claim rests on an undeniably successful product with excessive Kettering emphasis, resented perhaps by Cadillac engineers who had initiated original development.

The starter itself was covered by the two patent applications Kettering made during its development on April 17 and June 15, 1911, resulting in patent numbers 1,150,523 and 1,171,055, issued on August 17, 1915, and February 8, 1916.

Principal components were a motor generator and a 6-24 volt storage battery. The motor generator was a double-wound single unit operating on twenty-four volts as a starter motor and six volts as a generator for charging the battery. This required a series-parallel switching arrangement. The battery had twelve cells in three units of four each.

Mechanical arrangements comprised three assemblies: (1) a reduction gear-train movable axially, and a friction roller clutch at the rear of the motor generator; (2) a similar clutch on the

LAST OF THE FOURS: 1914

Swing-away steering wheels were thought to be original when Ford introduced them on the Thunderbird, but Cadillac predated their idea by over half a century, witness this 1914 hinged unit.

front of the motor generator, linking the generator to its driving shaft from the engine timing gears; (3) a controller, mechanically operated by a linkage which connected it with the starter pedal.

Operation was as follows: with the ignition switch "on," the circuit comprised a battery and shunt generator, operating as a six-volt motor, turning slowly. Depressing the starter pedal shifted (via the controller) the reduction gears into mesh with the teeth cut on the flywheel rim. At the same time the controller changed the electrical connections over from the six-volt circuit to the high torque twenty-four-volt series motor, cranking the engine. When the pedal was released the starting gears moved back out of mesh, and the controller returned, switching to the six-volt position. The motor generator was then driven by the engine as a six-volt generator — charging the battery and supplying current for ignition and lighting — with the battery "floating on the line."

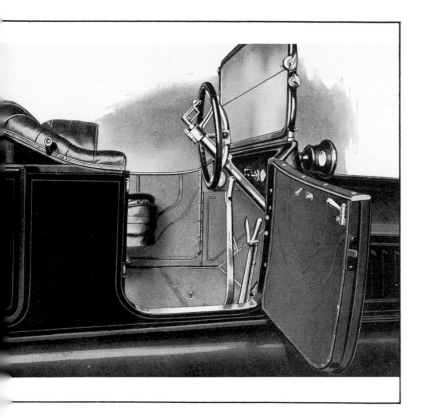

As mentioned earlier, the key feature in the success of automobile storage batteries was efficient regulation of the input charge. Here there can be no doubt about its introduction. Others had tried to regulate the input charge by variable-speed drives, slipping clutches, and even in one case a reservoir of battery acid and a hydrometer on the dashboard so the driver would know when to disconnect his dynamo! Kettering regulated current output by two means. An ampere-hour meter registered both the charge into and current draw from the battery and controlled contacts which cut a resistance into the field shunt or opened the shunt completely. Furthermore, the "differential compound" winding on the field meant that the series coil assisted the shunt for starting, but opposed it when the machine functioned as a generator.

Citing its "historical importance," Herbert Towle in the *Automobile Trade Journal* wrote that "the first commercial application of the variable-speed, regulated output principle was the Delco motor generator, first applied to the 1912 Cadillac late in 1911. Except for Delco, starting equipment came a year or two after the first lighting generators."

From the time of Benjamin Franklin, Americans had made notable contributions to electrical discovery. Joseph Henry and Dr. Page had provided, in the discovery of electromagnetic induction and the high-tension coil, much of the basis of electrical work that followed. The earliest American automobile pioneers also made contributions — Duryea and Haynes-Apperson with the dynamo-battery ignition even before 1900; Vincent Apple (later at Delco), who in 1908 used a dynamo and storage battery "floating on the line"; Homer Motzinger, who supplied his "autosparker" to Panhard et Levassor; Elmore with electric side and taillights in 1901; the Remy brothers with an advanced dynamo and storage-battery system before 1900; Olds and Packard with automatic spark advance around 1901; and Atwater Kent with his "spark generator" of 1905. But until the Delco system, America could not claim leadership over Europe.

The achievements of Kettering in 1910-1912 changed the position completely, and recognition in Europe was swift, at both academic and practical levels. After a test of a standard Cadillac involving 1,000 stops and starts using the electric starter in July of 1912, the Royal Automobile Club of Great Britain in 1913 awarded the Dewar Trophy for the second time to Cadillac — the only car up to then that had achieved the double distinction. In 1913 the Lanchester Company, renowned as one of Britain's most advanced technical organizations, adopted the Delco system. By 1916, ninety-eight percent of American models in production featured electric starting, and the trend became apparent in Europe after the war's end. Marc Birkigt, chief engineer of Hispano-Suiza and himself an electrical specialist, called "Le Delco" the "new thought," and standardized it on his cars. Robert Bosch's biographer later commented that magneto ignition appeared to be on the way out because "the Americans had abandoned magnetos and gone back to a very much more highly perfected battery-ignition system."

Actually, of course, most of the essential features were already there, pioneered by others before Kettering began his work. This fact, which is common to most technological advancements, has been used to "disprove" Kettering and Cadillac claims in this area. Some French claims have been put forward, but an interesting comment in this connection is made by Alec Ulmann: "It is the firm belief by all in France that a battery ignition can be collectively referred to as 'Le Delco'. . . . It makes no difference whether the ignition system is by any other make, the

French insist that it is the 'Delco' and that is that."

No debunker, however clever his research, can explain why the general revolution so closely followed the Cadillac announcement, rather than coming earlier; why no other system contained *all* the necessary features as early as Kettering's *and* as standard equipment; and why a European technical committee, sitting *at the time*, should have awarded an American firm the palm. Even though Kettering soon modified the Delco system, and others improved on it, introducing superior principles, the 1912 Cadillac marked a turning point in automobile design comparable with the advances made ten and twenty years earlier by Levassor and Maybach. For the first time, the automobile had a total electrical system.

The period of Delco innovations also saw interesting body and chassis developments at Cadillac. The most notable of these was the introduction of the closed body as a standard catalogue listing in 1910 and the introduction in 1914 of the short-lived two-speed rear axle. The former was much the more important, but the latter was technically interesting and had some extramural repercussions, and so deserves discussion too.

Closed bodies were not originated by Cadillac — there had been previous examples on both sides of the Atlantic — but the 1910 Cadillacs, it appears, could be bought off the dealer's floor complete with body — they did not need to be specially built to order.

The first closed body Cadillac was the Osceola-type coupé, which was offered in both single- and four-cylinder models in 1906. The same year, as mentioned in the previous chapter, the Model L limousine with roofed and screened driver compartment and fully enclosed rear compartment was available. By 1907 there was a Model H limousine at a considerably lower price — $3,600 — and by 1908, the Model G limousine appeared at $3,000. Standard finish of the G runabout was French gray with fine red striping and red leather upholstery. The G touring had a dark blue body with fine primrose (cream) striping, and wheels and axles in primrose with dark blue stripe. An option was Brewster Green body with red wheels and dark green striping. The G limousine had dark blue body panels with remainder in black, and dark blue running gear — a conservative ensemble for a formal car. The owner's compartment upholstery was in goatskin, with satin-trimmed ceiling. There were a speaking tube and an electric dome light. The chauffeur had to be content with black leather.

The Model H touring had a Brewster Green body, no striping and Brewster Green running gear with light striping, with an op-

tion of red running gear with dark green striping. The H limousine had a Brewster Green body with black trimmings and Brewster Green running gear with light striping. These styles were similar to the Model L, but a definite attempt was being made to bring down the cost. The first year's production of Thirty models seems to have been limited to open cars and touring top models, but in 1910 a limousine Thirty appeared with a style based on the previous L and H designs, but improved by having more glass and door area, which the increased wheelbase allowed. The price, however, remained at $3,000.

Prior to 1910, Cadillac closed bodies had been built by Seavers and Erdman, in a plant on Detroit's Jefferson Avenue. These bodies were all wood-paneled, but were soon supplanted by metal-paneled bodies, at first of aluminum, and later of steel. Henry Leland had foreseen the advantage of metal bodies, and eventually got Cadillac changed over to this practice. At first he had to overcome the resistance of Charles Nash, then head of Buick and very influential in General Motors policy. There were also technical difficulties with the construction of the bodies themselves, and both Lelands had to spend much time in the body plants solving construction problems in collaboration with the body builders.

Cadillac bodies were designed at the factory and first modeled in wax. From the wax pattern a plaster cast was made, and from this a die for stamping the parts out of sheet steel. Leland's collaboration with the stamping plants had improved metal processing and ductility to the point where splitting and other problems were overcome. For difficult shapes, several stampings were gas-welded together and ground smooth.

It is interesting that while Pierce-Arrow had investigated all body types of structure and decided on the cast aluminum variety as "far preferable," Leland, after his usual thorough examination, standardized on the built-up, hardwood-framed, steel-paneled body for open cars and used aluminum only for closed bodies, which then represented but a small percentage of production. Eventually steel was used for these also. Time ultimately upheld Leland's judgment, for although Pierce-Arrow built aluminum bodies quite successfully for many years, they eventually found, at the beginning of the twenties, that the disadvantages began to outweigh the advantages. Reluctantly they changed over to wooden framing, and finally to steel paneling, for standard production bodywork.

For open cars Cadillac supplied tops, which from about 1908 were made in their own factory. These were of two types, "rubber" and "mohair." The rubber top was a high-quality, rubber-

By 1914 Cadillac was offering these closed body styles: above, the Landaulet Coupé, three-passenger: $2,500. Below, the Inside Drive Limousine, five-passenger: $2,800, and the seven-passenger Standard Limousine, priced at $3,250 including standard equipment.

covered three-ply cloth, with heavy jean backing. Web-reinforced and padded with cotton wool, it held its shape and gave a smooth, distinctive top line which was typical of the quality American touring car. In contrast, the European cars (and some cheaper American cars), usually presented a "rag-bag" appearance because of the sagging, unpadded top line.

Cadillac mohair tops were also of top quality, in black mohair mackintosh cloth. These tops were priced at between $55 and $95, depending on type and model. This included side curtains and a cover for the top when stowed. Slipcovers for the car seats were also available, in light gray, made of heavy twill-back jean with rubber interlining.

"We manufacture our own tops because we want Cadillac users to have the best there is," said the company. "A Cadillac car is worthy of a Cadillac top."

These wooden bodies were soon supplanted by metal ones, which marked the advent of the Fisher brothers at Cadillac. Fisher body origins go back to the time when Fred and Charles Fisher learned the carriage trade in the carriage and blacksmith shop owned by their father, Lawrence Fisher, who was a wheelwright and carriage builder, and his brother Andrew, who worked as a blacksmith. Their father before them had been a wheelwright and blacksmith in Peru, Ohio.

At the age of twenty-four Fred J. Fisher, oldest son of Lawrence, came to Detroit to work as a draftsman for the Wilson Body Company, then working on automobiles — including Cadillac. He was later joined by his brother, Charles T. Leaving Wilson in 1908, the brothers, backed by their Uncle Albert, organized the Fisher Body Company with a capital of $50,000. The other brothers, Lawrence P., Jr., Edward F., William A., Alfred J., and H. A., subsequently joined and were taken into partnership as they came of age. The brothers all worked their way up, arriving first in the morning and leaving last at night. They all learned how to cruise timber (judging and selecting the proper quality in trees and milling stages) and served their time in all departments, taking part in woodcutting, purchasing, and processing, and actually working on the bodies until the completion of each job. The Fisher Company worked with many firms until its exclusive arrangement with General Motors and final absorption.

The newness of their company was an advantage, for the Fishers designed for the automobile from the start, instead of carrying over many unsuitable ideas spawned by the old horse-drawn coach. They were also fully alive to the possibilities of the closed car, realizing that "all-season" motoring, which would expand greatly the acceptance of the automobile, would come only with closed bodies. They pressed this point with car makers for two years, until the breakthrough finally came in 1910 with a Cadillac order for 150 closed bodies — the first quantity order ever placed in the United States. In December of 1910 this resulted in the formation of the Fisher Closed Body Company. Eugene Lewis, a salesman for the Timken Company, recalls in *Motor Memories* how he visited Cadillac in 1907 or 1908 and found Henry Leland and his engineers examining a coupé body made by Parry of Indianapolis. This body was installed on a Cadillac Lewis had ordered, and he commented, "It had a large plate-glass windshield with about three-quarters inch bevel all round its edges — which proved to be a wonderful idea to guarantee reflection. . . ."

Early in 1910 Lewis visited the Fisher plant at Piquette Street, Detroit, and asked them to build a closed body on his Cadillac. In his memoirs he claims this was the first closed body the Fishers ever made, and while this is open to question, his comments on the Fisher organization are of particular interest. He writes:

> They had a large blackboard at one end of the room where the complete picture of the body was drawn to scale on top of the chassis, the measurements of which were supplied in detail. We would sit in front of that blackboard drawing, and as suggestions and corrections were made, chalk lines would be erased and new ones put in until the general design was satisfactory.
>
> The process of making the body was long and tedious, especially with its multiple operations of pumicing, rubbing, and applying the numerous coats of paint. That body may not have been the best looking body ever made by the Fisher Brothers but they never made a better one. It was in use for years and when I finally sold the car, there was not a squeak or crack in the body.

Now to the second of Cadillac's noteworthy innovations of this period: the two-speed rear axle, presented on the 1914 models, introduced in July of 1913. It had two concentric pinions and bevel gears, giving two different axle ratios and six forward speeds. On direct drive the "high" ratio (low numerical) was 2.5:1, giving about 43 mph/1,000 rpm engine speed, while in "low" (high numerical) it was 3.66:1, giving 30 mph/1,000 rpm. Maximum speed on the 2.5:1 ratio was about 60 mph at just over 1,400 rpm.

Clutches engaged either set of gears, with an interlock preventing the engagement of both sets together. Selection was via electromagnetic latches with a switch in the driving compartment. Actual engagement was made by depressing the clutch pedal fully, as though shifting transmission gears, and a linkage attached to the clutch pedal lever pulled one set of gears into action while releasing the other set.

The Automobile was given a demonstration and reported that "the changing from one set to the other is a very simple matter and one which is quite noiseless. There was absolutely no noise connected with the changing of driving gears. Shifts from one set to the other were made at speeds of 25, 30, and 40 mph with equal facility, it being easier to tell when the 2.5 gearing was operating by the easier running of the engine and the general smoother operation of the car as a whole. There was a marked freedom from vibration when traveling at high speeds.

"The low drive is especially adapted for city driving, where starting, stopping, and slowing down are frequent and where cautious operation is necessary. Where speeds of about 16 mph or more are permissible and desirable the high ratio is of special advantage . . . effecting a saving of gasoline, while friction is due to slower operations of the motor."

Unfortunately, about twelve months after the announcement of this axle, Cadillac was sued for patent infringement by Walter S. Austin of the Austin Automobile Company, Grand Rapids, Michigan. Austin had introduced a similar design on his own car during 1913, having exhibited it at the Chicago Automobile Show in February, 1913, and having had a patent granted to him on March 31, 1914. Cadillac had been interested in his design and obtained a sample axle and drawings. But after examination they rejected Austin's arrangement of clutches and controls, and continued with their own design, which Henry Leland claimed had been originally considered in 1909 and had been one of several under development from that time. Austin, waiting until some 15,000 cars had been built and the takings were big enough, took the case to court late in 1914, and on January 8, 1915, at Grand Rapids, Michigan, District Judge C. Q. Sessions handed a decision down in Austin's favor. He allowed that the Cadillac design differed in the areas claimed, but that the improvement did not avoid infringement, and the Austin patent was valid. Cadillac appealed, but the Appeals Court upheld the first decision and substantial damages were awarded to Austin, with costs.

Although Cadillac had to pay up, the embarrassment was short-lived. Already they had abandoned not only the two-speed axle, but also the whole concept of the car that featured it. Four-cylinders were out. The era of the V-8 had begun.

Specifications in Brief

ENGINE—Four-cylinder, four-cycle; cylinders cast singly, 4½-inch bore by 5¾-inch stroke. Valve mechanism enclosed; cam shaft and generator shaft driven by silent chains from crank shaft. Five-bearing crank shaft, 2 inches diameter. Bearings, babbitt with bronze backing.

HORSEPOWER—40-50.

COOLING—Water. Copper jacketed cylinders, copper inlet and outlet water manifolds. Centrifugal pump. Radiator, tubular and plate type of unequaled efficiency. Fan attached to motor, running on two-point ball bearings; center distances of fan pulleys adjustable.

IGNITION—Delco improved Dual system. Current supplied by generator and dry cells. Single jump spark on magneto ignition; single jump or shower on dry cell ignition. Automatic spark control on both ignitions. Hand spark lever also provided.

LUBRICATION—Cadillac Automatic splash system, constant level; oil uniformly distributed. Supply maintained by mechanical force feed lubricator with single sight feed on cowl board.

CRANKING DEVICE—Cadillac Delco electrical, patented.

CARBURETOR—Cadillac, hot water jacketed. An electric heating device is provided which vaporizes gasoline in the carburetor before the engine is cranked, thereby greatly facilitating starting in cold weather. Single adjustment. Auxiliary air control on steering column.

CLUTCH—Cone type, large, leather faced, with special spring ring in flywheel. Clutch readily removable and exceptionally easy to operate.

TRANSMISSION—Sliding gear, selective type, three speeds forward and reverse. Chrome nickel steel gears. Chrome nickel steel transmission shaft and clutch connection shaft running on five annular ball bearings.

AXLES—Rear, Cadillac Timken, two-speed direct drive, patented, full floating type; special alloy steel live axle shafts; principal bearings, Timken. Front axle, drop forged, I-beam section with integral yokes; drop forged spring perches, tie rod ends and steering spindles. Spindles fitted with Timken bearings at upper ends. Gear ratio, 3.66 to 1 and 2.5 to 1. (See detailed description of rear axle.)

DRIVE—Shaft, to two sets of bevel gears of special cut teeth to afford maximum strength. Gears cut by us. Two universal joints, the forward telescopic, each enclosed in housing and running in oil bath.

BRAKES—One internal and one external brake direct on wheels, 17-inch x 2½-inch drums. Exceptionally easy of operation. Both equipped with equalizers.

STEERING GEAR—Our own patented worm and worm gear sector type, adjustable, with ball thrust bearings. 18-inch steering wheel with corrugated walnut rim, aluminum spider. Steering wheel hinged to swing downward, facilitating entrance to front seat at right side of car.

FRAME—Pressed steel, channel section, width 30 inches in front, 33 inches in rear.

WHEELS—Wood, artillery type, fitted with Q. D. demountable rims (option, standard Q. D. rims), special large hub flanges and special strength heavy spokes.

TIRES—36 inches by 4½ inches. United States.

WHEEL BASE—120 inches.

TREAD—56 inches. Option 61 inches.

SPRINGS—Front, semi-elliptic 36 inches long by 2 inches wide; Rear, three-quarter platform; sides, 54 inches long by 2 inches wide. Rear cross 39½ inches long by 2 inches wide.

CONTROL—Hand gear-change lever for transmission and hand brake lever at driver's right, inside the car. Convenient electric switch for rear axle gear control. Service brake, foot lever. Clutch, foot lever. Throttle accelerator, foot lever. Spark and throttle levers at steering-wheel. Carburetor auxiliary air control for starting, hand lever on steering column.

GASOLINE SYSTEM—Air pressure. Twenty-gallon tank situated at rear of chassis. Pressure pump operated from cam shaft.

OIL CAPACITY—6 quarts, sufficient for 600 to 900 miles.

UPHOLSTERING—Hand-buffed black leather over genuine curled hair and deep coil steel springs.

RUNNING BOARDS—Linoleum covered, with metal binding.

FINISH—Calumet Green with gold stripe.

STANDARD EQUIPMENT—Cadillac top, windshield, full lamp equipment, especially designed for Cadillac cars, black enameled. Gasoline gauge, electric horn, power tire pump, foot rail, robe rail and cocoa mat in tonneaus of open cars, tire irons, set of tools including tire repair kit. Warner Auto-meter.

PRICES on automobiles and parts are positively net f. o. b. Detroit.

No allowance will be made for any part of standard equipment if ordered omitted.

NOTE—The Cadillac Motor Car Company reserves the right to make changes or improvements at any time without incurring any obligations to install same on cars previously sold.

PENINSULAR ENGRAVING COMPANY, DETROIT

The 1914 Cadillac specifications and operating mechanism (right), with rear axle cutaway (below).

CHAPTER SIX

THE ARRIVAL
OF THE V-8

*The historic achievement which set the pattern
for all Cadillac engines to come*

In surveying the origins of the V-8 engine, it is worth quoting John Bentley in *Antique Automobile*: "The 90° V-8 was not in itself new; many automobile manufacturers had tried it before, but none had put into their design the care, forethought, and exactitude of detail felt necessary by Cadillac engineers. Hence no V-8 until then turned out a practical success in quantity manufacture."

By 1912 the four-cylinder engine in expensive cars had seen its best days. The six-cylinder commercially pioneered by Napier in England was superior in smoothness. It had passed through its initial stages of development, although its earlier years were far from trouble-free. The type suffered from a destructive torsional vibration period which proved very difficult to overcome and caused many crankshaft failures. Some American firms, such as Ford, tried the six and gave it up as an "odd number." Some put improperly designed sixes on the market and lost their reputations as a result; some, such as Cadillac, stayed clear of them altogether. Others persisted, solved the vibration problem, and evolved very fine machines which were technically and commercially successful. In America (which had built possibly the first six-cylinder car — the 1900 Gasmobile) the most notable were the Franklin, Chadwick, Packard, Peerless, Pierce-Arrow and Stevens-Duryea.

The more even torque and better balance of the new sixes made the four-cylinder Cadillac rather outmoded. Temporarily, the life of the Cadillac four was extended by the two-speed axle, but this was only a palliative. Moreover, Cadillac had been restrained from continuing it by the court decision in favor of the American Austin Company. Leland and his engineers had not been idle, however. The six was first examined as a type, and

discarded. Why not "go one better" with eight cylinders? The V-type eight had some definite advantages over the six, Wilfred pointed out: a shorter, lighter, stiffer crankshaft, a more compact engine, and lighter reciprocating parts allowing higher speeds. And since at least one maker had already built one in production, some existing experience was available to profit by.

As a type the V-8 dated back to 1903, when the Frenchman Clement Ader (an aviation pioneer) built one into a car entered in the light car class in the Paris–Madrid race of that year. The next V-8 was again a French racing car, the 24-liter ohv Darracq of 200 horsepower built in 1905, followed in the same year by the Rolls-Royce Legalimit and landaulet V-8's. In 1906 Marmon of Indianapolis exhibited a 60 hp air-cooled V-8 at the New York show, and in 1907 Hewitt displayed a V-8 limousine. Both had $5,000 price tags, but it is unlikely that their makers seriously considered production.

None of these early cars were genuine commercial propositions. In most cases they were merely experimental and contained serious faults. None was subjected to the proper research and development essential for series production. For instance, neither ignition nor carburetion were sufficiently developed to cope adequately with a V-8 engine in private hands at any time prior to 1910. The earliest attempt to make a commercially based, soundly conceived V-8 design was made by the old established firm of De Dion about 1909–1910, and although their commercial success is obscure and their design office vacillated constantly over the whole period of production, the De Dion V-8 marked a significant step. It gave Cadillac an outline to work on.

The idea for a V-8 had, as mentioned, been seriously mooted by Wilfred Leland in 1912. The Cadillac experiments started about

The Coming of The New Cadillac

THERE is one thought in connection with the coming of this new Cadillac which we would like you to grasp at once.

With the advent of this car, the Cadillac "Eight" enters upon its third successive season, with no radical change in the basic principles of its design.

This is perhaps the first time such a thing has happened in motor car development, and you will quickly see its significance as applied to the Cadillac.

Quite properly, we believe, the World has always looked to the Cadillac Company for advanced ideas, improved practice and progressive principles.

The fact, therefore, that the Cadillac car has proven itself beyond the need of radical change, is, in itself, too impressive and too illuminating to call for comment.

It does not by any manner of means, imply that the Cadillac process of refinement had come to a conclusion.

In a multitude of ways, this is a better, finer Cadillac than any which has preceded it—the subject of unremitting research and scientific betterment in scores of details.

What the absence of radical change really means, is that the underlying principles of Cadillac V-type eight-cylinder construction have been proven fundamentally sound by the performance of 31,000 cars.

It means that the Cadillac Company, with resources at its command probably superior to those possessed by any other motor car plant in the world, has arrived at the deliberate judgment that the *kind* of a motor car which it is now building, represents a higher degree of efficiency than any other in existence.

It means that this is the joint judgment of every expert mind associated with this Company. It expresses the judgment of 31,000 owners who cannot conceive of any respect in which Cadillac principles could be changed to their advantage.

The new Cadillac conforms to the finest Cadillac traditions, down to the least and last of details—and it advances them still more closely toward perfection.

It is a beautiful car to look upon.

The superior riding qualities, with which you are familiar, are enhanced and intensified.

The driving ease of last year and the year before, accentuated by the longer wheelbase of the new car, is more marked than ever.

It is doubtful if motoring can give rise to a situation which can successfully challenge Cadillac powers.

The old feeling that it is folly to seek further—the old sense of security that the Cadillac represents the uttermost in a motor car—will come over you more strongly than ever.

We are serenely confident of the exhilaration and enthusiasm which you will experience on the occasion of your first ride in this unusual car.

Specifications in Brief

ENGINE—Eight cylinder V-type, High-speed, High efficiency. HORSE POWER—S. A. E. rating 31.25; actual, more than 60. COOLING—Water. RADIATOR—Cadillac tubular and plate type. IGNITION STARTING, LIGHTING—Cadillac-Delco, improved system. LUBRICATION—Automatic pressure feed. CARBURETOR—Cadillac. CLUTCH—Multiple disc, dry plate type. TRANSMISSION—Selective type sliding gear, three speeds forward and reverse. AXLES—Rear, Cadillac Timken, full floating; Timken bearings; Spiral type bevel driving gears. Front axle, drop forged, I beam. DRIVE—Tubular shaft. BRAKES—One internal and one external brake direct on wheels, 17 inch x 2½ inch drums. STEERING GEAR—Cadillac patented worm and worm gear sector type; 18-inch steering wheel, hinged to facilitate entrance. FRAME—Channel section. WHEELS—Wood, artillery type, Timken bearings, fitted with demountable rims for straight side tires. TIRES—36" x 4½". WHEELBASE—125 and 132 inches. TREAD—56 inches. SPRINGS—Front, semi-elliptic; rear, three-quarter platform. CONTROL—Center control. GASOLINE SYSTEM—Twenty gallon tank with gauge at rear. STANDARD EQUIPMENT—Cadillac "one-man" top; windshield; full lamp equipment; Gabriel Snubbers; Clock; Warner Autometer; Electric horn; Power tire pump; Foot rail; Robe rail; License tag holders; Tire carrier; Tool box with locks; Set of tools; Tire repair kit; Handy lamp. Universal type fitting tool box, ignition and lighting switch and tire lock.

CADILLAC MOTOR CAR CO   DETROIT - MICHIGAN

Body Styles and Prices

The Type-55 Cadillac will be available with a complete variety of body styles, as follows:—

Open cars, 125 inch wheelbase; Seven Passenger with disappearing auxiliary seat $2080. Four Passenger Phaeton $2080. Two Passenger Roadster with two passenger disappearing rumble seat $2080. Four Passenger Close Coupled Roadster $2080.

Convertible styles, 125 inch wheelbase; Seven Passenger with Cadillac body (Springfield type) $2675. Four Passenger Victoria (convertible) $2550.

Enclosed cars, 125 inch wheelbase; Four Passenger Coupe $2800. Five Passenger Brougham $2950.

Enclosed cars, 132 inch wheelbase; Seven Passenger Limousine $3500. Seven Passenger Landaulet $3750. Seven Passenger Imperial $3750. Prices include standard equipment F. O. B. Detroit. Prices are subject to advance without notice.

Cadillac — Standard of the World

Though already two years old when the above ad was published, the V-8 was still viewed as a "coming" thing by Cadillac. And indeed it was: many motorcar manufacturers would not follow suit until well into the fifties. But at Cadillac the great new powerplant was reality early, much to the benefit of the company, as history showed. The architect of the engine was D. McCall White, right, a graduate of the Royal Technical College of Glasgow, Scotland, who had worked at Daimler and Napier before coming to America. Though sometimes held to be "a copyist rather than an innovator," White was said by Ernest Seaholm to be "in a class by himself," though "there was nothing puritanical about him" and he was thus not entirely acceptable to the conservative Lelands.

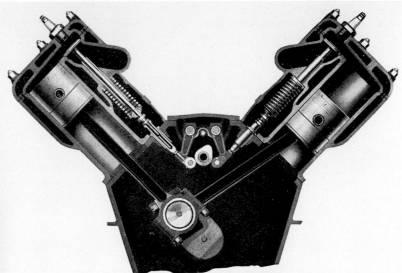

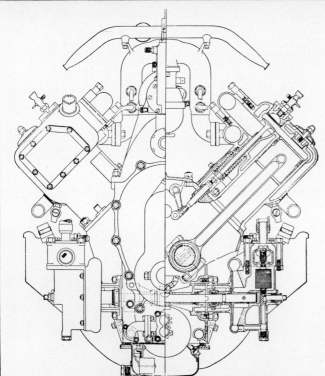

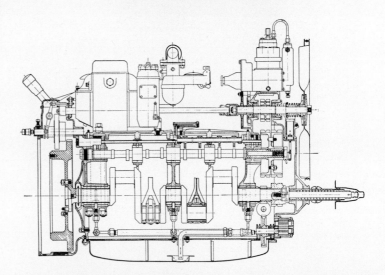

A variety of views of the Cadillac V-8. The engine itself, as it would be mounted in a car, is at top left, while a sectional view through the intake valves, showing details of the valve system, is at top right. Cadillac's poppet valves were forged from quality tungsten steel, and were of integral design rather than the built-up types with separate stems prevalent within the industry. Above are side and frontal cross section views of the Type 51 V-8 powerplant.

that year when Kettering and Deeds bought a De Dion V-8 after closely inspecting a show chassis at New York. This guinea pig was given grueling tests, dismantled, studied and thoroughly evaluated. Further experiments were carried out with a V-8 Hall-Scott aero engine designed by Col. Edward J. Hall (later of Liberty engine fame). The Hall-Scott engine was tested in an automobile chassis. As a result of this research, Kettering and Deeds, supervised by Leland, designed and built an experimental V-8 engine and chassis, incorporating some of the ideas from the De Dion and the Hall-Scott, in a new, improved Cadillac design.

Leland and his engineers were so impressed with its performance that H.M. gave the go-ahead to prepare a revised design for actual production, and placed D. McCall White in charge. White had graduated from the Royal Technical College of Glasgow in Scotland and had worked at Daimler and Napier before coming to Cadillac. His American associations probably began when he adapted the principle of the American Knight engine to production in Great Britain. Why Leland selected him is something of a mystery. He showed no greater originality than the existing Cadillac design group; indeed, Ernest Seaholm called him "a copyist rather than an innovator."

White did not arrive in Detroit until 1914. Definitive work toward a production Cadillac V-8 had started during 1913, probably about July or August; therefore it is chronologically impossible for him to have instigated the V-8. In fact it has been claimed by the Wilfred Leland faction that White was overrated as an engineer and incompetent in some respects. Mrs. Wilfred Leland told this writer that Frank Johnson recalled discussing V-8 drawings with White and was surprised at his inability to understand some of the details. According to Charles Martens, reports Mrs. Leland, there were arguments about White's unrealistic approach. White was unfamiliar with Cadillac standards, and tolerances specified by him had to be changed.

To be fair, however, one must temper these criticisms with the realities of White's entrance onto the Cadillac scene. It is unlikely that competent professional men like Johnson and Martens would take kindly to an outsider — and a Limey at that — being given an inside track in the design and engineering offices. White would have been familiar with Napier engineering standards, which were very high. If his practical engineering knowledge was limited compared with that of Leland's men, it is likely that he contributed more in the theory of certain specialist areas such as lubrication at high rpm and the breathing of engines with more than four cylinders.

Ernest Seaholm has provided some clues to the mystery.

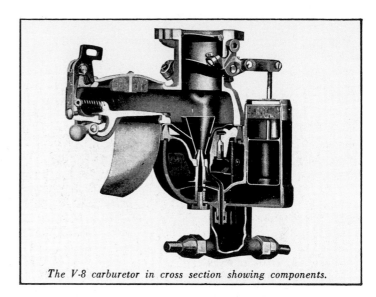

The V-8 carburetor in cross section showing components.

Despite White's tendency to copy rather than innovate, Seaholm told this writer that in some respects White "was in a class by himself," adding with a twinkle, "there was nothing puritanical about him and he was hardly the type personally acceptable to the family group. However, he had come at the right time for Cadillac. They had become inbred organization-wise and new blood was needed. In great secrecy, under White's direction, the V-8 took form."

The reasons for employing White can probably be summarized by citing two facts. First, he knew more about the theory of high-speed engines than any engineer at Cadillac. He was in touch with the latest continental developments, where engine efficiency in terms of specific output was more advanced than in the United States. This was to be a major consideration in the new engine, as the Cadillac engineering group had already decided the days of the refined but ponderous and inefficient big sixes were numbered. Even if White — like so many British engineers — was theoretical rather than practical, Leland's group would soon take care of that aspect.

And second, it was intended to make the V-8 a complete surprise. This would have been very difficult if the design project had been wholly in the hands of Kettering or the existing engineering group who were well-known to everyone in Detroit. Nothing could better throw the opposition off the track than to keep the regular Cadillac design group on the four-cylinder models, constantly improving and introducing new features such as the two-speed rear axle, which many thought was Leland's answer to the six-cylinder principle. Thus the fours continued to hold the limelight, while the eight secretly grew to reality at astonishing speed.

Tight security was maintained during the research and development period of the V-8. The Kettering-Deeds design was tested in Toledo, well away from Detroit, and the engine developed at Pelham and Drydock Avenues, near Detroit, using a concrete block building ostensibly housing "The Ideal Manufacturing Company," but actually owned by the Lelands. Cadillac employees were not permitted to enter the building, and even the wives of Leland's hand-picked engineering team were completely in the dark regarding the project. The new Cadillac model, known for no clear reason as the Type 51 (the model year in reverse, possibly), was announced publicly in September, 1914.

The concept of the V-8 was outlined in papers presented to the Society of Automotive Engineers in 1915 and 1919. Cadillac engineers felt that a touring car engine of that period should have an mep of 80 to 100 pounds per square inch at up to 2,200 rpm, and the Cadillac V-8 was designed to develop over 90 pounds from 800 rpm right through to 2,000 rpm. This was possi-

ble because of its high volumetric efficiency, light reciprocating and rotating parts allowing high mechanical efficiency, and high compression, permitting rapid combustion at high rotational speeds.

They aimed at an engine that would be sweet, silky, and silent when delivering power, and free from vibration at high speeds, yet had good torque at low speeds — opposing requirements that were not easy to meet. The L-head valve arrangement was favored because it allowed fairly large-diameter valves, had low reciprocating weight (no more than an overhead cam layout, which was considered far too noisy), and because the L-head "is the quietest type of valve gear that can be used in the touring car engine."

We will compare the Cadillac with the De Dion power units in some detail, because attempts have been made to belittle the Cadillac V-8 and its designers as mere copiers who built an engine in some ways inferior to the original. This is completely false.

Cadillac engineers found that while the De Dion engine structure was sound in some respects, it had a number of major and minor shortcomings. They adopted the fork and blade connecting

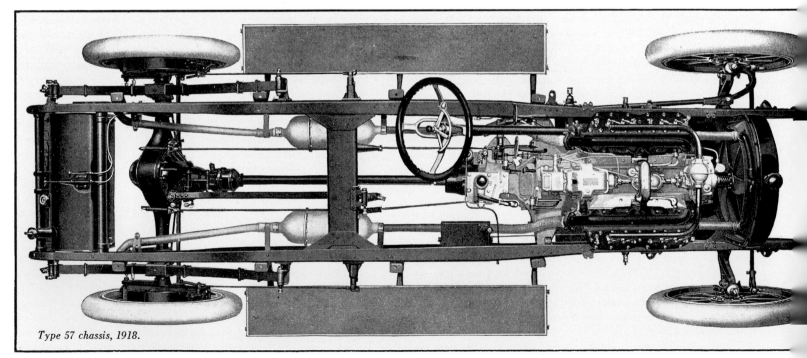

Type 57 chassis, 1918.

rods with nonstaggered cylinder blocks, favored because they equalized thrust, gave the shortest shaft and engine, and the least cams. The single central camshaft with rocker-fingers opening the valves, the chain-driven camshaft and fan, and the decarbonizing plugs in the cylinder heads were also taken from the De Dion. However, the De Dion main bearing layout was considered unnecessarily complicated and inaccessible. Apparently the engine had to be removed from the car before the main bearings could be inspected. The center main was installed on the crankshaft and was then bolted to a diaphragm or disc, split in the center and encircling the crankshaft. The crankshaft was then inserted into the engine lengthwise via the bell housing. The disc fitted inside a barrel-type web forming part of the crankcase structure.

Cadillac's main bearing design simplified things considerably, allowed removal of the shaft in the normal way, and lightened the structure. Similar improvements were made in the camshaft area. In the De Dion a separate camshaft chamber was formed by casting a wall into the crankcase V. On the underside of this partition ran an oil gallery for supplying the camshaft. The camshaft assembly was mounted above this horizontal wall and took the form of an unnecessarily complicated and heavy rocker box casting. Cadillac's design eliminated the separate camshaft chamber and considerably simplified the rocker-cam assembly. Lubrication was supplied from above.

The most serious shortcoming of the De Dion lay in its cooling arrangements. The exhaust ports for the two center cylinders of each bank were cored through the cylinder block so that considerable exhaust heat was retained in the cylinder casting. The end cylinders were not much better off. The exhaust manifolds were bolted up to a flat face cast full length along the water jacketing. Both the exhaust and water passages were restricted and as cooling was by thermo-syphon (*i.e.*, no water pumps), the whole design would have thrown a heavy load on the cooling system in a high output engine, although possibly satisfactory in the low output De Dion.

In the Cadillac generous water passages were provided throughout, and dual shaft-driven water pumps insured adequate circulation. The exhausts were large and the manifolds joined the head casting only at the bolting flanges, being taken upward and to the rear with full dual exhaust pipes. Each bank was treated as a separate four-cylinder engine with its own muffler and tailpipe. The headers were porcelained and the down pipes wrapped in asbestos. The De Dion's integral water jacketing was very advanced but apparently there were problems in the foundry and

irregularities in the castings. Without suitably large core holes and inspection plates, it was difficult to check the casting internally.

Automobile Engineering (a standard reference work compiled by a panel of SAE members), after commenting that the four-cylinder Cadillac had "one of the best" production designs of the old-type water jacket, noted the same thoroughness in the new Cadillac layout. "With integral jackets, in the best examples of design the core openings are very large, with plane faces, and are closed by screwed on plates, thus making the construction practically a compromise between the completely integral and completely built-on jackets.

"In such modern construction as Cadillac, a large plate will be noted on the end of the cylinders. This covers a tremendous core hole, by the use of which the internal construction is made practically perfect in the foundry. This also allows easy inspection and cleaning, the removal of the two end plates enabling a person to see right through the water jacket from end to end. This construction overcomes all objections previously raised against troubles with complicated water jacket cores."

Engineering thoroughness was not confined simply to the engine. The radiator was an efficient fin-and-tube type, not the honeycomb then considered best for high-class cars. The fin-and-tube radiator consisted of vertical tubular cooling passages and horizontal secondary surfaces or fins. The honeycomb, introduced at the turn of the century by Mercedes, had a great many double-walled hexagonal section tubes soldered together in a matrix. The air went through the tubes as the water circulated around them. The finned-tube core was cheaper to make, more robust, clogged less frequently, and when clogged was easier to clean. Moreover, the theoretically greater efficiency of the honeycomb was not true in practice. Cadillac obtained maximum efficiency by cowling the fan. The cooling system was completely sealed, with the overflow pipe terminating in a condensing tank so that all radiator overflow was automatically siphoned back again on cooling. Cadillac also incorporated an important innovation that was to become universally adopted. This was thermostatic control of the circulation. Each water pump had a thermostatic control valve which, when the motor was cold, shut off almost all water supply to the radiator until a predetermined "ideal" operating temperature was reached, then the valve permitted full flow. A small water flow was allowed to bypass the valve; this guarded against freezing the radiator.

The De Dion induction arrangements were at first glance advanced, with a dual throat Zenith carburetor, each half serving one bank. But the induction passages were pitifully small and the inlet ports, like the exhausts, were inefficiently designed. This nullified any advantage gained by the dual throat carburetor and rendered it a doubtful complication in the then primitive state of carburetion art. McCall White stated that Cadillac had experimented with dual carburetion, but there had been a *loss* in power, missing at high speed, and great difficulty in getting the engine to pull well under heavy load.

Cadillac used a single throat air-valve carburetor of their own design in which there were no problems of balancing and tuning one bank of cylinders against the other. This was possible because these early V-8's had a simple 180° four-cylinder crankshaft layout, which gave good firing-distribution pattern with a single carburetor. Efficiency was attained by using large, easy-flowing intake passages and ports, higher compression, better valve design, cam profiles and timing, and many other detail refinements which were the result of very thorough research.

Tests were made with a range of different timings until a standard setting was evolved which gave an almost ideal power curve up to about 2,800 rpm, yet good carburetion at low speeds and reliable starting in very cold weather.

The specially designed Delco coil ignition system was another point where Cadillac scored heavily. Magneto design increases in complexity with the number of cylinders, and early De Dions used two separate four-cylinder magnetos which, like the carburetion, required synchronizing. Later De Dions, circa 1913, used a single eight-cylinder magneto requiring four rotating poles and two geared-down distributors. Since the De Dion was not a high-speed engine, the usual magneto advantage — a hotter spark at high speed — was of no account, and it would certainly have inferior starting qualities. The Cadillac V-8's coil ignition using two sets of contacts in parallel (a system devised by Leland's electrical specialist, H. G. Schwartz) was tested at up to 4,000 rpm (engine speed) and ran a 400-hour test without adjustment. White commented, "I believe that it has been brought to a higher state of perfection than any other ignition."

At that time, too, the combined motor generator arrangement probably scored over others as a generally simpler, lighter, and more efficient arrangement for combining starting, lighting, and ignition. So far as the author knows, De Dion had no electric starter. That installed on the car in the Henry Ford Museum is nonstandard, and is an American Rushmore unit.

Battery ignition, starting and lighting equipment, though now three years old at Cadillac, was still an advanced feature to any contemporary. Such rivals as Packard, Pierce-Arrow, and Locomobile in America were still using magneto ignition, and Rolls-Royce had neither electric lighting nor starting as standard until 1919!

In the method of mounting the transmission Cadillac again scored over De Dion, as they combined engine, clutch, and gearbox in one unit in a manner that, although known in Europe, came to be accepted as "typically American" practice. The De Dion arrangement was, in contrast, "typically European"— a separate gearbox and exposed clutch, the two coupled by a short shaft.

The transmission was Cadillac's own design, made in their own factory using specially designed equipment. For instance, the gear teeth were bevelled or "backed off" on a beveler made by Cadillac and set up solely for this purpose. All gearbox components had to pass the usual tests of Cadillac's limit gauge system, plus other tests for silence, ease of shifting, and general refinement. The gear transmission shaft and clutch shaft were of highest quality nickel chrome steel, and the clutch connection shaft and jack shaft ran in annular ball bearings. The main shaft ran in roller bearings at its forward end and an annular ball bearing at the rear. For its time, the transmission was exceptionally quiet.

The clutch matched the refinement of the transmission. It had fifteen carbon steel plates and was unusually smooth and soft in operation. "A good example of Cadillac thoroughness," commented *Automobile Engineering*.

The drive was by open shaft to the rear axle, with two universal joints, and a V-shaped steel torque member took all drive and braking forces. The drive shaft joints were enclosed in spherical housings and ran in oil.

The rear axle was a full-floating Timken type with Timken tapered roller bearings throughout. The pinion was "straddle mounted," *i.e.*, supported on either side by Timken tapered roller bearings. The ring gear was supported by similar bearings, and the ring gear and pinion were of the spiral bevel type — "giving the efficiency of a bevel with the quietude of a worm." As with the transmission, the gears were cut in the Cadillac plant on special machinery, giving very high standards of accuracy in manufacture and silence in running.

The front axle also incorporated Timken bearings both in the wheels and also the chrome nickel steel steering spindles, which were fitted with Timken bearings on their upper ends. *Automobile Engineering* again praised this arrangement as "very excellent design."

The springing was exceptionally supple, with 42-inch semi-

The 1916 Type 53 roadster.

The 1916 seven-passenger touring.

The 1916 seven-passenger berline.

elliptics in front, and 54-inch platform rear springs, coupled by a 39½-inch cross spring with universal joint shackle mountings. This "platform" type rear suspension cannot be called advanced, and had been virtually abandoned in Europe. It must have had some merit, however, for Cadillac used it very successfully for about another decade.

The wheels were artillery-type, of highest quality, specially selected, well-seasoned, second growth hickory, and having demountable rims for straight-sided tires. This innovation in tire and rim design marked the end of the old "clincher rim" with beaded edge tires which had for years been detested almost as much as the crankhandle. The whole American industry at this time adopted straight-sided tires, although in Europe the beaded edge persisted well into the next decade.

Braking was on the rear wheels only, with expanding handbrake and contracting footbrake operation on the same drums, but separately linked, each linkage having its own equalizing gear. As with the suspension, it had little of note other than the soundness of design — workmanship and layout — using well-proven ideas.

The steering was worm and sector, and had a forward mounted track rod to place the tube and connections under tension rather than compression. All parts were of Cadillac design and make, to the usual exceptional standards of machining and fit. The sector teeth in mesh in the straight-ahead position were cut on a slightly smaller pitch radius to allow adjustment for wear, although due to the general quality of the mechanism play seldom developed until great mileages were reached. The worm was carried in two ball thrust bearings to reduce friction, and while the steering would be considered very heavy by today's standards, it was extremely accurate, and certainly among the best of the time. Steering met the standards even of the connoisseur, giving positive control for such a heavy and well-sprung car, plus a turning circle that was outstanding for such a wheelbase. The wheel had an eighteen-inch rim of corrugated walnut with an aluminum spider, hinged to drop open and permit easy entry for the driver.

The frame, in plan view, consisted of three main members, the two channel-section side rails and a massive central transverse member tying them together in an H-form. A number of tubular cross members completed the structure. The central member was filleted at the rail joints, giving it an effective width of about sixteen inches. This frame was another of the outstanding points of the car. The pressed-steel frame had been known since the first Mercedes, but for the first ten or fifteen years of the twentieth century very little progress had been made in frame design. Side rails were tied together with a small or large number of flimsy cross members, and "lozenging" of the frame was common because the majority of designs were not really a single rigid unit but two units linked together. A number of makers spent much time on this problem before World War I, and some good designs appeared during the teens and twenties. The Cadillac H frame was one of the earliest and best of these. It served the firm for two decades until the advent of independent front suspension, and inspired a number of imitators in the next decade.

A comparison with, say, the contemporary Locomobile 48 shows that the Cadillac had a much stronger frame and that the unit powerplant's compactness permitted this design. The Locomobile layout, with the separate transmission under the driver's seat, higher drive line, and universal joint further to the rear virtually ruled out a single substantial cross member.

The 122-inch wheelbase of the Type 51 was relatively short compared with that of some contemporaries. However, the compact V-8 engine gave Cadillac the body space of a comparable six-cylinder car on a 134-inch wheelbase. The V-8, in fact, occupied no more space lengthwise in the frame than the earlier, low powered, heavier Cadillac four-cylinder engine. The shorter frame, body space for body space, gave Cadillac a distinct advantage in frame stiffness in the vertical plane over makes using a longer in-line engine, and it was never necessary for Cadillac to resort to the ridiculous expedient of trussing the frame rails with underslung tie rods, which some high-class European makers were still doing even in the late twenties.

The overall frame rigidity allowed comparatively low-rate springs, and a soft ride without loss of good steering and handling qualities. This was a very modern outlook, well in advance of the general chassis practice of that day. The company's advertising copy made special note of these features, indicating how far they had come from the teeth-jarring singles of ten years earlier.

At its introduction, Cadillac offered the V-8 in ten standard body styles, three open and seven closed, prices ranging from $1,975 to $3,600. To present such a car at such prices on a profitable basis was a formidable commercial venture which would have been impossible without the manufacturing knowhow of the Lelands. While the car is chiefly remembered for its engine alone, it can be seen that the overall theme was very progressive. The advanced nature of Cadillac's unified electrical system had in the new V-8 been complemented by a similar design conception mechanically throughout the chassis. It was probably the first such car embodying characteristics of the later

vintage period to be placed on the market. A high quality car of this price and volume (15,000 units annually) had never been known before in the United States, and would remain beyond the comprehension of the European automobile industry for many decades. Leland in fact "did for the rich what Ford had done for the poor." While it was followed inside a year or two by a number of other advanced competitors such as the Peerless V-8, the Marmon 34, and the Packard Twin Six, it was the Cadillac V-8 which, said *The Automobile* in December of 1915, "ushered in an epoch." The magazine concluded: "Here is provided the harmonious blending of the highest engineering achievements with the utmost in designing art and coachbuilding skill."

"The engineers have provided an eight-cylinder motor of superlative smoothness," *The Automobile* explained. "The coachbuilders have provided a dignified and luxurious environment. The liquid smoothness of these cars is supplemented by a sense of complete seclusion; the seclusion by a sense of rest and relaxation; the restfulness by a sense of unexampled ease and elegance. . . . Buoyant springs, deep soft upholstery, appointments in quiet good taste but still almost palatial — all of these soothing influences bring supreme comfort to mind and

It is 1916, and President Woodrow Wilson is riding in a Type 53 Cadillac touring car en route to his second inaugural.

body, and leave you almost oblivious to the fact that you are being borne along by mechanical means."

Cadillac offered, as standard, body designs intended to equal in straight quality, from framework to upholstery, the best in custom coachwork. Enclosed cars had striped velvet upholstery laid in French plaits over the seat cushions and backs and lower side quarters below the arm rest. The upper work, ceilings and doors were dressed in plain and unplaited velvet of the same color as the lighter background of the striped material. This plush material, known as mohair velvet, was made from the fleece of Angora goat and was supplied by the firm of L. C. Chase. Carpet hassocks, interior door handles, robe rails, pull ropes, etc. were all covered with the same material. Miss Miriam Leland Woodbridge credits its introduction to her father, Angus Woodbridge, who was Henry Leland's son-in-law. Great attention was paid to weather sealing and rattle proofing. Limousines had speaking tubes for the driver and internal and external convenience lights, while speedometer, clock, ammeter, engine-driven tire pump and electric horn were all standard items.

Style had developed gradually over the previous five years into a pattern that, culminating in the V-8, would continue with little more than evolutionary change into the twenties. Up to 1912 the cowl had been nonexistent. Hood and body met abruptly at the vertical, square dash. In 1913 the pressed-sheet steel cowl appeared with its compound curvature matching the hood and "cockpit coaming" together in a semblance of flowing line. The driving compartment acquired low narrow doors — so light and easy to open or close, incidentally, that they feel like table tennis paddles by comparison with today's. The use of curved surfaces extended to the rear treatment of both roadster and touring models and accompanied the early body designers' attempts to cover up the machinery and merge the various unrelated bits into a unified whole. Fenders and running boards on the four-cylinder models had differed little from the singles until after 1908. Then had come the tangential downsweep of the front fender, and running board valances had bridged the unsightly gap between running board and chassis. Electric lights had assisted in cleaning up the appearance, as had inboard placement of brake and gear levers. Greater body enclosure saw the gradual departure of the early romantic age of the automobile when a ride was a real dress occasion wherein dust coats, goggles, cap, and gauntlets and, for the ladies, a hat scarf were essential adjuncts to be donned before departing.

Notable differences between American and European touring car appearance of this period, and for many years later, were the greater use of curved body surfaces, the running board valance which "filled in" the side elevation of the car, the enameled or varnished radiator shell instead of silver or nickel plate, and the use of wooden artillery wheels instead of wire spoke. All these features, and others, such as more complete touring equipment in general, gave the American car a distinctive appearance even before World War I. This reflected the different conditions of origin. The American had a far higher living standard and drove much greater distances, so he expected — and got — far more accessories and creature comforts than his poor European cousin. On the other hand, his road system was far less developed, and nickel-plated radiators and wire wheels were impractical except in city use. The American wooden wheel, criticized by European writers for its appearance, was actually the best wheel for most conditions outside Europe. The European (actually English) type of wire wheel was superior in lateral strength because of its triangulated section, was lighter and gave a more resilient ride — and looked more elegant. But it was more costly, more prone to damage and corrosion, and difficult to keep clean, and its protruding hubs were a menace in traffic. The American wooden wheel, of second growth hickory, was shown by actual test to be several times the strength of European wooden wheels of equal spoke size, and its felloe, made of whole stock by advanced methods under hydraulic pressure, was far superior to the European wood felloe, made by old-fashioned wheelwrights, cut from small pieces and prone to structural weakness. (Eventually, in the late twenties, America produced a wire wheel that eliminated several disadvantages of the European wire wheel and made it more suitable for general use.)

The preference of the American designer and buyer for practicality over style was also shown in the body. The rear of the high-class European touring car was stylishly low cut, but the height of the seat, terminating in the middle of the passenger's back, was far inferior in comfort to that in the American car, despite its smarter appearance. Yet there were some elegant bodies on the eight-cylinder Cadillac chassis as early as 1914. Their elegance, however, was formal rather than rakish, as exemplified by the landaulet coupé three-passenger, with its balanced design and curved glass suggestive of an electric brougham, or the two-door sedan with its large curved glass quarters, central entrance and stately rear lines, or even the limousine with its upright style.

The landaulet coupé had an aluminum body with back quarter and top of best grade bright finish landaulet leather. The top folded back directly behind the doors, with concealed landau irons giving the simple appearance of the fixed top. Inside there was a forward facing seat for three, and a small rearward facing drop-seat, with all upholstery in hand-buffed leather.

The limousine had Halo Cloth or green broadcloth upholstery and seating for five passengers. All closed cars had heavy crystal plate-glass windows. Quarter and dome lights were provided inside, with a pair of pillar lights outside. Lower body panels and doors were finished in Calumet green, with upper panels in black, as standard. The open drive limousine had the chauffeur's seat in waterproof cloth with protective side curtains and (this was before the windshield wiper) a "clear vision" screen with a hinged top half for visibility in rainy weather.

A special closed car built in 1919 for General John J. Pershing, commander in chief of the U.S. Expeditionary Force to Europe, was finished in suburban blue, with rich blue mohair antique upholstery to match the body, set off by gold background. Fixtures were gold plated — and a lady's vanity case and gentleman's smoking set with electric lighter were installed. The car's tools were nickel-plated.

The range of bodies was increased to eleven in the Type 55 for 1917, and although reduced to ten in 1918, it grew to thirteen in the early twenties, and fourteen for the V-63 line in 1925. One of the latter was the $3,650 five-passenger landau, "a design for those who desire a closed body of marked individuality." It had angled oval rear quarter windows, a "magic green" body finish trimmed in French gray beltline stripe, natural wood finish wheels and nickeled radiator, headlights, sidelights, and hubcaps. The interior was in mohair velvet, with silk roller shades.

Another was the Fisher coach, in green Duco with matched striping and taupe mohair upholstery. Equipment included rear view mirror, automatic windshield wiper, Fisher V-V windscreen, dome light, sun visor, and footrests. Several Fisher "customs" were also listed, with interiors in mohair velvet or broadcloth, walnut trimmed doors, walnut paneling, vanity cases and smoking sets with inlaid walnut panels.

During these decades the main style changes were domed fenders (1917), the raising of the hood line to give a more continuous flow-through at the cowl (Type 61), and the lowering of the car overall by a reduction in wheel size. Even then, in the early twenties, the Cadillac was a conservative car rather than a style-setter. Although certain standard models listed, notably the Type 61 phaeton, and some of the short-coupled closed bodies were classy enough, the more often seen standard models were vintage in appearance rather than classic, with considerable overall height and severely rounded fender lines. The trend

toward the classic would come with the Model 314 in 1925 and would be substantially realized in the 341 of 1927.

The new owner of a V-8 Cadillac had miles of pleasurable driving ahead of him. As finally announced, the Model 51 Cadillac V-8 — so designated in its first year — had a bore and stroke of $3\frac{1}{8}$ by $5\frac{1}{8}$ for a displacement of 314 cubic inches. On a compression ratio of 4.25:1, it developed 70 bhp at 2,400 rpm. Seven-passenger limousines on a 5:1 axle could do over 55 mph, and open models with higher axles were capable of 60 to 65 mph. Gas mileage averaged about 12 mpg. Acceleration figures in the 5-to-25 and 10-to-30 range were on the order of eight to ten seconds according to bodies and axles, with 10 to 50 mph in twenty to twenty-five seconds.

Among all automobiles in America at the time, the Cadillac V-8 and Packard Twin Six represented the most advanced thought in fine car practice. Each was the pioneer in its field and remained the most successful throughout its production span. Each inspired — or was followed — by numerous imitators. There were also some equally advanced contemporaries of differing concept. These were less successful but deserve mention, particularly the Marmon 34 and the Premier 6 with their light alloy engines, lightweight chassis, and electrically-selected transmission in the case of the latter.

The years 1914-1916 saw the American luxury car establish a technical leadership over the European car that was not wholly attributable to Europe getting itself into a world war and America — for the time being — keeping out of it. Postwar European designs, although showing some major technical strides, did not reestablish overall technical leadership and were certainly quite uncompetitive commercially. By 1916 America had produced a whole new breed of car in comparison with the earlier designs of the first years of the twentieth century. Great advancements had been made in the engines, chassis, bodywork, electrical apparatus, and accessories, so that these cars were far more reliable and much better equipped than their predecessors.

With their similarities and differences, the Cadillac V-8 and the Packard Twin Six are striking illustrations of the difficulty of building "the perfect car." Both had V-type, high-efficiency engines with unit transmission. Their chassis embodied lavish touring equipment, as shown in Kellogg tire pumps, trouble lights, cigar lighters, tilt beam headlights, and so on. There was, however, a discernible difference in their approach to engine design. Packard put refinement first and practicality second, with Cadillac the two were reversed. The Cadillac engine was never as smooth as the Packard, but the majority of prospects avoided the

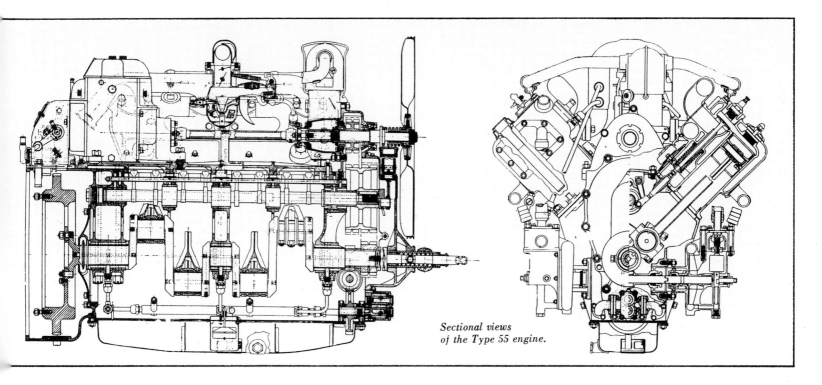

*Sectional views
of the Type 55 engine.*

complexity of twelve cylinders and settled for eight. Consequently average Packard sales during this period never equaled those of Cadillac, and ran between 4,000 and 5,000 per year. Even so, this was an amazing figure for a twelve-cylinder car, and underlines the writer's earlier comments about who was who in the luxury field among car-building nations. The Packard-Cadillac battle resolved itself in an interesting manner in the twenties, when Packard gave up twelve cylinders in favor of eight, and then outsold Cadillac!

Within three or four years of the introduction of the Cadillac V-8, there were on the American market at least twenty-two different makes listing V-8's. These ranged from the front wheel drive Homer Laughlin at $1,050 to the Richard, built in Cleveland, Ohio, and priced at $8,000. Between these extremes there was a range of V-8's good and bad. Some of them — such as the Peerless, an exceptionally well-engineered, well-built car backed by a distinguished quality maker — lasted a considerable period, and gave Cadillac substantial competition. But by 1921 only seven of these V-8's of the teens remained. They had been joined by three newcomers, only one of which would last into the

next decade. Two of these were Cadillac offspring — the Lafayette and the Lincoln. The former, named like its progenitor after an early Frenchman of significance to American history, had as chief engineer, McCall White, who left Cadillac in 1918. While the Lafayette was an excellent car, it lacked an adequate commercial organization and expired in 1924. The successful one was the Lincoln, sired by H.M. himself. It became Cadillac's most formidable competitor. A third, the Wills Sainte Claire, was out after 1926. Among all V-8's Cadillac occupied the first place. Its technical and commercial successes were immediate and long-lasting, and on a far greater scale than was true for any comparable car of the time. Production for the first year alone had totaled 13,000 cars, rising to 18,000 in 1916. By 1917, when the Type 57 was introduced, the V-8 had passed through models 51, 53, and 55 — and some 49,000 cars had been built. Compare these figures with, for example, those of Peerless, the closest of Cadillac's early V-8 rivals, whose normal figures were 5,000 per year, or approximately one-third the Cadillac output. The smaller manufacturers bear no comparison with Cadillac at all. Cunningham, for instance, never built more than a few hundred cars per year, while Daniels, who introduced a high-priced V-8 in 1916, announced after six or seven years of production that a total of 1,500 had been sold.

Comparison with the confused, vacillating, and mediocre history of the various De Dion models which came to an end in 1923 would be equally one-sided. On both counts — technical and commercial success — the Cadillac V-8 withstands the most critical inspection. Clearly it stands superior to the De Dion. Copying there was, but the final product was substantially different — and substantially better. Take the specific power output figures. These can be a controversial yardstick for differing engine types, but in this instance, where we have a similar layout, displacement, and application, they are meaningful:

Year	Model	Displacement	BHP	Specific output (bhp/liter)
DE DION V-8				
1910	50 hp	6,180 cc	50	8.1
1912-1914	26 hp	4,595 cc	38	8.3
1914	50 hp	7,770 cc	69	8.9
CADILLAC V-8				
1914	31.25 hp	5,140 cc	70	13.6

Cadillac's ability to get things right is illustrated by its selection of stroke-bore ratio. At 1.64 it differed from all De Dions, and it was obviously the optimum since it remained unaltered for thirteen years. De Dion, on the other hand, used no less than seven stroke-bore ratios over a similar period, ranging from 1.33 to 1.73.

Similarly, while Cadillac used one cooling principle and one carburetor and manifold layout, De Dion's use of two different cooling systems and three entirely different carburetor and manifold arrangements in the same period shows an impractical approach and inconsistency in the design office.

Significant of the transfer of design leadership within a few years is the fact that De Dion's postwar models showed considerable Cadillac influence, following Cadillac practice in their block casting, in the unit transmission, and in the electrics — with a motor generator for starting and lighting. However, De Dion made no attempt to follow Cadillac's "high speed, high efficiency" concept, and retained thermo-syphon cooling and sedate power outputs, along with such other dated features as magneto ignition and fixed cylinder heads.

Among automobile engineers themselves, it was realized that Cadillac had produced a giant killer. David Fergusson of Pierce-Arrow admitted to his directors that the Cadillac V-8 would give their sixes "strong competition." This was an understatement, as

can be seen from the following figures for 1915 models:

	Cadillac V-8	Pierce 38	Pierce 48	Pierce 66
Bore	3⅛	4	4½	5
Stroke	5⅛	5½	5½	7
Displacement	314	414	527	825
BHP	70	65	78	101
RPM	2,400	2,000	1,800	1,600
Torque at RPM	175 1,600	205 1,000	233 1,000	465 850
Weight	4,000	4,300	5,020	5,450
Axle ratio	4.45	3.78	3.53	2.88
Price	$1,975	$4,300	$5,000	$6,000
Maximum speed (touring car, top up)	60	56	60	70
Minimum speed	2½	5	6	7
Maximum gradient high gear	11.5%	10.2%	9%	13.1%
Acceleration 10-30, high gear	8.7 (seconds)	9.8 (seconds)	11.1 (seconds)	7.6 (seconds)
MPG	11-12	10-11	8-9	8-9
Oil consumption miles per pint	80	60	60	55

W. R. Strickland, chief engineer of Peerless, later wrote: "The Cadillac set the pace and showed the limitations of the size of cylinders, pistons, and other engine parts. At the time of the introduction of the V-type eight the fine cars of America were called 38's, 48's, and some 60's. What happened? The many ad-

The 1918 Type 57 phaeton (opposite), the 1917 Type 55 touring (above).

vantages of the eight . . . led to complete change of thought. Eights (and twelves) began to multiply and displace the older large bore engines." Strickland later put his views in practice, and produced an excellent new V-8 to replace the older Peerless sixes, which were similar to the Pierce line detailed above. The new V-8's sounded the death knell of the dinosaurs.

From its inception the Cadillac V-8 won immediate praise for its fine road performance. American journalists were markedly impressed, and English road tests echoed similar sentiments. The editor of *The Motor* wrote: "The engine is no doubt the *pièce de résistance* of the car, and its running is a revelation. The word flexibility takes on a new meaning." While *The Autocar* commented, "It is really difficult to convey on paper any idea of the delight of the running — one may indulge in superlatives and fall short of producing anything like the real impression of satisfaction." *Country Life* said: "Of the Cadillac 8's behavior on the road it would be difficult to speak too highly. The engine's acceleration has to be experienced to be believed."

Famous British automotive engineer W. O. Bentley, then working as an aero engine designer, had an interesting reminiscence of the period: "During the 1914-1918 war I bought an open four-seater Cadillac V-8. This was a very remarkable machine in many ways . . . one of the most flexible cars in top gear that I have ever driven, and astonishingly quiet. While some firms today boast that the passengers in their cars can hear only the clock at 100 mph, the only mechanical sound from the Cadillac at a very creditable top speed was its fan. I used to love to take it to Derby and, starting it in top gear, drive it at a slow walking pace round the

Rolls-Royce works to show off its flexibility. This leg pull used to exasperate those present."

The 1916 Model 53 had an enlarged intake manifold — 1½ inches instead of 1¼ — and a power increase of ten percent to 77 bhp at 2,650 rpm. In September, 1915, its increased performance was demonstrated at Chicago Speedway. Under the official observation of the technical committee of the Automobile Club of America, two fully equipped standard touring cars were tested over 100 miles for speed and fuel consumption. One car had already been used for some time by the Cadillac experimental department, while the other was a new car direct off the line, its only mileage being that between Detroit and Chicago. These figures were remarkably uniform:

Car No. 1	100 miles	84 minutes 16 4/5 seconds	71.19 mph
Car No. 2	100 miles	82 minutes 46 seconds	72.49 mph

Fuel consumption tests showed consumption ranging from 19 mpg at a constant 20 mph to 9 mpg at a constant 65 mph. At speeds between 40 and 50 mph, or normal fast cruising speed, gas mileage was surprisingly good — between 12 and 14.5 mpg.

In May the following year Cannonball Baker and W. F. Sturm, with a Cadillac V-8 roadster, broke their previous transcontinental record made with a Stutz Bearcat. They cut four days off the Bearcat time, covering the 3,741 miles from Los Angeles to New York in seven days eleven hours fifty-two minutes. Their daily average was 463 miles — not bad considering the deplorable weather and bad roads. In Missouri on one occasion the car took two hours to cover ten miles.

A week later T. J. Beaudet set a new Los Angeles-San Francisco record, averaging 48.4 mph over the 450 miles. He drove through the night, beating the fastest train by several hours.

The Cadillac V-8 had been announced almost simultaneously with the outbreak of World War I, and its performance in that war was as notable as any of its peacetime successes. Early in the war the French requested a number of Cadillac limousines for the French General Staff; the English and Canadian war departments used large numbers, particularly as ambulances; and Leland offered the V-8 engine as a power unit for various purposes. Then came the time to adopt a standard seven-passenger car for the United States Army. In this case the selection of the Cadillac was based mainly on two factors — its previous performance in a Mexican border incident with Pancho Villa in 1916 and the results of competitive tests made at Marfa, Texas, in July, 1917. Marfa, at the extreme southern border of Texas with Mexico, had no paved or graveled roads, and its sandy ruggedness roasted under a hot sun year in, year out. Here the

Left to right: drafting room, special machine working on both ends of an axle at once, quietness test of Timken bearings, pouring aluminum molds.

Left to right: testing five-bearing camshafts for alignment, testing the transmissions, riveting frames, drilling fifty-four holes at once in side bars.

Left to right: mounting body on chassis, testing chassis on dynamometer, painting the complete assembled chassis, assembling the wooden body frame.

108

Left to right: constructing tops, finishing new fenders, cutting teeth in spiral bevel driving pinions, testing pistons and rods for right alignment.

eft to right: finishing wheels, engines on dynamometer stands, testing an engine on the dynamometer, fitting components to and assembling chassis.

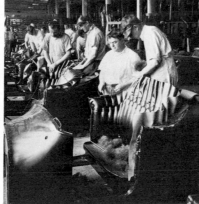

Left to right: cowl and body assembling, upholstering, rubbing down bodies between coats of paint, sandblasting before painting. All views circa 1915.

War Department tested several of the leading United States makes in a 2,000-mile run. In charge of the tests was Capt. F. L. Case, U.S. Army.

After it emerged the favorite, the Cadillac completed a second test of 5,000 miles, making 7,000 miles in all. During the test a total of only one and a half gallons of water had to be added to the radiator, and gas mileage averaged twelve to the U.S. gallon. The only repair part was a new fan spring (for the friction drive) costing thirty cents.

The Army took the Cadillac touring car as it stood, without changing a line or altering a dimension. A emergency fuel tank on the running board, tire chains added to the equipment, and olive drab finish — the car was unchanged.

Cadillac made a pointed comparison with America's aviation unpreparedness and hastily designed Liberty engine when they commented: "When it came time for the U.S. Army to adopt a standard seven-passenger car, it was not necessary to call the engineers of the country together to design and build one. The car was there — fit for the supreme test."

A total of 2,095 were shipped overseas, 199 to various posts and camps in the United States, and 221 to the Canadian government. A further 300 standard limousines were slightly modified for officer use, having leather upholstery instead of mohair, canvas blinds instead of taffeta, a cocoa floor mat and a map desk. In addition to the Army, the United States Marine Corps adopted the Cadillac as their standard officer's car.

An outstanding example of the car's performance in France was on the mail routes out of Paris, relieving the railroads. These runs varied from 150 to 200 miles, and the cars ran daily for months on end, averaging up to 55 mph. On one run from Bordeaux to Paris, Colonel Mullaly, brigade commander of the California Grizzlies, saw some fellow officers onto the Bordeaux-Paris express. All were to attend a reception for Belgium's King Albert in Paris the following day. More than an hour later, after supper, Colonel Mullaly and his driver left Bordeaux in their Cadillac, driving overnight to Paris. The express was on time, but when the officers reached the University Union to check in, they found Mullaly's Cadillac outside!

Colonel Hall, co-designer of the Liberty engine, wrote: "I believe these cars from my observation gave better service than any other make of car in France. I used Cadillac cars from fourteen to sixteen hours a day and most of the driving was done around an average of forty miles an hour. I was never held up on car trouble at any time. Furthermore, I never saw a Cadillac tied up for trouble of any kind. Many officers would delay their trips until they could get Cadillacs whereas there were many other makes of foreign and American manufacture available. One of the first things I did on my arrival home was to purchase one for my own use."

Lt. Col. George H. Johnson of the Canadian Army wrote that his Cadillac 44582 was the first Allied car to cross the Rhine, on November 18. Second Lt. W. Proctor of the Allied Expeditionary Force wrote: "Have sent fifty Cadillacs over to Paris to meet President Wilson. Nothing but Cadillacs in his convoy. Some car."

One sergeant noted that in seven months, from May to November, 1918, his car had traveled 21,000 miles, while another suggested, "If I were Pershing I would decorate the Cadillac with the D.F.C."

Besides supplying staff cars, Cadillac produced a searchlight unit using a Cadillac V-8 chassis of 145 inches. It weighed complete some 11,000 pounds less than the former unit, and could travel at 50 mph compared with the 15 to 20 mph of its predecessor. The sixty-inch searchlight had a range of fifteen miles.

The V-8 engine-transmission also powered the U.S. Army's 2½-ton artillery crawler tractor, 1,157 of which were built, and a balloon winch unit mounted on trucks.

One other application was noteworthy even though it was a "one-off" which never entered active service. This was the Davidson-Cadillac armored car of 1915, developed by Maj. (later Colonel) Royal P. Davidson, Commandant of the N.W. Military and Naval Academy in Wisconsin. Today it is recognized as one of the great early, pioneering armored fighting vehicles. Major Davidson had as early as 1898 built a powered three-wheeler with Colt machine gun. From then on his activities were continuous, notably with the three Cadillacs in 1909-1910 which he designed for anti-balloon work. One of them ran through a Glidden Tour! He followed these in 1911 and 1912 with Cadillac machine-gun vehicles carrying both wireless and powerful searchlights. Guatemala bought four of these vehicles, supplied by Cadillac itself.

Following the development of the armored vehicles for World War I, Davidson — in 1915 — produced a fleet of eight Cadillacs providing all the requirements of an armored force. There was a scout car with periscope, two wireless-equipped communications cars with telescopic antennae, a kitchen car with electric ovens supplied by a Delco generator, a hospital car, quartermasters' car, a balloon destroyer, and — the *pièce de résistance* — America's first full armored car.

A Cadillac staff car bearing Canadian officers enters Germany, 1918.

"The 1915 Davidson-Cadillac Armored Car was similar in layout to some of the early Royal Naval Air Service armored cars built in October, 1914," writes the English historian B. T. White, "Armored all round, with controllable radiator doors, the rear had an open top where the Colt machine gun with armored shield was mounted just behind the armored head cover for the driver. . . . The Cadillac was a much better designed vehicle than the RNAS cars, with a lower center of gravity and a better cross-country performance. It was capable of 70 mph on good roads."

Davidson, with picked cadets, in June, 1915, carried out a proper military exercise over long distances and later in the year participated in Army maneuvers. These demonstrated the versatility of the force and possibilities of mechanized warfare.

Cadillac's other major war effort was the production of the Liberty aero engine, although the circumstances were ironic. When Cadillac originally joined General Motors, William C. Durant assured the Lelands that they'd receive "no directions from anyone." The promise was observed by Durant, and after he left General Motors the arrangement continued, Cadillac operating as an autonomous company. But in 1916 Durant returned to control of General Motors. Relations this time between

the Lelands and Durant were not so cordial, as it was largely due to the Lelands' negotiations with the bankers that Durant had originally lost control of the organization.

Leland wanted to take on aero engine production, for which he was prepared to convert a new body plant, but Durant, a pacifist, refused. Leland was appalled at this, particularly since the nation was at war. Unable to move Durant, he and Wilfred resigned — and founded the Lincoln Motor Company for the express purpose of building Liberty aero engines, at which they were conspicuously successful. Many Cadillac employees followed the Lelands to join the new company, a number of important engineers and executives among them.

There was sadness on both sides at the break with the founder, but his work had been so well-done that the company never faltered. Richard H. Collins, a former salesman for John Deere, and later with Buick, was appointed the new president.

Ironically, Cadillac got into Liberty production not long after Leland left. Durant had had to change with the mood of the times. Realizing his error, he tried to get the Lelands to come back and direct Cadillac production of the aero engine, but they were already committed to their new company.

Cadillac and Cadillac people played significant roles in
World War I. Above is a V-8-powered winch, used
to raise military personnel for observation of the enemy,
then to lower them upon the approach of any
hostile aircraft. Below the wheeled searchlight,
towed by a Cadillac chassis fitted with army vehicle body.
At left on facing page, Wilfred and Henry M.
Leland, both now departed from Cadillac, flank the
first Liberty engine at its testing on July 4, 1917. Their
ex-rival Packard shows its flag behind H.M. On the
right is General Pershing (after the war) with 1920 staff car.

The Liberty engine was a joint product of the American automobile industry, but major credit for its design and development belongs to Packard which "had the vision to see the need for a fighting engine, . . . struggled through the developmental stage alone and smoothed the way for others." The chief designers were Jesse G. Vincent of Packard and E. J. Hall of the Hall-Scott Company. While Hall was vital to the project, Lt. Col. Phillip S. Dickey of the U.S. Air Force writes, "If any one man can be granted primary credit for the success of the Liberty, he is Vincent."

However, Cadillac's contribution was notable. They had two draftsmen on the design team, and in the paper stage the design was checked by outside experts, including George M. Layng and D. McCall White of Cadillac, as well as Henry Leland, who had only just left the company. Design started on May 29 and the first sets of prints from the engineering drawings were ready by July 5 — and an engine actually built by then. Ben Anibal of Cadillac, who had been in on the original design personally, took the prints back to Cadillac. The first twelve-cylinder prototype was running a fifty-hour test in August, and the first flight of a Liberty-powered plane took place the same month. The connecting rods and rocker arms for the first engine had come from Cadillac. Production of the engine was the overall responsibility of Kettering's Delco partner, Col. Edward A. Deeds, and among

the staff, coordinating design changes with production, were Wilfred Leland and White. In addition to designing and manufacturing the prototype connecting rods, Cadillac influenced the Liberty in other areas. It used Delco battery-generator ignition, with the patented Cadillac dual-contact arrangement first used on the Cadillac V-8, and when production began in the Holbrook Avenue plant Cadillac introduced improved methods of manufacture and testing. Most notable of the latter was the calibration of standard "club" propellers for all Liberty manufacturers. These club propellers eliminated the need for costly dyno testing of each engine.

The first production Liberties, tested in February, 1918, showed up very unsatisfactorily on load, and the whole lubrication system had to be redesigned. When these and other changes were made, the power plant emerged as one of the finest aero engines constructed. The first Cadillac-built Liberty was tested on May 13, 1918. GM production was shared with Buick, the corporation building about 2,528 engines in all, of the 20,478 produced by the U.S. automobile industry as a whole.

The Liberty has been criticized by English writers as "a fairly bad job, too heavy and unreliable," and "a 'nonstarter' so troublesome that not a single engine was able to contribute to the Allied cause." The facts, as given by the Smithsonian Institution and other reliable sources, are that: (1) By the armistice nearly

800 Liberty-powered DH-4's were *in service* with the American Expeditionary Force *alone* in France, and that even though these were reconnaissance and not fighter aircraft, they had already shot down fifty-nine enemy aircraft. Large numbers of Liberties also went to the British and French. A few more months of war would have seen several thousand DH-4's in service; 3,431 had been built but had not time to reach the front because, as Henry Leland commented, "The Kaiser ran away." (2) The Liberty had one of the best power-to-weight ratios of any water-cooled engine of its day or for a good many years later. It was substantially lighter per horsepower than, for instance, the Rolls-Royce Eagle, its closest rival. (3) Although it equaled or surpassed the best French and English engines in general efficiency, it was substantially simpler and cheaper to make in proportion to its horsepower. (4) Properly developed production versions were claimed by Vincent to be equal to the best French and English engines in reliability. Vincent, of course, can hardly be called an impartial authority, but it is a fact that he put his own beliefs to the test and personally flew thousands of miles behind Liberty engines during 1918. This was very rare among engine designers at that time, and the only other Allied designer with similar faith in his own powerplants is believed to have been W. O. Bentley.

It is also worth pointing out that the Liberty powered the very first Atlantic flight, the first nonstop trans-America flight, and

the first round-the-world flight, among many other notable exploits. No one in his right mind would have attempted such flights with an inherently unreliable engine.

All this considered, the most devastating commentary on this controversy is that the English themselves put the Liberty back into production during World War II to power British tanks!

The years of America's involvement in World War I had found Cadillac automobile development settled down to a pleasant consistency. There were only detail changes in the V-8's general design. *The Automobile* commented on the "really remarkable foresight in planning of both the design and the manufacture of the car." The Type 57 for 1918 featured detachable cylinder heads, a higher radiator and hood, and other minor changes. This design continued for two years as did the next series, the 59.

By now, writes John Bentley, the "Cadillac name represented not only the yardstick by which accuracy of American manufacturing methods were gauged in the automobile industry, but also the symbol of smooth and luxurious travel."

Wartime service had put the seal on what would prove to be the most significant model Cadillac had built, and the most successful luxury automobile in history. One French officer called it *"cette grande et si merveilleuse automobile Americaine!"*— while an American Air Corps officer, searching for a superlative to describe an aircraft, dubbed the Liberty-engined DH-4, "The Cadillac of the Air."

Now the Lelands were gone. Their departure marked the end of an era at Cadillac. Wilfred had made substantial contributions of his own and had been almost de facto general manager for years, but as his widow told this writer, "He was content to be his father's shadow."

In any summary the spotlight must be aimed at Henry Leland himself. No marque has ever had a more illustrious founder. He fully conforms with all the classic definitions of greatness and genius. Historically he was a decisive figure, yet unlike many famous men he had an impeccable moral code and private life. His mental alertness even at an advanced age was astonishing and was matched by an almost incredible physical toughness. On his eightieth birthday, for instance, he walked downstairs from his office to accept flowers and gifts from friends on the ground floor, then walked back upstairs to his office again. It was on the twenty-second floor of the Dime Building!

Henry Leland's technical achievements have been covered earlier; they need no further recounting. Let us instead close this chapter with the simple but telling tribute made by his associate, Ben Anibal: "He was a great mechanic. He understood quality."

The PENALTY OF LEADERSHIP

IN every field of human endeavor, he that is first must perpetually live in the white light of publicity. ¶Whether the leadership be vested in a man or in a manufactured product, emulation and envy are ever at work. ¶In art, in literature, in music, in industry, the reward and the punishment are always the same. ¶The reward is widespread recognition; the punishment, fierce denial and detraction. ¶When a man's work becomes a standard for the whole world, it also becomes a target for the shafts of the envious few. ¶If his work be merely mediocre, he will be left severely alone—if he achieve a masterpiece, it will set a million tongues a-wagging. ¶Jealousy does not protrude its forked tongue at the artist who produces a commonplace painting. ¶Whatsoever you write, or paint, or play, or sing, or build, no one will strive to surpass, or to slander you, unless your work be stamped with the seal of genius. ¶Long, long after a great work or a good work has been done, those who are disappointed or envious continue to cry out that it can not be done. ¶Spiteful little voices in the domain of art were raised against our own Whistler as a mountebank, long after the big world had acclaimed him its greatest artistic genius. ¶Multitudes flocked to Bayreuth to worship at the musical shrine of Wagner, while the little group of those whom he had dethroned and displaced argued angrily that he was no musician at all. ¶The little world continued to protest that Fulton could never build a steamboat, while the big world flocked to the river banks to see his boat steam by. ¶The leader is assailed because he is a leader, and the effort to equal him is merely added proof of that leadership. ¶Failing to equal or to excel, the follower seeks to depreciate and to destroy—but only confirms once more the superiority of that which he strives to supplant. ¶There is nothing new in this. ¶It is as old as the world and as old as the human passions—envy, fear, greed, ambition, and the desire to surpass. ¶And it all avails nothing. ¶If the leader truly leads, he remains—the leader. ¶Master-poet, master-painter, master-workman, each in his turn is assailed, and each holds his laurels through the ages. ¶That which is good or great makes itself known, no matter how loud the clamor of denial. ¶That which deserves to live—lives.

Cadillac Motor Car Co. Detroit, Mich.

Its leaders after leaving Cadillac, 1919. Left to right: Frank Johnson, Walter Phipps, Wilfred Leland, Ernest Sweet, Henry M. Leland.

CHAPTER SEVEN

TECHNOLOGY IN THE TWENTIES

A remarkable cadre of talented engineers combine to further Cadillac's mechanical preeminence

The end of the war in November, 1918, presented Cadillac with no great reconversion problems, as car production had been continuous. Many of the 2,600 Cadillac employees who had joined up for military service returned, and in 1919 production was 19,851 cars. But production of components involved seventy-seven different buildings around Detroit, so Cadillac decided on an entirely new manufacturing plant at Clark Avenue, on a site originally selected by H. M. Leland. The old Cass and Amsterdam plant was sold to Fisher Body and later razed. The site is now a parking lot opposite Dalgleish Cadillac.

An enormous building program actually continued through most of the twenties, and its final phases were not carried out until 1927. In September of that year the new $600,000 administration building was opened, concluding the final stage of the $25,000,000 project. Begun in 1925, this last stage included, besides the office building, a new foundry unit covering seven acres of ground, a new 750 by 126-foot assembly building, and additions to the Cadillac distribution facilities.

The administration building occupied a central position among other plant buildings. It had a frontage of 321 feet and a depth of fifty-six feet. It was thoroughly fireproof and was four stories high above basement, with provision for a fifth floor when needed. Architecturally it conformed with the remainder of the plant. Exterior was of ornamental brick and Bedford limestone. Interior finish was in keeping with the highest construction standards. The entrance was wainscoted ten feet high with French Tavernelli marble, with ceiling in decorative plaster paneling. The main staircase was done in Tennessee marble. Chief executive offices were in American walnut, with walls paneled eight feet high. The remaining offices were done in fumed oak.

The car offered in those first postwar years — 19,790 were produced in 1921 — did not differ greatly from earlier models. All the requirements of peace and rigors of wartime service had proved the soundness of the design, and a seller's market existed that discouraged radical changes that would have interfered with production. There was also the interruption involved in moving manufacture into the new Clark Avenue plant, which reduced production to only 11,130 cars for 1921. When the new factory was opened that year it was regarded as the most modern in the world.

"The site of the main plant now covers more than forty-nine acres, and the buildings provide over fifty-five acres of floor space," ran a contemporary description. "The new factory is flooded with daylight, and a splendid forced ventilation system now provides a constant supply of pure air. Much of the machinery was designed and built specially to meet the requirements of Cadillac. . . . The buildings are in two groups: the manufacturing section, in which the parts of the car are prepared, and the assembly building, where these parts are put together. . . . This factory has an annual capacity, without night shifts, of 30,000 Cadillac cars."

In the last year of the Type 59 — 1921 — the wheelbase was increased to 132 inches. The Type 61 was announced in September, 1921, and Cadillac made an important carburetion advance, standardized on these 1922 models. Mixture control was now by thermostatic means, entirely automatic throughout the speed range, and other than the choke button used for starting, the driver was relieved of all carburetion adjustments. More efficient carburetion and driving convenience were the advantages, as well as safety, for the driver could give more attention to road

After the war Cadillac was ready for major growth, and began at once to build their new plant at 2860 Clark Avenue. The view above shows progress made as of June 12, 1920. Production dipped to 11,130 units for 1921, when Cadillac was moving in, but soared with the rest of the economy during the twenties. At left and right are two Presidents from the era, motoring in Cadillacs, Woodrow Wilson being greeted in Boston in 1919 on his return from Europe, and a top-hatted Calvin Coolidge in Florida with Miami mayor Sewell.

and traffic conditions.

The 61 was changed in appearance, with a higher radiator having fuller shoulders, and a fuller hood, while the change from thirty-five- to thirty-three-inch wheels lowered the car and its center of gravity. Axle ratios were changed and 4.9, 4.5 and 4.15 were offered. Smartest of the line, and very desirable today, was the rakish four-passenger "sport phaeton," capable of seventy to seventy-five miles an hour.

Production for 1922 was back above the 20,000 mark for the first time since 1915, setting a calendar year record of 22,021 cars. Total production for the high-low years of 1921-1922 was 32,635, which averaged out to 16,318 cars — roughly the Cadillac norm over the first decade of V-8 production. Prices ranged from $3,000 to $5,000.

The volume of Cadillac output was a constant source of amazement to European automotive authorities. They could not understand, and in many cases flatly refused to believe, that a car built in such quantities — equal to the largest European *mass* producers — could equal in quality their finest automobiles — handbuilt at a rate of a few hundred units per year, and several times the price of a Cadillac. But a study of Cadillac technical literature and a tour through the plant would have silenced any doubts.

"The Cadillac steering arm is made from a high quality chrome nickel steel alloy," read one booklet. "Tensile strength 150,000 lbs. per square inch. As a check on their correct composition and heat treatment, a small nipple is forged on each arm, later to be removed and examined.

"The steel in the axle drive shaft must show a tensile strength of 175,000 lbs. per square inch. Every forging is sand blasted before inspection to make sure that no defect may be hidden by dirt or scale, and *every* single forging (not one in a hundred) is submitted to the Brinell hardness test.

"While the principle of progressive manufacturing is recognized in the Cadillac factory with reference to the orderly movement of materials and parts in a general direction, the ordinary method of engine assembly on a production line does not conform with the requirements of Cadillac. . . . One man, an expert, is made responsible for the assembling of each Cadillac engine. The parts and sub-assemblies are brought to him as a complete set, conveniently arranged on a movable rack designed for that purpose. By this practice each engine is individually built and the assembler has a powerful incentive to maintain a high standard of excellence. His work is keyed and can be identified years afterward. . . . After being completed and passing its preliminary inspection, each engine is tested on the block for six hours. Operating against electrical resistance, it is run at a gradually increasing speed with a corresponding increase in load. . . . At the conclusion of the block test, the crank case is opened, all lubricants removed, and the interior of the engine subjected to careful inspection. After being restored to operating condition, it is bolted into position in the chassis and undergoes a further test against resistance for two hours, the load being supplied by rotating drums in contact with the rear wheels. In addition, the chassis undergoes a final test on the road.

"All dimensions in manufacture are controlled by an elaborate

A 1921 Cadillac 59 touring.

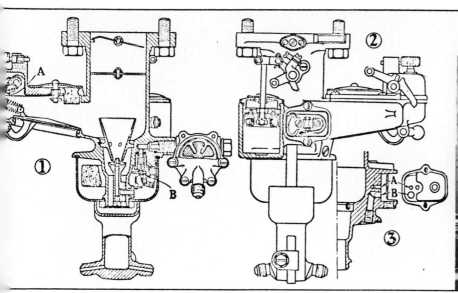

Left: a carburetor, 1923, shows air valve (A), needle valve (B), throttle pump (2), uncovered ports (3). Right: 1922's on line.

system of exact measurements. The minute variations permitted are finely graduated in accordance with requirements of the respective parts. More than 1,000 dimensions are held to limits of one one-thousandth of an inch, and more than 300 dimensions are held to one half-thousandth. . . . For this purpose 20,000 precision instruments are available, and 14,000 are constantly in use. . . . The accuracy of these precision instruments is constantly tested, the piston pin gauges, for example, being checked twice every day. The ultimate measure of accuracy is the Johansson gauge, the last word in mechanical measurement."

These gauge blocks were in three grades: the AA, accurate to ± two one-millionths of an inch, block length; the A, accurate to ± four one-millionths; and the B, accurate to eight one-millionths. The AA grade was used only to make an occasional check of the A grade blocks and was kept in temperature-controlled vaults, never touched by human hands.

The A grade blocks were used to frequently check the B grade or working blocks. The B grade blocks were used to check other measuring instruments such as micrometers, or to check the dimensions of finished work when the tolerance was very small. Another system was the Hokc gauge, developed by Major William E. Hoke of the National Bureau of Standards. He had originally improved the Johansson gauges by devising mechanical methods of production that reduced costs and made them practical for widespread use. With the Hoke gauge there

were two main types instead of three as with the Johannson. The higher or "laboratory" grade was similar to the Johannson AA grade, and the lower fell between the A and B Johannsons, being accurate to five one-millionths of an inch.

Turning from mechanical items to the car bodies, the booklet continued: "Bodies for Cadillac cars are built at the body plant and then finished at the assembly building. The body is twenty-eight days passing through the paint shops, where it receives eighteen coats of paint and varnish. [This, of course, was before Duco lacquers.] The body is dried after each coat, and after the color varnish, the body is upholstered, rubbed, striped, and finally covered with clear varnish. This care is the reason for the beautiful luster of the finished cars.

"From the clear varnish room, it goes to the final assembly line, on the first floor of the assembly building. Here all the parts are put on, such as windshield and instruments. The body is then placed on the chassis and is ready for final testing. . . . After the final assembly is made the car is given a road test and then prepared for shipping. . . . It is given a thorough cleaning, covered with linen to keep away dust, and then placed securely in a box-car for transportation."

From the time that manufacture got underway in the new plant, production records were set as the ground lost in the changeover was made up. Schedules ran at over 100 cars daily, maintained through the winter season. The factory payroll reached

Photographs from Ernest W. Seaholm show Cadillac in test roles and climbing Pikes Peak during the early post-World War I years. From lower left, proceeding in clockwise direction on this page, and quoting Mr. Seaholm's own comments: "test in mid-winter, mud, more mud, climbing Pikes Peak and at the crest of the peak." Aside from the convincing photographic evidence of the rigors its maker put the Cadillac through is the accurate view of what "highways" were like in those early days, and what a driver put up with as a matter of course on cross country runs such as these. Not all of the car manufacturers were ready to put their products to these tests. Cadillac, on the contrary, was.

8,000. General sales manager, Lynn McNaughton, announced in June, 1922, that a record of 150 Type 61's had been completed and shipped in one twenty-four hour period. More than half of these were closed cars, worth a total of over $700,000. A large increase in exports was shown to all parts of the world — 213 percent in Buenos Aires, thirty-seven percent in Norway, 135 percent in London, 420 percent in Sidney, 651 percent in Utrecht.

The following year McNaughton was made a vice president of the company. He said that sales for the previous twelve months exceeded any previous period both in unit number and total value. This was accompanied by strengthening of the dealer organization, improvement in service facilities, and erection of many new buildings by distributors and dealers.

In February, 1923, Cadillac announced standardized parts prices throughout the country, eliminating variables such as war tax, freight, and handling charges, and also introduced a system of standard rates for various repair jobs — the beginning of the Flat Rate principle.

In 1921 R. H. Collins left Cadillac, taking a number of engineers and executives with him, first intending to produce a Collins car, but later taking over Peerless. H. H. Rice succeeded him as Cadillac general manager in 1921. Rice had been a Cadillac salesman in Providence, Rhode Island, in 1903. Later he served as advertising manager and president of the Pope Manufacturing Company, afterward joining GM in 1916.

General Motors itself was reorganized in 1920 after Durant

Cadillac test crews took their brand-new cars everywhere in a steady effort to prove them better than the competition and to try out new components or equipment. Above we find the three cars shown on the facing page posing for their "proof of the pudding" photograph at the top of the peak, an automotive challenge often accepted by a manufacturer anxious to impress the world with the tenacity of his products. Apparently one car has been washed; the rest still show the accumulations of the trip up. At left below, one of the same trio poses for posterity in a sizable storm puddle; at right, among sequoias.

became involved in a big financial crisis for the second time. As on the previous occasion, Durant's debts were paid off by outside financiers, who assumed virtual control and compelled Durant's resignation. The new regime, headed by Pierre S. du Pont and John J. Raskob, was wholly beneficial, for a complete reorganization took place under the executive vice president, Alfred P. Sloan.

"Essentially, Sloan gave General Motors the staff-and-line pattern of a military organization," wrote Professor J. B. Rae in *American Automobile Manufacturers*. "The separate companies were transformed into operating divisions, each with virtually complete responsibility for its management. The staff functions, such as research, financial policy, and sales policy, were organized separately, with their services available to the whole General Motors family, but without direct authority over the operating divisions. The effectiveness of this plan may be judged from the fact that it has lasted without substantial alteration to the present and has been imitated by General Motors' competitors."

Despite the stability of Cadillac, there had been a period of frequent changes in its engineering staff during the First World War and afterward. First there was the departure of Henry M. Leland and a number of engineering associates; then D. McCall White left, to be succeeded by Benjamin Anibal, who in 1921 went with R. H. Collins to Peerless, and later worked at Oakland to produce the new Pontiac.

At this period a new name became prominent at Cadillac — Ernest W. Seaholm. Under the regime of this brilliant man, who

Beautiful as is this V-63, Two Passenger Coupe, its true greatness lies in more vital qualities —in the smoothness and quietness of its harmonized and balanced V-Type, 90° eight-cylinder engine; in its riding comfort; in the safety of Cadillac Four Wheel Brakes.

These qualities can be gauged by no former standards; they are unique and can be appreciated only by actually riding in the car.

Take this ride, in the Two Passenger Coupe or in any of the new V-63 models, and learn the full significance of Cadillac's invitation to you to *expect great things*

CADILLAC MOTOR CAR COMPANY, DETROIT, MICHIGAN
Division of General Motors Corporation

At left, R. H. Collins. At right, Herbert Rice.

C A D I L L A

THE FOLLY *of* UNSELLING

℺ If a man truly deserves a high destiny, he will attain it. Time spent trying to thwart him is worse than waste time because it corrodes the spirit of the one who makes the attack. Effort against another rarely succeeds unless that other has already failed. ℺ If your adversary is vulnerable it is permissible perhaps to press home your own superiority. ℺ But, again, if he deserves and is deserving of his high destiny—you wound yourself when you seek to injure him. ℺ There are those men, and those artistries, and those business institutions, which never relax their integrity and never lose their title as leaders. ℺ They do not lose their leadership because they strive with mind, heart and soul to continue to deserve it. ℺ Wise men do not waste time tilting at such high peaks as these. ℺ More especially, wise men do not seek to alienate the millions who have bestowed the leadership. ℺ When men in the mass have conferred fame and glory upon a name, it becomes in a sense their name, and they guard it jealously. ℺ They are, as we say in the colloquialism of commerce, 'sold' on that name; which means that they believe in it implicitly. ℺ And, of all the follies of selling, there is no greater folly than that of seeking to unsell that which is well and truly sold in the minds of men. ℺ Unselling fails a thousand times where once it wins a hollow victory. ℺ It delays, and distracts, and stirs up the muddiest depths of anger and envy. It poisons the sources of mental and creative activity and diverts them from their honest and healthful purposes. ℺ The excitement and the enthusiasm it engenders in the salesman who has undertaken the thankless task is a false and artificial emotion, born of unworthy motives. It punishes him whose one desire is to inflict punishment. ℺ Meanwhile, the man, or the thing, or the business house, of high destiny goes on unperturbed. ℺ If that destiny is deserved, it will be attained and maintained.

CADILLAC
Division of General Motors Corporation

succeeded Anibal as chief engineer in 1921 and remained in that position for twenty-two years, there came a flood of important technical achievements rarely equalled by any automobile manufacturer.

Although never the center of personal publicity like Leland and Kettering, Seaholm was a dedicated professional man whose identity was submerged in the product. He represented the kind of talent that enriched America from abroad; his parents came from Lidköping, Sweden. They landed in New York in July, 1889, when he was a little over one year old. From there they went to Hartford, Connecticut where, as Seaholm recalls:

"Father worked as a cabinetmaker and I attended public schools. In 1903 we moved to Springfield, Massachusetts, and it was here that I attended what was then known as the Mechanics Arts High School, graduating in June, 1905. This school, at the time, was more or less an experimental venture, which over the years became the Springfield Technical High School. I was in the second class to graduate — fifteen members (boys). Our course had included English, French, history, physics, chemistry, woodworking, pattern-making, machine shop, and mechanical drawing. Looking back, it was an excellent foundation for a fellow who couldn't go to college, in those days, and needed to make a living.

"On graduation, I freelanced for awhile as a mechanical draftsman — then was hired by Mr. Clark W. Parker, a New England inventor who was developing among other things an automobile transmission. He incorporated and promoted a com-

At left, William R. Strickland. At right, Ernest W. Seaholm.

pany known as the Parker Transmission Company. I was his designer. It failed, but meanwhile Mr. Parker had made the acquaintance of Henry Leland, who contracted with him to join Cadillac for development work. He asked me to come along, which I was happy to do, and beginning September, 1913, I was on the Cadillac payroll.

"Mr. Parker failed to find a niche for himself in the Cadillac organization of the day. Strangers seemed unwelcome. As for me, there was a lot of work to be done and in my echelon it seemed to be accepted. Offside, I obtained some valuable experience in tool design working for their tool engineer, getting ready for their new revolutionary V-8 production, and learning about their precision standards and shop practices. Then in 1916 Mr. Parker embarked on a new venture, the Parker Rust Proof Company. He made me an offer to go with him, which I accepted. It proved to be a transitory connection. After a little more than a year I was back at Cadillac.

"When I returned in 1917 we were in the war. The Lelands had left to found the Lincoln Company, and to concentrate on production of the Liberty motors; Cadillac had a new manager, R. H. Collins — D. McCall White was chief engineer, and Ben Anibal headed up design. I was on his staff.

"Car production during the war years, except for military usage, was at a standstill. The manufacturing of Liberty motors, cylinders, blocks, connecting rods, and camshafts was our main concern. For this a new plant had been erected and equipped throughout with the latest in the way of machinery. D. McCall White sent me over there — a strange territory — with the simple instructions, 'Make yourself useful.' Later D. McCall became a member of a congressionally appointed committee to investigate failure of the early Liberty motors, and, in turn, he assigned me along with others to get in on the testing. It was an experience — operating behind a protection barrier — opening the throttle and seeing the connecting rods exploding through the crankcase.

"The Liberty was designed 'overnight' by Vincent [of Packard] and a committee of which D. McCall White was a member. Ben Anibal had a part as the designer of the forked connecting rods — chosen for his knowledge of similar Cadillac V-8 rods. The engine itself, it seems, was partly patterned after a hydroplane engine in use on the west coast, and the designer of this engine, E. J. Hall, played a big role in its design. Its lubricating system was the cause of its failures. This was a splash system (no pressure) with some scuppers on the crankshaft scooping up the oil. The congressionally appointed committee to

The 1926 314 unit (above) was an inherently balanced V-8 engine. This was achieved by crankshaft balancing weights shown opposite.

investigate and report included Vincent, White, and the chief engineer of Franklin, John Wilkinson. Henry Crane was prominently on hand during the actual tests, as were a couple of British Admiralty and a couple of Italian officers. Crane may have been part of the appointed committee, I never knew. Fenn Holden and I were there along with several others of the testing crews, and, as it turned out, didn't have too much to do. There were several motors tested over a period of time, each test covering a matter of minutes except the last, which had incorporated a pressure lubricating system like the Cadillac V-8. Cadillac bearing material was also adopted, and then we got them to survive the fifty-hour test. Eventually came Armistice Day. I was back at my drawing board, happy it was over."

Seaholm continued with his recollections of the leading personalities in Cadillac engineering at this period. First, of course, was the "big boss."

"Henry M. Leland — I never recall meeting him personally. I was on the lower rung and he was at the top — and had some sort of sanctuary of his own in which he worked. He was an outstanding individual — very tall, gray hair and beard, a veritable patriarch, still riding around in an old single-cylinder Cadillac fitted with a coupé body . . . and almost high enough to enter standing up. He worked long hours. I learned this when I first arrived — for when he worked into the night, all salaried men worked into the night — and I was one of these.

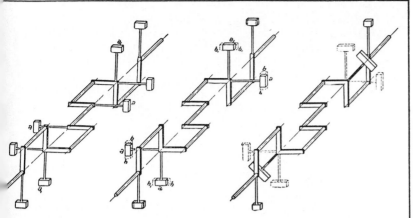

FIG. 5—HOW THE BALANCING WEIGHTS APPLIED TO THE CRANKSHAFT WERE DEVELOPED the Left the Weights Are Shown Divided and Applied to the Prolongation of the Checks Adjacent to the nkpins To Facilitate Practical Construction. In the Next Step the Weights a in the Central Drawing Are laced by the Weights b and To Produce a Symmetrical Weight Symmetrically Arranged on the Intermediate cks the Weights b, Are Added to the Weights a, and the Size of the Pair of End Weights Is Reduced as Shown the Dotted Lines. The Final Arrangement Is Shown Diagrammatically in the Drawing at the Right in Which Two Weights on the Intermediate Checks, Which Are Represented by Dotted Lines, Are Replaced by the Resultant Weights Shown in Full Lines and the End-Check Weights Are Reduced

"Fundamentally, he was a craftsman. Excellence and quality were something that he preached and insisted on — and strangely its attainment has been the goal ever since — to this day in fact; standards are higher today than ever.

"His organization was like a tight little family group. It wasn't easy to get accepted and those in the circle had apparently been around together for some time.... Ernest E. Sweet was his right-hand man. He, to my knowledge, didn't have a title, but seemed the man who coordinated things engineering-wise and production-wise generally and was closest to Henry M.

"Frank Johnson was the designing engineer and had played an important part in bringing Cadillac up through its early days prior to the advent of the V-8.... Fenn M. Holden was research chief. He had joined Cadillac in 1908, served as assistant research engineer for five years, and became chief of that department in 1913. I was with him on the Liberty program, and then he was selected as a member of the Bolling aircraft commission to Europe. After the war, Holden returned to Cadillac research and also did work for the aircraft division of GM."

Seaholm outlined the upheavals at Cadillac during this period, which culminated in his "appointment" as chief engineer in July, 1921:

"When the Lelands left in 1917 to form a company to manufacture Liberty motors — subsequently this became the Lincoln Company — with them departed their key men — Sweet,

Johnson and numerous production men.... In 1918, D. McCall White followed suit, leaving, in high hopes, to found the Lafayette Company — taking with him designers and draftsmen who had been working with him at Cadillac.

"Then (in 1921) R. H. Collins left and with him Ben Anibal and three other department heads to resurrect Peerless — Holden, Milner and Schwartz, heads of experimental, body and electrical departments.... You can imagine things looked dark. It was catastrophic, like suddenly losing your backbone. All the leaders from the top down were gone and those of us left were confused and anxious. In a short period of time we had two different managers, and then things settled down and a new organization took shape.

"This phase is a story in itself. Officially I was never designated as Chief Engineer. When the new managers came in, both unfamiliar with the operating of an automobile plant, I, due to my seniority possibly, and knowing my way around in this area, became the man that they contacted on engineering developments. No questions were asked and, in time, I found myself in charge. This went on for twenty years.

"William R. Strickland was the first in accession, in October, 1922. With the Cadillac men taking over, he had lost his position at Peerless, and for us it was almost providential to have him join up. He was of a bit older generation with a rich experience in the design of quality cars and while he was with us he was my assistant chief."

Born in Cincinnati in 1875, Strickland had gained a B.S. degree at MIT in 1898. Serving in the U.S. Navy in the Spanish-American War, he followed with eight years in civil engineering. In 1908, Strickland joined American Radiator Corporation as assistant manager, later moving to Peerless Motor Company as assistant chief engineer. Later as chief engineer, he introduced the famous Peerless V-8, after which he became vice president of the company.

Seaholm continued with his account of the research work of the twenties, the first fruit of which was the inherently balanced V-8 engine.

"About this time Kettering was getting the GM Research Laboratories under way. He had assembled a group of scientists and technologists for research and development beyond that within the [usual] scope of the automobile factories.... He had a way of asking questions for which no ready answers were available and then working out the solution. Among them: why do some fuels 'knock' in an engine and others not? This set in motion endless experiments that culminated in Ethyl gas with all its benefits." Although not the father of the Cadillac V-8, Ket had always taken an avuncular interest in it.

"So out of a clear sky came the question: 'Why does the Cadillac V-8, in spite of weighing of reciprocating parts and careful balancing of the crankshaft, have this annoyingly rough period?' Here his mathematicians went to work and came up with the crankshaft we now use and which has made this powerplant so desirable.

"It was one of the most important and fundamental developments in V-8 history.

"Kettering, brilliant engineer, scientist and inventor, was also a superb salesman, and so once he had solved this question, the heat was on to incorporate it in the Cadillac car. Unintentionally, possibly, we dragged our feet. The answer had come rather late. We were in the process of releasing next year's model so why not wait another year, etc.? He just wouldn't take 'no' for an answer and, while Herby Rice and I were in Europe for the automobile shows, he got to Mr. Sloan and they ruled it a must. When I returned Strickland had it well in hand. During this phase he had been virtually seconded to work at GM Research on the new shaft."

Kettering's mathematicians who worked on the two-plane shaft were T. P. Chase and Roland V. Hutchinson. The latter was associated with the Dayton work and with some done at Detroit shortly after the experimental engine was delivered to Cadillac. Hutchinson had some interesting comments:

"The first design and installation of a 'quartered' crankshaft for Cadillac was made under my supervision and to my instructions at the GM Research Laboratories in Dayton, Ohio, around 1921. Wright Aeronautical Corporation was reputed to have independently so converted an obsolescent 300 horsepower Hisso aero engine about the same time. . . . The scheme, set forth in *Balancing of Engines* by Sharp in 1907, was mentioned as a possibility in works published in 1916 with which I had been familiar since early 1918.

"Most builders of the old flat-crank V-8's soon realized the advantages of the new engine, not only in balance, but in avoiding the heavy loads on the center main bearing inseparable from a mirror symmetrical crankshaft, and so making a shorter and more compact engine."

"Hutch," commented Maurice Olley, "had a long span of engineering work, from about 1912-1913. He is a prime source of information on GM engine development, his background on engines reaching farther back than the GM Corporation — back to the Dayton-Wright Company prior to World War I, to Orville Wright, and Charles Kettering at Dayton. His grasp of engineering design problems, and of the mathematics to them, is of a very high order. He made quite an impression on the whole development of engines between the wars."

The technical problem and its solution were as follows:

Cadillac, like all V-8 makers up to that time, had used a simple four-cylinder type crankshaft in which the throws were 180

Left on the facing page, New Zealand's Newman Brothers service car in 1929. At right, Newman's royal convoy for Duke of York, 1927. Above, checking a 314 for nighttime visibility and glare. In the historic photograph below, standing behind the 1927 LaSalle are, from the left: Boston distributor Danforth, L.P. Fisher, sales managers Dunivan and Stephens, assistant general manager Lynn McNaughton, Harley Earl, H. Batchelor and R. Jose of Sales. E.W. Seaholm is behind the wheel. Seated next to him is factory manager Bert Widman.

degrees apart, or in a single plane. This worked well except that there remained the secondary out-of-balance force normal in a four-cylinder engine. In the 90 degree engine this force from the set of pistons in each bank combined to produce a horizontal resultant 41.4 percent greater than one set of pistons, the vertical components neutralizing one another but the horizontal components combining in the ratio of $\sqrt{2}$ to 1. At the critical speed — about 2,000 rpm in the Cadillac, or a road speed between forty and fifty miles an hour — this horizontal shaking force produced vibration.

In the first seven years of production this "period" was accepted as a small price to pay for the generally improved smoothness of the V-8 torque pattern over the six, and the majority of the cars sold had been open touring models in which the vibration was not as apparent as in a fully enclosed body with more panel work to "drum." However, during that seven-year period the production of closed cars increased from seven to fifty-four percent of the total. Something had to be done. The solution finally devised — the two-plane shaft — was described in detail by Seaholm himself in the *SAE Journal* for January, 1924.

Seaholm pointed out that the two-plane method was not new in theory and had been discussed in textbooks and the technical press over the years. Cadillac had, however, produced the first practical solution and had also solved a problem unresolved in the text books: how to eliminate the couples that arose with a two-plane layout. "With these forces present," Seaholm wrote, "complete smoothness cannot be realized. [We] arrived at a solution through the employment of compensating weights properly proportioned and disposed along the crankshaft."

With this crank and balance disposition, the engine was balanced as four ninety-degree V-twins, and the primary forces were counteracted by the revolving masses. Secondary balance was perfect because the adjacent pairs of pistons in each bank worked on cranks at ninety degrees, and the secondary forces equalized throughout, the sine wave of one secondary force being at all times ninety degrees out of phase with the other (i.e., a cosine) and thus perfectly opposing it. The couples were balanced out by the compensating weights. The result was, for the first time, perfect dynamics in a V-8 engine.

Following Seaholm in the *SAE Journal*, Cadillac design engineer D. E. Anderson explained the practical balancing aspects for production shafts. Parts were graded by weight on scales accurate to four one-thousandths of a pound, marked in hundredths of a pound and complete piston rod assemblies held within one-eighth of an ounce of each other per engine. The shafts were balanced on a specially-designed machine combining static and dynamic balancing, and correction was made by drilling the counterweights. This machine, which later became popular with a good many manufacturers in various countries, enabled a mere three men to handle over one hundred crankshafts per day.

The smoother running of the new engine required more careful balancing of the clutch and driveshaft assemblies, and machines for this purpose were developed. Static and dynamic tests were made on every unit at speeds up to 3,000 rpm, before they were passed for assembly into each car.

The new V-63 model (the "V" emphasized engine development) was announced in September, 1923. It featured eleven new bodies, restyled radiator, headlamps and fenders, and four wheel brakes on the Perrot system, which GM had already adopted on the Buick earlier that year. The Perrot system was a method of applying brakes to the front wheels mechanically, and used rods

or cables connected to short universally jointed shafts — called "Perrot shafts" — which could be adapted to the turn of the wheels in steering, yet transmit brake torque at the same time. But the main interest, at least to engineers, lay in the V-63's engine.

Maurice Olley, at that time chief engineer of Rolls-Royce of America, recalled foreseeing that "the quartered-crank V-8 would make obsolete all long crankshaft engines," and David Fergusson, chief engineer of Cunningham, issued to his own engineers and salesmen a bulletin which dwelled on the engine in the highest possible terms. Expressing admiration for Cadillac as builders of "one of the best cars in the world," who "have done most to popularize the V-8," he wrote that in 1914, while chief engineer at Pierce-Arrow, he had realized the V-8 would give the then dominant six-cylinder "strong competition." He had actually designed a V-8 at the time, but remained faithful to the six because of the flat crank V-8's vibration period. Even so, he had

THE CADILLAC CHASSIS FOR 1927

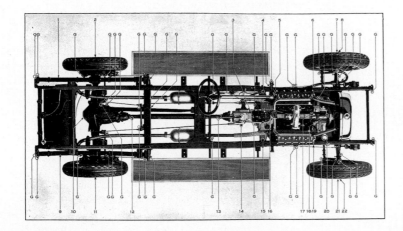

The 1927 chassis with lubrication points shows a "G" for each grease gun connection. Each number indicates a lubricating point. Lubricating points that are visible in the diagram are surrounded by circles, while others are indicated by arrows. There are sixty-five points.

POWER FOR HARLEY EARL'S CLASSICS

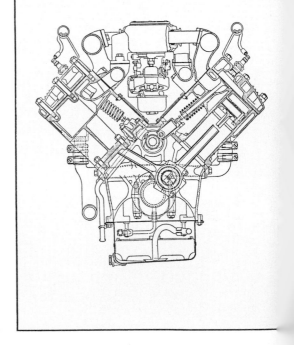

been aware of the six's shortcomings. "In sizes not over three and one-half inches bore it gives splendid results, but above this size, the long shaft twists unduly, and very large diameter shafts must be used to keep this down. Vibration is experienced and unless dampened produces a very objectionable tremor.

"With the acceptance of higher speed engines, the desirability of a greater number of cylinders than six became evident. The old, large-diameter, long-stroke sixes ran very smoothly at low and medium speeds. But they developed excessive vibration, and heating trouble, and wear when run twenty-five percent to thirty percent faster. To hold its own in acceleration, hill climbing, and speed, a still larger six had to be used, giving trouble by its greatly increased weight and excessive vibration due to the great length of the crankshaft. This was advisedly abandoned years ago, after it was recognized as an out-of-date proposition and a move in the wrong direction.

"The vertical-eight cylinder is an improvement over the six in small sizes, yet in larger engines of appreciably over three and three-eighths inches bore the excessively long crankshaft vertical-eight develops a most objectionable torsional vibration.

"This new V-8 arrangement gives perhaps the greatest perfection it is possible to attain. The smoothness of its running has won the admiration of all automobile engineers and all discriminating drivers. The shaft is so short that without great diameter there is scarcely any torsional vibration. . . . The compactness and rigidity cannot be approached by a straight eight. It would appear that this is the ultimate point in multiple cylinder construction as the twelve-cylinder has been abandoned."

The V-8, he continued, allowed a shorter vehicle for the same body space, and a lower center of gravity. He predicted with confidence that it would ultimately predominate as the engine for luxury cars.

Thirty-five thousand V-63's were built during its two-year run (1924-1925) and in its second year Cadillac announced that their

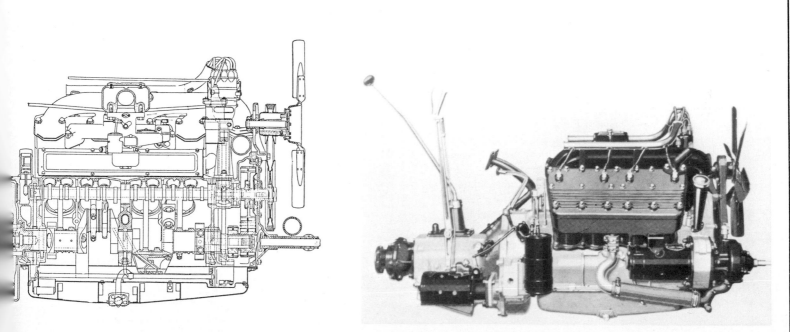

Fitted to the new 1928 Earl-designed Cadillacs was the new 341 engine.

total V-8 production had passed 180,000 units and *"not one of these engines has ever been replaced by the factory for any reason."* (Italics added.)

In August, 1925, for the 1926 model year, the new "314" model was announced. This was an "interim" design, bridging the gap between the first generation of the V-8's and the second. The engine retained the bore-stroke dimensions, crankshaft assembly, and structure of earlier models, but had some major differences in cooling and electrics. One pump only was used, and thermostatic radiator shutters replaced the valve type. A Delco two-unit electrical system, with vertically mounted starter-motor and separate generator, replaced the single unit. Crankcase ventilation was featured.

The main chassis change was the introduction of longitudinal, semi-elliptic springs at the rear in place of the old platform suspension. This lowered the car, and, in comparison with earlier models, the "314" was "sleeker, well-groomed, low-crouching." The frontal appearance was distinguished by a rounded radiator shell of attractive design. New car production for 1926 was 27,340 as compared with Packard's 34,907.

The engineer group responsible for the "314" consisted of E. W. Seaholm, chief engineer; W. R. Strickland, assistant chief engineer; Frank Johnson, assistant engineer, engine and transmission design; H. H. Gilbert, research engineer, laboratory and testing; G. E. Parker, designer; and W. N. Davis, body engineer.

In 1927 an important change occurred. Frank Johnson, one of the old Leland "family group," had left Cadillac in 1917 with the Lelands, and remained with them at Lincoln until September, 1921, when he returned to Cadillac. At first with George Layng in manufacture, where his experience in tool design was put to good use, he was soon back in the engineering department under Seaholm, who had a healthy respect for Johnson's ability as one of the ablest engine designers in America. Johnson's second spell at Cadillac lasted about five years, until in 1926 Thomas J. Litle, chief at Lincoln, shifted to Marmon. Johnson then went back to Lincoln, while his place was taken at Cadillac by Owen Milton Nacker, who had been a consultant with A. P. Brush.

Born in Highland, Michigan, in 1883, Nacker was in his middle forties when he came to Cadillac. "I have no recollection of the circumstances accompanying his arrival at Cadillac," Ernest Seaholm commented. "As near as I can tell, he just emerged. He had been hired as an engine designer — something we sorely needed after Johnson's departure, and really came to my attention when his performance marked him as a man of ex-

Cadillac advertising bespoke the halcyon days of the late twenties.

ceptional ability and one whom those working with him looked up to and accepted as a leader.

"He had been in the industry more years than any of us except Strickland (who was nearing retirement). As an engine designer he was 'tops.' Under his leadership our engines 'matured,' as Olley would say, and so did some of the young men who had become part of his team. Among them were Jack Gordon, Eddie Cole, and Harry Barr."

It was under Nacker's direction that the magnificent 341-353 series engines were developed, and the V-12 and V-16 were conceived. Ernest Seaholm considered Nacker's engines the finest that Cadillac produced up to World War II:

"They were quite a different animal from that inherited from the departing group back in 1922. Developmentally speaking, the latter was loaded with troubles. In the two-plane version we went to a 16-lobe cam to relieve the rather heavily-loaded cams, each of which served two valves. The 314 was an interim design, because at that time it was easier to balance the rotating couples out with opposite cylinders in the same plane. Shortly after, it was found possible to balance out satisfactorily even with offset blocks. As these gave the desirable plain rod, side by side, this

MacManus continued to handle Cadillac's ads with the above examples.

design was adopted for the new 341 series engines.

"Over the years we had persistently strived to make our engines better—never satisfied—and it paid off."

The first car with the new series engine was the LaSalle, introduced in March, 1927, after some two years actual preparation following surveys and planning that dated back to 1923. The LaSalle is remembered primarily as a stylist's car, but it was also important to the Cadillac engineering story. It was practically all new from the 328 engine (with model 314 electrics) to a new transmission with torque-tube drive to a new rear axle, underslung springs front and rear, a new frame and new brakes. The engine was designed for the new Ethyl fuel (another product of Kettering's Research Laboratories), and while 4.8 was the standard compression ratio, 5.3 heads were optional, so the LaSalle's performance was as snappy as its appearance. Styling, of course, was its keynote.

Of the LaSalle, Ernest Seaholm recalled, "I remember this so well! This LaSalle model marked Harley Earl's entrée as a stylist in the automobile production field and led to his appointment later by Mr. Sloan, to head up and organize the GM Styling Section. He came to Cadillac first, at the request of L. P. Fisher,

from California. There he had been a designer and builder of custom jobs, a field that was gradually disappearing.

"Up until this time Fisher Body Division had been the absolute dictators of body design and zealously guarded their prerogative. Theirs was a simple approach — a full size line drawing on a blackboard — take it or leave it.

"L. P. Fisher . . . recognized that the time had come for something better and that Harley could probably bring it about. So, we teamed up with him in our engineering shop, and out of it came this LaSalle. It was a beautiful job even by today's standards. We were unable to get it ready in time for the New York Show but arrangements were made for its premiere at the Boston Show shortly after.

"During the festivities we posed for [a] picture outside the Copley Plaza Hotel. Preparations had been carefully made. A couple of uniformed police were on hand to keep away the expected crowd of onlookers. And lo and behold — no one stopped to give even a passing glance! Knowing Harley, I doubt if he ever again went to Boston."

The LaSalle's styling, married to the new 341 series engine and chassis, saved the day for Cadillac. Packard had been making a substantial mark in the eight-cylinder field since the introduction in June, 1923, of the admirable Single Eight, designed by their longtime chief engineer, Colonel Vincent. From June, 1923, to February, 1925, they had produced 12,755 eights, and from December, 1923, to February, 1925, 9,611 Single Sixes. Though this total of 22,366 cars is difficult to compare with Cadillac's 1924 total of 17,748, because Packard's series runs did not follow a twelve-month cycle, they were obviously hitting Cadillac hard. In 1925, according to A. P. Sloan, Cadillac was displaced as overall sales leader in the luxury field. They still remained ahead on the basis of eight-cylinder sales, but Packard's combined Six and Eight production for an approximate twelve-month period in 1925 was 46,000 units. Cadillac production of 1925 models was only 22,542. Although it could be argued that more than 40,000 of the Packards were sixes, which were not really comparable to the Cadillac eight, the hard fact remained that in the over-$2,500 class, Packard, and not Cadillac, was now sales leader by more than two to one. And the influential General Motors stockholders didn't like it.

"One day," Ernest Seaholm remarked, grinning, "the seven Fisher brothers filed one by one through Herby Rice's office and told him what they thought of him and his management. Shortly after, Herby stepped down and Lawrence P. Fisher was made president."

This at first sight would not seem likely to bring much improvement, for, ironically, the Fishers were as responsible as Rice for letting Packard get into the lead. They were master body builders and skilled craftsmen, but as Ernest Seaholm has already pointed out, they had little or no imagination where style was concerned. Nor had Cadillac any style-consciousness of its own — Henry Leland had known nothing and cared less about that aspect, and his influence still lingered. The Cadillac was an engineer's car and its chassis feared no comparison with any other automobile, but style was now starting to sell cars. Cadillac's lines were stodgy and the wealthy buyer had to look elsewhere for style. Where else in the American car field could he find it? The three P's, Locomobile, Lincoln? Assuming quality, refinement and other practical factors to be equal, which of these cars was the best looking? And in a time of recovery from postwar depression, which company was soundest and best managed? "Packard" was the obvious answer. Once the junior of the three P's (before 1912 they were able only to offer four-cylinder cars against the Pierce and Peerless big sixes), Packard had forged ahead in 1916 with their magnificent Twin Six, the world's first production twelve-cylinder car. Against this, Pierce continued to offer only their traditional and by now outdated six-cylinder models, while Peerless, as we have seen, emulated Cadillac with an excellent V-8, but failed to match their rival's commercial success and offered nothing better than Cadillac in appearance or style. Locomobile followed a similar course to Pierce-Arrow and fared no better. The new postwar Lincoln, while a superb vehicle mechanically, suffered again from the "Leland look." In the postwar depression, it was common knowledge among car buyers that all these famous makes were in serious financial trouble. The bulk of the trade, therefore, was shared between Packard and Cadillac. In their Twin Six, Packard had the smoothest and the most refined automobile in the world, and it sold well for a number of years. All this admitted, the Twin Six was still an over-complex answer to the requirements of the luxury-car buyer, and sales declined after 1920. Nevertheless, it had given the Packard image an aura of super-refinement, which was automatically attached to the new Single Eight. While the latter was a simpler and more practical design, it retained the Packard connoisseur appeal. Thanks to advanced engineering principles it was only slightly inferior in smoothness to the Twin Six, and in style the Single Eight marked a new era for the American production automobile. Over a period of many years, the classic Packard radiator and long, distinctively-creased hood had been refined and supplemented by other styling

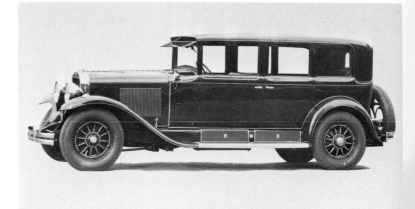

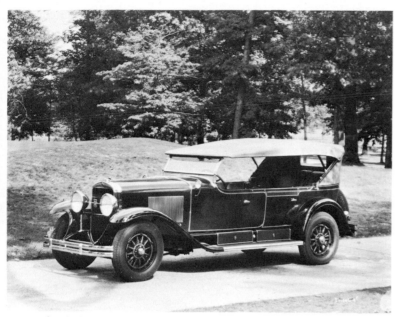

On the facing page, top to bottom, are a late 1926 convertible coupé and sedan of 1929 and New Zealand Railways Road Services' Series 341 at a Wellington wharf, 1935. Above and below, two distinctive 1929 Cadillacs.

features to make up a beautifully-integrated ensemble resulting in the most elegant American automobile ever to take to the road up to that time.

The men at Packard were smooth professionals who had gauged very accurately what the current generation desired in a luxury car. Colonel Vincent was both a brilliant engineer and a connoisseur who wanted a design to feel and look right. The knowledge that the wealthy buyer liked a long hood partly influenced Vincent's decision in favor of a straight eight, which he said "gave all the qualities of appearance that were desired," Cadillac's V-8, although it had some technical advantages, gave a shorter hood, which was an appearance handicap.

"The Packard of that day was a 'classic' — aesthetically and otherwise," recalls Seaholm. "It was our bogey for many years, and Vincent's stature as a designer was well earned."

Alvan Macauley, the Packard chairman, was an excellent businessman with impeccable taste, and his training as a patent lawyer gave him insight in mechanical matters rare in a business executive. So far as luxury cars were concerned, the management-engineering team at Packard was unsurpassed in the industry, and comparable in expertise with that at Pierce-Arrow prior to World War I.

Lawrence Fisher knew he had a tough nut to crack. He never did crack it during his ten years at Cadillac, although he did lay the foundations for ultimate recovery of sales position number one. Of the seven clannish Fisher brothers, he was definitely best-fitted for the post. Although retaining some of the family reticence he was gregarious, generous, and friendly, and known as "Larry" to a host of friends. A handsome and well dressed man, he was a "gay bachelor" typical of the Roaring Twenties. He did not marry until he was over sixty. His beautiful home at Grayhaven on the waterfront at Lenox Avenue was the center for many parties where he entertained his set lavishly.

Born in Norwalk on October 19, 1888, L. P. Fisher was only thirty-seven when he became general manager of Cadillac in April, 1925. He went on a tour of Cadillac dealerships in California and met Harley Earl in Los Angeles. Although Earl (then in his twenties) was considerably younger than Fisher, they were both of a time-of-life when youthful ideas and a fresh outlook were shared. It was this combination, and Ernest Seaholm (only a year older than Fisher) who provided the backbone of Cadillac's management-engineering-styling team for the exciting years to come. Their joint talents were initially — and beautifully — expressed in the LaSalle.

In September of 1927, the new 341 Cadillac was announced,

Earl A. Thompson and his Syncro-Mesh transmission.

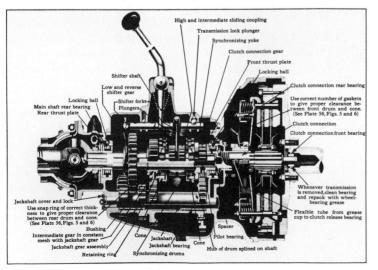

along the general lines of the LaSalle both mechanically and in appearance, but on a longer wheelbase and with a larger displacement, more powerful engine of 341 cubic inches (3 5/16 by 4 15/16 bore and stroke), providing ninety brake horsepower at 3,000 rpm with maximum revolutions of 4,200. Although transmission gears and bearings were similar to the earlier 314 the former aluminum housing was changed to cast iron. This was to ensure damping of any transmission noise transmitted by the new (to Cadillac) torque-tube drive. The higher engine torque allowed "faster" axles, the sedan model ratio, for example, being changed from 4.91 to 4.75. Springs were underslung, lowering the car overall, and further enhancing its fine lines. Twenty-six models in Fisher custom and Fleetwood lines were offered, ranging from $3,295 to $5,500. The bare chassis was priced at $2,800.

This "New Cadillac," with LaSalle, pressed Packard hard now, production totaling 34,811 in 1927 and 41,172 in 1928. In the United States, new car registrations were 29,719 and 36,888 — indicating a large export ratio. Packard's production was 36,480 and 50,054 for the same two years. In 1928 they dropped their sixes entirely and introduced a new Standard Eight as an answer to the LaSalle. In 1929 this model set a production eight-cylinder record of 43,130 cars, and may even have won over several thousand Cadillac/LaSalle owners, for production of the latter, combined, dropped to 36,698 units. Packard's U.S. sales were 44,634 in 1929, compared with Cadillac/LaSalle's 35,226. Total sales over the three years of 1927-1929 were 118,879 for Packard and 101,833 for Cadillac/LaSalle.

For 1929 there were power increases for both Cadillac and LaSalle engines, safety glass, improved brake design, double-acting Delco shock absorbers on Cadillacs, and various body refinements. But the outstanding feature was the clashless Syncro-Mesh transmission. Since 1912, many advancements had been hailed by various makers as the greatest step in driving ease since the self-starter, but this one genuinely merited that title.

"The new transmission," wrote A. F. Denham, "entirely eliminates any attention to relative engine and propeller shaft speeds when shifting either up or down, between intermediate and high. A down shift also involves no double de-clutching. It thus enables a quick shift into intermediate for traffic conditions and steep hills."

The second speed gear rode on a bronze bushing splined to the mainshaft, and was free to turn. It was in constant engagement with the corresponding gear on the countershaft. The driveshaft pinion was similarly arranged. Each of these gears had a tapered bronze cone, which when shifting engaged with a steel drum in a clutch action. The drum, splined to the mainshaft, forced the second speed gear to turn at the same speed as the main shaft, and shifting from low to second was easy and clashless. Similar provision was made for the shifts between second and high, up and down. To ensure perfect timing, a hydraulic plunger detent mechanism was used.

The "Syncro-Mesh" — so written and spelled for trademark purposes — was the brainchild of Earl A. Thompson. A brilliant transmission specialist originally trained as a hydraulics engineer, Thompson had worked on power stations in Oregon before coming to Cadillac.

"His history with Cadillac was an interesting one," recalled Ernest Seaholm. "He first dropped into my office along with a younger brother who was a Cadillac dealer on the west coast — somewhere in Oregon I believe. They had just arrived, having come cross-country in a Cadillac equipped with what later became known as a Syncro-Mesh transmission, synchronized in all three forward speeds and on which he had patents. He had come to Cadillac in view of his brother's sales connection, hoping to have it considered favorably and for possibly some sort of deal. The gear box was full of a sort of bewildering assortment of mechanisms that had been whittled out in some local machine shop in his western state. It lacked a professional touch in design, but it worked — and intrigued me. Accordingly I introduced him to the Corporation's New-Devices Committee, recently formed to handle matters of this sort for the Corporation as a whole rather than through our individual companies. They too manifested interest and some agreement was reached pending check-up on patents and other details.

"From here, for a time, the going was not smooth. He was referred here and there, but no one was interested in taking on the development. So, one day, he showed up in my office, this time discouraged and ready to pack up and go back home. This shocked me, for it seemed that here we had something of great potential and could not afford to let it slip through our fingers, and we made an agreement for him to stay on until together we could bring out a couple of production prototypes of his transmission.

"Before we launched it in full production (August, 1928), we tested altogether ten variants, in twenty-five different cars, stop-go, stop-go, up-shift, down-shift, run for 1½ million miles at the Proving Grounds.

"Thus the Syncro-Mesh was born, and it seemed no time at all before it was standard equipment throughout the whole industry."

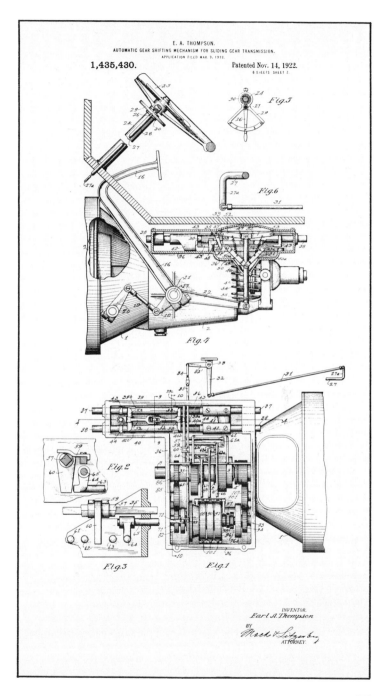

CHAPTER EIGHT

CONQUERING THE CONTINENTS

Those incredible feats around the world, from Arabian sands to the American range

After World War I America bestrode the automotive world like a colossus. The important makes exported huge numbers of cars all over the globe, where they pioneered new routes in Greece and Guatemala, the Gobi Desert or Patagonia, in Nova Scotia and New Zealand. Regardless of their claims to be the source of fashion and new ideas, the Europeans were completely overshadowed. They failed to get the balance right between low and high priced cars, and a plethora of expensive makes struggled for the limelight at the salons, while a few major producers such as Austin, Morris, Renault, Citroën, Fiat, and Opel attempted to emulate American mass-production methods. The results at either end bore little or no comparison with the United States and, so far as market penetration was concerned, the European car in most parts of the world was unsuccessful. The European who asked the American visitor what he thought of the "plant" was likely to be told "that ain't a plant mister, that's a weed." Offhandedly, Alvan Macauley told Alexis de Sakhnoffsky in 1928 that Packard exported "only" five percent of its production to Europe — so why should Packard care what Europeans wanted. Yet that five percent represented well over two thousand cars — a figure equaling several years entire production at, say, Rolls-Royce or Hispano-Suiza.

American success could not be attributed solely to low selling price — the result of making what the English and European apologists called a "cheap and nasty car." On the contrary, European engineers found the American car full of technical interest. Porsche designed a Mercedes "Nurburg" model on Packard lines (and prompted an English critic to comment acidly "Only Packard can build a Packard.") Armstrong-Siddeley's postwar "Thirty" was largely an anglicized Marmon 34. Rolls-Royce based their first postwar model on the Buick, and after 1923 began changing to American cars for research study "to gain the maximum amount of advanced technical information."

"The automobile industry in the United States had undergone a revolution," writes W. A. Robotham, former chief engineer of Rolls-Royce. "They began to produce quality cars in quantity." He further comments that it was difficult to pinpoint the precise moment when this occurred — a question not difficult for a Cadillac V-8 enthusiast to answer!

When Louis Coatalen took over direction of Sunbeam-Talbot-Darracq engineering in 1920, he was particularly interested in the Darracq V-8 designed by Owen Clegg. Clegg had based the design on the Cadillac V-8's, which he had seen at firsthand with the U.S. Army in France, and both he and Coatalen were fascinated by the Cadillac's technical features and its smoothness, flexibility, and refinement.

Another personality, upon whom the Cadillac V-8 made a lasting impression, was about fifteen years old and at the time in Smyrna, Turkey. He saw a Cadillac V-8 owned by a Standard Oil Company executive. Recently he recalled, "I was absolutely enthralled with it and became great friends with the chauffeur, because he would take me for short rides whenever no one was looking. This car ran with no noise at all; he used to drive it with the tires on the tramlines, which were just the right gauge, to avoid the rough cobbles. It was then perfection — not a sound. In those days I was not even aware of the existence of the Rolls-Royce."

The fifteen-year-old boy who "stole rides" because he was fascinated by automobiles became Sir Alec Issigonis, later director of engineering at British Leyland.

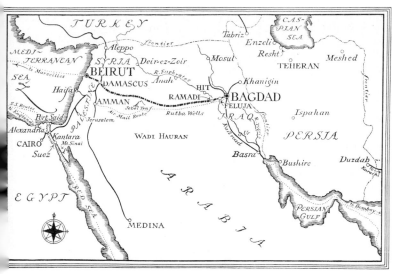

The
ESERT MAIL

Sand dunes and palm trees, camels and sheiks, look on at left while in the distance Gerald Nairn's Desert Mail cars take on the tortures between Beirut and Bagdad, from an illustration in a General Motors Export Company pamphlet, circa 1925. The route used is shown on the map above, from the same brochure. At upper right, one of the Cadillacs is about to leave Beirut, with J. Reid at the wheel and Gerald Nairn standing at right. On the car's hood, in both Arabic and English, are the words, "Nairn Transport Co. Overland Desert Mail. Bagdad-Beirut." At right center is a Cadillac prior to another trip, with lady passengers reasonably unconcerned about the prospects. At right below, at a temporary stop between Damascus and Rutba (see map), the quagmire is the least of concerns to the intrepid Nairn, who has halted only long enough to change two spark plugs, but the photograph proves deserts aren't always hot.

Smyrna is just across the eastern end of the Mediterranean from Syria. Of all the Cadillac's conquests of time and distance, none is more romantic and colorful than its association with this region. The Arab-Israeli war has directed today's attention to the Middle East, but, in fact, it has been the center of the world stage in many previous eras, and was the cradle of Western civilization itself. For romantic appeal there is no phrase more arresting than "Damascus to Bagdad!" Damascus — claiming the title of the world's oldest living city, center of the Arab world in the Middle Ages and a seat of Caliphs, Biblical history, the birth of Christianity, and Islam. All this, and much more besides, make the region a fascinating backdrop to the epic of the Nairn brothers and their Cadillacs. They came from a country half the world away from Syria, brought half a dozen luxury automobiles from the New World to the Old, and in the area that had previously known only the "ship of the desert" — the camel — they made modern transportation history.

Norman and Gerald Nairn were the sons of a doctor in a small town of Blenheim, New Zealand. Prior to the First World War they partnered a motorcycle business in their hometown, where some old-timers recall their high-spirited trick riding and stunts with these vehicles. They enlisted in the army when war broke out, Gerald in New Zealand and Norman in England, where he was on business connected with their motorcycle trade. Meeting in Palestine, they served during the war in the Middle East, in the motorized units of General Allenby, and instead of returning to New Zealand after the Armistice, decided to try their fortune where they were. Though they had no money, a Syrian financed them and they began in business in 1919 buying surplus army vehicles and selling them in Beirut. A year of this provided them with the capital to begin in Egypt as automobile importers, and in 1920 they started a mail and passenger service between Beirut and Haifa.

This appeared promising, since Haifa was an important Palestine seaport and Beirut was the "gateway to the Levant," entry point and commercial administrative center for the territory of Syria. Syria, formerly under the Turks, had been mandated by the League of Nations to France after World War I. The French understood the possibilities of this pleasant region at the opposite end of the Mediterranean, and it flourished commercially under their rule. They even established a French university there.

The only city with which Beirut was connected by road was Tyre. From Tyre to Akka the route was through ploughed fields, requiring the assistance of draft horses during the winter. From

Akka to Haifa it ran along the beach, and timetables were thus subject to the tides. Two rivers had to be forded, the one nearer Akka requiring an Arab pilot to take the cars across the sand bar. The 110 miles from Beirut to Haifa took nineteen hours.

Because of the difficult route and some competition backed by considerably greater resources, the Nairns' service was closed down after not much more than a year. The brothers were of two minds as to whether they should return to New Zealand, or perhaps try some other field, when the British liaison officer at Beirut and the British consul at Damascus approached them and proposed that they start a motor service to Bagdad — across the Syrian Desert. They were offered guides and other assistance and were soon making preparations for the great adventure.

Bagdad, capital of Iraq, was the administrative center for the British civil command, rulers of Iraq under a mandate from the League of Nations in the same way that the French reigned over Syria. Oil had been discovered and the area was becoming important. Many Englishmen stationed there traveled home at regular intervals. The only route open to them and the mails, other than by camel train, was from Bagdad to Basra (a port near the Persian Gulf), thence from Basra to Bombay in India, then via the Suez Canal to Great Britain, a journey of several weeks. If, however, a service car route across the desert could be opened and maintained, a trip home could be cut to ten days.

There had been British plans for a railway from Bagdad to

Passengers look on while Nairn attaches tow chain to bogged Cadillac.

Haifa on the Mediterranean coast, but they had fallen through for lack of finance. An air route between Cairo and Bagdad was established in the early twenties, but it was expensive travel, and only operated fortnightly.

Prior motor crossings of the Syrian Desert had been few, painful, and discouraging. In 1919 Lord Allenby had journeyed from Beirut to Palmyra with Rolls-Royce armored cars, but had traveled no farther. About a year later a Major Holt is said to have made the crossing from Damascus to Bagdad via Deir-ez-Zor down the Euphrates River. He started out with ten Model T Fords, of which only four finished the trek. In June of 1921 RAF Crossley tenders and Rolls-Royce armored cars had twice struggled over the desert from Amman and Bagdad while carrying out the railway and air surveys — there was then no thought of a service car route — and it was then estimated that the whole painful, arduous journey would take from eight to twelve days under the most favorable conditions.

German trucks during World War I had driven from Aleppo to Bagdad via Deir-ez-Zor and Mosul on the Tigris. After 1920 Syrians had used the Deir-ez-Zor/Euphrates and Mosul/Tigris routes for smuggling contraband between Syria and Iraq. But all these routes had serious disadvantages.

Beirut-Damascus-Palmyra-Muhaiwar-Rubaisa-Hit-Euphrates-Bagdad had been an ancient caravan route. It had adequate water supplies, and although indirect it was much shorter than the more northerly detours, it had actually been crossed once by Major Holt with his Fords. However, Bedouin raiders, noted for robbery and murder, were liable to strike at any time. Parties were attacked almost daily. The Deir-ez-Zor and Mosul routes were far too long, arduous, and dangerous to be considered and the same objections applied to the Amman course.

The only other path, the direct crossing of the Syrian Desert from Damascus via Rutba and Ramadi, had been avoided because it was desolate and almost waterless and without any human habitation in the five hundred miles between Damascus and Ramadi. The only usable water was at Rutba and Ramadi, with none in the two hundred miles between them. Another well existed halfway between Damascus and Ramadi but the water was unfit for any use. There was an almost complete lack of suitable spots for caching supplies of food and water, practically no landmarks, and no human help anywhere handy in case of misadventure.

Despite this there was one constant user of the route, an Arab sheik named Mohammed Ibn Bassam, who regularly made crossings between Damascus and Bagdad with a camel train. He was,

in fact, a gold smuggler, but was seldom bothered by Bedouins as he was wealthy enough to pay them sufficient "protection money." Ibn Bassam had already thought of using motorcars instead of camels, and, during January and February of 1923, sent two car convoys to Bagdad via Deir-ez-Zor and the Euphrates, but found it too long and liable to local raids from the wandering tribes. He then thought it might be feasible actually to run cars across the camel route he had been using. Despite its disadvantages, there were some things in its favor. The desert was not a sand desert but hard, sun-baked soil or gravel, and in dry weather the surface was good for cars. Under these conditions the only "soft going" was the forty-mile sandy section west of Ramadi, and although there were hills on either side for part of the way, the going was flat. Although in wet weather the surface was mud for miles in all directions, much of it under water, with numerous gullies and wadis presenting hazards after dark, it was possible that cars driven fast enough would master the difficulties. Ibn Bassam had approached the British consul in Damascus, Mr. C. E. S. Palmer, and put the idea to him. The Arab knew of the British interest in any possible desert route, and was anxious to keep in with the ruling power and forestall any possible rival. Palmer was enthusiastic, and soon the British liaison officer in Beirut, Captain D. McCallum, was ordered by the Foreign Office and Air Ministry to accompany the expedition and send in a detailed report of the crossing.

The Nairns supplied three cars — a six-cylinder 27 horsepower Buick, an eight-cylinder Oldsmobile and a Lancia, all standard touring cars. The drivers and mechanics were Nairn employees, Ted Lovell, chief mechanic of the Nairn Transport Company, being in charge. McCallum's wife accompanied her husband, and one of Ibn Bassam's Arab guides also went along. A ten days' supply of food and drinking water, plenty of water for the radiators, and sufficient oil and gasoline for the round trip were taken. A very comprehensive set of tools, plus blocks of wood for jack supports and for use in case of spring-breaking were also carried, plus rifles, shotguns and revolvers. As little as possible would be left to chance.

The convoy started from Damascus on April 2, 1923, and after one or two misadventures reached Bagdad three days later. They had come a total of 603 miles in three days and proved the route was entirely suitable for service vehicles.

After the return to Damascus, the Nairns made five more desert crossings, between May and August, including one in July, the hottest month of the year, but could find no more suitable route than the original one taken in April.

A convoy pauses before flat horizons during a desert crossing. The cars usually travelled in reasonably close company, but would spread out at night. Once a following car found its predecessor circling aimlessly, its driver asleep!

When they approached the Post and Telegraph Director of Iraq with proposals for a mail service, he was favorable, but pointed out the great danger due to the predatory tribesmen. A guarantee of security would be essential to the signing of all mail contracts. Unable to obtain assistance from the British High Commissioner, who had serious doubts about the practicability of the project and the safety of the persons involved, the Nairns managed to find the help they needed from Mohammed Ibn Bassam, who undertook to guarantee them freedom from tribal raids and provide guides and interpreters. His fee for this service was two thousand pounds in gold, annually.

The choice of cars for operating the service now had to be made. The Buick, Oldsmobile, and Lancia had performed satisfactorily on the original crossing, but the Lancia was not considered to be rugged enough for continuous travel and was sold. Sound as the other two cars were (and the Buick continued to serve the Nairns for many more years), the brothers knew that the backbone of the service they intended to develop required the ultimate in touring cars, the utmost ruggedness and dependability — a simple design, easily maintained, with adequate comfort and speed. Yet to be a commercial proposition it must not be inordinately expensive to buy or run. From their experience of British vehicles in Allenby's units the Nairns knew that their ideal car was not a British make. In fact, no European car offered a suitable combination of the right qualities. So Norman Nairn visited Detroit.

Soon new Cadillac Type 61 and 63 seven-passenger touring cars joined the Buick and the Oldsmobile to establish what eventually became the most famous desert service in the world.

The center seats of the Cadillacs were replaced by a sixteen-gallon water tank, and a twenty-gallon fuel tank was mounted on each running board, linked by a three-way cock to an Autopulse electric fuel pump (an advanced idea in the day of fuel tanks pressurized from an engine-driven air pump). In this form the cars carried one or two drivers and three or four passengers, with mail bags and baggage loaded on the running boards, fenders, and hood. Rations for a week were always taken — two full kerosene tins, and the extra fuel tanks enabled the cars to go right through without refueling. Small refrigerators, two spotlights mounted on the windshield, and asbestos-lined hoods were also part of the special equipment.

In the late summer of 1923, the Nairn Company was granted a five year contract for the carrying of the Iraq government mails between Bagdad and Haifa. (At Haifa the mails were transferred to a train for Port Said.) The conditions of the contract were strict. Mails from Bagdad had to reach Port Said every week within sixty hours or the Nairns would be fined. But the firm easily met the challenge, and their efficiency so impressed the French that they also granted them the Damascus-to-Bagdad mail contract, which began in October of 1923. Letters which had previously taken twenty-four days to reach London from Bagdad by sea, now began arriving in nine days. Passengers found that they could travel from the capital of Iraq to the Mediterranean coast more comfortably and far cheaper than by air, and just as quickly. The single fare by car from Beirut to Bagdad was £30. The equivalent air journey, Cairo to Bagdad, cost £150 per passenger. Considering the conditions of aviation development in 1924, it is not surprising that the car was considered more comfortable. As for two-thirds of the desert journey the terrain allowed "flat-out" cruising of up to seventy miles an hour, the aircraft did not prove any faster. (On one occasion Gerald Nairn left Rutba at the same time as an Imperial Airways Airliner, which was taking off after refueling, A headwind held the plane back and the Nairn Cadillac outpaced it to an Iran Petroleum Company Station about sixty-five miles away.)

Both Iraqi and Syrian governments forbade single cars to attempt the crossing because of the possibility of breakdowns.

The Nairns in any case knew the desert far too well to disregard this rule, and the convoy was standard practice. Their cars ran under rigid instructions to keep together, and by 1925 up to eight, nine, or a dozen cars would be keeping company. They kept to the original tracks as they became established, and avoided wells and wadis where Bedouins might be lurking. When a convoy left a staging station, a wireless or telegraph message was sent to the next station, which in turn informed the previous stopping place that the convoy had arrived.

The run of 550 miles between Damascus and Bagdad took a total time of twenty-four hours when there were no incidents. At first, as arranged with the sheik, Arab camel drivers went along to act as guides, being seated beside the driver, with the three passengers in the rear. Unaccustomed to the speed, the guides proved no use in a car and were soon dropped. From then on the Nairn cars were driven by compass, and at first two drivers were carried on each car, one relieving the other. Later one driver was found sufficient.

A contemporary article titled "The Desert Mail" described the trip: "Leaving Beirut and the colorful seacoast behind, the cars climb over the Lebanon Mountains. One passes Bedouins and Syrians driving strings of gaily decorated, heavy-laden camels, and quaint high-hooded carts drawn by teams of mules. From the top of the Anti-Lebanon Range, the road drops gradually to the oasis around Damascus. Steering due east, the oasis is left with startling suddenness and the travelers find themselves for the first time on the real desert. For some five hundred miles in the direct line of travel, there is not a human habitation.

"Fast traveling at forty to sixty miles an hour, under the hot sun over a limitless space resembling the flat horizon of a calm sea becomes very monotonous, and exercises such a hypnotic effect that it is only with great effort that the drivers are able to keep awake.

"Although Bagdad is 1,200 feet or so lower than Damascus, the descent is so gradual as to be imperceptible in the desert. Three hundred forty flat and uneventful miles out from Beirut is the Wadi Hauran, a dried up watercourse of considerable extent and uninviting aspect. Here are the Rutba Wells, the only known place on the desert where water, though of an unattractive color and taste, may be obtained if absolutely necessary. At Rutba the travelers catch their first sight of the air furrow — a line ploughed by the British Royal Air Force across the desert from Amman to Bagdad for guiding pilots of the Cairo-Bagdad air mail machines. Marks on the floor of the desert are visible from the air at great altitudes.

"From the Wadi Hauran the cars follow the air furrow to Ramadi — a little town on the Euphrates. Thence to Feluja and the cars cross the Euphrates by a bridge of boats — that is, if the bridge happens to be there.

"Two hours more level desert, then in the distance, the golden domes of Bagdad, glittering in the sun, lift themselves over the straight horizon. Gradually the cars enter a cultivated countryside; green surrounds them once more, behind it the minarets of the City of Caliphs. Through the noisy repair yards of the Iraq Railway, across the Tigris by the Maudi Bridge, the cars roll up to the hotel. There is a slight flurry, loiterers appear — then an official or two. The desert mail has landed."

Originally the cars started at five in the morning, drove all day and parked up for the night, continuing early next day. As the tracks became established, and the drivers got to know the route, this schedule was reversed, the cars starting about three or four in the afternoon and driving through the night. Thus, most driving was done in the cooler temperatures, which was easier on the vehicles and their occupants.

The cars traveled in a strung-out convoy formation, and at night the leading car would, at regular intervals, turn back until the headlights of the next car were seen, turn again, and continue on its original course. The second car would repeat this check on the third and so on down the line. On one occasion the leading car was unable to locate the second car for a time, and then the occupants saw headlights circling in the distance in an odd manner. Driving up, they discovered the Cadillac turning circles with the driver and passengers fast asleep! Only after much shouting and horn blowing were they awakened.

The Nairn drivers were more familiar with the Gilhooleys than Gilhooley himself. (A Gilhooley, named after the practitioner, consists of turning a car end-for-end remaining on its wheels.) About thirty miles out of Damascus, and again between Rutba and Ramadi (about 250 miles from Bagdad) were vast mud flats, which in the summer were as smooth as a billiard table with a thin film of dust on top. The gazelles roaming the flat invariably ran across the path of anything approaching, so that the driver swung to avoid them. The surface after light rain was so greasy that the three and a half tons of laden Cadillac would turn end-for-end several times from fifty or sixty miles an hour before the driver could get on course again — his passengers still open-mouthed!

Weather permitting, the cars kept a tight schedule, and one of the legends that grew up about this famous service was that locals, lacking any other method, set their clocks by the arrival of the Nairn cars. Heavy rain, however, involved a 150-mile detour through Mafrak.

The company's main aim in the early years was the high-class passenger trade, the mail service, and a small amount of urgent freight. "Their target was the traveler who wanted speed and comparative luxury, compatible with safety," wrote J. S. Tullet.

An early record night run made between Bagdad and Damascus did a lot to boost their reputation among European and American businessmen in the Middle East. It arose from a discussion between Norman Nairn and Sir Arnold Wilson, a senior executive of the Anglo-Persian oil company, then on his way from London to Persia where his company was doing exploration. Norman told Sir Arnold that he could have him in Bagdad sixteen hours after leaving Damascus, and Sir Arnold bet him that it was impossible. A Cadillac, tuned by Gerald Nairn and Ted Lovell, was made ready. Watches and the clock in the car were synchronized, and carrying only Norman Nairn, Sir Arnold and his personal luggage, the car swept out of Damascus at 11 P.M. The journey through the dark was made as fast as possible in the limited visibility, then as dawn broke and light spread, Norman opened the Cadillac up to top speed on the gradual downward run to Bagdad, seventy miles an hour and more. Sir Arnold, clutching for support in the swaying car as it swept down into the Wadi Hauran, saw the speedometer swing around past the end of the scale, which meant they were doing perhaps eighty miles an hour or more. He wondered how they would ever survive the trip. When they arrived at Bagdad, where news had been radioed of their impending arrival, they were met by a large crowd. Pointing to a local clock, Sir Arnold triumphantly shouted, "Sixteen hours, fifty-three minutes! You've lost, Nairn."

"*Fifteen* hours, fifty-three minutes," said Norman. "Look at your watch."

Reminiscent of Phileas Fogg in *Around the World in Eighty Days*, Wilson had forgotten a difference in the time zones. He paid up. Later, with typical British understatement, he described the trip in two words: "Pretty wild."

Once an Anglo-Iranian oil company director, Sir John Cadman, a friend of the Nairns, offered them double the normal fee for a car, if he could be taken to Beirut in time to catch a steamer, and nothing if they failed. Norman Nairn and Jack Reid drove, taking extra fuel, and giving the passenger an empty gasoline can for a fairly obvious reason. The trip involved an extra sixty-five miles and a climb of 1,500 feet through the Lebanon Range, but the Cadillac cut out the 615 miles in fifteen hours —

an average speed of forty-one miles an hour. The oil company official caught his steamer with an hour and a half to spare and the Nairns got their money.

Gerald Nairn himself once drove from Beirut to Bagdad and returned — 1,230 miles — in forty-eight hours without sleep or even a relief driver.

In the Syrian Desert operating conditions were, of course, exceptionally severe. In the summer temperatures were so high — to 123°F. — that the tubes would vulcanize themselves to the tires, and tires were even known to catch fire. Drivers had to change the tires with gloves on. There were dust storms that lasted six to eight hours and reduced visibility to ten feet, making it necessary for someone to stand on the front bumper and direct the driver. Winds blew hats away so fast that a car had to do fifty miles an hour to catch them rolling on their brims.

In winter, despite using up to ten different tracks, the cars often bogged down to the axles in mud. The drill was then for all to get out, including the driver, who would tie the throttle wide open. Heaving and pushing, using shovels and mud mats, with breaks of driving, then heaving and pushing again, up to thirty miles might eventually be covered in this manner with the car flat out in low gear much of the time. Sometimes the cars would bog down so badly that the party would have to wait up to two days for the mud to dry before they could get going again.

"Yet we never boiled a Cadillac," Gerald Nairn recalled to this writer. "They had excellent radiators and cooling systems generally — one of the major reasons we selected them in the first place for this route. We ran right through to Bagdad and back without topping up the radiators. They were, of course, always kept in tip-top shape by their drivers, who washed, maintained, and serviced the cars, and during the run fed the passengers and attended to their comfort.

"The drivers in the old Cadillac days were a great bunch, tough but good. They never let their passengers down, and their fidelity and endurance were known throughout the Middle East. We all packed a gun in those days. There were New Zealanders,

A Buick upsets on the run between Bagdad and Damascus. Note the interesting items strewn on the ground, showing the nature of the spare parts carried.

Aussies, British, Americans, and Canadians. Among the characters was John Reid, with one eye, who once, in a Cadillac, chased a cheetah down and shot it, and of course, Ryan, the Aussie who was very fond of the bottle. Passengers often complained he had been drinking, but I could never catch him or find liquor in the car. Finally I discovered that his chargals [water bottles with straws] were full of arrak — a powerful Lebanese booze made from grapes!

"Sometimes a car would get shot up by the Arabs and to get drivers to go out with a relief car and bring it in we would have to drag them out of hotels or brothels. So we gave them a house to live in and a girl each."

The Arabs could be very troublesome. On occasions the cars got home with bullet holes through the radiator temporarily plugged up, while on other occasions two Buicks were stolen, the drivers and all mail being left in the desert, lucky only that they were not stripped naked. As a crowning insult, the Arabs later made raids with the stolen cars, which were never recovered. Fortunately a Cadillac was never lost. Once a convoy car was held up and the driver called upon to deliver arms. He refused, and the bandits searched the car and found a fully-loaded revolver in one of the pockets. Challenged, the driver said it was unserviceable and of no use. A bandit then held it to the driver's heart and pulled the trigger. The only thing that saved him was that the safety catch was in position, and the Arab did not know how to render the weapon ready for firing. Because of these in-

cidents, it was often questioned whether it was wise to carry arms or not.

"We carried rifles ourselves, but these were chiefly for shooting at gazelles and a possible last resort," commented Mr. Nairn. "We never indulged in gun battles because of the passengers. Sooner than get passengers killed, we would hand over the items the Arabs might demand. We never lost a passenger, but did have one wounded on one occasion."

The only death occurred during the unsuccessful Druse rebellion in 1925 against the French. A British driver was shot and later died in Damascus. After a French escort accompanying the Nairn convoy was shot up, the French authorities gave the Nairns permission to go after the leaders of the attack, with arms. They ran the Arabs down in a couple of Cadillacs, and the tribesmen jumped off their winded camels and took off on foot. When their ammunition ran out, they surrendered to the Nairns, handing their knives over, as they said, to cut their throats. The Nairns, however, took them to the French, and saw them publicly hanged.

At one time the French were forced to close down the route because of the depredations of these tribesmen, and this called for a new and much more arduous route hundreds of miles longer, through Jerusalem. But the French were very helpful throughout the Nairn era in Syria, allowing them to import equipment from the United States free of duty and even granted a small subsidy. They had recognized the importance of the service from its in-

Shortly after the righting measures shown on the previous page, a Cadillac makes tracks for home port with one battered Buick in tow.

ception in October of 1923, when they had granted the Nairns their overland mail contract.

The cars underwent extraordinary punishment after the Druse Rebellion of 1925. A new route to avoid the unsettled area was taken — Beirut-Haifa-Jerusalem,Dead Sea-Amman-Rutba-Bagdad, a distance of 750 miles. On this route, between Amman and Rutba, were situated several lava beds up to five miles-wide, strewn with large boulders too close together to be avoided, giving a riverbed surface for miles on end. There being no alternative, the cars had to bump painfully over this frightful surface at a crawl, and as this route was used for six to eight months, the vehicles eventually had structural troubles. Chassis frames developed cracks near the front axles, springs broke and radiators leaked.

The chassis were reinforced by welding extra angle section steel inside the frame channels, and as a precaution, a rib was welded on the bottom of the banjo housing. Springs were roped up so that if one broke a car could still get home. Tires, of course, suffered severe wear, lasting only a couple of trips on this route, but they were regarded as expendable. Nairn himself told the writer that he doubted whether many other cars could survive continual lava bed crossings at all, and in 1930-1931, when another railway survey was made in the area, other cars could only cross the lava regularly after a road had been cleared by digging down to the earth beneath.

An interesting picture of this Trans-Jordan route, as seen by a passenger, was written by a British member of Parliament, Sir Douglas Newton, in 1926. At the beginning of the journey from Jerusalem there was a quick descent from an altitude of 2,000 feet above sea level, via a "mountainous and precipitous" route to Bethlehem and the Good Samaritan Inn. This hostel was in "a sad state of dilapidation and incapable of providing anything other than a very modest refreshment." After this, the descent continued until the Dead Sea was sighted, and the cars reached Jericho, standing in the great depression near the shores of the Dead Sea, 1,292 feet below the level of the Mediterranean. "Certainly one would wish one's enemy no worse fate than that he be sent to Jericho," commented Sir Douglas. "The atmosphere is appalling — hot and oppressive — and the dirt, dust, and flies are intolerable. It would seem to be the most unhealthy, and it is certainly one of the most unattractive and unpleasant spots in the countryside."

The convoy then crossed the River Jordan, "a dirty, turgid stream," and into Trans-Jordan, where the climb to Amman began. This little town, capital of Trans-Jordan, had only a few

months ago seen a great fight between the Wahabis and the small British outpost at Amman. News of the unprovoked attack about to be made reached the garrison less than two hours before the battle, but the troops captured the enemy's standard and defeated him with heavy casualties. "The lesson was a wholesome one," wrote Sir Douglas, "and has not been forgotten."

"Nevertheless," he continued, "in that quarter trouble may arise at any time. Bedouins are by instinct marauders, and the womenfolk of the desert tribes are still branded on their faces with tribal marks for identification, and recovery after raids."

From Amman the cars continued to climb, and after a few miles the Druse Mountains — "bare, precipitous, and forbidding" — were seen, and the convoys began passing Druse cattle watering at springs near the route. Low lying hills of volcanic origin were crossed. These were thickly studded with rounded block boulders of all shapes and sizes, varying from a few pounds weight to several hundredweight. Little or no deviation could be made from the regular track at any point, and as this would make an attack easy, armored cars were stationed in this area.

After a few miles the desert was reached, with its surface quite unlike the loose shifting sands of the desert of Egypt. "In places the traveling is the reverse of pleasant. It is amazing that cars can be built to stand up to the work. One section of the track is so bad that it has been named 'Biscay.' When crossing it, the car rocks and sways violently and continuously like a small ship tossed in a great gale at sea." Punctures, leaky radiators and damage to the chassis and springs were frequent in this area. In contrast were other sections where the surface, formed by the mud of dried-up pools and lakes, was as smooth as glass, and just as hard, and maximum speed could be held for hours.

The journey was not monotonous, as there was plenty to see and do. "Clinging to the seat to prevent being thrown up through the roof is strenuous exercise when continued for several hours," commented the narrator. There was a wooden bow in the Cadillac top just ahead of the passengers, and this could cause a condition known locally as a "Nairn nose" if the car hit a deep pothole at speed and passengers were caught unaware and thrown up off their seats. After one or two incidents of this kind the bows were always wrapped in blankets.

Common sights were one or two dead Bedouins lying by the side of the track; graceful gazelles bounding across the desert; sand grouse so abundant that the sky would seem black as they suddenly arose in front of the cars — twenty or thirty being knocked down at a time by the speeding cars and the windscreens in danger of being smashed. Ostriches were also seen, and hyenas, foxes, badgers, jackals, and a host of smaller animals of the rat family. Some of these animals were far from harmless, as witness the incident when a driver broke a hyena's back with a rifle shot only to have the animal mount the running board and take the muzzle of the weapon between his teeth. Another shot down the throat finished him, but the strength of his jaws was shown by the teeth marks left on the end of the gun barrel!

Nature designed these animals for their element, despite the inhospitable desert. The sand grouse, for instance, has a pouch under its mouth for carrying water many miles to its young.

Mirages were a constant puzzle. Amazing views of forests surrounded by great pools of water would vanish as the car proceeded, as mysteriously as they appeared. Sand storms appeared in the distance with whirling columns of sand reaching high into the sky, and at night a continuous and impressive electrical display could sometimes be seen.

"Whatever charges can be brought against the Syrian Desert, and they are many, it cannot be argued that it is uninteresting," commented Sir Douglas.

After mentioning the methods of operating the convoy and keeping in contact, he continued, "Occasionally there is a flavor of hunting about the journey. The leader of the convoy will perhaps lose the track during the night; then all the cars will gather around him like a well-trained pack of hounds. Wide casts are made until suddenly wheel tracks are espied, when there is a loud blowing of horns and the whole convoy once more dashes ahead down the trail."

Short stops only at irregular intervals were made for food, supper being usually eaten about 9:30 P.M., after which the convoy drove continuously until fatigue compelled a short sleep on the desert sands during the early morning, accompanied by hosts of hungry sandflies. It was not considered wise to stop for long as the Bedouins, though generally friendly, might be tempted to act otherwise.

The whole journey of 700 miles was made at an average speed, including stops, of fourteen miles an hour; but the first 480 miles from Bagdad were made at an average of over thirty miles an hour.

"The drive provides an endurance test of no mean order for drivers, whose aim appears to be complete the journey in the shortest possible time. The Cadillac and Buick cars, which make up the convoys, are called upon to convey astonishing loads. In addition to a full complement of passengers they each carry some sixty-eight gallons of petrol and sixteen gallons of water, together

with food and luggage strapped onto every available place. For those who must . . . go to Bagdad the new Jerusalem route is practicable. It cannot, however, be recommended. It is not, nor can it be made, a good route without the expenditure of labor and money. Even if this be done it will always take longer and prove a more arduous journey than the Damascus route. A great saving in time, however, is effected by traveling by either overland route as compared with the journey by sea. The 700 miles of desert travel short-circuits a journey of some thousands of miles, and it saves some seventeen or more days of hot and enervating travel via the Red Sea, Indian Ocean, and the Persian Gulf."

A new route came into use before long — this being Beirut-Homs-Palmyra-Rutba-Bagdad — with a rest house at Rutba, halfway across the desert. Thus, the lava beds were avoided and the distance reduced to 650 miles; later they returned to the direct Damascus-Bagdad route. Rutba doubled as an airport and car staging point, and a hotel, aerodrome, fort, and other facilities were built there.

By 1927 nearly 4,000 desert crossings had been made by the Nairn cars. Twenty thousand passengers and 4,500 sacks of mail had been carried, but the proudest boast of the company was that, despite all hazards, no passenger's life had been lost. The organization and running of the service was superbly efficient. Its reputation and prestige were world-wide, and after only a year of operations, in November of 1924, a Nairn convoy had been entrusted with the transport of the Shah of Persia and his suite across the desert.

The noted historian, Professor Arnold Toynbee, wrote: "The effective opening up for the first time in history of the direct trans-desert route between Iraq and the Mediterranean coast of Syria was one of the most important developments of the postwar age."

Eventually the Nairns, absorbing a rival firm, extended their operations beyond Bagdad to Persia, running five hundred miles right through to Teheran, near the Caspian Sea. This route involved climbing steeply through the Zagros Mountains to a hotel stop at Kermanshah, a mile above sea level. Next day the route led through winding gorges and along steep, narrow, deeply-rutted roads, and then over the eight thousand-foot Asadabad Pass to Hamadan, followed by a long run to Teheran.

But whether it was the endless mud of the desert's rainy season, its shimmering heat in summer, or the freezing blizzards and snowdrifts of the Asadabad in winter, year in and year out the Nairn drivers found their Cadillacs virtually invincible.

Nothing, it seemed, could stop these super cars.

The Nairn Transport Company had its ups and downs, but it became a model to the world in its field, introducing specially designed buses as traffic increased beyond the capacity of the cars. On these vehicles it pioneered some important developments — notably air conditioning — now in use in buses around the world. Eventually, in the thirties, the Cadillacs were pensioned off. Each one had covered between 200,000 and 250,000 miles.

Some thirty odd years later, in his beautiful home at Sunshine Bay, Picton (New Zealand), Gerald Nairn recalled "the old Cadillac days" with the warmest of nostalgic affection. "Those Cadillacs *made* us," he said. "They were the finest cars in the world."

Whether it was Asia Minor or Australasia, the record of the Cadillac in pioneering new road routes over undeveloped terrain was a magnificent if scantily-acknowledged chapter in automobile history. It was the long-distance, cross-country touring car *par excellence*. Total mileages by individual cars might range from five hundred thousand up to one million — much of it at cruising speeds of forty, fifty, and even sixty mph over indifferent roads. In the earliest touring car period, travelers took rain, dust, sun, and windburn in stride, luggage lashed to fenders, running boards, and anywhere suitable on the car. Later the closed car made travel far more comfortable.

Undoubtedly much of the Cadillac's adaptability came from the simple facts of life in its country of origin. Conditions there and in the rest of North America duplicated almost everything the motorist was likely to encounter in the rest of the world: the

Syrian Desert or the Painted Desert, the Dead Sea or Death Valley. When Ernest Seaholm kindly gave this writer some priceless photographs he had taken during Cadillac transcontinental runs with his own test crews, they were found to be difficult to distinguish from similar photographs donated by Gerald Nairn!

Seaholm offered an insight into what testing was like in the early 1920's: "We kept a careful check on our rivals," he said, "and I personally did a lot of driving. In the early days, before the Proving Grounds were in action, our favorite areas were in the hills of Pennsylvania, where we spent much time. Here in these hills we worked on brakes, detonation, handling, clutches, riding, and so on. There seemed to be no end to problems.

"On our way down, occasionally we would stop in Dayton, where Ket would come aboard and join us. He was an inspiration — enthusiastically facing whatever at the time seemed insoluble and hopeless. He would make a hillbilly wisecrack to give us a laugh — suggest some fresh approach — and we would get back to work with fresh heart. . . . Incidentally, Ket wasn't the world's best driver by quite a bit!"

T. A. Boyd, Kettering's longtime associate and biographer, had described Kettering as an excellent driver, and this writer approached him for a reconciliation. Mr. Boyd's reply: "I think it might be more accurate to describe him as a skillful driver rather than as a good driver. With this I think Ernie Seaholm would agree. In all of Kettering's miles and miles of driving I never heard of his having an accident of any consequence. But although he was a skillful driver, he was sometimes given to

Much as the Conestoga wagons of the early pioneers, Nairn's Cadillacs and Buicks circled together wherever they paused.

chance-taking in his rigorous and tough testing of any equipment to discover any weaknesses. He would sometimes drive on the inadequate roads of that time so fast and with such seeming disregard for safety that some engineers found reasons not to ride with him."

"Occasionally we took off cross country to the west coast," Ernie Seaholm recalled, continuing his reminiscences, "and along the way I would join up with the caravan. A trip such as this was an adventure — high mountains (we would climb to the top of Pikes Peak, cross the Rockies and through the Grand Tetons) — desert, heat, rugged terrain, sand storms, broken springs, punctured tires and so on! It was a test of men as well as cars!"

One run under the direction of Strickland was a good example. During 1927, the assistant chief engineer and Ernest C. Garland, service engineer, made a run to the Pacific coast and back with two of the first ten cars off the production line that year of the new Cadillac and LaSalle models. The trip was a test check, since more than 200,000 miles of testing of the new Cadillac in its final form had already been completed at the General Motors Proving Ground and in cross-country runs before the cars were placed in production. It was also the consummation of a series of tests on Cadillac and LaSalle cars carried on mostly at the General Motors Proving Grounds during the past twenty-six months and totaling nearly a million and a half miles.

The route selected for the transcontinental drive avoided the good highways. Bad roadbeds, rough going, steep grades and wide variations in temperature and climate were imperative to the test, and they were sought by the use of by-ways and circuitous routes.

For a test on mountain grades and at various altitudes the party seesawed back and forth through the backbone of the Rocky Mountain region, using every mountain pass available from Independence Pass, Colorado, at a height of 12,095 feet, to the district around the Salton Sea, where the road is 200 feet below sea level and the thermometers were registering a blistering heat well over the hundred mark. In all, twelve passes were crossed, ranging in height from 5,000 to 12,000 feet.

To illustrate the ordeals to which the cars were put, in the desert sands at a temperature of 106°, both cars being heavily loaded with baggage, testing apparatus and photographic equip-

Well loaded and liberally mudded cars pause briefly on one of the better roads between Beirut and Bagdad (left), while drivers check water ahead.

"The drivers . . . were tough but good. They never let their passengers down, and their fidelity and endurance were known throughout the Middle East."

ment, one car was made to tow the other. With five passengers and equipment and with the towed car in low gear, the lead car plowed the sands at twenty miles an hour. It did the same at forty miles an hour with the tow in second gear, and at sixty miles an hour with brakes partially set. Quite a performance!

"After the Proving Grounds got under way," Ernie Seaholm continued, "we had accurate information on competitive cars — performance, measurements, appearance, and other items. But up to then — and in contrast with today's facilities — highly sophisticated laboratories and proving grounds, and endless research information — our approaches were most primitive and time-absorbing. They did, however, have about them a spirit of romance and excitement. Not knowing any better, there was a thrill to being behind the wheel of the then conventional touring cars, unheated in the winter, uncooled in the summer, with side curtains flapping, taking whatever came along in our stride."

As noted at the beginning of this chapter, Uncle Sam was in the driving seat of the automobile industry, supplying practical vehicles for world needs, from the Ford and Chevrolet through the Chrysler and Buick up to the Packard and Cadillac. The latter had their rivals in the luxury field, chiefly Lincoln and Pierce-Arrow. But Cadillac's and Packard's market acceptance put them in the forefront. They were, however, cars of different emphasis. The Packard crossed deserts and continents too, but it was primarily "a gentleman's car built by gentlemen" — most of all at home on Sunset Boulevard, Fifth Avenue, or Bond Street in London. Plenty of Cadillacs were, of course, seen in Hollywood, Park Avenue, and Paris as well; yet for years "The Standard of the World" was a down-to-earth workhorse designed by hard-headed engineers for men in their shirtsleeves. The catalogue acknowledged that "fashion counts," but stressed that "ability is essential. . . . In the Mesabi Range country, at Gallup, on the sandy route to Bagdad, they feel out the accelerator, step hard on the brakes, ask about the cooling."

While the latter was Cadillac's first objective, Packard ignored certain practical, underhood aspects for the sake of eye-appeal alone. In comparison with the utilitarian Cadillac design, Packard's engine was an aesthetic masterpiece — but achieved at some sacrifice of serviceability. For symmetrical appearance, the distributor was placed squarely in the middle of the cylinder head. To decarbonize a Packard, first the distributor had to be removed before the cylinder head, and then retimed on reassembly. By contrast, Cadillac heads were removed alone. Again, for "clean design," Packard squeezed the water pump into the end of the block behind the fan. This was a source of trouble

in several ways. The Cadillac pump was placed to one side in a less artistic but much more satisfactory position.

Although Cadillac's pragmatic engineering philosophy had many practical advantages in service, eye appeal remained an important factor for a certain class of luxury buyer. The Packard owner was proud to lift the hood and impress the bystander with the beauty therein.

Aesthetics came to Cadillac with Harley Earl, as we have already seen, but had been confined to the external appearance of the car as a whole. Now they were to be applied to the engine room also. An entirely new powerplant was taking shape. It was, however, no mere styling exercise. From an engineering standpoint, it was unprecedented.

A 1934 ad expresses Cadillac's international reputation.

CHAPTER NINE

CYLINDERS THE RAGE

Sixteens and twelves power Cadillacs silently, effortlessly, if not pragmatically, through the thirties

The very phrase "sixteen cylinders" implies something super-excellent; it is suggestive perhaps of the sibilant whisper of the great engine itself. Cadillac advertising copy made the most of this impression in a series, each one dramatically headed "SIXTEEN CYLINDERS." Even its model designation — the 452 — connoted its probable market, the Four Hundred. And, as Dave Holls has pointed out, the engine was a classic in its own right judged by its styling alone.

Nowadays people who have never seen or even heard of a sixteen-cylinder car are more inclined to question why such a super-elaborate power unit was ever put into a mere automobile in the first place. The answers can be found in "Reasons for the 16-cylinder V-Type Cadillac Engine," a paper read by William R. Strickland to the Detroit section of the SAE in April, 1930, and later published in the *SAE Journal*.

"With the continual development in smoothness and power of the Cadillac V-8 went the research work into greater and finer attainments for the future," he began. "Improvements called for a survey of the possibilities of advancement in engineering design . . . preceded or paralleled by a survey of the demands of the more enlightened engineers and car owners."

He noted the increased weight and size of cars, brought on by the desire for more grandiose custom bodies and luxurious equipment, plus wider three-passenger seats requiring increased power at high speed. Yet at the same time the luxury car owner demanded that this car "must accelerate in traffic with or ahead of the jam, must take all main roads over hills or mountains with ease and at highest permissible speeds, and maintain high speed on the new superhighways multiplying rapidly all over the country."

To adequately meet the demands called for a power increase of at least forty percent, Strickland continued. How was this to be done — by increased displacement? Higher compression? Supercharging? Could a four-speed transmission give an effectively higher performance? The latter two were completely rejected. The supercharger was practical only for racing cars. The "so-called" four-speed transmission, he said rather scornfully, was generally so arranged that it was in effect a three-speed, as no one used the low speed, and the car was underpowered.

"We did not believe it possible to obtain the increase of power by any known design of combustion chamber, either L-head or overhead valve, although we have followed with research work all the celebrated suggestions. Higher mean effective pressure can be of value only if smoothness, especially at low speeds, is not interfered with."

Simply enlarging the V-8's displacement meant larger bores and certain thermal problems. (Evidently the engineers felt that while the Duesenberg was obtaining very high power from an eight, it lacked the refinement demanded by Cadillac clientele.) Moreover, a bigger V-8 would require a new transmission and rear axle, and Cadillac was reluctant to design and introduce new ones when their existing drive line had proved wholly satisfactory. Reliability might suffer and costs certainly would.

By the process of elimination, more cylinders, a larger displacement, and higher compression was the solution arrived at. With a bore/stroke of 3 by 4 inches displacement was 452 cubic inches. Sixteen-cylinder torque characteristics meant that peak stresses in the transmission and axles were no higher than with the V-8, thus allowing the existing V-8 units to be used. Overhead valves were selected mainly for accessibility with the 45° V, but

WORKS OF THE MODERN MASTERS

e Very Finest
of its kind

right you see a camera portrait of a mechani-
sterpiece—the Cadillac 16-cylinder V-type
    Among automotive power plants, it
uniquely alone—not only the *first* of its
o be produced, but entirely unchallenged
he standpoint of its general excellence.
here is nothing surprising in this fact—
illac is unquestionably the very first
y on the V-type engine. It has now been
a years since Cadillac began to concen-
clusively on V-type design. During all
ears, the Cadillac engineering staff has
engine problem aside from the improve-
f this one type of design. Hence, their
and their talents have gone toward
n, rather than in the direction of general
entation. Consequently, they have
he V-type engine to a point of excellence
ached in the field of automotive design.
l this is equally true of manufacturing.
s entire equipment for engine building
on V-type design. Its engine craftsmen
oled in this design alone. And its

materials are selected for their exclusive fitness
to this particular type of engine. . . . When you
drive a 16-cylinder Cadillac, you will see how
really important this vast experience is. For
there is no power plant in any motor car so
smooth, so quiet, so flexible—or so generally
satisfactory—as Cadillac's 16-cylinder engine.
Truly, it is a masterpiece—the very first of its
kind. . . . Naturally, the same experience and
the same skill that go into the creation of the

V-16 are back of the great engines that Cadillac
builds for its other cars—the V-8, the V-12 and
the La Salle. Whichever of these cars you select,
you will find its engine as outstanding, by comparison, as is the V-16 in that market which so
peculiarly belongs to it. In their silken smoothness, their almost complete quietness of operation,
and their instant and unhesitating response to
the throttle, they contribute immeasurably to
the unending satisfaction of Cadillac ownership.

Cadillac A GENERAL MOTORS VALUE

*right, "Boss Ket" poses with the 1930 V-16. The advertisement
above hails the engine as an art form, for physical beauty
was as much a part of its makeup as technical prowess.
Nevertheless, it was performance that captured the imagination of
the press. "Designed for enormous acceleration, unheard of
hill-climbing ability, and more speed than perhaps
any man will care to use," said Motor, "the sixteen cylinder
Cadillac initiates a new trend in motor car design. Rather than
state the actual performance figures, Cadillac prefers
to let the new car speak for itself." It most certainly did that.*

appear to have given some gain in specific output, and with a compression ratio of 5.5 to 1 torque went up to more than 300 lb/ft, and horsepower to 160 plus. These figures gave all the performance desired, and the level of silence and smoothness set the world's highest standard of luxury car refinement — criteria, in fact, equaled in their time by only Marmon, and probably never surpassed to this day. Strickland said modestly that "the smoothness of operation gives the term a new significance; silkiness would be a more appropriate word. The pick-up, the running on the road, and the overrunning are all smooth and quiet." As we will see later, he was understating it.

It was interesting that after years of decrying the straight-eight principle, Cadillac had virtually adopted it, for the V-16 had a 2-4-2 (Packard type) straight-eight crankshaft and each cylinder bank with its own manifolding was a straight-eight. However, the short-stroke (4 inches compared to 5 inches for the contemporary eights) and the smaller bore (3 inches against 3½ inches), coupled with a five-bearing layout completely nullified the usual objection to long crankshafts. The V-16 shaft was actually 3½ inches shorter than, for example, the Pierce straight-eight, and slightly (one-quarter inch) shorter than the Pierce V-12! Consequently torsional effects were very small and the harmonic balancer on the front end of the crankshaft had very little work to do. In any case, it was a GM Research design of the leaf-spring type and required no maintenance.

Such in brief was the technical story of Cadillac's first V-16 engine. In its chassis it followed the same engineering pattern as the V-8, and many parts were interchangeable. The frame was heavier and longer, and other differences were a dual-exhaust system, a larger radiator, longer drive shaft for the longer wheelbase, heavier springs, larger clutch, and greater braking area with a vacuum power brake assister.

Complete secrecy was insisted on during the car's creation. "Many of the people on the lower levels of engineering and particularly outside suppliers," wrote N. F. Uhlir, "thought Cadillac was doing some design work for one of the other GM divisions because many of the design requests and blueprints referred to the vehicle as 'Bus' or 'Coach.' [However] Sloan, Fisher, and other top officers dropped in often to check on progress. A 'sight' model was built for approval. It looked so real that by adding a little oil, gas and battery power, it might have run."

"Following customary body practice" wrote W. R. Strickland, "wood and clay models were made and installed on a chassis, and the external details were worked out with simplicity,

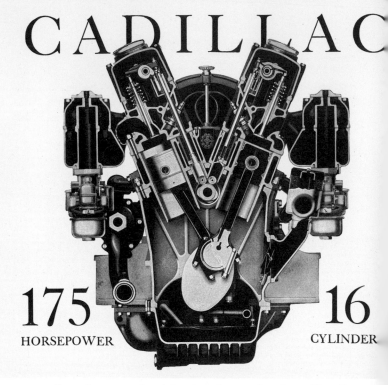

CADILLAC

175
HORSEPOWER

16
CYLINDER

Frontal cutaway view (above) and restored engine at Harrah's.

serviceability, and appearance uppermost in mind, so that when experimental models came through nothing had been left to chance. The appearance of the models completely confirmed the preliminary studies and the program for experimental production."

This part was directed by Ernest Schebera at Fleetwood, who was devoted to meticulous construction of bodies, but also appreciative of Harley Earl's modern thoughts on style. Thus, the two worked well together, and since Fleetwood was within the General Motors organization, total security was maintained in this area also. Thus the car was designed, engineered, prototypes handbuilt, and hundreds of thousands of miles testing carried out over more than three years, without public knowledge.

The publicity accompanying the V-16's introduction was proportional to the size of its engine. Since maximum security had been maintained throughout its development, the new V-16's debut would be doubly dramatic. In the second week of December,

1929, radio announcements were made, while simultaneously, L. P. Fisher sent form letters to Cadillac dealers to confirm the news. The first showing was staged at the factory on December 27, after the first three models had been built and made ready for the January New York show. Fisher had telegraphed invitations to friends, business associates, and their families, resulting in virtually public "private showings."

Public shows were equally sensational, and orders so far surpassed company expectations that production priorities were revised. Originally it was intended that dealers would receive their first cars in April. Actually, by April 8, the factory announced that the thousandth V-16 had been shipped.

In April alone, 576 left the factory, in May 445 — twenty percent of Cadillac's total unit sales of 2,219 cars. By June, shipments reached 2,000. L. P. announced that sales volume had reached 13½ million dollars — a total "far in excess of our expectations."

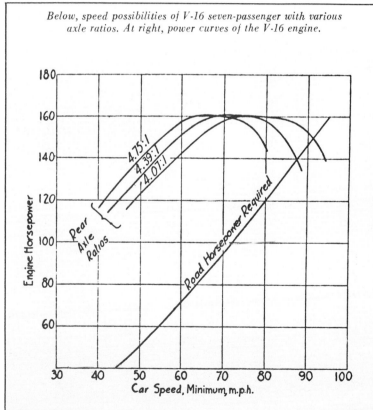

Below, speed possibilities of V-16 seven-passenger with various axle ratios. At right, power curves of the V-16 engine.

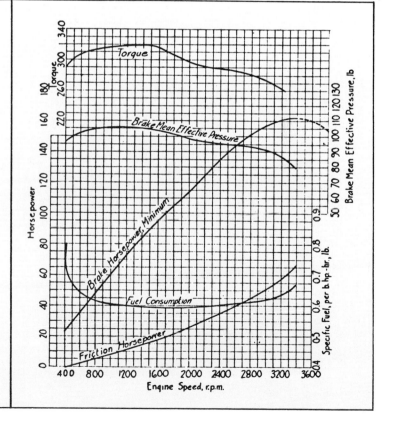

In June a "caravan" of V-16's went to Europe to make an introductory tour, including a visit to the ancient seat of the Cadillac family in France. In July they won prizes in Vienna. Cars, exhibited at London's Olympia, were priced at £1,500 (chassis), £2,450 (Imperial Limousine), and £2,860 (Imperial Brougham), prices that were practically double those of the V-8's on the same stand. The motoring press called it "a really magnificent car de luxe . . . of outstanding technical interest . . . the last word in automobile design in America."

One English road tester commented: "The outstanding feature is undoubtedly the engine, which is so smooth and quiet throughout its range as to make it seem incredible that the car is actually being propelled by exploding gases.

"The minimum speed on top gear was 2¼ mph. From this speed the car will get away quite smoothly if the throttle be suddenly opened wide. In London traffic the flexibility and instant acceleration on top gear make the car delightful to drive, and the same qualities produce very effortless travel in the country."

Despite this, the V-16's performance has been criticized in more recent years as "not startling". . ."not up to the Duesenberg." It had, they say, "a surprisingly low top speed . . . falling short of the Marmon 16." Moreover its "poor mechanical efficiency" resulted in "high fuel consumption" sometimes quoted as low as four miles to the gallon! Probably the most astonishing claim is that the smaller Cadillac V-12 would "outperform its larger brother!"

Stemming from a sports car "complex" in one instance and plain misinformation in the others, these comments are loaded against the V-16. As an instance of obvious bias, one of these sources calls the occasional sticking of a carburetor float hinge-pin an "appreciable shortcoming of the engine!" It also calls "fast" a rival car whose mean maximum of eighty-seven miles an hour is identical with the V-16, even though this car — the Rolls-Royce Phantom III — was six years later in arriving on the market. The V-12 versus the V-16 claim shows a failure to apply proper scientific standards of comparison, since body style for body style, GM Proving Ground data reveal the V-16 to be seven miles an hour faster than the V-12.

Diameter of the V-16's outside clutch (above) was increased 30% to eleven inches. The V-16 chassis is at upper right, the V-12/16 carburetor at far right below. Immediately to the right, the adjustable valve action.

Let us examine the subject in detail. In the first place, it is essential to realize that the superior and, in some cases, impossible figures often claimed for rival cars are based merely on wishful thinking by enthusiasts or owners, or a specially modified car with, say, minimum bodywork, the highest possible axle ratio, mild or wild tuning, and a speedometer reading on a one-way run, maybe downhill with a tailwind. These claims bear about as much relation to the reality of GM Proving Ground figures as wartime propaganda does to postwar examination of national archives.

Even reputable makers put their best possible foot forward in certain instances, so that a misleading impression became "official." Several figures quoted for the Duesenberg either will not stand critical examination or should be qualified when compared with the V-16. The peak horsepower figure forever advertised for the Model J — 265 at 4,200 — was impossible with the single torque curve that has been published. Similarly, the top speed of 116 mph appears to relate to a speedster only and was probably unattainable by a full-sized sedan.

In Europe, it was common practice to supply the press with roadsters or "speed models" whose figures were then quoted as typical — even though closed models with heavy bodies and "slow" axles would inevitably show lower figures. Typical instances of the V-16's day were the Rolls-Royce Phantom II Continental model, the V-12 Hispano-Suiza, and the 8-liter Bentley. All of these, as tested, had the lightest possible bodies of their type and the highest axle ratios available. Their minimum dimensions also lowered wind resistance — at the expense of interior space.

Cadillac seldom mentioned actual performance figures. Their main aim was silent, effortless propulsion over an adequate range — not at an unusually high top speed. Being a Detroit maker, with a large market, their standard basis of comparison was the five- or seven-passenger sedan. With adequate interior space for maximum comfort, the bodies were big. Figures from the factory graph show that with these large, heavy bodies and resulting high drag, the true top speed of the V-16 was as follows:

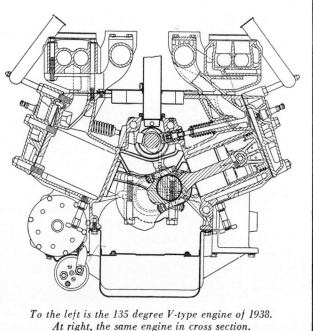

To the left is the 135 degree V-type engine of 1938. At right, the same engine in cross section.

Axle	Speed	Remarks
4.75	84 mph	Normally used only on V-8 models. Not recommended for V-16 except on seven-passenger models used in cities where steep hills must be negotiated in traffic—such as San Francisco.
4.39	87 mph	Standard
4.07	91 mph	Fast

Open models with the following ratios were faster because they had less wind drag. There was also a high-speed ratio (3.47) supplied only on special order, supposedly (though not always) limited to the roadster. Open models, therefore, produced these figures:

Axle	Top Speed
4.39	90+
4.07	95
3.47	100+

GM Proving Ground figures for the seven-passenger sedan with the 4.39 axle are on the conservative side. Actual test figures recorded by a competitor show that even with heavy bodies and the "fast" 4.07 axle option, the V-16's acceleration was still outstanding:

5 to 25 — 7.88 seconds
10 to 40 — 11.95 seconds
10 to 50 — 16.15 seconds
10 to 60 — 21.10 seconds
10 to 70 — 27.86 seconds
10 to 80 — 36.70 seconds

The same source (Lycoming Motors) estimated a true top speed of 95 mph, thus amply confirming Cadillac's own figures and making the car one of the fastest on the market in 1930.

For 1930 all Cadillac transmissions had a faster second gear (1.48) and this ratio permitted speeds over fifty in the V-8 and well over sixty in the V-16. From carefully controlled GMPG tests and authentic owner experience over extended mileage the fuel consumption was 8.8 mpg at forty miles an hour, 8.0 mpg at sixty–sixty-five miles an hour, and about 8.5 mpg on an average.

To summarize, while fuel consumption was certainly not light, it was not as heavy as some writers claim. Four miles to the

gallon can only be the result of an engine in faulty condition, badly tuned, and with carburetion unsynchronized, or a leak from vacuum tank to induction system. The performance figures, as a whole, could be bettered in 1930 by only one American car, and there were very few examples of it on the road. The Model J Duesenberg, announced a year earlier, had been in production for only eight or nine months (since April or May, 1929) and with average annual sales of about fifty cars. No other car anywhere in the world could both equal the V-16 figures *and* the refinement that went with them. In fact, up to that time, all overhead valve engines — including the push-rod type — had been noisy. The quietest were side valves, and Rolls-Royce, for instance, had to accept a slightly higher noise level when the ohv

Phantom I replaced the Silver Ghost. With the V-16, however, silence hitherto unknown was achieved, because, as Ernest Seaholm recalled, "It was here we used hydraulic zero-lash adjusters for the first time."

As Cadillac specialists point out, "the critical 'listening test' for the V-16 specifies that you hear nothing more than the spark of the contact points at idle," while John Bond has written, "At cruising speeds the only audible sound was from the fan and the two carburetors pulling air through their large air horns."

Within a few years, several of Cadillac's most famous rivals — Packard, Pierce-Arrow, Lincoln, and Rolls-Royce — went to hydraulic valve adjustment to match the V-16's silence. Two of them (Packard and Rolls) used a similar design, the two others used the now-standard hydraulic tappet — which Cadillac itself later adopted. Both types had been explored at Kettering's research laboratories, but the first type had been used in the V-16 because it was well suited to ohv and reduced the reciprocating weight of the valve gear. The principle of hydraulic valve adjustment had been attempted earlier by others, but the V-16 is the earliest known example successfully put into production.

The only other car to equal the V-16's refinement level was the Marmon V-16. Some actually question whether it did in fact do this. The writer has driven both cars, but found it hard to decide because conditions were different and precluded an immediate comparison. Still, Paul Schinnerer quotes several enthusiasts who, after driving both cars, agree that the Cadillac was

Undaunted Cadillac V-16's on a test tour at the Tetons (left), and Yellowstone (right).

smoother and quieter. Three things might account for this — Marmon lacked hydraulic valve silencers and a counterweighted crankshaft, and all-aluminum engines are usually noisier (in this case — less silent) than cast iron blocks and heads. But granting the Marmon V-16 equal refinement and admitting its greater power, acceleration, and top speed, it is obvious that (particularly when commercial considerations are ignored) any competent engineering group should be able to produce a technically improved car given another fifteen months in which to do it. The Marmon's advantages over the Cadillac were only of academic interest to all but a few buyers. It arrived on the market well over a year after the Cadillac, when the market was starting to collapse. So was Marmon, and the production of the Marmon V-16 did nothing whatever to stave off impending disaster for the company that produced it. It was, in fact, a luxury that Marmon could not afford. Its sales were about 130 annually over three years, compared with Cadillac figures of 2,000 in the first six months of production, and since its price was of a similar order, it is impossible to see how the company could have shown a profit on the car.

Cadillac's major rivals, Packard, Pierce, and Lincoln, took two years to reply to the V-16. They were all twelve-cylinders, all announced for the 1932 model year. Although none could quite match its refinement, in some design areas they were (as they should have been) improved over the V-16. For instance, all three V-12's had downdraft carburetion, Packard had a unit-block casting, and the Lincoln had the edge in performance. Judged overall, they were simply cars of the same order, and the V-16 scores on the two-year lead it had established. However, the Packard, Lincoln, and Pierce V-12's impress one as more typically "American" than the V-16, simpler in design, with adequate refinement and performance, and somewhat better from the serviceability angle. The V-16 needed more attention to keep it in proper tune and was probably more temperamental than the V-12's mentioned. It thus showed slightly un-American tendencies, particularly in comparison with the Cadillac V-8.

In comparison with more important rivals, we can summarize that the V-16's performance upon its introduction far outclassed any American car except the Model J Duesenberg, that the Marmon V-16 was the only car to match its refinement *and* surpass its performance, but that these cars were little threat saleswise. The only cars that were — the Lincoln, Packard and Pierce-Arrow — were much later in arriving, and not a major advancement when they did, so far as new car buyers were concerned.

SIXTEEN CYLINDERS

The Cadillac sixteen-cylinder engine goes far beyond the contemporary conception of brilliant performance. It multiplies power and subdivides it into a continuous flow ... constantly at full-volume efficiency ... flexible ... instantly responsive. This, plus complete individuality in styling, is — in brief — the story of the "V-16"

CADILLAC MOTOR CAR COMPANY   DIVISION OF GENERAL MOTORS

SIXTEEN CYLINDERS

Custom-built...the most highly
personalized of all motor cars

CADILLAC MOTOR CAR COMPANY . . . DIVISION OF GENERAL MOTORS

*Cadillac advertising for the V-16 was simple, refined, elegant,
bespeaking themes which those for whom it was intended
would instantly recognize: the hunt, the theatre, the social
"do," the country club — the world of the very rich, and very few.*

Among European contemporaries, the only comparable concepts were the Maybach V-12, announced about the same time as the Cadillac's V-16, the Hispano V-12, which came out contemporary with the Marmon V-16, and the Grosser Mercedes. The sales of these cars, even in Europe, were extremely small, and only a few have ever reached the United States — probably as much the result of postwar "collecting" as any sales when new. The Hispano V-12 has had a great deal of fulsome praise from several English writers in the past, but more realistic appraisals of it have been appearing recently. While it could outperform the V-16, several authoritative English sources consider it an overrated car, with clutch, transmission, chassis, and steering far short of the standards of its engine. The chassis remained undeveloped through its production life. Even the engine is open to criticism from a service angle, with its fixed cylinder heads, pinned big-ends and the inevitable problems of light alloy, wet-liner construction. W. O. Bentley tested it and called it "a surprising disappointment."

The Maybach V-12 and Grosser Mercedes are of academic, technical interest only. The latter was seldom ever seen except at ceremonial head-of-state functions, and only 117 cars were sold from 1930 to 1937. The Maybach's production was similarly limited, and both cars were good examples of the Teutonic tendency to add complication to a design complicated to start with. Even then their chassis development lagged behind — except the 1938 770K. In reviewing them alongside the V-16, which was built to similar standards but sold nearly 4,000 units, it is difficult to take the German cars seriously at all.

For six years all that Rolls-Royce engineering had to offer were the outdated Phantom II series, and (particularly after studying the report of W. O. Bentley) E. W. Hives, and W. A. Robotham of Rolls-Royce engineering concluded that their own car was no longer the quietest or most comfortable vehicle, nor was it very easy to handle. Among other things, W. O. Bentley commented that the mere word "automobile" was inadequate for the V-16.

Italy's only contender, the Isotta-Fraschini, was an ancient design and, from all accounts, a far inferior car to the V-16. It has been summed up by one English critic as "a very bad car in the grand manner." Undoubtedly this arose from the simple fact that the Italians have never shown the expertise in building big cars that they undoubtedly possess in other directions — the Alfa Romeo for instance.

From 1930 to 1933 the V-16 and the V-12 power was unchanged, although weights and gear ratios increased. From 1932, axle ratios became:

V-16	V-12	Remarks
4.07		
4.31	4.60	Fast
4.64	4.80	Slow

These continued until 1937. The bhp in 1934 became 185 for the V-16 and 150 for the V-12, both at 3,800 rpm. Tire-wheel size was reduced one inch in 1932 (7.50 by 18) and another in 1933 (7.50 by 17). The latter continued until 1937. The effect of all these changes indicates that the slowest cars would be 1932-1933 models, but that from 1934 onward performance was brought back to original standards.

Even the seven-passenger limousine, according to W. O. Bentley, would reach 90 mph. The car he tested for Rolls-Royce at Brooklands appears to have been a 1934 or 1935 model, and would have had either a 4.31 or 4.64 axle. These would have required 4,100 or 4,400 rpm respectively, speeds which may seem high for such a big displacement engine, at least by European standards. There is no doubt, however, that these engines were capable of well over 4,000 rpm. The original stress calculations and graphs were based on 4,200 rpm, and Strickland mentioned that the ignition system still worked correctly at speeds "considerably exceeding 4,000 rpm."

At this time, David Fergusson, chief engineer of Cunningham, was wondering how on earth he could make their ancient V-8 competitive. He calculated that the V-16 was probably still developing 180 bhp even at 4,100 rpm, "a speed which they can safely use due to their stroke being 1 inch less than ours, also due to their smaller reciprocating weights of pistons and connecting rods, they can still further increase these engine speeds compared to ours." He mused on his notepaper: "This, with the greater gear reduction and smaller tires, gives them much better performance, acceleration, hill climbing and speed than the Cunningham."

Fergusson pondered whether a supercharger might be the answer — plus a .705 to 1 Warner overdrive! This would keep the 473-cubic-inch Cunningham V-8's rpm down to a safe level, while the supercharger would give nearly as much horsepower as the V-16. This interesting project never materialized for several reasons — one being that the selling price of such a car would be "not less than $9,000."

Despite its size, the V-16 was easy to drive, and Paul Schinnerer writes of his 1930 model: "I think Cadillac realized that

The 1931 Cadillac V-16 limousine.

The 1931 Cadillac V-16 dual-cowl phaeton.

The 1932 Cadillac V-16 two passenger coupé.

buyers were not especially interested in sheer speed as much as smooth, quiet and well performing cars. My car is a very good performer . . . cruises nicely at 70 . . . seems a little slow at slow speeds unless you wind it up through the gears, but at 50 it starts to accelerate and just keeps going up to around 85, then begins to taper off. No other car of that year can match it except the Duesenberg."

Schinnerer feels, as does this writer, that the best performers were the '30's and '31's, but Norm Uhlir makes the interesting comment that "needless to say, the lighter Fisher bodied '32's would go like blazes. One friend of mine had his '32 convertible V-16 timed at over 105 mph at Sebring." This seems an unusually

high speed, but may have been possible with a standard car in exceptional tune and 3.47 axle fitted.

No power increases were made after 1934, as sales did not justify spending much on development. The potential was there, however, and hot rodders allegedly raised output as high as 250 bhp in four-carburetor versions. Uhlir's own V-16, with drastically raised compression and downdraft carburetors, has "the most startling performance" of about twenty ohv's he has tried.

"I can't compare later sixteens in performance because there isn't known data," he continued. "I've driven many, but tune and condition generally make it impossible to determine whether it is typical. Only one Proving Ground report was written on the V-16

Miss Alice Bliss and L. P. Fisher, 1933.

The 1935 Cadillac V-16 convertible sedan.

The 1936 Cadillac V-16 town car.

The 1937 Cadillac V-16 seven-passenger sedan.

in 1930. I've never seen any other comprehensive test report on these cars. They cost too much to lend out for independent testing and I'm sure the dealers didn't want to risk their being damaged. Therefore, comparative test data is based on the sedan with an axle not selected for high speed. However, the 4.07 as well as the 4.39 provided excellent acceleration and 90 or more top speed."

Probably the best example of what the V-16 could do occurred in May, 1931, when the so-called "M-B-D Scientific Expedition" was carried out. According to the official report of the "Expedition," the purpose of the trip was rather indefinite — it was to be decided on the return of the explorers. They wanted "to

TWELVE CYLINDERS

The new Cadillac V-12 is powered with an engine of the same type and built to exactly the same standards as the Cadillac V-16—in fact, a duplicate of this engine in pattern and appearance, but having twelve instead of sixteen cylinders. Coachwork and interiors of rare beauty by Fisher and Fleetwood

Ten body styles; wheelbase 140-143 inches. Prices from $3795 to $4875, f. o. b. Detroit

CADILLAC MOTOR CAR COMPANY   DIVISION OF GENERAL MOTORS

The V-12's advertising followed traditional form.

prove: that the world was flat; to get away from all telephones; to see Havana by moonlight; to get a good restful vacation; and to prove that Dr. Behneman could really get away from his business."

Behneman was one of the three members of this unusual expedition, the others being H. L. Menke, owner of the car, and Clarence J. Dixon, service manager for Don Lee Incorporated, Cadillac distributors in San Francisco. Menke acted as "pilot, cinematographer and chief hand-shaker," Behneman was "navigator, chief surgeon and accordion teaser," and Dixon was "chief engineer and scout extraordinary." None were professional racing drivers.

Extraordinary was the word for their trip. The car was a V-16 sedan with 17,000 miles on it at the start, and twenty-four days later its odometer read 27,000 miles. Leaving San Francisco at 4 A.M. Saturday, May 2, they drove first to Los Angeles, covering the 450 miles in 8¼ hours. From there they continued to El Paso, arriving seven hours ahead of the *Sunset Limited*, fastest train from San Francisco. After a quick side trip to Juarez, Mexico, and back, they were on their way to New Orleans. On this leg they covered one stretch of 300 miles in exactly 300 minutes. Leaving New Orleans a day and a half later, they caught a ferry to Cuba on the Wednesday. Arriving on the Friday, they drove around the island and left for Key West the following Tuesday. Driving up to New York, they continued into Canada and returned to the United States at Detroit. A three-day stay there included a visit to the Cadillac factory and was followed by a run to Chicago. The last leg from Chicago to San Francisco, via Omaha and the Victory Highway, was made over some poor roads, especially from Salt Lake City to Reno. This "held them down considerably" and as they also spent six hours in Salt Lake City and Reno, their elapsed time of sixty hours forty-two minutes was "no better than the fastest train time." They arrived in San Francisco Monday, May 25.

Their normal cruising speed had been sixty to sixty-five miles an hour, and their overall gas mileage was 8½ mpg, with an oil consumption of 150 miles per quart, measured over the 10,000 miles.

The entire trip started as a vacation and ended that way. Whenever there were sights, they stopped as long as they wished, and about twelve of the twenty-four days were sightseeing — including a rainy day in Reno. "If we had wanted to do a record trip" said Dixon, "I believe we could cut the time in half.' They took turns at driving, riding and sleeping in the rear compartment. After the first day, no difficulty was experienced in sleeping, and they reported:

"The easy riding qualities of the V-16, the roominess and lack of bouncing and jarring made sleeping quite comfortable. We saw plenty of traffic cops — in fact more in California than all other states put together, but so unostentatiously did the V-16 slide along the road that not once were we stopped for a speeding violation."

Menke wrote to the factory: "Other cars and drivers under stress might equal the figures, but not with the ease and comfort that marked our trip as an outing for pleasure. For comfort under all driving conditions, the V-16 has completely won me. The car ran like a top, in fact, so well we would love to do it all over again."

Refinement was not confined to the V-16's engine alone. John Bond has commented that "supreme silence and clashless shifting made the transmission a delight to use, while the clutch functioned smoothly under all conditions." Perhaps the best comment on the transmission was made by the English *Motor Sport*. Sampling a V-16 in *1964*, they recommended that a well-known English maker study it as providing a lesson in silky operation even by modern standards!

Like its performance and fuel consumption, the V-16's brakes have been criticized. Despite the increased braking surface and power assist, brakes on the early models left something to be desired in stopping from high speeds. Apparently the friction characteristics of hard-linings (chosen for durability and lack of fade) coupled with high-carbon steel drums, were the reason for this inadequate stopping power. A change was soon made to electric furnace molybdenum cast iron drums which were a big improvement. This was just as well, and not only from the safety angle. The special equipment for making the drums cost Cadillac some $200,000. The drums were machined all over using carboloy tools, ground within seven-thousandths of an inch for concentricity, highly polished, and carefully balanced. Another improvement was an aluminium brake shoe which on repeated application expanded sufficiently to maintain lining contact with the drum. "The result is that Cadillac brakes are just as good at the bottom of a long hill as when first applied at the top," said the Service Manual.

In discussing brakes today it is well to remember that braking standards have improved out of all sight since the twenties and thirties. Although some brakes of the time were very good even by modern standards, under certain conditions, they left something to be desired in stopping from very high speeds because of the limited ability of the materials and the tremendous inertia of vehicles weighing 6,000 pounds or more, and capable of up to one hundred miles an hour. This failing, incidentally, was not confined to American cars. Various European top class makers from time to time offered models with braking inadequate to their performance — one example being the

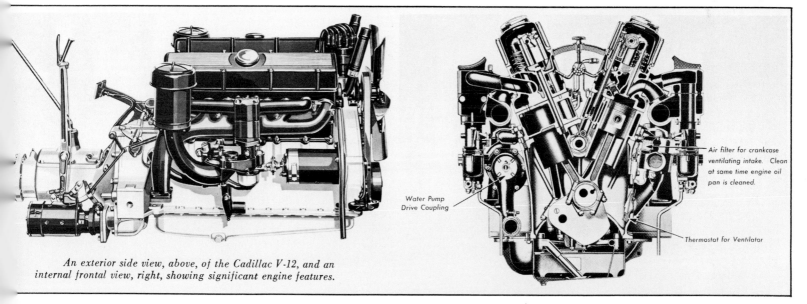

Air filter for crankcase ventilating intake. Clean at same time engine oil pan is cleaned.

Water Pump Drive Coupling

Thermostat for Ventilator

An exterior side view, above, of the Cadillac V-12, and an internal frontal view, right, showing significant engine features.

The 1931 Cadillac V-12 two-passenger coupé.

The 1931 Cadillac V-12 sedan.

Mercedes 36-220 and 38-250 series. Even the mechanical-servo types used by Hispano-Suiza, Rolls-Royce, and Pierce-Arrow, although probably best for high speed work, had their drawbacks and among other things, did not fully live up to the makers' claims that they were absolutely "fade-free." W. O. Bentley cites this in connection with Rolls-Royce, and the writer found it the same with Pierce-Arrow. Although more powerful and stable than the vacuum-servo, these "fade-free" brakes can lead to overconfidence, and, as W. O. observed, continuous use is followed by "very sudden fade." These brakes are also definitely not at their best at low speeds, and in the case of the Hispano, disconcertingly ineffective in reverse.

Cadillac engineers pointed out the following reasons for selecting a vacuum-boosted, self-energizing principle in preference to the Pierce or Rolls system:

1. Direct connection between pedal and all brakes regardless of power unit functioning or not. (Pierce-Arrow relied on the handbrake operating four wheels for emergency, while Rolls-Royce had pedal linkage to the rear brakes only.)

2. No "lag" as with the mechanical servo. (Although not noticeable at speed, this involves perceptible allowance when parking a car.)

3. Cadillac brakes did not "hang-on." If the driver wished to decrease deceleration slightly, he merely reduced foot pressure, instead of being forced to almost release the pedal, then apply at reduced pressure.

4. Better control on slippery or icy roads.

5. Because of its simplicity Cadillac engineers believed the vacuum assister more reliable than the servo-motor.

6. Uniformly self-energizing despite wear. This, the engineers claimed, was not the case with the nonwrapping mechanical servo type.

However, the last two were denied by Pierce-Arrow, who claimed *their* servo-unit was more reliable and that their brakes were more consistent in performance. From study of and experience with both systems, the writer feels that Cadillac's first three (and possibly four) claims were correct, but that the last two were disputable. Particularly in the case of the fifth, a vacuum system is more likely to be temperamental in use than a straight mechanical system because the former relies on seals and valves that can eventually deteriorate. The mechanical servo, on the other hand, as used by Pierce, was virtually indestructible, sealed in oil, and practically good for the life of the car. Some consider it superior to the "dry" type used by Rolls-Royce and Hispano, but wet or dry, the mechanical servo was very costly and had to be specifically designed into each car.

Time proves all things, and on this score Cadillac (and all vacuum-servo exponents) eventually won the argument. Pierce, and ultimately Rolls, abandoned their mechanical servo. To make this comparison fair, it should be noted that Pierce-Arrow, although they had pioneered vacuum boosters for the United States in 1927, had only Bendix-type self-energizer brakes without booster during 1930–1932, turned to the friction servo in 1933, and returned to vacuum again in 1936. Also, Rolls, who stuck to mechanical until the 1960's, went over to a hydraulic system — not a vacuum.

Like Pierce, Packard, Lincoln, Rolls, and a number of others, Cadillac was then "afraid of hydraulics" — used at that time by such rivals as Duesenberg, Stutz, and Chrysler Imperial. Cadillac claimed their system was more positive and reliable than hydraulic and just as frictionless because needle roller bearings were used in no less than fifteen places. Of course, eventually, like everyone else, Cadillac abandoned the mechanical system in favor of hydraulics.

Paul Schinnerer, who has owned several V-16's, comments, "The brakes work very well up to 70 mph but when driving any faster, it is a good idea to leave plenty of room between cars as 6,200 lb. is a lot of car to stop fast!" Without actual stopping distances for the V-16 and its rivals under comparable conditions, we have to leave the matter at that. The V-16's brakes, while perhaps less powerful at high speeds, were probably better than the Pierce, Rolls, and Hispano types for city traffic, with a stand-off between them at medium speeds. In this the V-16 was no better and no worse than such rivals as Marmon, Lincoln, and Packard, so overall must be accepted as satisfactory in the context of its time.

On July 30, 1930, L. P. told a group of distributors in Detroit that yet another model was on the way — a V-12! In October that year, J. C. Chick (newly appointed general sales manager in succession to Lynn McNaughton, who had retired September, 1930), entertained Cadillac distributors at the factory and showed them the V-16's younger brother. Its engine was a sixteen less four cylinders, with 3⅛-inch bore, distributor, crankshaft, camshaft, and induction and exhaust systems for twelve cylinders, the only changes. This gave a 370 cubic-inch displacement, 135 bhp at 3,400 rpm and 284 lb/ft at 1,200. The V-12 was very compact, with crankshaft length just under thirty-six inches. Although this was eight inches longer than the V-8, there was room in the eight's engine compartment for the V-12, and it used the same 140-inch chassis. Although not as fast as the V-16, it soon gained a reputation for its ability to rev high in complete smoothness, and was a fine performer. Its top speed was not high (eighty mph for the seven-passenger sedan with standard axle), but cruising speeds of sixty to seventy miles an hour were completely quiet and turbinelike.

"So," laughed Ernest Seaholm, "we wound up with: a LaSalle V-8, a Cadillac V-8, a Cadillac V-12, and a V-16! We must have been mad!"

Madness or not, others were keen on the idea, and as already outlined, Packard, Pierce-Arrow, and Lincoln followed after a considerable pause — with a range of eights and twelves that

Willard Rader paces the 1931 Indy 500 in a V-12.

The 1932 Cadillac V-12 convertible coupé.

The 1933 Cadillac V-12 sedan.

must have strained their resources just as much, if not more, than Cadillac's. Packard had two sizes of eight and one twelve.

Actually, Cadillac's "saturation bombing" was rational enough. From an engineering standpoint, there were really only two cars, the L-heads and the over-heads. The LaSalle and Cadillac V-8's were practically identical. The V-12 power unit was simply adapted from the V-16, and used the biggest V-8 chassis. And since the basic chassis design existed from 1927 to 1928, the only big new development was the ohv engine. This explains how Cadillac was able to out-general their opponents and produce the four different cars without prohibitive cost. The others, Packard, Pierce, and Lincoln, had to produce new transmissions, axles, and chassis to go with their new engines. And, in tribute to Nacker's ability as a designer it should be noted that V-16 developments were remarkably trouble-free, few changes were required during test and development, and also after the engine got into production. On the other hand, the others struck problems. Marmon's first V-16 design had to be scrapped during the development stage. Packard experimented with a twelve in line which was quite useless, and had to rely on an outside design for its twelve, produced by Van Ranst. This in turn, required substantial alteration before production could begin. Pierce's early twelves had to be revised to give satisfactory performance. Lincoln showed inconsistency in planning two quite different V-12 designs, so that one was replaced by the other after only two years production. Admittedly, all these engines proved excellent designs when fully developed, but Cadillac comes out of the comparison very well.

The only possible criticism is that after 1930, the Cadillac twelve may have stolen sales from the sixteen. It sold 1,984 units in its first six months — better sales than the V-16. But it would be difficult to judge which of the twelve's buyers were sixteen prospects and which Packard, Lincoln, or Pierce! Undoubtedly, the major factor in decline of V-16 sales after the first year was the growing effect of the depression. The overall drop in sales for all makes proves this — forty-two percent down in 1931. (In the worst depression years, the mere mention of sixteen cylinders was enough to deter some buyers.)

In 1930, 2,887 V-16's were built, nearly 2,500 being sold at retail. But only about 750 were sold in 1931, and dealers were already offering heavy discounts by the spring of that year. About half of these were cars left over from 1930 production, with an actual 364 new cars built in 1931. In 1932, 300 were sold, each being built virtually to special order. This became official policy in 1933 when Cadillac announced that only 400 sixteens would be built. Actually, serial numbers indicate that no more

The 1933 V-12 shows its beautiful front ensemble.

The striking convertible sedan V-12 from 1933.

The engineer who created the V-16, Owen Nacker.

than 126 were built that year, halving to 56 in 1934. Total production for 1934–1937 was only 212 cars, and the fifty cars built in 1935 can be taken almost as an average for most years. Total production altogether was 3,878 cars over seven years, some twelve percent less than the 4,425 indicated by serial number. The 508 flathead sixteens built in 1938–1940 bring this to 4,386

V-12 figures show a trend from the V-16 and toward the V-12 from the latter's inception. The drop in sales as the Depression worsened, was noticeably greater for the V-16, and never really recovered. The V-12 outsold the V-16, suffered less in the lean years, made a substantial recovery in 1936 compared with 1935, and in 1937, the final year for both ohv's, it outsold the V-16 nearly ten to one. Total sales V-12/V-16, 1930-1940 were 15,207, far surpassing either the Packard V-12 or the senior Lincoln V-12 line, and almost equalling both together.

The V-16 was technically successful in that it was a sound design, and commercially successful in that its initial sales exceeded company expectations. (Production had to be stepped up four times in the first year.) It was also psychologically successful in that it scooped its real rivals by a substantial time lead, and was not subsequently overshadowed by them. It set an "ultra" seal on Cadillac's engineering reputation matched only by Duesenberg. All this, achieved during the two years 1930–1931, was a shock to Packard in particular. Until then they felt they were in command of the bulk of the connoisseur market, but Cadillac had shown it had not only the desire but the ability to beat Packard at their own game.

The V-16, of course, marked a departure from Cadillac's pragmatic philosophy, and the concept was abandoned after only one decade. Maurice Olley dismissed it as "mere elaboration." Yet, like an earlier analogy (the Packard Twin Six), it would seem to have been worthwhile. Its glamorous aura did something for Cadillac. As John Bond writes: "Few would say the car was a mistake. It is one of the seldom-mentioned reasons for Cadillac's success in the prestige market. While obviously impossible to assess in exact terms, the prestigious image now enjoyed by Cadillac undoubtedly owes much to this fabulous sixteen cylinder. . . . A visible tribute to men possessed by the desire to build a motor car to the most exacting standards, . . . it established the make for the wealthiest of drivers."

But of all the accolades, I favor the one Ernest Seaholm himself jotted down for me: "A dream of the Roaring Twenties . . . materializing at the time the bottom dropped out of the stock market — advertised for the '400' — who were now in hiding — and finding instead only empty pocketbooks. Be that as it may, it was an outstanding piece of work."

PRESERVING THE HERITAGE

*A portfolio in color
of Cadillac
and LaSalle motorcars*

A prominent new leisure time activity has arisen in recent years that traces its origins decades back, to the founding of the Veteran Car Club of Great Britain in 1930 and the Antique Automobile Club of America in 1935. These two small groups became the bases for the modern hobby of restoring, preserving, and researching the history of the automotive flyers of yesterday. The pastime today is no longer looked upon — as it once was, incorrectly — as one pursued only by the very rich or the slightly eccentric. It has come of age. Clubs, publications, whole businesses exist to cater solely to a hobby which conservatively involves upwards of 200,000 people in North America alone, from every age and income strata imaginable.

Among collectors, Cadillac was relatively late to gain acceptance. Perhaps this was due to its continued presence among us. There is something of the underdog in automotive names long expired, and all Americans love underdogs. This manifestation once led collectors to subconsciously seek out cars no longer built, leaving marques like Cadillac — in many vintages superior to most of their rivals — off the want lists. But no more.

Today Cadillac is an intrinsic part of the restoration boom, and becoming more important all the time. Throughout the history of the movement Cadillac remained, if not always the preferred choice, a recognized leader, a standard of excellence. Yet almost from the beginning, single- and four-cylinder and early V-8 Cadillacs appeared among the ranks of the Antique Automobile Club of America, the Veteran Car Club of America, and the Horseless Carriage Club. In England, as we have seen, the British V.C.C. was among the sponsors of Fred Bennett's return trial fifty years after the original — in the same car.

When the Classic Car Club of America was founded in 1952, an impressive proportion of pre-1942 Cadillacs and LaSalles were cited with the distinguished "classic" designation, just as many fine post-1945 Cadillacs are being named to its rolls twenty years later by The Milestone Car Society. The Contemporary Historical Vehicle Association, concentrating on the 1928-48 period, counts Cadillacs of all varieties on its roster, and for the true Cadillac aficionado — the specialist — there is the Cadillac-LaSalle Club for all pre-1949 Cadillacs and LaSalles, which embraces a fine cross section of models ranging from one to sixteen cylinders.

Thus we find the marque amply represented among today's enthusiasts, themselves backed by a growing industry offering the restoration services, research sources and rare old parts and technical manuals which make the gallery of historic Cadillacs presented here such a splendid one.

This collection of Cadillacs and LaSalles, while most likely the best color portfolio of these marques ever put together, is only a sampling of what collectors have accomplished. The models range from the antique to the contemporary, from the one-cylinder to the modern V-8, from an age of dusty, meandering carriageways to the day of rolling Interstates. And yet certain themes are common to them all: engineering excellence, styling distinction, consistent quality, exuded steadily for seventy years by the Standard of the World.

—*The Editors*

1903 Model A runabout │ *Pollock Automotive Collection*

1907 Model M coupé | *Pollock Automotive Collection*

Inset: 1907 Model K roadster | *Owner: J. Renzulli*

Above: 1910 Model Thirty touring | *Owner: Tom Patris*   *Below: 1912 Model Thirty "Torpedo" sport touring* | *Owner: Sheldon Ball*

1912 Model Thirty coupé | *Harrah's Automobile Collection*

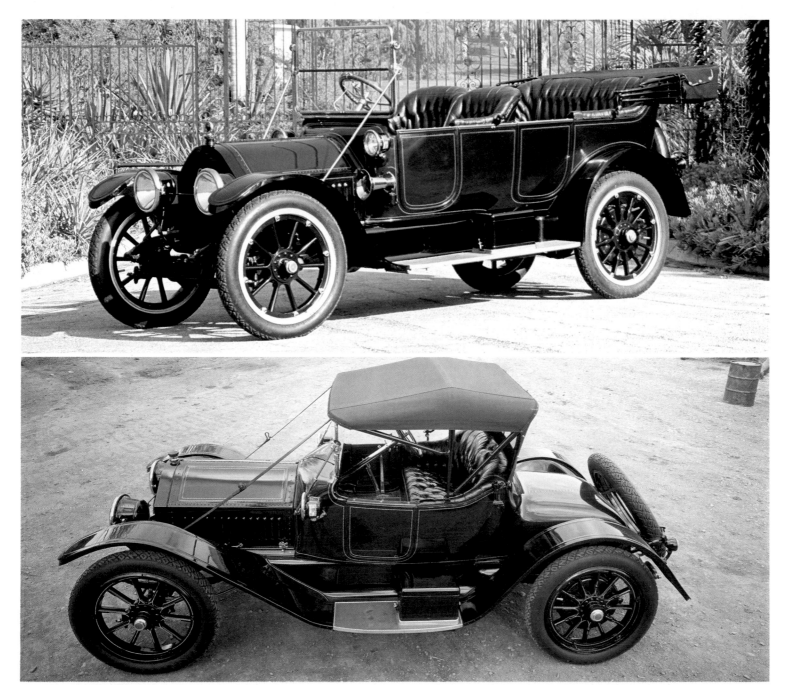

Above: 1913 Model Thirty touring | Owner: B. Greene   *Below: 1913 Model Thirty roadster | Harrah's Automobile Collection*

Above: 1914 Model **Thirty** *touring* | *Harrah's Automobile Collection*

Below: 1915 Series 51 5-passenger sedan | *Owner: Al Carroll*

174

1916 Series 53 touring | *Owner: Herb Sculnick*

Above: 1918 Series 57 7-passenger touring | *Owner: Ray Williams*   *Below: 1921 Series 59 7-passenger touring* | *Owner: Rubin Jurman*

176

1925 Series V-63 4-door brougham | *Owner: Mrs. G. Bauer*

Above: 1923 Series 63 touring | *Owner: J. D. Forney*

Below: 1926 Series 314 7-passenger sedan | *Owner: Mrs. G. Bauer*

178

1927 Series 314 dual cowl phaeton | Owner: Thomas J. Dawson

1928 Series 341-A dual cowl phaeton | *Formerly A. N. Rodway Collection*

Above: 1929 LaSalle 328 convertible coupé | *Formerly A. N. Rodway Collection*   *Below: 1929 LaSalle 328 convertible coupé* | *Owner: Rob Johnson*

Above: 1929 Series 341-B-7 passenger touring | *Formerly A. N. Rodway Collection*   *Below: 1930 Series 353 Fleet roadster* | *Owner: Thomas J. Dawson*

1930 Series 452 5-passenger Imperial Landaulette by Fleetwood | *Owner: Dave Towell*

Above: 1930 LaSalle 340 sedan | *Owner: Stephen Nicas*   *Below: 1930 Series 452 touring* | *Owner: Joe Runyan*

184

1931 **LaSalle** *345-A convertible coupé* | *Owner: Donald Klusman*

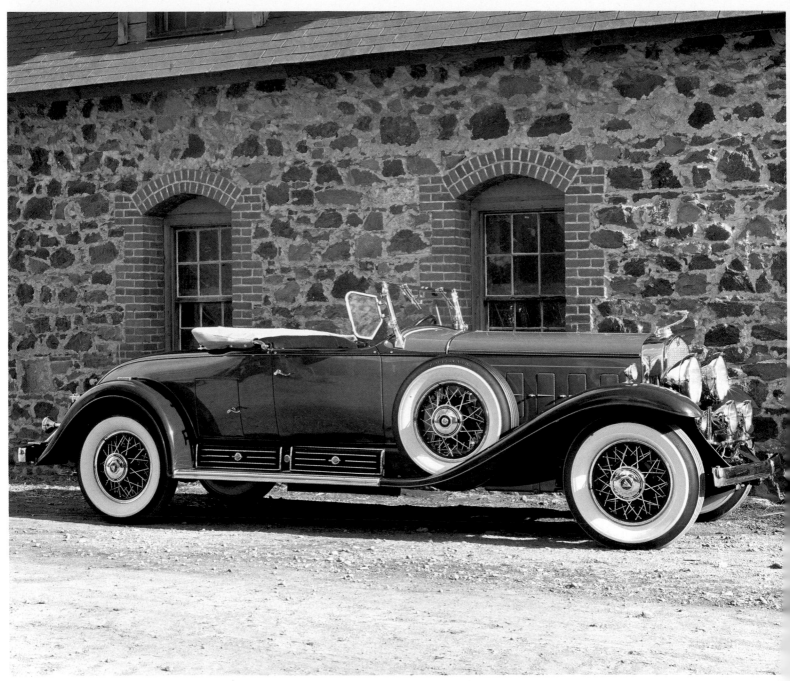

1930 Series 452-A roadster by Fleetwood | *Harrah's Automobile Collection*

1931 Series 355 7-passenger touring | *Owner: Ed Schnaidt*

Above: 1931 Series 355-A sports roadster by Fleetwood | *Formerly A. N. Rodway Collection*   *Below: 1932 LaSalle 345-B sedan* | *Owner: R. Brown*

1932 Series 370-B deluxe sport phaeton | *Owner: Milford H. Gould*

1933 Series 452-C all-weather phaeton by Fleetwood | *Harrah's Automobile Collection*

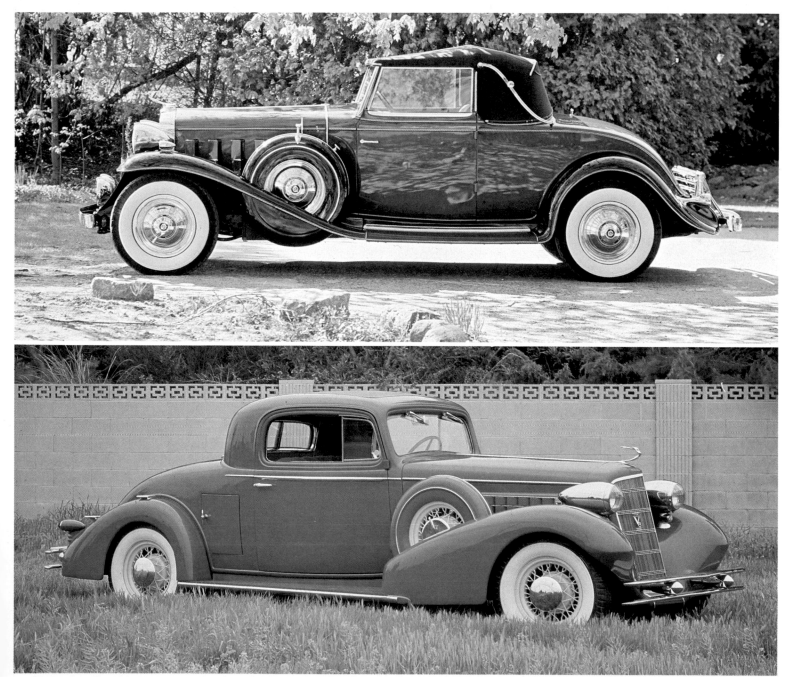

Above: 1932 Series 355-B convertible coupé | *Owner: Dave Holls*   *Below: 1934 Series 355-D coupé by Fleetwood* | *Owner: C. R. Currey*

Above: 1935 Series 370-D town car by Fleetwood | *Owner: E. O. Nance*　　　　*Below: 1936 Series 90 7-passenger sedan by Fleetwood* | *Owner: W. Podsed*

1936 Series 80 convertible sedan by Fleetwood | *Owner: J. Longo*

1936 Series 75 convertible sedan by Fleetwood | *Owner: Dr. W. W. Stanton*

ve: 1940 Series 60 Special sedan by Fleetwood | *Owner: R. D. Blake*   *Below: 1940 Series 75 town car by Fleetwood* | *Owner: M. Caire*

1940 Series 90 formal sedan by Fleetwood | *Owner: Mills Lane*

Above: 1941 60 Special town car by Fleetwood | *Owner: R. Leibendorfer*   *Below: 1941 60 Special sedan by Fleetwood* | *Owner: R. J. Brelsford*

Above: 1941 Series 62 convertible coupé | Owners: Linhardt/Gilbert   Below: 1941 Series 62 convertible sedan | Owner: Cal Moxley

1941 Series 62 custom estate car by Coachcraft | *Owner: Hollis G. Weihe*

Above: 1942 Series 63 sedan | *Owner: Bob Dunham* *Below: 1942 Series 60 Special sedan by Fleetwood* | *Owner: Luther Jones*

1947 Series 62 Coupe | *Owner: Robert J. Brelsford*

1949 Series 62 Coupe (sedanette) | *Owner: Ray Carmody*

Above: 1950 Series 62 sedan | *Cadillac Motor Car Division*   *Below: 1953 Eldorado convertible* | *Owner: Don Davidson*

Above: 1954 Eldorado convertible | *Cadillac Motor Car Division*   *Below: 1954 Series 62 Coupe de Ville* | *Cadillac Motor Car Division*

Above: 1956 Eldorado convertible | Cadillac Motor Car Division   Below: 1957 Eldorado Brougham | Cadillac Motor Car Divison

Above: 1957 Eldorado Seville | Cadillac Motor Car Division

Below: 1958 Eldorado Brougham | Owner: Jere C

210

Above: 1963 Sedan de Ville | *Cadillac Motor Car Division*   *Below: 1964 de Ville convertible* | *Owner: Hollis G. Weihe*

212

1966 Fleetwood Brougham | *Cadillac Motor Car Division*

Above: 1965 Calais coupé | *Cadillac Motor Car Division*

Below: 1967 Eldorado | *Cadillac Motor Car Division*

Above: 1970 Sedan de Ville | *Tate Motors Incorporated*

Above: 1973 Eldorado coupé | *Cadillac Motor Car Division*

Below: 1974 Coupe de Ville | *Cadillac Motor Car Division*

Above: 1975 Eldorado Coupe | *Cadillac Motor Car Division*

In two- and four-door versions and with a slightly lower profile, the clay model called "LaScala" which was completed September 17, 1973.

Leading to Seville. Fiberglass "LaSalle" prototype with Hooper-Daimler overtones, April 6, 1973. Notchback fiberglass prototype, June 26, 1973.

The final fiberglass model, based on X body components and bearing again the "LaSalle" name, which was completed June 5, 1974.

Now called the Seville, the car was given its official debut on May 1, 1975—with production having begun a month earlier, on March 26.

Above: 1976 Eldorado Coupe | *Cadillac Motor Car Division*

Above: 1976 Eldorado Convertible | *Cadillac Motor Car Division*

Above: 1977 Fleetwood Brougham d'Elegance | *Cadillac Motor Car Division*   *Below: 1979 Eldorado Coupe* | *Cadillac Motor Car Division*

THEMES IN CADILLAC ADVERTISING

How these cars were promoted

As one wanders among displays of Cadillacs such as the foregoing, he finds it relatively easy to recall the division's exhortation of The Product through the years, under the direction of Theodore F. MacManus since 1915 and later the merged D'Arcy-MacManus firm. Led by *The Penalty of Leadership* of 1915, Cadillac publicity developed to become respected throughout the advertising industry.

Before 1915 Cadillac ads had sold lots of cars, but hardly represented the ultimate in sophistication. They were, as the reader can see from examples in early chapters, blocks of data, news items, performance comparisons, running costs. The "fireside chat" style was typical of the brass age. *The Penalty of Leadership* changed that forever.

This legendary advertisement, suggested by Wilfred Leland and written by Theodore MacManus, appeared only once, yet millions of copies have been reproduced. As Julian Lewis Watkins wrote in *The One Hundred Greatest Advertisements* decades later, "hardly a week goes by that either Cadillac or its agency do not get requests for copies." In compiling his book, Watkins wrote to fifty leading advertising men for nominations. *The Penalty of Leadership* was listed by every one of them. "It is," said Watkins, "perhaps the greatest of all advertisements."

After *The Penalty of Leadership*, Cadillac advertising followed a variation of the Pierce-Arrow theme — artistry, subtlety, implication. As Ned Jordan said, "to hell with the mechanical chat-

ter." An air of effortless superiority, almost condescension, began to creep in. "Modern advertising would seem to make all cars pretty much alike," said one layout. "Of course a moment's thought immediately disposes of the idea." Another ran, "Wherever the admired and notable congregate, observe the overwhelming preference for Cadillac and LaSalle." The theme was that a Cadillac had *benefits* rather than mere features, which when you look at it is probably a more pragmatic approach than critics of Cadillac's "snobbishness" would care to admit. When Theodore MacManus was followed by Jim Adams the message continued. "I don't sell mechanism," he said, "I sell a state of mind." His ads, *Fortune* commented, exude "elegant pictorial backgrounds and velvet language, bespeak prestige and status."

The "By implication" theme reached its peak in association with old time arts and crafts — antique gun collections, manuscripts and first editions of great books, quality jewelry, china or glass: "The silver gilt ewer is a triumph of Roman craftsmanship, 17th century, and bears the inscription of . . ." intoned Cadillac catalogues. "The chalice, a gift of J. P. Morgan to the Metropolitan Museum of Art, is of gold and enamel, German, about 1609. . ."

Such backgrounds, despite their opulence, usually managed to highlight, not overpower, the car itself. The strain of consistency was maintained through the years, and today the Cadillac advertisement maintains an aura of quiet, dignified luxury, in tribute to the cars themselves.

THE UPHILL DECADE

The practical approach, technical progress, and consolidation a keynote during a difficult era

Whereas 1932 marked the peak point of the American "classic" tradition, the "coach appearance" and concept, and its constructional practices, simply had to go. However much classicists decry the fact, the modern automobile could never have developed any other way. With 1933 as a transition year, 1934 saw the beginning of the modern automobile in both style and engineering. "Modern" ideas, trends, and practices had existed since the beginning of the industry, of course, but this period saw a notable increase in their general application to mass produced cars, and usually, but not always, their general acceptance by the public.

Symbolizing this was the Chrysler Airflow, commercially a flop, controversial in appearance, but full of advanced ideas later accepted. These ideas were fully practical and proven, and integrated beautifully engineering-wise, regardless of what superficial critics say about the car. The Lincoln Zephyr was another example, commercially more successful than the Chrysler. Other makes were less radical, but definitely began moving in the same direction. It was, as Maurice Olley remarked to this writer, paradoxical:

"A great deal of the credit for the advances of the 1930's must go to the stock market crash of 1929 and the subsequent depression. This demanded real improvements in the product and discouraged mere elaboration, like sixteen cylinders.

"Next I think we have to give credit to the stylists, who integrated the whole passenger car design by shoving the entire sprung mass about twenty-eight inches forward on the wheelbase. (Independent front suspension helped this immensely.) This shift brought the rear seats ahead of the rear wheels, adding a foot or so to the true seat width, and allowing the seats and roof to drop about five inches. At the same time the running boards could disappear, and the trunk became part of the body and no longer an appendage. The passenger car came of age."

All this of course took a decade or more to achieve, and some of the major features had arrived years prior to 1934 while others were yet to come. Olley continued:

"Synchromesh, automatic transmission, hypoid rear axles, and in engine design the enormous improvement in plain bearings from massive and costly bronze shells with ridiculous thick white metal to super-accurate steel pressings with a mere plating of anti-friction metal all deserve credit."

Many of the advancements were pioneered by others beside Cadillac. Of the above mentioned, Packard introduced hypoid gears in 1926, and Studebaker the steel-strip bearing in 1931. But Cadillac's record was nonetheless impressive, as one would expect of a leader. Its most notable contribution in 1934 was the "flat ride." No doubt many expected to read "independent front suspension," but there is an important difference. I.f.s. had been known since the early days, ever since that remarkable French designer, Amédée Bollée, had used it on a steam carriage in 1873. Several European makers used it in actual production before World War I, and even in the United States there had been one or two examples, notably on the Christie front drive. Probably the first reasonably engineered production i.f.s. was the 1922 Lancia design which Ford's chief engineer, Harold Youngren, said "aroused great interest in the United States. I.f.s., however, was not adopted by American constructors until 1934, and the delay is explained by the lack of real need, for until this time most used their cars for comparatively short journeys and women did

Aboard Mr. Sloan's yacht. Standing, from the left: Harold Youngren, chief engineer of Oldsmobile; E. W. Seaholm; Ben Anibal, then chief engineer of Pontiac; A. P. Sloan. Seated: "Dutch" Bower, chief engineer of Buick; Henry M. Crane, Sloan's technical assistant; C. F. Kettering; Ormond E. Hunt, formerly V.P.-engineering at Packard and chief engineer of Chevrolet, and at this time of General Motors; Jim Crawford, chief engineer of Chevrolet; Alfred J. Fisher, chief body engineer, Fisher Division.

not often drive . . . . Since then there has been a mounting need for a better ride, which can only be provided by i.f.s. to the front wheels."

Maurice Olley was the man chiefly responsible for the trend in the United States. He had been supervising engineer at Rolls-Royce of America, and knew Seaholm's family in Springfield. On the collapse of Rolls-Royce of America in 1930, he left for Detroit seeking an interview with Seaholm. The latter recalled that Olley "dropped in one day with a letter of introduction from my sister, looking for a job. Her letter gave him an entre and we talked on. He was a mild, unassuming sort of person, but there was something 'Rolls-Royce' about him that impressed me. Finally — pointedly — I asked, 'Mr. Olley, what do you think you could do for us, given the opportunity?' 'I think I can improve your ride and handling' — or something to that effect — was the answer. This struck a responsive chord, for riding in those days was a continual struggle with springs and shock absorbers — endlessly

Henry M. Crane, Sloan's technical assistant.

getting nowhere.

"And so he came with us on a sort of probationary basis — given a place to work, along with whatever help he needed. He concentrated on riding and handling — approaching the problem step by step — analyzing, designing, building, checking, developing formulae, etc. — finally coming up with the solution — the suspension now used. In his area he was a genius."

Some Rolls techniques were introduced at Cadillac by Olley, although it is interesting that whereas he credits Robotham of Rolls-Royce with solving a shimmy problem by bump-rig, Robotham himself credits one (unnamed) American manufacturer with solving it first!

Olley himself continued the story. He did not always agree with some of the popular history on the subject. At Cadillac, the whole question was a much larger one than the merits of one particular design over another, reduction of unsprung weight, or even the whole principle of i.f.s. itself.

"We were not particularly interested in i.f.s. per se," he remarked. "About this period the air seemed full of i.s. designs for front or rear, generally without a clear idea of the reasons for using them. In the little design group at Cadillac in 1931, we were concerned with getting a 'logically comfortable' ride. We found that to avoid throwing the rear passengers and get a 'flat ride,' we'd have to lower the front ride frequency to about half the currently accepted practice. Instead of an effective front spring deflection of two and a half to three inches we needed a deflection of ten or twelve inches.

"Our K^2 rig of 1931 aimed to answer all the ride questions by actual road-testing with quick change comparisons. The car, a seven-passenger Cadillac V-12, had leaf-springs front and rear, the fronts softer and the rears stiffer than standard, to provide basically equal deflection, (i.e. load/rate ratio) at the two ends. By shifting weights we could vary the K^2 and we could change the relative deflection front and rear. The basic idea was that by making the K^2/ab* equal to 1.0 and having *equal* deflection front and rear, we could produce the condition of only one ride frequency in pitch and bounce. It was at once apparent that this was *not* the answer! Under this condition the car had no typical 'action.' It 'shambled.' But by shifting all the weights forward, thus making the front frequency definitely *slower* than the rear, we got our first experience of a really flat ride."

* K^2/ab is a formula for assessing a car's suspension behavior. "K" is the radius of gyration, or the distance from the car's center of gravity at which a specific mass would equal the moment of inertia of the entire sprung mass. The letters "a" and "b" represent the distances from the center of gravity of the sprung mass to the front and rear axle centers. Together, a + b always equals the wheelbase, but do not necessarily equal K^2. Hence the ratio varies from car design to car design, with corresponding variances in road behavior.

It is interesting to note that this was established in research with solid axles — thus confirming Olley's opening contention that most i.f.s. designers of that period actually knew very little about suspension characteristics and vehicle dynamics. "We turned to i.f.s.," he continued, "to gain freedom from the shimmy cycle and brake windup, accurate steering geometry, and roll-understeer." This development has its legends. One is that the term "SLA" as applied to the wishbone suspension design ultimately standardized, means "Short and Long Arm."

"This is such a logical legend that one might as well accept it, though it ain't so. The K^2 rig was followed by design developments of what were hopefully called 'Stream-Lined' cars. These had independent suspension front and rear. The first bunch of three were the 'SLA's.' The SLB's were never built. That's what SLA meant then."

Another legend is that the Frenchman André Dubonnet "was responsible for causing the industry to change its mind," and "brought about a new era in front-end geometry in the United States." This, of course, is only partially true, for Dubonnet had no influence on the decision of Cadillac to set up a special investigation of automobile suspension behavior. Experimenting at Cadillac had already started by the time Dubonnet's suspension patent was granted in May, 1931. Actually designed by Chedru, Dubonnet's layout was a logical development of Georges Broulhiet's "chandelle" design, which in turn had been inspired by the Lancia. Since Lancia's design is believed to have been originally inspired by the American Christie suspension we have a classic example of the wheel turning full circle!

Dubonnet came to the United States in 1932 with his suspension built into a very fast Hispano-engined "special." James Zeder stated that he first went to Chrysler, but they turned him down. Olley, however, was at first attracted by the Dubonnet concepts. "In the 'fireplug' design (so called from its appearance) that we evolved at Cadillac, it had all sorts of ad-

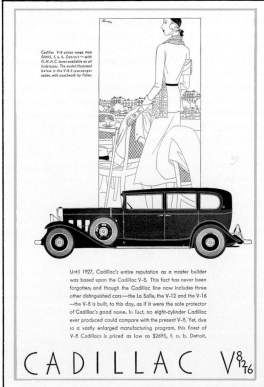

Until 1927, Cadillac's entire reputation as a master builder was based upon the Cadillac V-8. This fact has never been forgotten; and though the Cadillac line now includes three other distinguished cars—the La Salle, the V-12 and the V-16 —the V-8 is built, to this day, as if it were the sole protector of Cadillac's good name. In fact, no eight-cylinder Cadillac ever produced could compare with the present V-8. Yet, due to a vastly enlarged manufacturing program, this finest of V-8 Cadillacs is priced as low as $2695, f. o. b. Detroit.

Cadillac advertising in the early half of the thirties continued in the pattern of simplicity and elegance established in the beginning of the classic period. Not until the decade began to close on World War II were any Cadillac promotions easily mistaken for those of another manufacturer. Layouts were of the traditional pattern abroad as well as at home; the example to the right appeared in L'Illustration, the prestigious French magazine, in its issue of March 22, 1930.

SA LIGNE DE TOUTE BEAUTE AJOUTE
AU CHARME DE CES MAGNIFIQUES AVENUES

CADILLAC • PRODUCTION DE LA GENERAL MOTORS

vantages . . . weather-proof, free of all wheel-fight; steering accuracy, ground clearance, etc. It was wonderful in crosswind, but had heavy steering on corners. What really condemned it for a heavy car like the Cadillac was that it was not a good structure for holding the wheels upright, whereas the wishbone type provided excellent structure."

So the coil-wishbone or so-called SLA suspension was designed. Here there are some more legends. One book on suspensions states that this design "originated on the drawing board of W. J. Davidson at GM Research and was adapted to the Cadillac by Maurice Olley." The same book also implies that ride comfort was *not* Olley's primary objective, and that "it took many years for Olley's findings to reach production cars."

None of this is correct, and Olley states flatly "Wm. J. Davidson was not a researcher. He was, at the time in question, active in critical appreciation of automobile products, reporting to A. P. Sloan and to Henry Crane. Actual drawing board designs for the early GM independent suspensions came from Robert B. Burton, who headed design on my small group at Cadillac."

Another belief, open to much question, is that the Cadillac wishbone-type i.f.s. was copied from a Mercedes-Benz design. The writer first encountered this legend nearly twenty years ago in discussions with the late Laurence Pomeroy, Jr., of *The Motor*, when quoting Alec Issigonis as crediting the major development of coil-wishbone front suspension to the United States (a belief also shared by George Lanchester). Pomeroy claimed that "the first car to use this system was the 1932 Mercedes 3.8 litre. One of these cars was imported into the United States by General Motors and the whole of their line of i.f.s. copied from it." On the same topic an ex-Oldsmobile engineer wrote that he had worked in Lansing in 1933 and seen the Mercedes parts used by the Olds drawing office. Later, however — much later — he admitted he had not joined Olds' until 1935 and had only "been told" this story.

Further investigations — consulting various sources, the more notable of which were Olley, the GM Technical Center, and Rudolf Uhlenhaut of Daimler-Benz — disclosed that: (1) No "1932" Mercedes-Benz 380K model was ever marketed. An experimental chassis was built *toward the end* of 1932 and first publicly displayed at the Berlin Motor Show in February, 1933. Confronted with this, Pomeroy then admitted it to be a "1933" model. (2) Even though described as a "1933," again displayed in the Paris Show in the fall of 1933, and listed in the press that year as a current model, the 380K remained experimental until the end of *that* year, Uhlenhaut remarked. He added that

In a Cadillac in Grand Rapids, President and Mrs. Franklin D. Roo

...ute to a speech on administration housing projects in October, 1936.

"Various early experimental types in the early months of 1933 were made [and] after successfully meeting extended tests, series production at the *end of 1933* was begun." (Italics added.) (3) The experimental Cadillacs with i.f.s. (one Dubonnet, one wishbone) were fully operational by the beginning of 1933 and road demonstrations were actually given to the GM Technical Committee by Seaholm and Olley in early March, 1933.

From this it seems a physical and chronological impossibility for any Mercedes to have undergone examination in the design offices at Cadillac before their own suspension was produced. Comparisons may well have been made later, but when questioned Olley replied: "I cannot recall having actually seen the Mercedes suspension."

Of course, they were well acquainted with it from descriptions, patent applications, etc., but then parallelogram linkages were used by Lanchester in the early 1900's, and coil springs just as early. One or two continental makes were using or advocating parallel links around 1932, but with transverse leaf springs. So the combination only was new, and Olley says:

"At Cadillac, the short and long arm design was more or less fortuitous. A nine-inch upper arm was convenient length for an arm-type shock absorber. An eighteen-inch lower arm was convenient for a steering-linkage layout, which should be free from geometrical errors, without excessive ball-joint angles. And there was the fact that if the arm lengths varied inversely as their height from the road, the wheel track remained constant as the wheels moved up and down. The really practical feature of the SLA i.f.s. was that it permitted the entire sprung mass assembly to move forward 'on its wheelbase.' "

Alfred P. Sloan in *My Years with General Motors* discusses both the Dubonnet and wishbone systems, and while acknowledging the former as a design from outside, clearly refers to "the wishbone type, *we had developed.*" (Italics added.) Seaholm, recalling the incident, stated, "Mercedes had a similar system, but it was Olley who mastered the technique in this country."

For further proof that the Cadillac design originated in the Cadillac design offices, let us study some of the differences between the two designs:

1. Short and Long arm. While true for Cadillac which used a 2:1 ratio, this is almost a misnomer for the Mercedes, which had about a 10:9 ratio giving near parallel motion. "Almost equal" describes the Mercedes more accurately than "unequal length."

2. Mercedes used ball-joints (later abandoned and so credited to Citroën in 1934). Cadillac used threaded bushes.

3. Mercedes used horizontal compliance. Cadillac had none.

4. Mercedes apparently had no hydraulic shock absorbers. Cadillac's were designed in, and formed the upper arm anchor — totally different from that in Mercedes.

5. Steering layouts were quite different.

6. Almost every aspect of detail design was different.

7. It appears that the Mercedes suspension was much "stiffer" and Olley comments "Merc and continental makers generally, have been slow in accepting the need for soft front springing."

8. The whole application to the car was different, so far as sprung mass was concerned. Perhaps for aesthetic reasons, or out of sheer conservatism, the radiator on the Mercedes was still over, or even *rearward* of the front wheel centers, with all that that implies in weight distribution. Cadillac's was eight inches *forward* on the V-8 engine of 1934.

Actually, *Mercedes* eventually learned a good deal from *Cadillac* in this area—abandoning the ball-joints as too difficult for production, lengthening the lower arms, adding a stabilizer bar and hydraulic damping with end-to-end discharge (lever-type shocks were more durable than the telescopic "flit-gun" kind), and eventually moving the sprung mass of the car forward.

Since Mercedes built only sixty 380K's and 254 type 500 and 540K's during 1934–1936, the vast field experience of GM's application on many thousands of cars (Olds and Buick, as well as Cadillac) in the first year, probably more than offset any advantage Mercedes might have claimed from the so-called laboratory of Grand Prix racing. Of the latter Issigonis wrote in *The Autocar*: "It is apparent that the Mercedes-Benz designers did not appreciate the fact that low unsprung weight is **not the** only necessity for good wheel adhesion. Good dynamic stability of the sprung mass of the vehicle is vital. . . . [Their] early cars were being run backwards . . . the pair of wheels softly sprung were at the wrong end of the vehicle. A car will not ride flat unless the front suspension has a lower period than the rear."

The experimental Cadillacs also had independent rear suspension, but this was not adopted on production cars. At first a De Dion system had been considered, but this was ruled out because of its cost and complexity. Three i.r.s. systems appear to have been tried, as follows:

1. The Dubonnet system at the front matched by parallel trailing arms at the rear, with one-quarter elliptic spring per arm shackled forward. Despite use of massive malleable iron castings, the "couple" in this layout (similar to Dubonnet) gave too many deflections in this linkage, Olley commenting: "We learned from this never to drive through parallel arms— too much tire wear."

2. The next layout used splayed trailing arms to cut down tire wear and raise the roll center. "We wanted some of the characteristics of swing axles without their undesirable characteristics."

3. Parallel transverse arms were also tried, and "gave a delightful ride" but brought on problems in tire wear and handling because of track changes and poor camber respectively.

So independent rear suspension was abandoned — and by revising spring mounting to give roll understeer, adding a rear stabilizer bar and changing from torque tube to Hotchkiss drive,

Cadillac's independent front suspension, 1934.

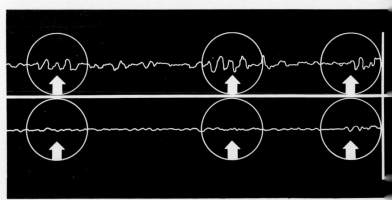

"Ride-o-graphs": that of Cadillac's is below.

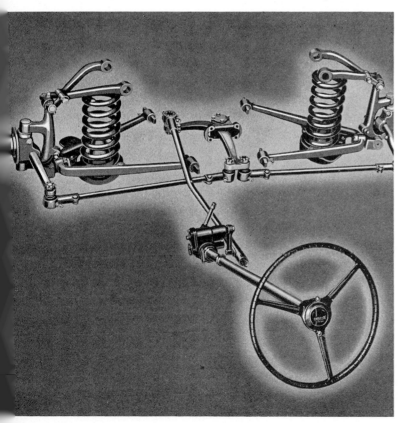

Power steering's father, Francis W. Davis. Center Point Steering below.

the rear end behaved satisfactorily with the good old live axle.

The important thing was that now the Cadillac owner, as well as his chauffeur, had a smooth ride. (Olley, a small man with impish humor, said that under the old conditions, the owner merely acted as a harmonic balancer for his chauffeur, who had the most comfortable seat in the car!) Cadillac literature pointed out the various advantages: unsprung weight was reduced from 460 to 360 pounds, but most important, "the softer front springing practically eliminates pitching, with proportional improvement in the back seat ride."

W. O. Bentley noted that the Cadillac V-16 was the only car in which a rear-seat ride could be taken in perfect comfort around Brooklands track at eighty miles an hour. Gone was the terrible rear-end "ejector seat kick" resulting from the intersection of bounce and pitch curves; in its place was a slow, easy, comfortable motion, properly controlled. Scientific suspension had arrived.

While the central figure in the new development, Maurice Olley generously praised the work of Cadillac's engineering group and the Research Laboratories as a whole:

"It was very far from a one-man show, and owes a great deal to Henry Crane, Ernest Seaholm, Kettering, Nacker, and a number of Cadillac and Buick engineers. Also the tolerance and constant support of L. P. Fisher, who accused me at the time of being the first man in GM to spend a quarter of a million dollars in building two experimental cars!

"We owed a lot to Henry Crane, and his persistent road testing. Front roll stabilizers were introduced at his urging, to improve handling. Ket, too, was a great help and I still remember his statement — in the middle of the Depression — and cutbacks everywhere — 'It seems to me we can't afford *not* to do it.' Seaholm, of course, was magnificent, and a joy. He was my constant supporter . . . a quiet, friendly giant, dominating through friendliness. His ideal for the Cadillac was that it should be the unquestioned high quality car of the GM line."

At Seaholm's request, Olley was granted a substantial increase in salary. He went from strength to strength in GM engineering, which benefited from his talents for the next quarter century, until his retirement in 1955.

Olley, however, was not the only genius working at Cadillac in this period. During the development of the wishbone suspension, Olley's group ran into shimmy and steering problems. One man he remembered well in this area was Francis W. Davis, whose name in the power-steering field parallels Olley's in suspension.

Davis, formerly chief truck engineer at Pierce-Arrow, had come to Detroit in 1926. He had demonstrated a hydraulic power-steering gear he had designed and built into his own Pierce-Arrow runabout. In October, 1926, he showed the car to Strickland, Gilbert, and Prentis of Cadillac. Gilbert was in charge of laboratory and testing, and Prentis supervisor of steering, shock absorbers, and frame design. All were enthusiastic and GM Research acted on their recommendations. After a conference with engineers and patent counsel, an option agreement was agreed on in January, 1927. From then until 1934 Davis worked with Cadillac on power steering.

During the first year GM built a truck gear which performed very well with a Saginaw coal company. The driver loved it because he could back to unload using two fingers on the wheel. Following this, a Cadillac power steering gear was built, and there was a lengthy development period suiting the gear to the Cadillac engine, working out bugs, and redesigning parts to reduce costs and simplify assembly.

Continual improvement was necessary because manual steering gear makers were not standing still. When Davis began his pioneer work in the twenties, screw-and-nut and worm-and-sector gears were normal practice. These were comparatively crude principles with overall efficiency of no more than thirty to forty percent. But in the late twenties the steering gear firms began to come out with roller bearing contacts — which could be preloaded and led to efficiencies of seventy to eighty percent. Cadillac itself was a pioneer in this trend.

"So," recalled Davis, "we were battling against conditions where they were improving the manual gear, and at the same time we were trying to sell them something which would compete with the earlier type gear."

However, the factors of larger, lower-pressure tires and Olley's movement of the engine forward, putting more weight on the front wheels, all argued in favor of power. So did Charles Kettering, who drove the first power-steered Cadillac and enthused over it. Davis states that Kettering had one of the most penetrating minds he has ever encountered, and the ability to sum up situations with witty little epigrams. The two men had a long conference, and Kettering said he would pay one hundred dollars to have power steering on his car — a large sum to add to the list price of a car in 1930. Then, Davis recalls, "Ket" made one of his little quotes.

"When you look at a piece of work and you think the fellow is crazy, you ought to pay some attention to that. One or the other of you may be crazy, but you better find out which one it is. It makes an awful lot of difference."

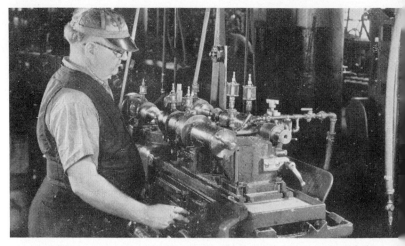

Diamond boring connecting rods, above. Crankshaft/piston grinding, below.

A second, improved Cadillac gear was built, as well as a bus gear, and by 1932 Saginaw had an advanced design under test in an eight-cylinder Cadillac, and in 1933 in a twelve-cylinder model as well. These performed so well that the engineers passed them as fit for production. But when Seaholm asked for the tooling cost from the Saginaw Division, back came a figure that was to set power steering back for nearly two decades. The depression was at its worst; Cadillac planned to build less than 15,000 cars for 1934, most of them straight-eight LaSalles which would not use the power gear. In such small quantities tooling costs would be very high and the cost of power units would result in excessive retail price. The depression had cut Cadillac's research budget in half. Both Cadillac and the Central Office under O. E. Hunt refused to meet the cost. In January, 1934, Davis' license agreement was cancelled. A new agreement relieving GM of paying the yearly minimum was not acceptable to Davis, so he left.

He worked for some time at Bendix, but by 1939 was back at GM with his power steering again — this time at Buick. Here there was a serious chance of production until Pearl Harbor put a stop to that. However, while the war shut one door on power steering, it opened another, and Davis units were installed on Chevrolet armored cars built for the British Army in 1940.

After the war Davis built another improved unit into his 1946 Cadillac, and had another conference with General Motors. But they were now having trouble keeping up with the postwar com-

Center Point Steering and ride stabilizers on 1938 Cadillac.

petition, let alone tooling up for power steering.

This time the situation was opposite that of 1933 — a seller's instead of a buyer's market — but the GM answer was just as negative. "Then, in 1951," Davis recalled, "Chrysler came out with a power steering based on some of my early patents which had expired. I didn't collect any royalties from Chrysler, but I didn't worry, because it was the best news I'd heard. It had turned to a buyer's market, and General Motors called me out. How soon, how fast, how many?" Thus in 1952 Cadillac appeared with power steering on the principles that Davis and they themselves had proven ready for production twenty years earlier!

W. R. Strickland had been president of the SAE for 1929. In August, 1930, although aged only fifty-five, he retired in ill health. Though he later recovered and lived until 1958, some of the aura of 1930 lingered, for his obituaries mentioned "the once-famous V-16." In his place as assistant chief engineer, Seaholm appointed Earl Thompson, designer of the synchromesh transmission. Thompson continued to work on the miscellany of production and engineering problems present.

"Then," said Seaholm, "while abroad for the London Auto Show, I was attracted by the new Daimler — among other details featuring a fluid flywheel. It seemed worthwhile to have one in Detroit to look over and so I placed an order and eventually it showed up. To my discouragement it aroused little interest here in design circles except in Thompson. With him the fluid flywheel unleashed a whole new line of thought and next thing I knew he came up with a carefully worked out drawing of a 'brain box' as you call it. Thus the birth of the Hydramatic.

"We could find nothing wrong with the design and approval was had for further developmental work. We were well along with the first working model when the far reaching effects of the depression years had their impact. Our engineering budget was cut in half and we were not financially in a position to complete the development. Meanwhile we had progressed far enough so that the Corporation recognized its value. They picked it up where we left off, forming a new division which subsequently put it in production. Thompson went along as did a group of younger men who had come of age, as it were, working with him — to make history in bringing out one of our greatest innovations since the beginning of the automobile — Thompson was a genius."

One of the "younger men" was Oliver K. Kelley, an M.I.T. graduate who had worked with Thompson since 1927 — "when I was just a cub engineer out of college," as Kelley recalled. "But I was closest to Thompson. He was big, six feet two inches, broad shouldered, tough, honest and had no excuse for poor work. He would put his arm round you and say 'Don't make mistakes — know what the hell you're doing.' Yet he was a very fine person and a terrific teacher who kept your nose into it until you understood."

Work on the automatic transmission started in 1932, and progressed so favorably that in March, 1933, Thompson was made "special-assignments engineer" to head a new department at Cadillac concentrating solely on shiftless drive. Nacker was appointed assistant chief engineer, succeeding Thompson.

Edward N. Cole has a lighthearted recollection of this period.

"During the development of the automatic transmission at Cadillac, there was a problem with the seal on the clutch end of the transmission. At this stage we were using a standard Cadillac transmission in development work. It was leaking and allowing oil to get on the clutch disc. This caused the clutch to slip.

"They gave me the job of setting an engine and transmission up on the dynamometer to find and observe the oil leak with a spinning clutch in place. Since the environment was quite different when it was on the dynamometer than when it was in the car as far as pressures were concerned, Earl Thompson asked me to take an air hose and pressurize the transmission slightly at the vent. I did, but the result was more than we expected. It was like an undercoating gun taking off!

"This forced 600W oil from the seal spraying everybody there — including Earl Thompson, Mr. Seaholm and Mr. Parker, who were all down at the vent trying to see where this oil was coming from. It thoroughly coated all of these top engineers with this very thick oil. I looked at Tommy, who was blinking his eyes, and wondered if I should beat it right out of there. Of course, I felt it was completely my fault and that my next job was going to be picking up my tools and leaving the organization.

"They were all very gracious about it — they were all nice fellas — but in about two weeks I got shifted over to engine development! I recalled this to Tommy a few years ago and he got quite a kick out of it, laughing, 'I shoulda fired you!'"

By 1934, the Cadillac transmission group had a step-ratio gearbox that would shift automatically under full torque. Further design work was carried out by the same men at GM Central Research in 1935, and in 1935–1936 pilot transmissions were built and handed over to Oldsmobile engineers for widespread tests. A semi-automatic transmission on these lines called the "traffic transmission" was offered in Olds and Buick models for 1937 and 1938, and by 1939 the Hydra-Matic had reached its essential form, with fluid-coupling, planetary gearset, and the Thompson "brainbox" providing full automatic control. As such it was first offered on Oldsmobile's 1940 models, followed by Cadillac the next year.

As with other great forward steps, Hydra-Matic contained ideas applied much earlier. Planetary gearsets had been used in the earliest Marmons, as well as Cadillacs and Oldsmobiles in both two- and three-speed form, and also in England by Lanchester and Wilson. It was Wilson, in fact, who had a good deal to do with the preselective transmission used in the Daimler that attracted Seaholm's attention. Similarly, fluid couplings had been used for marine purposes prior to World War I. Charles R. Radcliffe, associated with the Long Distance Automobile Company in 1904–1905, had a considerable number of patents covering hydraulic drives of various sorts, and formed the Radcliffe Turbine Drive Company of New York, which developed a fluid flywheel particularly designed for Studebaker and displayed in a Studebaker chassis at the 1919 New York Show. However, although it was listed as an option at the stated price, it is not believed that the Radcliffe fluid flywheel was ever used in production on any automobile. Credit for this must go to the English Daimler Company, whose engineer, L. H. Pomeroy, adapted a fluid flywheel (designed for buses by an Englishman named

Harold Sinclair) to the Wilson Transmission and installed it in Daimler cars around 1930. None of these, however, were "automatic transmissions" — they were, rather, "pre-selective" and still required "three-pedal driving." They lacked a "brain."

"We need to get rid of the clutch pedal," Thompson had said, and Kelley recalled "E. A. T. and I used to drive back and forth from work to home discussing it in the car, and decided that a hydraulic pressure-sensitive control was the answer. . . . The no-creep fluid coupling (which had a torus and drive sequence quite different from the Daimler) was my contribution, but the main credit really goes to Thompson. The SAE wanted to nominate me for the Elmer A. Sperry Award, but I told them E. A. T. deserved it."

This award was made to Thompson by the SAE in Cobo Hall, Detroit in 1964. Thompson died in March, 1967, aged seventy-five.

With Nacker as assistant chief engineer, work began on a series of new engines to replace the aging V-8 and the complex and costly V-12 and V-16. Chassis-wise, the new suspension was good for many years, but new frames, transmission, and axle design was also underway. Nacker was now known as "the Sheriff" because of a battered Stetson which he reputedly wore even in the bath. Apart from his talent for engine design, he was famous for his ability at ride evaluation — using the seat-of-the-pants method.

New men were now coming to the fore, Seaholm recalled. "Just as our engines had 'matured' under Nacker, so did some of the young men who had become part of his team. They had drifted in — it seemed — in the drafting room, in the laboratory, asking for opportunity only. I remember them so well — loyal, eager, tireless, enthusiastic. They stood out from the run of the mill and many of them in following years went right to the top. Among them were John Gordon (later President of GM), Ed Cole (also a GM President), Harry Barr (a vice-president), Fred Arnold (recently retired chief engineer of Cadillac), Carl Rasmussen (late chief engineer of Cadillac) and many others who have contributed to the development of the automobile.

"It's a source of great satisfaction to have been associated with men such as these. Someone recently complimented me on the fine training these men must have received under my tutelage. Really there was no training — I just turned them loose. I didn't make them — they made me."

CADILLAC CRAFTSMANSHIP

On the facing page, final tear-down and inspection of each engine after its hours of running in. Above, piston inspection (left) and fitting to engine (center) after final inspection of matched sets (right) of piston, piston pin, rings and connecting rods; in all, a careful process.

John F. Gordon succeeded Nacker as supervisor of engine design. Born in Akron, Ohio, in 1900, he graduated from the U.S. Naval Academy in 1922, and earned a Master of Science degree at the University of Michigan in 1923. That year he joined Cadillac as laboratory assistant. In 1928 he became assistant foreman of the experimental laboratory, and foreman a year later. When he was appointed chief engine designer, he was only thirty-three years old.

Of this period, Edward N. Cole reflected: "Owen Nacker was not only an outstanding motor engineer, but also had a very good understanding of the suspension, transmission and overall vehicle characteristics, particularly handling. He worked closely with Maurice Olley in connection with the development of the SLA front suspension.

"I also worked quite closely with Mr. Nacker in the development of the Cadillac engine program, including the straight eight (LaSalle), V-8, V-12 and V-16 engines. I was close to the flathead 135° V-16 and did a considerable amount of design work on this engine, as well as run the laboratory dyno tests.

"Mr. Gordon was involved in all the engine programs. In fact, Jack Gordon was the one who persuaded me to stay on with Cadillac when I had an outstanding offer from a competitive company. Mr. Gordon was responsible as the motor engineer for the 322 LaSalle V-8 and the 346 Cadillac V-8 which were developed during the period 1932-36. At that time, I worked in the dyno lab and ran many tests on both of these engines and the developing of the structure, as well as improving the overall engine efficiency.

"Fred Arnold at that time was my boss. He contributed greatly with many ideas towards the success of these engines. He should be given credit for the pressed-in wrist-pin which, up to that time, had been floating. Fred suggested the pin be locked into the rod by a press fit which would eliminate the locking rings or other methods of retaining the wristpin. Eventually every motor manufacturer attempted this system. Fred Arnold was an outstanding developer of young engineers and had fellows like Harry Barr, Harold Warner and many others who have attained prominence in GM working for him at one time or another.

"Harry Barr and I worked side by side for many years and this very serious individual . . . was always very concerned about getting his job done and making a contribution to the success of Cadillac. That is one of the reasons why he moved up to eventually become the Vice President of Engineering of the whole Corporation."

Above, piston pin grouping, 1/10,000th-inch limits. Below, crankshaft balancing (left); matching/testing transmission gears by sound (right)

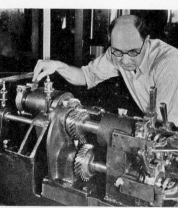

During the eight years from 1928 to 1935, the bmep and horsepower per cubic inch of the Cadillac V-8 had steadily climbed, while the stroke-bore and lb/hp ratios had correspondingly decreased. The design, however, had become outmoded, particularly the three-piece block crankcase structure, with light-alloy case and cast iron blocks. A unit block was better, in one material. This principle had first been applied way back in 1916 by the Ferro Foundry, Cleveland, in a line of V-8's and V-12's designed by ex-Cadillac engineer Alanson Brush. They were used by several makes, notably the Hollier, built by Lewis Spring & Axle Company in Chelsea, later Jackson, Michigan. General Motors had already built such an engine for the V-8 Oakland and Olds Viking models during 1929-1931. These actually preceded the Ford V-8; thousands were built, and from a foundry point of view the castings were completely successful. As R. V. Hutchinson said, "the Olds' block was an excellent production design, *no* experimental castings were lost and production foundry scrap was less than one half of one percent."

The cars failed to find a lasting market, so Ford deserves full credit for their brilliant design which, apart from monobloc construction, had downdraft carburetion and advanced manifolding, giving equal distribution to all cylinders. The latter had been a problem with V-8's since the ninety degree crank in 1923. Cadillac had been reluctant about downdraft carburetion but it was now well established.

Thus, in 1936 a brand-new Cadillac V-8 appeared with downdraft carburetion and unit-block construction. The engine, although all iron, was only twenty pounds heavier (due to thin wall techniques) than the previous V-8 with aluminium crankcase, and was far more rigid. This engine was the basis of all V-8 activity at Cadillac (including outstanding wartime service) right up to 1949.

There were two versions in 1936 of this new engine: a 135 hp, $3\frac{1}{2}$ by $4\frac{1}{2}$, 346-cubic-inch size for the long wheelbase (131 and 138 inches) V-8, the 70 and 75, which shared chassis with the V-12; and a 125 hp, $3\frac{3}{8}$ by $4\frac{1}{2}$, 332-cubic-inch size for the new 121-inch wheelbase Series 60.

The latter car had a chassis similar to that of the LaSalle, and the GM "B" body shell shared with Buick. Weighing only 4,200 pounds, its performance put an end to complaints from owners whose older V-8's had been "honked and passed" by a mere Ford. (An embarrassment shared by owners of several other prestige makes at the time.)

Maximum speed of the sedan was over ninety-two miles an hour, ten to sixty in high took only 17.6 seconds, cruising speed was exceptionally high, yet the car would idle to a walking pace in high gear. Its hydraulic brakes, adopted by Cadillac for 1936, matched the performance and were reported as giving the highest deceleration of any car, competitive or otherwise, tested at the GM Proving Grounds up to that year.

In comparison with its rivals, the Packard 120 and the Lincoln Zephyr, it had a higher acceleration and top speed — at the cost of a higher fuel consumption. Actually the Packard was only two-thirds the price and a comparison is perhaps unfair. The Zephyr, at $1,320 was closer to the 60's price ($1,695) and here the comparison is interesting. The Cadillac had a better engine and suspension than the Zephyr — although the Zephyr's unit construction body and styling were more advanced. Within a couple of years, however, its style leadership was to be challenged, as we shall see shortly.

The Series 60 had a new, rugged, fast-shifting gearbox that later became the hot-rodder's joy, and one (a LaSalle) was driven for 500 miles at the Indianapolis track at an average speed of eighty-two miles an hour, in completely stock condition.

The LaSalle for the years 1934, 1935, and 1936 was virtually a high-class Oldsmobile straight-eight, with special styling by Jules Agramonte under Harley Earl's direction. It had a striking, tall, narrow grille as a key feature. This decision to move away from the "junior Cadillac V-8" idea was a depression retrenchment, since there was not enough room in the high-priced range for both, and little brother had to step down. Success was moderate only, but at least the make was preserved for what appeared to be a recovery in 1937. This year it again became a lower priced Cadillac V-8.

The performance of these new V-8's was amazing, and the cars were also very "roadable." Consequently there was little that could live with them for fast, effortless, long-distance travel.

One *Autocar* correspondent writing from France noted how remarkable it was to see so many Cadillacs used for long trips in "the home of the Bugatti and the Hispano," while David Scott-Moncrieff writes, "A friend of mine left his hotel in Switzerland, and drove his Bugatti as fast as he could to Paris. As he drew into the Liotti, grimy and exhausted, he was followed by a chauffeur-driven Cadillac containing two American matrons. They and their chauffeur were as fresh as paint and showed no signs of fatigue. They had been staying at the same hotel as my friend in Switzerland and had left it an hour after he did!"

In *Motor Sport*, August, 1944, Squadron-Leader J. M. Boothby, R.A.F., D.F.C., told of his motoring experiences with a LaSalle.

Sound-proof room test of differential carrier assemblies.

He had owned a "Prince Henry" Vauxhall, a GN, Morgan, Salmson, Lancia Lambda, Brescia Bugatti, Delage, Bentley, and 38-250 Mercedes, and had had experience with the three-litre Sunbeam and Alvis Silver Eagle models. He wrote:

"In Canada I bought a Ford V-8 as a stop-gap. A month later I found what I wanted and exchanged it for a 1938 LaSalle, with the very potent Cadillac V-8 engine. I had 1/16 inch milled off the heads, a 2.9 crown wheel and pinion cut, and obtained a special set of valves and springs. To help the steering I doubled up on shocks all round. When finished I had a car with a timed maximum, four ways, over a half mile, of 107.2. Zero to 60 took 10.2 seconds. Over the magnificent roads of Ontario I was able to cruise at 85–90 all day long. With two specialist navigators on board with synchronized chronometers, I clocked two hours, twenty-seven minutes for the 167 miles from Royal York Hotel, Toronto, to the gates of Port Albert, the last twelve miles being over dirt roads. The steering was infinitely superior to that of many very expensive British luxury cars, and it carried heater

and defroster gear. It would have cost in America with modifications, about £285 new, which makes you think. I covered 27,000 odd miles, much of it over the worst dirt roads, gave my new born twins their first taste of three figure motoring at five weeks old, and toured in the Northern Ontario backwoods. My total repair bill amounted to $12.50 and I only sold it when it ran out of tires, then unobtainable."

Since the performance of the new V-8's surpassed the V-12 and equaled or bettered even the V-16, neither of the classic ohv's was seen after 1937. Yet a remarkable decision was made — to design an up-to-date replacement for the old sixteen. Since the market had practically dried up and no comparable designs had appeared from other American makers for four or five years, historians have speculated on the reasons for this surprising development. The general feeling is that Cadillac wanted to emphasize its leadership in the fine-car field with another "super-engine." Like the first V-16, it shared the V-8's chassis and transmission, so its development costs were not prohibitive. There was also the hope that the engine might be suitable for naval PT boats, and therefore ultimately pay its way. Packard, however, won that contest with a fine ohv marine twelve.

Seaholm recalls that one of the sponsors of this application was C. V. Crockett, "one of our most brilliant and versatile boys — filling in wherever assigned. Among other things he handled all accessions and contacts wishing to use our power plants for speedboats and other purposes. He retired in the 1960's after a time in Germany representing the United States in the design of a tank for general use by NATO."

The motto was now "Simplicate and add more lightness" — at least as far as sixteen cylinders could be simplified. The twelve idea was out altogether, and the new V-16 was a completely fresh angle on sixteens — literally. The angle between the banks was 135°, the layout resembling a horizontally opposed engine. Seaholm listed the original requirements:

"Our idea as to the characteristics of the new automobile were well defined, hence we knew in a general way what was required of its powerplant:

1. More than eight cylinders and as much power as the current sixteen.

2. Reduced in length compared with the current twelve and sixteen.

3. Lighter than either.

4. More economical to produce and simple to service.

5. The engine must, of course, meet the high standard of performance and serviceability required of high-priced

At left, balancing of brake drums. At right, balancing of propeller shafts. This series of manufacturing photographs was taken at Cadillac in 1931.

automobiles.

"Sixteen cylinders were chosen because of the greater smoothness . . . and increased durability since it would have less piston travel. Increased manufacturing expense and complication were objections . . . we believed, however, that we could develop a simplified design in which sixteen-cylinder advantages could be realized in an engine having fewer parts than either the sixteen or twelve then in production. The final design justified this belief."

Simplicity dictated L-heads, this in turn indicated a 135° angle to give equal firing intervals and room for manifolding and downdraft carburetors inside the Vee.

"The weight of the vehicle had been estimated and power requirements determined from which we fixed engine size at about 430 cubic inches. Other factors were determined by laying out four different designs. Number four was eventually chosen. Its integral all-iron structure was based on the design foundry technique and experience gained with the 346 cid V-8 and 250 pounds lighter than the old V-16 and 115 pounds lighter than the old V-12! It required only half the number of parts yet developed the same power with even greater smoothness. It had nine main bearings against the older engine's five, yet was six inches shorter. And despite its wide cylinder angle it occupied less than two-thirds the volume of the old V-16. Duplication of accessories — two eight-cylinder distributors and carburetors — actually simplified servicing," said Seaholm straight facedly, "because a four-barreled carburetor or a sixteen-cylinder distributor might frighten a mechanic unused to sixteen-cylinder parts."

Engineering-wise, the engine was far superior to that in the first sixteen, and gave the car tremendous performance, maximum of over one hundred miles an hour, with acceleration and flexibility, smoothness and silence superior to the V-8's. This, of course, makes nonsense of claims that the engine was "no match" for the mechanical excellence of the older V-16. These claims are superficial and based merely on the appearance of the two engines. Aesthetically, the old engine had it all over the new one, of course, but it was designed when an engine's eye appeal was important. Now high fender catwalks and general styling features, and accessories such as the separator bowl air-cleaner, precluded any clear view of the power unit. Cosmetics no longer counted. Now they interfered with accessibility and cost too much money. We will cover the last point in more detail shortly, but first a quote from the French automobile engineer Gregoire:

"At the risk of making the reader jump six feet in the air, I consider a number of American engines, surrounded as they are by forests of wires, accessories, and bits and pieces, and designed without thought for line, nearer to beauty than the elegant Bugatti engines . . . mechanical beauty corresponds to the best use of material according to the actual state of technique.

"An engine in which the manifolds are hidden in the cylinder head, the wiring is concealed behind covers, and the accessories lurk under the crankcase, all for the sake of beauty, is less good-looking than a motor where all the manifolds are clearly seen and checkable and where the wiring, accessories, and apparatus are accurately located and accessible."

The "villain" in this area at Cadillac was Nicholas Dreystadt, from Cadillac's service branch in Chicago. Appointed general service manager in 1926, he succeeded Albert V. Widman as factory manager on the latter's retirement in April, 1932. In June, 1934, L. P. Fisher transferred to GM's Operating Division, and Dreystadt succeeded him as general manager of Cadillac.

"He was a real hustler, tough, and didn't make many friends, but he really lined us up where costing was concerned," recalled Seaholm. "We had never worried about costs at all — or not much anyway. In the twenties you could sell at very high prices and the sixteen was conceived under those conditions, and that's how we wound up with all the different models. This proved far too costly in the thirties."

"Far too costly" was something of an understatement. Cadillac, along with their traditional rivals, were in a bad way. The losses were so heavy in this division, with no end in sight, that top management was seriously considering eliminating Cadillac altogether unless they came up with an answer that enabled them to pay their own way. The answer proved to be Nick Dreystadt.

"Nick made us look closely at everything, in comparison with any part anyone else was making. If someone else made a part for two dollars — why did ours have to cost three or four? We had a tough time proving it! Detailed studies were made. Not only that, he went through the whole manufacturing operation all the way, cut it down so that we wound up with only two floors in our present factory, and, of course, only two models. He was a tough man to work with, as anyone in his job would have to be, but he was fundamentally sound. Looking back, he did one of the most constructive jobs any man ever did at Cadillac.

"From there we really looked ahead. Packard cut costs too, but they didn't do as good a job. They went down among the cats and dogs, and that cost them their name."

Apart from the new V-16, high points of the 1938 range were the 60 Special (analyzed elsewhere by Dave Holls), restyled Cadillacs, and LaSalles, increased body room, longer wheelbases, lower chassis (hypoid axles were now on all models after their debut in 1937 on the LaSalle 50 and Cadillac 60) and steering-column gearshift.

With the dropping of the V-12 and the V-8 70, the 1938 line had the LaSalle on a 124-inch wheelbase, with 322-cubic-inch engine (unchanged) and a choice of five Fisher bodies. The Cadillac V-8 — models 60, 65 and 75 — were on wheelbases of 127, 132, and 141 inches (versus 124, 131, and 138 inches for 1937), and were powered by the 346-cubic-inch engine. The 60 offered only one body style (Fisher, four-door), the 65 offered three Fisher bodies, and seven Fleetwood bodies (the same number as in 1937).

The V-16 had the same body range and was on the same wheelbase as the 75 — 141 inches. It used the same transmission as the V-8's, for the same reasons as in 1930 — the low individual cylinder impulses and zero torque vibration gave no more stress than the V-8. "We had so worked on our transmissions over the years," Seaholm has commented, "that we came up with one, as I recall, lighter and smaller than the Chevy, yet it could easily handle the torque of the V-16."

Another V-16 advantage was its unbelievable compactness. The flat cylinder angle enabled the toeboard to be placed *over* the rear blocks, so that although the engine was no longer than in the old V-12 (!), the radiator-dash dimension was three inches *less* than in the V-12 — thirty-nine versus forty-two inches.

One collector has summarized the later 16's as follows:

"Although all V-16's are rare because of their limited production, some seem to be sought after more than others and some are more unusual than others. This phenomenon appears to be even more true of the later V-16's — 1938 through 1940.

"In the eyes of the so-called 'serious' collector, the late sixteen somehow has not had the 'glamour' of the early sixteen, yet we have all noticed recently that they are becoming 'worthy' of attention and meticulous restoration. Perhaps the late sixteens have been considered too 'modern' or too 'comfortable' or too 'easy' to drive. Yet these attributes are used to describe luxury classics and are the characteristics that made any classic stand out.

A Cadillac "first" was the concealed spare tire, in 1934. Note bullet-type bumper guards, found only on the 1934 Cadillac models.

"Actually, the late sixteens are rarer — only 508 (514 engines) compared to the 3,889 early ohv sixteens. In fact the late sixteen is rarer than the almighty Duesenberg and certainly more comfortable and dependable. The flexibility and smoothness of the Cadillac V-8's of that period also contributed to the rareness of the V-16 during the late 1930's. After all, why should anyone pay such a premium for twice the cylinders to get only a measly 50 more horsepower? Smoothness? Yes! Torque? Yes! Actually 'prestige' was the only really valid answer. It gave instant prestige to its owners and its owners gave their prestige to the marque. It was truly rare, unusual and distinctive — even in its own day."

On the 60 Special, height (including floor height) was reduced three inches below that of 1937 by a new double-drop frame. Even with large kickup over the rear axle and side rails *reduced* in depth, the frame stiffness was substantially *increased* by an exceptionally sturdy X-member. John Bond has written: "The Duesenberg frame, for all its massive appearance, was still somewhat flexible. No really stiff frames appeared until the Cadillac '60' Special." He considered that "something similar" would still be rated adequate twenty-five years later!

The 60 Special's visibility was a marked improvement, coming from a larger windshield and narrower pillars all-round, with reduced radii. Its lower silhouette, absence of running boards, its

integrated trunk and smart "convertible flavor" doubtless influenced the later Lincoln Continental, and set a standard in car styling that endured for decades. The writer recalls that in one of his many arguments with the late Laurence Pomeroy, this car enabled him to score a point. Pomeroy, characteristically maintaining that the main trend of design was ever European, instanced the work of Jaray on the 1934 Adlers, "culminating in its prewar aspect in the 1940 Brescia BMW, designed by Touring." He continued, "This in turn leads on to the Packard Clipper, and Packard, owing to America not being at war, were able to put this style on to the production map for the first time."

The writer then cited the Cadillac 60 Special as probably having more influence on the Packard Clipper than the BMW ever did. Pomeroy then admitted that this had "given him a bone to gnaw on," but made no further reply and the subject was dropped.

Many years later, however, confirmation came via a source hardly open to question even from the ghost of Laurence Pomeroy. It was a confidential memo from the Packard engineering department to the Packard president, dated August 30, 1944. Headed "Notes on Packard Styling Problem," it concerned future programs and reviewed the styling development of the Clipper. It read in part:

"Present Clipper styling should not be viewed as being a new

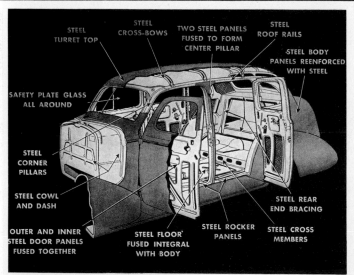

By 1936 the concealed spare tire lay flat, allowing more luggage access. At right, Fisher's "Unisteel" turret-type body for the 1938's.

243

style *trend* established by Packard, but rather as what it really is — a very good evolutionary development of a *trend* clearly established by GM and which we improved upon and still retained the very necessary Packard identity. We must not give ourselves credit for establishing a new style trend with the Clipper design, but rather credit ourselves with having been good at evolution of a trend already established by GM, [who] have recently been style trend dictators for the industry."

The 1939 range was restyled (except for the V-16), but otherwise changes were minimal. Models for both years, incidentally, featured blinker directional signals as an option, but they were not much in demand. Self-cancelling, they were operated by a column-mounted lever with flasher in the dash — as today. In 1940 sealed beam headlights were adopted — an industry-wide change — and that year Cadillac introduced Saginaw's new recirculating-ball steering. As mentioned earlier in regard to Davis and power steering, Cadillac was a pioneer in low-friction gears. In 1926 they had introduced the Saginaw worm-and-roller type, and in the late twenties the hourglass worm and sector. The efficiencies of these gears were far superior to the older types then in general use. The recirculating-ball again represented a new order in frictionless operation, using a very modern application of the old traveling-nut principle with dozens of small balls circulating internally, providing a ball-bearing principle and exceptionally low-friction operation. The disassembled pieces of this unit were studied very carefully by other makers including, eventually, Rolls-Royce and Mercedes-Benz. The principle is today widely used.

The 1941 models saw a complete reversion, for the first time in a decade and a half, to the principle of "one make — one engine." The LaSalle and the V-16 disappeared, and the line became six series in three wheelbase lengths — the models 60 Special, 61, 62, and 63 on a 126-inch wheelbase, the 67 on a 139-inch wheelbase and the 75 on 136 inches. All had the 346-cubic-inch V-8 on a 7.25 compression ratio, horsepower now raised to 150 from 140 in 1939–1940. Three axle ratios were offered, 3.77 and 4.27 standard, with a 3.36 economy option on any 126-inch wheelbase model.

The already outstanding performance was improved, and maximum speed was one hundred miles an hour, with zero to sixty in fourteen seconds, zero to eighty in twenty-three seconds — and still better hill-climbing qualities. Gas mileage with the 3.77 and 3.36 axles was also remarkable for such a powerful car, particularly when compared with the 1936 model 60, which had been the first of the new V8's.

The Cadillac Fleetwood convertible coupé for 1934.

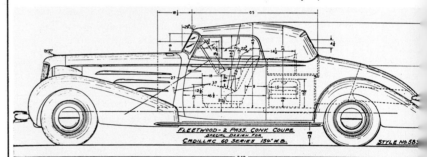

Fleetwood sketch of convertible coupé measurements.

Sixty-first Shrine Conclave official car, a 1935 V-8.

CADILLAC LUBRICATION CHART

CAUTION: *Never run the engine in a small closed garage.*

Check the engine oil every 150 miles

Rear Spring Shackles

2 each side

Apply chassis lubricant to connections, with grease gun.

Every 1000 miles

Storage Battery

Add distilled water to bring level up to bottom of filler tubes.

Every 1000 miles

In warm weather check level every two weeks.

Pedal Shaft and Connections

Apply engine oil with oil can to holes in pedals and to all clevices.

Every 1000 miles

Clutch Release Fork

Refill grease cup with wheel bearing grease and turn down.

Every 1000 miles

Steering Gear

Add steering gear lubricant to bring level up to filler.

Every 3000 miles

Engine Oil Filler

Check oil level and add oil as required.

Every 150 miles

Drain crankcase and refill with oil of correct grade.

Every 2000 miles

Front Wheel Bearings

Each front wheel

Remove bearings, clean, repack with wheel bearing lubricant and readjust.

Every 6000 miles

Carburetor Air Cleaner

Remove filtering unit, clean in gasoline, dip in SAE. 50 engine oil and reinstall.

Every 2000 miles

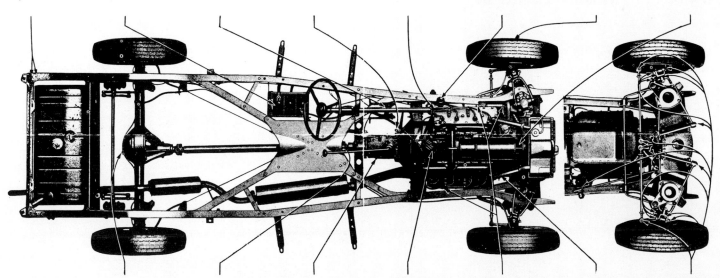

Body Hardware

Apply a few drops of light oil to door hinges and apply a small amount of vaseline to all door striker plates and wedges.

Every 1000 miles

Rear Axle

Add rear axle lubricant to bring level up to filler hole.

Every 3000 miles

Change to winter grade lubricant for cool weather.

Universal Joint Splines

Apply chassis lubricant to connection with grease gun.

Every 1000 miles

Transmission

Add transmission lubricant to bring level up to filler hole.

Every 3000 miles

Change to winter grade lubricant for cool weather.

Timer-Distributor

Apply water pump lubricant with grease gun.

Every 1000 miles

Starter and Generator

1 oil cup on starter

2 on generator

Apply a few drops of engine oil with oil can.

Every 1000 miles

Water Pump

Remove fitting and apply water pump lubricant with gun.

Every 1000 miles

Front Wheel Suspension

20 points under chassis

Apply chassis lubricant to connections with grease gun.

Every 1000 miles

Even in 1936, Cadillac lubrication needs were not excessive.

MPH	3.77	3.36	4.10	(1936)
20	21.2	22.2	14.6	(MPG)
30	19.0	20.2	15.0	
40	17.4	19.0	14.0	
50	15.8	17.3	12.9	
60	13.0	15.2	10.7	
70	11.9	12.7	9.3	

Cadillac pointed out that if a '40 and '41 were driven across the continent, the '41 would make it, but with the same quantity of gas the '40 would run dry 400 miles short of New York.

The 1941 models introduced factory air conditioning, following Packard by a year. Only about 300 units were installed. Like early power steering and various other accessories, the layout was bulky, crude, and inconvenient to use. It had no electromagnetic clutch and ran all the time the engine was operating. Disconnection required removal of the drive belt; the various units in the system were strung throughout the length of the car, and weighed something over 300 pounds. Consequently the air con-

TRUST THE INSTINCT WHICH IMPELS YOU TO CHOOSE FROM
the Royal Family of Motordom

More conventional advertisement and engine, 1936.

Cadillacs for 1938: 60 Special five-passenger above; a limousine below.

ditioning never caught on at that time, but deserves mention as a pioneer move. (Packard's had similar drawbacks.)

The same year Hydra-Matic transmission was available — much more advanced in its state of development than air conditioning, but still susceptible to improvement, it was the first fully automatic automobile transmission. Although offered one year earlier on Oldsmobile, its primary origins were Cadillac, which had thus made the two greatest transmission advances in both decades between the wars.

But the end was at hand for LaSalle and the V-16. These had become great traditions, and many regretted their passing. The demise of the V-16 had fairly obvious reasons — it was now possible to build cars with half that number of cylinders which could virtually equal its performance and offer such high refinement that the extra cost and complexity of the sixteen was no longer justified.

The LaSalle's end is not so easily explained, but was just as inexorable. It was priced fairly close to the Cadillac, yet low enough to have competition from Buick, which was GM's

A Cadillac sedan for 1938, and a convertible coupé, below, for 1939.

strongest medium-priced make. For prestige purposes, with Packard, Lincoln, and Chrysler getting more and more involved in the medium-price field, it was good psychology for Cadillac to abandon it altogether and go all-out to conquer the high-price field, which they soon did. And, although the cars were very similar, the existence of the LaSalle still meant, as Ernest Seaholm remarked, "just one more car to engineer and style." So on August 26, 1940, a four-door torpedo sedan, serial No. 4333589, left the factory — the last production LaSalle, and the last example of a memorable style setter called the "cat's pajamas" and "America's sweetheart." Cadillac was on its own again.

The Cadillacs of 1938 to 1941 form an interesting contrast to their predecessors. Noting the revolutionary change in style and taste and the elimination of cosmetic finish on the engine, the older classic diehards have wagged their heads at the "decline in standards," and one English critic has even written that the Cadillac "lost all its character." But another gets nearer the mark by commenting: "Just before the war Cadillacs may have looked a bit agricultural under the bonnet, but they were very definitely and unequivocally very fine cars which did their job magnificently . . . as engineering they were first-class. . . . There was nothing of their day and age which could touch them for a fast, comfortable ride over bad or indifferent roads. The Rolls-Royce Phantom III, which indeed wore front suspension made under General Motors' license, ironed out the bumps just as well, but the Cadillac was eight to ten miles an hour faster, while with the Rolls one was psychologically exhausted from having pasted its beautiful hand-built coachwork."

The fact was that these Cadillacs were "modern" automobiles in the sense that they had more features in common with postwar practice than any other car. Driving them is an interesting, even memorable, experience. In the context of their contemporaries, they have tremendous power, acceleration and hill-climbing ability, very high cruising speeds with notable economy, extreme refinement and comfort, outstanding ease of driving and good riding and handling qualities. All this *and* their completely "practical" nature make the expensive handbuilt, high-class "classic" automobile seem not merely anachronistic, but something of a sham. (Similar comments apply to the all-new 160 and 180 series Packard straight eights introduced for the 1940 model year. These were certainly Cadillac's most formidable competitors and, according to one Packard engineer responsible for their design, could actually outperform the Cadillac V-8.)

As to the charge that Cadillac has "lost its character," the writer's considered opinion is that the 1936-41 V-8 marked a closer approach to the pragmatic Leland ideal than did the V-16, which for Cadillac was a departure from the optimum high-class automobile. The Leland V-8's were not "cosmetic," because he believed beauty was more than skin deep, and the V-8 was always a more practical car than the V-16. Judged by these criteria, then, the Cadillac V-8 still aimed to be "Standard of the World," and its basic character was unchanged.

Shortly after December 7, 1941, Cadillac went into military work for another world war. Peacetime production stopped in February, 1942, and fifty-five days later the M-5 light tank started to come off the line. In the spring of 1941 Cadillac engineers adapted the V-8 engine and Hydra-Matic transmission to tank work, using two per vehicle. Each engine-transmission unit drove on one track, steering by twin throttle levers. The Ordnance Department testers were impressed with the engine's performance, maneuverability, easy starting, smooth low-speed operation, plus the ready availability of its power-transmission unit familiar to thousands of automobile mechanics. These factors made it one of the most effective armored vehicles of the war, and its chassis was later adapted to the M-8 howitzer carriage. This was followed in 1944 by the M-24 light tank, and in 1945 by the M-19 anti-aircraft vehicle.

Probably the most glamorous wartime production remained for another GM division — Allison — building precision parts for the famous (and widely utilized) Allison aero engine. Known as the V-1710 from its piston displacement, each one cost $16,500. Cadillac made camshafts, crankshafts, con rods, piston pins and reduction gear assemblies for these engines, which were used in P-38, P-39, P-40, P-51, and P-63 fighter aircraft.

Allison Engineering had been founded in Indianapolis in 1915 by James A. Allison (one of the builders of the Indianapolis Speedway). Early machine-shop work for racing cars was followed by marine engines and reduction gears for aircraft and marine use. Allison worked on Liberty production in the war. Conversion of the Liberty engines during the 1920's led to the development of high-quality steel strip bearings which Allison sold extensively in the twenties. When James Allison died in 1928, his chief engineer, Norman H. Gilman, succeeded him as president, and stayed after the GM takeover, arranged by L. P. Fisher in 1929.

By this time the leading American liquid-cooled aero engine, the Curtiss V-12, was becoming outmoded, and Gilman decided to produce a successor for the armed forces. The first engine ever designed for ethylene-glycol coolant, the original V-1710, ran in

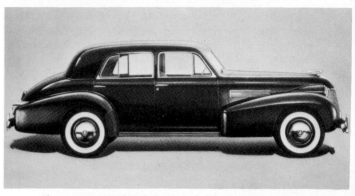

Above, a 1939 60 Special sedan; below, a 1941 convertible sedan.

August, 1931, and developed 650 horsepower, which was raised to 750 the next year. Both these figures were maintained in fifty-hour tests, but in 1932 the military requested a target of 1,000 hp, and a new design (the V-1710-C) was produced. In 1935 it ran fifty hours at 1,000 horsepower. Then the military asked for full power for 150 hours, and this caused so many developmental problems that GM assigned Ronald M. Hazen, an outstanding research engineer, to the job. In April, 1937, the V-1710 became America's first aviation engine to pass all the Air Corps tests at 1,000 horsepower, and in March, 1938, when a P-40 won the Air Corps fighter race at forty miles an hour more than the previous winner, the V-1710 came into its own. The U.S. government ordered more than 800, and in May, 1939, construction of a new plant at Indianapolis was begun. More orders followed and by December, 1941, Allison was building 1,100 per month.

Allison-powered aircraft served in the Atlantic, Mediterranean,

Above, the 1941 60 Special; below, a Raymond Loewy custom convertible.

African, Continental European, Russian, and Pacific fronts in a wide variety of applications. The Curtiss P-40 was the earliest Allison-powered fighter, being converted from the radial-engined P-36 of 1936. Therefore it became outmoded during the war. Nevertheless it became world famous, particularly because of the "Flying Tigers," and nearly 14,000 were built. The Bell P-39 Airacobra was the first production fighter with engine behind pilot, a layout which has many advantages and has now become standard for jet fighters. Although unsuccessful in western Europe, the P-39 was highly regarded in Russia as a low-level fighter and in ground attack, as was its successor, the P-63 Kingcobra. The Russians considered these aircraft tougher and better suited to their conditions than any other Western fighter. Nearly 13,000 were built, of which half went to Russia.

Most outstanding of all was the P-38 Lightning, one of the fastest combat planes of the war. P-38's were named "Der Gabelschwanzteufel" (Two Tailed Devil) by the Germans, were the favorite aircraft of such famous pilots as the Frenchman, Saint-Exupery, and the top U.S. aces, Bong and McGuire. Over 10,000 Lightnings were built.

Perhaps the peak point of the Lightning's combat career came in the spring of 1943. The U.S. Navy had managed to obtain the details of the Japanese naval code. This enabled them eventually to organize "the most extraordinary man hunt in the entire Pacific war." The objective was Admiral Isoroku Yamamoto, master strategist behind the Pearl Harbor attack, and operational commander-in-chief of the Imperial Japanese Navy which in a few months had crippled the U.S. fleet and swept the Dutch and British fleets clean out of the Pacific.

Yamamoto was on a tour of naval bases in the Solomons area to boost Japanese morale, which was starting to sag under repeated heavy losses and reverses. A message containing his inspection itinerary was intercepted and decoded by the U.S. Navy. In a marvel of military organization and timing, sixteen Lightnings took off from Guadalcanal, flew the 550 miles to Kahili, intercepted the Japanese air squadron of eight aircraft (two bombers and six Zeros), and shot down both bombers to make sure of Yamamoto, plus one Zero.

Flown by crack pilots, the admiral's fighter escort went frantic, and many more Zeros took off from Kahili airfield below like angry wasps. But, using their tremendous speed, the Lightnings pulled up in a vertical climb so fast that the Zeros were left behind, their controls stiffened by the speed, unable to keep up for fear of folding their wings. The Lightnings returned to Guadalcanal with the loss of only one aircraft. The Zero pilots must have felt like either following them or diving into the sea. The blow to Japanese morale was terrific — one admiral, on receiving the news, went straight to his cabin, locked himself in and refused to speak to anyone for a whole day.

The late G series Allisons attained an emergency combat rating of 2,250 hp at 3,200 rpm. This equaled the rating of the much-vaunted Rolls-Royce Merlin and represented one of the highest specific outputs (1.31 hp/c.i.d.) of any wartime aero engine. Seventy thousand Allisons had been produced for the U.S. fighters already mentioned when manufacture stopped in December, 1947. Then available at less than one hundred dollars each as war surplus, they became favorites for 200 mph Gold Cup racing and for attempts to shatter the world's water speed record.

Despite this record, the Allison has been attacked (in the same way as the Liberty) as "a dreadful engine." The classic instance quoted is its replacement by the Rolls-Royce Merlin in the P-51

A military awards ceremony, above, and an Allison engine, below.

Mustang. Actually, after the first P-51's were supplied to the British, they *doubled* their order to more than 600 aircraft because they were impressed with the Allison's "excellent low-altitude performance," and these aircraft, used in action by the R.A.F. from July, 1942, quickly acquired a good reputation.

The reason for the changeover to the Merlin was that the British required a high-altitude, long-range fighter. Their own Spitfire was a short-range aircraft, but the Mustang built specifically to British requirements looked very promising. The Allison engine had never been developed for this purpose, since the U.S. Army had mistakenly thought most fighting would take place at low to medium altitudes. The Allison, therefore, had a simple, single-stage supercharger. With Britain's whole future at stake in the war, the Merlin had already received intensive development, regardless of cost, while the Allison was still being developed with peacetime funding until 1942. The Merlin had an advanced, two-stage, two-speed supercharger and originally outperformed the Allison, particularly at high altitudes, so its being chosen for an American aircraft originally designed to British order is hardly surprising.

When developed under the same wartime pressure as the Merlin, the Allison equaled the British engine's performance, and in the last version of the Mustang it actually replaced the Merlin. This was the Twin-Mustang, which later became the first aircraft to destroy 'an enemy in the Korean war, and eventually flew nearly 2,000 sorties in that area. Also, the P-51 J Mustang with the Allison V-1710-119 well equaled the best Merlin Mustang (the P-51 H) but came too late to see service in World War II. The P-40 F and L had a Merlin instead of an Allison to improve high-altitude performance; nevertheless 300 of these were later replaced with Allison V-1710-81's. The P-40N-1 series with Allison V-1710-81 engine equalized the P-40F with Packard Merlin, and the P-40Q with Allison V-1710-121 was the highest-performing P-40 ever built. A Curtiss replacement, the P-60, was built and tested with both Allison and Packard Merlin engines and again the Allison equalized the Merlin version. Neither the P-40Q nor the P-60, however, were put into production because the Army Air Corps favored the P-47 and the P-51. The turbo-supercharged Allisons (as in the P-38) had better power at altitude and possibly better cruise economy than the Merlin. The Merlin, on balance, was the better engine for single-engined fighters, mainly because its integral blower-unit was lighter and more compact than the bulky GE turbochargers, but the Allison must still rank among the most outstanding aero engines of the war.

An interesting development of the V-1710 was the W-3420,

which was two V-1710's geared together to produce an engine in the 3,000 hp class. This arrangement was used in the Fisher XP-75, the Lockheed XP-58 Chain Lightning, and one version of the B-29 Superfortress. These aircraft were, however, experimental and did not see service.

One top Packard engineer — who would hardly overrate a GM power unit and whose aviation experience dates from World War I — told this writer that, aside from a certain fire hazard due to magnesium components, "the entire Allison design was super excellent. The V-1710 was a highly successful design with outstandingly low weight per horsepower. It provided fighter performance which far exceeded any of the available air-cooled engines [and] played a very important part in winning the war."

Cadillac contributed to the design as well as the manufacture of Allisons. The first production engines brought problems, and in July, 1940, Owen Nacker, John Gordon, and Ed Cole from Cadillac engineering, plus John Dolza from Buick, transferred to Allison in Indianapolis. There they ironed out difficulties with crankshafts and blower-gear drives, and produced two-stage supercharging by adding a second blower driven by a fluid coupling. These improvements raised the Allison's altitude power to 1,125 hp at 15,000 feet and 1,100 at 28,000 feet.

Another interesting development was a turbo-compound version which alternately increased power by twenty-five percent or reduced fuel consumption by twenty percent.

Nacker was at Allison for a year, then to Chevrolet, retiring in 1947. Gordon, however, returned to Cadillac in 1943, to become chief engineer when Seaholm retired in July, 1943.

Seaholm's "early" retirement — he was only fifty-six and could have remained another eight years — was explained to the writer by Seaholm himself: "I went to a Swedish party once where the host announced at 11 P.M. that 'The party is over.' He had previously explained that happy memories remained if a party terminated at its peak, whereas dismal ones prevailed as the merriment subsided in the morning hours.

"I had a similar philosophy on retirement. The time to step out — if you can afford to — is when you are at your peak, and everything considered, this was the time for me. I had been working since I was seventeen without a let-up. I had been chief engineer for over twenty years with little time off. I had been most fortunate — far beyond my dreams. I was comfortably fixed. I had no social ambition or any great desire for power and prestige. I had an idyllic place up in the country. Ahead, after the war, I visioned a period of restaffing, need for men trained in science and technology, etc., etc. Why outplay your luck? And so I retired. The twenty-five years since have been most rewarding — busy ones in activities that pay nothing in money, but much in satisfaction."

Seaholm "retired to devote time to personal affairs," but these personal affairs were actually community matters. He was an avid civic worker, devoting much of his time and money to religious and educational institutions. He served on the Birmingham school board and has the Seaholm High School named after him. He was more than a mere engineer or executive: he was a public-

Cadillac began war production just after Pearl Harbor, and for four years its halls echoed to the roll of tanks like these.

spirited citizen, and like the Lelands, a man of very high moral standards and character, yet free from their sometimes oppressive Puritanism.

In his prime Seaholm was six feet tall, strongly built, and weighed nearly 200 pounds. Yet he was a quiet, soft-spoken man who seldom raised his voice. He was an exceptionally good organizer and communicator, spending a lot of time among the people he supervised. When we met, several years ago, he was by then slightly stooped under his eighty years, but still an impressive figure, still very active. If he has a fault, it is his excessive modesty. Time and again he would say, "I had very little to do with that," or "I just turned my men loose on it," when the writer knew from both extensive research and the comments of some of his associates themselves that Seaholm had a great deal to do with it. Moreover, he claimed that "writing is not my forte," yet his letters are concise, expressive, and sometimes so beautifully phrased that a professional writer would be proud of them.

He struck this writer as a very relaxed man, at peace with himself, withholding nothing, offering no protests, excuses, recriminations, or self-justifications, which is in marked contrast to some other engineers and executives of the period. He nostalgically recalled the classic era at Cadillac with a quiet sense of humor that relished Kettering's hillbilly wisecracks and Olley's dry wit. By all accounts he was a man easy to get along with — provided you pulled your weight.

Because of his retiring nature, and the brilliance — even genius — of some of the figures who worked under him — such as Nacker, Thompson, Olley, and Davis — Seaholm's name is practically never mentioned in automobile literature. Yet he is, after Leland and Kettering, probably the most important man in Cadillac's engineering history. His twenty-two-year tenure was the longest of any Cadillac chief engineer's — much longer even than Leland's association. It saw the rather primitive open touring cars of the early twenties evolve into the smooth-riding, silent, scientifically designed cars of the forties.

Seaholm took over Cadillac engineering when its best men had gone. Its management was shaky, its morale low, its designs outmoded, and sales leadership was about to pass to Packard. Certainly he was able to rely on GM resources, but it was Seaholm who rebuilt the Cadillac engineering department into one of the finest in the industry, while maintaining the "group technology" originally established (in primitive form) by Leland. Alfred P. Sloan had said, "Mr. Seaholm — I don't want you to just design cars — I want you to train men." Ernest Seaholm had

indeed done that — and considerably more.

A man of patience and imperturbable calm, he directed without dominating, gently guiding the talent that made Cadillac a leader. Several of his men were the world leaders in their field, but "loners" in the sense that they were interested only in their own special line of research. They had little ability to coordinate or time for administration or training. It was Seaholm's job to give all this a unified purpose and he did. Moreover, his own engineering ability was still influential and decisive. Francis Davis recalled him as "a very pleasant, intelligent person and very receptive to new ideas in the automobile field."

The current president of General Motors, Ed Cole, also had a fine tribute for Seaholm: "He was one of the most significant men in Cadillac's engineering history and is a very fine man personally. I've said many times that he was probably one of the most outstanding men for whom I've ever worked. He had both concern for and interest in the individual and was quick to ex-

press appreciation for a job that had been done well. He had unusual ability to make good judgments and evaluate engineering projects — to determine whether they were worthwhile efforts or just promotions of individuals.

"He was responsible for developing and bringing up through the organization more top engineering talent than any other man I know of — Harry Barr who later was GM vice president in charge of the Engineering Staff, Jack Gordon who became president, and another man, who did, too.

"Ernie Seaholm is one of the men that really put the character in the Cadillac. This is a reflection of his own personal character and integrity."

Admittedly Seaholm had greatness thrust upon him — he referred to his appointment as chief engineer as an "accident" — but he proved equal to the task. Let his personnel file card have the last word: "Ernest W. Seaholm. A first class engineer and designer. Cadillac quality in every respect."

General Douglas MacArthur in his Cadillac Series 75 staff car is on the facing page. Above, the final Cadillac-built M-24 tank goes out the door at the close of the war. At the right is one of the many awards to Cadillac for its war effort.

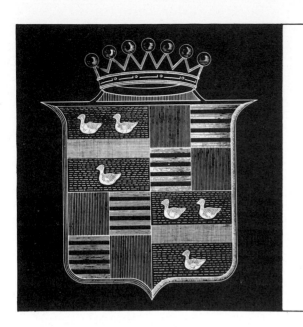

GOLDEN AGE OF THE CADILLACS

Cadillac's ascendancy as a designer's — as well as an engineer's — automobile began in the late twenties and reached a climax in 1941, setting standards in the process that brought it permanent and continuing acclaim through the thirties. The forties brought Cadillac permanent dominance of the luxury car field, and the crucial role of styling in the combination of factors which brought this about may be largely traced to a Californian named Harley Earl.

Earl was born and spent his early years near Hollywood, where his father had a carriage works. He graduated from Stanford in 1918, and had intended to enter law, but his innate talent for automotive styling was irrepressible. When his father's illness necessitated his lending a hand in the family business, Harley began attracting repair work from the owners of some of Hollywood's fine motorcars. As each vehicle arrived, he would spend hours taking careful notes on its laudatory styling treatments.

The elder Earl returned to find, as Harley later recalled, "a glorified hotrod shop" where his carriage works had been, and voiced reluctance over his son's plans to move into this field. As a result the works was sold to the Don Lee Corporation, Cadillac distributors and custom body builders, for whom Earl, Jr. became chief designer and director of the custom department. He worked on Packard, Pierce-Arrow, Crane, Rolls-Royce, Bentley, Renault,

and Stevens-Duryea chassis as well as those of Cadillac, gradually building an international reputation.

Earl finally attracted the attention of Cadillac general manager Lawrence P. Fisher who, along with GM chairman Alfred P. Sloan, Jr., shared the belief in the importance of appearance. The growing strength of Packard, which was already being "designed" to a certain extent, convinced Fisher a change was needed from the old "Leland look," which many customers felt was awkward and old-fashioned, and L. P. paid a visit to Earl in California.

The advanced new methods of Harley Earl — modeling in clay instead of wood or metal, blending all components of a design, emphasizing lower, longer looks, impressed Fisher immediately, and he invited Harley to Detroit to compete for the design of the forthcoming LaSalle.

Earl produced a LaSalle design — four separate clays for different bodies — in about three months. The GM executive committee — John J. Raskob, John T. Smith, Charles Kettering, George Whitney, and Charles Fisher, in addition to Larry and Fred Fisher, accepted the design, and sent Earl to Paris where he "filled five notebooks" with ideas gleaned from the builders of Europe's luxury cars. In the wake of LaSalle's enthusiastic reception, Alfred Sloan proposed a GM design department under Earl named "Art and Colour," which Harley thought a "sissy name."

That aside, it turned out to be an inspired decision.

Earl started slowly at GM, knowing he would have to move gingerly to avoid antagonizing proponents of the Old School. He recruited and trained those he called "fundamental fellows," notably Vincent Kaptur, who took over blackboard and engineering details, and Bob Lauer from Cooper Union. Earl was an inspiring and dynamic leader. His great height and physical and athletic prowess, combined with his Hollywood background and flamboyant but tasteful dress, made him a standout in any company. What he wrought for Cadillac was miraculous, a sudden and beautiful change for the better.

While the first products of Art and Colour — the LaSalle and 1928-29 Cadillacs — were impressive for their day, it wasn't until 1930 that the department's work really came into its own. Earl designed dynamic-looking cars — the best, most advanced, wildest things he could think of. He leaned on Hispano-Suiza to a degree, as well as some of the ideas of Hibbard and Darrin (who filed suit as a result but were mollified by being given some prototype work by Earl and Sloan.) Once he had gained the confidence of management, Harley took off on his own, and any charges of copying ceased abruptly.

The V-16's were good examples of Earl's flair. Cadillac needed something pretty impressive to compete with Packard in those days, and Earl's design, which reached its zenith in 1932, was the flowering of the classic style — the final blooming of the fully open fenders, sweeping lines and blending-of-components type of car. On Cadillac it was a fabulous vintage, more serene in detail from the flamboyance of 1930-31, opulent, done to perfection, with cost no object. It was the year that Harley said he liked most of the classic era.

Around 1933 Earl started doing Fleetwood work in higher volume, beginning the transition toward the envelope body. In 1934 Cadillac passed the rest of the luxury car industry decisively, with modern, streamlined luxury cars which gradually evolved to another high in 1941. Nineteen thirty-four also saw a lovely, revitalized LaSalle, which convinced the board to retain the junior line, an important step in that LaSalle continued to influence Cadillac styling through the turn of the decade.

The V-8's and V-12's of the thirties were significant too, though not as much as the V-16, which was good enough to be carried four years without change. From 1935 through 1937, Cadillacs became a trifle ordinary, looking like the big versions of standard cars, but in 1938 the "Cadillac look" was forcefully back, supplemented by another great achievement, the 60 Special. The latter was Bill Mitchell's first big assignment from Earl — a smart new car which injected still more prestige to the Cadillac line.

255

Cadillac's classic age begins with LaSalle, the first car done by Harley Earl. The first (1927) LaSalle had strong overtones of Hispano-Suiza, especially at the front — in fact there was a LaSalle clay model at the studio that almost duplicated an Hispano. Harley (behind the wheel of the 1927 LaSalle, above on facing page) was striving for a very flamboyant car but one with impeccable taste — and he succeeded. The 1928 Cadillac (town car shown below on facing page) bore a very direct relationship to the first LaSalle. There were modifications — fine side louvers and minor frontal changes — but already we see custom influence in the V-windshield, a configuration common only to custom body builders. The windshield was an important element for Earl, and on some Cadillacs he'd done for Don Lee he used wrapped windshields which actually presaged those of the fifties. Another unique aspect of Cadillacs from 1928 through the early thirties was the molding treatment, going down the center of the hood and continuing along past the cowl and side-mounted spare — a very dashing line, almost the reverse of the Duesenberg's which picked up the same motif ahead of the louvers.

At left above is a 1928 phaeton, a very popular style at the time, which came with or without the read windshield. The little wicker motif on the rear door was popular with Earl on 1928-1929 cars, which are quite easy to differentiate by the placement of the parking lights. On the 1928 models the parking lights are mounted on the automobiles' cowls, while on the 1929 Cadillacs they were fender-mounted. A 1929 town car is at right above, again very flashy. Note the engine-turned aluminum hood. Also visible on this automobile are Buffalo wire wheels, with stainless steel spokes, a trademark of Cadillac's which we'll see more and more. At left below is another very elegant 1929 formal sedan. This fine design is a precursor to the Madame X, with specially built Fleetwood body showing rectangular window frames and V-windshield. A 1929 roadster by Fleetwood with the popular high engine compartment and low tapered rear (a style also favored by LeBaron) is at right below. Significant on this car are stanchion-mounted spotlights and the lack of a hood ornament, though the latter didn't really gain full favor until the thirties.

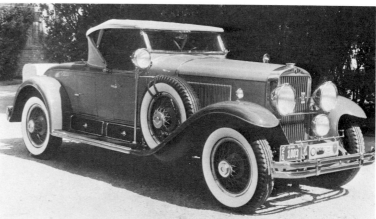

These cars represent the 1930-1931 series. This is the height of opulence in the classic Cadillac. At left above is a more or less standard V-16 model in the popular sedan style, a strong and solid, but trifle heavy, design. Beneath is another V-16, a true Madame X, distinguished by its very slender door and windshield pillars and chrome edge moldings. Notice here the windshield slant—a beautiful sedan and Fleetwood's answer to the custom body builders. There were also four-window sedans and coupés offered in the Madame X configuration. The grandiose hood sweep molding of previous designs was deleted on Madame X bodies, which offered instead a so-called Hibbard and Darrin type molding that came down and rolled up, and in some cases, across the cowl. On this car it goes straight up the windshield. Note the very custom-looking door handles. A slightly smaller running mate, the V-8 sedan of 1930, is shown at the left below, with its shorter hood and conventional body. On the left immediately below is another V-16 four-window sedan with padded top, clearly displaying the V-16's scaled-up headlights and radiator, plus many individual items specific in a period when cost was no object. Again we find stainless steel spoke wheels with painted rims, regular for 1930-1931. (The Buffalo wire wheels ended in 1929.) Present—and most popular at the time—are chrome-plated hood doors, another well liked accessory actually begun by Hibbard and Darrin, who had some unkind things to say to Earl over their presence here. The car immediately below on the right is a 1931 V-16 sport phaeton. This car is not a dual cowl, as Cadillac had some complaints about egress and entrance on these models. This was their answer—a unique style of their own. The cowling goes up behind the rear seat, encompassing a lowerable windshield. Above on the facing page is a V-16 roadster, a most popular style among collectors, again with stainless steel spoke wire wheels. It uses a fabric sidemount spare tire cover and optional mirrors. Below left on the facing page is a V-12 all-weather phaeton, a style first introduced in 1927, with double beltline molding to break up the side while retaining a clean look. To its right is a 1931 V-8 convertible coupé (cabriolet), with optional chromed louvers and golf bag door opening which emptied into the rumble seat compartment.

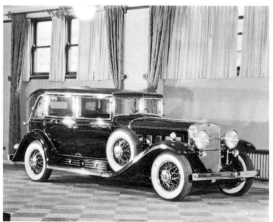

At left above is a 1932 Cadillac V-8 six-window sedan, a new body without fender wells, symbolic of the merging of some components with other GM cars to cut costs during the depression. On Cadillacs this policy resulted in the "clam shell" fender and curved running board, smaller wheels, more bullet-shaped head and tail lights.

Generally, the 1932 models were smaller in dimension and "softer" in line. The all-weather phaeton at center left is shown with Cadillac's first grille — the screen is not separate but integral with the radiator shell, possibly inspired by the six-cylinder Mercedes radiators. Also new are the wind splits on the head, parking and tail lamps. This particular car has chrome spokes. All 1932 models retained doors on the sides of the hood. Harley Earl was fondest of this vintage, and it was probably the epitome of his classic career, for after 1932 he was attempting to do a different type of car. The town coupé at lower left was a unique Fleetwood style introduced for the 1932 model year — what we would call a "coach" today — with fender wells and lacking the earlier style valance in which the body side descended to the running board. The body now completely covers the frame rail. The car is physically lower as directed by Earl, who once said his entire life was spent promoting the rectangle at the expense of the square.

Directly above is a V-16 convertible coupé without the fender wells, which is rather unusual though designers were searching for clean, simple lines and really preferred to omit them, as the Europeans were already tending to do. Many foreign cars actually used rear-mounted spares in this period, as exampled by one Bugatti Royale, which had long sweeping fenders and no side mounts, although one or two builders reverted briefly by mounting the spare tires on the sides in the late thirties.

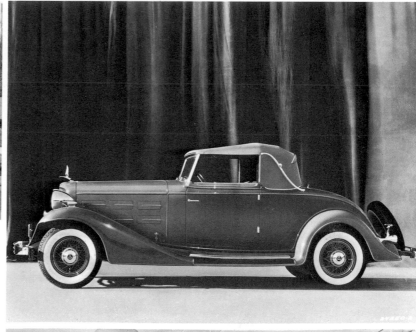

Nineteen thirty-three was an intermediate year of transition between the pure classic look and what later evolved into the streamlined or envelope body. Cars continued to use the new body introduced in 1932, but with more streamlining influences, such as the skirting of fenders on all models and Vee-ing of radiators. In this they were drawing away from the car as an assemblage of parts toward a more complete, integrated unit. It was an evolving period after the "clam shell" fender, and Cadillac quickly moved to a newer fender design which appeared the following year. There was a change in the bumper between 1932 and 1933, the result not unlike the Cord of a few years later. The hood ports or vent doors are horizontal, just another expression of the flowing motion, streamlined theme which was beginning to have its effect throughout the industry. This is also the first year for the wing windows on closed models, referred to as "no-draft ventilation" at the time. Introduced by Cadillac in 1933 they were removed in 1966 on the original Buick Riviera and Toronado. Coming into greater use also was the full wheel cover, introduced on Cadillacs the year previous, an attractive chrome disc as an option to stainless steel spoke wheels or wooden artillery wheels — the last being a concession to the ultra conservative buyer. Immediately above is a 1933 V-8 sedan, exhibiting most of the changes mentioned, the body lines appearing rather confused in comparison to those on the V-8 of the previous year pictured at upper left on the facing page. A 1933 convertible coupé is at right above, a very pretty body style similar in most respects to the 1932 models, though still obviously evolving rapidly. At right below is a 1933 V-12, basically the same size as the 1932, in six-window sedan form, again more streamlined and with the mildly skirted fenders, but otherwise close to the 1932 model.

Above is a 1933 V-16 six-window sedan, a decided departure from past Sixteen designs. It has an entirely new styling motif from the standard car, with different fenders and horizontal louvers on the sides of the hood. This is a feature that began on the 1933 V-16 and was retained right up until its demise: long fairings on the sides of the hood with slots underneath for the air to enter. Functionality is not implied, of course, in the smaller louvers as they appear on the fenders—simply as trim. This car is a prototype; a smaller duplicate of the hood louvers appeared on production fenders rather than the design as shown. Also visible are "Hollywood" wheel discs with spinner blades initiated by Cadillac and popular on smaller cars throughout the thirties, a very dynamic sight in motion along the road. The blade was so placed on these to allow the owner to remove the wheel cover by hand rather than with tools, and thus was functional as well as beautiful. The bumper on this car is also unique, being a multiple-bar affair which the Chrysler Airflow designs introduced the following year. Note that the headlight shells are painted, rather unusual considering the Sixteen's high price bracket, but an indication of the designers' ardent desire to eliminate the old chrome extra pieces. Among other departures were the concentric ring horns mounted on this car, while design themes already established included the flat windshield, Vee-d radiator shell and flat headlight lenses. The small parking lights painted in the body color had originated in 1932 and 1933.

Above is a V-16 dual cowl phaeton of 1933. Here again is a case of the Fleetwood designers producing a car every bit as attractive as what custom body builders across the country were doing at the time. It provides visual evidence to back up Cadillac's preference for using their own Fleetwood people to handle even the special one-off orders for Cadillac motorcars. They had a good argument with this dual cowl phaeton. This car features horizontal louvers on its front fenders as well as on the sides of the hood, and again the "Hollywood" style wheel disc puts in a distinctive appearance, with its twinkling handle-spinner decoration. The popularity of these spinner affairs was to extend all the way into the postwar years. They became prominent in every catalogue of virtually every accessory house in the country, and rare indeed was the hot-rodder or customizer who failed to at least pause lengthily over their illustrations in those booklets. This car carries the justly famous Cadillac goddess ornament, redesigned in 1933 for the sixteen-cylinder series only. The V-8 and V-12 models were given the heron ornament, which had been available optionally with an earlier, thinner goddess on all models the year previous. This redesigned goddess was given a more massive look than its predecessor, and it ranks as the most long-lived of all Cadillac mascots. In fact a goddess-type hood ornament, an evolution of the pre-1933 design, remained available on Cadillacs until 1956. The three motifs on the goddess carry out the forward motion. In all its various guises the figure seemed very appropriate to Cadillac.

Above is a 1934 Cadillac, the production car version of the 1933 Chicago World's Fair car described in forthcoming pages among the specials and show cars. Streamlining is very much in order now. The fender is completely separate from the car, and moreover is pointed in the front. The headlamp pods are painted to encourage the flowing look of the design, and the car bears a side molding of bright metal just as the World's Fair show car did the year before. The headlights are long and bullet shaped to further accentuate the streamlined look. The wheels on this car are novel, inasmuch as they involve hub caps covered with wheel discs. A most unusual feature — which lasted only a year — is the bumper design, those rather famous, or infamous, biplane bumpers (two bullets plus two horizontal bars) which were subsequently discontinued when their fragility became all too apparent. Below right is a 1934 V-12 town car which contains most of the elements of the coupé above, being very well streamlined throughout.

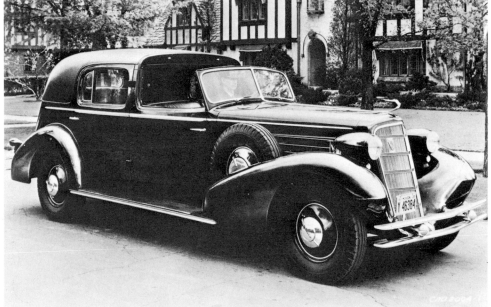

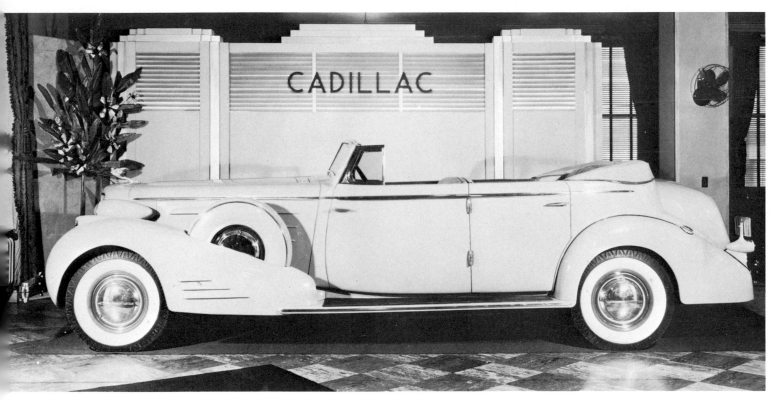

On the facing page are two V-16 sedans. The 1934 model (below) displays Cadillac's first assembled egg crate grille and symmetrical or bullet-formed fenders. Flat or Vee-d windshields (the latter shown on the 1935 model above) were available in both years. These cars are mainly distinguished by the 1934's unique one-year bumper unit.

A 1936 convertible sedan is immediately above, while Cadillac's largest seller for that year, the V-8 Series 60 sedan, with the roundest windows ever to appear on a GM car, is left below. A 1936 Series 60 convertible coupé, with Cadillac's straight-bar grille and, interestingly, deeply buried side-mounted spares is shown below right.

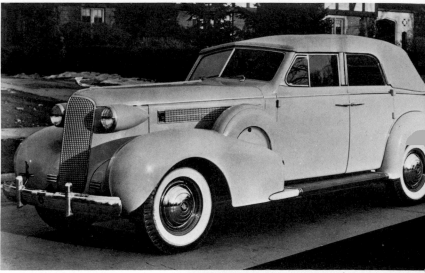

At left above is a 1937 Fleetwood Series 70, its
major change being a die cast, egg crate type grille and new bumper, along with an entirely
new side molding treatment. The bumper now employs a Cadillac crest at center between two sets of
vertical bars; the following year the crest would yield to the name
"Cadillac" in script. Lacking side mounts or fender-stanchion headlamps, this
model gives a good view of the bullet-formed fenders.
Their symmetry reflected the amount of hand finishing that Cadillac would tolerate
at this time; they had to piece these rather convoluted forms together and metal finish them.
General Motors could not afford this, obviously, on less expensive automobiles. There
was a considerable amount of metal finishing required — fenders
had to be assembled and welded to look like one piece — but the kind
of manpower required was cheap in the middle thirties, at least for an expensive
automobile — and that the Cadillac was. At right above is a 1937
convertible sedan, more refined in line, no doubt reflecting Bill Mitchell's involvement
in styling during this period. Though it's a fastback convertible sedan, trunk-back versions were available
at the same time. The running board was becoming more closely integrated, with
the body-colored extension joining the rubber mat section to the
fenders. The year before had seen an entirely different motif, with the trim running
all the way from the rear wheel to the rear of the front wheel cut, whereas in these 1937 models an
attempt was made to give a more fluid flow to the cars. By 1938 they were able
to eliminate the running board altogether. At right
center is the large 1938 V-8 model, showing much detail on the die cast egg crate
grille. This same body was used on the V-16 of that year. Note the way in which
the headlights are mounted now, on fender stanchions rather than horizontal posts extending out from
the hood. At right below is the 1938 V-16 convertible sedan. The large hood louvers are
retained exactly as they were when introduced in 1933.
They proliferated on 1938 model Cadillacs, however, for on the
V-16 they appeared on the rear fenders as well as the front. In comparing this car to
the 1934 V-16 series, one notices that the hood is dramatically forward; the fenders were
placed well out in front of the radiator on the 1934, while on
this model the hood is moved forward. There's a more vertical motif and the car is quite massive in 1938.

Nineteen thirty-eight was a very significant year in the history of Cadillac, for a number of new cars were introduced, as well as a new sixteen-cylinder engine. But with regard to style, the 60 Special was the main attraction: a notch-back sedan with convertible-type styling around the windows, obviously meant to be owner-driven. It was slightly smaller than previous Cadillacs and didn't require the usual trim of most motorcars of its era — there was no chrome or belt molding along the side, just clean sheet metal. There was no running board either, and the traditional egg crate front was replaced by a masterful horizontal motif that was to become very popular with Cadillac customers. The 60 Special was the first mass-produced American car with a distinct "upper and lower" — the roof form was placed on a lower body form. It would become quite common throughout the industry in time. The trunk was no longer a form pulled out of the body but rather an extension of the body itself, and here again we can see those individual fenders, almost tear-dropped in front but with a sharply vertical emphasis in the rear, a design that also appeared on other cars for the 1938 model year. At left above is the original prototype for the 1938 series 60 Special, featuring more vertical and numerous horizontal chrome hood louvers than the final production car. At left center is a later prototype quite close to the end result, although the license plate is still on a stanchion over one of the rear tail lights. At left below is the 1939 model Cadillac, again a new styling effort and a certainly broad departure from the past, eliminating the egg crate in favor of a more pointed frontal aspect. At one time this was meant to be a "catwalk cooled" car, i.e., the panels below the headlights were designed to admit cooling air and the center part of the grille was meant to be just a shape painted the color of the body. At center below is the standard sedan. The new body was called the B-O-P style, and marked the entry of product analysis men into Cadillac company planning — but the design lasted only into some 1940 models. Customers, it seemed, wanted considerably less static lines, and it took very little time for Cadillac to react accordingly. At right below is the facelifted 60 Special for 1939. Only the front end and minor details were changed, and it is still a very lovely car.

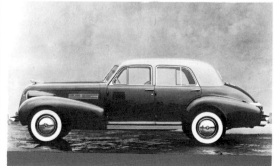

At left are two views of the original body that was introduced in 1940. The top one is a coupé which previewed in California, with a new and much bolder grille compared to previous models. No longer was Cadillac shy about putting chrome up forward. This car had more road value than the 1939 model, which had a tendency to "black out," as the stylists say, from a distance. This car, by contrast, had good road value. Most people felt it was a facelift that made for a much improved car. Below left is a styling prototype for the sedan, then called a "torpedo," though later that word was used so diversely it's become difficult to call it that now. Fender skirts prompted considerable effort at the time and on this car the rear fender appears almost lacking a skirt cut line. It wasn't until the spring of 1940 that a convertible sedan and convertible coupé joined this offering in showrooms. Above is the 1940 Series 60 Special, with its new front. Actually certain 60 Special influences can be seen in the "torpedo" sedan. The notchback quality is there with a little more flow and no side chrome. Visually both cars are in the same family, having almost the same size graphics with, of course, variations. Below is the Series 75 limousine for 1940, the last model year for the V-16, which used this body but carried over the vertical, massive grille of 1938.

At right above is the Cadillac for 1941, an extremely important year. The face of this car set a pattern for years to come, a heritage that was to remain Cadillac's own for many years: the egg crate, horizontal effect and elimination of the vertical grille for a time, though it was brought back later. Many of Cadillac's top competitors were hesitant about embarking on a similar kind of evolution and subsequently found it was so late they almost didn't know how to do so. Lincoln and Chrysler floundered for years trying to come up with a facelift but weren't successful. Cadillac at least had set some ground rules and were constantly refining, until a number of factors solidified in this particular car. Both GM and Cadillac had a very controlled ability to detail an automobile that was lacking in the competition. The discipline of Earl's designers showed nowhere more clearly than in this car. It marked a return to a well organized "power" look, suggesting what dwelled beneath the hood. At the time the designers wondered if this was really the way to go, but Earl was convinced that it was and eventually everyone fell in love with it. Beneath the 1941 model is a '42 —the last year before the war that cars were produced. The same basic theme of the 1941 grille was retained and carried over after the war. It's bolder, larger, more typical of postwar developments, with the first of the bullet-shaped bumper guards which grew into the infamous "Dagmars" of the fifties. A few of these cars were built with grilles painted over the chrome. At center left is a 1941 coupé Series 62, with the optional fender skirts, a very lovely car much in demand today. Below it is a much changed 60 Special, despite its retaining of the 1938 body. This car introduced for GM a new fender line that flowed through the door. At center right is the 1942 60 Special, which introduced the standard C body used on Buick-Oldsmobile-Pontiac cars later. The fellows in styling — it can now be recalled — didn't particularly like putting that many vertical louvers on the final version (below right), and all aspects considered, it certainly was not a 60 Special that could compare to those which had gone before. It wasn't until the 1948 restyle that Cadillac was able to produce a unique 60 Special again.

Here are some very early custom Cadillacs done by Harley Earl for Don Lee in California. The style of the car above was known as "sport-formal" — all the elements of a distinguished type of body were combined with very modern motifs. The 1928 town car below is particularly significant in that it represents typical custom touches put on the basically standard Fleetwood cars by Art & Colour. It has a V-windshield, engine-turned hood and no doubt a lavish interior.

A Type 59 Cadillac with traditional styling for formal motorcars is shown above. The razor-edge features were common to many Cadillacs built by both Fleetwood and other custom body companies and were clearly quite popular. Below is one of the first American non-Fleetwood custom Cadillacs, by the Murphy company of California on a 1920 chassis. Note the extremely slender door and window pillars, a Murphy characteristic matched by Cadillac's Madame X.

Cadillac, as we know, was the only builder of
luxury cars in this country who shied away
from special custom coachbuilders. They wanted
to handle custom bodies exclusively, mainly
because of their large interests in Fleetwood.
When a special order car was made, it would
be produced through Fleetwood by Cadillac,
and would thus remain with the GM family. The
ultimate motive, probably, was to keep
control over the design — not so much for
financial reasons as much as because of Harley
Earl. He wanted that control, and GM wanted
him to have it. The car at the immediate
right is another early creation of Earl's
before his arrival at GM. It's a limousine
with a center entrance door. Wicker is
carried completely around car and windshield,
which is one of those curved varieties
which represented Harley's attempts at a
wrap-around design that finally blossomed in
1954. Combined with the square cut windows,
it bears testimony to Earl's sensitivity
for proportion and form. At right below
is an influential Hibbard and Darrin design of
1928, with a roof treatment created to
effect good lines regardless of the position of
the top. Just behind the front seat was a
windshield which lined up with the shape of the
rear window, providing a tidy appearance
with both windshields up, and top either up or
down. Hibbard and Darrin had introduced
a similar body on a Minerva at the Commodore
Salon in 1927, but 1928 was probably the
first year for production convertible sedans or
all-weather phaetons with roll-up windows.
This Cadillac was among the first body designs
to carry that theme. Incidentally, the
V-shaped pillar between the windows was licensed
to a number of other body builders, and
one finds many other cars with this motif,
but Hibbard and Darrin originated it.
The concept was a weighty influence in the
much later design of the 60 Special, which
serves to illustrate how farsighted the idea was
at the time. This car is also equipped with
wheel discs. These were fairly common in Europe,
but rare in the United States; though Packard
had introduced discs during this period,
they hadn't the effect of a new idea.
Cadillac offered discs a little later, covering
the wire wheels. Some say this was to make
cleaning easier for the chauffeur, but it's
more likely that the motive was to be modern
and smooth. Yet for some time the wheel
disc appeared generally on custom cars only.

At the immediate right is another special Fleetwood done on a 1929 chassis, distinguished by a most unusual roof treatment, one utterly flamboyant compared to typical Fleetwood practice — and one of the first instances of the use of two colors cutting across the hood and around the spare tire. Rear-seat passengers in this convertible victoria were enclosed within and under the top. With its rather high section and windows, it's more like the standard convertible victorias, which hadn't felt the influence of the low, long, four-passenger look, but it has the Cadillac requirement for headroom and flush-folding of the top. Here, as in the standard bodies, are the Buffalo-type wire wheels with stainless steel spokes. At right center is the 1930-1931 series V-16, source of a number of specials, this dual cowl phaeton being one of them. Cadillac was building the separate cowl with roll-down windshield but this is more typical dual cowl style, with the second cowl lifting to allow access and then folding down over the occupants' laps. This was not uncommon in Lincolns and Packards, but was most unusual for 1931 Cadillacs. Another V-16 sport phaeton appears at left below, a styling prototype which features a complete absence of flow-through side moldings. It was one of the first plain-sided cars built by Fleetwood. At center below is a razor-edge town car reminiscent of the earlier Harley Earl efforts for Don Lee discussed on previous pages. This type of elegant, formal, razor-edge style was highly popular with luxury car clientele. It is very elegant, conservative and without styling excess — and executed with extraordinary good taste. The same car, basically, is shown at right below, but this version includes canework around the sides and back, changing the outward appearance from the conservative to the flamboyant. Incidentally, this is the motorcar taken around Europe when the V-16's made their grand tour. The canework was meticulously applied by brush strokes, using special roller brushes. It would be applied at varying angles, each creating a different depth. The effect was amazingly imitative of real cane, even if one examined it closely. Moreover, this process offered the very positive attraction of not deteriorating, peeling, or breaking off the body. Real cane had a poor record of longevity — a decided disadvantage — and consequently little "canework" was really genuine. The battery covers, by the way, open on the side of this motorcar.

On this page we have two studies in contrast which symbolize the extent
of variety available to the Cadillac buyer despite the company's desire to order most
of its non-standard bodies from the Fleetwood company.

At the immediate left is probably the most unusual custom ever seen on a Cadillac chassis, done by the Italian body builder Pinin Farina. The configuration is that of a boattail speedster, but unusual in that the rear compartment completely disappeared when closed, giving the effect of a single seat, two-passenger boattail. When opened the body suddenly became a dual cowl phaeton. It appears to be rather narrow, and the seating was probably very tight. This particular body style was executed occasionally in Europe, but rarely in the United States. Farina, who was born in Turin in 1895, was at the time of this car's construction associated with his brother Alessio in their coachbuilding firm of Stabilimenti Farina. Later, in 1930, Pinin struck out on his own, though the much more familiar name form, "Pininfarina," was not legally combined until the early sixties. This car is particularly unique in that the fenders are all cycle types, with no running boards, and a louvered valance panel covering the frame. The spare is cowl-mounted in the position where one would expect to find the side-mounted spare, the windshield is Vee-d, and the lines of the doors are quite rakish. At left below is another good example of individual order Cadillacs. This particular 1932 Cadillac V-12 was basically a standard sedan. However, the customer evidently wanted more distinction in the roof area, so it was padded and bestowed with landau irons. This car also has special wheel discs in the body color with chrome edges on wheel covers. Noticeable too is an extension of the body color to the rear shell as well as to the headlights and parking lights, not a standard practice on 1932 Cadillacs, which offered chrome in those areas. Cadillac is one of the few manufacturers who offered, through 1932, two different emblems, and the heron (the alternate was the goddess) shown here was very popular that year. In 1933 the heron became standard for the V-8 and V-12; the V-16 received the goddess. The 1932 cars retained the doors on the sides of the hood (instead of louvers) throughout the model range. Another detail feature of this vintage is the utilization of little engine numbers — V-8, V-12 or V-16 — in the centers of the wheels, the V-16 having begun this practice two years before. These designs were done in paint rather than cloisonné, though cloisonné was retained for the front radiator emblem. Generally the custom touches which distinguished this particular car from the standard line offerings are small. It does, however, retain a distinctive look, which no doubt is exactly what the client was seeking. Typical of Cadillac practice, the body was built by the company through Fleetwood. And, again, this year marked the last for the "pure" classic style of Cadillac body.

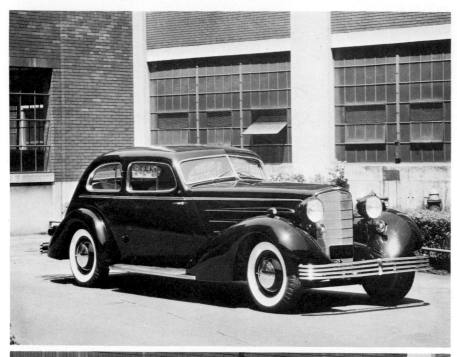

At left is the 1933 Chicago World's Fair show car, a V-16 fastback coupé that is remembered as one of the great styling triumphs of the period. Its all-steel roof was something the designers considered imperative, because this car was to be completely new, free of many of the old hang-ups. The studio wanted individual fender shapes and the body flowing through the hood in one graceful form. They were determined not to have fender wells, in order to keep the form simple, lithe, and smooth. The spare was concealed in the trunk — really GM's first built-in trunk with hidden spare tire. Along with the Pierce Silver Arrow, Cadillac was the first to accomplish these objectives in a truly graceful way. The front end was retained close to stock car form, simply to insure the presence of the Cadillac image at the World's Fair. But the rest of the car was a totally different style. At the rear, the recessed license plate with the light above it was radically new, as was the gas filler built into the top of the tail light, a feature which appeared on stock models in 1941. We see chrome window edges showing up again, and the addition of the chrome belt molding is significant in marking an early attempt to create the first flow-through automobile with integrated hood and body. Here's a case in which the designers really struck a blow for the totality of the body shape, drawing a bright line along the side of the car. Progress toward this end was mentioned regarding the design of the 60 Special on earlier pages, and we've also seen examples in which they took the moldings off, and again in which they put them on, so this was a transitional period for learning the best way to handle the concept. The Cadillac fenders represent a crucial step in this regard. Others were putting skirts on fenders, but Cadillacs were much later than 1933 in form and were carried right up to 1936 by most of the industry. It was fine styling — if you hold your hand over the front end and look at the car from there back, you begin to see a fair resemblance to the Cord Beverly. At the same Fair, Pierce had their Silver Arrow, a more extreme design, perhaps, than this Cadillac. Packard had a Golden Packard by Dietrich, actually a carryover from Dietrich lines put into production in 1932. Duesenberg had Gordon Buehrig's Twenty Grand, in a sense a closed version of an earlier Brunn torpedo phaeton. The Cadillac and the Silver Arrow were the most modern of the four, especially by comparison to Packard. This was a time that saw Cadillac begin to make bold, yet careful steps toward change, while Packard hung tenaciously onto its long heritage, making only limited changes. A lot of people went along with them at the time, but the practice established a position, and they were stuck with it, later on with disastrous results.

At right above is a V-12 formal sedan of 1934, built on a standard convertible sedan chassis with a fixed roof covered with leather. Unusual here are the bank vault or piano-type hinges on the side of the car, which are somewhat alien to the design, a graceful example of a combination of standard body style with formal features. These hinges were a favorite of Gordon Buehrig, who at the time had left GM to work for Duesenberg. Overall, this car is absolutely delightful in its proportions and in the complementary shapes of top and trunk. Immediately above is a V-16 town car of 1935 by Brunn, a good example of why Cadillac was concerned with special bodies by outside firms. Here Brunn has used pontoon-style fenders like the 1933 show car, but combined them with extreme razor-edge styling. Others had done it too, Lincoln rather regularly and even later than this. Cadillac naturally would take exception to this combination. Still there is no doubt about its quality — Brunn was among the best of U.S. coachbuilders. The two cars to the right are renderings, shown to indicate how modern Cadillac wanted to become with their custom designs. The drawings were done by GM Styling — two extremely wild shapes with corresponding astronomical price tags. Both have disappearing tops, exhibit no chrome, their designs relying on totality of body form rather than excesses on fender skirts with imitation wheel discs. They are extremely clean designs, indeed their cleanliness is almost flawless.

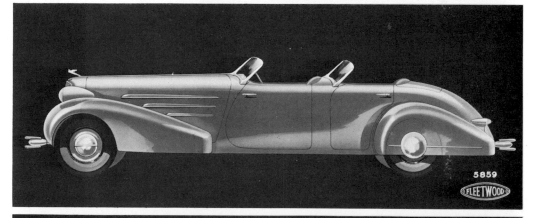

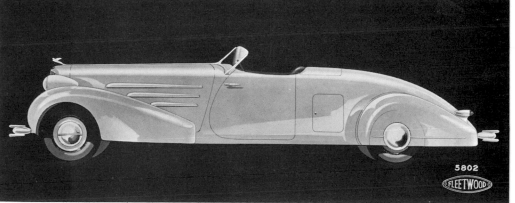

At the immediate right is a V-16 special built by GM Styling
for William Knudsen, president of Cadillac at the time.
It is significant in being a rare fastback sedan built during
this period, and is strictly a one-off, though it does
exhibit a number of 60 Special overtones. Features of note
include its general cleanliness of line. It has no belt molding
but does employ chrome window edges. The net effect
was that of a very elegant, yet dashing, formal Cadillac.
Below is a little convertible coupé from 1936, the model year
during which Cadillac introduced a smaller, lighter model —
as well as a new flathead V-8 which was to prove
one of their nicest prewar engines. This car was done for
Bunkie Knudsen, William's son, who was later to become general
manager of Pontiac and for a brief period president of the
Ford Motor Company. The convertible top on the car is completely
concealed when lowered, definitely a custom feature,
and we again see the hub-cap-on-skirt motif similar to the GM
drawings on the preceding page. The chrome-plated headlight pods
were also custom touches at this time. Note as well the lack
of running boards, and verticals on rocker panels — a European
touch. At right below is another 1936 Cadillac convertible,
in this case a victoria club convertible by Vanden Plas which
sports a small rear seat. Cadillac had a two-passenger convertible
coupé at the time. This configuration provided capacity for
two additional passengers and was quite common for the Belgian
coachworks. The rumble seat convertible, which had peaked in
popularity, was generally being replaced by the four-seat body
style, which was generally known as the "club convertible."

At the immediate left is the special V-16 for Knudsen which is described on the facing page. Beneath it is a special by Bohman and Schwartz on a 1940 convertible coupé chassis, an excellent example of the type of custom body building that was beginning to appear on the West Coast. With most coachbuilders, sadly, defunct by then, Hollywood backed firms like Bohman and Schwartz, who produced entirely new, extroverted shapes, this being probably the farthermost example of their style. The molding cutting through the body side, and right through the fender skirt, is rather avant garde for the time. Howard "Dutch" Darrin was doing the same thing, basically, with Packards, but these men were doing it with a slightly different twist, and it produced quite an unusual car. Below at left is a 1938 Cadillac V-8 by Franay of Paris, an extremely impressive coachbuilder. Franay was a European master of the formal — though somewhat ostentatious — body style, and mounting it on an American car was perhaps not out of context. It is typical of his work, with extreme contrasts, using a light yellow or cream body with a darker color on fenders and roof. Franay was noted for the ever increasing dropped belt line, and most of his work had a very smooth, elegant look to it. Below at center is another "sport formal," really a convertible town car with less than the customary rather stiff formal treatment accorded to most of its variety. This is a 1940 Cadillac by Brunn of New York, one of the more radical town cars built in this country, created in black with cream accent stripes. Brunn was not noted for this kind of ostentation — indeed the company was quite the opposite in approach — so this was apparently produced for an individual order. Nevertheless, it does make for a striking car. Below at right is a fastback V-16 coupé from 1940 built by Derham of Rosemont, Pennsylvania. It represents a most awkward approach at the rear. Cadillac was not offering a fastback at the time, and Derham's client no doubt expressed the desire to have that interpretation on his V-16. The body is completely changed in character, however, even though Derham retained the standard hood and fenders of the Cadillac. Another rather unusual, and not too tasteful, feature is its padded top — quite a rarity for a fastback body style. The side-mounted spares are combined with the pontoon fenders too. It's another example of why Cadillac didn't like their cars tampered with by outsiders, and there's a safe bet that GM Styling was properly vexed when they saw it. They knew how to do a much better fastback, though they didn't really get the chance to do it until the 1941 models reached the design stage.

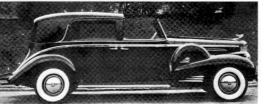

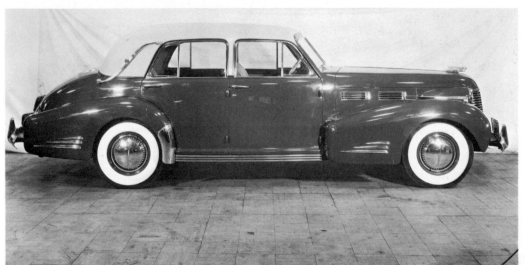

A 60 Special done on executive order is at left, one of about ten made between 1938 and 1941. Unique wheel discs, V-16 fender louvers and metal stone guards are custom features. Below is a 1941 Coachcraft convertible, extremely clean, an example used by postwar customizers to point up the advantages of lowered bodies, flow-through fenders and shaved hoods. On the facing page are postwar specials by Coachcraft. The car above is a very fine piece of work, a shortened, de-chromed and beautiful little formal coupé. Beneath it is another distinctive town car credited to Maurice Schwartz, though he was working for Coachcraft at the time. It's identical to but more successful than the coupé above. Its clean styling worked much better on a long wheelbase. The car's surfaces are rather full, and thus when it's stretched out to this length it comes out quite well. All in all, a very elegant car.

CHAPTER ELEVEN

TAIL FINS AND HIGH COMPRESSION

Postwar developments carry Cadillac to unparalleled supremacy in its field, a position not since challenged

In 1942 Cadillac introduced a substantial restyling which, although looking altogether new, was basically the successful 1941 body shell. Continued was the coffin-nose hood introduced in 1941. Added were a wider, more massive grille and bullet-shaped front and rear fenders on Series 61, 62, 63, and 60 Special models. On these the front fenders flowed into the front doors and the rear fenders had low wheel openings with fender skirts. On the 60 Special the body shell was elongated four inches over the standard model 62, there was an unusual roof-drain molding which was separate for each door opening, and a series of somewhat garish chromium louvers across the bottom of the fenders. The 60 Special was available on special order with a formal divider window between the front and rear compartments. The 1942 models were rounded out by the model 75 long-wheelbase formal limousine and the relatively rare model 67 "streamlined" limousine, both of which were nine-passenger cars when optional jump seats were ordered.

Following the war, the 1946 models were substantially 1942 models with detail changes. The grille and front parking lamps were somewhat altered, as were small dashboard details, and wrap-around bumpers were added. The poor-selling models 63 and 67 were dropped in the process.

There had been improvements in the Hydra-Matic transmission resulting from wartime experience, but Cadillac found that advertising their postwar cars' "battle-proved" engines and transmissions was a mixed blessing. Distributors, dealers, private owners, sawmill operators, and boat builders constantly queried the factory about using war surplus units, and finally the general service manager wrote: "Individuals have experienced considerable expense and loss of time in trying to adapt military

engines and transmissions to civilian use. . . . The purchase of such material should not be encouraged.

"Here are a couple of typical cases in which the results obtained were certainly not those expected: (1) An owner of a past series Cadillac had an M-24 tank engine and Hydra-Matic installed in his car, and after the installation had been completed, he found that the car could not be backed up because there was no reverse unit in the transmission. (2) A sawmill operator installed a tank engine and Hydra-Matic as the power unit in his small sawmill. This man wanted to know how to eliminate the downshift of the transmission with resultant changes in saw speed every time the saw struck a knot in the green lumber being cut."

There followed a lengthy listing of "only some" of the items non-interchangeable with passenger cars, such as electrical units, cylinder heads, crankshaft and flywheel, manifolds, fuel pump, water pump, and various other vitals, including, in some cases, the cylinder block casting itself! But they underestimated the zeal of Cadillac collectors, and many Cadillacs *have* been successfully converted by restorers — although pages would be needed to describe the changes and adaptations necessary.

The popular "fastback" body styling in the form of two-door coupés was continued in 1946. This was available in two series, the model 61 on a 126-inch wheelbase, and the model 62 on a 129-inch wheelbase, the latter being particularly racy looking.

Despite material shortages, production increased from 28,144 in 1946 to 59,436 in 1947. Even at that, there were 96,000 unfilled orders, and Cadillac set itself an unprecedented production target of 100,000 cars annually. They were helped by a GM decision, said *Fortune*, "that if there were going to be more

NUMBER ONE
Regular Production Car
1946 CADILLAC
OCTOBER 17-1945

General Motors vice-president B. D. Kunkle and Nick Dreystadt (left), Cadillac general manager, greet first postwar car.

customers than cars, it might as well be generous with the division that could return the most dollars per pound of steel."

The demand for Cadillacs was so great that in Los Angeles, Eugene Jaderquist noted, "Cadillac fever is of epidemic proportions. Dealers are becoming acquainted with the 'pool.' Two, three, and sometimes five or six people of moderate means pool their resources for the specific purpose of buying one Cadillac. Ownership rests with the group as a whole, but actual use of the car rotates in whatever pattern the members have been able to agree upon. As far as can be discovered only Cadillac enjoys this unusual tribute. Pools don't consider the big Chryslers, Lincolns, or Packards. In Hollywood, for years, Ciro's night club has reserved its main parking lot for Cadillacs only, other breeds being relegated to another hardstand a few doors west on Sunset Boulevard."

During these years Cadillacs were something of a bonanza for GM executives entitled to purchase them at cost. After driving them for a year, they were usually able to sell the cars for more than they had paid.

The 1948 models brought the controversial and imitated tail fin treatment, adapted by Harley Earl and his assistant, Julio Andrade, from the Lockheed P-38 Lightning fighter of World War II. The concept had originated when the Earl team had a look at an early (and secret) P-38 well before Pearl Harbor. Some of the

Cadillac convertible of 1941 carries Harry Truman, 1946.

proposals that followed included other aspects of the aircraft as well as its tail fins — pontoon fenders, airplane-like cockpits, propeller-shaped noses. Fortunately, only the tail fins were carried through to production.

Regardless of criticism, the tail fins had fantastic public appeal. "Cad Fins," wrote Jaderquist, "quickly became a symbol of grace, beauty, prestige. Imitation fins popped up in accessory shops all over the country; for a few dollars you could give your Chevy or Olds' that Caddie look. Custom builders in California, Florida, wherever they might be, were plagued with orders for the little magic rudders on every sort of stock car. The Cadillac fin has proved a stroke of styling genius."

This writer agrees with Jaderquist and the mob on this topic, while maintaining some reservations about the heights the fins later attained. The cries of purists and aficionados were typically biased. Actually, the fins were striking, original, and distinctive. Moreover, having done so much to power the P-38, Cadillac was as entitled to a mark of the association as, say, Hispano-Suiza was after World War I, when that company wore the flying stork of Guynemer's squadrons.

The new body style was Harley Earl's answer to Kaiser-Frazer's and Studebaker's fenderless, full-width concept, though it did not entirely do away with fenders. It was first introduced on the 1948 models with the exception of the Fleetwood 75, which retained the older styling through the 1949 model year. The new look was found on four-door sedans, coupés, and convertibles, and similar treatment was applied to other GM lines, Buick in 1948 and Oldsmobile, Pontiac and Chevrolet in 1949. *The Motor* commented that "their form, like that of a salmon, is entirely suited to smooth travel in one direction. Static pictures can do scant justice to their natural look as they glide along the road."

The 1948 Coupe, later nicknamed "sedanette," was beautifully done, and the Bentley Continental of several years later bore more than a passing resemblance to it. Rear bumpers were "built-in," and the gasoline cap was hidden under one tail light hinged for that purpose — an innovation which actually had its beginnings in the 1941 models. Low pressure (24 p.s.i.) tires became standard equipment and ninety-five percent of production was Hydra-Matic-equipped.

Discussing the early postwar models in *The Motor*, Laurence Pomeroy wrote that they were "Top Class . . . [The Cadillac is] acknowledged to be America's finest car today; fitted with fully automatic gear changing and 150 hp engine, it is a good example of balanced design in the Transatlantic manner." Pomeroy's words were echoed in Italy by Fabio Rapi of Isotta Fraschini, who was then designing "a new intercontinental car of high quality, which might be able to compete with the Cadillac." Donald Healey, visiting the plant in 1948, afterward remarked, "Detroit, the home of Cadillac, that wonderful piece of luxury motorcar that sells for less than a thousand pounds."

Nineteen forty-eight was the last year for the rugged L-head V-8, and in January, 1949, an all-new 331-cubic-inch, short-stroke, high-compression overhead valve engine was introduced. The 1948 chassis was continued but body styling was altered in the form of a new massive grille and a revised dashboard. In addition, on the models 61 and 62 sedan, the rear trunk lid was altered in mid-year with a more pronounced squareness to give better luggage accommodation, but the new engine was the big news and was to prove as great a landmark as the 1914 and 1923 V-8 designs — and become "the engine an industry adopted." For some reason, early announcements (or overenthusiastic journalists) called it "the Kettering engine." The legend took root, and Kettering is often still credited with its design.

Actually, as John Bond wrote in *Motor Trend*, "This new engine is not the so-called Kettering engine, which was a small six of 180 cubic inches. While the Cadillac was developed concurrently with the GM Research 12.5 to 1 compression engine, it is considerably different."

Bond selected Cadillac as the outstanding "car of the year" on the basis of its engine, pointing out that while the Olds engine concurrently announced was similar, "the engines are not by any means the same. The Cadillac, with 10 percent more piston displacement, develops 18.5 percent more bhp and weighs a few pounds less."

The actual design and development work on this V-8 was carried out by Cadillac engineers under the supervision of John F. Gordon, and later, Harry F. Barr and Edward N. Cole. Barr (later to become vice-president in charge of engineering for the whole GM complex) was born in Enid, Oklahoma, in 1904. Graduating from the University of Detroit, he joined Cadillac in 1929. Cole (president of General Motors since October, 1967) was born in Marne, Michigan, on September 17, 1909. In 1923 he bought his first car, a Saxon, "promptly converted it to a hot rod and burned up the back streets of Marne." Then followed a succession of Model T's until he enrolled in the GM Institute in 1929, when he "prudently purchased a new 1929 Chevrolet." Cole alternated between engineering courses in Institute classrooms and paid work at Cadillac, which sponsored his studies. He soon equipped the Chevrolet with Cadillac V-16 rocker arms, three carburetors and an exhaust reputedly made up from "a four-inch furnace flue." With William E. Burnett, a fellow Cadillac technician (who later became chief passenger-car engineer for Ford), Cole rigged up a drag race with the head of the Cadillac dyno

The 1946 (left) and 1947 Series 62 sedans were basically similar. Script nameplate replaced block letters on 1947's fender.

lab, Fred Arnold. Arnold had a Cadillac V-12, well known for its fine tune, but Cole left him standing in Clark Street, in front of the factory.

This was typical of Cole, dynamic, extroverted, enthusiastic, and an engineer respected by all. "Ed Cole is quite a guy," says Karl Ludvigsen. "He's a man's man. His men would do the impossible for Cole, even without being asked." Some of his thinking can be gauged from the fact that he liked reading letters on automobiles "written by those obviously under twenty-one" — and when his son (an engineering student at the time) wanted to buy an old car to fix up, Cole discouraged him and bought him a new Chevrolet "so he could go on from there." On power units, Cole believed that "an engine must be made to hang together under any circumstances."

Development of the new engine actually began before the war, in 1937. Experiments with the new 346 L-head engine showed that the limit of compression with that layout was not far off. Higher compressions were not feasible much above 8 to 1, because the cramped head and transfer passage caused a loss in volumetric efficiency. Also combustion roughness started. Yet higher compressions were necessary to get the best use from higher octane fuels, which promised higher efficiency. (During the same period, Ethyl Corporation experimented with a supercharged Cadillac V-8, and without any change in design or materials, obtained 234 bhp — an increase of fifty percent.)

The first step at Cadillac was a five-bearing crankshaft, to see if higher compressions were possible, with smoothness, using the existing L-head. This halved crank deflection and raised its peak from 2,600 to 3,700 rpm. While this reduced crankshaft vibration, air-flow checks and roughness studies showed that at 8 to 1 with a head design giving satisfactory flow, even the five-bearing engine was still too rough. The next step was an overhead-valve, five-bearing engine which had many features later adopted in the 1949 production model, such as a shorter stroke than bore, slipper pistons, wedge combustion chamber, and general layout. This engine was running before the war.

A major factor in the success of the overall engine design was the so-called "slipper" piston, which had cutaway skirts to lighten the piston and thereby reduce reciprocating weight. The pistons traveled lower between the crankshaft counterweights, allowing a shorter rod which further reduced reciprocating weight and lowered the block height, resulting in a lighter and more compact engine. The slipper design was the work of Byron Ellis, a piston specialist, who was first a consultant, then part of the Cadillac engineering staff, where he helped develop aluminum pistons for the 1934 line. Ellis started on the slipper idea around 1938, continuing his work even during the war.

Julio Andrade (above), assistant to Harley Earl, stands among Cadillac prototypes for 1948 restyling, inspired by the Lockheed P-38 fighter of World War II. Many features of the airplane were considered in addition to tail fins: pontoon fenders, bullet-like noses, cockpit-shaped greenhouse designs. But the tail fins were in the end the only major P-38 influence on what became, on the 1948 Cadillacs, one of the remarkable postwar automotive designs. Since Cadillac styling was handled at Earl's studios, which developed the lines for all GM products, certain features seen here eventually were applied to Cadillac's sister makes. The complex curved, widely wrapped windshields, for example, were common to many GM cars by 1959, and the pillarless "hardtop" design made its appearance on Oldsmobile and Buick, as well as Cadillac, for 1949.

Engine work during the war was concentrated on the military needs of the existing 346 engine. After the war, Cole and Barr reviewed the situation in the light of advice from Ethyl, and decided to design for an ultimate compression ratio of 12 to 1, but to introduce the engine at 7.5 to 1. This was to take advantage of 88-octane fuel while allowing for octane levels as low as 84. Cars exported to countries where only low-grade fuel was available would have a compression ratio of 6.7 to 1. Provision for the higher ratios required no major machinery for tooling changes. Other objectives were better fuel economy, reduced weight and size, smoother operation, clean design appearance, good accessibility, increased performance, improved durability.

All these objectives were achieved. Although smaller in physical size and displacement, the engine developed 160 hp bare, 133 net, a gain of seven percent; torque was up from 260 net to 270, and specific fuel consumption was improved by fourteen percent, which translated to a gain of two miles per gallon at all speeds between twenty and eighty miles an hour.

The new engine did all this, and more. Its weight (699 pounds dry) was 188 pounds lower than the L-head. However, since it was thermally more efficient, its radiator and coolant requirements were also smaller, so the total weight saving was 221 pounds. Even the overhead valve gear had been lightened by ten percent compared to the previous L-head! High-speed durability was also improved. After 131 hours at 4,250 rpm, the bearings of the 1948 head engine were in fair condition and good for more running, but showed signs of wear. But after 541 hours — four times as long — at the same speed, the 1949 engine's bearings were still in perfect condition. As installed in the car, sustained piston speeds over 2,500 feet/minute were virtually impossible, coming at 104 mph with the 3.77 axle and 96.5 mph with the 4.27. This further made for durability.

Time magazine, announcing the new model on October 25, 1948, said that the new engine could "drive the heavy Cadillac from standstill to 80 mph in 30 seconds," but was economical and quiet as well, because two things had bothered general manager John Gordon:

"Gordon, who first began working on the engine when he was Cadillac's motor design engineer, had wanted more fuel economy — he remembered the old gag of the filling station man telling the big car owner: 'Shut off your motor, you're gaining on me.' The new engine is so quiet, Gordon swears that in road testing it he was bothered by the noise of the dashboard clock, had it redesigned to give the motor's purr a hearing."

There had been a decrease in maximum speed of several miles an hour from the one hundred of 1941 to ninety-three–ninety-five in 1946–1948, due to the combined power losses in the Hydra-Matic and low pressure tires. The new ohv engine restored the

one hundred top speed.

Characteristically, GM Proving Ground figures showed a conservative 98.5 mph top speed, but when *The Motor* tested a car supplied by a private owner, they recorded 99.7 mph mean time, four ways over the measured mile. This car had not been specifically tuned in any way prior to the road test, and had just completed a journey to Italy and back.

In March, 1949, describing the new model, *The Motor* had speculated that the "rakish combination" of two-door Coupe de Ville body and Series 61–62 chassis "would make one of America's fastest production cars." Confirmation of this came in 1950, when Briggs Cunningham ran two Series 61 Cadillacs at Le Mans, one with an aerodynamic body, one a standard Coupe de Ville.

The aerodynamic version was nicknamed "Le Monstre," and was indeed formidable looking, low and squat, yet three inches narrower than the stock coupé. The streamlining was designed by Howard Weinman of Grumman Aircraft, and chromemoly steel tubing was employed for the body-frame to reduce weight. Brakes were stock Cadillac with aluminum cooling fins, bonded on by the Alfin method. A novel feature was the Link two-way radio, used to maintain contact between driver and the pits.

Although the engine for "Le Monstre" was specially prepared by Frick-Tappet and boasted no less than four carburetors, a strictly stock chassis was used and the transmission was Cadillac's own three-speed manual. Despite a few skids into various sandbanks, loss of all gears save top, and a weak battery, the streamliner clocked an average of 81.33 mph for the twenty-four hours and finished an amazing eleventh overall.

More impressive yet was the performance of the other Cadillac entry, a near-stock Coupe de Ville driven by Sam and Miles Collier. Once again, the chassis and transmission were stock, though Marchal driving lamps were fitted along with, of all things, a manual wiper-turning lever that could be operated from inside the car to conform with French road regulations! In practice the Colliers were hitting about 117 mph in the Tours straight. In the real thing, the amazing de Ville finished tenth overall, ahead of the streamliner, with an average speed of 81.54 mph. "We doff our hats," said *Road & Track*, "to Briggs Cunningham and his team for their outstanding contribution. . . ."

The Motor was "particularly impressed by their silence and stability at high speed," and although some of the stability doubtless came from Cunningham modifications, the silence was strictly Cadillac's.

It was a good year for the new GM ohv V-8's, for an

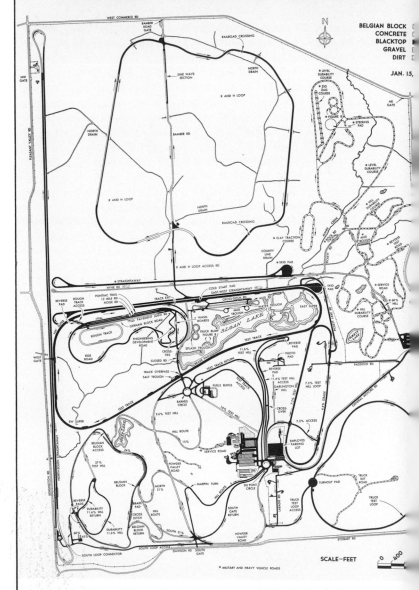

A 1949 model, on the facing page, at Milford's banked test track.

Oldsmobile driven by Hershel McGriff won the Pan American road race, and Tom Deal (Cadillac) came second. (Although Cadillac never won, they consistently placed well in the Carrera Pan Americana through the years.) The 1950 Grand Canyon Mobilgas economy run also saw Cadillacs taking first place in classes G and H, and their figure of more then twenty-seven miles a gallon was only a mile or two less than the lightest cars competing.

When it came to checking out their beliefs with an actual road test a year later, *The Motor* used as a test car a four-door sedan supplied by Briggs Cunningham. "A make which ranks as one of the world's best," their report read, "impressive, well-balanced, and with sheer scale effect that lends a certain majesty.

"Performance was of an extremely high order . . . which few makes can rival, fewer still surpass. The Cadillac is a vehicle manifestly designed to cover long distances at a high cruising speed whilst demanding the absolute minimum effort from the driver and imposing the smallest possible distraction on the passengers . . . outstanding overall silence. . . . Conversation in ordinary tones can be maintained at between 80 and 90 mph. The combination of high acceleration with a comfortable cruising speed of not much less than 100 mph results in exceedingly high overall speeds, and 60 miles in the hour may be considered on reasonably straight roads."

With this went remarkable economy and 15-17 mpg was an overall average for a 160-mile test that included much cruising between eighty and ninety miles an hour.

The car caused a sensation among Temple Press executives (publishers of *The Motor*) and Laurence Pomeroy later wrote: "This car was extensively driven by most members of the staff, and reactions ranged between 'the perfect car' through 'super transport' to 'wouldn't have it at any price.' Moreover, opinions were so fixed and furious that only the fact that the staff is in truth a band of fellow travellers kept them on speaking terms."

Pomeroy himself criticized the car's size, brakes, steering, transmission, suspension, and a number of minor details ranging from finish on the window cappings to the lack of a cocktail cabinet. Nevertheless, he conceded it was "a remarkable car, fast and economical, making little demand on the skill or physical effort of the driver, with many practical features such as the most efficient heating system I have ever encountered, which includes positive demisting of the front windows as well as the windscreen." Summarizing, he called the car a "Transatlantic Apotheosis" and drew a nautical analogy, "regarding the Cadillac as the *Queen Mary*, in which the captain lives in comfort, has all modern aids to navigation, but can only exercise remote control."

His co-tester, Joseph Lowrey, commented: "The Cadillac represents a peak of American automotive development, although it was not prevented by its size or suspension flexibility from travelling fast on European roads."

A year later *The Autocar* published a similar road test and reaction. "Once inside the car," they said, "it did not take long to realize that in the Cadillac, General Motors have really 'got something'. . . . a car with outstanding performance. . . . Indeed one run of just under a hundred miles was covered at an average speed of 52 mph without apparently hurrying, and at a fuel consumption of 14–16 mpg.

"The car handles extremely well at speed, and possesses a certain 'quality' feel. On corners there is a minimum of roll and the car feels 'solid.' One is impressed most of all by its extreme silence. . . . It is a most pleasing car to drive. Judged by any standards of performance, comfort or maneuverability, this car would fulfil the needs of a most critical driver."

Visiting a large British factory the following year, *Autocar* testers were impressed to find "the very latest" in V-8 Cadillacs

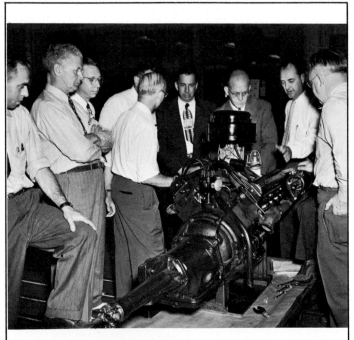

Cole (dark suit), Gordon and Barr (to his left) with new V-8.

under study by "the backroom boys." They thought this a good answer to critics "who like to aver that British firms are backward in studying foreign competitors." Years later, the magazine's Grand Old Man, S. C. H. Davis, rated the Cadillac as one of the six outstanding cars of the first *and* second postwar decades.

In January, 1950, GM put on a "Mid Century Motorama" at the Waldorf Astoria in New York City. Cadillac's exhibits were the most lavish, and its gold-plated "Debutante" convertible reputedly cost $30,000. Seats, floor, and side panel trim were in leopard skin, selected from 187 imported Somali leopard pelts. Lower seat backs, cushions, and lower sides were in opalescent gray nylon satin, with armrests in gray leather. Every unpainted metal surface in the interior was gold plated, even to the ignition key and chain. The yellow buff exterior blended with the tone of the leopard skins and the paint had a pearlescent fish-scale base giving a brilliant pearl-like luster.

Whether this car was inspired by the Broadway stage hit, *The Solid Gold Cadillac*, later made into a film, or vice versa, is unknown to this writer.

Specials were not restricted to show cars. One Chicago family, the Gaylords, had chief engineer Cole build them two special 1950 models with substantially modified engines, racing-hydramatic transmissions, 140 mph speedometers, and built-in tachometers. In 1953, when Cadillac had made Hydra-Matic standard, Edward Gaylord had Cole supply him with a 1953 Series 62 coupé with three-speed synchromesh and 3.07 rear axle, the only one built that year.

Even the 1950 models, Gaylord recalled, were very fast. "The 1950 160 h.p. Cadillac Series 61 with three-speed standard shift and 3.77 ratio was the fastest car made in the United States and perhaps the fastest accelerating stock car in the world; I owned one of these and a new Jaguar XK-120 at the time, and the Cadillac was the fastest car up to about 90 mph. My Cadillac set what was then a stock car record at the original quarter-mile drag races in Santa Ana, California. . . . The only competition Cadillac had in acceleration was from the small 135 h.p. Olds' 88 coupe, but the Cadillac engine was substantially more efficient both in performance and economy. Actual timed top speed for this Cadillac was 107 mph, while the Olds 88 with 3.90 rear end would do 103 mph. The Cadillac could out-accelerate the Olds' by two car lengths from zero to sixty."

Cadillac began the fifties with a range of eight models, the Series 61 four-door sedan and two-door coupé, the Series 62 four-door sedan, two-door convertible, coupé, and Coupe de Ville, the

Series 60 Special Fleetwood four-door sedan, and two Series 75 Fleetwoods.

The 61 was the cheapest model, upholstered in two-tone fabrics with Morocco brown door trim panels and window moldings. The coupé style, similarly upholstered, had a rear quarter window and pillar that pivoted backward out of sight.

Series 62 convertibles were, of course, all-leather, with five individual colors or two two-tone options. Chrome hardware and hydraulic top controls were mounted in a light-toned insert in the front door. The power-operated top was available in either black or tan. The rear quarter and side windows, as well as the seat adjustment, were hydraulically operated. Model 62 coupés and sedans had two-tone cloth with heavy dark wool-pile carpet to match. The Coupe de Ville had two-tone top-grain leather and cloth upholstery with dark carpeting. The interior was brightened by chrome trim including simulated chrome top bows.

The 60 Special had a longer 133-inch wheelbase, larger rear deck and rear fenders. Upholstery choices were in four color tones, either plain or patterned with trim, carpets and moldings to match. The Series 75 had remained unchanged in body styling

—even retaining exposed, rubber-covered running boards—from 1941 through 1949, but by 1950 model year it was new throughout. Available either as a seven-passenger sedan or as a limousine with division, it had "luxurious fabrics and trim," but these were not considered equal in quality to those in prewar models nor even contemporary Packards. The ideal American enthusiast's car of this period, in fact, might well have had a Cadillac engine and transmission, Chrysler brakes, a Hudson "step-down" body frame, and Packard standards of interior quality and finish.

About this time the new Cadillac engine made its presence felt in sports car racing, and the English Allard company standardized on the Cadillac engine and transmission for their famous J2 sports car. One of the outstanding competition cars of the decade, the J2 had placed third in its first major appearance at Le Mans in 1950. In February, 1951, *The Motor* published a road test which said in part, "On rare occasions, cars produce figures and comment which make history. . . . The figures which we obtained from the Cadillac-engined Allard are in several instances unique. . . . Acceleration through the gears is in most instances the best ever recorded in the history of our road tests."

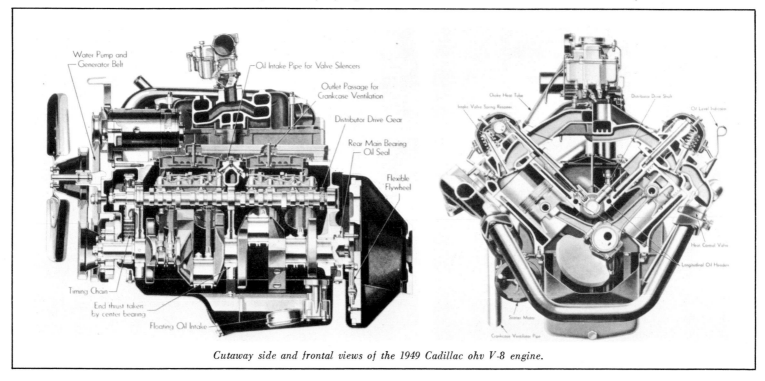

Cutaway side and frontal views of the 1949 Cadillac ohv V-8 engine.

However, despite the "tremendous, extraordinary, astounding" power, the road test continued, the eight-cylinder engine "propels the Allard in a manner more docile than most family saloons . . . completely without temperament. . . . Engine flexibility makes turning around in a wide road in top gear a smooth operation. . . . There is a very great fascination about the ultimate in high performance. . . . [Driving this car] is one of the most memorable experiences which a motoring enthusiast can achieve."

Fortune made a survey in June, 1950, selecting at random 5,000 of its readers "to insure an accurate sample, geographically distributed, of high income *Fortune* families." While Cadillac rated fifth in number among this ownership, it shared first place with Oldsmobile in answer to "What make do you think you will buy next?" And among the expensive makes, Cadillac was overwhelmingly voted "best looking" and "best value," receiving in both cases more votes than all its competitors combined.

Cadillac's popularity in this poll doubtless reflected the progress since 1936, when the division overtook Packard (with forty-eight percent of sales above $1,500) and began to dominate the quality field. In 1939 more than half of "fine car" sales over $2,000 were Cadillac, and in 1950 the division had produced over 100,000 cars for the first time in its history. Even at that, production lagged behind sales. From then on, six-figure annual production became the norm — an achievement comparable with the production of the original V-8 in 1915, the first quality car to establish a five-figure level.

Cadillac's first postwar general manager came straight from the engineering ranks. When Nick Dreystadt moved to Chevrolet in 1946 (he died of cancer two years later), his replacement at Cadillac was John F. Gordon. Gordon's successor as chief engineer was Edward N. Cole, whose own post of assistant chief was filled by Charles Frederick Arnold — the same Fred Arnold who had lost the Clark Street drag race to Cole some years before. With these three in the top posts at Cadillac it is easy to see why the 1949 model was a shining achievement.

Because of Gordon's accomplishments in engineering and his leadership at Cadillac, he was selected as head of the General Motors Engineering staff in July, 1950. A year later he became a group vice-president of GM, and in September, 1958, he was named president of the Corporation. At Cadillac his successor was D. E. Ahrens, whom *Fortune* described as "looking like a typical, well-groomed Cadillac owner." Ahrens had previously been sales manager.

In 1950, during the Korean War, Cadillac opened up a new tank plant in Cleveland, and Cole went there as its manager. Later he headed Chevrolet engineering and, ultimately, General Motors itself.

Fred Arnold became Cadillac chief engineer in January, 1950. Born in Harrison, Ohio, in 1900, he was educated at Harrison public and high schools and received his degree in Mechanical Engineering at the University of Cincinnati. After two years at Studebaker as a project engineer, he joined Cadillac as laboratory assistant in September, 1925. He became assistant laboratory foreman in 1932, supervisor of the experimental laboratory in 1936, product improvement engineer in 1938, quality and product control engineer in 1941, and section engineer in October, 1943. In his fifteen years as chief engineer, Arnold saw several management changes.

Don Ahrens was followed in 1957 by J. M. Roche, another Cadillac sales manager who had joined the division thirty years before as a statistician in the Chicago sales and service branch. By 1928 he was already assistant to the branch manager, and in 1933 he came to Detroit as assistant business manager. Heading that department in 1935, he became personnel director in 1943, and in 1949 director of public relations. An avuncular type whose "quiet voice was like the purr of a Cadillac engine," Roche left in 1960 to become a GM vice-president, and later chairman of the board. He was succeeded in 1960 by Harold G. Warner, whose

previous position — general manufacturing manager — had been the culmination of a career that began on the production line many years earlier.

Model year 1951 brought four new models providing a total range of eight. Carried over from 1950 was a single-piece curved windshield in place of the divided one, with a flat-topped roofline giving a severe "frowning" effect. Changes carried over from 1950 were the vee-d grille and a broken fender or belt line at the rear, emphasized by the dummy vertical "air-intake" at this point, which one observer called "a chrome bandage."

Cadillac production reached 110,340 cars in 1951, but that year brought the Chrysler V-8 with hemi-head, improved semi-automatic transmission, disc brakes on some models, and power steering. Its homely styling notwithstanding, the Chrysler was an outstanding car, and Cadillac decided to revise their chassis to remain fully competitive. In 1952 came Cadillac's Golden Anniversary models with Saginaw power steering, and power increased to 190 bhp at 4,000 rpm. The power steering, based on Bendix-Davis patents, differed from Chrysler's Gemmer gear in having a preload to give road feel. The engine featured a quadrijet, four-barrel carburetor developed by the Rochester Division of GM. This unit gave better fuel distribution and high-speed breathing while retaining economy at lower speeds. A progressive throttle linkage opened only the two primary barrels until half-throttle was reached, then cut in the secondary barrels for maximum power. This principle had been used many years before on the Peerless V-8 of 1916, but with two barrels instead of four.

The new Dual-Range Hydra-Matic provided manual control over third and fourth gear as required, allowing a "hold" in third for city traffic or mountain work, thus avoiding "lugging" and retaining engine braking.

Motor Trend found two areas in which the Cadillac fell short of previous standards: ride and economy had both suffered from engineers' efforts to improve power and handling. Nevertheless, they summarized, "through the years, the name Cadillac has been synonymous with the word Class, although it may be questioned how long Cadillac can hold their leadership on the basis of class alone, *Motor Trend* road tests indicate that the prestige factor should enable them to stay out front for a long time to come." Later, the magazine selected Cadillac as Car of the Year.

Star of the 1953 line was the limited edition Eldorado, a custom convertible produced as Cadillac's version of the ultra-luxury cars typified by the Packard Caribbean, Kaiser Dragon, Buick Skylark, and Oldsmobile Fiesta. Only 532 Eldorados were built for 1953, all convertibles. The line boasted Cadillac's first wrap-around windshield, cut-down doors, and special interiors in posh leathers and cloths. Factory delivered price was similarly exclusive — $7,465. The Eldorado continued in this guise

On the facing page, the 1949 Series 62 sedanette. Above, a 1949 Coupe de Ville and, above right, a 62 sedan. Right, drawing for 1950 75 restyle.

Cadillac engines powered this variety of strong competitors in the early
fifties. Above, Briggs Cunningham's basically stock Coupe de Ville
for the 1950 Le Mans, and his special bodied "Le Manstre"
for the same race. At right, the legendary Cunningham C-3 sports
car, powered by the 331 c.i.d. Cadillac and extremely fast. On the facing
page, an Allard J-2 under Cadillac power at British rallye.

through 1955, whereupon it became an upper Cadillac series, still limited, for 1956, in both convertible and hardtop form. Still later it was to spawn the Eldorado Brougham of 1957–1960 and the front wheel drive Eldorado of the sixties.

The horsepower race was well under way by 1953, and Cadillacs were boosted to 210 bhp at 4,150 rpm to keep pace. The power increase and new electrical system represented all required changes, but except for a rise in compression to 8.25 in 1952 and an altered combustion chamber in 1953, alterations were confined to the breathing system — four-barrel carburetor, larger exhaust valves, dual exhausts, altered valve timing and lift. Fred Arnold stated, "The revolutionary technical idea Cadillac embodied in the first high compression engine of 1949 was that it be designed for change. . . . Design innovations were arranged to allow two important types of change: (1) increasing compression ratios year by year to take advantage of fuel octane improvements; (2) modifications of combustion chambers without basic redesign of the engine."

It seems from the specifications that the 1953 and 1954 models were actually identical in power output, although 230 bhp at 4,400 rpm was announced for the 1954 model, a twenty horsepower increase over 1953. "The 1953 engine was in-

tentionally underrated," wrote Evan Aiken in *Automobile Topics*. "The tooling, parts production, and assembly changes made in 1953 served a second year without interruption. All that had to be changed was the advertising."

Edward Gaylord took his stock engined 1953 Series 62 coupé to the Santa Ana, California, drag races. Even with the ultra-high axle ratio of 3.07, it set another stock car record. With its three-speed synchromesh transmission, it could do 65 mph in first, 113 in second, and 116 in high. These were timed speeds, not speedometer readings.

Chrysler Imperial models had 235 bhp in 1954, adopting a four-barrel carburetor with split intake manifolds, dual exhaust and large valves. The compression ratio remained at 7.5, and Cadillac engineers admitted that "the best ultra high speed power was obtained with a hemispherical head with vee valve arrangement." However, they maintained that these speeds were seldom in the operating range of passenger cars, and that the wedge head gave better combustion control. "The hemispherical chamber," wrote Cadillac engineer, Harvey L. Mantey, "has a higher peak pressure and is more sensitive to ignition by compression; and has no quench area to cool the last part of the charge. Extremely high rates of pressure rise occur at low engine speeds with resultant combustion roughness."

Restyling came again in 1954, with wrap-around windshield and the upswept "Dagmar" bumper with suppressed center section standard on all models. This was the first all-new body since 1950, with height reduced by half an inch, wheelbase increased by three inches, but overall body length the same. The grille changed to a fine texture type, thus starting a long tradition. Directional signals were repositioned and the air vents placed in the cowl directly under the windscreen — safe from traffic fumes. The wrapped windshield dominated the styling of the car, but other points were lowered relationship of the hood front to lights and grille, heavy emphasis on the rear deck, larger rear window to match the windshield, squared fins and round exhaust ports in the rear bumper, and air conditioning intake scoops behind the rear window on either side. The heating system was rearranged, with louvers at the sill line. Auxiliary controls for the air conditioning were placed on the rear package shelf. Automatic windshield washers were now standard. One push on the button started their cycle — squirt and wipe, water cut off, six more wipes and then stop. Power steering was also standard.

Science and Mechanics commented, "In the public mind a Cadillac represents — with good reason — just about everything that a motor car should be. The only trouble with staking a claim to the title of 'the finest' is that you have to start competing with

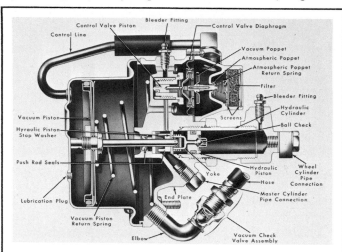

Above, the 1952 power braking system. Below, Cadillac's Debutante convertible complete with Somali leopard skin upholstery for the Motorama. At right, a bejeweled advertisement for the '50 model.

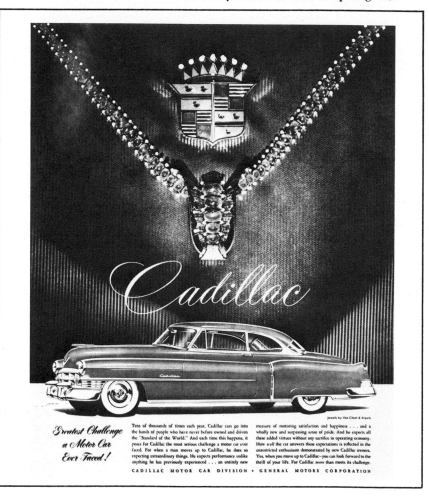

perfection itself — a hard task for any product. However, the Cadillac didn't fall too far short of the total performance ideal.

"Perhaps the most striking overall feature of this car is the manner in which all the functioning parts go about their tasks with such hushed and elegant competence that you're barely aware you're driving a complex machine. The silent engine, the almost inaudible wipers, the driving and operating controls doing their jobs quietly but surely, add up to true driving luxury."

Significant features included a four-way power adjusted front seat, air conditioning with switch-controlled engagement, power window lifts, the quality of the radio, "Autronic Eye" headlamp dimmer control with override for overtaking, and the safety-pad-

ded dash. Roadability was rated high: "You name the road — bumpy, rocky, washboard or whatever, and the Cadillac will take it in stride with a minimum of shock and vibration. Not a top performer on cornering, but its ability is good for a car of this size."

As so often happens with cars and humans, the Cadillac had put on weight with the years. Whereas the 1949 Series 62 had weighed around 4,200 pounds, the 1952 car scaled 4,500 and the 1954 model's *Motor Trend* test weight was 5,100. Nevertheless, because of the increased power, the performance considerably exceeded that of 1949 versions. The 1953–1954 models were the highest performing cars, despite air conditioning and other power

The Inaugural parade, January, 1953: President Dwight Eisenhower, his First Lady, and the Cadillac Eldorado.

accessories making them up to 600 pounds heavier. Zero to sixty in 1954 was 11.0 seconds, whereas in 1953 it was 13.2. The power was there!

Nineteen fifty-four production was limited to nine months because of a fire in GM's Hydra-Matic plant, but by converting to Dynaflow for the time being, it was possible to build 123,746 cars for the 1954 calendar year.

During the fifties, Cadillac built a number of experimental cars for those gaudy carnivals of girls, glitter, and gladiolas, the Motoramas. Notable among these were the Le Mans, Orleans, El Camino, La Espada, and Park Avenue. The Le Mans was the styling forerunner of the 1954–1956 line. The 1954 Eldorado limited production convertible closely resembled the Le Mans, though it was already in production in 1953, as previously mentioned.

Motor Trend's staff actually got to drive the Le Mans "sports prototype" at the GM Proving Grounds and reported "moderately sensitive steering and good roadholding, but definitely too heavy and spongy for competition." Its fiberglass body and 115-inch wheelbase made Le Mans 400 pounds lighter than a standard convertible, and a 9 to 1 compression with 250 horsepower at 4,500 rpm gave "surprising performance." *Road & Track* called the Le Mans "that thing," but felt the El Camino and La Espada were "beautifully done."

As the 1955's had the 250 hp rating of the experimental Le Mans, the Eldorado was boosted to 270, thanks to a carburetor arrangement of two four-barrel units. Even so, *Motor Trend* showed the standard sedan to accelerate marginally better, a half-second quicker from zero to sixty and one tenth of a second faster in the standing quarter mile.

While the Eldorado was priced at $6,331, prices for other models started at $3,927 for the 62 coupé. The Eldorado, however, came with all accessories standard except air conditioning. This cost $620. Sales for 1955 were a new high at 150,134 cars, with production at 153,334, another record.

Styling changes were slight: the "Florentine curve" roofline on the coupés was extended to the sedans, the chrome door strip line turned up at right angles on the rear door. The bumper bombs were bigger this year, and caused many complaints — from other car owners — due to parking damage.

This year Packard introduced its long-awaited new model with updated body styling, V-8 engine, and the revolutionary Allison "Torsion Level" ride. Packard's was acknowledged the best ride of any 1955 model, with good stability as well, and the cars maintained the usual Packard quality finish. But Packard

performance fell short of the Cadillac in acceleration and top speed, fuel economy was slightly inferior, and the new engine and suspension had more teething troubles than buyers were prepared to stand for — particularly from a Packard. The engine had a reputation in some quarters for "stabbing rods through the block." Despite the promise of its design, Packard was by now, unfortunately, not long for this world.

The 1956 Cadillacs introduced two new bodies, the Sedan de Ville four-door hardtop and a Vicodec cloth-covered hardtop version of the Eldorado named the "Seville." The Eldorado convertible was renamed the "Eldorado Biarritz," and both Eldorados featured an entirely different fin treatment, larger and longer, with both tail and directional lights on a paired housing at bumper level with fadeaway fairing into the fenders. (Someone at the A.M.A. name registration bureau must have slipped up this year, as DeSoto's Fireflite four-door hardtop also sported the "Seville" nameplate.)

The regular line compromised on Eldorado styling, with tail lights still in the fins, but directional signals at bumper level, oval in section, with fadeaway housings. Other features were the

On the facing page: 1953 Eldorado; LeMans show car with Ahrens driving, Roche standing. Above and below: a 1953 convertible, the LeMans.

twin-finned hood ornament on Eldorados and simulated spoke Kelsey-Hayes wheels. A new instrument panel and brocaded interiors on several models were also featured.

In 1956 production reached 140,873, and Cadillac built its millionth postwar car. The division had built the first million over forty-five years, but the second million had taken only seven!

For 1956 there was yet another advertised power increase — 285 bhp in the standard models, 305 on the Eldorados. This was obtained by a 3/16th-inch bore increase to four inches. Displacement was now 365 cubic inches. This was the first alteration in the original 1949 engine dimensions.

For 1957, the chassis had a new tubular X-type frame without side members, reminiscent of Mercedes designs, that allowed a three-inch height reduction in sedan models. Bodies were also completely new, incorporating many features of the Motorama Cadillacs and having a leaner, more attractive look in place of the ever-fatter, ever-bulkier models of the previous few years.

Particularly striking was the opposed angle of the windshield pillar at the front and the rear quarter panel at the rear door and

window. The grille texture was changed and the cowl vent recessed. All models now had low-mounted tail lights, with bare fins as on the 1956 Eldorados. Two different rear-end treatments were featured, the Eldorado's cigar-shaped in elevation with trunklid matching the line and inboard fins and the regular models with buttress-line fin and fuller trunklid style. Rubbertips on bumper bombs, like black bras, showed a belated concern by stylists for the other car's safety.

Ball-joint suspension with anti-dive geometry, same wheel tread front and rear with wider set rear springs, and the stiffer frame (sixteen percent over the old) gave improved handling with no loss of the happy compromise between soft and firm ride that had been notable on the models of the previous few years. The new frame carried the body on outriggers instead of its own frame rails.

Internally there was "safety-think," with recessed knobs, padding on the instrument panel, dished steering wheel, and floor-mounted parking brake. The fascia itself was much improved in layout, with the controls easier to identify, including power windows, washer-wiper, and air-conditioning knobs were better placed. (Air conditioning was now fully mounted under the cowl). Even the trunklid had an unlocking button on the dash, with warning light and two-way power assist. The radio fender antenna was also power operated.

A few years earlier, Cadillac workmanship had been criticized, but the standards of these models proved that Cadillac had mastered the difficult task of reproducing custom-type quality finish in a quantity produced car. Options and combinations of color and upholstery were sufficient for virtually any taste, and quality control excellent.

The biggest news for fans of mid-fifties gimcrackery and engineering innovation was the Eldorado Brougham, which had been announced for the 1957 model year after a lengthy gestation period. Actually the Brougham was preceded by the Park Avenue and Orleans show cars of 1954 and 1953. Cadillac had been watching Lincoln's plans to revive the Continental, and the Eldorado Brougham was their counter. Whereas the Continental was "modern formal" in concept, the Brougham was to be "modern technological."

Harley Earl had noted that while 1953 Motorama crowds had surged around the Le Mans, those who could "back up their approval with a check" paid closer attention to a less showy car over in a corner. This was the Orleans, America's first truly pillarless four-door sedan. The majority of prospects said they wanted four doors, four seats, and a metal roof. At the 1954

Show cars: the 1953 Orleans, left, a pillarless four-door, and the first (1955 Motorama) four-door hardtop Eldorado Brougham.

Motorama, reaction was similar — crowds surrounded the El Camino coupé and the La Espada roadster, but the well-heeled were interested in the Park Avenue show model. Earl made up his mind in the first half of 1954, recalling, "The first minutes of meetings concerning the Eldorado Brougham were recorded on May 4, 1954, and included preliminary specifications of the passenger compartment. The four-passenger seating was tentatively agreed upon as well as general seating dimensions. Shortly afterward the wheelbase and treads were pegged and a seating buck was fabricated with seats, steering wheel, and foot controls installed in accordance with our full-size layouts. At the same time I gave approval to start immediately on a full-size clay model."

The Cadillac studio under Ed Glowacke carried out the development, taking the upper structure of the Park Avenue with its brushed-aluminum (later stainless-steel) roof, but eliminating the side pillar and allowing the window frames to drop with the side glass. Vent panes were absent, their presence made less needful by integral air conditioning with heater as standard equipment.

"By August 10, 1954," continued Earl, "most major changes had been made. Rear overhang was reduced several inches to gain compact proportions and improve handling and parking. . . . Aircraft type air scoops were modelled on the upper front fender surfaces for pressurized ventilating. The model, at this point, was moved under wraps to the Styling Section auditorium and previewed by top management. The usual adjustments of major lines and surfaces were noted and the model was returned to the Cadillac studio for further refinement."

Meanwhile drawings of the various interior components, layout and trim were made, and seat contours designed. These were oversized and gave a feeling of extreme luxury enhanced by the selection of materials made from a variety of domestic and foreign suppliers. The interior clay buck was started in late September, 1954, and assembly began on November 6, when Cadillac delivered the special chassis and underbody to the studio. This was only seventy-four days before the Motorama.

The car was ready for paint on January 10, 1955, but was still in Detroit getting finishing touches on January 17, two days before the New York Motorama opened. Earl recalled "the thrill of seeing the finished car being hoisted into the van as the shipping deadline approaches, craftsmen still applying the finishing touches." His joy was hardly amplified when the car fell off its jacks at two in the morning of Show day. Some "pretty frantic" panel beating followed on the damaged fender and bumper. Yet when the invitational preview began — "a nice private little party of five thousand people" — the car was revolving quietly on its turntable as though nothing had happened. Public reaction ensured production of the Brougham, but tooling and design changes delayed announcement until December, 1956.

Typical of the Brougham's advanced thought was the brushed stainless-steel roof, quadruple headlight system, and air suspension. Of these, the lighting and suspension were the most influential. Quad lights permitted ideal design of each pair of lamps for one purpose — dip and high beam — instead of the compromise focus previously necessary, and the improved cooling allowed much higher wattage for better overall lighting. In 1958 quad lights became optional throughout most of the industry's

Predecessor to the Eldorado Brougham was the Park Avenue, left, of 1954. At right, a special 1954 for a Reynolds Aluminum president.

models.

The air suspension was literally the first in production anywhere, because Citroën's contemporary system, introduced in October, 1955, was hydro-pneumatic. Actually the Cadillac suspension went back further in origin, being based on the experience gained by GM's bus division. There, air suspension had been in use since 1952. The principle was old and experiments extended back many years earlier in several countries, but GM and Citroën were first to actually go into production.

The Cadillac air suspension was developed from a design produced by L. J. Keyhoe and V. D. Polhemus at GM's Technical Center. Both these men were Cadillac-trained, Keyhoe having joined GM in 1927 as a GM Institute co-op student sponsored by Cadillac, where he worked after graduation until 1940 on various studies, including high-speed handling problems. Polhemus had joined Cadillac in 1933 with a degree in mechanical engineering from Cincinnati, and worked at Cadillac as a laboratory assistant on engine function studies and transmission development. He and Keyhoe studied the GM Coach spring but decided it was unsuitable for scaling down into a passenger car. They produced a diaphragm-type spring which gave "reasonable cost and size, was capable of long life, adaptable to any type of suspension, its stroke could be varied easily and it produced the desired spring rate characteristics." Since longitudinal and lateral positioning were lost, a four-link rear axle location was devised for Hotchkiss drive cars. This system was then adapted to the Eldorado Brougham.

The Brougham's air suspension was designed by Lester D. Milliken and Fred H. Cowin, both at Cadillac. Milliken was a long-time Cadillac staff engineer. Cowin had joined Cadillac in 1941 as a laboratory technician. In 1946 he became a project engineer on brakes and ride engineering, and in 1950 assistant staff engineer supervising transmission, brakes, suspension, and steering developments. Later he was concerned with the tubular X frame, and low-profile tires in conjunction with the air suspension.

As laid out and developed by Cowin and Milliken, the system had at each wheel an air spring consisting of a dome air chamber, a rubber diaphragm, and a piston. Other principal components were an air compressor and accumulator, air piping, leveling valves, and solenoid controls. This provided a constant car height regardless of load, used the ride clearance more effectively, and made possible ten percent lower ride frequencies for greater passenger comfort.

The existing Cadillac front suspension was modified to accept either coil springs as before, or new air springs. The rear was entirely new, and also accepted either coils or air springs. The rear-link design in either condition had new advantages — independent control of roll center, lateral stiffness, and acceleration squat. It was superior to the previous arrangement. The Cadillac design differed from the central GM design in having a yoke in place of the upper two rear links and in using an open-type air system, where the inlet air for the compressor was taken from the atmosphere via the engine air cleaner, and exhausted to the atmosphere. This eliminated the low-pressure tank and plumbing required by the closed-circuit system. Although the standard coil-spring Cadillacs were built at the rate of 600 per day and the air-sprung Brougham at the rate of only three per day, the interchangeable design enabled both cars to be built on the same line.

Both American and English testers were impressed with the new air suspension, but not overly so, because as Joseph Lowrey wrote, "There was not, of course, a huge difference, for the ordinary Cadillac is by no means ill-sprung!" This applied to good roads, but on rough roads there was a "real, even amazing improvement," and *Motor Trend* said that the only other suspension that could equal it was Citroën's. Probably the most worthwhile gain was the constant-level ride, which applied to all conditions and not to just some.

Another was the "quick jack-up." By operating a handle under the dash the driver could actuate the lift-valve, fully pressurize the suspension, and so raise the car to clear deep rutted road centers and back easily out of steep driveways. Eventually, however, the air suspension was abandoned. It had some bugs arising from its "air-breathing" principle — moisture and freezing were two, and while it had certain advantages, the overall result did not justify the cost and complexity. One payoff, however, was the rear suspension linkage, which was retained with steel springs and improved the rear-end road behavior of the car. It continues to this day. Another, revived a few years later, was the constant-level ride feature, based on air-suspension experience, but used with steel springing.

After only four years, however, air suspension was dropped. Ed Cole comments: "As far as the system was concerned it gave outstanding capability [in] ride leveling and damping. The only problem was with air leaks, usually around the fittings or valves, which let the car's suspension relax and bottom out. Further, it became quite complicated and costly for the benefit it provided in leveling and riding comfort. Therefore it was abandoned."

The Brougham was produced for four years, during which less than 1,000 cars were built — 400 in 1957, 304 in 1958, 99 in 1959, and 101 in 1960. The original price was scheduled at $8,500, but the ultimate figure was $13,074, well above even the Continental Mark II's $10,000 and a record price for a postwar American car. This figure was probably the major reason for its low sales, and the Brougham can be written off as a corporate engineering, styling, and prestige exercise which Cadillac might never have put into production except for the Continental Mark II. It was usually underplayed in Cadillac catalogues, which described it only briefly and referred prospects to dealers for details.

For the first and second years, Broughams were entirely hand built in Detroit, but after that and following a styling change, the

Two show cars: the La Espada, above, and the El Camino, below — 1954.

crated chassis were shipped to Italy for bodies by Pininfarina. These 1959 and 1960 Broughams were actually only a token retention of the Brougham line, with minor identification to separate them visually from other Cadillacs, and somewhat more luxurious interiors. Whether the switch to Turin was to take advantage of cheaper Italian labor, or to avoid tying up the Fleetwood plant with a special body produced only in a trickle, or to give the car's image a lift with a foreign accent, is not clear. The cost saving of foreign labor would probably have been offset by the shipping expenses, and even when Broughams returned from Italy, they still required final touch-up in Detroit where they were given finishing lacquer, polishing, and tune. An interesting commentary on the difference in workmanship and execution is reflected in the prices paid by collectors years afterward. Fleetwood-built models fetch four or five times the price of Turin-bodied versions, which are considered far less distinctive and desirable by enthusiasts — as indeed they are. Also worthy of note is the fact that only the 1957–1958 Brougham, not the 1959–1960, has been cited by The Milestone Car Society, which is dedicated to the distinctive domestic and foreign motorcars

From top: 1956 Eldorado, de Ville, show town car.

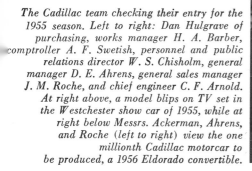

The Cadillac team checking their entry for the 1955 season. Left to right: Dan Hulgrave of purchasing, works manager H. A. Barber, comptroller A. F. Swetish, personnel and public relations director W. S. Chisholm, general manager D. E. Ahrens, general sales manager J. M. Roche, and chief engineer C. F. Arnold. At right above, a model blips on TV set in the Westchester show car of 1955, while at right below Messrs. Ackerman, Ahrens, and Roche (left to right) view the one millionth Cadillac motorcar to be produced, a 1956 Eldorado convertible.

built during the first two postwar decades.

Summarizing the Brougham technically, its list of "firsts" is impressive. In addition to those already mentioned, it featured an early version of the "wide oval" tire (a low-profile, standard-width section giving improved steering), automatic trunk lid, automatic "memory" seat, and air conditioning as standard. One owner, calling it "the most luxurious and complex automobile ever built in America," admitted that he was glad he was an automotive engineer. But he refused to part with his car.

Actually, standard Cadillac models during 1957–1960 shared most of the Brougham's "exclusive features," and this period saw the introduction of "Cruise Control," high-pressure cooling (15 p.s.i. and 245° operating temperature), two-speaker radio with automatic signal-seeking tuner, and automatic-release parking brake.

Styling changes for 1958 were confined to revised front and rear ends with altered body trim. Quad headlights, redesigned bumpers with lower bumper guards, a new grille texture, and rear slanting fins on all models were the main changes. Power window controls now extended to the front vent windows, and four-door models had power-vent windows in the rear as well. Electric door locks were optional on power window models and new molded fiberglass headliner was used on the hardtops. Stylish, practical, and easy to clean, it made the interior quieter with its sound-absorbent qualities.

The Biarritz and Seville Eldorado models had distinctive styling features — special trim on the rear quarter panels and their own bumpers. Cape Buffalo leather in grained or metallic finish, or combinations of leather and metallic threaded nylon upholstery options were available on these models.

On the Fleetwood Series 60 Special, an extruded aluminum panel across the rear quarter, repeated on the rear deck, and a stainless-steel rocker sill molding below the doors were identifying marks.

The Eldorado Brougham had its own styling/technical features, such as a rear quarter panel window which automatically slid back to ease passenger entry when the door was opened, returning when the door was closed. It could also be opened from the inside in the usual way. The Brougham's mouton carpeting and high-quality broadcloth upholstery were matched in the trunk by nylon frieze material which covered the entire interior — deck lid, spare tire, and battery cover included.

In 1959 engine size went up to 390 cubic inches, with two different horsepower ratings. There were improvements in the shock absorbers and power steering, and fourteen models in four series were available. This year saw the tail fins reach a literally ridiculous height, from whence they began a gradual decline starting in 1960, reaching a subdued form by 1964. The fins had plenty of critics, including this writer, as did the dummy rear grille featured that year, and they were dropped quickly. Nevertheless the 1959's, overall, were excellent and some of their styling features were successfully carried forward into later models. As cars — rocket fins or not — they were undeniably excellent.

The 1960 line came in thirteen models in three standard and one custom series. The 62 coupé and sedan, the Coupe de Ville, and Eldorado Seville, all had the same upper structure as in 1959, with the sweep-down rear window line. The 62 models were offered with interiors of fawn, blue or gray Cortina cord, and also turquoise, green, Persian sand, or Black Caspian cloth. All had Florentine grain vinyl bolsters in complementary colors. The 60 Special offered a handfitted fabric roof cover and a choice of ten interiors. The Sedan de Ville offered combinations of Cambray cloth and leather, and the Eldorado Seville had a textured vinyl fabric top. Eldorado models were available in fifteen standard and five special colors. Interiors were available in cloth and leather. The 62 sedan and Sedan de Ville had a new single rear window curving completely around the rear quarter panels and a straight-topped roofline overhang. De Villes offered Chadwick cloth interiors, while convertibles were upholstered in Florentine leather in single or two-tone combinations, or in one-tone Cardiff leather.

The Fleetwood 75 limousine offered passenger accommodations in Bradford cloth and wool or Bedford cord and wool. The chauffeur's compartment was trimmed in Florentine leather.

Car Life, in rating Cadillac "the best buy in the luxury field," commented that the marque was "still the champ." Tester Jim Whipple complained about rear seat exit and entry that "required planning," and conceded that quantitatively — in ride, handling, and performance — there was little to choose between the Cadillac and a Lincoln or Chrysler Imperial. "The differences which put Cadillac ahead are qualitative — a matter of fit, finish, and workmanship. Cadillac is my pick in the way it is made." The paint job was "near to perfection. . . . Quality of metal finishing and fit of panels and trim strips is unequalled. . . .

Upholstery is without peer this side of the Atlantic. This true quality of product in the Cadillac makes it the best buy."

In England a year later, *The Autocar* ran an extensive test on a Series 75 nine-passenger limousine weighing over 6,000 pounds with air suspension. "The Cadillac," they said, "follows the tradition of fine cars in seeming to grow progressively smaller the farther one drives. It has a precision and ease of control which make it simpler — and much more enjoyable — to drive than many a car of lesser dimensions. . . . In almost every respect the mechanical behaviour of the Cadillac conforms with the highly civilized luxury of its appointments. It cruised at a true 100 mph with less noise than any car we can remember and reached 120 mph without vibration or stress. . . . At such speeds it ran true as an arrow."

The Brougham was a "lead" to the styling of the next year's Cadillacs, although air suspension was dropped for them, and the 1961 models adopted the 1960 Brougham's general lines. The wrap-around windshield was replaced by the Brougham design, which was actually similar to the standard model rear window of 1960.

Only the Fleetwood 75 retained the wrap-around windshield. In addition to a new upper structure, changes were made in the lower panels, front-end treatment, and rear fenders. A beveled-side style was adopted and continued around the rear, which had horizontal oval tail-light clusters. Some interiors on closed cars were finished in Canberra or Chilton cloth, with similar Cambridge cloth options on the 60 Special, Covington Coronel or Cromwell cloth on the Coupe de Ville, and Calais cord or broadcloth on the Fleetwood 75. Open cars had Florentine leather in eight selections or ostrich grain leather in eight selections and twelve different colors.

The 1962 models were little changed from 1961 in appearance, but featured cornering lights and dual-circuit braking. This year saw a production run of 158,528 units.

Despite the steadily climbing production, quality of manufacture was carefully watched. In 1960, Harold G. Warner, Cadillac general manager, gave a detailed description of the manufacture of Cadillac cylinder heads, and *Automotive Industries* reported that "Cadillac manufacturing methods on engine production equal virtual aircraft engine specification refinement." Warner pointed out that this was necessary to obtain the closest control of combustion and insure uniformity in all cylinders.

"Our cylinder head development involved planning a closely controlled process which would give us extreme precision and a high degree of finish. The first operations are the rough and finish machining of all areas, including combustion chambers, to good commercial tolerances. The matter was not allowed to rest here, however. Another group of machines was added to precision re-machine the combustion chambers and joint surfaces. This gave us finishes, volumetric and surface accuracy beyond those normally associated with automobile manufacture."

Immediately preceding this finishing operation, the cylinder heads were put through an automatic parts washer of the latest type in order that no metal particles from previous operations could interfere with the accurate locations or mar the finishes. Following the finishing operations, they were again washed, completely checked with precision air gauges, and assembled. For absolute cleanliness each head assembly, after inspection, was placed in a covered container where it remained untouched until delivery to the engine assembly point. As another example of quality workmanship, the valve guide bushing inside diameter and valve seat were precision machined in the same operation. This assured concentricity of valve stem and valve seat and a perfect valve seal. In the same process, the cylinder head spring surface was finish machined to control a precision tolerance from the valve seat to the spring seat — thus ensuring equal valve spring load throughout all valve springs.

Contemporary Rolls-Royce advertising was stressing quality and precision in manufacture, citing the well-publicized "walnut husk powder" blasting of oil passages in their license-built version of Cadillac's Hydra-Matic "brain box," along with other examples of Old World craftsmanship. Warner was asked by the press how Cadillac and Rolls-Royce manufacturing standards compared. Although experienced in the British auto industry, having worked at Vauxhall, Warner was reluctant to be specifically critical. He merely said that "eyebrows had been raised" at Cadillac over the walnut husks, and forebore mention of the disastrous results of Rolls-Royce efforts to "improve" the Hydra-Matic. (In this episode, the British engineers finally admitted that the Hydra-Matic was the world's best engineered automatic transmission — just as it stood.)

Pressed further on the subject of "hand-finishing," Warner retorted, "The best hand-finishing cannot equal the precision machine tool, either in initial accuracy or from the standpoint of consistently repeating that accuracy." Regarding the lengthy "running-in" of engines as favored by Rolls-Royce, Warner remarked, "We run an engine long enough to check if everything is OK, and no longer. The only reason for lengthy running-in these days is because you didn't build the engine well enough to begin with." All Cadillac engines were run on the dynamometer,

A 1957 Eldorado Brougham contrasts with outline of 1941 Cadillac.

From top: 1957-59-60 Eldorado Broughams. Below: 1958 Sixty Special.

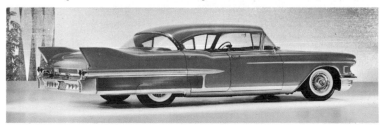

Design phases of the 1959 model: above and below, sketches; right, wood mock-up.

...ve, the 1959 undergoes structural tests. Below, the 1960 Fleetwood Sixty Special.

but mainly for performance checks and adjustments. Normal dyno time was fifteen to twenty minutes, but up to four hours might be spent on a particular engine if required. Running-in was unnecessary because of the super-precision manufacture of all bearing surfaces. The cars could be safely driven at any speed on delivery, although it was suggested that the new owner vary his speed in the first hundred miles to ensure ample lubrication.

Indirectly confirming Warner's claim, John R. Bond later wrote, "The bores for the five main bearing inserts are machined three times: rough bore, finish bore, then honed! Bearing tolerance is only four ten-thousandths inch per inch diameter — undoubtedly the closest fit in the industry."

Dan Cordtz in *The Wall Street Journal* wrote that while Cadillac's own officials admitted to him that replacements of faulty transmissions in one year had cost the division plenty, James Roche's claim that "quality-consciousness" permeated the whole organization was not merely sales puff:

"Most of the professional authorities who test Detroit's products agree that Mr. Roche and his organization attain their goal," he wrote. "Cadillac aims for greater-than-average quality by special attention to detail, closer tolerances in all specifications, more thorough training of workmen, and more assembly-line inspectors (15 percent of the staff) than in lower priced car divisions. The car's engine, for example, meets U.S. Commerce Department aircraft specifications.

"The name, of course, is used to identify the best in many fields and foreign friends and foes alike use Cadillac as the symbol of American wealth and materialism. GM's prestige car rolls serenely along in good years and bad — an international symbol of success. In spite of the strongly running trend to economy in transportation, it's a safe bet that one out of every 40 cars sold in the United States this year will bear the familiar crest. . . . In 1959, a mediocre car year, 133,733 Cadillacs were sold — more than double the total volume attained by all other high-priced cars ($5,000 and up) put together, including such imports as Rolls-Royce and Mercedes.

"Cadillac in recent years has withstood industry slumps better than most other makes. In 1958, for example, total new car registrations dropped 22 percent from 1957, but Cadillac's decline was only 13 percent."

Why is Cadillac so successful, he asked — answering himself by saying the question was complicated, but that the main reasons included prestige, genuine comfort and luxury, generally excellent quality of construction, good performance and relative economy, and a very good resale value.

CHAPTER TWELVE

MAINTAINING THE STANDARD

The key to success: dedicated personnel at every level, a great car every year

Cadillac is traditionally the best car in America," wrote the great English technical journalist Laurence Pomeroy. "Built to high standards both mechanically and in respect of coachwork, and fitted with every conceivable refinement including air-conditioning, it is a car particularly recommended for the international driver who wishes to cruise quietly at 100 mph."

Pomeroy was describing the 1962 models, which took the original 1949 V-8 engine to its limit. Despite redesigns and refinements since, the general layout remains even today a recognizable development of the 1949 design—"a remarkable tribute," wrote John Bond, "to the perspicacity of its original designers."

The first major overall change came in 1963. Although the bore and stroke remained unchanged at 4.000 by 3.875, all components excepting valves, rocker arms, cylinder heads, and rods were new. The change came as a result of two coincident lines of thought — production men who were ready for all-new tooling, and engineers of the design staff who had fresh ideas for another step forward in powerplant practice.

The initial step was an all-new cylinder block, lower, shorter, stiffer, and lighter. Accompanying this was a new crankshaft, cast in GM ArmaSteel, much stiffer because of its 3.000-inch main bearings (increased from 2.625 inches) yet eleven pounds lighter. The entire accessory layout was redesigned for accessibility; it was grouped at the front, made of die-cast alloy and saved weight and space. Many detail refinements were also introduced throughout the engine and its auxiliaries. All these changes resulted in an engine more rugged and efficient than before, easier to make, and which reversed weight growth, back to a point actually lower than that of 1949. The original 331-inch engine had weighed 612 pounds, and had grown to 652 by 1962.

The 1963 390-inch engine weighed only 600 pounds. Although cast iron, it was actually one hundred pounds lighter than the smaller (380-cubic-inch) Rolls-Royce "light alloy" V-8!

Despite the very large diameter main bearings, production engines showed no increase in friction losses, John Bond noted, attributing this to "super accurate machining and rigid construction." Much of the engine assembly area was air conditioned to maintain a constant temperature, and give maximum precision in measurements. "The secret is superior manufacture and assembly," wrote Roger Huntington. "It's a well-engineered engine that's built right."

One interesting test comment was that while the new engine made the car smoother and quieter inside, it was slightly more audible outside than previously, mainly because of a more definite exhaust note at idle.

One owner-enthusiast friend of the author reported that contemporary Cadillac folklore held that a weakness of the cars of 1960 lay in the cylinder heads, which were prone to give trouble in time, especially when raced; that the '63's weakness was in the pistons (if pushed hard enough for long enough); and that the 429 motor was markedly less economical than the 390 and earlier engines. All were agreed, however, that all engines were good for high mileages.

"For years," he commented, "I was strongly anti-Cadillac on the theory that they were enlarged, better trimmed and more expensive Chevrolets. I've changed my mind. I got one because I wanted a big car to drive east across the country and it amused me to confound my friends, who are still horrified by my fall from small-car grace. The experience of driving this one has convinced me it is a better car. It swoops one along the highway in

At left, the Cadillac for 1962 at the General Motors Proving Ground. At right, interior views of the 1962 convertible.

silence and reminds me of the overdrive cars I've owned in the sensation of gliding you get on the open road.

"In one day we drove from Billings, Montana, to Seattle, Washington, 842 miles, arriving eleven P.M. Through Southeastern Oregon I covered seventy-eight miles in one hour. We had covered 10,852 miles in less than six weeks. I'm afraid that even flow of power tempts me too often to use it to the detriment of economy, but the mileage never went below ten mpg even though it was driven fast consistently and most of the time the air conditioning was on. We had a heavy load — eight suitcases, a tent, six sleeping bags, cooking gear and food, dishes, a portable icebox, propane stove, and the host of odds and ends for six people going camping."

In 1964 the bore and stroke became 4.00 by 4.13 (429 cubic inches) and power and performance went up with displacement. *The Autocar* tested a 1964 Coupe de Ville and recorded a mean top speed of 121.5 mph, with a best run at 123 mph in "contemptuous ease." The standing quarter mile was covered in seventeen seconds, and one hundred miles an hour came up in just under thirty. Yet this performance was achieved with "very little mechanical fuss or disturbance. . . . Inertia that pulls one back firmly in the seat is the main evidence that one is being rushed from a standstill. The big V-8 engine is a paragon of unobtrusiveness, with a surge of power always in reserve . . . an almost silent source of energy that one can regulate at will." *The Autocar* was particularly impressed with the "outstanding precision and sensitivity" of the power steering, the stability in both straight lines and cornering, and comfort on normal roads. They were less happy with the suspension over rough going, and found the braking powerful but prone to fade under repeated hard usage. "But," the magazine continued, "these are special circumstances that cannot take precedence over the car's usual

The 1962 Series 62 four-window sedan.

The 1964 Cadillac Coupe de Ville.

The 1961 Cadillac six-window sedan.

The 1964 Fleetwood Eldorado convertible.

habitat, when it would be difficult to better for restful motoring."

Another criticism was detail body finish, which although "not so meticulous as European equivalents," was qualified in relation to retail price, "which in this country and with a stiff import duty included, is still far below what must be paid for the classiest home product. Moreover, it has several luxuries that cannot be had at any price in European cars." Several of these — six-way adjustable steering wheel, special lighting equipment, cruise control, and other "sophisticated gadgets" — were cited, but Comfort Control headed the list as "surely the most outstanding of all Cadillac's contributions to motoring well-being." The driver had only to dial-a-temperature, and never need touch the control again. Thermisters, based on the principle of analog computors, cleaned, dehumidified and maintained air temperature automatically.

Of ten German, British and American luxury cars tested by *The Autocar* over a lengthy period, the Cadillac was rated as "the most comfortable and easiest to control. Difficult to better for restful motoring, the car feels smaller than it is. Things have progressed somewhat since those first single-cylinder Cadillacs of the early 1900's," they concluded, "but one has the impression that behind all the gracious motoring and flashing performance of this great car, the hardware's just as good as ever. As a dynamic object, it represents the highest standards attainable in most important respects."

The continuing sales climb demanded factory expansion and in December, 1962, general manager Harold Warner announced a project adding 411,000 square feet of floor space and the conversion of over 200,000 square feet to manufacturing. Space was cramped, and so was room to expand — the confined area occupied for more than forty years dictated that if Cadillac stayed at the old stand, the only way to go was up. Modernization of key

The 1965 Fleetwood Eldorado convertible.

buildings had to be carried out while they continued in operation. So executives worked in various warehouses and cubicles, and others of the office staff were spread along hallways and in storerooms. Cadillacs were built to the sound of construction cranes, pneumatic hammers, and cement mixers. A 300,000 square-foot engineering center was built on an old parking area. Half at a time, the administration building was stripped and rebuilt, and a fifth floor added to both administrative and manufacturing buildings. The old engineering building was converted to assembly operations and a new paint shop built on top of the manufacturing building. Seven and a half miles of conveyors were installed, a new floor-type final assembly line was built, and engine facilities extended twenty-five percent by relocating in a newer building that was formerly a press shop. These arrangements gave Cadillac an almost self-contained facility, the only outside division section being a parts warehouse, a press plant, and the Fisher Body Fleetwood plant some miles away on Detroit's west side. The last 1964 model built actually left the line as cutting torches and excavators for the new conveyor pits moved in. Six weeks later, on August 24, the first 1965 model came off the line.

There were many changes for 1965. The engine was the same, but the X-frame was replaced by a perimeter-type based on other GM designs already in use, but structurally different. Fully boxed from front to rear, it was still 300 pounds lighter than the previous frame. Rolling with the punch, it was deliberately made more flexible and the body phased to vibrate at a different frequency so that the worst road shocks could not produce a phased and therefore exaggerated vibration. Instead of one big vibration, there were two smaller ones. Handling remained satisfactory in spite of the change, since there were various suspension and steering improvements, a wider front track and improved tire design.

A new Turbo-Hydramatic combined the best features of the 1964 Turbo, plus the dual-range braking of the older Hydra-Matics, and various other improvements. The engine-transmission unit, carried on "pheasant-tail" mounts, was six inches further forward in the frame — without, it was claimed, disturbing previous weight distribution. A single-piece driveshaft replaced the earlier two-piece shaft. The rear suspension linkage was redesigned, and the Delco superlift shock absorbers had automatic height control with pneumatic adjustment via a leveling valve, vacuum-operated compressor and air reservoir.

A restyle almost eliminated the famous fins and made the car look lower and longer. The new grille was broader and bolder and the rear treatment all new. Eleven body styles were offered, using the same basic shell as the Buick Electra but in the distinctively chiseled Cadillac style.

Overall, the car continued its traditional compromise approach, in a very successful attempt to offer the best all-round balance of automobile excellence. One experienced driver commented: "We couldn't actually rate the car as the best we've driven in any one major aspect. Chrysler's 300 L is a better road car, Lincoln provides greater driver comfort and Imperial has a roomier passenger compartment. But the Cadillac is above average in every one of these areas. If each of its competitors can surpass it on individual points, it can equal or better them in its combination of qualities." One consumer magazine, stating at the outset that it was against the whole luxury-car idea, since its primary attraction was prestige and not practical factors, still admitted that while some of the Cadillac's features were over-elaborate, its standards of mechanical excellence and luxury were so high that they were a positive enjoyment to the driver, regardless of his reasons for buying the car. Slyly, several magazines even complained that the level of luxury was too high, and became soporific. They recommended a pin for the seat-warmer, to jab the driver occasionally and keep him awake, or a Cruise-Control that would sometimes reach out and tickle the driver's foot. "Silky-smooth, utterly obedient power and luxury has become as much a Cadillac trademark as the name itself," said *Car Life*. "It is a road tester's cliche to describe in dazzled awe the Splendid Sensations of Driving a Cadillac — and yet the car's silence, responsiveness, and sheer comfort exist and must be recognized."

One example of the lengths Cadillac was prepared to go was the "mink test." Mink swatches were rubbed over all new upholstery materials and checks made to determine whether the fur was caught, discolored, or unduly worn. Mink-dressed models were taken for fifty-mile rides during which the girls got in and out, lounged, sat up, and did all manner of acts to check compatibility of materials. How far Cadillac test drivers participated in these "tests" has never been revealed, but materials which failed to pass muster were out, naturally.

The three millionth car was built on November 4, 1964, and production for 1965 was 181,435 cars. But, with the options available, Cadillac publicly claimed that it could build three years' full production without exactly duplicating a single car. Each one was made to order, with customers specifying color, equipment, and interiors. There were 171 interior trim combinations with extensive use of leather, which was specified in

thirty-eight percent of all Coupe de Villes. Air conditioning was standard in eighty-three percent of 1965 production. Since Harold Warner was a hi-fi and stereo enthusiast, it was inevitable that Cadillac would be equipped with one of the finest AM-FM stereo radios available, with four speakers and of concert quality.

The electric seat warmer, which held a temperature of 100° F, was first offered optionally on the 1966 models. Standard was variable-ratio power steering, with increasing response to left or right and only 2.4 turns lock to lock compared with 3.6 the previous year. In this year the demand for air conditioning increased to eighty-eight percent. The 75 limousine, which had retained the X-frame and had not had a major body change since 1959, got both a new body and a perimeter frame, while the Fleetwood Brougham became a new, twelfth model. Styling changes on the regular line were minor, but new sales and production records were set.

To combat the oohing and aahing going around the automotive press over the superior engineering and workmanship of some imports, Cadillac publicity eased up on its symbolism and snob appeal, began to let a little substance into its ads, even allowing technical data to leak out. This, of course, was calculated to do the same for Cadillac's image as the earlier approach, only aimed at aficionados rather than matrons and bankers.

Cadillac pointed out that the exhaust vents for its air conditioning were selected only after wind-tunnel tests revealed the correct low-pressure areas, that its universal joint was an expensive nylon-sealed, double-cardan, constant-velocity type to

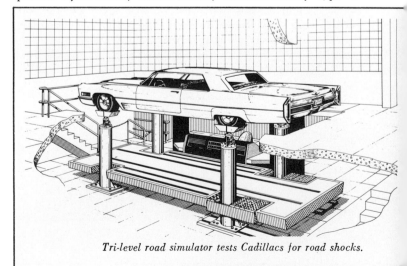

Tri-level road simulator tests Cadillacs for road shocks.

eliminate variations in driveshaft speed, that the chassis had Teflon inserts at every friction point, that there were hard gold contact points in the voltage regulator to eliminate sticking, that wristpin installation was accurate to five one-hundred-thousandths of an inch, that the accelerator pedal shaft was stainless steel to avoid sticking from corrosion by road salt, and that intricate air gauges were used to check the accuracy of the cylinder bores and pistons. Harold Warner claimed that the engine was so well balanced (electronically), it never stopped twice in exactly the same place in its cycle. He also mentioned testing of the Climate Control — cars were taken to a cold part of Canada, then driven to Texas and Florida. In this variation from 28° below zero to 90° above, the unit had to maintain temperatures within three degrees of the setting, measured at ankle height and at head height. Humidity was maintained at fifty-five percent inside even when reaching ninety percent outside.

The "difference" even extended to the Cadillac paint shop, where filtered air directed downward kept things so clean that "a Cadillac painter wearing a white shirt can paint black cars all day and stay nice."

After visiting Cadillac's facilities and seeing, among other things, a $250,000 road simulator which held the car on four pistons and could reproduce any road surface in the world by tape, without the car even moving out of the garage, one independent European tester revised his views on the merits of "certain top luxury cars from across the pond who wouldn't even begin to afford the facilities Cadillac has." Later, another

authority confirmed the point by admitting, not too readily, that a certain German maker was adopting certain Detroit development techniques that had been in use at Cadillac for years.

Despite all the sophisticated technology, however, Warner claimed that Cadillac's 10,400 employees were its greatest asset. They tended to be long-service types, above average in experience, and were given twice as long to do their jobs on the assembly line compared to workers on lower-priced makes. This seems true. For example, the writer, visiting the plant, watched women aiming headlights. They did the job unhurriedly, efficiently, yet still had time to spare before the next car came along.

The human element was still used when it counted, said manufacturing manager George Elges. After being electronically balanced, the crankshaft was further checked by a veteran skilled worker, who turned it over by hand. "If it doesn't feel right to him," said Elges, "we'll turn it down."

Warner even went so far as to say that only Cadillac workmen could build a Cadillac — a comment that no doubt could be made with equal sincerity by several of Warner's opposite numbers — at Lincoln, for example. Nevertheless, much of this professional pride had a sound basis. Of Cadillac's 10,400 employees, 1,500 are of twenty-five years tenure or more, and 1,500 do nothing but inspection work. Every car passes 23,000 inspection checks — not too great when its 15,000 or more components are considered — 300 checks as a complete car, and a roller test. Additional checks include a Final Car Audit of a

Testing methods. Left, observing response to road simulator. Right, using radioactive isotopes to check Cadillac oil consumption.

1966 De Ville convertible and Fleetwood Brougham (right).

percentage of cars selected at random by the Reliability Division, another check for all cars at the shipping area, and a constant program of "take-home" checks by company executives daily. Before World War II, every car was road-tested on the highway by plant test staff, but with today's production such tactics, even if feasible, would hardly meet the approval of Detroit's traffic authorities. Methods have therefore been introduced that eliminate the necessity for road testing, and even the dealer, who could easily assist in this area, normally has no more to do than remove the utility shipping carpets and replace them with the proper ones stowed in the trunk. That and any minor adjustments are usually all the dealer need do. Many cars, usually about thirty daily, go straight from the plant to owners taking delivery on the spot. One Detroit reporter gibed that the owners' lounge at the plant reminded him of the delivery room in a posh hospital.

Many visitors follow conducted tours around the plant to see how a Cadillac is made. There are places they do not see, of course, where Cadillacs are engineered and designed. Engineering is carried out at the 339,000-square-foot, two-story engineering center at the plant itself, while styling is done at the GM Technical Center in Warren, Michigan. Both interior and exterior Cadillac design originates at Warren, sketches and air brush renderings eventually becoming clay. Fiberglass models complete with chrome and glass follow, and then the main plant engineering staff takes up the thread of development. Full-scale drawings are made in the huge central drawing office, where a Calcomp computerized drafting machine assists the designers in preparing detail drawings for the wood models, metal shop and space buck. From the wood "Keller" models (so named for a practice originated by a die-maker named Keller), plaster and fiberglass molds are prepared for the manufacturing dies.

Meanwhile, the engineering groups have been developing their various designs under separate specialist headings — engine, body, chassis, transmission, and electrical components. These are tested under laboratory and dynamometer conditions, including eleven different dynamometers for engine work alone, the "hot" test room, the "cold" test room, ad infinitum. Prototype cars go to the GM Proving Grounds at Milford, Michigan, and Phoenix, Arizona. Analysis of field recording is quickly made up by the computer application group. Following this, when a design has passed its field testing, the production group have their say in making the prototype specifications a manufacturing reality.

Manufacture of a Cadillac is a lengthy process. From five to seven days is spent in processing and building a Cadillac body to order. This order, from the dealer via the factory sales distribution department, is actually the genesis of a car. While the standard bodies come from Fisher Fleetwood only three miles away in Fort Street, Eldorado bodies come from Fisher Body in Euclid, Ohio. Each body, coded with a "broadcast number" teletyped to all departments involved in its building, is ready for final assembly when it arrives at Clark Street.

The engine is the next longest a-building. Blocks arrive from

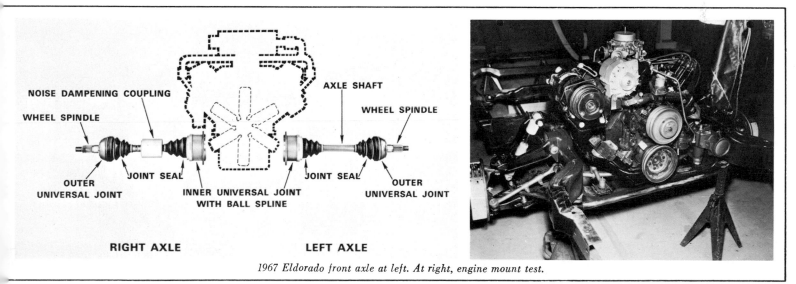

1967 Eldorado front axle at left. At right, engine mount test.

the Ohio Central foundry and are cleaned by a large filtration system. All machining is done in the plant, as is assembly, balancing, inspecting, testing, tuning, and final adjustment. At some fifty or sixty engine bays men start each engine and check against their standard test sheets. Defective items such as carburetors are relegated to the reject stand with tags reading "floods," "no adjustment," etc.

Chassis are inverted for ease of assembly of suspension linkage and rear axle, then turned over. The engine and drive line are installed, followed by gas tank, exhaust, and wheels. Then the body — with dash, trunk lid, doors, seats, and upholstery and all wiring, firewall equipment and brake booster — is dropped on. Radiator and air conditioning equipment go in. Other body parts such as hood and fenders are then attached, followed by grille and bumpers. Clearances and alignments are checked at appropriate points.

The completed car, filled with gas and water, comes to the end of the line and has its roller tests, where wheel alignment, steering and braking are checked, including simulated high speeds in reverse. After that it visits the "Minor Repair Area," for work involving one or two hours only. Anything longer goes to the "Major Repair" section. Signs suggest "Let's Do The Job Right First Time," and "Teamwork Does The Job Well." Each mechanic is allowed as much time as is required to get the car perfect. After that come cleaning and final inspection, and the new Cadillac is ready for trucking to the dealer or for factory delivery to its actual owner.

In 1965, chief engineer Fred Arnold retired. The holder of nine patents, he had long been a member of the SAE and the Engineering Society of Detroit. Arnold also took an active interest in community activities and devoted himself to a variety of charitable institutions and civic endeavors, notably the Michigan Cancer Foundation, the Boys Club of Detroit, and the Detroit Department of Streets and Traffic. He was succeeded by Carleton A. Rasmussen. Born in Clintonville, Wisconsin, Rasmussen was a graduate of Purdue University and joined Cadillac in 1940 as a laboratory technician. The following year, Harold Warner was succeeded as general manager by Calvin J. Werner. Born in Dayton, Ohio, in 1907, Werner earned a degree in electrical engineering at the University of Cincinnati and joined Delco in 1923 as a tool-maker apprentice. From Delco he became general manager of Moraine Products Division in 1955, and of GMC Truck and Coach Division in 1959 before coming to Cadillac.

Nineteen sixty-seven saw the introduction of the Eldorado

Above, full size clay model of XP-727 #2, an Eldorado forecast, 1961. Below, a four-door exercise, XP-727 #3, highly finished, 1962.

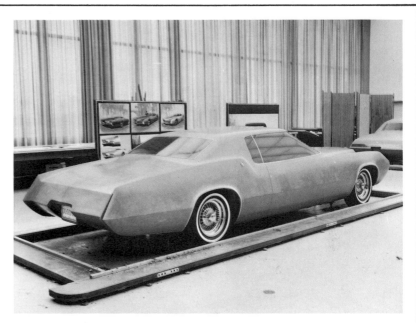

The fiberglass shell (left above) from which production Eldorado dies were made was developed from the XP-820 (right above) begun in late 1963. Other interim design proposals included the XP-784 (left below), the first design conceived from the outset for F.W.D., and XP-825 (right below).

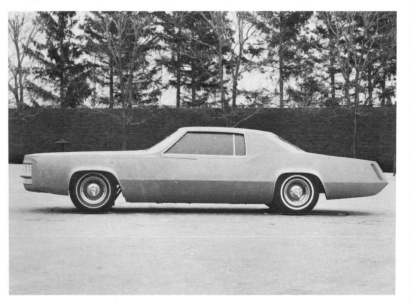

front-drive "personal car." Like the Olds' Toronado introduced the previous year, it used the f.w.d. package developed by GM Central Research. Staff engineer Lester Milliken, a specialist in vehicle dynamics and handling, and other members of Cadillac's design group, had worked with Central Research on the project. The Eldorado, however, actually began at Cadillac during the period of the Eldorado Brougham. In 1959, assistant chief engineer Dan Adams and assistant general sales manager Tom La Rue worked out their ideas for a personal car to succeed the Brougham. While the Brougham ended in 1960, it was another six years before the successor appeared. After approval by Harold Warner, experimental and development work started in the fall of 1959. During that winter a prototype with front wheel drive was tested on an airport at Grayling, in northern Michigan. It was here that front wheel drive showed some advantages over rear wheel drive in ice conditions; Maurice Olley told about one driver who in testing found he could safely travel on glare ice at about double the speed of a rear drive car. A V-12 with single overhead cam per bank was rumored to have been projected for the package at one stage.

While the engineers worked on chassis development, the styling section evolved designs suitable for either front or rear drive in case the former failed to make good. They began in October, 1959, with "XP-727," dropped it a few months later, and followed with "XP-727-2," which reached finality in August, 1961. Then came "XP-727-3" during 1961–1962. When it was definitely decided that a front wheel drive approach would be used, "XP-784" was begun and occupied the stylists from May to August of 1963. The following month came "XP-820," which by December had evolved into "XP-825," and a fiberglass version of this virtually final production form was shown to the management in May, 1964. This was approved and the next two and a half years were spent getting it ready for production: tooling-up and laying down a separate line (for the first time in Cadillac history) in the former Clark Street foundry building. This move apparently fooled the skeptics who had argued against rumors that a new Cadillac model was in the offing by pointing out that the regular line already had as much as it could comfortably handle.

Oldsmobile's Toronado had stolen the front-wheel-drive limelight a year earlier, so the Eldorado met with more restrained, although still enthusiastic, reception from the automotive press. This actually reflected Cadillac's own wishes, which have always presented the car in a relatively low key from the start. "It was a temptation," said Charles Adams, "but our advertising approach has always been that a Cadillac is a Cadillac whatever

Phases of Cadillac production include chassis line and body drop (above), final assembly and paint baking (below).

Eldorado prototype assembly.

The 1967 Eldorado and De Ville convertible.

the model, whatever the year." After a couple of years production, however, the Cadillac touch was evident. The extra year's development allowed Cadillac to refine its front wheel drive over that of the Toronado, making it softer riding and quieter, and with fewer teething troubles. The Eldorado sold 20,728 cars in 1967 and increased its sales in 1968, whereas the Toronado, after high first year sales (50,000) dropped off thirty-three percent in 1967. In 1968 Eldorado deliveries rose to over 23,000, and Toronado fell to 25,000. In 1969, the Eldorado climbed again to over 26,000, while the Toronado remained almost static. The lesson seems to be that luxury specialty cars can be built by others, and in greater numbers, but Cadillac retains its sure touch and gets the success it wants regardless of opposition. It aimed the Eldorado at ten percent of its own market and at a lower age group than the usual Cadillac buyer. Production and sales figures, and owner surveys, bear this out in practice. Ad copy called it "the world's finest personal car" and in the inimitable — or infuriating — Cadillac manner, declared that it was the only car that could make a Cadillac owner look twice. This advertisement showed one of the regular models and an Eldorado above the caption, "While longtime Cadillac owners, accustomed to the finest, may prefer one of Cadillac's traditional models, they have high regard for the spirited glamor, admire the bold concept of the Eldorado."

Automobile buffs, even the skeptics, were inclined to agree. Said *Car & Driver*: "The Eldorado's appeal is based on the technical aspect of motoring and on automotive verve . . . a certain mystique from front wheel drive." *Car Life* commented: "Eldorado seems beyond the scope of today's luxury/specialty car concept; rather it appears to be the sort of visually distinctive, tastefully luxurious, enormously expensive, individualistic conveyance which characterized the Classic Era of automobile design."

Automobile Quarterly gave the Eldorado its "Design and Engineering Excellence" award, pointing out that despite the tremendous power, far greater than any other front-wheel-drive car excepting the similar Toronado, all the traditional unpleasant characteristics of front-wheel-drive cars had been eliminated. The variable-ratio power steering made the car feel much smaller than its size and the handling and controllability standards were so high that "it could take bends at speeds that will send many so-called sports cars skittering wildly out of control."

Predictably, however, *Car & Driver* struck a sour note. Having expected a Detroit Mercedes, they said, it was disappointing to find just another Cadillac! Concepts of handling evidently differed from tester to tester, one contradicting the other. Nevertheless, all but *Car & Driver* agreed on the impressive handling qualities — *Motor Trend* even asserting that if a corner was taken faster than intended, "powering through the turn was quite safe — front tires will make a lot of noise, but the car will stick."

In construction the Eldorado supposedly shared the GM "E"

The Coupe de Ville is a body style dating back to 1949 and Cadillac's first hardtop. Here, a 1967 (left) and a 1968 model.

body shell with the Buick Riviera and the Toronado, and the mechanical package was rather similar to that of the Toronado, with chain drive, side-mounted transmission, torsion-bar front suspension, and single-leaf rear suspension with quad shocks and beam rear axle. The rear suspension and axle were at first sight crude, but actually so light that unsprung weight rivaled that of independent systems, and the car surpassed many of them in consistency of rear axle behavior. "The layout rendered independent rear suspension quite unnecessary," Maurice Olley commented.

Stylewise, the Eldorado looked quite different from the Toronado, with its Cadillac grille and creased rear window, and its general sheet-metal treatment was so distinctive as to raise the question of just what commonality of "E" body parts was supposed to exist between it and the Toronado. However that may be, its effect was dramatic. Said one observer: "Sight and touch say Eldorado is a classic — made in a modern manner of modern materials. By being both briskly and solidly constructed, Eldorado imparts the same sort of feeling as a carefully machined block of platinum."

In 1967 Cadillac introduced a restyled regular line, characterized by the "leaning forward" grille and raised, sharp-lined haunches. Production (including Eldorados) reached 200,000 for the first time, and total deliveries were 213,699 cars. The whole Cadillac range remained in short supply despite the unprecedented production level, and dealers' stocks of Eldorados were limited to less than a week's supply. Two shifts were work-

The 1969 Fleetwood Eldorado (foreground) and Sedan de Ville.

ing on the regular line, and one on the Eldorado. Management was reluctant to employ added shifts and overtime, ostensibly for fear of endangering quality, although there were also suspicions that Cadillac actually encouraged a certain scarcity as good sales psychology.

In 1968 came a new enlarged engine: its 472 cubic inches made it the largest in the industry. Carl Rasmussen explained that the car needed no more performance than it already had, but the profligate demands of the many power accessories left them no option but to increase displacement. Air conditioning required ten to twelve horsepower alone. Little was interchangeable with the old engine, and a complete retooling was required for its production. Its main theme was attention to a multitude of detail refinement, with the philosophy that "trifles make perfection but perfection is no trifle." A major attribute was provision for growth in displacement, even beyond 500 cubic inches. The "tremendous trifles" showed up in an amazingly low engine weight of 600 pounds, despite displacement and extras such as air conditioning, far in excess of the original 1949 engine.

A new grille and detail alterations were the only styling changes for 1968. Air conditioning was now practically standard, since all but four percent of buyers specified it. Power windows were also standard through the line.

Production reached 230,000 for the year, and on June 10, 1968, Cadillac built its three-millionth postwar car. A survey showed that more than 1,650,000 Cadillacs of all ages were still on the road.

Models for 1969 featured major styling changes in the standard line, minor changes in the Eldorado, and complete new interior styling in all models. They had restyled front and rear ends, with repositioned headlights, new grille texture, and chisel-tip fenders. "Safety features" dominated the restyle, but there were some other changes: redesigned frames, disc brakes as standard features on all models, with new vacuum booster, larger-capacity automatic climate control, sealed-engine cooling system, and elimination of the vent windows. Production fell to 223,000 but new car registrations reached nearly 245,000, or 2.58 percent of the total market. The Eldorado maintained its approximate ten percent share of Cadillac output and the breakdown of 1967 models was Calais: 12,432; De Ville: 180,487; Fleetwood: 21,709; 75 and chassis: 4,664; Eldorado: 24,613; making a total of 243,905. These figures far exceeded those of all Cadillac's "rivals" together, the nearest being Lincoln, whose combined total of Continental and Mark III sales was 58,835. While the Mark III might be considered a success comparable to the

Eldorado, the Continental at 38,384 was no match for the regular Cadillac line, although the Lincoln, in its turn, outsold Imperial, Mercedes, and Rolls combined in the United States.

The undeniably impressive statistics for Cadillac appear to be unwelcome to some members of the automotive press. Every car has its "antis," of course; as Emerson noted, there should always be a minority unconvinced. The anti-Cadillac element within the automotive press undoubtedly stems in part from "the grass is always greener (in Europe)" syndrome, fostered by that at times appealing tendency of journalists to stand themselves apart from the crowd. This inevitably dictates opposition to a successful product, simply because it is generally accepted. Consequently Cadillac has more than its fair share of critics, and one finds that there is not always a general agreement among them. The attitude toward Cadillac can vary from time to time even within the same publication, presumably depending upon which individual happens to be writing up the final draft of the test report at the time. One favorite technique, dear to some of the press, is to credit the car generously in areas where its excellence is just too obvious to be denied, and then introduce a heavy slant in the opposite direction in other areas where the car falls short of its rivals, or in some abstract or abstruse scale of values personal to the tester or his group thinking. This is then used as the decisive factor in an overall summary, and the Cadillac — according to the report — emerges, of course, as an admittedly

General Managers Harold G. Warner, left, who arrived in 1960, and Calvin J. Werner, who arrived in 1966.

remarkable piece of modern technology, but nevertheless a failure by the standards of the tester, or at best, lacking in what is really wanted. Admittedly, no human being, or even a committee, can be completely impartial. Positive judgments are preferable to the inconclusive, and some purpose and sense of direction are desirable. There is, however, a certain amount of fallacious argumentation involved. These journalistic critics like to imply that they have a higher standard of overall judgment, analysis, and criticism than Cadillac's own clientele, or its executives, designers, engineers, salesmen, and dealers — or for that matter, its own rivals who as one journalist complained "hold Cadillac in the same esteem as their own best products." Yet among those automobile enthusiasts whose theoretical and practical knowledge, expertise and experience, are the equal of the most scholarly of Cadillac critics there can be found adequate testimony to the contrary. The late Ken Purdy, for instance, quoted the eye-opening case of Phil Walters, "for years probably the best road circuit driver in America." Walters was asked what kind of car he would like best for a long trip. "His starry eyed questioners," wrote Purdy, "expecting that he would cite some exotic, fussy, hard sprung, gear-howling European model, were nonplussed when he said: 'An air conditioned Cadillac, what else?' "

Consider, too, Abner Doble, the American steam-car proponent and builder, certainly possessed of one of the most brilliant minds ever applied to the automobile, despite his offbeat approach. During the 1950's as he and his patent attorney, Marcus Lothrop, were reviewing the possibility of a future steam-car revival, Abner commented: "Well, Marcus, I guess I've still got one more design left in me even yet. But [pointing to his own Cadillac parked in the street] how can I hope to compete with that?"

Such certainly heady testimonials to the marque could easily be followed by many others. But somehow they suffice. On the success scale of luxury marques Cadillac stands quite alone. No other car can match its production or approach its position in the luxury market. In the overall sales picture, not even Lincoln, Imperial, and all Mercedes imports taken together constitute any real threat to Cadillac, let alone singly. And for 1972 Cadillac scheduled a production of no less than 250,000, by far the highest in its history and a completely unprecedented figure for a car of this class. Even the skeptics have to be impressed.

With the seventies have come new Cadillacs. For the 1970 model year, apart from the larger 500-cubic-inch engine in the Eldorado and the optional computerized rear braking, there were few changes — thus presaging the major styling and engineering alterations for 1971. These included a new, low horizontal frontal treatment, new body shape, and a modern roof interpretation of the Brougham which, the factory proudly claimed, was reminiscent of the classic V-16's of the thirties. Safety had been a major feature for 1969, while for 1971 anti-pollutant measures predominated. All '71's had a combined air-injection reactor and controlled combustion system for exhaust emission control. Engines were redesigned to operate on unleaded or new low-pollutant fuels, and had lower compression. (Because the spark was retarded in first and second gears to give better smog control, '70's had been slightly inferior in acceleration to the '69's.) Interesting for 1971 was the inclusion of net and gross horsepower and torque figures — the net figure being to SAE specifications J245. These compared as follows:

Gross	Net	Gross torque	Net torque
		STANDARD	
345 @ 4,400	220 @ 4,000	500 @ 2,800	380 @ 2,400
		ELDORADO	
365 @ 4,400	235 @ 3,800	535 @ 2,800	410 @ 2,400

There has been a lot of discussion about the high horsepower claims made during the horsepower race, and Cadillac's 375 hp figure of 1968 was certainly suspicious. But through 1964 and the 325 hp figure, the claims seem reasonable, as gross outputs.

In 1949 both net and gross figures were specifically stated in the Barr-Cole paper to the Society of Automotive Engineers. The graphs with correlating horsepower and torque figure curves were published with details as to how they were obtained. The net figure was under GM test code conditions (stiffer than SAE conditions by four percent) with 100° F. underhood temperatures, and all accessories operating. This was the only time the net was given for the next twenty-three years. Horsepowers published from then on were gross. The claimed increases, however, were actually borne out by improved road performance figures in independent road tests for a good many years. Today the cars are twenty-five percent faster, and this indicates greatly increased power output even allowing for lower drag bodies and possibly more efficient transmission.

The writer was present when one race car builder in the fifties was told the results of an independent dyno test for a standard Cadillac 230 hp engine he had imported for a racing car. The test figure was 242 bhp — or twelve above that claimed by the factory. The driver later won an important road race with it, and

even knowledgeable skeptics admitted, "He's certainly getting that advertised horsepower."

By 1949 net/gross standards, a 325 hp engine should deliver 265–270 horsepower net. The latter figure was obtained once by Aston Martin engineers on a Cadillac test, but unfortunately with the 375 hp engine, which should have shown over 300 net! However, there is the factor of lowered compression ratios (down two full ratios from 10.5 to 8.5) for unleaded fuel operation. Undoubtedly this lowered peak power outputs. After giving both net and gross in 1971, today the company states SAE net figures only. These, incidentally, are equal to a slightly higher DIN figure, i.e. a 225 hp SAE car is equal to a 229 hp DIN car.

To summarize, the probability is that Cadillac gross figures were for many years accurate, but in the final stages the advertising department added some paper horsepower of their own. This is scarcely a phenomenon singular to Cadillac. Its American contemporaries have indulged themselves similarly, and in eras past and present a number of reputable European manufacturers have claimed more horses for their cars than were delivered. Legend to the contrary, the horsepower race is not an all-American one.

For Cadillac's seventieth anniversary year — 1972 — the factory provided styling refinements and a number of engineering improvements, including improved bumper-crash absorption and transistorized rear braking available on all models.

George R. Elges, left, succeeded Werner in 1969. Robert D. Lund, right, followed Mr. Elges in 1973.

Now three-score years and ten, Cadillac is nevertheless as vigorous and firmly entrenched as it ever was in the past. Why is it so far ahead of what, as roadtester Tom McCahill once wrote "might laughingly be called its competition?" And why has it so convincingly survived in an area where there have been so many failures and so few lasting successes? The author remembers asking himself these questions a few years ago in three different parts of the United States. On Cleveland's Quincy Avenue, while photographing the one-time Peerless plant (converted to a brewery—still existing), a new Cadillac sped past. On Detroit's Jefferson Avenue, we drove past the downtown depot that had once serviced gleaming Packards. Its windows were broken and it was as silent and forlorn as the Packard plant in East Grand Boulevard, which we visited a few minutes later — in a Cadillac. At Buffalo, on Great Arrow Avenue and Elmwood, we had paid respects to the former Pierce-Arrow plant — again to the whisper of new Cadillacs in the background. In Rochester, we had driven past the Cadillac dealership, housed in the former Pierce-Arrow distributor's building which had been built for this purpose in 1929 at immense cost. What happened to the "three P's," once the pride and glory of American autodom, and almost all their famous counterparts?

The Cadillac survival, it seems, is a typical American success story based on a typical American philosophy — pragmatism. Pragmatic engineering, pragmatic management. At some stage or other, its rivals lost sight of the fact that such thinking and its application are essential for lasting success in American business. One by one they caved in. Locomobile, Peerless, Marmon, Pierce-Arrow, Duesenberg, finally even Packard. In each case, management decisions — or lack of them — inflexibility and the reluctance to move with the times and nourish new talent, catastrophic errors of judgment, had resulted in virtual corporate suicide. Cadillac had itself come close on occasions, but the situation had never been allowed to get completely out of hand. Always there has been a realistic appraisal at some decisive point, from which the division recovered and went forward. Because engineering and management are so all-important in automobile design and manufacture, their balanced interplay is crucial. Cadillac has always been blessed in this respect. There are cases to the contrary but as a general rule, from the time of Leland himself, Cadillac engineers have been good managers, and its managers good engineers. The result is that Cadillac has *always* built a good product, one that usually found a secure and profitable market. Its few commercial failures have been far outweighed by its overwhelming successes. Technically, as Mark Howell once

remarked, "Cadillac have never built a bad car," a belief shared by so experienced a critic as W. F. Hillstead of the old Bentley company, who writes that in fifty years of international motoring he could "never remember a bad Cadillac."

This tribute to the consistency of Cadillac standards of manufacture can be matched by a remarkable tribute to Cadillac pioneering and innovation. In 1958 *Popular Mechanics*, advised by a panel of five distinguished automobile historians, selected the most significant automobiles in American history, basing the choice on engineering and styling features of outstanding merit. In a list compiled from several thousand makes and whittled down to a mere sixteen automobiles, Cadillac rated a unique four mentions — twenty-five percent of the total: the 1908 single cylinder ("Parts Interchangeability"); the 1912 four cylinder ("Self Starter"); the 1915 V-8 ("Forerunner of Today's Power Plants"); the 1929 ("Synchromesh").

The only other makes to score more than one mention were Ford (three), Chrysler (two), and Oldsmobile (two). It is interesting that Leland was associated with one Oldsmobile model mentioned, the curved dash, and that the other Olds gained a listing from its introduction of Hydra-Matic transmission — which was, as we have already seen, primarily a Cadillac con-

The 500-cubic-inch Eldorado engine for the 1970 line.

tribution anyway. Furthermore, one Ford mentioned was the early V-8, which also owed much to Cadillac and GM influence in its engine design.

It is worth speculating on other notable Cadillac contributions that could have been classed with the above — the "flat ride" of 1934 is certainly one. Like synchromesh, and automatic transmission, it is a development that could well have qualified for the Dewar Trophy, since its application has since become almost universal even down to the cheapest cars. While not of universal application, the inherently balanced V-8 of 1923 and the high-compression, short-stroke V-8 of 1949 were also major advancements that have become generally adopted in the luxury-car field and further down as well. In styling, the LaSalle, though admittedly derivative, was also a major step forward, as were the Cadillac 60 Special and the novel '48 lines.

The list of Cadillac's technical advancements is in fact almost endless. What is most significant is that so many of these advancements have eventually been generally adopted both in the United States and abroad. Judged by this standard, many of Cadillac's rivals claiming "advanced features" do not show up so well. For instance, the Cadillac inherently balanced V-8 and the Mercedes controllable Kompressor came out about the same time,

A new option was the electric sun roof on 1970 hardtops.

but there can be no doubt about which was the more significant advancement. Similarly, at a time when multi-range transmissions and free wheeling were the rage, and thought to be the new trend in ease of shifting, Cadillac pioneered synchromesh and wiped them out. Although Cadillac cannot claim a monopoly in such advancements, and in other cases the comparisons can be reversed (specifically hydraulic brakes — Chrysler and Duesenberg) its record is so outstanding that it makes complete nonsense of a claim that "General Motors is interested only in mass-produced junk" or that "Europe always leads, America always follows." Cadillac has been one of the greatest of all innovators. This policy began to change to some extent in the thirties, when Oldsmobile was selected, by a central decision, to be the pilot for many new GM ideas. However, that had nothing to do with the Cadillac Division's inherent ingenuity or ability, but was based on hard economic facts of life. To gain the most return on a new device that may have cost millions in research and development, the trend was to first apply it to a higher volume car. Then after a year or so of proving in field experience, Cadillac would bring out its own perfected, bug-free version, and maintain its "refined" image. Thus Hydra-Matic and the Toronado. Even so, innovation has continued at an impressive rate.

Whatever may be the special claims of its rivals in the luxury-car world, and whatever its own shortcomings, Cadillac remains The Standard. It represents, as *The Autocar* said, "the highest standards attainable in most important respects" — a level which rivals must at least attempt to equal, if not strive to surpass. Even then, it is still rough going. As one Lincoln executive told *The Wall Street Journal*, "There have been times when we knew we had a better car than the Cadillac, but we could never convince the public. They have the kind of public acceptance that just rules out debate on the merits."

Cadillac's total market penetration, between two and three percent, remains virtually the same today as it was in the early years of the V-8, which entirely changed the concept of fine cars in America, and ultimately the world.

Reviewing the Cadillac, what it has done and represents, comes down simply to men and cars. So far as origins go, we start with the grand old founder, Henry M. Leland, "Master of Precision" — the commander-in-chief — the one indispensable man. With micrometer in one hand and Bible in the other, he preached the ultimate standards in matters mechanical and moral. He was one hundred percent American, but he and his son Wilfred were also reminiscent of the patricians of ancient Rome in that they felt that what they did was as much for the good of the Republic as it was for themselves. In an ever-more hedonistic, materialistic, and godless age, it is heartening to reflect that these men had no difficulties reconciling Christianity with Science, and that Henry Leland could combine noble idealism with complete mastery of practical matters — even to qualifying as America's original "hot-rodder."

Charles F. Kettering equaled Leland in stature and his brilliant unorthodoxy beautifully complemented Leland's rigid traditions, to the inestimable benefit of Cadillac, General Motors, the automobile industry, and mankind as a whole. He has been aptly called a kind of twentieth-century Benjamin Franklin.

Likewise, we can easily discern two more early giants —Fred Bennett and Harley Earl. Bennett's influence in establishing Cadillac overseas and ensuring the successive Dewar Trophy triumphs made him the most influential Cadillac man outside the United States. The beneficial publicity of these awards, backed up by Bennett's own resourceful promotion, was of enormous value to the marque.

While Earl came much later than the other three — Leland, Kettering, and Bennett — in respect to his area of influence he was just as much a pioneer, and certainly equally dynamic and colorful. Nor can the tough, competent Fisher brothers be ignored, although perhaps we can symbolize their contribution in the personality of L. P. Fisher.

Deeper analysis of the engineering record discloses some very important men. First the two Ernests, Sweet and Seaholm, earnest by name and nature — calm, competent, utterly reliable — and almost utterly unknown. They were the forerunners of the later professional automobile engineer-executives, like Arnold and Rasmussen, virtually anonymous but virtually indispensable. Then there have been the brilliant specialists — designers and technicians, men like Johnson, McCall White, Strickland, Nacker, Thompson, Olley, Davis, and a multitude of others — too numerous to mention — through latter-day stalwarts like Barr and Cole.

Of general managers, the first two to follow Leland — Collins and Rice — lacked particular distinction but Lawrence Fisher was capable and colorful, and Nicholas Dreystadt, though lacking Fisher's glamour, was one of the most efficient and influential men ever to hold the post. Looking at his successor, John F. Gordon, one may question the theory that giants existed or were needed only in the early days, for Gordon rose from the job of helper in the laboratory to the posts of chief engineer and general manager, and finally became president of General Motors itself. Ahrens, Roche, Warner, Werner, and Elges have all maintained a traditional competence of management that has kept the

The elegant Cadillacs for 1971 included the Fleetwood Sixty Special Brougham, left, the Coupe de Ville, right. On the facing page is the Eldorado in Sable black given by President Nixon to the Soviet leader, Mr. Brezhnev, on his visit to Russia. This, of course, is a 1972 model.

division in a highly satisfactory position.

These, of course, are the leaders, but mention should also be made of the unknown thousands. Cadillac workmen are above average, better trained, more experienced, and more stable; they stay longer on the job and take more pride in their work than the general run of industry personnel. As one brochure says, "Cadillac is People. . . . With the greatest continuity of employment in the industry, these quality-minded people do their jobs each day . . . in the Cadillac way." And they do.

Viewed in retrospect, the cars too take on their own personalities — the hardy, pioneering little singles, challenging the world to match their standard of manufacture, and finding no takers. The admirable four-cylinder models, duplicating their forerunners' technical achievement with another great step forward. Then the momentous entry of the V-8, most important and enduring type in the whole history of the marque. The fabulous, magnificent, myriad-cylindered twelves and sixteens, evocative of a golden age of classicism that will never return. Along with them, the glamorous and nostalgic LaSalle. The 60 Series that charted a new course for Cadillac and served as well in war as in peace, followed by yet another trend setter — the fine overhead-valve V-8, and its lineal successors. Plus the styling tour de force of 1948, the limited-production Eldorado of 1953

and beyond, the Eldorado Brougham of the late fifties, and the Eldorado front-wheel-drive of the late sixties — models for connoisseurs, and now for collectors who covet significant cars of the postwar era.

One of the most lasting impressions gained from any lengthy study of Cadillac is the association of names and the symbolism of the marque itself. Probably only Rolls-Royce has been so widely used in the same connotation.

Fortune in 1968 called Morgan Stanley and Company the "Cadillac of Wall Street bankers," and in the same year their article on Cadillac itself parodied Gertrude Stein's tribute to the rose with the title "A Cadillac is a Cadillac is a Cadillac." Elaborate caskets seen at funeral homes are dubbed "Cadillac coffins," while *Car & Driver* commented, "You've heard of the Cadillac of lawnmowers and the Cadillac of fishing reels." While typing this we heard a TV commercial advertising the "Cadillac of guns." In 1969 King Ibn Saud's newspaper obituaries described him as the monarch of a land of Cadillacs and Camels, and when New Zealand's famous guide Rangi died, a leading newspaper reporter reminisced about her "Cadillac tourists." From the days of "Happy Cadillac" to "The Lady from Twenty Nine Palms" and Eartha Kitt's "Old Fashioned Millionaire," the car, of course, has been featured in song, and one musical com-

position is titled simply "Cadillac."

All this, perforce, is a tribute to the symbolism of the marque, and to return to the rose, already mentioned, it is interesting to speculate what the image might have been had the name been something else. One long-time American Rolls-Royce owner, a patent attorney, half seriously once remarked that he believed Detroit became the center of the auto industry because General Motors' foremost car was named the 'Cadillac.' His Cleveland dealer, with the local river in mind, joked, "I can't imagine it ever succeeding if they'd built it here and called it the 'Cuyahoga Eight.'"

Certainly the euphony and associations of the name leave little to be desired, although one objection might be that while it does a lot to perpetuate the original founder of Motor City, it does nothing to even recall the man who founded the make itself.

What would those two men have made of the modern Cadillac? Le Sieur Antoine, perhaps, would have felt it only right that such a symbol of leadership and association with luxurious elegance should bear his name and no other. Leland's austere personality, on the other hand, might well have frowned at the sybaritic connotations his car has acquired, and its occasional flamboyant styling lapses. But he would, no doubt, have nodded approval of its continuing record of engineering triumphs, the precision of its manufacture, and its fulfillment of the promise implied in his original slogan by so convincingly establishing itself as the world's most successful luxury car.

Above all, certain visions are outstanding. Henry Leland in his top-heavy "Osceola," Bennett at Brooklands, Pershing in his staff car, the Nairn brothers sweeping across desert wastes in their touring cars, Al Capone in his armor-plated version — and J. Edgar Hoover in his, J. Paul Getty traversing the Communist Balkans in his "long shiny symbol of capitalist wealth." William Francis Gibbs driving down in his black limousine to await impatiently the return of his creation, the *S.S. United States*, after another triumphant crossing of the Atlantic. President Nixon, presenting as a token of good will a new Cadillac to Leonid Breshnev. Astronauts and electronics experts . . . fashionable women alighting along Park Avenue South. Rented cars loaded with tourists, ambulances with victims — or funeral cars with coffins. More than four million Cadillacs have been built — their variety is endless. All a far cry indeed from cobbling shoes, the Colt revolver, and a little brick foundry on Trombley Avenue, Detroit, many years ago. Yet a tenuous link is there. The Cadillac is certainly a very substantial part of the American heritage. And chances are that it will stay that way.

The 1973 Sixty Special Brougham, above, and Sedan de Ville

The 1973 Eldorado and, on the facing page, the Coupe de Ville

CHAPTER THIRTEEN

THE CONTINUING STANDARD

Three quarters of a century from genesis -- Cadillac in the Nineteen Seventies

Since the foregoing history was concluded, the story's subject, of course, has continued its successful career. And it's grown some too. Extensive plant modernization and expansion at Cadillac Division began in late 1972 and continued into 1974. It ranged the gamut from research into color schemes to select those most likely to boost staff morale, to new tunneling for car delivery from the final paint repair operation to the shipping department. Everything at Cadillac, it seems, is done in full measure.

There were personnel changes too. In December, 1972, general manager George Elges announced the appointment of Robert J. Templin as chief engineer, succeeding Carlton A. Rasmussen, who was obliged for reasons of ill health to take medical leave of absence after thirty-two years at Cadillac. Templin, born in 1927 and a graduate of Rensselaer Polytechnic Institute, had served at Cadillac previously. Joining General Motors in July of 1947 as a chemical engineer at the Research Laboratories in Detroit, he became project engineer at Cadillac in 1950, moving that same year to Cadillac's Cleveland Tank Plant. In 1954 he was appointed assistant staff engineer, and a year later staff engineer, of the tank plant. Returning to Detroit in 1957, he carried several engineering assignments, then was named Cadillac's assistant chief engineer (chassis) in May, 1965. Some four years later, in September of 1969, he was transferred to GM's Research Laboratories—and at the time of his reappointment to Cadillac was special assistant to the president (engines), having made intensive study of the Wankel principle.

Tall, well-built, square-jawed, ruggedly handsome, nonchalant in manner and with a rather sardonic sense of humor, Templin may be the signal for dramatic change at Cadillac. One veteran employee, a classic car fan steeped in Cadillac history, said quietly but seriously, "I think we may see another Seaholm era."

At the same time as he was announcing Templin's appointment, Elges was preparing to leave (reluctantly, he told this writer) for Buick, "where I'm needed more than here." Although a Cadillac man from 1941, he had served at Buick previously—1964-1965—which accounted for his recall to that division, despite his own desire to remain with Cadillac. This, one thinks, is typical of the very real esprit de corps at General Motors' premier division, reflected in the comment of various Cadillac dealers who had previously, for example, handled Chevrolet. Their new appointment they likened to "dying and going to Heaven."

Elges was succeeded at Cadillac on the first day of 1973 by none other than the former general sales manager of Chevrolet Division, Robert D. Lund. Having risen through the ranks at the division and in the field since 1946 when he joined Chevrolet as Minneapolis district sales manager, Lund was a go-getter. In 1971 he had set a record of three million Chevrolets sold, which some commentators attributed to a Lund selling philosophy hearkening back to his football days in the early Forties as a "hard-charging guard" for the College of St. Thomas in St. Paul, Minnesota. (Though be it added that his credits also included a B.A. in business administration at St. Thomas—and post-graduate work at Harvard University Graduate School of Business.) The tall, distinctively featured Lund has said, "the way to win is to get out in front and improve your position. When you're green, you're growing, but when you're ripe, you're next to rotten."

Whether or not he was referring specifically to Cadillac's continuing success breeding a dangerous complacency, Lund made his presence felt immediately. Also his sense of humor. Very shortly after he arrived at Cadillac, it became known that a monthly record of some sort, and of no particular import, had been set at the divi-

There were numerous changes at Cadillac in the early seventies—and not all of these were concerned with the car itself. Others pertained to the environment in which it was built. Expansion and modernization projects began in late 1972 and continued into 1974. Unveiled in November that year was a new automobile shipping facility, a 54,000-square-foot building on a fifteen-acre site adjacent to the division's Detroit final assembly plant. It is a marvel of computer age technology, as illustrated herewith. Just a few feet from the last assembly inspection point, the completed Cadillacs are assigned computerized traffic control instructions and designated holding spaces (above left). The cars are then placed on a computerized conveyor system for the 1,200-foot trip to the new building, where upon arrival they are unloaded (above right) and relocated in their computer assigned sections for ultimate shipment nationwide either by truck, tri-level railcar or stac-pac railcar. With regard to the latter, the new shipping facility includes eleven on-site railheads (below right) for the loading of cars to be sent stac-pac, a shipping concept comprising a completely enclosed metal container holding three cars. Stac-pac shipped cars are mechanically loaded in the new facility, with the loader unit wired to the main traffic control computer system to assure that the appropriate car is put in the appropriate place.

sion. Although he obviously hadn't been on the job long enough to have contributed to the record—however insignificant—he ordered cakes and coffee and shut down the line for a short jocular celebration. And it was then he announced his own goal: a 300,000 sales year. It had never been done before. It was his "magic number."

Lund missed no opportunity to promote Cadillac in the public eye, and while some of his efforts might have seemed more appropriate perhaps to Chevrolet than to Cadillac, he took care to emphasize the latter's traditional image at the same time. The accountants and stockholders were delighted with the monthly sales figures the Lund regime was producing, and aficionados simultaneously nodded approval at the appearance along Cadillac halls and stairways of elegant old-time advertisements, placed there to revive interest in the marque's past.

The marque's present—on the twenty-seventh day of June, 1973—provided a demonstration of Cadillac Division's quantity-production expertise. The five millionth car built rolled out of the factory. A blue and white De Ville sedan, it was the center of a brief ceremony attended by the employees who had a hand in its building, general manager Lund and the car's purchasers, the Scharffin family of Indianapolis, who were guests of Cadillac for the occasion. The acceleration of Cadillac popularity down through the years was indicated by the ever-shortening periods between each millionth car, nine years between the first and second, six years between the second and third, five years between the third and fourth, and only four years to build the fifth million.

A month earlier, two other Cadillacs had provided the marque additional publicity—in the city for which the five millionth car was destined. They arrived in Indianapolis for the 500. The first—used to open the track for time trials—gave the crowd a glimpse of what a pace car for the first Indy 500—had there been one—might have looked like. It was a 1911 four-cylinder Cadillac originally shipped to the McAllister Brothers Car Company of East Liberty, Pennsylvania on May 15, 1911—and made available for the event by the car's current owner, Francis Burns. The second car, supplied by Cadillac Division and used to pace the 500 itself, was a white 1973 Eldorado convertible. It was driven by the 1960 Indy winner (and Cadillac dealer in Melbourne, Florida) Jim Rathmann. An ebullient Lund pointed out that "our engineers must have had a premonition of participating in the 500, having given the Eldorado a 500-cubic-inch engine." He did not say, but it was well rumored and never officially denied, that the pace car had its emission control removed and the engine tuned accordingly, so that it would be equal to any demands on it in pacing the roaring pack. This being true or

not, it marked the fifth 500 for which a Cadillac paced Indy, the others 1927, 1931, 1934 and 1937.

Indianapolis was not the only competitive event during these years in which the name Cadillac merited mention. There was the Cannonball Baker Sea to Shining Sea Memorial Trophy Dash as well, an event inaugurated in 1970 and staged ostensibly to demonstrate that competent drivers, using the national highways and driving basically stock cars, could safely cross the United States at higher speeds than posted limits. In its second running, 1971, the victor was a Ferrari, but the performance put up by Larry Opert and Ron Hasko driving the Cadillac Coupe de Ville that placed second "and might have won if [Opert and Hasko] hadn't stopped to talk with so many cops" caused much comment.

What happened the year next prompted the race sponsor—Brock Yates of *Car and Driver*—to lament that he had "spent two thousand dollars toward building the best, American genre, interstate GT car in order to get blown off by a dead stock Cadillac." Yates had entered a specially prepared Dodge Challenger. The winners—Steve Behr, Bill Canfield and Fred Olds—by contrast, had taken a fresh-off-the-production-line Coupe de Ville, and beat out not only Yates but such esoterica as Ferraris, Panteras, Mercedes, Alfa Romeos, et al., as well as specially hopped-up vans and American sedan competition. Cruising at 80 to 100 mph where possible, the

A grinning Robert Lund "hooks" a production record setter as it's "reeled" off the line by a Cadillac worker in July of 1973.

trio covered the 3,000 miles in 37 hours 16 minutes elapsed time at an average speed of 80 mph. "Like it or not," commented *Motor Trend*, "after that Cadillac owned a not-so-subtle performance image." Steve Behr mused, with the approval of *Car and Driver*, "Maybe it's all right for Cadillac to call itself 'Standard of the World.'"

Whatever conclusions might be drawn from such an event, Behr's comment was subtly reflected in automotive ad copy and lore 'round the world. Car buffs on both sides of the Atlantic used Cadillac's slogan to describe past and present rivals, like Duesenberg and Rolls-Royce. In advertising copy from two of Cadillac's most prominent rivals—Lincoln and Mercedes—"the standard" became a popular term. And in an article entitled "Which Size Car For You?," *Road & Track* took "the roomy Cadillac as a standard for the other cars measured."

Other sometimes veiled—and sometimes not flattering—tributes to the Cadillac mystique followed. *Business Week*, critical of the United Auto Workers efforts to shut Japanese cars out of the American market, satirically echoed Marie Antoinette by heading its column on the subject, "Let 'em drive Cadillacs!" Black leader Rap Brown quipped pungently, "The White man don't like nothing black but a Cadillac." One Zurich call girl distinguished herself from the run-of-the-mill by taking the professional name of "Erika

Robert J. Templin, left, who became chief engineer in 1972. Edward C. Kennard who succeeded Lund as general manager in 1974.

Cadillac."

A more fitting reference certainly—from Cadillac Division's point of view—was actor Richard Attenborough's confession that "as a real film fan, the most exciting thing for me was driving down Sunset Boulevard in a Cadillac." And artist Vladimir Tretchikoff's admission that despite being "a Bohemian at heart . . . I like to live like a capitalist—rather drive a Cadillac than pedal a bicycle."

The Cadillac that Tretchikoff would have been driving in '73 was a congenial facelift of the '72 model, as the '74 would be of the '73. Indeed most press coverage—as well as Cadillac p.r. itself—focused these years on bumpers front and rear, styled for aesthetics certainly, but most importantly for adherence to mandatory government regulations. The cars were Cadillacs in the Cadillac tradition, but neither they nor the marque's mystique nor the Cadillac word of mouth, the compliments either straightforward or backhanded, would provide Robert Lund the goal he sought. But he was agonizingly close. Sales for calendar year 1973 totaled 289,233 cars.

There was the matter of an energy crisis. It came late that year—an Arab oil embargo in October, the gasoline crunch in November—and resulted in quite adverse publicity for a car like the Cadillac. A Pentagon general here, an assistant secretary of state there—to the accompaniment of headlined news stories—ceremoniously discarded their Standards of the World, to set an economy example ostensibly. And one classic cartoon depicted a Cadillac owner, hand over his eyes, pointing a revolver at his Eldorado.

Cadillac sales for '73 provided a record, but it was 10,767 units short of the magic number Lund was aiming at. Production, at 307,698 cars, did exceed it incidentally—and soon after the first of the year the Cadillacs not sold during the height of the energy crunch would begin moving again. Sales for February of '74 were but 11,581 cars. Sales for the first twenty-one days of March were but 7,894. Then the oil embargo was lifted. During the last ten days of March, Cadillac sales soared to 10,000 cars. America hadn't decided against the large car after all, it seemed.

It was a breathing-easier-now Robert Lund who introduced the new '75 Cadillac in September of 1974. The nine models in the three series—Calais, De Ville and Fleetwood—all had GM's catalytic converter for the sake of pollution and, concomitantly General Motors said, fuel economy. They all now carried the Eldorado's 500-cubic-inch V-8. And they boasted as well a new grille, hood, front fenders and front lights, and various other distinguishing refinements.

Bob Lund watched over Cadillac for the next two months. On Monday, November 4, 1974, with 182,467 Cadillacs having come off the line since the beginning of the new year, Lund found himself in a new chair—and watching over car production in the millions. He was promoted to general manager at Chevrolet.

Moving into his spot at Cadillac—fairly enough—was someone from Chevrolet, the general assistant sales manager, a gentleman as Texan as the Alamo. Born in Anderson in the Lone Star State and a graduate of the University of Texas, Edward C. Kennard was a school principal in a three-teacher school in Carlos and an IBM specialist in San Antonio until after the war, when he happened to send a Christmas card to a wartime acquaintance. It was 1946 and the recipient of the Christmas card happened to work for General Motors. In January of 1947, Kennard found himself in Chicago as parts stock manager for Buick. Now, twenty-seven years later, having served GM in many cities and many capacities, he was at Cadillac. An affable, easy going man with an engaging Texas drawl that has never left him, Kennard remains a bit of a country boy to this day. He has a working cattle ranch just outside Anderson to which he returns for respites from corporate cares. It wasn't long after he joined Cadillac, however, that he sighed wistfully, "I don't get back nearly as frequently as I'd like to." There was much to do.

The lifting of the oil embargo hadn't erased the energy problem. It remained—joined by rising inflation—and the talk around Detroit, indeed the entire country, was the small car as the coming thing in America. Cadillac had an idea.

That's not exactly accurate. Better to say, perhaps, that some people at Cadillac had an idea. In 1970 the division had circulated a questionnaire amongst Mercedes and Cadillac owners, relating to the idea of a smaller Cadillac. This was not the first time such a survey had been made, but it was the first time Mercedes owners had been approached. Previously, shrinking Cadillac's size had backfired. Stylist Chuck Jordan recalled, "People kept saying, 'We've got to have a small Cadillac,' so we did it—and you couldn't give those things away."* Bill Mitchell pointed out, "When you do it, you've got to be very careful . . . you could have a helluva time getting a fellow to trade in his car." Both scorned the idea of the basic Cadillac becoming smaller. But a smaller *addition* to the line —"that," Jordan remarked, "would be something to look at." As to looks, said Mitchell, "nobody's buying Mercedes for looks."

In April, 1973, Gordon Horsburgh was brought to Cadillac from Chevrolet by Lund. His task as director of marketing would be to develop a marketing rationale supporting the need for a smaller Cadillac. This would be done in a series of meetings with Cole, Estes, Terrell and other corporate executives, Cadillac representatives usually including Lund, Templin, Horsburgh, comptroller Lee Busch and manufacturing manager Bud Brawner.

---

*Jordan was referring to a car of the late 1950's, called the Park Avenue, wherein Cadillac—in response to client requests for a car that might fit in their garages—lopped about seven inches off the back of their standard model and termed the result a short-deck sedan. It didn't fare well.

Cadillac, the official pace car for the Indianapolis 500 in 1973, left, and the Fleetwood Eldorado Coupe for 1974, right.

What exactly would be the point of a small Cadillac? The point was Mercedes. From about 22,500 deliveries in the United States in 1968, the marque had doubled sales to about 44,000 by 1973—versus a forty-three percent increase for luxury cars as a whole. Moreover, Mercedes was attracting a different kind of U.S. buyer, the sort of purchaser who, when asked what his second choice would have been had the Mercedes not been available, tended to answer "none" or "don't know." Demographically, more Mercedes buyers were younger, female, better educated, and "more upscale" in occupation than the average domestic car buyer. The marque was essentially unchallenged in a market niche it had carved out for itself. Cadillac dealers recognized that as heartily as did Cadillac management. In the spring of '72, general manager Elges had swung round the U.S. and found dealers voting 3.5 to one for a smaller luxury car. A year later the vote was six to one—and, even more ominous, an increasing number of Cadillac dealers were adding smaller car franchises, many of them imports, some of them Mercedes. That wouldn't do.

What to do. Certainly there was much to be said for the Mercedes package dimensions in terms of maneuverability, parking space and efficiency. But internally at Cadillac there was dissension. "The struggle to get this car," Bob Templin remembers, "was pretty much between the guys who say you can do this on a high priced car and the guys whose marketing expertise tells them that anything that is smaller has to be perceived as less value. You know, they ride a Mercedes and they say why would anybody pay $18,000 for that? But our class of customer has been traveling in Europe and he sees that nice cars can be built in smaller packages. I spent a lot of time running around the world motoring in these different cars of smaller size—Mercedes didn't invent the dimensions—and I came to appreciate them. There aren't many people in General Motors who have tried to drive an Eldorado through the Swiss Alps. It's an impossible situation. The rest of the world is just not compatible with our size of cars."

With the naysayers conquered—or at least subdued—there was one parameter set immediately. There would be none of the oh-a-small-Cadillac-here's-my-chance-to-own-one aura to the car. The theme of all-out quality and luxury was a topmost priority from the first. Lots of people in Detroit still remembered the Packard One Twenty, and although the efficacy of Packard's producing that model remains a hotly debated point to this day, Cadillac quickly decided a cheaper Cadillac was simply not the way to go.

By the time Bob Templin had arrived on the scene as chief engineer—January of '73—the project was at "the will-it-fly stage . . .

The Fleetwood Brougham for 1974.

The Sedan De Ville for 1974.

The Coupe De Ville for 1974.

Refined in both styling and engineering, with nine models in three series, the 1975 Cadillacs were introduced in September of 1974.

it was a conceptual thing, but what the product was going to be was not. We got into the hot and heavy breathing on the thing about June." Initially, everything was tried: body frame integral, full separate frame, front drive, rear drive, a rotary engine—"all the combinations, mostly trying to search out, was there some magic bullet . . . with no thought then to tooling costs because it wasn't clear what the hell the whole picture led up to." The body. Templin and his assistant, Dan Evans, looked at taking the car off the existing corporate intermediate body; no, too heavy, incorrect proportioning. They looked at taking the car off the '73 corporate compact body; no, that wasn't right. They looked at the Holden Statesman in Australia, the Opel Diplomat in Germany, the latter more intently. Templin again: "We brought Diplomats over and reworked them. We looked at the logistics of it and, as you might suspect, with the currency exchange going the way it was and the compromises that are necessary to bring out a body built to European practices, and they *are* different from the U.S. . . . when you add all that up, plus the 3,000-mile supply line, and all that, it just didn't wash."

Nor did the idea of having Pininfarina design the body, also considered. Having the car overstyled and determining who would produce the body were among the Cadillac concerns. Finally, because the division was in this new market segment for the "long haul," and because there was so much at stake, Cadillac executives concluded that, despite the cost, they really had to design an all-new body, styled by the General Motors Design Staff.

K Car was the code name assigned, that letter of the alphabet being free, having previously been assigned a John DeLorean project to produce a low-price Camaro which had died aborning.

"I got a sort of sinking feeling in the stomach when we were awarded that letter," Bob Templin recalled.

There was little opportunity thereafter for feelings, sinking or otherwise. Now came the seven-day weeks, the ten-hour days. Gordon Horsburgh was asked by Lund to coordinate an interstaff committee to meet almost weekly for the purpose of making a doublecheck on all K Car activities and as a means of keeping the general manager fully informed. The range of topics included engineering changes, manufacturing plans, public relations, merchandising and other promotional activities, moving in importance from the former to the latter. Critical path scheduling was the name of the game. The result was to be the introduction of the car in sixteen months from final corporate approval—two months faster than any previous all-new product development.

The news of the project traveled quickly. It was welcomed by Cadillac dealers, but there were rumors of friction between the GM high command and Cadillac division itself. The former wanted to take time to test both car and potential market (plus its effect on other division sales, Buick in particular) but Cadillac was insistent that the car be put in production as early as possible, the 1975 model year being the target date.

Cadillac market research people had conducted a major product clinic involving K Car prototypes in Anaheim, California in July, 1973. Seven hundred luxury car owners went through an exhaustive two-and-a-half-hour evaluation of the prototypes versus other luxury cars on the market. Several owners were involved in additional hour-long group sessions. Many Cadillac executives heard comments first-hand. At the completion of the clinic, Cadillac knew it had a go proposition and a pretty good handle on volume as well.

Among the offerings for '75 were the Sedan De Ville, far left, the Fleetwood Talisman, center, and the Fleetwood Brougham, right.

Betimes, things had started falling into place. The engine. An oversquare design, 4.057 by 3.385 bore and stroke, 350 cubic inches, an Olds' based V-8 with Electronic Fuel Injection. With a displacement only seventy percent of the De Ville, and a compression ratio of 8.0 to one against the De Ville's 8.5, it produced 180 bhp at 4,400 rpm compared to the De Ville's 190 at 3,600. Torque was also proportionally superior, a figure of 275 lb/ft at 2,000 rpm translating to seventy-seven percent that of the larger engine's 360 lb/ft at the same revolutions. Relevant to engine size, this made the Seville ten percent "better." Top speed would be around 115 mph.

Electronic fuel injection was not an innovation, Mercedes having used such a system for several years and the idea having originally been pioneered by Chrysler with the Bendix "electrojector," the father of all such systems, as far back as 1958. Cadillac, of course, could scarcely be expected to make mention of that. What Bob Templin said privately was, "There wasn't a system around that was worth a damn, so we started a program with Bendix to pull this thing off—and the result was the first system we thought we wanted to bet our money on." For official consumption, he explained its workings: "It utilizes a solid state pulse timed, manifold injection fuel delivery via eight injectors onto the intake valves. The electronic sensors monitor a wide range of factors necessary for desired performance characteristics, feeding this data to an analog computer, called the Electronic Control Unit (ECU) which computes the fuel required for optimum performance, and in turn controls the fuel delivered by the length of time the injectors remain open."

Innovative certainly for the new car was the Delco "Freedom" battery, never requiring water replenishment, this accomplished "by switching from antimony to calcium in the plates, resulting in

improved charge acceptance, decreased thermal runaway and reduced self discharge even during storage." Unusual for the new car too was the 80 amp generator, justified by the increased electrical load of the two electric fuel pumps, yet another unusual feature.

Perhaps unusual too—or at the least surprising—was the use of a Hotchkiss drive with live axle and semi-elliptic leaf springs. Independent rear suspension was not considered worth the extra cost and complication, this decision made in the light of substantial General Motors experience with i.r.s. over the past fifteen years on several of its makes and similar experience with the alternative de Dion type axle on the Opel Diplomat, as well as the Cadillac experimental work dating back as far as the 1930's about which the reader has learned in chapters previous.

Independent rear suspension is obviously more sophisticated than a live axle, and since the new Cadillac was to be an expensive car and a highly refined one, its rejection was particularly intriguing. Bob Templin explains: "We had looked at front and rear drive. We would have liked to have gone front drive, but unfortunately the only front drive hardware was too big, and to do a whole new front drive would have been a king's ransom. We just couldn't cut that kind of hardware for this volume a car. So with the decision to go rear drive, next came the question of what kind of rear suspension would we put on for handling. It sort of answered itself. All our simulation work [Cadillac's computer technology is probably the most sophisticated in the business] has shown that the only reason to put an independent rear on a rear drive car is for trunk space; you sure don't get anything out of it handlingwise. When you get right down to the nitty-gritty, the factors of compliance in the sus-

Preparing the way for Seville, workers completing new chassis pedestal conveyor, left, in the former Eldorado assembly area.

pension bushings and with radial tires and so on, if you do a job of matching up your compliances and look at the system rather than the individual features, you can't tell the difference from an independent rear on virtually any kind of road."

The pronounced American preference for live rear axles remains, of course, a lively topic for discussion in the motoring world. Maurice Olley, one of the world's greatest authorities on suspensions and queried on that subject by this writer several years ago, noted that "a rear axle tramps because of its low $4K^2$/track 2 ratio, i.e. the mass concentrated at its center. But today's *lighter* axle centers with heavier wheels and brakes have reduced the trouble of unsprung mass at the rear." He pointed too to the desirable features of a live axle seldom attained with i.r.s.—the rear wheels are always parallel and axle and road noises are insulated from the chassis and body by the springs. The most advanced independent rear suspensions have to accept great complication to match non-independent systems in these qualities, as witness Rolls-Royce and Mercedes-Benz.

Independent systems have also come into disfavor with some eminent contemporary engineers. One in particular is Giulio Alfieri of Maserati who, after designing high performance luxury cars with all types of rear suspension—i.r.s., de Dion and live axle—strongly preferred the latter as "giving smoothness and insulation from road noise that cannot be matched by i.r.s. or de Dion systems, and at practically no loss in handling qualities." Likewise, Opel's chief engineer has scored independent rear axles for complexity and allied servicing problems, factors in which he was joined by another prominent engineer, Maurice Platt, who has remarked: "One of Maurice Olley's 'dicta' in his last years was that it was a mistake to drive wheels which did not maintain a reasonably camber-free relation to the road—main objection being rapid tire wear. I don't believe i.r.s. is worthwhile for anything other than a real high performance car likely to be driven by really expert and critical people —it just isn't appreciated by the average owner. . . . The whole

Finishing the new chassis floor conveyor and putting in new lighting, center, and preparing delivery conveyor for components, right.

subject is both complex and interesting—no easy answers." And it shall doubtless be debated for some time to come.

The rear suspension for Cadillac's K Car was refined in details, with a rear stabilizer bar rubber mounted to the lower spring clamps and attached to the underbody structure with articulating rubber bushed links. Shock absorbers with pliacell gas chambers and large diameter bushings would serve to isolate road disturbances, the pliacell chamber preventing mixing of shock oil and reservoir air. As Bob Templin summarized, "we ended up with a multi-leaf rear which to the purists sounds like a step back to the Dark Ages but again handling and noise were our principal objectives that had to be met and this met them best of all. We modified the leaf rear by a very simple technical breakthrough—teflon interliners—and we got a very good leaf spring rear that doesn't suffer from all the choppiness and variable ride characteristics that leaf springs of the rear in the past have suffered."

Up front, the wheels, suspension and engine transmission unit were attached to a steel subframe. This subframe was connected to the body-sheet metal structure through a special mounting system consisting of six "Isoflex" cushions and two hydraulic dampers similar to those in the car's rear suspension. These dampers, mounted between the front sheet metal structure and the subframe along with the Isoflex cushions, dissipated impact energy and would provide an exceptionally smooth and quiet ride.

General Motors' three-speed Turbo-Hydramatic transmission was fitted to Cadillac's new car. The standard axle ratio (a "performance option" would be made available) was 2.56 to one compared with the De Ville's 2.73. For braking, Cadillac decided upon discs with ventilated cast iron rotors and single piston calipers at the front, drums at the rear. Bob Templin again: "We like to stop a car under high speed conditions and all that just like anybody else, but we likewise don't accept any squeaks, groans, grunts, rattles or stutters on the kind of driving most people do—so we looked at everything available and the weight of this car and said, okay, we can do a job that is 99.99 percent as good as four wheel discs and with fewer problems via an eleven-inch front disc and an eleven-inch drum rear."

Outside, Cadillac's K Car would be better than two feet shorter, eight inches narrower and a half a ton lighter than other Cadillac models, with its wheelbase set at 114.3 inches, overall length at 204 inches, width at 71.8 inches and weight at 4340 pounds. Its height (54.7 inches) and ground clearance (5.4 inches) would be virtually identical with its bigger brother.

As Bob Templin remarked during its development, the K Car had to veritably "ooze luxury." Structural integrity was paramount, anti-corrosion protection was incredibly extensive, and the sound absorbent padding throughout was simply monumental. Standard equipment would be lavish, ranging from automatic climate control, automatic level control and power door locks to washer fluid level indicator and warning chimes for the seat belt system. A buzzer would doubtless be beneath the Cadillac image, or as Ed Kennard would comment, "Chimes remind rather than order you to buckle up." Optional equipment would run the gamut from a dealer installed engine block heater to avoid cold starts and prolong engine life to a power seatback recliner, from cruise control to a limited slip differential, and from a theft deterrent system to a sun roof.

As for the car's looks, the new Cadillac had been fairly accurately predicted in a Harry Bradley drawing appearing in *Motor Trend*'s October, 1974 issue. It showed a distinctively straight-line treatment with ample glass area and wasn't far off in general, though in particular it didn't hit the mark. For some time previous, of course, Cadillac stylists had been evolving a variety of treatments: initially new sheet metal front and rear on a production Opel Diplomat body, which went to full-size rendering only; then to fiberglass models on a second car with strong Hooper-Daimler overtones and a third car with notchback. Both of these were shown to the board of directors in June of '73, together with two clay models, one a variation on the Hooper-Daimler theme, the other a variation on the notchback. New ideas in a clay model came by September of 1973, and the final fiberglass model followed in June of '74. Wayne Kady was heading the Advanced Studio when the Hooper-Daimler prototype was designed and when he left there for the Buick studio, Stan Parker took over the project and carried through to the final prototype, under the direction of Jack Humbert and Irvin Rybicki.*

Almost from the beginning, the new Cadillac was planned as a four-door car. As Bob Templin explained, "If we'd had our druthers, we'd have done a coupé and a four-door both. It depends on marketing. You see, we were not going after the traditional Cadillac buyer here. There's no point in spending all that money just to swap customers, or just take the same customers and swap their choices.

*These prototypes are shown in the color section of this book.

The first K Car prototype in test analysis, left, on West Coast highways; auto writers look over the Seville at Milford, right.

We want to conquest the guy who's buying the foreign imports, or luxury cars of some other description. If you're going to do any new car, you do a coupé traditionally. It has a bigger appeal and would make the car appeal more to the younger buyer. You can make a pizzazz-ier image out of the thing, and that was the tack we were on first. But other people in the organization felt that if you were going to conquest the foreign import, the sedans are the prime candidate. So let's go with the sedan, and if it has the acceptance we think it will, we'll bring in the coupé later. So that's the tack we went on."

What resulted finally was a car which, in contrast to the current crop of American Mercedes look-alikes, remained very Cadillac in flavor. The new hood design was a break from the traditional Cadillac raised hood. Squared quad headlights with corner illumination, the Cadillac grille with its egg-crate texture and various other touches made the new car a Cadillac to be sure, but one in its own right. Semi-circular wheel arches, a unique rear quarter treatment, the square-cut side windows, the tapered flute effect flanking the rear deck, the simplified V-front with staggered headlights— all were characteristic to the new car. A functional, uncluttered rear styling approach continued the design theme, the taillamps wrapping around the rear corners and incorporating the side marker lamps and side and rear reflectors. It looked a handsome package.

Meanwhile, as Cadillac engineering and styling was working its magic, marketing director Horsburgh was wrestling with another matter seemingly as complex, and fraught with problems as knotty. Obviously, Cadillac's new vehicle couldn't be called the K Car forever.

"Naming the car was an experience by itself," Gordon Horsburgh would reminisce. "Naming a car is definitely more difficult than naming your own child. There's a lot of emotionalism, ego-maniacal attitudes that come forth, and there were strong feelings within General Motors about the name for our new baby." And there was considerable discussion too regarding how closely to associate the car with the Cadillac name. At one time, during the energy crisis, it was suggested that all "Cadillac" designations be removed altogether—"that if the big gas-guzzling car became really an ugly thing, we might be better off" without the marque association. Ultimately, however, cooler heads prevailed, and everyone agreed that the strongest intangible the new car had going for it was its Cadillac parentage.

The other decision, the name itself, was not so congenially arrived at. Virtually everyone at GM was involved—suggestions were requested from Engineering, Manufacturing, Financial, Public Relations, Personnel, Reliability, Purchasing, the Corporate Design Studio and elsewhere within the corporation. Gordon Horsburgh set up some name selection guidelines, among them: "pref-

The Seville on the track at Milford, and being admired by two key engineers, Robert W. Burton, left, and Daniel M. Adams.

erably associated easily with Cadillac so would not have to spend lots of money in advertising for the association process"; "meaning is reasonably apparent, so won't have to define through advertising (Chevrolet had a difficult time with Vega in this respect)"; "no negative meanings—either distasteful, in general, or insulting to an ethnic or racial group. Sometimes, the main meaning can be positive (e.g., Concord—a patriotic association), but another meaning negative or inappropriate (e.g., Concorde is a big, supersonic plane); "no braggadocio, as the car's essential definition is one of understated elegance"; "a French name would, of course, be appropriate . . ."; "possible suggestion of worldwide appeal"; "possible tie-in with patriotism"; name has to "look right on car and in advertising" and be "legally available and not associated with a competitor's product."

Suggestions followed by the droves. Merlette, Sierra, La Mancha, Canterbury, l'Eclipse, Urbana, Le Nouveau, DeIntegro, Medici, Debonair, Berkshire, Caravel, Road America, Concept II, Americus, Leland, Minuet, Camelot, Renaissance, Counselor, De Ville— among hundreds of others. Some were rejected out of hand, others took some thought for the inappropriateness to become apparent. "Merlette" is French for duck, which winged creature appears on the Cadillac crest, though the duck seems scarcely the bird of a feather to the image the new car was designed to enhance. "Leland" had a commemorative nicety to it, but it was pointed out that Cadillac's founder "eventually ended up at Lincoln." "Renaissance" meant rebirth, which the Cadillac marque, its standard lines selling well, didn't need. And apparently in the frenzy of things one suggester had forgotten that Cadillac already had a De Ville in its lineup, although the name (meaning city car in French) would have been appropriate.

Names with any potential at all were evaluated by a committee comprised of Cadillac sales, merchandising and advertising heads and chaired by Gordon Horsburgh. "Rather intensive discussions ensued," he remembers. Interestingly, among the twenty-four "Preferred Names for 'K' Car" totted up in a memo dated June 7, 1974, not one was the name of the Spanish town which one GM staffer had suggested be spelled "Se Ville" for the new car.

Gordon Horsburgh was becoming discouraged: "I would frequently go to a meeting not feeling very good. I didn't have the name—it never zinged me. Then you find out nothing ever does zing you. It's just one long tedious work process."

The process was winnowed to seven names by late 1974. Earlier, "good name" candidates had been inserted in several of the marketing department's ongoing research studies. Now, one final and

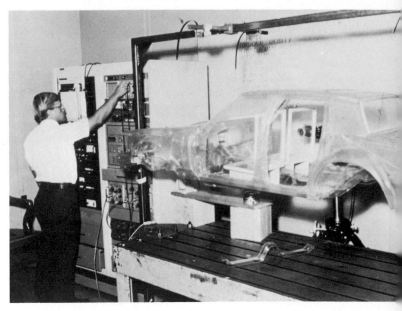

Plastic scale modeling, above, quickened the Seville's development period, enabling engineers to determine performance parameters while the design was under way. An automatic fast fourier analyzer, below, provided the method for dynamic structural analysis.

The Seville hoods, fenders and bumpers—new dies all for this new size Cadillac—were stamped out on Conner Avenue, above, and a conveyor took completed subframe, engine and rear suspension on two pedestals to the body drop area for final assembly, below.

more exhaustive survey was made with the seven finalists by D'Arcy-MacManus & Masius. The purpose was "to determine the connotations of each name that are most closely associated with the product's positioning and attributes." The method was a personal interview with 100 male owners of luxury cars (half Cadillacs, the other half Lincolns, T-Birds, Imperials, Rivieras, Toronados, Mercedes, Jaguars, et al.) in the Los Angeles and Baltimore areas. The seven finalists were Allegro, Couronne, DuMonde, Envoy, LaSalle, St. Moritz, Seville.

A 100-plus-page report resulted. The conclusion: "LaSalle and St. Moritz are generally superior to the other five names. . . ."— the former running away with a +187 score, the later a distant second with +97. Placing third with +35 was Seville.

Why then, one might ask, did LaSalle finally lose out? According to Horsburgh, the name was controversial. In its favor was the positive support it elicited, the nostalgia of a grand old name (several older Cadillac dealers still referred to their dealerships as Cadillac/LaSalle Sales & Service outlets), the fondness particularly among car buffs with which the LaSalle was remembered ("Gee, our old LaSalle ran great," Archie and Edith Bunker sing on *All in the Family*)—and "if Lincoln were to get rather pointed about the idea that the original LaSalle was dropped, we could remind them that the name Continental was dropped in 1948."

On the negative side, there was the simple fact that the old LaSalle had been dropped. It had been an astounding aesthetic success, but somewhat less than that commercially—and, moreover, the historic LaSalle was a less expensive car than the Cadillac, which the new car would not be. As Gordon Horsburgh remembers, "LaSalle would have alienated some people—maybe even thirty percent of our management and dealers—but the other seventy percent would have loved it."

As for St. Moritz, though three-quarters of the luxury car owners in the D'Arcy-MacManus survey correctly pronounced the name, the people at Cadillac concluded that the general populace wouldn't —and pronounceability, as any student of marketing knows, is a prime factor in name selection. Among the top contenders, that left . . . Seville.

The Seville name had been used before too, on an Eldorado coupé for model years 1956 through '60—and though its "positive thrust" was minimal, it had no negatives. The ultimate decision was entrusted to Ed Kennard and top corporate management. And when the decision was made, everyone decided that William Shakespeare had been right all along—and what's in a name was not nearly as important as what's in the car. And they were convinced they had a winner.

With the name of the new car chosen and made public, the media guessing game now revolved around the smaller Cadillac's price. Leaks to the press put the figure at between $11,000 and $13,000. The Seville would come in at $12,479. "There was nothing magic about that decision," Gordon Horsburgh remarked, "We took our normal markup, the normal dealer discount, although there was some consideration of using a slightly smaller dealer discount—sort of consistent with the car-size/discount relationship that exists in the industry (the smaller the car, the smaller the discount), and the fact that Mercedes and Jaguar do tend to have smaller dealer discounts. But we didn't. Our dealers spend an awful lot of money in their own quality checks and in their follow-up service. So, we went with the traditional Cadillac dealer discount because we wanted the initial quality of Seville to be just right."

However the price was arrived at, it slotted in nicely with the competition, the final figure of a similar order to the Mercedes 280 six-cylinder four-door, a somewhat smaller car than the Seville, and only two-thirds that of the four-door Mercedes 450 SE ($22,000) which was the car most assumed the Seville to be aimed at first and foremost. In Cadillac's own range, the Seville's price tag was topped only by the limited production Cadillac Seventy-Five sedan ($14,231) and Seventy-Five limousine ($14,570).

Money, however, seemed not a deterrent for potential Seville purchasers in any case. Well in advance of production, Cadillac dealers began reporting ample interest in the car by customers prepared to back their enthusiasm with cold, hard cash—people division officials described as "the usual celebrities, doctors, lawyers and board chairmen!" In Chicago, for example, one dealer held fifteen orders ($4,500 deposit each) a month before any customer had seen the car, or even knew what it looked like.* To the west, in affluent Sherman Oaks, California, Warren Swem of Casa de Cadillac reported 179 orders already by announcement date, with 300 prospects. And in Dallas, Texas, D. A. Bell, sales manager of Lone Star Cadillac announced: "The price tag hasn't scared anyone away. We have fifty solid commitments for the Seville, sight unseen, and another twenty deposits. They don't care what it looks like, what color it comes in, the interior, or anything. They

---

* The first photo to reach the press was a non-factory shot by Bob Irwin of the Detroit *News*. The Associated Press acted quickly and that photo, a three-quarter front shot, was already in newspapers as far away as New Zealand, *before* the Seville was officially announced.

just want the car."

Meantime, the press had been given a look at the Seville. In what was described as "the first preview ever conducted for the enthusiast press by Cadillac," the division made a number of the cars available to the media at the GM Proving Grounds in Mesa, Arizona. The event was held in March, 1975—and every key Cadillac executive from general manager Kennard down devoted two full days to driving and candidly discussing the Seville with motoring writers. The latter came away impressed.

Making two laps of the five-mile test track at 111 mph, Robert R. Tripolsky of *Mechanix Illustrated* reported: "You couldn't hear the wind whistling past or the roar of the engine. That's quiet and performance." "The Seville doesn't ride, it *GLIDES*," commented Mike Lamm in *Popular Mechanics*. "It's glass smooth, yet the suspension is firm enough so there's hardly any lean in sharp turns. Handling is one of this car's very strong points; quick, precise, predictable."

Motor Trend editor Eric Dahlquist was impressed to find Cadillac making available at the test track both a Seville and a Mercedes 450 SE sedan for no-holds-barred comparison purposes—"obvious proof of their convictions." "The new Seville," Dahlquist concluded, "is a smash. Make no mistake about that."

Karl Ludvigsen felt it was "the best Cadillac in twenty-six years [since the 1949 ohv model]." Driving the new Seville he found an "unexpected, pleasant surprise." The steering was light, but with enough feel, the ride smooth yet firm without a trace of wallow, while the cornering—he stated emphatically—was the best in Cadillac history and equal to many of the world's finest sedans. Regarding the invited comparison with the Mercedes 450 SE, Ludvigsen pointed to the difference in emphasis, Mercedes aiming for the ultimate in all-out performance and sporting capabilities, Cadillac showing best in the driving range most commonly used by luxury car owners. Cadillac owners, he explained, are "more concerned with silence at 80 mph than hearing an overhead cam engine." In appearance, Ludvigsen noted, the Seville succeeded as an obvious challenger in the Mercedes-Benz market, without even hinting at "the heavy Stuttgart style. . . . Clean lined, the Seville's styling will easily pass the test of time . . . artfully and subtly formed . . . delicate, bold and pure Cadillac at one and the same time."

A telling point was made by *Road & Track* merely by its inclusion of a Seville road test, a driving report of a Cadillac never before having appeared in *R&T* because it was felt the marque was not of particular interest to its readership. Now, the magazine

The Only Way

No matter what we say or show in our advertising efforts, or what others have said in praise of Seville, it is only in the driving that you will fully understand what kind of car it is.

No amount of words or pictures can come close to describing the new experience that is Seville.

So, please, drive one. Your Cadillac dealer will be pleased to make one available at your convenience. It's really the only way.

Seville
BY CADILLAC

THE CADILLAC SEVILLE, COMPARATIVELY

Rating the Seville vis-à-vis the larger Cadillac, the Rolls-Royce, the Mercedes was almost a mandatory exercise for various leading automotive magazines during 1975. The following table is a compilation of their findings.

MAKE & MODEL	CADILLAC SEVILLE	CADILLAC DE VILLE	MERCEDES 450 SE	ROLLS-ROYCE SILVER SHADOW
Price in U.S.A.	$13,700	$9,500	$19,500	$34,350
Top speed (miles per hour)	115	120	130	115
Standing quarter (seconds)	18.7	17.9	17.7	17.9
Braking 70-0 mph (feet required)	226	202	210	203
Cornering power (g)	0.67	—	0.70	0.67
Fuel consumption (miles per gallon)	15–15.5	11.5–12.0	11.5–13.5	11.5–12.5
Interior noise (decibels) at 70 mph	66	66	72	70
at full throttle	67	71	74	75

The new Seville—advertised, compared, and photographed.

noted: "Cadillac . . . one of the world's oldest luxury car manufacturers, and certainly the most successful, [have] set out after
the Mercedes and Jaguar market . . . significant is the fact that . . .
what they came up with . . . is a Cadillac . . . a very good Cadillac
indeed. . . . The Seville excels in those areas in which Cadillac
for a long time has set the standards; notably, almost total silence,
a high degree of comfort, numerous power accessories, lavish
interior appointments . . . an exceptionally smooth ride . . . one of
the highest standards of quality control of any manufacturer in the
world . . . very low frequency of repair rate, and excellent dealer
service." The Seville decision was a wise one for Cadillac, the
magazine concluded. It was a car which competed with the Mercedes and Jaguar, yet was distinctively different. It would add to
Cadillac sales instead of cutting into the bigger models' following,
and would undoubtedly increase the size of the total market for
smaller luxury cars.

In addition to the Mercedes 450 SE, *Car and Driver* included a
look at the Seville versus the Rolls-Royce Silver Shadow, the latter
the world's most expensive sedan, nearly three times the price—in
America—of a Seville. "What we uncovered in this comparison,"
C&D commented, "was how truly impressive the Seville is!" While
the Rolls triumphed in such areas as quality of finish and elegance
of walnut trim, the Seville's superior technology gave it the edge
in ride, silence, air conditioning, electronic fuel injection. "The
Cadillac Seville is a totally up-to-date car, with every convenience
the product planners can think of to insulate you from the hard-
ships of driving," the magazine remarked. "Yet it would make an
ideal Cannonball Baker racer, for it has the comfort, speed and
room, to move a relay team of drivers coast to coast without wrin-
kling their driving suits." (As mentioned earlier, a standard Coupe
de Ville had done just that already.) "The Seville," concluded
C&D, was "better than a Rolls in many important respects . . . the
Silver Shadow, a precious yardstick by which to measure any car,
pinpoints the Seville as a mass produced automobile cultivated to
an unsurpassed level of comfort . . . an American accomplishment
worthy of international esteem."

The Seville-Rolls comparison was ventured in England too, by
that venerable British motoring institution called *Autocar*. As
might be expected, with British nationalism in this case playing its
role, the Seville scored less impressively—though, again, the very
presence of such a comparison in an English magazine was noteworthy. Though the Rolls headed off the Seville in many particu-
lars, there was admission that the Seville was "more modern in
line and styling," it was softer in ride and quieter running, "but

Sporting new wheel discs, the Fleetwood Eldorado Coupe for 1976.

tauter in feel than the average American car." In quality of
finish, it was "a very different animal from the average mass produced American car"—though exceeded vastly in this regard, of
course, by the Rolls. Still, noting that the Seville, landed in
England, was priced at less than £10,000 with all options, whereas
the British car was priced at nearly £17,000 for the home market,
one of the *Autocar* journalists was moved to question, "Is the
Rolls £7,000 better?"

Subsequently, another British journalist suggested unabashedly
that "though rather doughty in appearance, [the Seville] gives
the buyer everything the Rolls Camargue has to offer, but at a
fraction of the price"—and pointedly noted that the *Autocar*'s
carping wouldn't affect "one jot" the Seville's sales prospects in
England.

Certainly the initial results proved this out. Lendrum and Hart-
mann, Cadillac concessionaires in London, advised that every
Seville it had been allotted—a year's quota of one hundred—was
sold before its arrival in England, and L&H executives were at
work on a feasibility study for a right-hand conversion which, they
estimated, would mean sales of "over 500 cars a year in Britain
alone."

All this was in the future, if in mind already, on the day of the
Seville's official debut—May 1, 1975, when the car was introduced
in dealerships. Production had begun a month earlier—March
26th—with 18,000 units planned for the remainder of the introductory year and a targeted 55,000 to 60,000 cars for 1976. That in
itself was an accomplishment. Although Cadillac didn't make its
dreamed-about model year '75 introduction date, the Seville did
move into production very quickly. Setting up a new production
line to produce a new car is no easy matter in any event, and with
the necessity of speed in so doing, general manager Kennard was

Among the nine other models in four series in the lineup for 1976 were the Sedan De Ville, left, and the Calais Coupe, right.

confronted with awesome logistics problems. Not the least of these dealt with the United Auto Workers; with a new line an old worker might not necessarily find himself in the same position, "bumped off" in labor parlance by someone with more seniority. Ed Kennard solved this by negotiating an agreement with the UAW whereby the men on the Eldorado line would remain intact to produce the Seville. Then he took the Eldorado, which was front drive, and the standard Cadillac, which was rear drive, and meshed them into one line, again with the full cooperation of the union. The Seville took over the Eldorado's old line. And to acquaint both labor leaders and the workforce with all problems involved, management arranged meetings to explain the situation and took the un-precedented step of showing them a full-size prototype of the car before even the press was invited to see it.

Initial Seville production was scheduled at eleven to fourteen cars per hour (as compared to the standard Cadillac's fifty-seven) —and the first 2,000 cars (one slated for each of the 1,600 Cadillac dealers) were uniform, silver in color with silver grey interior decor and identically equipped. The men on the line hadn't yet been trained for option fitting. Everything moved smoothly.

The picture wasn't entirely rosy, however. The Seville was introduced in the midst of the worst economic period in the United States since the recession of '58. On the day the car was announced, for example, Chrysler Corporation had voted to omit its regular dividend for the second consecutive quarter. GM had trimmed and American Motors had cut their regular dividends as well.

Moreover, the Seville itself had been greeted with some com-plaints—mostly from those who had been hoping for an in-metal confirmation of early rumors which had projected the car as a Wankel-engined front wheel drive design, instead of the stereo-typed layout finally adopted after the Wankel project was shelved.

As *Motor Trend* put it: "The criticism was, for the most part, not directed at the car's tangible properties, but more in reflection of unfulfilled expectations. People were expecting something *new*. What they got was a distinctive skin stretched over an existing skeleton."

Some of this criticism rankled the fellows at General Motors. As Gordon Horsburgh fumed, politely, "Some people have said that Seville is a takeoff from the corporate compact body—the Nova type. Well, as I understand it, all we have in common with that body is a floor pan and one door hinge. If you think that is too much commonality, you might want to consider that the all-new Rolls-Royce Camargue, at about $70,000, utilizes a GM Turbo-Hydramatic transmission!"

Sales, as always, would tell the real Seville story. There would be no fuming from Cadillac in that regard, for the Seville came out, in the graphic word of a former champion boxer, "smokin'." For years Monterey, California had boasted a disproportionately large quota of imported cars, particularly Mercedes models. The first day the Seville was available there, the local dealer reported four Mercedes taken in trade on the new Cadillac. "Monterey, that nut that Cadillac committed itself to crack," wrote automobile journalist Leon Mandel, "is definitely showing signs of becoming Seville country."

Comparison with Mercedes sales figures was inevitable, of course —and was in a way what the game was all about.* From May,

---

* A comparison with Rolls-Royce would be meaningless since that company has a total production of about 3,000 cars a year—and though Jaguars were among those cars Cadillac was enthu-siastically reporting as trade-ins on Sevilles, Mercedes remained the obvious target.

1975 through April, 1976, retail deliveries totaled 44,475 Sevilles (including export and Canada), 45,353 Mercedes—enticingly close figures, if a little misleading. Most of the Mercedes sales were diesels—forty percent—or other lower powered models not comparable to the Seville except in price. (Mercedes wisely gives the impression that its V-8's are big sellers in the Cadillac and Lincoln league. This they are not and never have been. In fact, the sales of its most prestigious V-8 model, the 600, have proved an acute disappointment to Mercedes.)

How the Seville has actually fared against the Mercedes 450 is not very clear from comments of company spokesmen on either side. Cadillac marketing director Horsburgh claimed "conquest business," while a Mercedes spokesman pointed to an 18.6 percent rise in Mercedes sales in 1975 over 1974. However, again, most of this increase was in diesels, and although Mercedes sold more of the low volume V-8, SEL and SLC models, its widely promoted V-8 (the 450 SE) suffered a drop. The Mercedes people blamed themselves for this, having introduced a competitive 280 S model—and attributed Cadillac's success to the Seville "creating its own little niche." An interesting admission certainly, since the "little niche" for this single Cadillac model was virtually equal to the complete Mercedes line; indeed by March/April of 1976, Seville sales had not only approached the figures for the *entire* Mercedes line, but had passed them! There was a note of authority in Gordon Horsburgh's voice as he lilted, "We're definitely influencing Mercedes. If you ask people what they would have bought had the Seville not been available, thirty percent mention a luxury import. The majority of those are Mercedes."

And then there is the tantalizing prospect of export. Calling the Seville "international" size was more than an exercise in rhetoric. As far as Bob Templin is concerned, he's now got his Cadillac for the Alps. Gordon Horsburgh can barely contain himself: "People see Seville as taking on Mercedes on the streets of New York, Miami or Los Angeles but why not on the streets of London and Paris and Frankfurt? We're not going to make sudden leaps but we're going to add some meaningful export business and that's all pure conquest. It will be a struggle, but GM Overseas is reorganizing its marketing thrust and the potential is certainly there."

And the plans are ambitious. In pre-Depression years, Cadillac exported as much as fifteen percent of its production, and the marque continued to be internationally popular for years thereafter, though the economics of small production had led to the discontinuation of right hand drive models and the abandonment after 1960 of the special export (crated, knocked down) sedan. In

The end of an era, 1976, the last American convertible comes off the line.

recent years, Cadillac export has totaled only about a thousand cars—"about half of one percent," as Gordon Horsburgh figured it, "and that's not very impressive for 'The Standard of the World.'"

During the Seville's first year of production—to the end of April, 1976—two thousand Sevilles were marked for export. This was merely a test—which was passed beautifully—but it was an effective doubling of Cadillac export already. Projected now for the long term is an increase in export volume to between five and ten percent of total production by the mid-1980's. As Gordon Horsburgh enthuses, "If we can increase our export volume to, say, 30,000 units, and, at the same time, divert 30,000–40,000 luxury import sales, that is a net swing of some 60,000–70,000 cars and, with a $10–$11,000 wholesale price, that's a three-quarters of a billion dollar shift in our nation's trade balance that equals the net export of the U.S. tobacco industry." For a small car, the Seville is a portent of big things.

There is no question but that the Seville has helped Cadillac in every way. Certainly it contributed to the sales increase for calendar year 1975, though, at 267,049 units, '75 was not as good a year as the Lund regime's 1973 had been. The continuing eco-

Later, Albert E. Collier, Gordon Horsburgh and Bill Knight look it over.

nomic malaise was being felt in GM's premier division, as it was throughout the corporation and the industry—but not as much. Early in '76, Cadillac could point to the three previous quarters in which the division gained nineteen percent over the year preceding, while the overall market suffered a five percent decline. Asked by newsmen to explain the why of these figures, general manager Kennard offered several reasons: first, Cadillac buyers are not as affected by economic downturns as other segments of the market; second, they may tend to look upon the Cadillac as an investment; third, moving up to Cadillac was no longer as difficult a jump as previous since price increases in smaller car lines had narrowed the gap; and fourth, with the GM announced intention to scale down their lines in the future, a number of aficionados perhaps were motivated, in Ed Kennard's words, to get "one last big Cadillac before they lose the chance."

The big Cadillacs for '76 were given, optionally, the Electronic Fuel Injection introduced on the Seville, there were styling refinements for all three of the traditional lines—Calais, De Ville and Fleetwood—and the Eldorado received four wheel disc brakes as standard. Perhaps most significant, however, was something that

couldn't be seen, even if one looked underneath or lifted the hood.

In 1974, tests at the proving grounds in Mesa had shown a typical standard Cadillac delivering 15.8 mpg at a steady 55 mph —provided the air conditioning was turned off. At 70 mph, the figure fell to 12.3 mpg. By detail refinements thereafter to combustion chamber, camshaft, clutch fan, air conditioning, et al., plus adoption of steel belted radial tires, electronic ignition and Electronic Fuel Injection, the figures were much improved. By 1976, respective EPA ratings were: for 500-cubic-inch V-8 models, Federal 12 mpg (city), 16 mpg (highway), California 11 mpg (city), 15 mpg (highway); for the Seville, Federal 15 mpg (city), 21 mpg (highway), California 13 mpg (city), 19 mpg (highway). This wouldn't, of course, plunge the small car makers into catatonia but the figures were noteworthy.

Still the big news for '76—and it turned out to be even bigger than Cadillac imagined—was a different announcement altogether, the fact that the marque, after holding out longer than any manufacturer in America, had decided to abandon production of a body style which the advent of air conditioning, hardtops and vinyl roofs and federal rollover standards was making pretty much obsolete in this country. As one owner of a '71 Cadillac model mused, "I love the bugs in my face in April, the cold drafts in January, the big back seat in June, and the way it makes me long for air conditioning in July." Fourteen thousand Eldorado convertibles, so Cadillac said in the fall of '75, would be built for the '76 model year—and that would be it. That would be the end of the American convertible.*

Probably not since Henry Ford announced the end of the Model T was there a more instantaneous reaction—or one more pleasantly rabid. Everybody, it seemed, now wanted an Eldorado convertible. By February of '76, sales were running better than double the '75 pace—and more than a few Cadillac enthusiasts began ordering the cars in quantity, for their posterity, just as diehard Model T fans had a half century earlier. A seventy-two-year-old businessman in Nebraska bought six, someone in Kansas bought seven—and an enterprising dealer in Louisiana bought three used Eldorado ragtops "at unreasonable prices" one week and sold them the next, to one buyer.

Dealers began besieging Cadillac and other dealers with offers of a thousand or two extra dollars bonus just to get one—and the factory stopped taking orders. William H. Leland II of Northboro,

---

* American Motors had built its last convertible in 1963, Chrysler in 1971 and Ford in 1973.

Massachusetts got his only after writing the Boston zone manager that he was a grandnephew of Cadillac's founder—and this word was passed to Detroit. And into Detroit, too, came countless requests from Cadillac fans that they be given the opportunity to buy the last convertible built, with all manner of reason—long-time devotion to the marque, et al.—why they should be chosen for the honor. It was all rather getting out of hand.

Befitting perhaps the dashing rakehell image of the convertible itself, a Knight came to the rescue, William J., director of public relations for Cadillac. In January of '76, he was chosen to chair the "Last of the Convertibles" committee. And he veritably—forgive the pun—charged into the project. Among other decisions, the committee quickly realized the dangers of building and designating a "last car." They decided instead on 200 last cars—each identical, white, with white top, white accented wheel covers and a red and blue "Bicentennial" hood accent stripe, each with an instrument panel plaque attesting it to be one of the last of the U.S. production convertibles. This seemed to solve one problem, though obviously these 200 cars would not be sufficient to supply the demand. "No way would I take one of the last ones," Ed Kennard would tell a WWJ-TV reporter in Detroit, "too much criticism, saying 'you wouldn't give me one, but you take one for yourself!'"

And, of course, there *did* have to be a "last" Eldorado convertible. Wisely, the people of Cadillac concluded that the car belonged to the marque itself—and it would be retained by the division for historical purposes. The other 200 were sold among Cadillac's 1,600 dealerships.

As those last 200 convertibles began rolling off the assembly line, there settled over the plant a haunting eeriness. The workmen began to sense the import of what they were doing, and employees from other departments began to drift in to watch. Men who had retired came back for a look as well.

And then there was the last day and the last car itself. It was April 21, 1976. Many of the men who had worked the previous shift stayed over to see the last convertible come off the line. Some made signs saying good-bye, some were wistful, others choked with emotion. Perhaps the notion that a car is just a car isn't true, not at Cadillac anyway. Not that day.

The fellow who affixed the hood said simply, "It's great to be a part of history," and a co-worker painted the dolly that carried car body to chassis red, white and blue for the occasion. It was a little after ten o'clock that Joyce Harlston, feeling "really proud," put the finishing touches—a label on the windshield wiper fluid

tank and a couple of knobs on the radio-tape system—and it was exactly 10:12 that the finished car rolled off the line. Ed Kennard was behind the wheel, general manufacturing manager Bud Brawner and Detroit mayor Coleman Young were in the front seat, several line workers were in the back—and cheers were heard all 'round. Some of the Cadillac people weren't convinced—or didn't wish to be—that this was really the last. Woodrow Powe, installer of fender braces on the line, said that in "three or four years we'll be building 10,000 more."

Perhaps. But it's unlikely. The figures tell the story. The convertible car market at Cadillac had shrunk from its ten percent norm to less than three percent by 1975. As GM board chairman Thomas A. Murphy remarked, "If as many people who say they really wanted a convertible would have been buying them, we'd still be building them."

Cadillacs for 1977, the Seville as refined, above, and the completely redesigned, inside and out, Fleetwood Brougham, below.

All this was reflected in the media coverage of what seemed to be the automotive event of the season. Journalistic wags made reference to "going 'topless' for the last time" or "top goes up on convertible era." Television stations across the country sent reporters and cameramen to Detroit, and newspaper editors from coast to coast found the subject worthy of nostalgic editorials. Some remembered back to the evocative "somewhere west of Laramie" advertisements of Ned Jordan when the open road and the open car was the only way to travel if one had romance in his soul, others remembered that the car Judy Holliday stepped into in the last reel of one of the few movies ever to bear a car's name was not only a solid gold Cadillac but a convertible too.

Ed Kennard allowed that Cadillac had parts on hand to build another thousand cars, though they would be retained for service, to keep these last convertibles on the road as long as possible. And

Refinements to embellish the Eldorado Coupe for '77, below, a new size, weight, and new styling for the Sedan De Ville, above.

everyone in Cadillac management promised to build a convertible again—if a viable market reappears to warrant production. Perhaps it says something about Cadillac too, that of all American carbuilders, it held to the convertible the longest, and gave it a farewell that will be long remembered.

In the meantime, of course, Cadillac goes on. Its 1976 model year saw 309,139 cars built—a record—and Ed Kennard's only lament was that he hadn't the facilities to build 20,000 more—he could have sold them. He doesn't cotton to the idea that the American consumer has turned away from impressively sized cars—"small cars are in for real trouble," he commented in June of '76. Recent figures would appear to prove him right. As long as there is fuel available, there will be buyers for the Cadillac, be it "international" or full size. That spring the division had a mere twenty-seven day supply of cars on hand, half the industry average.

This does not mean that Cadillac is unaware of industry trends. The marque has been scaled down some in recent years, first by the Seville addition—and for 1977 the big Cadillacs in the De Ville and Fleetwood series (the Calais line was dropped) were pared some too, via a new and lighter 425-cubic-inch seven-liter V-8 engine and with the lopping off of nine inches from the restyled De Ville and twelve and eight inches respectively off the brougham and limousine models. But it scarcely seems a concession. The cars are still Cadillacs—and all that the name implies.

One cannot imagine it being otherwise. On the writer's visit to Cadillac several years ago, this was brought effectively home. Descending a stairway in the engineering building, I was struck by the great wall-mounted replicas of the classic era's artwork, the almost impossibly elegant ladies with their Cadillacs. The ads had seemed nine feet tall even on quarto-sized magazine pages, here they *were* nine feet tall, and although it was 1973 and not 1933, they looked neither anachronistic nor out of proportion. Further along the stairway, in the company of Cadillac's chief engineer, I was shown a small plain wooden box. It held the original set of Johansson gauges. "We're getting them ready to put on display," Bob Templin said, aware, as was I, that here, symbolized in several dozen tiny polished steel blocks, was the essence of more than seventy years of a tradition in building automobiles to the highest standards of manufacture.

Nothing that has happened since the publication four years ago of the first edition of this history alters the conclusion regarding the marque presented then. The Cadillac is certainly a very substantial part of the American heritage. The chances are better than ever that it will stay that way.

CHAPTER FOURTEEN

ENGINEERING TO THE FOREFRONT

New Standards for the Seventies and Eighties

Entering the door of Cadillac's reception lobby, your eye will be taken by three striking exhibits: on the right, the last convertible of 1976, in gleaming white; in the center, a 1903 single-cylinder; on the left, a magnificent 1931 sixteen-cylinder sport phaeton, both of the latter finished in red. After taking in this magnificent display, you descend the stairs to the basement, where there is a selection of large-scale models, trophies, and other exhibits to highlight the story of Cadillac from the turn of the century down to the nineteen-seventies. As you depart the lobby to be escorted on a guided tour of the plant, you walk down a long gallery, lined with hand-painted color portraits of twelve great Cadillacs of the past—from the first of all Cadillacs with period-dressed couple, to the 1977 Sedan de Ville with a contemporary tennis group. There is the 1912 Cadillac with the second Dewar Trophy, a wartime staff car with General Pershing, the first LaSalle with a "flapper" of the Roaring Twenties, a sixteen-cylinder roadster with golfer in plus fours. Coming to more recent times, a 1938 town car with uniformed chauffeur, the 1958 Eldorado Brougham with jet-set business executive, the 1967 Eldorado front drive with yachtsman, and the 1976 Seville with a debutante.

These and other significant cars selected from Cadillac's rich heritage, plus the exhibits mentioned in the chapter previous, epitomize the factory's nostalgic tribute to its past.

The historical display reflected the influence of then general manager R.D. Lund and public relations director Bill Knight, but it also showed the touch of chief engineer Robert J. Templin, a man who is an enthusiast, an innovator, and a go-getter. "He's the best thing that has happened to Cadillac in years," one employee told me. "A lot of people around here, me included, hope he will become general manager." Although he has scathingly referred to some automobile publications as "penny dreadfuls," Templin has given correspondents

good value, with lucid explanations and adequate information. Motoring editors have found, with mingled amazement and delight, that under Templin's direction, Cadillac has moved in their direction.

"Surprise! Opulence can be fun," wrote David E. Davis, Jr. in the *Car and Driver* road test of the 1978 Coupe de Ville. Continued Steve Thompson: "With older Cadillacs, you gave orders to the helm . . . rang down for more steam. Damn the Datsuns! Full speed ahead! But that's all gone . . . the new Coupe de Ville is a civilized, decent performer."

"A solid piece of machinery that left me favorably impressed," added Don Sherman. "A revelation," concluded Larry Griffen.

"We may not be the people the Cadillac designers had in mind when they engineered the de Ville series," summarized Davis, "but it's a little startling to realize how far they've shifted their product focus in our direction."

The focus had, in fact, been in evidence some five years earlier, when I visited the plant in June, 1973 to see the five-millionth car come off the line. At a memorable luncheon later, in the executive dining room, I recall the owner of the car, one Howard Scharffin of Indianapolis, discussing with the Messrs. Templin and Lund, and myself, some of the characteristics, and the market, of the current crop of luxury cars—Lincoln, Mercedes, and Rolls. Lund dealt with the marketing aspect (mainly Lincoln, with some Mercedes figures jotted on a blotter I later pocketed). Templin took the cars apart, noting in particular that Cadillac, while aiming for the maximum luxury, prefers to keep some road feel in the car, while it is Lincoln's aim (he and Scharffin both felt) to isolate the occupants from all sensation of mechanism. Thus the comment in *Car and Driver*: "Cadillacs have rather sensitive controls, with quite a lot of 'feel' fed back to the driver. Lincolns are Novocain numb: no feeling, no sensitivity, just

A styling comparison, the 1977 Sedan de Ville, fitted with the 1978 upper grille texture, side by side with the 1979 "C" car body.

A new and bolder design grille, as well as new rear bumpers with vertical taillamps, distinguished the De Villes and Fleetwood Broughams for 1978.

softness and silence."

However, there was no more likable "driver's car" in the Cadillac lineup for the seventies than the Seville. Before driving it, I was told "it's a sweetheart" and "you'll fall in love with it," and this proved true. Responsiveness and feel, and the precision of the handling were a delight. (An added bonus was some mileage in a diesel version which performed as a Cadillac diesel should—quieter and smoother than any other, and as admirable in acceleration, in fact, as the legendary 1949 Cadillac.) In England, Ronald Barker and *Car* magazine were Seville-impressed. Barker, scuttling round Welsh border lanes, found the Seville better braked, and easier to place accurately, than a Bentley Corniche.

"Positive and not too light, with no appreciable lost motion, the Seville's steering lets you use every inch of a narrow road with precisely," he wrote. "There is so little body roll that passengers are scarcely aware of it, and the all disc brake system is beyond criticism."

Car commented: "The Cadillac has very good steering, the gearing is excellent and the feel adequate. It directs the car accurately, the chassis responding with consistency to strong understeer, so that it imposes its engineer's will on the driver." (Take a bow, Mr. Templin!)

"It has more natural poise than the Rolls," the magazine continued, "and is easier to hurry . . . when many drivers will find it preferable to the Rolls."

Comparing it with the Daimler Double Six Vanden Plas (which rated tops in the four-car comparison), Rolls-Royce Silver Shadow II, and Mercedes 450 SEL 6.9, *Car* found the Seville attained "quite remarkable heights of refinement," was "obviously a very good buy"

in its own country, yet (despite right-hand drive adding $2,000 to the retail price for the English market) "a fairly good buy in Europe, too." It was, in fact, "a surprisingly nice car," and because it came from the hands of the world's most adept production car stylists it did not really look out of place in Europe, either in size or appearance. "It has put the seal of desireability on a new era in American car design."

"Cadillac have an enviable reputation for models among the most refined and luxurious in the world," began the *Motor*, in a comparison between the Rolls, Mercedes and Seville. That magazine's conclusions, in a special eight-page article, were that the Mercedes was ahead in handling and performance, the Rolls tops in finish, but that the Seville was unsurpassed in silence, smoothness, comfort, and furnishings— and in completeness of equipment it was clearly "best value."

On the Continent, in an article titled "The Cadillac Crest Confronts the Mercedes Star," Gero Hoscheck of *Auto Zeitung* observed that "the Caddy is on course for Europe." Making direct comparison with the Mercedes 450 SE, he found that the Seville was the "sportiest Caddy" in existence. From 0-60 the Seville accelerated faster than the 450 SE, he noted, although the Mercedes was superior above that speed:

"The Mercedes has considerably better handling on curves, nevertheless the Seville can be quite quickly steered round narrow curves with the acceleration pedal and the agreeably direct power steering. At top speed (180 kph or 112 mph) the car holds the road well . . . not worse than the Mercedes."

"General Motors Nobel Marke is compact and luxurious, and has a restrained elegance," commented the Swiss *Automobile Revue.*

From the left: the Coupe de Ville, Fleetwood Brougham, Sedan de Ville.

"Engineering is standard but refined. Noteworthy is insulation against noise. The small 'Cadi' has better fuel economy (13-17 liters/100 km) than its sister models, and ought to be more economical than comparative U.S. cars. Maximum speed is about 180 to 190 kph (112-118 mph)."

The Continental critics were happily free from the pique evidenced in some sections of the British press, where the Seville's handling and steering were attacked as mediocre, where blatantly inaccurate road test figures were published, and where at least one basic premise was completely false. For example, the Seville's top speed was listed at a mere 103 mph, and its *between-walls* turning circle was compared with the *between-curbs* circle of rivals. The "basic premise" that "the Seville was intended purely for U.S. home consumption" was a curious description for a car advertised by Cadillac as "international-size . . . at home anywhere in the world." On a par, in fact, with another publication which, after admitting the Seville was "sumptuously-upholstered," and the most completely-equipped luxury car in the world, then labeled it "pseudo-luxurious."

Back home, as competitors from Lincoln and Chrysler duly appeared, the domestic press concentrated on comparisons among them. Michael Jordon wrote, "The Lincoln Versailles, the Chrysler Le Baron and the Dodge Diplomat . . . have their own marketing strategies . . . but the standard of reference is the Seville."

"Detroit's answer to the luxury imports continues its incursions into that market," noted John Ethridge. "During the two years since its introduction, some 77,500 examples have been sold. Not only has it been well received by luxury car buyers, but it has been carefully

watched by the whole auto industry. One thing for sure, Cadillac has a good thing going in the Seville."

A good thing going in America, a good thing going in Europe, and a good thing going, too, in the Middle East. In February, 1977, it was announced that General Motors Iran Ltd. had plans to begin assembly of Sevilles in March at a rate of 1,000 per year.

The arrangement was a partnership between the Shah, GM of Iran, and a local investor. Styling remained unaltered, but some chassis modifications were made in this "export" model. Most emission controls were deleted, and the compression ratio increased, while suspension settings were made firmer to suit local roads.

As the Seville had become an especially sought-after commodity in the Middle East, the plan for local manufacture helped Iran to keep more of its oil money at home. (One oil sheikh, the Sultan Qaboos Bin Said of the Gulf State of Oman, was currently reported to have ordered not one or two, but six Sevilles, cut and lengthened seventeen centimeters to accommodate desks, bars, and glass sunroof.)

More plaudits for the Seville came from industrial stylists. *Fortune* magazine, in consultation with a group of eminent designers and architects, named the Seville as one of the twenty-five best-designed of all products available in the United States. And it was chosen one of the world's ten most beautifully designed cars of the past fifty years by the Dean of the Parsons School of Design, David C. Levy. Said Levy: "Not only does this automobile, with its exceptionally clean and understated line, easily outclass any Cadillac built since 1940, it handily surpasses both its American and European competition. It is, in fact, the best looking American car I have seen in years." The Seville, in fact, had already established its character in motoring lore.

For example, in an amusing skit entitled "The Cradle of Sevillization," Ted West complained that the "august, beautifully engineered car" he was driving "really had no use for him." It had, he said, the cool, mortician-like self-sufficiency of "the proper butler" and considered him to be "essentially redundant."

In the 1978 model range a new Seville appeared, the Seville Elegante, which Cadillac said was "luxurious, versatile, elegant and sporty at the same time." Available in two-tone shades of brown, and black with platinum, it displayed distinctive script, had full wire wheels, and specially-styled exterior moldings.

"The interior," noted Cadillac, "is luxurious even by Seville's demanding standards." Leather/vinyl seat and door trim with segments of perforated leather and suede-like accent stripes were offered in gray or saddle. The steering wheel was wrapped in matching leather. The center console featured folding armrest, interior light, rear floor courtesy lamps, writing tablet and provision for a tape storage cabinet or telephone.

General manager Kennard commented, "The Elegante was researched at auto show displays for two years, and received with great enthusiasm by our most discriminating prospects and owners. We plan to build 5,000 Seville Elegantes during 1978." Kennard also announced that for 1978, "we're again planning to personalize between thirty-five and forty percent of our Eldorados with the Biarritz optional package. Easily recognized by its uniquely-designed roof, special body moldings, opera lamps, Biarritz script, special accent stripes, and color co-ordinated wheel discs, the Biarritz interior highlights plush appointments with 50/50 pillow type leather/vinyl seating."

Mechanically, there were two noteworthy additions to the Seville for '78. One was the Trip Computer, a high performance electronic device which Karl Ludvigsen called "something that's sure to be the envy of every other luxury car maker in the world. Not since the first car radio has anything this entertaining decorated a dashboard."

More matter-of-factly, chief engineer Templin announced that it was "the latest state-of-the-art technology in onboard computer systems." Preprogrammed, it computes and displays operational information in three separate instrument panel areas. A typical example is miles per gallon, which can be obtained at the press of a button, for any and each continuous instant of driving. It will show, for example, the effect air conditioning has on the car's fuel economy. These, and many other items of information available instantaneously, bear out Templin's statement that it "provides important benefits for the Seville owner by accurately displaying functional information, which, before this unit, was a calculated guess at best."

"By using the information provided," he continued, "drivers will be able to form more efficient, fuel saving operating habits."

The Trip Computer was Cadillac's own offering (made by Delco), but the other major addition, also with an eye on fuel economy, came from Oldsmobile. This was the diesel V-8, which, in addition to its economy, met emission standards without a catalytic converter or exhaust-gas-recirculation valve. Approximately 1,500 diesel-powered Sevilles were scheduled to be produced during the 1978 model run, with an EPA mileage certification of 21 mpg (city) and 30 mpg (highway). This gave an average rating of 24 mpg—nearly fifty percent better than the gasoline-powered Seville.

Comparison with domestic competitors centered mainly around the Lincoln Versailles, announced in May, 1977—nearly two years after the Seville. Whereas the Seville had broken entirely new ground in styling, the Versailles emerged as a scaled-down Continental Mark V. While built with the care traditional at Lincoln, there remains the question as to whether scaling down a large luxury design is wholly successful. Packard attempted it with indifferent results in 1936, and Lincoln would seem to have fared little better in 1977. "Chunky" and "stubby" were frequent criticisms, and whether or not this affected

sales, there is ample evidence that marketing of the Versailles did not match up to Ford Motor Company aspirations, at least in the first year. Doubtless strong corrective measures will be taken. Meantime, a look at general specifications for the two rivals:

	Seville	Versailles
Basic Price	$13,359	$11,552
Engine	350 V-8	351 V-8
Wheelbase, inches	114.3	109.9
Length, inches	204	201
Weight, inches	4406	3956
0-60 time	11.5	11.1
Gas mileage	14	18
(EPA Combined)		

The introductory year of the Lincoln Versailles also saw an important personnel change at Cadillac. The popular Bill Knight who, among many other things, was a constant help in the original compilation of this Cadillac history, left Cadillac after twenty-two years to take up the post of General Motors public relations manager for the North Central Region, in Chicago.

Succeeding him was Patricia Montgomery who, as the new director of Cadillac public relations, became the first woman to head any of GM's five car divisions in such a capacity. Patricia, a journalism graduate from the University of Missouri, worked for United Press as a reporter and feature writer, then held writing and editing positions with the *Chicago Daily News* and *House & Garden* magazine, followed by a thirteen-year stint in public relations with American Airlines in New York and subsequently the position as director of public relations for GM's New Departure-Hyatt Bearings Division. Women have always been in the picture at Cadillac—quite literally as sophisticated figures in advertising, back through the thirties, the twenties, even the teens. On the production line, where they make up thirty percent of the payroll, or as cool-super-efficient secretaries, women count at Cadillac. Patricia Montgomery's appointment symbolized all that they had done to make Cadillac what it is.

But 1977 was also tinged with sadness where Cadillac personalities were concerned. Bob Templin had earlier pointed out to me that no less than seven successive chief engineers of Cadillac were still living. With his interest in tradition, he hoped to assemble them all for a group photograph. Regretably, during 1977, this happy situation no longer obtained. That year saw the passing of Benjamin Anibal, Ernest Seaholm, and—unexpectedly—Edward N. Cole. Anibal and Seaholm received routine obituaries—both men were over ninety—but the death of Ed Cole, in a plane crash in May, came as a shock to many. "He had twenty good years ahead of him," his widow Dollie remarked,

For 1978, the Cadillac Seville (above), the Seville Elegante (below).

as tributes poured in from across the country.

In any listing of Cadillac engineers, Cole ranks as one of the "greats," the equal of Seaholm, if not comparable with Kettering or Leland himself. In "retirement," he had become involved with several projects whose scale suited his own dynamic stature. One such, a Cadillac for a king, was largely left in the capable hands of his wife Dollie. This was to design and produce an official limousine for King Khalid Ibn Abdul Aziz of Saudi Arabia. This car, to be four feet longer than standard Fleetwoods (it measured twenty-five feet two inches overall) required special interior appointments to suit the perquisites and duties of government and to make it the official transportation and home-away-from-palace of King Khalid.

"The terminology, 'fit for a King,' suits," recalled Dollie Cole. "This unique automobile was designed for delivery to one of the world's few remaining Kings and had to be the best."

After a visit to Saudi Arabia as guest of the King, Mrs. Cole drew up a list of requirements and ordered a Fleetwood limousine. Upon advice from some Cadillac dealers, the Wisco Corporation of Ferndale, Michigan was selected to carry out the conversion. This began with cutting the car apart, about which Mrs. Cole philosophized: "It must take a special brand of guts to put a saw and torch to a brand-new $15,-000 car right behind the driver's seat. The cut was made and there it

sat—a front end and a back end. Oh my God! was my only thought."

The interior was removed and extra insulation installed to assist the air conditioning in maintaining the requisite 55⁰ internal temperature in the Arabian 125⁰ ambient, also to muffle noise from the specially designed heavy duty electrical system and booster pumps. Modified suspension coped with the additional four-foot length and 1,800-pound weight, with additional stabilizing to cut road sway in the rear end. Drive train, air conditioning hoses, and brake and fuel lines were extended four feet. Special order, larger, steel belted radial tires were supplied by Uniroyal, each with a load rating of 2,500 pounds. The car had the world's longest padded vinyl roof, stretching nearly fourteen feet, and all windows were special one-way mirror glass.

Internally, seating for ten was provided with four individual Fleetwood Brougham Talisman seats in the rear compartment, trimmed in luxurious dark-blue crushed velour "Medici" cloth. A needlepoint replica of the royal emblem in gold and green was affixed between the rear seats. Nearly fifty hours of hand workmanship went into this decoration alone.

Moslem religious scruples prohibited a bar, nor was a television set

Celebrating assembly at South Gate, the Fleetwood limousine for King Khalid.

356

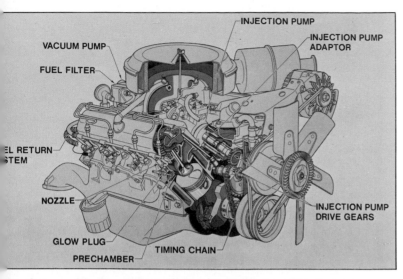

Cutaway of the General Motors diesel engine, Cadillac's new Trip Computer.

requested, although an eight-track stereo sound system and telephone were provided. A writing desk which folded out of sight in the center armrest was installed for the King's personal use. The entire project required five men and two women working a total of more than 3,000 hours, and the cost was reportedly "over $100,000."

"Every element in this outstanding car," wrote Dollie Cole, "was included to provide the King with the finest possible transportation befitting his position. It is elegant and pure class—it will provide the King a royal ride."

Turning from one King to a "King" of another kind, 1977 also saw the passing of the one and only Elvis Presley, "King of Rock." Press releases the world over somberly related how "ten white Cadillacs led the funeral procession out the gates of his mansion today, as thousands of mourners burst into tears at the sight of his copper coffin."

Presley had always been a Cadillac fan, and news reports placed his current collection at from four to six cars. In 1960 he had flamboyantly commissioned the creation of a "Golden Cadillac" that could stand comparison even with that of King Khalid. The car, a 1960 Fleetwood 75 Limousine, had been custom built for Presley by Barris Kustom City of North Hollywood. Inside there were such conveniences as an ice machine, an electric shoe buffer, and swivel television. The floor was carpeted in white mouton fur and all metal trim was finished in 24-karat gold.

Be it oil King or rock King—or affairs of state—Cadillac continued in the limelight. On the occasion of Henry Kissinger's retirement, at least for the moment, from political life, a correspondent of the London *Times* noted that an era had ended. "The crowd that used to hang around hotels and airports for hours just to catch a glimpse of the United States Secretary of State—or at least his famous armored Cadillac—are missing now," he wrote.

On the other side of the Channel, French President d'Estaing, in a Bicentennial Message to America, began his address with the words: "America has always held an attraction for France . . . French names bear witness to an ancient presence: Detroit, Cadillac . . ."

International publicity of this stature remained the envy of almost every other marque; to the "Standard of the World," it was taken for granted.

Turning from affairs of state to the antique saw more favorable publicity attend the Cadillac name: the "Bay to L.A. Run" in Los Angeles. This eighteen-mile event for pre-1918 cars witnessed a 1906 single-cylinder Cadillac take the Trophy for Best Performance. It was driven by its eighty-eight-year-old owner, Russell L. Squires, accompanied by his wife. "It was just another daily drive down Wilshire Boulevard for the Squires," commented Robert J. Gottlieb dryly. "He deserved the trophy, although he had an advantage over all other participants. The Cadillac has been in his family since new, and it is

Squires' only transportation. He drives it daily to market, on errands, and is a popular spectacle in the Santa Monica to Los Angeles area each and every day of the year."

Across the Atlantic, England's *Motor* celebrated its seventy-five anniversary. The editors selected twenty significant cars from this period to represent motoring's "Greats." First in the lineup was the single-cylinder Cadillac—chosen because it "demonstrated that the days of the hand-built car were numbered." The magazine tried out a 1903 model from the National Motor Museum at Beaulieu, and commented that it was "well designed and excellently made . . . the workmanship throughout is sound." A run in it proved "splendid" and brought its passengers back to London "comfortable and happy, free from any feeling of fatigue, and [hoping] to repeat our experiences under circumstances equally pleasant."

After that, it appears further comment on the Cadillac mystique

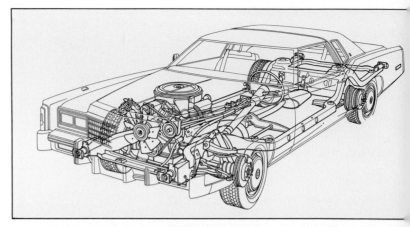

Cutaway drawing of the 1978 Eldorado (above), the Eldorado Biarritz (below).

The Eldorado for 1978 (below), the special "Custom Biarritz Classic" (above).

would be rather superfluous. Let us return instead to technical matters of the present day.

When the 1977 models made their bow, Cadillac announced "the next generation of the luxury car . . . taking advantage of the most advanced automotive technology." This brought heckles, particularly when Bob Templin laid these comments on the staff of *Car and Driver*. Yet the results of an impartial comparison test among the Cadillac and its three closest rivals indicated the claim could not be taken lightly. Least of all by *Car and Driver*, since that magazine was responsible for the test. Briefly, the box score was:

	Cadillac Coupe de Ville	Lincoln Continental V	Mercedes Benz 280 E	Rolls-Royce Silver Shadow
Price in U.S.	$13,375	$15,500	$16,290	$44,225
Top speed (MPH)	108	106	107	106
Max. in second	89	84	90	65
Standing quarter, seconds	18.2	18.2	18.9	18.7
0-80 mph, seconds	18.5	20.3	22.2	23.3
0-100 mph, seconds	37.9	NA	NA	NA
Braking 70-0 feet	207	262	223	203
Fuel consumption MPG	16-17.5	12-12.3	15.5-16	11.5-12.5
Interior noise DB. at 70	67.5	66	72	71
at full throttle	79	70	77	75
Turning circle	34.1	NA	37.0	38.4

Performance figures for the 1977 Rolls-Royce were from *Road & Track*. All other figures derived from *Car and Driver* for 1977-1978 models. Criticism could be voiced of a performance comparison between a three-liter Mercedes and a seven-liter Cadillac, but this is countered by the economy comparison, which should favor Mercedes. In any case, that Cadillac—of all cars—should take a full-page ad in the *Wall Street Journal*—of all journals—titled "Mileage" indicates the changing times more forcefully than a public statement by the President himself.

To sum up, any car that can show to advantage against such esteemed rivals as tabled here is certainly not lacking in "advanced engineering." Nor, it would appear was the front-wheel drive Eldorado which, after more than a decade of production, remained a more advanced design concept than any that Cadillac's traditional rivals had in

Cadillac in production, 1978, above from the left: body delivery from Fisher, body wiring, component part painting, engine installation.

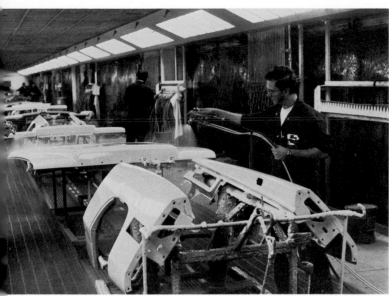

Below from the left: tire mounting, electrical inspection, the Seville body drop, the Cadillac body drop, the new cars ready for shipping.

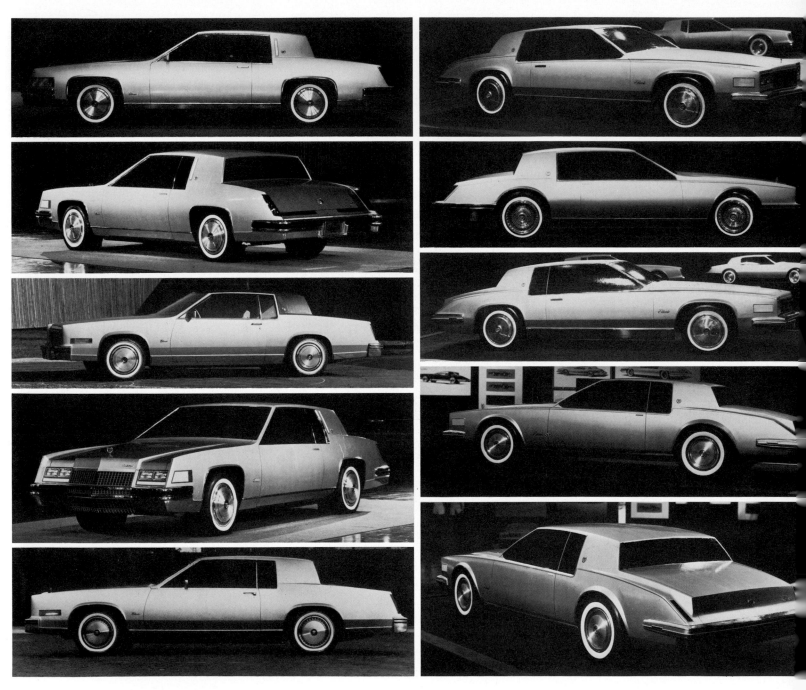

Variations on a theme, prototype proposals for the 1979 Eldorado.

General sales manager Lindley B. "Braz" Pryor.

Director of public relations Patricia Montgomery.

production. The Panther company in Britain certainly thought so. During 1977 it announced its extraordinary two-seater grand touring "Super Sixer," a 600 hp, six-wheeled sports car, with a top speed of over 200 mph, and capable of reaching 100 mph in seven seconds from a standing start. When questioned about the design of this "Ferrari-Killer," its engineer, Bob Jankel said that he decided at the outset, "that if he was to combine shattering performance with real ease of driving, he had no choice but use a big American V-8 . . . the eight-liter Cadillac Eldorado . . . with the advantage of its front drive transmission adaptable to a mid-engined layout."

Motor, which had already selected Cadillac to lead off its parade of twenty motoring greats, chose the Cadillac-powered Panther Super Sixer to close it.

The publication in England of Stanley Sedgwick's *Motoring My Way*, the automobile memoirs of the founder of the Bentley Drivers Club, was also of interest to Cadillac owners. Sedgwick, internationally famous for more than thirty years in the motoring world,

wrote: "There will always be room for an American luxury car in my Stable—an assertion which may seem odd from one so keen on Edwardian cars, Vintage sports cars and high performance thoroughbred cars, but I know what I like when it comes to comfortable, safe and speedy transportation."

After some pointed criticism about "uninformed prejudice" against American cars, Sedgwick detailed some of his experiences with "top quality American cars, represented by Lincoln, Cadillac and Chrysler Imperial." After some Chryslers, his first Cadillac experience was in 1950 when he was Le Mans pit manager for Briggs Cunningham. "Briggs lent me his latest Cadillac, which was being used by Donald Healey. It was a revelation in transportation to me," he recalled, "and I found its performance quite staggering. It was the first time I had driven a car with Hydramatic, and as a result, came to the conclusion that two-pedal motoring would oust the stick shift. I could scarcely believe that all this could be had for the equivalent of £1,000 in the States."

Congratulations for a job well done extended from Ed Kennard to a Seville worker.

Then, after several years of highly satisfactory motoring with a Lincoln Continental, Sedgwick had a unique opportunity to buy a Cadillac Fleetwood Brougham from Rolls-Royce Motors, that company having been carefully evaluating this example of "the best their Transatlantic competitors could produce." Sedgwick found the Cadillac an enjoyable means of transport and, with it, made his "one and only trip from home [Surrey, England] to the south of France in a day . . . a running average speed of 73.5 mph over 855 miles, accomplished in air-conditioned, fatigue-free comfort."

After a similarly satisfactory interlude with another Lincoln Continental, Sedgwick bought a 1974 Eldorado. "Do I like the car?" he asked. "Yes. Everything has worked faultlessly—except the never-used electric sunroof. The air-conditioning is superb. The Cruise Control is consistently accurate and the many other aids to effortless driving and comfortable travel work well. The quietness of the engine ranks with the best. And it was not long before I perceived the advantages of front wheel drive."

The advantages of front wheel drive had been engaging the attention of chief engineer Templin since the early 1970's. When the Seville was first mooted, several compact cars had been designed, prototypes built, and some testing done. The initial move was made prior to Lund and Templin, under George R. Elges. He had some styling prototypes built, and tested dealer reaction, which was generally favorable. During 1973 running prototypes were engineered, some around extensively reworked and restyled Opel Diplomats, including a three-rotor Wankel version. Front wheel drive was tried, and independent rear suspension replaced the Opel De Dion which Bob Templin particularly disliked as having the most drawbacks and least merit of all systems. Independent rear suspension with front drive was the way to go, he said. In one case, he recalled, "we built a front-drive independent rear car as short as 188 inches with the same room as the full size Cadillac. You can build a much more flexible line of cars."But, as Templin himself stated at Seville debut time in 1975, to put these cars into production at that time would have been too costly even for General Motors. The concept had not been abandoned, however, and it was now possible some three-and-a-half years later, to announce the car Cadillac had always wanted in the first place.

On September 20, 1978, Cadillac revealed its all-new Eldorado for 1979: "It retains the classic Eldorado look, handles better than its predecessors, has more passenger room and features sophisticated engineering advances." The new generation Eldorado presented a combination of engineering features not found in any rival—front wheel drive, four wheel independent suspension, four wheel disc brakes, electronic fuel-injected V-8 engine with diesel option, and electronic level control. It was Seville-size, twenty inches shorter in overall length than the old Eldorado, ten inches shorter in the wheelbase, and eight inches narrower. Yet internal room had been actually increased. Head room, leg room, knee room, front and rear, were greater, and there was also more usable trunk space.

The new Eldorado was 1,150 pounds lighter than its predecessor, and although using the 350 engine, actually outperformed the 1978 car with 425 engine. Gas mileage was dramatically improved. EPA estimates were: 22 highway, 14 city, with a composite of 17, a gain of nearly five miles per gallon over 1978. Diesel option Eldorados were, of course, better still: 29 mph highway, 21 city and 24 composite.

How was this miracle achieved? "We engineered the weight out, retained structural integrity and made the car more efficient," said Templin. "We designed the Eldorado chassis for efficient utilization of weight/space. Chassis weight is reduced by 224 pounds, we have an all-new transmission lighter by 56 pounds, and the power steering has been reduced in size and weight by use of a smaller pump and gearbox."

"There is over three inches more leg room than 1978, over one inch

For 1979, the Eldorado (below) and the Eldorado Biarritz (above), distinguished by its stainless steel roof cap and cast aluminum wheels.

The 1979 Eldorado, in cutaway illustration, interior view, and undergoing tests in the cold room to check out the window defog vent system.

more rear knee clearance, more than one inch rear head room improvement, yet the car's turning circle is lighter by over five feet, curb to curb and wall to wall . . . . The 1979 Eldorado has more usable trunk space, thanks to a new independent rear suspension that makes it possible to locate the rear wheels ten inches further forward. This, combined with a vertically-mounteed spare tire, increased trunk space."

The combination of independent rear suspension with the most advanced front-drive design yet produced enabled a lower car of reduced frontal area and less weight, Templin continued. Passenger space was increased and weight reduced by the elimination of the driveshaft and universal joints, and the tunnel housing. Elimination of the rear axle also improved passenger and trunk space, and gave better riding qualities. And—"The Eldorado also rides smoothly on new tires characterized by an aggressive tread that improves gripping ability on grooved highway surfaces and has all-weather traction qualities."

The independent rear suspension selected was the splayed trailing arm type first used on the Lancia Aurelia during 1950-1954. Although replaced with retrograde De Dion layout by Lancia, BMW adopted it for 1962 on their 1500/1800 models, where it was so successful that it has subsequently been adopted by Triumph, Mercedes-Benz, Rolls-Royce, and others.

Cadillac, however, was perhaps the first to experiment with this suspension layout. During the thirties, as mentioned in Chapter Ten of this book, an experimental Cadillac with splayed trailing arms was designed, built, and tested. The idea was to combine some of the best features of the parallel trailing arm and swing axle layouts, without their disadvantages. (Parallel trailing arms have a low roll resistance, and are liable to deflect unless extremely rigid mounting is provided. Swing axles have no structural deflection problems, a high roll resistance, and structural simplicity. However, their camber changes caused undesirable tire scrub and unpredictable cornering.) The design objectives were achieved at Cadillac in the nineteen thirties, but the complexity of the design in a rear-drive car caused it to be abandoned. From that time Cadillac engineers held that with rear drive, the marginal ride improvement with i.r.s. was not justified by

With the '79's and the press, Ed Kennard (far left and right), L.B. Pryor (left).

The 1979 Coupe de Ville (above), its interior (below left) and that of the De Ville d'Elegance (below right); prototype ideas for '79 (page opposite).

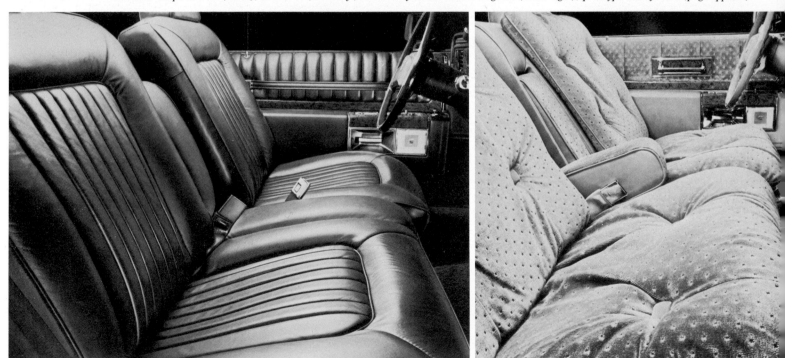

the cost and complication. With front drive, of course, the objections disappear, and in the new Eldorado the three objectives of excellent ride/handling qualities, maximum space utilization, and simplicity of design have been achieved to an extent unmatched by any rival.

The car declared its heritage in "clear, crisp, functional lines." The long hood and front fender lines were readily identifiable Eldorado characteristics. The Cadillac image was seen in the broad, low look, and traditional cross-hatch grille design framed by headlamp modules.

The frontal statement was reminiscent of some of the Cadillacs of the classic era—in particular, the 1941 models (note photographs on page 269) with a similar textured grille flanked by rectangular parklights. Also, the mitred cap of the 1938 V-8, V-16 and LaSalle (refer to pages 200, 266, and 404).

A new flush-mounted windshield both reduced wind noise and enhanced the frontal aspect. Its backlight profile reminiscent of the Seville, the new Eldorado featured rear quarter panels capped by vertical taillamps, and a clear sloping deck and bumper treatment retained the classic Cadillac look from behind. Available as a "special edition" Biarritz option was a brushed stainless steel roof—first used, Cadillac recalled, twenty-two years earlier on the classic Eldorado Brougham.

Enhancing the car's appearance was a new cast aluminum wheel, regular equipment on the Biarritz and optional on the standard model. It saved eighteen pounds of weight per car.

Internally, Cadillac called the new Eldorado "a car that is the ultimate in personal luxury and elegance."

The interior was "all Cadillac." The split front seats, with fold-down driver armrest, were available in a fashionable array of leathers and fabrics—eleven shades of leather, six of cloth. Also available were three combinations with white leather seats and black, blue or carmine instrument panels and carpets. Door trim complemented the seating decor, and carried simulated burl walnut to match the dash. The full width instrument panel was "functionally co-ordinated" with driver-only controls on the left, shared controls on the right. A center control and display area gave both driver and front passenger easy access to the new, electronically-tuned stereo radio and climate control. Other controls such as wiper/washers, headlamp and cruise controls were on the left of the steering wheel. A new two-spoke steering wheel improved instrument visibility. Also new was a combination dome lamp with fixed dual map lamps, located on the roof headliner above the front seat back. A cloth-trimmed sail panel with courtesy lights gave the finishing touch to the new, all molded cloth headlining.

The instrument panel upper cover incorporated outlets each side of the car to defog the side windows, a new feature. The cover extended beyond the panel itself, appearing to be part of the door trim, and creating the wide classic image of an integral "hooded cowl."

The Biarritz interior was a tufted seat trim design, in blue knit cloth or a choice of five Sierra Grain leather/vinyl colors. Included were a leather-trimmed steering wheel rim and plush floor covering "with the appearance and feel of fine fur."

Finally, to further reduce maintenance and enhance long life, wheel bearings were pre-adjusted, greased, and scaled at the factory, never requiring lubrication. Cadillac's best efforts also went into corrosion control. Bolted up fender design allowed complete phosphate and prince coating on the backside. The lower fender was wax dipped against road splash, as was the chassis frame. The lower half of the rear suspension arms was galvanized, and the entire assembly wax dipped. One-side sincrometal was used on the front fenders, and the inner wheelhouses were plastic, with integral, non-corroding battery trays. Molding either had gaskets or was non-corrosive bi-metal in all locations, and all visible underhood features had polyseal coatings.

Sophisticated quality control in manufacture included a 100 percent on-line check for the electrical system, computerized wheel alignment equipment for both front and rear wheels, and computerized torque control for critical fasteners.

With an overall length of 204 inches, on a wheelbase of 114.3 inches, and with a 350-cubic-inch V-8 engine inside, the Cadillac Seville for 1979.

Such was the all-new Eldorado. A car magnificent. An engineering and styling masterpiece. An American standard for the world. General manager Kennard was actually being modest when he announced: "The 1979 Eldorado rides and handles better than its larger predecessors, yet has the feeling of a big car. Our new Eldorado will fit well into the growing luxury car market, and be a distinguished companion to our international-size Seville."

Making similar announcements for Cadillac too was Lindley B. "Braz" Pryor who was appointed general sales manager on March 1, 1978, succeeding F.T. Hopkins who retired after serving nearly forty-two years with General Motors. Braz Pryor's career with GM began in 1947 with the Chevrolet Division sales organization in Dallas, and in the thirty years following he climbed the corporate ladder, with Chevrolet zone managerships in New Orleans and Oakland (California), was named dealer relations director in 1969, was promoted to an executive position on the marketing staff in 1971, and joined Cadillac sales in 1973.

Because of the ever-increasing demand for Cadillacs, 1979 saw the Eldorado with its own assembly facility in Linden, New Jersey. The home plant in Detroit continued to produce Coupe de Ville, Sedan de Ville, Fleetwood Brougham, Limousine models, commercial chassis and the Seville. And at South Gate, California, General Motors Assembly Division produced Coupe de Villes and Sedan de Villes.

Cadillac production for 1978 was a new record at 350,813 cars, well up even on 1977's 335,785, the previous record. The end of the 1978 model year saw production of the first-generation Eldorado total 464,650 cars—a record for American front-drive models. Accounting for approximately two-thirds of the domestic deliveries during the 1978 model year, the Coupe and Sedan de Ville maintained their popularity. Kennard said that the resized De Villes and Broughams were appealing to a younger type of buyer.

Fleetwood Brougham sales in particular rose from 28,000 in 1977 to 36,800 in 1978—a thirty-one percent increase. The de Villes were the most popular full-size luxury cars in the West, and South Gate was a natural assembly plant to fill the demand. Continuing the California phenomenon, San Francisco deliveries were consistently better than the rest of the nation. Over the last five years Bay City sales increased fifty-nine percent compared to twenty-six percent nationwide. Over the 1978 model year, San Francisco deliveries were up ten percent, and Cadillac's share of the luxury market grew from thirty-three percent to thirty-eight. From May, 1978, the Seville outsold the entire Lincoln line in the Bay area. Deliveries of Broughams doubled from 2,000 to 4,000, 1976 to 1977, and for 1978 increased a further fifty percent.

The Seville with metal-painted roof (left), the Seville Elegante (below) offered in a two-tone color combination of Slate Firemist and Sable Black.

Sharing dimensions with the De Ville series (221.2 inches overall length on a 121.5-inch wheelbase), the Fleetwood Brougham for 1979, and its interior.

A record 53,000 Sevilles were sold in 1978, up twenty-nine percent from the 41,000 of 1977. In Los Angeles, the import car mecca, Seville sales were up fifty percent over 1977. Nine thousand more Sevilles were sold than the entire Mercedes range of ten models, diesels and all, through 1978, in the United States.

"Current research tells us there's a strong feeling among luxury car owners that the smaller Seville represents the right size package for now and the future in luxury automobiles," said Kennard. "Since introduction, the Seville has consistently increased in international reputation and sales success against the luxury imports. Seville is doing exactly what we hoped it would do, diverting luxury import sales and outselling Mercedes by 23.6 percent through July of this model year." He predicted another record sales year in 1979.

A realistic sales projection through 1979 would indicate Kennard's prediction to be a likely one. If the relatively stereotyped Seville could outsell Mercedes, what of the new Eldorado, which excels Mercedes in engineering advancements and sophistication, matches it in quality, and substantially undercuts the equivalent Mercedes models in price? To add to the possibility that the Mercedes heyday in the American market may be over, the diesel Cadillacs have arrived as an extra threat. Kennard announced that not only would the diesel Seville continue, but there was a similar diesel option in the Eldorado, and that

The 1979 Special Edition De Ville Phaeton, and its "convertible-like roof covering," available in three color combinations as either coupe or sedan.

later in the model year, the same diesel option would be offered in the larger Cadillacs—the de Ville and Fleetwood Brougham. Not to mention, of course, plans still further ahead to "front-drive" the Seville, and eventually, the entire Cadillac line.

The European market, too, is certain to see more of the new Cadillacs. Sales projections for the next few years are high. Said Ed Kennard: "There's a lot of interest in Europe, and we have been doing reasonably well in that area. But it's been a minimum figure, primarily because we are taking care of our own home market first, and we have been somewhat capacity restrained in our Seville production, because we have a separate dedicated facility there [Iran] for the assembly of that car .... Overseas we are pretty excited about the E car—the Eldorado—and we have looked at developing a European riding package, just as we did for the Seville, and in Iran."

"We think there is a very big opportunity for our cars in Europe," said Peter Wallace, newly named GM director of sales with headquarters in Antwerp. "We find that our new designs are more acceptable in Europe and our cars are attracting more attention. Taxi owners are buying the Oldsmobile diesel instead of Mercedes." With the fall of the American dollar, European customers in the upper half of the car market find American cars great bargains. Always possessing a good reputation for ease of maintenance, their recent sales growth in

Europe has been strongest in northern Europe—the Netherlands, Belgium, Germany, Switzerland, the Nordic countries—where personal incomes are highest. The opportunity here for GM's quality marque is undeniable.

"In Germany," said Gordon Horsburgh, "we introduced the Seville head-on in terms of deutsche marks, in terms of dollars. With the change in currency we have got as many as eight to ten DM advantage vis-à-vis the 450 SEL in Germany. We are much more competitive than we were two years ago .... I can tell you that GM has taken a long term look-out to the mid-80's to really get Cadillac exports up by seven or eight times. As our cars get smaller and get the front wheel drive and independent rear design, in the ride and handling package, this is going to be the most exciting part of the business. Over the next decade, we are really going to begin burying those guys overseas."

Thus Cadillac, now moving toward its eighth decade, long the backbone of the American luxury car industry, has stayed ahead of its domestic competition, met, countered and outflanked the foreign invasion, and stepped in front with a new automotive concept that removes, at one dramatic stroke, any doubt about its leadership in the field. As the 1979 brochure so eloquently stated, it is now, "more than ever, at the summit of the car makers' craft . . . an American standard for the world."

INTRODUCTION
TO THE
APPENDICES

Despite the encyclopedic nature of the foregoing history, the editors felt it impractical to present in the desired depth the various specialty areas of particular interest to the Cadillac enthusiast. We therefore elected to rely heavily on the salvation of the historian, the Appendix—and we hope the following sections will serve to round out the history you have just digested, especially if you are a devoté of these interesting aspects of the Cadillac company lore.

Because of the esteem in which AUTOMOBILE *Quarterly* holds the leisure-time historian—the efforts of those whose avocation is the study and perpetuation of motorcar lore should ever be lauded—we open in Appendix I with a listing of the enthusiast organizations which welcome and revere Cadillacs and LaSalles today, headed by the outstanding group which has done so much to advance the preservation and enjoyment of the marques, the fourteen-hundred-member-strong Cadillac-LaSalle Club.

Appendix II deals with the story of LaSalle— the most complete history of Cadillac's companion car ever assembled, by a man particularly qualified to assemble it, Mr. Jeffrey I. Godshall. Therein you will read of the birth of the LaSalle, its important contributions to the Cadillac story, the great LaSalles of the classic era, and how the marque was almost dropped for 1934, only to return with a fine new streamlined design, but to die again, finally, in 1940. This appendix also contains the prototypal LaSalles for 1941, as well as the short-lived experimental LaSalle II sports car of 1955.

In Appendix III are assembled notes by the author on the coachbuilding activities of Fisher and Fleetwood. This section delves into the incredible efforts expended by these builders, the products which resulted, and what they were like, inside and out. Among the grand marques, Cadillac is distinct in having so many of its bodies crafted by its own coachworks. In this appendix the wisdom behind that practice is, we think, suitably revealed.

We are especially proud of the assemblage of Cadillac and LaSalle heraldry (and a few close copies from other sources) compiled in Appendix IV by Mr. Harry Pulfer, the recognized dean of automotive heraldic research. Mr. Pulfer has been of inestimable value to restorers for years, supplying to their specifications nearly every type of automotive badge, and from his detailed files our artist, Mr. Joe Trainor, reproduced the full heraldic history in this section. We urge anyone with specific questions on reproduction or coloration of these Cadillac or LaSalle badges to contact Mr. Pulfer at 2700 Mary Street, La Crescenta, California 91214.

Appendix V lists the key men in Cadillac's history from 1902 to the present: general managers, directors of engineering, design and sales. Appendix VI presents from the author's research a thorough summary of the specifications of every Cadillac motorcar ever built. In the interests of readability, you will find that the latter lists changes in specifications whenever they occur, but avoids presenting the same figure over and over when it remained unchanged in successive models or years.

The exact quantities of each model built have always
fascinated automotive enthusiasts, and we are confident that
Appendix VIII, by William R. Tite and the editors,
will be of interest to readers. Presented is the full record
of Cadillac and LaSalle production from 1902
through 1978, broken down by individual model and,
when available, by body style. Each year is accompanied
by two grand totals, one for calendar and the
other for model year, these being rarely identical except in
the early years of the Cadillac Motor Car Company.

In Appendix VII, there is a special page for Cadillac
wordsmiths, a glossary presenting the derivation
of some of the various model names used by the marque.

And Appendix IX, titled "Notes on the Chapters,"
presents additional information on Cadillac motorcars
which has resulted from correspondence and further research
accrued since the publication of the First Edition.
Finally, we have included two Indexes to this volume,
one of a general nature containing references
to all subjects covered in these more than four hundred
pages, the other an index of illustrations to
assist the reader in quickly locating photographs of
particular models in which he may be specifically interested.

No appendices would be complete, however, unless mention
was made of the many sources of reference available
to the Cadillac enthusiast without whose help this book
would have been, obviously, quite an impossible
undertaking. At the head of this list is the Cadillac Motor
Car Division itself, Department of Public Relations,
2860 Clark Avenue, Detroit, Michigan 48232, which has
a large file of readily available photographs for
the restorer or researcher. Among the many comprehensive
public collections available for the use of the
enthusiast, we should like to recommend two: the
National Automotive History Collection, Detroit Public
Library, 5201 Woodward Avenue, Detroit, Michigan 48202
—and the Automobile Reference Collection which
is located in the Free Library of Philadelphia,
Logan Square, Philadelphia, Pennsylvania 19103.

ORGANIZATIONS FOR THE ENTHUSIAST

CADILLAC-LASALLE CLUB
3340 POPLAR DRIVE, WARREN, MICHIGAN 48091
(CADILLACS AND LASALLES THROUGH 1952)

This worldwide organization dedicated to the history and restoration of Cadillac and LaSalle motorcars came into being in the summer of 1958, when Detroit enthusiast Norman Uhlir answered a newspaper ad by Kenneth Baldwin, who was in search of a speedometer for his 1931 Cadillac V-12. The speedometer exchanged, three meetings resulted in an interplay of ideas and the founding of an organization designed to help Cadillac-LaSalle enthusiasts communicate, locate parts, and obtain technical knowledge and assistance. The club has been a success story ever since.

The first publication, in August, 1958, was called *The Standard*, and included a roster of four members. Today, though the organization makes no attempt to advertise, it counts approximately 2,100 on its membership rolls. *The Standard* gave way to the *Club Bulletin* in November, 1958, when it was discovered that another group had already been using the title. Since February, 1959, it has been called *The Self Starter*. While resisting the inclusion of commercial advertising, *The Self Starter* has remained a refreshing, well edited monthly crammed with Cadillac lore and technical data.

The Cadillac-LaSalle Club does not require ownership of a car for membership, and accepts all Cadillacs and LaSalles after they are twenty-five years old. Specialists are available to assist members in specific areas and an annual directory of members and cars is published. Emblems and regalia produced by the organization "meet the Cadillac criterion for styling, durability and quality."

"Matching the reserve and dignity which has been character-

istic of the company that built the marques," says co-founder Norm Uhlir, "has been a goal of the Cadillac-LaSalle Club since the beginning." With membership scattered around the world, it has not been possible to utilize car meets as a cohesive activity. Rather, it has been the well performed task of *The Self Starter* to accomplish that goal. Cadillacs and LaSalles have been prominent for a number of years now in their successes at multi-car club meets across the country. The activity during the past few years "down under" in Australia and New Zealand has also been startling. "We are proud of our club because it has stuck by its original purpose of encouraging automobile enthusiasts to band together for mutual benefit in the preservation, restoration and enjoyment of the Cadillac and LaSalle." Applications for membership may be obtained from the membership secretary at the above address.

ANTIQUE AUTOMOBILE CLUB OF AMERICA
501 WEST GOVERNOR ROAD, HERSHEY, PENNSYLVANIA 17033
(CADILLACS AND LASALLES THROUGH 1951)

The oldest and largest historic car organization in the United States, the Antique Automobile Club of America now numbers over 35,000 members. Of its nine national meets, by far the best known is the Eastern Division National Fall Meet held in Hershey every October, with its huge concours and flea market, that despite a new record every year seems to become larger yet a year later. The AACA also sponsors the annual Glidden Tour, holds a national convention in Philadelphia, and publishes a bi-monthly magazine, *Antique Automobile,* plus an annual roster of members. Dues are $8.50 per year for a single membership, or $11.50 per year for a joint membership. The only requirement for membership is an interest in antique cars.

Horseless Carriage Club of America
9031 East Florénce Avenue, Downey, California 90240
(1915 limit for voting members; later cars accepted)

Founded in Los Angeles in 1937, the Horseless Carriage Club of America is dedicated to the preservation of motor vehicles of ancient age and historical value, their accessories, archives and romantic lore. Membership is open to all who have a sincere interest in the hobby and support the purposes of the club; ownership of an antique car is not required. A national convention is held in January of each year. In addition, the national club sponsors, during the touring season, two annual tours—one for single- and two-cylinder cars, the other for larger cars, both limited to vehicles of 1915 vintage or earlier. The HCCA has seventy-eight regional groups throughout the United States, and one in New Zealand. Generally, social activities such as local tours, swap meets, car shows, etc. originate at the local level within the regional groups. A subscription to the bi-monthly *Horseless Carriage Gazette*, the club's official publication, is included with membership, with classified advertising of a noncommercial nature free to members. A new roster of members is published approximately every third year. General membership includes husband, wife and all children under eighteen, and some 7,000 families are currently on the rolls. Annual dues are $15.00 per year in the United States, $20.00 per year elsewhere. A subscription to the *Gazette,* without membership, is $12.00 yearly in the United States, $18.00 yearly elsewhere.

Veteran Motor Car Club of America
15 Newton Street, Brookline, Massachusetts 02146
(Various classifications from turn of century to 1960's)

Those familiar with the antique car hobby usually recognize at once the colorful *Bulb Horn,* bi-monthly publication of the Veteran Motor Car Club of America, an organization founded in 1938 and now numbering over 4,000 members in fifteen regions and seventy-five chapters. The VMCCA has no fewer than nineteen classifications of cars, under several of which Cadillacs and LaSalles through 1942 are included, plus its Class 16 for "Classic Cars" as included by the Classic Car Club of America and its Class 19 for "Milestone Cars" as included by the Milestone Car Society. Along with the *Bulb Horn,* the club publishes a bi-annual roster of cars and members. Annual dues are $14.00, and the ownership of an antique car is not a requirement for membership. A variety of meets, tours, and social events on local, regional, and national levels are scheduled by its many chapters,

including the Glidden Tour. All correspondence should be addressed to The Veteran Motor Car Club of America, Dr. Robert H. DeHart, Executive Secretary, 105 Elm Street, Andover, Massachusetts 01810.

Classic Car Club of America
Box 443, Madison, New Jersey 07940
(Limited to "classics," 1925-1948)

The Classic Car Club of America was founded in 1952 to further the restoration and preservation of distinctive motorcars produced in the period from 1925 through 1948. Its classification procedure for the "classic" rank is based on objective factors such as f.o.b. list prices, production figures, classic components such as Bijur systems, power equipment, engine displacement, custom bodies and other concrete factors. The 4,000-member organization publishes a quarterly magazine, *The Classic Car,* along with a news bulletin and an annual handbook and directory, including rosters of cars and members, classification procedures, a current list of approved classics, judging rules and by-laws. Presently recognized within the "full classic" rank are all Cadillacs from 1925 through 1935, all V-12 and V-16 Cadillacs, all V-8 Series 70, 72, 75, 80, 85 and 90's, all 1938 through 1941 Series 60, all 1946 through 1948 Series 75, and all LaSalles from 1927 through 1933. Membership dues are $17.00 for regular members, $3.00 for associate members. Ownership of a classic car is not a requisite for membership.

The Milestone Car Society
Box 1166, Pacific Palisades, California 90272
(Limited to "Milestones," 1945-1964)

Celebration of the distinctive cars of the 1945-1964 period is the objective of the society, which was founded in 1972 and reached a 2,500 membership two years later. Cars are recognized as "milestones" on the basis of design, engineering, performance, innovation and/or craftsmanship. Each must exhibit excellence, relative to its era, in at least two of these categories. Approval is based on the opinion of a nominations committee including designers, journalists, engineers, and historians active in the period, plus ratification by members. Currently recognized are the 1948-1949 Series 61 and 62 sedanet and convertible, 60 Special, and the 1957-1958 Eldorado Brougham. MCS publishes a quarterly, *The Milestone Car,* and a bi-monthly bulletin, *The Mile Post,* along with a roster/manual. Research consultants are available for each model recognized, and dues are $12.50 per year, or $15.00 for an entire family.

LaSALLE: THE CADILLAC COMPANION

by Jeffrey I. Godshall

Against a seventy-year record of successful competition, Cadillac is obliged to recognize its one failure — the warmly remembered LaSalle. Despite a promising beginning, despite generally brilliant styling and obvious high quality, despite determined efforts to make the car a success, the LaSalle slipped quietly out of production in the summer of 1940, its passing scarcely noted by the automotive press. LaSalle's beginnings, however, were far more dramatic, stretching back twenty years earlier.

The sharp economic recession of 1920–1921 had a profound effect on the automobile industry and on the General Motors Corporation in particular. In the 1920 panic William C. Durant lost control of General Motors for the second and final time and left the corporation to begin again with his own Durant Motors. When he left, GM was a polyglot of unrelated companies with little central control and a confused product lineup. GM cars garnered only twelve percent of the 1921 U.S. market, compared with Ford's sixty percent, and the situation was becoming critical. In April of that year the GM Executive Committee set up a special committee of the Advisory Staff, headed by Alfred P. Sloan, Jr., to study the corporation's product policies. From that study came a report that would have far-reaching results. Sloan found that only Buick and Cadillac were established, money-making automobiles. The rest of the line was shaky at best and some, like Sheridan and Scripps-Booth, were real dogs. Sloan made plans to improve all lines and introduce new products where necessary, so that GM would have a competitive car line in every price class.

Sloan's study indicated that a car was clearly needed to fill the $1,000 gap between Buick and Cadillac, and in 1924 he requested Cadillac to study the possibility of producing a family-type car to sell around $2,000. At the time Cadillac was progressing in a steady but unremarkable fashion, clearly established as a leader in the high-priced field yet lagging behind Packard. Since the proposed new car was to be a quality product and since Cadillac production volume could stand a shot in the arm, Cadillac was a logical choice to build the new car. When Lawrence P. Fisher assumed the general managership of the Cadillac Motor Car Company in 1925, one of his first programs was the inauguration of a $5,000,000 expansion program which increased Cadillac production capacity to 60,000 cars annually in anticipation of the division's forthcoming entry into a lower-priced field.

So it was that Cadillac embarked on the design and manufacture of a junior edition of the "Standard of the World." The choice of a suitable name was no difficulty. Since Cadillac itself was named in honor of Antoine de la Mothe Cadillac, founder of Detroit in 1701, the choice of another explorer's name to grace the new car was indeed appropriate. That explorer was Rene Robert Cavelier, Sieur de la Salle, who claimed all of Louisiana for King Louis XIV of France in 1682. Unfortunately, the explorer LaSalle came to a sudden end, killed by his own men while leading a disastrous march through east Texas in 1687. Considering the subsequent career of the LaSalle automobile, the choice of names was unknowingly prophetic.

Yet the birth of the LaSalle was an event of considerable pleasure for Cadillac and of lasting significance for the automotive industry. Introduced in March, 1927, the LaSalle emerged as a companion to the prestigious Cadillac, aimed at the owner-driver as a man looking for an automobile of high quality and unquestioned value in a smaller, less expensive, more

A LaSalle on test attracts Santa Fe onlookers (left), arrives in Gallup, New Mexico, with same e.t. as "The Chief," in the background (right).

maneuverable package. No effort was made to conceal the LaSalle's Cadillac heritage and the car was unabashedly advertised as a "blood brother to the Cadillac" and of "genuine Cadillac calibre." The hoped-for target of $2,000 was not reached, but at $2,495 to $2,685, the LaSalle slipped neatly between the most expensive Buick ($1,995) and the cheapest Cadillac ($2,995). The price class the LaSalle was entering included some tough competition, namely the Chrysler Imperial 80, Elcar 8-90, Franklin 11-B, Hupmobile E, Jordan Great Line 8, Kissel 8-75, the little Marmon, Packard 6, Paige 8-85, Peerless 6-72, and the Roamer 8-88.

As nearly everyone knows, the LaSalle was the first production car to be designed by a stylist, and that stylist was Harley Earl. Earl grew up with his father's coach and carriage business in the years leading up to World War I. He was serving as draftsman and later as designer while still in his teens, conjuring up lavish and/or bizarre coachwork for the likes of "Fatty" Arbuckle and Tom Mix. After the war the Earl Carriage Works were purchased by the Don Lee organization, also of Los Angeles, and Earl was put in charge of the elaborate customizing and coachbuilding works. Earl now rapidly began to make a name for himself.

By the mid-1920's his fame had spread to Detroit, attracting the attention of Lawrence Fisher who was aware that many of Earl's successful designs had appeared on a Cadillac chassis. Fisher was impressed with Earl's approach to car design. Among his innovations was the use of modeling clay to develop the forms of the diverse components. In some of his creations Earl was also designing the complete automobile, molding the hood, fenders, lights, and other ingredients into a unified whole rather than a collection of unrelated parts. AUTOMOBILE *Quarterly* asked Earl for his memories of his first association with the LaSalle project. Here, in his own words, are some of those recollections, beginning in March, 1926:

"About 1926 Cadillac thought of coming through with the LaSalle and several people had worked on it to create what they wanted. They had a price on the car and they wanted it not to be quite as conservative as the Cadillac. They were shooting at more of a two-car family, that was their philosophy. Fred Fisher recommended that they permit me to do one, just to get a different angle. That's when Larry Fisher came into the picture and he asked me to come back to Detroit and talk to him about it. I was just to be a consultant to Cadillac.

The same LaSalle in Mojave Desert, February, 1927.

"When you are a designer, you kind of think, 'Well, if I were building one for myself from the chassis up, what would I do?' The Hispano was a car I was deeply in love with, from stem to stern. I didn't want to take too big a chance and do something that didn't look like anything.

"So I went back and sketched some stuff for them and they asked me to stay and finish it. The models and sketches took about three months, from sketch to mock-up. Mr. Sloan brought in the heads of the departments and asked if they saw anything that would be a problem, like tearing the dies and salvage problems. They went over it very thoroughly and said they would make some little dies and stretch metals. They didn't have any trouble. After a full-size dog was completed, Mr. Fisher gave me a trip to the Paris automobile show as a sort of token. It was my second trip abroad.

"When I came back I stopped to see if there were some little things that needed to be made — sometimes they get into slight changes after tooling. Fortunately, there weren't any, so I went back to California after completing the 1928 Cadillac for Fisher.

"About a month later Mr. Sloan asked me to come back to New York to discuss a permanent job in the new styling depart-

ment which was to be called the Art and Colour Section. I started that, and then the thing sort of grew...."

Indeed it did, and from 1927 onward the presence of the stylist became increasingly apparent in the design of American automobiles.

Fortunately for Earl and Cadillac the LaSalle was a handsome automobile indeed. There was a strong Hispano-Suiza look about the car (even to the winged radiator emblem), reflecting Earl's knowledge and appreciation of the most advanced of European design. Until the LaSalle arrived on the scene, most American cars were heavy and clumsy-looking, square-cornered and somewhat overbearing. The LaSalle, with its smooth hood sides and graceful tablespoon fenders, was a move away from the heaviness and toward the fleetness and grace of the mid-classic era. Detailing was equally impressive with a high, handsome radiator, headlamps mounted on vertical stanchions, and side windows on sedans reproportioned for a fleeter look. Corners were smoothed off wherever possible, and on some cars, the hood and cowl were painted a darker shade than the bodies for a unique look. The result was a very impressive car of unrivaled appeal to quality buyers.

The 1927 LaSalle chassis (above) and engine (below).

Customers had a choice of eleven body types in the standard line. Eight of these — the two passenger roadster, coupé, and convertible coupé; the four-passenger phaeton, dual-cowl phaeton, and victoria; and the five-passenger sedan and town sedan — were mounted over a 125-inch wheelbase, seven inches shorter than the smallest Cadillac. Three special bodies — a seven-passenger sedan, Imperial sedan, and five-passenger Imperial sedan — came on a larger 134-inch chassis. All came with Fisher bodies. Also available was a series of Fleetwood styles for those with more demanding tastes, including a two-passenger coupé and five-passenger sedan, town cabriolet, and transformable town cabriolet. The LaSalle represented good value. A dual-cowl phaeton with folding rear tonneau windshield, searchlight, six-wheel equipment with fenderwells, and a dashing appearance (to say nothing of Cadillac quality) could be had for under $3,000.

In engineering the new LaSalle was essentially a lighter, smaller Cadillac. Its 90° L-head V-8 had a 3⅛-inch bore and a 4¹⁵⁄₁₆-inch stroke. Total displacement was 303 cubic inches; brake horsepower, seventy-five. The 90° V-8 was introduced by Cadillac in 1914 and refined and developed down the years. Thus the new car benefited from the parent company's experience gained in building over 250,000 V-8 engines. The LaSalle engine was quite different, however, from the Cadillac's, being a completely fresh design which, in a larger-displacement/bigger-bore version, was introduced later in 1927 as the new 341 series Cadillac.

With the new engine, the LaSalle's connecting rod big ends were placed side by side for each pair of cylinders, a major departure from the interlaced forks used by Cadillac until then. The three crankshaft bearings were 2⅜ inches in diameter. Interchangeable bronze-backed, babbitt-lined, split bushings were used for main bearings. Connecting rods were ten inches long between centers and the big-end bearings were cast in. Unlike the previous design which placed cylinders in left and right banks opposite each other, and used a forked connecting rod on one side, the new layout moved the right bank of cylinders forward 1⅜ inches and placed two connecting rods side by side on the same crank pin. The detachable cylinder heads were ribbed for "cooling," a neat touch, actually for appearance.

There were two Morse silent chains forward, driven from sprockets on the crankshaft. One drove the centrally located camshaft, situated on the V of the engine directly over the crankshaft. The other chain drove the water pump and generator.

The single unit carburetor was Cadillac designed and built,

located between the manifolds and carrying a raised "LaS" emblem. Fuel was fed to the carburetor from a vacuum tank, a devilish device remembered well by our forefathers. Vacuum from the intake manifold was supplied to a vertical cylinder which induced gasoline to flow from the fuel tank at the rear of the car. Its advantages were complete independence from mechanical and electrical failure, but it was apt to go thirsty on a long uphill climb, when manifold vacuum dropped to the vanishing point. LaSalle sought to overcome this fault by incorporating a supplementary vacuum pump driven from an eccentric on the camshaft, which worked much in the same way the auxiliary vacuum pump on a latter-day mechanical fuel pump operates. A one-way valve was included in the system to make sure that the pump's efforts were confined to the vacuum tank.

The Delco ignition system featured a dual-point distributor with centrifugal spark advance, which Cadillac engineers claimed made the steering-wheel spark adjustor unnecessary, so that control was moved to the instrument panel. It was to be used only during hard cranking or when anti-knock gasoline was unavailable, when the car had the optional high compression head.

Engine temperature was controlled by external shutters which were operated by a thermostat in the header tank. Thermostatic temperature control was pioneered by Cadillac in 1914 in their first V-8. The advantage over the internal-thermostat, open-radiator system was that the entire cooling system, including the coolant in the radiator, was kept above freezing temperature during winter months. Cooling-system capacity was five gallons, and airflow through the radiator core was ensured by a six-blade, twenty-inch fan.

Lubrication was conventional; connecting-rod bearings were pressure-lubricated through a drilled crankshaft, and the timing chains were oiled by the overflow from the oil-pressure regulator. One feature that was new at the time was the provision for lubricating the valve stem from small oil passages extending from the cylinder walls.

Two famous conveyances of 1927.

The 1927 Series 303 Fleetwood seda:

The 1927 sedan (below), and its coupé line mate.

387

Braking was accomplished by two independent systems much in vogue today, though their actuation was by mechanical means as GM (and Ford) were still somewhat uneasy over the possible consequences of hydraulic line failure. The front shoes were internal expanding while external bands contracted about the rear drums. The handbrake operated through internal shoes on the rear drums only. This arrangement was identical to the Cadillac braking system. The conservative policy of remaining with mechanical brakes was perhaps unjustified, since other makes like Peerless, Reo, Paige, and Chrysler Corporation had switched to hydraulics. Indeed it was not until seven years after its introduction that LaSalle was finally to get hydraulics.

It would be a mistake to conclude that the LaSalle, for all its staid heritage and engineering, was an uninspired performer. Three months after its introduction a standard production roadster was taken out to the 3.78-mile track at the GM Proving Ground for a little high-speed work. Fenders and running boards were removed, along with the windshield and headlamps. A slightly higher compression ratio, a hotter camshaft, and a longer rear axle were the only mechanical alterations — but they were

Scenes from Bill Rader's GM Proving Ground high-speed testing with a stripped LaSalle roadster. On the facing page, Rader laps the 3.78-mile track and pits for refills. Below, the pits record a quick circuit, while, above, the tired driver finishes. His tires are below.

enough to reduce a lot of impressionable newsmen to open-mouthed astonishment. "Big Bill" Rader of the Cadillac experimental group and ex-dirt track racer Gus Bell were to serve as driver and riding mechanic.

The test run began at six-thirty in the morning, as the little roadster stormed off into its first lap, leaving behind an agglomeration of spare wheels, tires, fuel, mechanics, timekeepers, and hopeful GM executives, including Harley Earl. Within a few minutes the hopes of all were to be realized beyond their wildest dreams. Rader was lapping the track in the high nineties and hitting well over a hundred miles an hour each time around. It seemed unthinkable that a harmless little touring car could survive this kind of treatment for long.

Soon the first stop for fuel and tire inspection was due, and Rader slid the car to a halt as mechanics swarmed over it. A Cadillac bulletin described it thus:

"Comes the drone of the LaSalle as it roars up to the pits. The car stops, but the engine is kept 'reving,' the corps of mechanics rush each to his appointed task. Water in, gasoline filled, oil replenished simultaneously with the jacking up of the car; off comes the old wheel and on with the new — a drink of water for 'Big Bill' Rader, face blackened with grime and dust. Ready? Let her go. Engine accelerates with a roar, clutch goes in, wheels shriek and skid violently, and she's off again like a shot from a gun."

Rader made nine such stops and covered 951.9 miles at an

More test work in tandem on the dirt, 1927. Bill Rader at the wheel as W.R. Strickland looks on.

amazing average of 95.3 mph before an oil line fractured and put an end to the run after ten hours. The figures speak plainly enough for themselves, but they become downright uncanny when one considers that the 1927 Indianapolis 500 was won by a 160-hp Duesenberg at a mere two miles an hour faster — and over half the distance!

And LaSalle stamina was not reserved solely for the racetrack. In another remarkable test of LaSalle quality, twelve cars were picked at random from the production line and driven over 300,000 miles during a four-month period at the Proving Ground. To everyone's surprise not a single failure of a major component was recorded.

Beautiful lines, great performance, and a quality-car heritage made this first LaSalle a real winner and the public responded by taking 26,807 of the 1927–1928 Model 303. During the first year of LaSalle production, Cadillac was obliged to build nearly 21,000 more cars than it had ever built before during any single model year. Cadillac and Messrs. Sloan and Earl had good reason to be highly pleased with their new baby.

Part of this success may be attributed to the efforts of one Captain Edward V. Rickenbacker, who joined General Motors on January 1, 1928, as a sales "trouble shooter" for Cadillac-LaSalle. One of his accomplishments was the upgrading of Cadillac-LaSalle dealerships whose service departments were, in Captain Eddie's words, "in awful shape. Garages were dirty, the tools lying around everywhere. This slackness frequently spread

A well restored 1927 touring.

throughout the entire operation." Improvements were promptly undertaken.

With LaSalle selling so well only minor changes appeared on the 1928 model. Hood sides were changed to accept twenty-eight smaller vertical louvers, replacing the twelve coarser louvers of 1927. As with any successful automotive product, there was the inevitable urge to expand the line and Cadillac succumbed. Three additional models were offered in the standard LaSalle range, including five- and seven-passenger family sedans and a four-passenger coupé, all of which was accompanied by an average $155 price reduction. The Fleetwood line was greatly enlarged to include a four-passenger victoria, two-passenger business coupe, five- and seven-passenger Imperial sedans, and a five-passenger sedan and fixed transformable. Apparently Cadillac felt the day of the small, high-quality luxury car had really arrived.

One advantage in having a fine car like Cadillac as a sponsor was that when Cadillac engineers came up with any significant improvements the LaSalle was quick to benefit. So in 1929 LaSalle quietly adopted Cadillac's silent synchromesh transmission, introduced on the parent car a year earlier. The "Clashless Synchro-Mesh" was, of course, a major advance, enabling even the most novice driver to change gears smoothly and silently. Before full-scale production was realized, ten variations of the Synchro-Mesh were tested in twenty-five different cars run over 1,500,000 miles at the GM Proving Ground, indicative of Cadillac thoroughness. Other 1929 advancements included improved internal four-wheel brakes (again mechanical); safety glass; adjustable front seat; and that future darling of the stylist, chromium plating. The engine was rebored to 3¼ inches, resulting in a larger displacement of 328 cubic inches and sixteen additional horses.

The LaSalle lineup was reorganized so that all closed and convertible bodies were mounted on the larger 134-inch wheelbase while the original 125-inch chassis was reserved for the roadster and phaetons. Prices ranged from $2,345 for the two-passenger

The 1930 LaSalle convertible sedan.

roadster to $2,875 for the four-passenger phaeton, with Fleetwoods up to a whopping $4,900! Production held steady at 22,961 units, which meant that during three model years the division had built nearly 50,000 editions of a brand-new, relatively expensive automobile, quite an achievement for even General Motors.

Yet despite that apparent success one has to question how much faith Cadillac had in its original concept. For scarcely three years after its introduction, LaSalle had moved away from the compact luxury car concept. With the 1930 models *all* LaSalles, from the two/four passenger roadster to the seven-passenger Imperial sedan, were mounted on the 134-inch chassis, nine inches longer than the 1927 series. Whereas in 1928 there had been a difference of fifteen inches in wheelbases between LaSalle and the smallest Cadillac, there was now but six inches difference. True, the LaSalle's price range remained constant, meaning that the buyer was getting a bigger, more spacious car for his money, but is this what he really wanted? Perhaps

Cadillac felt compelled to up the wheelbase of the LaSalle as a result of competitive pressure. Many of LaSalle's competitors — the Packard 733, the Pierce-Arrow 133 Standard Eights, the Peerless and the Graham Custom Eights — all had models with wheelbases 134 inches or longer selling directly in LaSalle's price range. Once again, the traditionally American "bigger is better" philosophy triumphed.

Not that the 1930 LaSalle was a bad car. Mounted over the now-standard 134-inch chassis were new Fisher/Fleetwood bodies, styling being altered by making the radiator 2½ inches higher than previously. The six-model Fleetwood line used names like "Fleetcliffe" and "Fleetshire" to designate the custom coachwork. On the mechanical side bore was upped again to 3 5/16 inches, while the stroke remained the same, the result being a new displacement of 340 cubic inches. Horsepower was now ninety. But with Cadillac's immense 452-cubic-inch V-16 receiving the acclaim of the motoring press, LaSalle dropped out of the limelight it had enjoyed since its introduction. More importantly,

A two/four passenger Series 340 Fleetwood roadster.

Above is a 1930 five-passenger coupé. At lower left, an interestingly paint
four-door sedan of 1932, and at lower right, a 1931 Series 345A
two-passenger coupé. On the facing page, affording a close comparison
of different body styles for 1932, are a coach (above)
and a coupé (below), both in formal black with the heron hood mascot

production dropped sharply, only 14,995 of the 1930 Model 340 LaSalles being assembled. Wall Street had laid its famous egg and car buyers could sense the impending depression. Luxury cars (of any size) were the first to feel the effects of the slackening economy.

Management's reaction to economic despair and falling production was a curious mixture of advancement and retreat. To further entice the remaining luxury-car buyers a new 368 CID V-12 was brought out under the Cadillac nameplate as the LaSalle was simultaneously stripped of its separate identity. The 353-cubic-inch Cadillac V-8 was adopted as the LaSalle powerplant, and was to remain so through 1933. In an effort to promote greater interchangeability of parts among all Cadillac-produced cars, the LaSalle became, in every way possible, a mechanical twin of the Cadillac V-8. In addition, the wheelbase of most of the V-8 Cadillac models was reduced to 134 inches, so the two cars shared identical chassis as well. The main difference was the higher prices on the Cadillac (at least $500). Available in twelve body styles, the LaSalle's $2,195–$3,245 price range represented an average drop of $180. Detail improvements included single-bar bumpers and moving the battery under the front seat from its former position under the running board apron. Production fell again to 10,103 units, not as much as might have been expected. Still, on the registration lists more Cadillacs than LaSalles were sold to buyers, a situation that existed during 1930 as well.

During 1932 and 1933 seasons LaSalle offered an interesting car both aesthetically and mechanically. Body styling was new with more rounded lines and graceful "flying wing" fenders. Following the lead of Graham's famous "Blue Streak" model, LaSalle fenders were skirted in 1933. Also adopted that same year was a vee-d radiator grille and famous No-Draft ventilation as Fisher ended an era of drafty sedans and stuffy coupés. Once again management fiddled with the wheelbase, the 1932–1933 line comprising four models on a 130-inch wheelbase and three additional styles on a larger 136-inch chassis.

Engineering changes included an improved synchromesh transmission with silent helical gears in all forward speeds, six-point engine suspension cushioned in rubber, and two-way hydraulic shocks adjustable by the driver. Offered also was that automotive fad of the early 1930's, free wheeling, combined with a vacuum-operated automatic clutch. The driver could disengage the clutch by pressing a conveniently located button below the clutch pedal, while letting up on the accelerator at the same time. Gear changing could then be accomplished and the clutch re-engaged by releasing the button or stepping on the gas. The clutch pedal could also be used in the regular manner if desired. During the two model years horsepower was upped again to 115.

As with most companies General Motors was engaged in a continuous program of testing and evaluating competitive cars. This included the company's own cars as well. At the Proving Ground a 1933 Series 345-C LaSalle five-passenger sedan was duly tested and the crew's opinions make interesting reading. While the No-Draft ventilation was found to be practical and efficient, the car's overall performance was rated below average. The crew was especially critical of the lack of rigidity in the front end structure, which shook badly and even caused the spare wheels in the

The sporty 1932 convertible coupé.

fender wells to vibrate. Chatter bumps caused shivers throughout the car. The report frankly stated that the problem might "hinder sales." A far greater hindrance of course was the depression and production collapsed to 3390 cars in 1932 and 3381 in 1933. Consequently, LaSalle fell to twentieth place or worse on the registration lists.

What was happening was obvious enough. The automotive market had changed completely since the LaSalle's introduction and luxury cars had become just that — a luxury that most people could not or would not afford. The LaSalle had been conceived in the expansive mood prevalent during the 1920's, along with such upper and middle priced makes as Viking, Marquette, DeSoto, Pontiac, Roosevelt. Of all of these aforementioned autos only Pontiac and DeSoto had managed to get securely established despite the deepening depression. Most of the new entries never had a chance.

Even at GM the Depression caused retrenchment. Chevrolet and Pontiac production lines were consolidated, as were Buick and Oldsmobile. Pontiac, Oldsmobile, and Buick sales and dealer organizations were combined into a single division. The short-

From 1933, the convertible coupé (above), and imperial sedan (below).

lived Viking and Marquette and even the venerable Oakland were unceremoniously dumped and there was talk of liquidating the entire prestigious but money-losing Cadillac-LaSalle operation. The GM management team, headed by Sloan, was a hard-headed, unsentimental bunch. Despite a promising start the LaSalle was clearly on its way out, at least in its familiar form.

The story is told (which may be apocryphal) that the decision had already been made to kill the LaSalle when Harley Earl persuaded management to look at what he had in mind for the nameplate for 1934. The officers came, they saw, and then gave their enthusiastic approval, ordering the car into production. However, it is unlikely that anyone at General Motors made the decision so lightly. Something was needed to pull Cadillac out of the red and put it back on a solid financial footing. It was decided to continue building cars under the Cadillac name for the remaining luxury market while also producing a cheaper car that would hopefully increase production to a profitable level. This car would bear the LaSalle name and the target price was $1,000 below the cheapest Cadillac.

This was achieved by clever use of off-the-shelf parts from other GM divisions. Replacing the expensive V-8 was an improved version from Oldsmobile's L-head straight eight block, introduced in 1932, with Lynite aluminum Lo-Ex pistons and a thermostatically controlled automatic choke. A counterweighted crankshaft was fitted with a vibration dampener at its front end. The five main bearings, connecting rods, wrist pins, camshaft bearings, and timing drive chain were all pressure lubricated. With a three-inch bore and a 4¼-inch stroke, the 240.3-cubic-inch engine developed ninety-five horsepower at 3,700 rpm. Wheelbase was slashed to 119 inches, making the new series not only the smallest LaSalle ever but also the cheapest ($1,595–$1,695).

The most significant engineering innovation was the "Knee-Action" independent front suspension which was new to this country, although it had been used on European cars for some time. Chief supporter of the change from the solid front axle was Maurice Olley, although credit must also be given to Henry Crane, Ernest Seaholm (Cadillac chief engineer), Charles Kettering, Owen Nacker, and a number of unheralded Cadillac and Buick engineers.

Olley came to Cadillac from Rolls-Royce in November of 1930, and concentrated his efforts on developing a better riding car. Early in 1932 a seven-passenger limousine, nicknamed the "K-2 Rig," was constructed which enabled the engineers to alter various aspects of a car's springing by movable weights. In this way they could test various "rides" and so found that a flat ride was highly desirable. Attempts were made to achieve this by using extremely soft front springs with a conventional front axle. But the result was shimmy and lack of stability, as the Proving Ground crew found when they tested the 1933 LaSalle.

With the support of Lawrence Fisher, two experimental cars were constructed at Cadillac at a cost of over a quarter of a million dollars. These cars had two different types of independent front suspension, one designed by French engineer André DuBonnet, who was collaborating with GM, the other one a "wishbone" type developed at Cadillac. Independent rear suspension was also tested, Olley feeling that the time had come to get rid of the conventional rear axle as well. After much development work the cars were ready for demonstration.

In March of 1933 the members of the GM Technical Committee, including Sloan, Kettering, and high division executives, assembled at the Cadillac Engineering Building to ride in the two experimental cars and a conventionally sprung Buick. The three cars were run to Monroe, Michigan, and back, a distance of seventy miles. However, within two miles of the Cadillac plant, the ride had sold itself. Olley hoped that Cadillac would be granted exclusive use of the new suspension for the first year, but the vastly improved ride was so impressive that every division wanted it. Even Chevrolet could not be turned down. So all GM cars had Knee-Action on their 1934 models, Chevrolet and Pontiac using the Dubonnet system and the others, including LaSalle, the wishbone type.

As used on the LaSalle, the system featured a kingpin carried on a vertical support arm, to the top and bottom of which were attached V-shaped or "wishbone" links, which were in turn hinged to the top and bottom of the frame. With the upper link the shock absorber was bolted to the top of the frame and acted as the frame hinge. The lower link was hinged to the frame with threaded bolts and bushings to take end thrust. The same kind of bearing hinge was also used at the upper and lower ends of the vertical knuckle support arm.

The wishbone links completely controlled wheel motion, permitting the wheel to move up and down in an almost vertical plane and also absorb side thrust and brake torque reaction. Coil springs were employed, since if a leaf spring had been used it would have had to be extremely long to give the required softness without overstressing the spring. To guard against bottoming with the softer coils, rubber bumpers were installed inside the coils. Alternately, overexpansion was prevented by placing another rubber bumper on the frame where the upper link might make contact if it swung down too far. Individual tie rods to the

The much-altered 1934 LaSalle.

wheels were required to obtain proper steering geometry. Torsional stabilizer bars were used at the rear to help prevent side sway, resistance to which was lessened by the softer coil springs.

Eventually this wishbone type proved easier and cheaper to manufacture and more trouble free, and was adopted by all General Motors cars. Actually, the Olley-designed independent front suspension is the basis of many of today's modern suspension systems and in the designer's opinion a similar treatment for the rear wheels is long overdue.

The other important mechanical change was the adoption (finally) of hydraulic brakes. Hotchkiss drive was also adopted, replacing the torque-tube construction which characterized Cadillac products for the past six years.

To top off this new package, Harley Earl and the Art and Colour Section came through with another styling triumph equal to that achieved on the 1927 model. Body lines were completely

The 1934 sedan with bullet bumpers.

Thermostats for
Exhaust Heat Control Valve

Thermostat in
Water Outlet

Crankcase
Ventilating Outlet

Combination Fuel
and Vacuum Pump

New straight-eight power for 1934.

The 1934 Series 34-50 convertible coupé.

new, modern, and dramatic. All traces of the old "classic" styling vanished under Earl's supervision, replaced by smooth, clean, almost austere body planes. Even the spare tire disappeared, concealed in the fastback trunk, though fenderwell spares were available. The smoother look was relieved by such accents as porthole louvers on the hood sides and open, double-bar bumpers with telescoping spring mounts, a system returning to favor in face of the upcoming Federal bumper requirements. Wire wheels were covered to resemble discs. Pontoon fenders and the streamlined bodies gave the car a much more substantial look which was to influence heavily all GM car lines during the 1930's. But the focal point of the new styling was a very narrow, vertical radiator grille. This slim-nosed look was to serve as LaSalle's trademark through the 1940 model.

By boldly striking out into a new design direction, LaSalle stood clearly above its competition, most of whom were still trying awkwardly to adjust to streamlining. The model line was reduced to just four body types — sedan, club sedan, coupé, and convertible coupé — all by Fleetwood, with "unlimited" choice of color schemes.

With its new lower price the LaSalle moved into a different market entirely, competing with such cars as the Auburn V-12, Nash Ambassador 8, Reo-Royale 8, Buick Series 34-90, and the Airflow Chrysler Imperial.

The LaSalle was an impressive car and caused considerable stir among the more knowledgeable figures in the industry. One of these was Duesenberg president Harold Ames, who began planning a lower-priced Duesenberg using cheaper Auburn parts, in a frank imitation of the LaSalle concept. Ames got Gordon Buehrig to design a body for the experimental Duesie chassis and it was that car which ultimately emerged as the Cord 810. Strangely, Buehrig's concept was one Harley Earl had rejected during Buehrig's brief tenure at GM.

But the motoring public was unfortunately not as impressed. Perhaps the depression was still too fresh in buyer's minds. At any rate, only 7,128 1934 LaSalles and 8,653 of the similar 1935 model were produced, which must have come as a tremendous disappointment to Cadillac officials. In the meantime Packard was introducing its "120" line, which not only undercut the LaSalle's price but also carried the immense prestige of the Packard name. Nearly 25,000 Packard 120's were produced and sold during 1935, which cut deeply into LaSalle's market.

Bill Rader pacing Indy, 1934.

Detail alterations on the 1935 LaSalles included lengthening the stroke on the straight eight to 4 3/8 inches, increasing displacement to 248 cubic inches. Horsepower was upped to 105 at 3,600 rpm. Though styling remained virtually the same except for cheaper bumpers and a vee-d split windshield, Fisher's new all-steel "Turret Top" bodies were mounted on a wheelbase one inch longer. In response to Packard's bold thrust, prices were reduced so the cheapest LaSalle was now $1,255. This car was carried through 1936 substantially unchanged, except for minor styling changes and front doors hinged at the front for greater safety.

But Cadillac received some further bad news in the form of increased competition, this time from a new $1,275 Lincoln-Zephyr V-12. It seems as if every remaining luxury-car producer was getting the same idea at the same time. Another price cut to $1,175 base enabled Cadillac to produce and sell an encouraging 13,004 LaSalles, yet LaSalle still ranked behind the Zephyr (at 15,482) and far behind Packard's 120B (55,042). While a Proving Ground report on the Series 36-50 LaSalle stated it was a "very good appearing car with fair riding and good handling characteristics and considerable in-built quality," the public just

Above, the 1935 Series 35-50 convertible coupé. The mid-thirties styling mock-up below predicted much of the 1936 shape.

The 1936 Series 36-50 coupé.

wasn't responding with enough orders.

It became clear that the straight-eight LaSalle, however brilliantly styled, was failing to achieve the hoped-for production volume, so another try was made for 1937. A V-8 engine was returned to the car, this time borrowed from the 1936 Cadillac Series 60. This L-head V-8, which was to serve LaSalle to the end, had a $3\frac{3}{8}$ inch bore and a $4\frac{1}{2}$ inch stroke for a displacement of 322 cubic inches. Peak horsepower of 125 was developed at 3,400 rpm and the compression ratio was 6.25 to 1. The increased power made possible a reduction in the axle ratios, so that pistons in the 1937 V-8 traveled only 2,100 feet during one driving mile compared with 2,360 feet in the former straight eight. Other mechanical advances included an improved engine-mounting system, a carburetor with two float bowls to avoid fuel starvation on sharp turns, oil-bath air cleaner, hypoid rear axle, and a new exhaust system with a single large muffler instead of the two

smaller units used before. Oscillation rates of both rear springs and Knee Action units at the front were changed to produce a softer ride at low speeds and a smoother ride at higher speeds. Roadability was improved by the use of a torsional stabilizer at the front and a Panhard-derived track bar at the rear. Waxed liner inserts between the leaves of the rear springs guaranteed permanent lubrication.

Wheelbase was lengthened to 124 inches and the frame was lowered and stiffened by the use of added X-members. Styling was typically GM — massive and well detailed. The bodies, with their narrow side windows, were shared with other upper-line GM cars. Five body types — two- and four-door sedans, coupé, convertible coupé, and convertible sedan — were priced at an exceedingly low $995 to $1,485. The longer chassis gave increased passenger room and great attention was given to more luxurious interiors.

The 1937 Series 37-50 convertible sedan.

The new model was heavily advertised as the lowest-priced LaSalle ever and *completely* Cadillac-built. It worked — the new styling, V-8 engine and advertising together with an improving economy, resulted in the production of 32,005 units, the highest production ever achieved for the marque. One result was that Cadillac divisional deliveries at retail reached a record high. Yet this placed LaSalle only slightly ahead of Zephyr and still far behind Packard's cheaper cars. The new model was carried into 1938 with minimal styling changes and mechanical improvements like a column-mounted gearshift and alligator hood. Assemblies declined to 15,501 in the face of an economic recession that killed Pierce-Arrow and fatally weakened Hupmobile and Graham.

LaSalle was caught in a difficult position, facing increased competition not only from the small Packards and Lincolns but also from a fast-rising Buick with its popular Century series. Time was running out on the junior Cadillac, but the LaSalle was

given an additional two years to prove itself in the marketplace.

In common with other GM cars, new bodies were introduced on the 1939 LaSalles. One of the chief complaints on previous models was the narrow slit windows which cut driver visibility, so glass area was increased twenty-seven percent on the new series. This change not only resulted in a lighter, more modern look but also contributed to safer driving. The trademark radiator grille was narrowed even further, becoming a slim column of brilliant chrome flanked by lower catwalk grilles. Apparently the sales people could not agree on a suitable chassis as the wheelbase was cut back to 120 inches, only to be increased three inches in the final year. Running boards disappeared except as options and in the convertible coupé, all four passengers sat inside under a common roof, eliminating the drafty, uncomfortable, dangerous — and sometimes delightful — rumble seat. On closed cars the customer could choose a "Sunshine

Roof" option featuring a retractable metal panel over the driver's compartment. While this feature is currently enjoying a comeback, the original versions leaked so badly they were withdrawn after a short time. Redesigned pistons cut oil consumption and the rear suspension was altered. Assemblies increased to 23,028 for the model year.

Nineteen-forty was to be LaSalle's final year and, let it be said, the marque went out with a flourish. Styling was refined with new sealed beam headlights nestled into the fenders. Standard bodies included two- and four-door sedans, coupé, convertible coupé, and convertible sedan, but the highlight of the line was the Special Sedan and Special Coupé. In mid-year a sleek convertible sedan and convertible coupé were added to the Special line. These cars, with their gently rounded "torpedo" forms and restrained detailing, were among the handsomest LaSalles ever built. Prices on the nine-body line began at $1,240 and went up to $1,895. Throat diameter of the dual downdraft Carter carburetor was increased one-eighth inch, resulting in 130 horsepower for the final V-8. Refinements in engine and chassis provided quieter operation and improved riding. Production in that final year totaled 24,133 as against 90,000 small Packards and 22,000 Zephyrs.

There was a 1941 LaSalle program and Styling went ahead with its development, including full-size finished mockups. Photographs of these cars reveal that the 1941 model would have been merely a Cadillac with LaSalle grille and hood ensemble. Since the LaSalle had failed to garner the desired number of customers despite vigorous efforts to make it successful, division officials quietly discontinued the car at the end of 1940 after fourteen years of honorable service.

For the 1941 season a lower-priced Cadillac Series 61 was introduced at $1,345 to $1,535 to fill the gap left by LaSalle. It must have been the right move since the division's production jumped from 37,162 to 66,130 in 1941, a new record. Cadillac became busy with handsome profits and the LaSalle was quickly forgotten.

All in all, over 205,000 LaSalles were built from 1927 through 1940, an average of only 15,000 cars a year. As a money-making

Various LaSalles from 1938 (left and below) and 1939 (above).

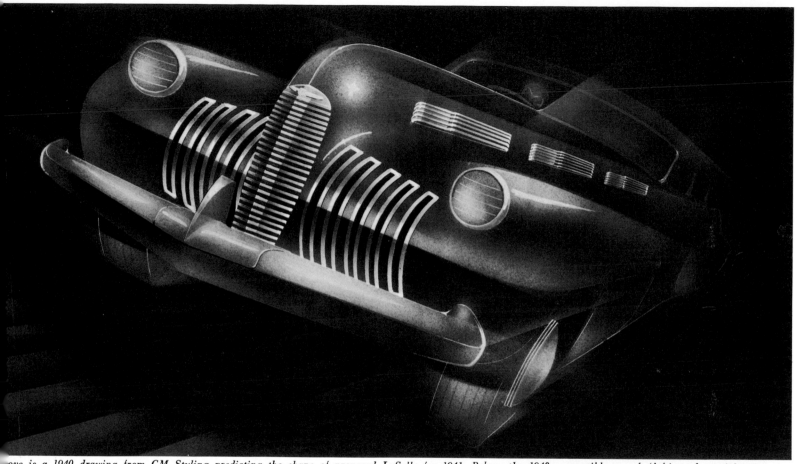

ove is a 1940 drawing from GM Styling predicting the shape of proposed LaSalle for 1941. Below, the 1940 convertible coupé (left) and special sedan.

405

The 1940 drawing on the previous page evidently
was of considerable influence on the new
program for the 1941 LaSalle, prototypes of which
are shown here. Above and at the right
are views of the fastback four-door sedan model.

At left and below are views of the notch-back sedan
proposal for the 1941 LaSalle. Among several
interesting features are the thin horizontal parking
lights, return of the traditional LaSalle
radiator badge/crosspiece, and spinner hub caps (above).

venture the LaSalle was a failure and its production therefore came to an end. But why did it fail? After all, it had "everything" — distinctive good looks, solid engineering, and the backing of the world's largest automobile company. How could it lose?

The classic 1927–1933 line was doomed by the depression. The market for smaller luxury cars collapsed along with the market for all luxury cars and LaSalle suffered with the rest. You couldn't sell $2,500 cars to people out of work and those who had jobs were more interested in $500 V-8 Fords. Although the 1934–1940 cars were excellent values in their price field, the LaSalle name actually hurt sales. The cars were Cadillacs in everything but name, but that was the key factor. Remember that both Packard and Lincoln marketed their cheaper cars under their own names, thus lending the prestige of the luxury cars to their medium-priced running mates. Despite Cadillac's strenuous efforts to promote the LaSalle nameplate the public generally preferred to buy Packard 120's and Lincoln-Zephyrs with their big-car names and status.

By 1941 Cadillac had finally realized what was happening and imitated their competitors by putting the Cadillac name on the division's cheapest car, something they probably should have done in 1934. When Cadillac's medium-priced car was named LaSalle it was a commercial failure. When it was finally graced with the magical Cadillac name the result was the greatest year in Cadillac history up to that time, proving once more you can't beat the sales appeal of a well-known and well-respected marque.

In the years following the LaSalle's demise there have been some wistful hopes for a LaSalle revival. One such faithful soul was observed by the writer while vacationing with his parents during the 1940's and 1950's. To reach our destination each year, we had to pass through the small anthracite town of Mt. Carmel, Pennsylvania, passing the streetfront showroom of the local Cadillac-Olds' dealer. Year after year, a large neon "LaSalle" sign hung in that showroom window in the forlorn hope that the car might someday return. We often thought about stopping to talk to the dealer about the sign but never did. Then one year, the sign was gone. And so, finally, was the LaSalle.

The LaSalle II sports prototype, 1955.

FISHER AND FLEETWOOD

notes by the author

Without the resources and modern machinery for steel fabrication, which became more important in body manufacture each year, custom bodies could not have kept pace with the rapid improvement in design and construction except at prohibitive prices. The alliance of Fisher and Fleetwood — one of the leading body manufacturers with one of the world's greatest custom design firms — permitted the best styling, fabrics, fittings, distinction, and comfort to be combined with economical production and advanced construction methods.

Special facilities were provided at Fleetwood for the various preliminaries in connection with the design of all custom bodies as well as their fabrication and finishing. The artisans of Fleetwood designed, painted, upholstered, and fitted bodies with a skill fully equal to the finest of the independent coachbuilders. The demand for Fleetwood bodies heavily taxed the Pennsylvania plant, however, and it was enlarged. Eventually, in the thirties, a Detroit-Fleetwood plant was established on West Fort Avenue. Many of the Pennsylvania staff moved to Detroit, and it became the center of Fleetwood-Cadillac activities. The Pennsylvania facilities, however, continued to handle Cadillac chassis and were also available to other makes, such as Stutz.

This appendix is designed to examine some of the methods used in creating these excellent Cadillac bodies, in greater depth than was covered in the text, for readers who are particularly interested in this phase of Cadillac history.

Although lacquering had greatly simplified body painting, many operations were required before the lacquering of a body was completed. Most of these operations had to do with preparing the body to receive lacquer. The metal body was first cleaned with an acid solution to remove all dirt, grease, and oil — then washed with boiling water, after which it was air dried, wiped off, and sent through a drying oven maintained at 190° F. to evaporate all moisture. The first coat was a primer of red oxide. After this was applied, the body passed through an oven held at a temperature of 185° — a very slow journey which required three and one-half hours. Depressions made by screw heads were then filled with special putty which became an integral part of the body. Another coat of "rough stuff" filler was then sprayed on, after which the body passed through yet another drying oven. In all four coats of "rough stuff" were applied, the oven drying operation between each coat requiring two and one-half hours. A crew of "rubbers" then massaged the body until its surfaces were thoroughly smooth. Inspectors carefully checked the body for surface defects, marking same with colored grease-chalk. This eliminated the chance of a defect passing, as parts marked with grease-chalk had to be rubbed in order to remove the marks.

The body was then ready for a Japan ground color, corresponding with the shade of lacquer used later. The ground color having been thoroughly dried, four to six (and sometimes up to thirty) coats of lacquer were applied, with a drying period between each coat. After another period of drying, the body was rubbed with oil and fine sandpaper until all unevenness resulting from the quickly drying lacquer was removed and the body was perfectly smooth to the touch. It was then polished, and the work of the paint shop was finished — unless the color design called for striping. Attempts to stripe bodies by use of stencils and other mechanical devices were failures, so striping was freehand, requiring the work of highly skilled specialists in this delicate art.

Drying periods were shortened through the use of special ovens in which a constant temperature was maintained by electrically

controlled thermostats. All the floors in the paint shop were oiled and cleaned regularly with vacuum cleaners to keep them free from dust. This was especially true of the final finish room where a small particle of dust could and did cause inspectors to reject the finish.

Turning to the upholstery, wool from Australian sheep was used for the finest cloth fabrics in the Fisher-Fleetwood bodies. The long fiber wool was selected through a careful process which weeded out unacceptable portions. Great strides had been made in developing fabrics combining the beauty of color and finish with durability and long wear. As the demand for different types of bodies increased, so did the demand for different fabrics suitable for their upholstery: Channel Bedford cords in two-tone colorings for owner-driven cars; hair line broadcloths and figured cloths for more dressy appearance; beautiful Doeskin broadcloth for the elegant, chauffeur-driven broughams and cabriolets.

Velvet, as developed for the automobile industry, was another durable and beautiful cloth, a pile fabric having a surface composed of upright tufts of fiber. This pile was woven through and locked into the backing or basic fabric. It would be mohair, worsted, cotton or a blended yarn in which two distinct fibers were combined. As pressure is applied to the ends of these erect, pliant fibers, friction is absorbed and the possibility of wear reduced to a minimum. Mohair, made from the long, silky fleece of the Angora goat, was the most beautiful and luxurious type of velvet. Mohair worsted varieties, especially developed for the motorcar body — with a pile composed of a blend of mohair and worsted fibers — combined the best features of both: the luster of mohair, and the covering quality of worsted. The result was a beautiful close-surface fabric. Cotton velvet, when properly constructed with closely woven short pile, was an excellent material, withstanding effects of hard usage.

Regarding construction, the factory claimed that "Fisher is not committed to any special type of body construction. Fisher bodies are of composite wood and steel construction, because up to the present time that is the only type of automobile body construction which permits the maximum strength, maximum resiliency and maximum safety." Actually, the Fishers were largely tied to investments in hardwood forests and their commitment was *not* unbiased, but they did have some good arguments for composite bodies, shared also by Packard, Pierce-Arrow, and Lincoln. Fisher for many years experimented with types of bodies other than those of composite wood and steel construction. They also applied comparative tests to their own composite wood and steel bodies, and to all-steel bodies. These tests, Fisher claimed, "proved the vast superiority of composite construction."

In one test, for instance, the strongest and best "so-called all-steel body" (so-called because it was actually twenty percent wood) was selected. For comparison there was chosen from the regular Fisher production a steel and wood sedan body selling at the same price. These two bodies were mounted on a platform inclined at forty-five degrees. Pressure (9,000 lb.) was applied to the upper right-hand roof rail in a perpendicular line whose plane of pressure was diagonally through the body from the upper right hand roof rail to the lower left hand sill.

Under this load the so-called steel body deflected a total of eleven inches. The roof was smashed, every panel of glass in the car was broken excepting the lower panel of the windshield which, though not receiving full pressure, sprung out of position on its frame. All doors were clamped tightly shut under pressure and could not be opened. Every door, window pillar, and rear quarter panel was buckled. The body damage was beyond repair.

Exactly the same pressure was applied in the same way to the Fisher wood-framed steel body, and under the 9,000 pound load there was a gross deflection of only four inches in its trueness. At this point four spot welds on the right quarter panel broke loose. This action broke in turn the two spot welds on the lower seam of the left quarter panel, and at the same time fractured the windshield glass in the upper left hand corner. But under pressure all doors remained true in their frames and could be opened and closed as easily as when the body was affixed to the

chassis. "Except for the windshield," stated the report, "no glass anywhere in the Fisher body was cracked and the body could have been made as good as new in any well equipped shop. . . Such tests as these prove conclusively that the steel-wood body is subject to about one-third the deflection of the so-called all-steel body and that it has more than eight times the resistance to return to normal after deflection."

"The strength of wood is not generally appreciated," said Fisher. "As a matter of scientific fact, some wood is actually stronger than wrought iron bar of the same size. No other substance combines resilience and strength as does wood; it has no substitute. Obviously, a body which affords the superiorities of both wood and steel is better than a body which does not employ both materials. . . The automobile body developed by Fisher is an expertly engineered product in which wood and steel are scientifically combined so as to obtain the utmost strength, resiliency and absence of noise."

At the same time that Fisher was publicizing the superiorities of composite bodies, the Budd Company, Chrysler, Hudson, and others were running one car of each type over cliffs to prove the opposite. The ultimate winner, of course, was the all-steel body, although at GM this did not come until 1935. The heavy Fisher investment in hardwood timber forests and their desire to amortize their wooden body tooling and plant undoubtedly influenced their attitude, but we should also note the following:

(1) The all-steel *sedan* was not finally realized by *any* maker until 1935, when GM introduced the turret top. Up to then Fisher's gibe about "so-called" all-steel bodies was partially true, for only touring "all-steel" bodies were truly *all* steel.

(2) The composite body was probably quieter than the all-steel body, and for luxury cars like Cadillac (as well as Packard, Pierce-Arrow, and Lincoln) this was a very important consideration. At that stage of development this outweighed the all-steel body's advantage of cheaper manufacture.

(3) Some sympathy can be felt for the Fisher brothers, master artisans in woodwork descended from a family of coachbuilding tradition. Their natural reaction to "this Budd upstart and his tin can bodies" can well be imagined. Psychology plays as much a part in automobile advancement as does science.

Full use was made of the 1,245 acre General Motors Proving Grounds in the testing and rating of body design and construction "by standards as definite as those which apply to chassis performance." The engineers assigned to these tasks devoted themselves to impartial, constructive fault finding, using scientific methods and apparatus to ensure complete accuracy. Body contours were compared by photographing the car against a great board, laid off in squares, so that the exact relation to each part of the outline of the car to each other part was checked and compared with scientific exactitude as to correct proportioning. Panoramic cameras were used to obtain data for designs ensuring maximum visibility. Special tests were made to check on reflection and dazzle. Scientific measurements were made to ensure anatomical correctness for maximum comfort.

Finally, test bodies took part in the road testing of the entire car, and in a month underwent more miles of road work and hard service than the average owner would put them to in his entire ownership of the vehicle.

Fisher employed more than 1000 production body inspectors. From the time timber was cut in their own forests until the finished body was mounted on the chassis, there was a series of inspections as the body progressed through the departments. This program insured that a bad piece of timber, steel, hardware or cloth was rejected before becoming part of the body. The material going into the plants was inspected before it went to stock and again before being installed. One department acted as a check against the other. After Fisher inspectors passed a body it then had to pass the scrutiny of Cadillac inspectors before leaving the Fisher plants.

Fleetwood always showed an imaginative approach and took a fresh line in design or decor at frequent intervals. One year its coloring of paint and upholstery based itself on "Nature's Studios" — familiar and unfamiliar colors in nature, from tropic to temperate zones. On another occasion inspiration was drawn from great works of the old masters. At the 24th New York Show Fleetwood's central display was titled "L'art moderne," featuring a Cadillac town car, beautifully finished in black lacquer and polished metal. Recessed hood and cowl panels were of polished aluminum, spot-buffed to give a Damascened finish. Base body moldings, window moldings, and top and back moldings, together with headlights, windshield frame, wheel spokes and trunk rack, were all bright chrome. A new rayon fabric for the seats was piped with silver leather. Plain rayon was used for side and headlining, and a cabinet for the rear compartment was inlaid with twenty-two different varieties of hardwood.

"Duco" (nitrocellulose lacquer) appeared as standard on the 1924 models. The story of Duco, which was the most important advance in body finishing in the history of the automobile, is another facet of the many sided genius of Charles F. Kettering. A large production bottleneck lay in the paint room, where methods dated from the carriage building days. Kettering arranged a meeting of paint manufacturers and told them that taking thirty-three to thirty-seven days to paint a car body was absurd. The time would have to be reduced. The paint men dove into the problem and reported proudly that they could reduce the time to thirty days. "Boss Ket" then staggered them with the reply that he was thinking of *hours*, not days — for the whole operation. The contretemps was unresolved until on July 4, 1920, a chemist at DuPont noted a chemical reaction that promised a paint revolution. A lacquer base with greatly improved pigment suspension and color brilliance was produced. It was fortunate that this chemist had decided to work during the holiday, for as a result cars would no longer look like they were all going to a funeral. (Oakland cars also used Duco from 1924 on.)

Kettering and the DuPont laboratories found that by adding small amounts of sodium acetate to a thick solution of nitrocellulose and storing the result, a paint was developed that was thin enough for spray application, making laborious hand brushing obsolete. After three years of experiments with many different gums, resins, plasticizers and pigments which were exposed on panels in all climes from New Jersey to Florida, a lacquer was finally developed which dried in minutes compared to hours or even days for color varnish. Duco's glossy, rock-hard, weather-resistant finish was superior in every way, and eventually swept the industry.

Associates tell a story of Kettering in this connection. Kettering asked one of the leading paint men to come to his plant prepared to spend some time with him. When the paint man arrived, Ket showed him a number of sample boards painted in various colors, explaining that he was trying to decide which might be the most acceptable to public taste. "In other words, which of these colors would you choose for your car?" he asked. The visitor indicated his choice. They talked paint, had lunch, and talked more paint. Finally the visitor said he must be leaving. Ket went with him out to the yard. His visitor could not find his car. Kettering asked what kind it was and was told it was a Cadillac. Ket then pointed to the only Cadillac on the lot and said, "This must be it." The paint man identified it as his car, but of course could not believe it had been refinished during the visit.

That demonstration was a clinching argument to the paint men that painting a car could be reduced from thirty days to three hours if the old techniques were discarded and they would proceed on the theory that "nothing is impossible" — Ket's lifelong working maxim. The paint breakthrough thus added to the already prominent standing of Fisher and Fleetwood bodies.

CADILLAC AND LaSALLE HERALDRY

Research by Harry Pulfer, Illustrations by Joe Trainor

Among automotive regalia there are many famous symbols, a goodly number of which are intrinsically fine works of art. The cormorant of Packard, the flying lady of Rolls-Royce, the three-pointed star of Daimler-Benz, and the soaring stork of Hispano-Suiza are among the more prominent of these. But the symbol that is probably best known among enthusiasts of any generation is the coat of arms of Le Sieur Antoine de la Mothe Cadillac, adopted for use on Cadillac motorcars in 1905 and registered as a trademark on August 7, 1906. For the Standard of the World this crest has been an enduring symbol. Its origins, though less known, are of particular interest to students of the marque.

Lacking direct family records, historians have ascertained only that Cadillac was born in Gascony on March 5, 1658, certainly to a family of quality, for only youths of high rank were granted commissions, as he was, in the Royal Army. His heroic adventures in the New World were climaxed by the founding of Detroit in 1701 and the governorship of Mississippi, in recognition of which Louis XIV, the Sun King, awarded him the rank of Chevalier of the Military Order of St. Louis. These events occurred, however, fully four centuries after the armorial bearings of his family had been set down in French heraldry. A translation of the original heraldic description is as follows:

"Arms: Quarterly (shield divided into four sections); first and fourth (quarters) gold, a fess (lateral band) sable (black) between three merlettes (small heraldic birds) of the same (black), posed two in chief (upper third of section) and one in base. Second and third (quarters) gules (red) quartering argent (silver) three bars (small fesses) azure (blue)."

Breaking the arms into their component parts we have:

The Couronne (Coronet). This symbolizes the six ancient counts of France. The pearls — these have varied in number on both family and automobile crests — signify descent of the family from the royal counts of Toulouse.

The Shield. In heraldry the shield, round or otherwise, is used to denote the courageous origins of a noble family, being taken from the shape of shields used by the crusaders. An original family seal found on a Cadillac letter in the Burton historical collection of the Detroit Public Library, which may predate the more typical shield, is round in configuration.

First and Fourth Quarterings. These display the arms de la Mothe. The birds or "merlettes" are heraldic adaptations of the martin, but are shown without legs or beaks. The ancient historian Guillame commented that merlettes are "given for a difference, to younger brothers to put them in mind that in order to raise themselves they are to look to the wings of virtue and merit and not to the legs, having but little land to set their feet on." When appearing as a trio, the merlettes also refer to the Holy Trinity. They were usually awarded by the School of Heralds to Knights making significant contributions in the Crusades. The color scheme — black against gold — denotes wisdom and riches. The "fess" or lateral bar was also an award for Crusader service, concerning which Guillame wrote, "This is a military girdle of honor," requiring that he who holds it "always be in readiness to undergo the business of the public weal."

Second and Third Quarterings. Historians agree from an interpretation of the red, white and blue colors, that this design

was added to the arms de la Mothe after a favorable marriage which increased their estates. The colors indicate "prowess and boldness in action" (red), "purity, charity, virtue and plenty" (silver) and knightly valor (blue).

In a 1922 description of the coat of arms, the Cadillac Motor Car Company remarked: "Apart from the purely heraldic aspect of a coat of arms is its historic aspect. Every crest is linked with a history in which is enfolded the origin, genealogy, deeds, services, honors and alliances of the family bearing it. In all France there are few families more ancient than the Cadillacs. In both dignity of design and significance of detail the Cadillac coat of arms speaks volumes in courage and honor for the forbears of the Father of Detroit."

Indeed the analogy is precise, for in all the world there are few marques more venerable than that of Cadillac. In their timeless dignity the armorial bearings witness the integrity and honor of a marque to which, as we have seen, they justly apply. One would suppose the mating of car and crest are only to be expected.

Mr. Harry Pulfer of La Crescentia, California, has made an avocation of automotive regalia and its reproduction for restorers. In the process of collecting and researching thousands of automotive heraldic devices, he has made extensive studies of their evolution and origins, particularly those of Cadillac. For the benefit of the casual reader as well as the restorer, this appendix presents a compilation of the various Cadillac and LaSalle heraldic devices and significant alterations from year to year. They revolve mainly, as will be seen, around the noble coat of arms above described.

TRADE-MARK.

No. 54,931.
REGISTERED AUG. 7, 1906

CADILLAC AUTOMOBILE COMPANY
AUTOMOBILES.
APPLICATION FILED AUG. 18, 1905.

Witnesses
O. B. Baeuziger
E. L. Schwartz

Proprietor.
Cadillac Automobile Comp.
By Newell S. Wright
Attorney

Though evidence exists that brass "Cadillac" script was used on some hubs
as early as 1904, the radiator scripts did not appear until 1906.
At left we have a typical variety; from top to bottom: the plain, slanted
script of 1911, the dated version of 1912, a catalogue variety
with motto from 1914, and the script as used on serial number plates from
1908. The arms, above, were not registered until August, 1906.

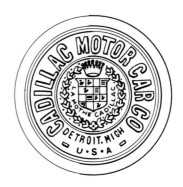

Although the Cadillac arms were not registered as a trademark until 1906, they were in use as early as September, 1902, in decal form on the Model A, and persisted in this guise until 1904. Early arms designs, such as the example at left above, were closely based on the registered design, with merlettes slanting down to the left and a wreath composed of tulip bulb-like flowerets arching up to a seven-pointed crown. Gradually this changed to the more graphically visible pattern shown at center above, with the slogan added upon Cadillac's receipt of the Dewar Trophy that year (1908) for achievements in standardization of parts. This succeeded the more complex design of 1906, at right above, which while retaining the basic badge format of the trademark registration had resorted to a more complicated wreath pattern. The 1906 hub insert design was maintained in 1907, giving way to the newer pattern for 1908. Note the nine-pointed crown on the 1908 hub device.

The hub insignia, reverting to seven points on the crown, was used in 1909, which also saw the same device as a radiator stamping. The "Standard of the World" slogan would be used for several years on hubs, though the radiator emblem was abandoned from 1910 to 1916. Script nameplates for radiators were optional in 1912. On the last Four, in 1914, hub caps showed eighteen-point crowns, but the cars remained badgeless and without radiator script. The advent of the V-8 in 1915 brought "V8" emblems to the hubs, and from 1916-1918 Cadillac used the radiator badge at left below — this time it was back to stay, tulip bulb-wreathed per the original trademark, but with nine points on the crown. By 1918 the crest was backed by German silver. The crown reverted to seven points and joined the crest in 1920, center below, but the birds seemed more like ducks now, with short necks. This crest persisted through 1925 while hubs, right below, retained the slogan.

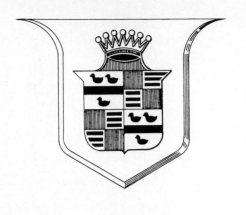

The radiator badge of 1925, left above, omitted the laurel (or tulip bulb) wreath but retained the same pattern with the short-necked birds which had arrived in 1920. Ads of the period often interlocked the Cadillac crest, with a more curved bottom, and the Fisher body emblem, as is shown at center above, with the famous coach that has persisted in that device to the present. After ten years of constant radiator emblems, Cadillac dispensed with the circular background for 1926, right above, substituting the shield backing shown, but using the same crest design they had used for some time without change, but this would only be used for this year, as a major change in both badge and car line-up was in the works for the '27's.

A novel application of the Cadillac crest was on the lube and maintenance record plates of this period, an example of which is shown at left below. With the 1927 model year came Cadillac's companion car, LaSalle, with its own hub design as illustrated at center below, using the interconnected monogram composed of the first three letters of its name encircled by the identity of its builder. The Cadillac emblem, at right below, now became a two-piece affair, black with gold markings, and this was continued along with the "Standard of the World" motto on Cadillacs through the 1929 models. Note that on this new badge Cadillac again used true swans, with crown topped by no less than eighteen pearls.

ENGINE. *Horsepower*: increased to 150 at 3400 rpm on all models. *Compression ratio*: 7.25 to 1.

TRANSMISSION AND CHASSIS. Standard gear ratio 3.77 for 126-inch wheelbase cars; 4.27 for the others, with optional 3.36 ratio. Hydra-Matic option. The 60 Special frame on all models was made. forty percent stiffer. *Wheelbase*: 126 inches for the 61, 62, 63 and 60 Special; 138½ inches for the 67; 136¼ inches for the 75.

BODIES. New bodies with four fastback styles. The 61 was available as a five-passenger touring sedan and coupé (fastback); the 62 as a five-passenger touring sedan, four-passenger coupé, convertible coupé and convertible sedan; the 63 as a five-passenger touring sedan; the 67 as a five-passenger touring sedan (with or without formal division for chauffeur driving) and a seven-passenger touring sedan (with or without Imperial division); the 60 Special as a five-passenger Fleetwood sedan available with sunshine roof or glass chauffeur division; the 75 Fleetwood as a five-passenger touring sedan (with or without formal division), a seven-passenger touring sedan (with or without Imperial division) and a seven- and five-passenger formal sedan.

PRICES. Base price for the 61, $1445; for the 67, $2595.

PERFORMANCE. Maximum speed 100 mph. Zero to 60 in 14 seconds.

SERIES 61, 62, 63, 60S, 67, 75 (V-8)
CURRENT 1942
ENGINE SERIAL Nos. 5,380,001 - 5,386,463 (61)
ENGINE SERIAL Nos. 8,380,001 - 8,386,560 (62)
ENGINE SERIAL Nos. 7,380,001 - 7,386,375 (63)
ENGINE SERIAL Nos. 6,380,001 - 6,386,375 (60S)
ENGINE SERIAL Nos. 9,380,001 - 9,386,180 (67)
ENGINE SERIAL Nos. 3,380,001 - 3,386,327 (75)

Similar to 1941 with the following exceptions:

CHASSIS. *Wheelbase*: changed to 129 inches for the 61-62-63; 133 inches for the 60S; 136 inches for the 67-75. *Weight*: 4525 pounds for the 67 and 75; 4115 pounds for all others.

BODIES. Restyled. Swept-back fenders, those in front extending into doors on all models except the 75.

SERIES 61, 62, 60S, 75
CURRENT 1946
ENGINE SERIAL Nos. 5,400,001 - 5,403,001 (61)
ENGINE SERIAL Nos. 8,400,001 - 8,418,566 (62)
ENGINE SERIAL Nos. 6,400,001 - 6,405,700 (60S)
ENGINE SERIAL Nos. 3,400,001 - 3,401,927 (75)

Similar to 1942, with the following exceptions:

TRANSMISSION. Hydra-Matic optional on all models.

BODIES. Facelift. Minor detail changes only. Series 63 and 67 eliminated.

PRICES. Base for the 61, $1920; for the 62, $2136; for the 60S, $2899; for the 75, $3891.

PERFORMANCE. Maximum speed 95 mph. Zero to 60 in 16 seconds.

SERIES 61, 62, 60S, 75
CURRENT 1947
ENGINE SERIAL Nos. 5,420,001 - 5,428,555 (61)
ENGINE SERIAL Nos. 8,420,001 - 8,459,835 (62)
ENGINE SERIAL Nos. 6,420,001 - 6,428,500 (60S)
ENGINE SERIAL Nos. 3,420,001 - 3,425,036 (75)

ENGINE. *Horsepower*: 150 bhp gross (130 net) at 3600 rpm. *Torque*: 275 lb/ft gross (260 net) at 1600 rpm.

TRANSMISSION. Gear ratios 3.77 and 4.27.

CHASSIS. *Weight*: 4138 pounds for the 61; 4201 pounds for the 62; 4351 pounds for the 60S; 4836 pounds for the 75.

BODIES. Facelifted. New grille (four bars instead of five); hubcaps and chrome gravel shield were the main changes. Others were confined to new color and upholstery schemes, semi-circular horn ring and winged trunk ornament on all models except the 60S, which carried "Fleetwood" identification.

PRICES. Base for the 61, $2060; for the 62, $2290; for the 60S, $2990; for the 75, $4095.

SERIES 61, 62, 60S, 75
CURRENT 1948
ENGINE SERIAL Nos. 486100001 - 486148663 (61)
ENGINE SERIAL Nos. 486200001 - 486252704 (62)
ENGINE SERIAL Nos. 486000001 - 486052706 (60S)
ENGINE SERIAL Nos. 487500001 - 487546088 (75)

Engine, transmission and performance similar to 1947.

CHASSIS. The wheelbase of the 61-62 changed to 126 inches. *Weight*: approximately 4100 pounds for the 61-62.

BODIES. Restyled for all except 75. Design was all-new and full-width, with straight-through slab sides and tail fins plus new drum type instrument nacelle.

PRICES. Base for the 61 sedan, $2833; for the 62 sedan, $2996; for the 60S, $3820; for the 75 sedan, $4779.

NOTE: For succeeding years, engine serial number designations followed the pattern set down with the 1948 models. That is, the first two digits represent the model year, the second two digits the series number.

SERIES 61, 62, 60S, 75
CURRENT 1949
ENGINE. Eight-cylinder ohv V-type (3 13/16x3 5/8, 331 cubic inches). *Horsepower*: 160 bhp gross (133 net) at 3800 rpm. *Torque*: 312 lb/ft gross (270 net) at 1800 rpm. Cast iron block and heads. Carter dual downdraft carburetor, Delco-Remy ignition, AC oil filter.

TRANSMISSION. Standard three-speed synchromesh; four-speed Hydra-Matic standard on Series 62 and 60 Special, optional on others. Hypoid axle ratios: 3.77 standard with synchro, 4.27 on Series 75; 3.36 with Hydra-Matic, 3.77 on Series 75. Hotchkiss drive.

CHASSIS. *Suspension*: independent front suspension with coils; semi-elliptic rear 54½ inches by 2 inches. Delco shock absorbers. *Steering*: Saginaw gear. *Brakes*: Bendix hydraulic duo-servo. *Wheelbase*: 126 in-

ches on 61-62; 133 inches on 60S; 136¼ inches on 75. *Weight*: approximately 3900 pounds for the Series 61 and 62.
BODIES. Facelifted. Grille lowered and widened. Coupe de Ville (hardtop) added to Series 62 in July. Drum type instrument panel replaced by simplified horizontal type.
PRICES. Base for the 61 sedan, $2893; for the 62 sedan, $3050; for the 60S, $3828; for the 75 sedan, $4750.
PERFORMANCE. Maximum speed 100 mph. Zero to 60 in 13.4 seconds. Gas mileage 12 to 20 mpg.

SERIES 61, 62, 60S, 75
Current 1950

Similar to 1949, with the following exceptions:
CHASSIS. *Wheelbase*: 122 inches for the 61; 126 inches for the 62; 130 inches for the 60S, 146¾ for the 75.
BODIES. Restyled. One-piece windshield, broken fenderline, and round park-directional lights were main features. The Series 75 was entirely restyled to conform with the rest of the line, the first such revision since 1941.

SERIES 61, 62, 60S, 75
Current 1951

Similar to 1950, with the following exceptions:
BODIES. Facelifted. Minor detail changes included new grille openings under headlamps. Warning lights replaced gauges for oil pressure and amperes. Series 61 discontinued at mid-year.
PRICES. Base for the 61 sedan, $2940; for the 62 sedan, $3528; for the 60 Special, $4142; for the 75 sedan, $5200; for the 62 convertible coupé, $3987; for the 75 Imperial, $5405.

SERIES 62, 60S, 75
Current 1952

ENGINE. *Horsepower*: 190 bhp (gross) at 4000 rpm. *Torque*: 322 lb/ft (gross) at 2400 rpm. *Compression ratio*: 7.5 to 1. Full dual exhaust system, four mufflers. *Carburetor*: two-stage four-barrel.
TRANSMISSION. Dual Range Hydra-Matic with manual control over third and fourth gear. Standard ratios 3.36 or 3.07.
CHASSIS. Saginaw power steering with built-in "road feel." Increased braking capacity. Autronic Eye automatic headlamp dipper.
BODIES. Facelifted. Broad chrome trim below headlamps, broader "V" emblems on hood and deck, built-in exhaust ports at rear.
PRICES. Base for the 62 sedan, $3684; for the 60S, $4323; for the 75 sedan, $5428. Typical optional equipment and accessories included windshield washer, $11.36; fog lamps, $36.91; heater, $113.66; radio with pushbuttons and rear speaker, $112.45; same radio with signal seeking feature, $129.22; power steering, $198.43; automatic window lifts, $138.64.
PERFORMANCE. Maximum speed 112 mph. Zero to 80 in 28 seconds. Gas mileage 16 mpg at 60 mph.

SERIES 62, 60S, 75
Current 1953

ENGINE. *Horsepower*: 210 bhp (gross) at 4150 rpm. *Torque*: 330 lb/ft (gross) at 2700 rpm. *Compression ratio*: 8.25 to 1.
TRANSMISSION. Axle ratio 3.07 for 60S; 3.77 on 62-75.
BODIES. Facelifted. Raised, enlarged bumper guards, chrome-lidded headlamp surrounds, dished wheel discs, one-piece rear windows. Eldorado limited production luxury convertible added, technically a part of the Series 62.
PRICES. Base for the 62 sedan, $3666; coupé, $3571; concertible, $4144; Coupe de Ville, $3995; for the 60S, $4305; for the 75 sedan, $5604, limousine, $5818; for the Eldorado, $7750. Wire wheels ($325) and power steering ($177) standard on Eldorado. Hydra-Matic remained an option on the 75 at $198. Air conditioning optional at $619.
PERFORMANCE. Maximum speed 116 mph. Zero to 80 in 27 seconds. Gas mileage 14 mpg at 75 mph.

SERIES 62, 60S, 75
Current 1954

ENGINE. *Horsepower*: 230 bhp (gross) at 4400 rpm. *Torque*: 330 lb/ft (gross) at 2700 rpm.
CHASSIS. Power steering standard. *Wheelbase*: increased three inches on the 62 and Eldorado to 129 inches; on the 60S to 133 inches; on the 75 to 149 3/4 inches.
BODIES. Restyled. Wraparound windshield with ventilator intake mounted across its base. Two hardtops now available on Series 62 as standard and DeVille.
PERFORMANCE. Series 62 (test weight 5100 pounds, 3.36 axle, air conditioning installed): maximum speed 113 mph. Zero to 80 in 24 seconds. Gas mileage 14 mpg at 70 mph.

SERIES 62, 60S, 75
Current 1955

Similar to 1954, with the following exceptions:
ENGINE. *Horsepower*: 250 bhp (gross), 270 for the Eldorado.
BODIES. Facelifted. Chrome side trim extended back from grille to form vertical simulated louver on rear fender on all but 75. Eldorado featured individual circular tail and directional lights.

SERIES 62, 60S, 75
Current 1956

Similar to 1955, with the following exceptions:
ENGINE. Bore increased (4x3⅝ to 365 cubic inches). *Horsepower*: 285 bhp (gross), 305 for the Eldorado.
TRANSMISSION. Auxiliary fluid coupling in Hydra-Matic for smoother shifting.
BODIES. Facelifted. Finer textured grille, parking lights moved below

bumper guards. On Eldorado, "Seville" hardtop added and convertible designated "Biarritz." Series 62 DeVille hardtop now with two or four doors.
PRICES. Air conditioning option down to $540.

SERIES 62, 60S, 75, 70
CURRENT 1957
ENGINE. *Horsepower*: 300 at 4800 rpm (gross), 325 for Eldorado. *Compression ratio*: 10 to 1 for first time.
CHASSIS. Tubular X-frame without side rails on all models. Center section of various lengths to give different wheelbases. Four-link rear suspension. Air suspension standard on Eldorado Brougham. *Wheelbase*: on 62 and Eldorado, 129.5 inches; on Eldorado Brougham, 126 inches.
BODIES. Restyled. Longer, tapering fins, black rubber tipped bumper guards raised to top of grille. Goddess hood mascot replaced by stylized double fins. Series 60 Special now a four-door hardtop. Eldorado Brougham added, designated as Series 70.
PRICES. Base for the 62 sedan, $4781; for the Coupe de Ville, $5116; for the Eldorado Seville/Biarritz, $7286; for the 60S, $5614; for the 75 sedan, $7440; for the Eldorado Brougham, $13,074.

SERIES 62, 60S, 75, 70
CURRENT 1958
Similar to 1957, with the following exceptions:
ENGINE. *Horsepower*: 310 bhp at 4800 rpm (gross). *Compression ratio*: 10.25 to 1.
CHASSIS. Optional air suspension on all four wheels. Central compressor and accumulator. Self-leveling, constant weight automatically maintained. Four-link rear suspension with either air units or coil springs.
BODIES. Facelifted. Wider grille with bumper guards lowered to just above parking lights. Four headlamps, smaller, less pronounced fins. Series 60 Special given an aluminum panel on the lower rear fender. Eldorado Brougham retained with little change. Extended deck Series 62 sedan offered, 8.5 inches longer than standard.

SERIES 62, 63, 60S, 64, 67, 69
CURRENT 1959
ENGINE. Stroke increased (4x3⅞, 390 cubic inches). *Horsepower*: 325, 345 on Eldorado (gross). *Compression ratio*: 10.5 to 1. *Carburetor*: standard four-barrel downdraft; three two-barrel version on Eldorado, optional extra on all other models.
TRANSMISSION. Axle ratio 2.94 standard, 3.21 optional (mandatory with air conditioning). For the Seventy-five, (now designated "67") 3.36 standard, 3.77 optional, 3.21 with air conditioning.
CHASSIS. *Suspension*: full air or coil spring suspension optional, air suspension standard on Eldorados. *Brakes*: power assisted and self-ad-

justing. *Wheelbase*: 130 inches on all models save the Seventy-five ("67") now at 149.87 inches.
BODIES. Restyled. Large tail fins and twin bullet tail lamps. Two distinctive roof contours and heights, six- or four-window versions, in the Series 62 sedan and Sedan de Ville series. The 60S returned to pillar construction. Options included cruise control, power windows and seats (standard on several models), Guide-Matic headlamp beam control, power door locks, E-Z-Eye tinted glass, automatic finger-touch-tuned two-speaker radio, with electrically operated antenna, air conditioning, heater and defroster, foglamps. All of the foregoing standard on the Eldorado Brougham. New factory numerical designations were 63 for the DeVille; 64 for the Eldorado; 67 for the Seventy-five; 69 for the Eldorado Brougham, the last now built in Italy for Cadillac by Pininfarina.

SERIES 62, 63, 60S, 64, 67, 69
CURRENT 1960
Similar to 1959, with the following exceptions:
BODIES. Facelifted. Lowered rear fins and deleted pointed front bumper guards. Full width grille. Automatic releasing (vacuum) foot-operated parking brake. Fender-mounted directional signal indicator lights.
PRICES. Base price for the 62 six-window sedan, $5080; for the Series 63 Sedan de Ville four- and six-window hardtops, $5498; for the 60S, $6233; for the Series 64 Eldorado Seville/Biarritz, $7401; for the Series 67 Seventy-five sedan, $9533; for the Eldorado Brougham, $13,075.
PERFORMANCE. Maximum speed 117 mph with the 3.36 gear ratio, 120 with the 2.94 ratio. Zero to 60 in 11.2 seconds, to 80 in 19.4 seconds, to 100 in 34.3 seconds. Gas mileage 11 mpg at 80 mph, 13.6 mpg at 60 mph.

SERIES 62, 63, 60S, 67
CURRENT 1961
ENGINE. Four-barrel carburetion only. Single exhaust system.
TRANSMISSION. Limited slip differential.
CHASSIS. Air suspension dropped. Rubberized front and rear coil springs used instead. *Wheelbase*: reduced to 129½ inches on the Sixty-Special and Sixty-Two.
BODIES. Restyled. New grille placed between headlights, wraparound windshield replaced by forward slanting pillars, straight, sharp-lined rear window treatment. Short-deck hardtop sedan added to Series Sixty-two. Eldorado Seville and Eldorado Brougham dropped, with Eldorado Biarritz convertible retained under Series 63.
PRICES. Air conditioning now $474, $624 for Seventy-five.

SERIES 62, 63, 60S, 67
CURRENT 1962
Similar to 1961, with the following exceptions:
CHASSIS. Separate front and rear hydraulic circuits in brake system.

BODIES. Facelifted. Fins lowered, heater/defroster made standard, cornering lights introduced. New Series Sixty-two Town Sedan added on 129.5-inch wheelbase.
PRICES. Base for the Sixty-two, $5213; for the Sixty-Special, $6366; for the Series 67 Seventy-five, $9722.

SERIES 62, 63, 60S, 67
CURRENT 1963
Similar to 1962, with the following exceptions:
ENGINE. *Horsepower*: 325 bhp (gross) at 4800 rpm. *Torque*: 430 lb/ft (gross) at 3100 rpm. New drive shaft with two constant velocity joints and one universal joint.
BODIES. Facelifted. Main styling package unchanged. Short-wheelbase Town Sedan dropped from Series Sixty-two. Six-position steering wheel. AM-FM radio offered as an option.
PERFORMANCE. Maximum speed 115-120 mph. Zero to 60 in 10 seconds, to 80 in 16.1 seconds, to 100 in 28.5 seconds. Gas mileage 12-14 mpg.

SERIES 62, 63, 60S, 67
CURRENT 1964
ENGINE. New design. (4 1/8x4 1/10, 429 cubic inches). *Horsepower*: 340 bhp (gross) at 4600 rpm. *Torque*: 480 lb/ft (gross) at 3000 rpm. *Compression ratio*: 10.5 to 1.
TRANSMISSION. Three-speed Turbo-Hydramatic with torque converter.
BODIES. Facelifted. Park Avenue short wheelbase sedan dropped from De Ville/Eldorado (Series 63). Fully automatic, thermostatic air conditioning or "Comfort Control." Headlight control called "Twilight Sentinel" allowed continuous headlight burning for a predetermined period after driver left car.
PRICES. Base for the Sixty-two, $5236; for the Series 63 De Ville, $5655; for the Sixty-Special, $6388; for the Series 67 Seventy-five, $9746.
PERFORMANCE. Maximum speed 122 mph. Zero to 60 in 9.7 seconds, to 80 in 17.1 seconds, to 100 in 29.8 seconds. Gas mileage 10.5 mpg at 80 mph.

CALAIS, DE VILLE, FLEETWOOD SERIES
CURRENT 1965
Similar to 1964, with the following exceptions:
TRANSMISSION AND CHASSIS. New Turbo-Hydramatic. New perimeter frame replaced tubular X frame used from 1957 through 1964. Automatic level control for all Fleetwood models except the Seventy-five. Tilt and telescoping steering wheel. *Wheelbase*: revised to 133 inches for the Fleetwood Sixty-Special.
BODIES. Restyled. Symmetrical tapered rear fender forms at both top and bottom, minimal fins. Grille design more unified. Traditional numerical designations dropped in favor of Calais, including four-door sedan, hardtop sedan and coupé; DeVille, including the three above plus a convertible; and Fleetwood, including a Sixty-Special hardtop sedan with "Brougham" trim option, an Eldorado convertible, and a (non-facelifted) Seventy-five sedan and limousine.

NOTE: With the model rationalization of 1965, Cadillacs were no longer distinguishable by the first two digits of their model number. New five-digit codes (see production list, Appendix VI), began with "68" except for the Seventy-five and, beginning in 1967, the Eldorado, which both began with "69."

CALAIS, DE VILLE, FLEETWOOD SERIES
CURRENT 1966
Similar to 1965, with the following exceptions:
CHASSIS. Variable ratio power steering introduced. Perimeter frame now applied to the Fleetwood Seventy-five limousine.
BODIES. Facelifted except for Seventy-five limousine, which received restyling, the first since 1959. Brougham now a separate model in the Fleetwood series, a more luxurious version of the Fleetwood Sixty-Special. Electric carbon-cloth seat heating pads were announced as an optional extra.
PRICES. For the Calais four-door sedan and two-door coupé, $5817 and $5632; for the De Ville sedan, coupé and convertible, $6227, $5985 and $6101; for the Fleetwood Eldorado, $7277; for the Fleetwood Seventy-five sedan and limousine, $10,474 and $10,683.

CALAIS, DE VILLE, FLEETWOOD SERIES
CURRENT 1967
The Fleetwood Eldorado now became a front-wheel-drive coupé, while the rest of the line was similar to 1966. Eldorado specifications:
ENGINE. As for standard line, with modifications for front drive. Rochester Quadrajet four barrel carburetor and new fan clutch in cooling system (also on other models).
TRANSMISSION. Three-speed Turbo-Hydramatic as for regular models, but mounted longitudinally alongside engine. Transfer case with chain drive. Morse Hy-Vo inverted-tooth silent chain, two inches wide. Rubber cushioned sprockets. No tensioning device. Drive designed for life of power transmission unit. Spiral bevel ring gear and pinion with planetary differential, 3.21 ratio. Constant velocity joints on drive shafts.
CHASSIS. *Frame*: boxed perimeter, integral. *Suspension*: Front suspension torsion bar and A arms. Telescopic shocks, stabilizer bar. Rear single-leaf longitudinal semi-elliptic springs. Four shock absorbers, two vertical, two horizontal. With front/rear weight distribution 61/39, spring rates 140 lb in front, 105 rear — compared with rear drive models' 86 front, 110 rear. Automatic leveling control. Laminated mylar printed instrument panel circuits (also on other models). *Brakes*: separate hydraulic circuits front and rear; vacuum boost, 100 pound pedal pressure equaling 1100 pound line pressure; four piston caliper and radially vented discs front, 11-inch diameter. Duo servo, 11x2 finned drums rear. (Front discs optional on other models). *Steering*:

power, variable ratio recirculating ball, rack piston with concentric valve, parallelogram linkage. Overall ratio 16.3; 2.7 turns lock-to-lock; 41-foot turning circle. Weight: 4800 pounds.
BODY. Shared General Motors' C-body used on Riviera and Toronado, but with distinctive styling.
PRICE. Base $6277; with all options, $8061.
PERFORMANCE. Maximum speed 125-130 mph. Zero to 80 in 15.3 seconds, to 100 in 24 seconds.

CALAIS, DE VILLE, FLEETWOOD SERIES
CURRENT 1968
ENGINE. Eight-cylinder ohv V-type (4.30x4.06, 472 cubic inches). *Horsepower*: 375 bhp (gross) at 4400 rpm. *Torque*: 525 lb/ft (gross) at 3000 rpm. *Compression ratio*: 10.5:1. Thicker cylinder wall sections. Major castings completely redesigned to include emission control air injection passages in cylinder head. Cast Armasteel connecting rods. Many bolt-on accessories now provided for on basic block. External dimensions similar to 1967 engines but new version 80 pounds heavier.
TRANSMISSION. Standard axle ratio 2.94; 3.07 for the Fleetwood Eldorado; 3.21 for the Fleetwood Seventy-Five.
BODIES. Facelift. Eldorado given a longer hood. Concealed wipers, nighttime side illumination on all models. Safety engineered interior: all new instrument panels, crushable structure, extensive padding, recessed controls, padded windshield pillars, breakaway inside mirror. Sedan with pillars dropped from Calais line.
PERFORMANCE. For the Coupe de Ville: maximum speed 120+ mph. Zero to 80 in 16.5 seconds, to 100 in 27.8 seconds. Gas mileage 12 mpg at 70-80 mph.

CALAIS, DE VILLE, FLEETWOOD SERIES
CURRENT 1969
Similar to 1968, with the following exceptions:
BODIES. Facelift. Horizontal dual headlamps; horizontal and vertical bars in grille. New roof line and sculptured rear deck and bumpers; new auxiliary light treatment front and rear.
CHASSIS. *Wheelbase*: 129.5 inches (Calais and De Ville); 120 inches (Eldorado); 133 inches (Fleetwood Sixty-Special Brougham), 149.8 inches (Fleetwood Seventy-five limousine).
PRICES. For the Calais two- and four-door, $6162 and $6338; for the De Ville two-door, four-door and convertible, $6399, $6632 and $6583; for the Eldorado, $7389; for the Sixty-Special Brougham, $7788; for the Seventy-five limousine, $11,657.

CALAIS, DE VILLE, FLEETWOOD SERIES
CURRENT 1970
ENGINE. New for the Eldorado. (4.30x4.304, 500 cubic inches). *Horsepower*: 400 bhp (gross) at 4400 rpm; others 375 bhp. *Torque*: 550 lb/ft (gross) at 3000 rpm; others 525 at 2800 rpm.

TRANSMISSION. New, heavier, stronger rear axle and differential. Ratios remained at 2.94 standard, 3.07 on the Eldorado, but changed to 3.15 on the Fleetwood Seventy-five.
CHASSIS. Trackmaster computerized anti-skid rear brake unit optional. New integral steering knuckle for greater dependability.
BODIES. Facelift. Vertical wing emblem very similar to 1941 models appeared on front fenders.
PERFORMANCE. For the Fleetwood Brougham: maximum speed 124 mph. Zero to 80 in 17.6 seconds, to 100 in 28.4 seconds.

CALAIS, DE VILLE, FLEETWOOD SERIES
CURRENT 1971
Similar to 1970, with the following exceptions:
CHASSIS. *Wheelbase*: 130 inches for the Calais and De Ville; 133 inches for the Sixty-Special Brougham; 126.3 inches for the Eldorado; 151.5 inches for the Fleetwood Seventy-five.
BODIES. Restyled. Headlight pairs set wider. Large vertical bumper guards added. Sedan with pillars and convertible dropped from De Ville series. Eldorado convertible added. Eldorado given a squarer grille, spring-loaded standing crest and laurel wreath hood ornament, tall and narrow side windows at rear. Options included all-systems lamp monitors, electrically operated sun roof, AM/FM signal-seeking stereo radio with separate pushbuttons for AM and FM stations, stereo tape deck.

CALAIS, DE VILLE, FLEETWOOD SERIES
CURRENT 1972
Similar to 1971, with the following exceptions:
BODIES. Facelift. Horizontal accent bars on grille and new lighting arrangement. Distinctive grille for Eldorado with vertical bar theme, as opposed to horizontal treatment on the regular line. Impact resistant bumpers with optional full width rubber strips.

CALAIS, DE VILLE, FLEETWOOD SERIES
CURRENT 1973
ENGINE. Additional emission controls to meet government regulations, and acoustic improvements in exhaust system *Horsepower*: 220 bhp, 235 on Eldorado (net). *Torque*: 365 lb/ft, 385 on Eldorado (net) at 2400 rpm. *Compression ratio*: 8.5 to 1 on all models.
CHASSIS. Additional frame strengthening.
BODIES. Vertical style grille and console style head/park lamps on all models except Eldorado, which uses egg-crate type grille. All grilles mounted to bumpers to allow them to retract upon impact. Tail lamps moved out of impact areas. Brougham d'Elegance option for Fleetwood series includes vinyl roof padding, Eldorado type hood ornament, special identification, richer interiors. Accessories include pillow and robe option, illuminated vanity mirror, electrically heated rear windows for all models except the Seventy-five, power operated automatic radio antenna, electrical theft deterrent device, outside temperature gauge mounted integrally in side-view mirror, expanded brands of steel belted radial ply tires on all but Seventy-five.

CALAIS, DE VILLE, FLEETWOOD SERIES
CURRENT 1974

ENGINE. Redesigned combustion chambers for faster burn, reduced cam overlap, altered engine mounts for better damping, new clutch fan, new intake silencer. Choke with vacuum re-indexer for better starting. Electronic ignition optional. *Horsepower*: to SAE specification J245—205 bhp, 210 on Eldorado (net) at 3600 rpm. *Torque*: 365 lb/ft, 380 on Eldorado (net) at 2000 rpm. *Compression ratio*: 8.25:1, lowered for use of low octane fuel.

CHASSIS. Rear stabilizer bar added on Eldorado. Mechanical lockout starter system. Steel belted radial tires optional, with space saver spare.

BODIES. Standard line featuring new lighting arrangement with headlamps closer together. Parking lamps (including turn indicators and cornering lamps) on outer corners of fenders, wraparound. New grille with bold square openings, above and below bumper. Rear quarter redesigned with all new panels having lower profile. New fixed rear quarter window on Coupe de Ville and Calais coupé. Wheel discs redesigned on all models. Twenty-one exterior colors, fifteen new. Ten vinyl and seven convertible tops available. Optional padded roof on Calais. Eldorado offered in convertible and coupé styles, with distinctive "fine-mesh" grille. New air conditioning with better distribution and control. Car length increased 2.2 inches on all models by new rear bumper, Delco telescopic, energy absorber design. Front bumper modified. Power operated antenna with all radio options. *Interiors*: All-new instrument panel on all models, extending in one continuous sweep across front compartment. Warning lights and fuel gauge in horizontal "condition information" band across panel upper portion—including precision crystal controlled digital clock. Speedometer, transmission indicator and turn signals in housing over steering column. Air Cushion Restraint System optional. New interiors including three color brocades, crushed velours, herringbones and leathers. Head restraints with matching seat fabrics in all cloth interiors (except Calais). Three new optional "Special Edition Cars"— Fleetwood Talisman, De Ville d'Elegance (sedan and coupé) and De Ville Cabriolet. Four individual seats, with reclining front passenger seat back in Brougham d'Elegance and Fleetwood Talisman.

PRICES. For the Calais coupé and sedan, $5997 and $6169; for the De Ville coupé and sedan, $6399 and $6631; for the Eldorado coupé and convertible, $7491 and $7812; for the Sixty Special Brougham, $7896; for the Seventy-five sedan and limousine, $12,344 and $12,478.

CALAIS, DE VILLE, FLEETWOOD SERIES
CURRENT 1975

ENGINE. All models, ohv V-8 (4.30x4.304, 500 cubic inches). *Horsepower*: 190 (net) at 3600 rpm. *Torque*: 360 lb/ft (net) at 2000 rpm. *Compression ratio*: 8.5:1. Electronic ignition standard. Optional electronic fuel injection. Recalibrated quadrajet carburetor, with electric choke. High spark advance vacuum spark unit improvements. Above changes, and raised compression ratio, to give improved fuel economy despite tighter emission control. All cars equipped with GM catalytic converter. Exhaust pollutants reduced.

CHASSIS. The 2.73 axle standard on all models except Fleetwood limousines, with 3.15 axle (optional on other models for trailer and mountain use). Steel belted radial tires standard.

BODIES. New grille, hood, front fenders and lights. Rectangular headlamps, fine textured grille on standard line, emphasis on "lowered" front end appearance. Calais and De Ville with new fixed quarter rear window, increased rear visibility. Twenty-one exterior paint colors, fourteen new—nine metallic, four firemist, eight non-metallic. Eldorado coupé and convertible continued; larger rectangular texture grille with bold vertical fins; redesigned front fenders and modified bumper; enlarged quarter window on Eldorado coupé; new rear wheel cutouts without covers; shortened "character line" body side moldings from front wheel opening. "Astroroof" optional on all series except Eldorado convertible and Fleetwood Seventy-five. Power operated sliding glass panel, tinted in harmony with car color scheme. Manual shade. Improved FM stereo radio. "Economy" theme in fuel panel lights, indicating most economical driving range. "Economy" setting on Automatic Climate control reducing use of compressor. Twenty-second "Illuminated Entry" feature optional on all models, operated by exterior push button, automatic switch off. Theft deterrent system improved, aimed by power locking doors with indicator light, warning (lights flash and horn sounds) activated if door locks, hood release or trunk lock opened by other than owner's key. Width, 79.8 inches on all models. Length, 230.7 inches on Calais and De Ville series, 233.7 inches on Sixty Special, 224.1 inches on Eldorado coupé and convertible, 252.2 inches on Seventy-five sedan and limousine. *Interiors*: All series with new cloth and leather trim. Calais, "Morgan" plaid cloth standard, "Morocco" matelasse cloth optional. De Ville, "Metamora" plaid, "Maharaja" (an Indian print), "Mardi Gras" and "Manhattan" striped velour, plus genuine leather. Eldorado, "Metamora," "Montecello" and "Mosaic" check plus genuine leather. Fleetwood Brougham, "Moselle" knit and "Monticello" velour, plus genuine leather, new softer type leather used. Special wood insert type door handles, new design distressed pecan wood grain.

PRICES. For the Calais coupé and sedan, $8197 and $8390; for the De Ville coupé and sedan, $8613 and $8814; for the Eldorado coupé and convertible, $9948 and $10,367; for the Sixty Special Brougham, $10,427; for the Seventy-five sedan and limousine, $14,231 and $14,570.

SEVILLE
CURRENT 1975, 1976

ENGINE. Eight-cylinder ohv V-type (4.057x3.385 inches, 350 cubic inches, 5.7 liters). *Horsepower*: 180 bhp (net) at 4400 rpm. *Torque*: 275 lb/ft (net) at 2000 rpm. *Compression ratio*: 8.0:1. Cast iron block and heads, five main bearings. Hydraulic tappets. Electronic fuel injection, pulse timed, solid state, control unit computes fuel requirements from data supplied by electronic sensors, and controls opening period of injectors. Manifold injection with fuel delivered onto intake valves. Two electric fuel pumps. Catalytic converter and high energy electronic ignition system. High capacity 80 amp generator. Delco "Freedom" battery, water never needing to be replenished.

TRANSMISSION. Automatic with part-throttle downshift. Torque converter with three-speed planetary geartrain. Transmission similar to

Turbo-Hydramatic in larger Cadillac, but nine inches shorter. Constant velocity joints in driveshaft, hypoid axle. Standard rear axle ratio, 2.56:1. CHASSIS. Unit body and chassis assembly, GM "K" body type but exclusive to Seville and not shared with any other GM car, only common sheet metal panel being trunk floor. Two-piece assembly, bolted together at firewall and tied below by subframe. Subframe mountings compliant, with hydraulic damping. *Suspension*: Front, A arms with coil springs, telescopic dampers and anti-roll bar; rear, live axle with semi elliptic leaf springs, telescopic dampers, with self leveling by automatic air compressor, anti-roll bar. *Brakes*: Vented discs front, 11-inch diameter; drums rear, 11-inch diameter, vacuum power assisted. *Wheels*: Steel disc, 15.00x6.00, with radial tires. *Steering*: Recirculating ball, power assisted, with hydraulic damper. Overall ratio 16.4-13.8:1; 3.2 turns lock to lock; 40-foot turning circle. *Wheelbase*: 114.3 inches. *Weight*: 4345 pounds, distributed 57/43 front/rear.
BODIES. Grille texture of large cross-hatch pattern. Rectangular headlamps with wrap-round bezels, wrap-round taillamps integrating side marker lamps and side and rear reflexes. New hood design with Cadillac script displayed on hood face. Fourteen exterior colors, eleven padded vinyl top selections, nine color accent striped selections. Standard wheel discs highlighted by modified wreath/crest ornamentation on center hub. Optional wire-type wheel disc and turbine disc. Overall length, 204.0 inches; overall width, 71.8 inches; overall height, 54.7 inches (twenty-seven inches shorter and eight inches narrower than '75 Sedan de Ville). *Interior*: Rosewood wood grain trim throughout. Knit "Mansion" cloth in seven colors, optional soft leather seat trim in eight colors. Front seats 50/50 divided with double pulldown center armrests. Sound absorbent padding and insulation throughout. Cadillac Fuel Monitor System standard. Illuminated Entry system, Theft Deterrent System and Twilight Sentinel optional. "Astroroof" and "Sunroof" optional after start of '76 production.
PRICE. $12,479 for sedan, only body style available.
PERFORMANCE. Maximum speed 115 mph. Zero to 60 in 11.5 seconds, to 80 in 22.7 seconds. Gas mileage 15.0 to 16.5 mpg.

CALAIS, DE VILLE, FLEETWOOD SERIES
CURRENT 1976
ENGINES. Electronic Fuel Injection optional. Optional 80 amp generator on all full size models, standard on Seventy-five series and Electronic Fuel Injected engine cars. Delco "Freedom" battery standard.
CHASSIS. Automatic level control standard on Fleetwood series, optional on others. Eldorado equipped with four wheel disc brakes and hydraulic powered brake booster as standard; front disc and rear drum brakes on other series.
BODIES. New grilles with cross-hatch motif, revised cornering lamps on Calais, De Ville, Fleetwood Brougham and Seventy-five series featuring chrome strip inserts, Eldorado taillamp one continuous red lens with large bezel frame. New wheel discs for Eldorado with black center hub. Optional wheel discs (including wire and turbine type) on all models except Eldorado. New automatic door locking system, locks all doors when shift lever in "Drive." Fifteen standard and six optional firemist colors, thirteen new. Eleven padded vinyl roof selections, seven convertible tops and eight color accent stripes. *Interiors*: Rosewood grain trim throughout. Carved gun stock pattern simulated wood trim in Eldorado. New trims comprising sporting plaids, plush velours, knits and eleven leather selections.
PRICES. For the Calais coupé and sedan, $8629 and $8825; for the De Ville coupé and sedan, $9067 and $9265; for the Eldorado coupé and convertible, $10,586 and $11,049; for the Sixty Special Brougham, $10,935; for the Seventy-five sedan and limousine, $14,889 and $15,239.

DE VILLE, FLEETWOOD AND SEVILLE SERIES
CURRENT 1977
ENGINE. All models (save Seville which retains Electronic Fuel Injected 350 engine) powered by new 425 cubic inch (7.0 liter) V-8. Electronic Fuel Injection optional on De Ville, Brougham and Eldorado models.
CHASSIS. Four wheel disc brakes on Brougham, Seville and Eldorado. Front disc, rear drum arrangement continued on De Ville and Limousine models.
BODIES. De Ville, Brougham and Limousine models redesigned, with full rear wheel openings and framed door glass construction utilizing body color with chrome accent molding. Cross-hatch grille with larger, horizontal pattern combined with headlamps placed at extreme corners of front fenders for wide stance. New bumpers, larger cornering lamps, extensive use of chrome trim. New vertical integrated tail, side marker lamp positioned on rear quarter end, backup lamps flanking license plate, sharply sculptured rear deck lid. Eldorado and Seville refined, the former with grille and headlamps unified into horizontal design, trimmed with brushed and bright chrome molding and accented by Eldorado lettering used on hood face. Vertical taillamps on Eldorado relocated at bumper ends. New grille design for Seville utilizing vertical styling, with amber park and turn signal lamps. Elk-grained padded vinyl roof retained on Eldorado; all others use new padded "Tuxedo" grain material. Sixteen vinyl roof color choices, three exclusive to Seville, painted metal finish top also available for latter. Fifteen standard and six optional firemist colors, eighteen of them new. De Villes, at 221.2 inches overall, nine inches shorter than previous; Brougham at 221.2 inches and Limousines at 244.2 inches, twelve and eight inches shorter respectively. Average weight reductions more than 950 pounds. New Cadillac Electronic Cruise Control option, including "resume" and "advance" features for increased flexibility. Optional automatic trunk release wired to ignition system and inoperable unless ignition switch is on. *Interiors*: New instrument panel, highlighted by center control area, speedometer cluster featuring both "miles per hour" and "kilometers per hour" markings, trip odometer simplified to reset at touch of button. Newly styled two-spoke steering wheel. New optional AM-FM stereo radio with 23-channel citizens band controls, also optional the stereo push button radio with digital display, weatherband feature, integrated stereo tape player. New trim selections include plaids, plush velours, knits and ten leather/vinyl choices. Eldorado offers "Edinburgh" plaid and four two-tone leather combinations, Seville "Dover" knit cloth as standard, leather as option.
PRICES. For the De Ville coupé and sedan $9654 and $9864; for the Fleetwood Brougham and Eldorado, $11,546 and $11,187; for the Seville, $13,359.

DE VILLE, FLEETWOOD AND SEVILLE SERIES
CURRENT 1978

Wheelbase, overall and interior/exterior dimensions and weights for all 1978 Cadillacs virtually identical to 1977 models.

ENGINE. All models (save Seville with Electronic Fuel Injected 350 engine) powered by 425-cubic-inch (7.0-liter) V-8 developing 180 bhp (net) at 4000 rpm, with torque at 320 lb/ft at 2000 rpm. Compression ratio: 8.2:1. The Seville's figures as follows: 170 bhp at 4200 rpm, torque 270 lb/ft at 2000 rpm. Transmission; Turbo-Hydramatic throughout line. Axle ratios: 2.28, 2.73, 3.08 for De Ville series and Fleetwood Brougham; 2.73, 3.07 for Eldorado; 3.08 for Limousines; 2.56, 3.08 for Seville. Smaller bore throttle body on Seville EFI for smoother throttle response. Seville EFI electronic control unit revised for improved high altitude driveability. Seville with new electronic spark selection added to HE ignition, giving electronic advance/retard and improving cruising economy by about a mile per gallon. All 425-cubic-inch engines available with optional electronic injection. Downshift speeds increased.

CHASSIS. Electronic load leveling system standard on Brougham, Eldorado, Seville and Limousine models, optional on De Villes. Electronic sensor activates load leveling. Instrument signal lights when "Level Ride" compressor is activated. Brake hydraulic booster from power steering pump on Eldorados. Tandem vacuum booster on De Villes, Broughams and Limousines. Single vacuum booster on Seville. Weight reduction in two major areas: new aluminum intake manifold assembly on Seville 31 pounds lighter than 1977, aluminum hood 45 pounds lighter than previous design, used on most Broughams and all California and EFI Sedan De Villes. (Cars able to stay within EPA 4500-pound weight class.) More use of aluminum hoods planned after evaluation in world service.

BODIES: Seven models offered: Coupe De Ville, Sedan De Ville, Fleetwood Brougham, eight-passenger Limousine, seven-passenger Formal Limousine, Eldorado Coupe, Seville Sedan. Two "Special Edition" offerings: Eldorado Biarritz and Seville Elegante. De Ville, Brougham, Limousine and Eldorado feature bolder horizontal cross-hatch grille. All except Eldorado use new rear bumper outers, Seville with new rear bumper guards. Exterior opera lamps available on Seville (except Elegante). Elk grain vinyl top on all models except Seville, with 16 color choices available. Total 21 exterior color selections, 15 regular and 6 firemist, 17 new for 1978. Biarritz with unique style vinyl top and other special decorative features and offered in five colors. Seville Elegante offered in two exterior paints (two-tone dark/light brown or black/platinum) with full wire wheels, painted metal roof, special Elegante script, unique body accent side moldings and car color bumper stubs. Optional wire wheels with integral locking device. New chrome-plated wire wheels with Cadillac center hub optional on De Ville, Brougham and Seville. Basic interior design unchanged from 1977; seven new interior colors and three new body cloths (Random velour, Hampton and Halifax woven cloths); leather-vinyl combinations available on all cars. AM/FM signal seeking stereo radio standard on all models; AM/FM stereo radio with 40 channel CB controls and integral eight-track tape player available. New radio option on Seville and Brougham models: precise electronic tuning and frequency selection, digital radio frequency/time display, eight-track tape and signal seeking/station scanning. Astroroof and Sunroof options available on all models except Limousines.

PERFORMANCE. Coupe De Ville with 2.73 axle ratio: maximum 108 mph; maximum in second, 89 mph; acceleration, 0-60 in 10.6 seconds, 0-80 in 18.5, 0-100 in 37.9; standing quarter mile in 18.2 seconds, 78.8 mph. Note: with 2.28 axle, top speed would be substantially higher. Fuel economy: 16 mpg city, 17.5 mpg highway.

PRICES. For the De Ville Coupe and Sedan, $10,399 and $10,621; for the Eldorado Coupe, $11,858; for the Fleetwood Brougham, $12,223; for the Fleetwood Limousine, $19,285; for the Fleetwood Formal Limousine, $20,000; for the Seville, $14,161.

SEVILLE DIESEL NOTES. 350-cubic-inch V-8, 120 bhp at 3600 rpm, torque 220 lb/ft at 1600 rpm; compression ratio 22.5:1; rear axle ratio 2.56. Price: $16,447, includes $150 for diesel option and $87 for HD diesel package. Acceleration: 0-60 in 15.4 seconds, standing quarter mile in 20.0 seconds. Fuel economy: EPA weighted average 24 mpg, *Motor Trend* road test 24.3 mpg, cruising range on full tank approximately 450 miles.

DE VILLE, FLEETWOOD AND SEVILLE SERIES
CURRENT 1979

Seville, De Ville, Fleetwood Brougham and Limousines retain general design characteristics and overall dimensions from 1978, as well as engine designs, horsepower and torque; and transmissions. Axle ratios, Federal and California: 2.28 for Coupe and Sedan De Ville and Fleetwood Brougham; 3.08 for Limousines; 2.24, 2.56 for Seville; 2.56 for Diesel Seville. California Seville designed for "closed loop" fuel control; exhaust oxygen sensor determines and controls engine air-fuel ratio for combined improvement in engine performance and emission control. Improved Seville ride balance from returned suspension; modified front spring rates and modified front/rear shock absorber valving. All 425 carburetor engines with exhaust gas recirculation tubes for better emission control and fuel economy. All diesel Cadillacs with Bendix "Hydro-Boost" hydraulic brake booster off steering pump. Tire pressures of De Villes and Brougham increased from 26 to 32 p.s.i. for better fuel economy. Ride qualities retained by sophisticated returning of structure—modified sheet metal and body structure, body mount rates and shock absorber valving. Outside left and right mirrors electrically controlled.

BODIES. As for 1978, except three "Special Editions" by addition of De Ville Phaeton, offered on Coupe and Sedan De Villes as an option, with convertible-style roof covering, wire wheel discs, accent stripe, redesigned smaller rear backlight, chrome pillars and other decorative features, available in three color-coordinated combinations. Seville Elegante offered in two new two-tone combinations (Slate Firemist/Black and Cedar Firemist/Red Cedar). New, lower profile, two-spoke steering wheel. De Ville, Fleetwood Brougham and Limousines feature newly styled cross-hatch grille with finer texture, accented with border chrome molding with engraved Cadillac script and black accent band. Total of 21 exterior colors, 14 regular and 7 Firemist, 13 new colors for 1979 (14 of the colors exclusive to Cadillac): 17 color coordinated Elk Grain and Tuxedo Grain vinyl top selections available. Sunroof and Astroroof option now made by Fisher Body Division, marking first time Cadillac sunroof option has been installed while body being assembled.

PRICES. For the De Ville Coupe and Sedan, $11,139 and $11,493; for the Eldorado Coupe, $14,240; for the Fleetwood Brougham, $13,446; for the Fleetwood Limousine, $20,987; for the Fleetwood Formal Limousine, $21,735; for the Seville, $15,646.

ELDORADO NOTES. 350-cubic-inch V-8, 170 bhp at 4200 rpm; compression ratio 8.0:1. Cadillac Open Loop Electronic Fuel Injection. Fuel tank capacity 19.6 gallons approximately. Transmission: THM-325, three-speed, automatic for front wheel drive. Dimensions: tread, front 59.3 inches, rear 60.5 inches; wheelbase, 114 inches; overall length, 204 inches; overall height, 54.2 inches. Shipping weight, 3792 pounds. Wheels, 15x6JJ, steel-belted radial tires P205/75R15, wide white stripe.

GLOSSARY
OF
CADILLAC MODEL NAMES

BIARRITZ. French seaside resort on the Bay of Biscay. Became fashionable in the era of Napoleon III following visits of the Empress Eugenie. Applied to convertible Eldorado models in the late 1950's and early 1960's—". . . rarely, and only to a supremely fortunate few, there comes an automobile the very sight of which summons forth visions of distant mountains, pounding surf and soft southern skies . . . this superbly crafted motor car makes every journey memorable, every arrival a special occasion."

BROUGHAM. Originally a horse-drawn carriage for four persons, with a box seat for the driver, and a footman. It was built as a specific design in 1838 for Lord Henry Peter Brougham (1778-1868), Lord Chancellor of England. Used since 1969 for one of the models in the Fleetwood series.

CALAIS. Seaport and industrial town on the French channel coast. One of the chief landing places for travellers from England to the Continent. Used for the lower priced Cadillac series, usually the first model for new Cadillac owners. (Calais, in Greek mythology, was one of the winged twin sons of Boreas, god of the North Wind, and Oreithyea.)

DE VILLE. French phrase meaning "of the city or town," Coupe de Ville translating as "town car." A recognized body style originally featuring a permanently closed rear compartment with an open front seat for the chauffeur. A smart style which emphasized the social difference between owner and chauffeur. A removable leather cover over the front seat for rainy weather was known as the "De Ville extension." Used for the sporty Cadillac convertible, the personal Coupe de Ville, the popular hardtop sedan and the spacious Sedan de Ville.

ELDORADO. Spanish for "the Gilded One." A legend from the time of the Spanish conquistadores, applied to a fabulous land somewhere in South America, believed to abound in gold and precious stones. The inspiration behind many European expeditions, including one by Sir Walter Raleigh. The name was applied both to the country, and its chief or cacique, who was believed to be a South American Indian leader whose body was sprinkled with gold dust and periodically washed off in a lake. Pizarro's lieutenant, Orellana, claimed to have discovered the land between the Orinoco and the Amazon. But the actual "city of gold" sought by the conquistadores is believed to have been Manoa, in Guiana. The term is still used today to signify fabulous wealth. A distinctive nameplate reserved exclusively for the most luxurious Cadillac models. It was first selected in a contest in 1953, having been suggested by a secretary in the Cadillac merchandising department. The first Eldorado was a sporting convertible introduced in 1953. The current model is the front drive series introduced for the 1967 model year.

FLEETWOOD. A custom coachbuilding house founded by Harry Uhrich in the borough of Fleetwood, Pennsylvania in the Nineteenth Century. With the advent of the automobile, the firm became specialists to Cadillac. (See "Fisher and Fleetwood" in Appendix II.)

SEVILLE. Province in Spain, with capital bearing same name, the city renowned for its history and treasures of art and architecture. During the Sixteenth and Seventeenth Centuries, the name was applied to a school of painting, with two of its masters, Velazquez and Murillo, natives of the province. Used during the 1956 through 1960 model years for coupé in Eldorado series. Name revived in 1975 for the new small Cadillac.

TALISMAN. Astrological charm, carved on stone or metal, and carried on the person to avert evil, protect from danger, safeguard health, et al. From the Cadillac catalogue: "Webster defines 'Talisman' as something producing apparently magical or miraculous effects! So does Cadillac." Used for a luxurious four-passenger Fleetwood model introduced in 1973.

CADILLAC PRODUCTION: 1902–1978

Research by William R. Tite

This table, compiled by William R. Tite of the Cadillac-LaSalle Club and the editors, includes production figures for all cars and chassis since the origins of Cadillac. Theoretically, the totals for model and calendar years should be identical after 1942, when production halted for the war, but those who check will find several thousand units difference in favor of calendar years. This is due to the fact that some Cadillac model year records are based on sales rather than production, which would decrease the totals in the model year column.

Please note also that only V-8 models, during the thirties, are differentiated between Fisher and Fleetwood, inasmuch as the V-12 and V-16 came with Fleetwood bodies except in the case of business sedans; also that the table omits certain models of the late thirties which Cadillac originally listed but did not build. Commercial chassis are grouped with the Series 75 or Fleetwood in later years for clarity, although they usually bore different identification numbers. The letter "X" appearing with some model numbers from 1948-1958, indicates electric window lifts, and "CKD" or "crated, knocked-down," refers to export models boxed in component form for overseas deliveries.

MODEL DESCRIPTION Name (cylinders-wheelbase)		PRODUCTION BY YEAR	
		Model	Calendar
1902			
Model A (1- 76")		0	3
1903			
Model A (1- 76")		2,500	2,497
1904			
Model A (1- 76")			
Model B (1- 76")	All models:	2,418	2,457
1905			
Model B (1- 76")			
Model C (1- 76")			
Model D (4-100")			
Model E (1- 76")	Model D:	156	
Model F (1- 76")	Others:	3,556	
		3,712	3,942
1906			
Model H (4-102")		509*	
Model K (1- 76")			
Model L (4-110")			
Model M (1- 76")	Models K, L, M:	2,150	
		2,659	3,559

MODEL DESCRIPTION Name (cylinders-wheelbase)		PRODUCTION BY YEAR	
		Model	Calendar
1907			
Model G (4-100″)		422	
Model H (4-102″)	*see 1906 total		
Model K (1- 76″)			
Model M (1- 76″)	Models K & M:	1,925	
		2,347	2,884
1908			
Model G (4-100″)		207	
Model H (4-102″)	*see 1906 total		
Model M (1- 82″)			
Model S (1- 82″)			
Model T (1- 82″)	Models M, S, T:	1,482	
		1,689	2,377
1909			
Model M (1- 82″)	questionable production		
Thirty (4-106″)		5,903	
		5,903	7,868
1910			
Thirty (4-106″)		8,008	10,039

MODEL DESCRIPTION Name (cylinders-wheelbase)		PRODUCTION BY YEAR	
		Model	Calendar
1911			
Thirty (4-116″)		10,018	10,071
1912			
"Thirty" (4-116″)		13,995	12,708
1913			
"Thirty" (4-120″)		15,018	17,284
1914			
"Thirty" (4-120″)		14,002	7,818
1915			
Type 51 (V8-122″)		13,002	20,404
1916			
Type 53 (V8-122″)		18,004	16,323
1917			
Type 55 (V8-125/132″)		18,002	19,759
1918			
Type 57 (V8-125/132″)		20,285	12,329

MODEL DESCRIPTION	PRODUCTION BY YEAR	
Name (cylinders-wheelbase)	Model	Calendar

1919

Type 57	(V8-125/132″)	20,678	19,851

1920

Type 59	(V8-125/132″)	19,628	19,790

1921

Type 59	(V8-125/132″)	5,250	11,130

1922

Type 61	(V8-132″)	26,296	22,021

1923

Type 61	(V8-132″)	14,707	22,009

1924

Type V-63	(V8-132″)	18,827	17,748

1925

Type V-63	(V8-132″)	16,673	22,542

1926

Series 314	(V8-132″)	14,249	27,340

1927

Series 303 LaSalle	(V8-125″)	10,767	
Series 314A	(V8-132″)	36,369	
		47,136	34,811

1928

Series 303 LaSalle	(V8-125″)	16,038	
Series 341/341A	(V8-140″)	40,000	
		56,038	41,172

1929

Series 328 LaSalle	(V8-125″)	22,961	
Series 341B	(V8-140″)	18,004	
		40,965	36,598

1930

Series 340 LaSalle	(V8-134″)	14,986	
Series 353	(V8-140″)	11,005	
Series 370	(V12-140″)	5,725*	
Series 452	(V16-148″)	3,250*	
		55,770*	22,559

MODEL DESCRIPTION	PRODUCTION BY YEAR	
Name (cylinders-wheelbase)	Model	Calendar

1931

Series 345A LaSalle	(V8-134″)	10,095	
Series 355	(V8-134″)	10,709	
Series 370A	(V12-140″)	*combined	
Series 452A	(V16-148″)	with	
	above	15,012	

1932

Series 345B LaSalle	(V8-130/134/136″)	3,386	
Series 355B	(V8-134/140″)	2,693	
Series 370B	(V12-134/140″)	1,709	
Series 452B	(V16-143/149″)	296	
		8,084	9,153

1933

Series 345C LaSalle	(V8-130/134/136″)	3,482	
Series 355C	(V8-134/140″)	2,096	
Series 370C	(V12-134/140″)	952	
Series 452C	(V16-143/149″)	125	
		6,655	6,736

NOTE: Production for V-16's between 1934 and 1937, and for most models from 1938 on, has received much deeper research than has thus far been possible with earlier years. Members of the Cadillac-LaSalle Club have analyzed company shipping invoices and other documents not available for other years, obtaining production data in minute detail which is incorporated in the figures which follow.

1934

Series 350 LaSalle	(8-119″)	7,195
Series 355D	(V8-128″)	2,015
Series 355D	(V8-136″)	2,729
Series 355D	(V8-146″)	336
Series 370D	(V12-136″)	683
Series 452D	(V16-154″)	56

V-16 Body Number, Style and Production:

5725	Town Cabriolet	4
5730	Imperial Brougham	1
5733	Imperial Town Sedan	1
5733S	Town Sedan, 5-pass.	2
5735	Convertible Coupe, 2-pass.	2
5775	Imperial Sedan	10
5775FL	Imperial Cabriolet	1
5775S	Imperial Brougham	5
5776	Coupe, 2-pass.	5
5780S	All-weather Phaeton	1
5780	As above with division	5
5785	Convertible Coupe	1

		Model	Calendar
5799	Aerodynamic Coupe	3	
6075	Imperial Sedan, 7-pass.	9	
6075S	Sedan, 7-pass.	5	
	Chassis	1	
		13,014	11,468

1935

		Model	Calendar
Series 50 LaSalle (8-120″)		8,651	
Series 10 (V8-128″ Fisher)		1,130	
Series 10 (V8-136″ Fisher)		1,859	
Series 10 (V8-146″ Fleetwood)		220	
Series 40 370D (V12-146″ Fleetwood)		377	
Series 60 452D (V16-154″ Fleetwood)		50	

V-16 Body Number, Style and Production:

5725	Town Cabriolet, 7-pass.	2
5730S	Sedan, 5-pass.	1
5733	Imperial Town Sedan, 5-pass.	2
5733S	Town Sedan, 5-pass.	4
5775	Imperial Sedan, 7-pass.	15
5775S	Sedan, 7-pass.	2
5776	Coupe, 2-pass.	2
5780	Convertible Sedan, 5-pass.	4
5785	Convertible Coupe, 5-pass.	2
5791B	Limousine Brougham, 7-pass.	1
6033S	Town Sedan, 5-pass.	2
6075	Imperial Sedan, 7-pass.	6
6075B	Imperial Cabriolet, 7-pass.	2
6075S	Sedan, 7-pass.	3
6075H3	Imperial Brougham, 7-pass.	1
	Chassis	1
		12,287	23,559

1936

		Model	Calendar
Series 50 LaSalle (8-120″)		13,004	
Series 60 (V8-121″)		6,700	
Series 70 Fleetwood (V8-131″)		2,000	
Series 75 Fleetwood (V8-138″)		3,227	
Series 80 Fleetwood (V12-131″)		250	
Series 85 Fleetwood (V12-138″)		651	
Series 90 Fleetwood (V16-154″)		52	

V-16 Body Number, Style and Production:

5725	Town Cabriolet, 7-pass.	1
5725C	Town Landau, 7-pass.	1
5730S	Sedan, 5-pass.	1
5730FL	Imperial Cabriolet, 5-pass.	3
5733S	Close-coupled Town Sedan	3
5735	Convertible Coupe, 2-pass.	2
5775	Imperial Sedan, 7-pass.	24
5775S	Sedan, 7-pass.	2
5775FL	Imperial Cabriolet, 7-pass.	1

		Model	Calendar
5776	Coupe, 2-pass.	1	
5780	Convertible Sedan, 5-pass.	6	
5799	Aerodynamic Coupe, 5-pass.	4	
	Chassis	3	
		25,884	28,479

1937

		Model	Calendar
Series 50 LaSalle (V8-124″/160″ commercial)		32,000	
Series 60 (V8-124″/160″ commercial)		7,000	
Series 65 (V8-131″)		2,401	
Series 70 (V8-131″)		1,001	
Series 75 (V8-138″/155″ commercial)		3,227	
Series 85 (V12-133″)		474	
Series 90 (V16-154″)		49	

V-16 Body Number, Style and Production:

5725	Town Cabriolet, 7-pass.	2
5733S	Close-coupled Town Sedan	2
5775	Imperial Sedan, 7-pass.	24
5775S	Sedan, 7-pass.	2
5775FL	Imperial Cabriolet, 7-pass.	3
5775SF	Imperial Brougham, 7-pass.	1
5776	Coupe, 2-pass.	4
5780	Convertible Sedan, 5-pass.	5
5785	Collapsible Coupe, 5-pass.	2
5791	Limousine Brougham, 7-pass.	1
5799	Aerodynamic Coupe, 5-pass.	1
	Chassis	2
		46,152	45,223

1938

		Model	Calendar
Series 50 LaSalle (V8-124″)			15,575
5011	Sedan, 2-door	700	
5019	Sedan, 4-door	9,765	
5019	As above, CKD	228	
5019A	Sun-roof sedan, CKD	72	
5027	Coupe	2,710	
5029	Convertible Sedan	265	
5067	Convertible Coupe	819	
5067	As above, CKD	36	
50	Chassis	5	
50	Chassis, CKD	75	
50	Commercial Chassis, 159″	900	
Series 60 (V8-124″)			2,051
6119	Sedan, 4-door	1,295	
6119	As above, CKD	12	
6127	Coupe	438	
6149	Convertible Sedan	60	
6167	Convertible Coupe	145	
61	Commercial Chassis, 159″	101	

| MODEL DESCRIPTION | PRODUCTION BY YEAR | |
Name (cylinders-wheelbase)	Model	Calendar
Series 60 Special (V8-127″)		3,703
6019S Sedan, 4-door	3,587	
6019S As above, CKD	108	
60 Chassis	8	
Series 65 (V8-132″)		1,401
6519 Sedan, 4-door	1,178	
6519F Imperial Sedan	110	
6549 Convertible Sedan	110	
65 Chassis	3	
Series 75 Fleetwood (V8-141¼″)		1,802
7519 Sedan, 5-pass.	475	
7519F Imperial Sedan, 5-pass.	34	
7523 Sedan, 7-pass.	380	
7523L Business Sedan, 7-pass.	25	
7529 Convertible Sedan, 5-pass.	58	
7533 Imperial Sedan, 7-pass.	479	
7533 As above, CKD	84	
7533F Formal Sedan, 7-pass.	40	
7533L Business Imperial, 7-pass.	25	
7539 Town Sedan, 5-pass.	56	
7553 Town Car, 7-pass.	17	
7557 Coupe, 2-pass.	52	
7557B Coupe, 5-pass.	42	
75 Chassis	16	
75 Chassis, CKD	8	
75 Commercial Chassis, 161″	11	
Series 90 Sixteen Fleetwood (V16-141¼″)		311
9019 Sedan, 5-pass.	43	
9019F Imperial Sedan, 5-pass.	5	
9023 Sedan, 7-pass.	65	
9029 Convertible Sedan, 5-pass.	13	
9033 Imperial Sedan, 7-pass.	95	
9033F Formal Sedan	17	
9039 Town Sedan, 5-pass.	20	
9053 Town Car, 7-pass.	11	
9057 Coupe, 2-pass.	11	
9057B Coupe, 5-pass.	8	
9059 Formal Sedan, 5-pass.	8	
9067 Convertible Coupe, 2-pass.	10	
9006 Presidential, 161″	2	
90 Chassis	3	
	24,843	27,613

1939

| MODEL DESCRIPTION | PRODUCTION BY YEAR | |
Name (cylinders-wheelbase)	Model	Calendar
Series 50 LaSalle (V8-120″)		22,001
5011 Sedan, 2-door	977	
5011A Sun-roof Sedan, 2-door	23	
5019 Sedan, 4-door	15,688	
5019 As above, CKD	240	
5019A Sun-roof Sedan, 4-door	380	
5019A As above, CKD	24	
5027 Coupe	2,525	
5029 Convertible Sedan	185	
5067 Convertible Coupe	1,020	
5067 As above, CKD	36	
50 Chassis	5	
50 Chassis, CKD	24	
50 Commercial Chassis, 156″	874	
Series 61 (V8-126″)		5,874
6119 Sedan, 4-door	3,955	
6119 As above, CKD	96	
6119A Sun-roof Sedan, 4-door	43	
6119F Imperial Sedan	30	
6127 Coupe	1,023	
6129 Convertible Sedan	140	
6167 Convertible Coupe	350	
61 Commercial Chassis, 156″	237	
Series 60 Special Fleetwood (V8-127″)		5,506
6019S Sedan, 4-door	5,135	
6019S As above, CKD	84	
6019SA Sun-roof Sedan, 4-door	225	
6019SAF Imperial Sedan, Sun-roof	55	
60S Chassis	7	
Series 75 Fleetwood (V8-141¼″)		2,065
7519 Sedan, 5-pass.	543	
7519F Imperial Sedan, 5-pass.	53	
7523 Sedan, 7-pass.	412	
7523L Business Sedan, 7-pass.	33	
7529 Convertible Sedan, 5-pass.	36	
7533 Imperial Sedan, 7-pass.	638	
7533 As above, CKD	60	
7533F Formal Sedan, 7-pass.	44	
7533L Business Imperial, 7-pass.	2	
7539 Town Sedan, 5-pass.	51	
7553 Town Car, 7-pass.	13	
7557 Coupe, 2-pass.	36	
7557B Coupe, 5-pass.	23	
7559 Formal Sedan, 5-pass.	53	
7567 Convertible Coupe, 2-pass.	27	
75 Chassis	13	
75 Commercial Chassis, 161″	28	
Series 90 Sixteen Fleetwood (V16-141¼″)		136
9019 Sedan, 5-pass.	13	
9019F Imperial Sedan, 5-pass.	2	
9023 Sedan, 7-pass.	18	
9029 Convertible Sedan, 5-pass.	4	
9033 Imperial Sedan, 7-pass.	60	
9033F Formal Sedan, 7-pass.	8	
9039 Town Sedan, 5-pass.	2	

Model	Name (cylinders-wheelbase)	Model	Calendar
9053	Town Car, 7-pass.	5	
9057	Coupe, 2-pass.	6	
9057B	Coupe, 5-pass.	5	
9059	Formal Sedan, 5-pass.	4	
9067	Convertible Coupe, 2-pass.	7	
90	Chassis	2	
		35,582	38,520

1940

Model	Name (cylinders-wheelbase)	Model	Calendar
Series 50 LaSalle (V8-123″)			10,380
5011	Sedan, 2-door	366	
5011A	Sun-roof Sedan, 2-door	9	
5019	Sedan, 4-door	6,558	
5019	As above, CKD	24	
5019A	Sun-roof Sedan, 4-door	140	
5027	Coupe	1,527	
5029	Convertible Sedan	125	
5067	Convertible Coupe	599	
50	Chassis	2	
50	Commercial Chassis, 159″	1,030	
Series 52 "Special" LaSalle (V8-123″)			13,750
5219	Sedan, 4-door	10,118	
5219	As above, CKD	132	
5227	Coupe	3,000	
5229	Convertible Sedan	75	
5267	Convertible Coupe	425	
Series 62 (V8-129″)			5,900
6219	Sedan, 4-door	4,242	
6219	As above, CKD	60	
6227	Coupe	1,322	
6229	Convertible Sedan	75	
6267	Convertible Coupe	200	
62	Chassis	1	
Series 60 Special Fleetwood (V8-127″)			4,600
6019S	Sedan, 4-door	4,242	
6019SA	Sun-roof Sedan, 4-door	230	
6019F	Imperial Sedan	110	
6019AF	Imperial Sedan, Sun-roof	3	
6053LB	Town Car, leather back	6	
6053MB	Town Car, metal back	9	
Series 72 Fleetwood (V8-138″)			1,526
7219	Sedan, 5-pass.	455	
7219F	Imperial Sedan, 4-pass.	100	
7223	Sedan, 7-pass.	305	
7223L	Business Sedan, 7-pass.	25	
7233	Imperial Sedan, 7-pass.	292	
7233F	Formal Sedan, 7-pass.	20	
7233L	Business Imperial, 7-pass.	36	
7259	Formal Sedan, 5-pass.	18	
72	Commercial Chassis, 165″	275	

Model	Name (cylinders-wheelbase)	Model	Calendar
Series 75 Fleetwood (V8-141¼″)			959
7519	Sedan, 5-pass.	155	
7519F	Imperial Sedan, 5-pass.	25	
7523	Sedan, 7-pass.	166	
7529	Convertible Sedan, 5-pass.	45	
7533	Imperial Sedan, 7-pass.	338	
7533F	Formal Sedan, 7-pass.	42	
7539	Town Sedan, 5-pass.	14	
7553	Town Car, 7-pass.	14	
7557	Coupe, 2-pass.	15	
7557B	Coupe, 5-pass.	12	
7559	Formal Sedan, 5-pass.	48	
7567	Convertible Coupe, 2-pass.	30	
75	Chassis	3	
75	Commercial Chassis, 161″	52	
Series 90 Sixteen Fleetwood (V16-141¼″)			61
9019	Sedan, 5-pass.	4	
9023	Sedan, 7-pass.	4	
9029	Convertible Sedan, 5-pass.	2	
9033	Imperial Sedan, 7-pass.	20	
9033F	Formal Sedan, 7-pass.	20	
9039	Town Sedan, 5-pass.	1	
9053	Town Car, 7-pass.	2	
9057	Coupe, 2-pass.	2	
9057B	Coupe, 5-pass.	1	
9059	Formal Sedan, 5-pass.	2	
9067	Convertible Coupe, 2-pass.	2	
90	Chassis	1	
		37,176	40,245

1941

Model	Name (cylinders-wheelbase)	Model	Calendar
Series 61 (V8-126″)			29,250
6109	Sedan, 4-door	10,925	
6109D	Deluxe Sedan, 4-door	3,495	
6127	Coupe	11,812	
6127D	Deluxe Coupe	3,015	
61	Chassis	3	
Series 62 (V8-126″)			24,726
6219	Sedan, 4-door	8,012	
6219D	Deluxe Sedan, 4-door	7,754	
6219D	As above, CKD	96	
6227	Coupe	1,985	
6227D	Deluxe Coupe	1,900	
6229D	Convertible Sedan	400	
6267D	Convertible Coupe	3,100	
62	Chassis	4	
62	Commercial Chassis, 163″	1,475	
Series 63 (V8-126″) Sedan, 4 door			5,050
Series 60 Special Fleetwood (V8-126″)			4,100

		Model	Calendar
6019	Sedan, 4-door	3,693	
6019A	Sun-roof Sedan, 4-door	185	
6019F	Imperial Sedan	220	
6053LB	Town Car	1	
60	Chassis	1	
Series 67	**(V8-138″)**		900
6719	Sedan, 5-pass.	315	
6719F	Imperial Sedan, 5-pass.	95	
6723	Sedan, 7-pass.	280	
6733	Imperial Sedan, 7-pass.	210	
Series 75 Fleetwood	**(V8-136″)**		2,104
7519	Sedan, 5-pass.	422	
7519F	Imperial Sedan, 5-pass.	132	
7523	Sedan, 7-pass.	405	
7523L	Business Sedan, 9-pass.	54	
7533	Imperial Sedan, 7-pass.	757	
7533F	Formal Sedan, 7-pass.	98	
7533L	Business Imperial, 9-pass.	6	
7559	Formal Sedan, 5-pass.	75	
75	Chassis	5	
75	Commercial Chassis, 163″	150	
		66,130	59,572

1942

		Model	Calendar
Series 61	**(V8-126″)**		5,700
6107	Coupe	2,470	
6107	As above, CKD	12	
6109	Sedan, 4-door	3,194	
6109	As above, CKD	24	
Series 62	**(V8-129″)**		4,960
6207	Coupe	515	
6207D	Deluxe Coupe	530	
6267D	Convertible Coupe	308	
6269	Sedan, 4-door	1,780	
6269D	Deluxe Sedan, 4-door	1,743	
6269D	As above, CKD	84	
Series 63	**(V8-126″) Sedan, 4 door**		1,750
Series 60 Special Fleetwood	**(V8-133″)**		1,875
6069	Sedan, 4-door	1,684	
6069F	Imperial Sedan, 5-pass.	190	
60	Chassis	1	
Series 67	**(V8-138″)**		700
6719	Sedan, 5-pass.	200	
6719F	Imperial Sedan, 5-pass.	50	
6723	Sedan, 7-pass.	260	
6733	Imperial Sedan, 7-pass.	190	
Series 75 Fleetwood	**(V8-136″)**		1,526
7519	Sedan, 5-pass.	205	
7519F	Imperial Sedan, 5-pass.	65	

		Model	Calendar
7523	Sedan, 7-pass.	225	
7523L	Business Sedan, 9-pass.	29	
7533	Imperial Sedan, 7-pass.	430	
7533F	Formal Sedan, 7-pass.	80	
7533L	Business Imperial, 9-pass.	6	
7559	Formal Sedan, 5-pass.	60	
75	Chassis	1	
75	Commercial Chassis, 163″	425	
		16,511	2,873

1945

		Model	Calendar
Series 61	**(V8-126″) Sedan, 4-door**	0	1,142

1946

		Model	Calendar
Series 61	**(V8-126″)**		3,001
6107	Coupe	800	
6109	Sedan	2,200	
61	Chassis	1	
Series 62	**(V8-129″)**		18,566
6207	Coupe	2,323	
6267D	Convertible Coupe	1,342	
6269	Sedan	14,900	
62	Chassis	1	
Series 60 Special Fleetwood	**(V8-133″)**		
	Sedan		5,700
Series 75 Fleetwood	**(V8-136″)**		1,927
7519	Sedan, 5-pass.	150	
7523	Sedan, 7-pass.	225	
7523L	Business Sedan, 9-pass.	22	
7533	Imperial Sedan, 7-pass.	221	
7533L	Business Imperial, 9-pass.	17	
75	Commercial Chassis, 163″	1,292	
		29,194	28,144

1947

		Model	Calendar
Series 61	**(V8-126″)**		8,555
6107	Coupe	3,395	
6109	Sedan	5,160	
Series 62	**(V8-129″)**		39,835
6207	Coupe	7,245	
6267	Convertible Coupe	6,755	
6269	Sedan	25,834	
62	Chassis	1	
Series 60 Special Fleetwood	**(V8-133″)**		
	Sedan		8,500
Series 75 Fleetwood	**(V8-136″)**		5,036
7519	Sedan, 5-pass.	300	

Model	Description	Model	Model (prod)	Calendar
7523	Sedan, 7-pass.	890		
7523L	Business Sedan, 9-pass.	135		
7533	Imperial Sedan, 7-pass.	1,005		
7533L	Business Imperial, 9-pass.	80		
75	Chassis	3		
75	Commercial Chassis, 163″	2,423		
75	Business Chassis, 163″	200		
			61,926	59,436

1948

Model	Description	Model	Model (prod)	Calendar
Series 61	(V8-126″)		8,603	
6107	Coupe	3,521		
6169	Sedan	5,081		
61	Chassis	1		
Series 62	(V8-126″)		34,213	
6207	Coupe	4,764		
6267X	Convertible Coupe	5,450		
6269	Sedan	23,997		
62	Chassis	2		
Series 60 Special Fleetwood (V8-133″)				
	Sedan		6,561	
Series 75 Fleetwood (V8-136″)			3,329	
7519X	Sedan, 5-pass.	225		
7523L	Business Sedan, 9-pass.	90		
7523X	Sedan, 7-pass.	499		
7533L	Business Imperial, 9-pass.	64		
7533X	Imperial Sedan, 7-pass.	382		
75	Chassis	2		
76	Commercial Chassis, 163″	2,067		
			52,706	66,209

1949

Model	Description	Model	Model (prod)	Calendar
Series 61	(V8-126″)		22,148	
6107	Coupe	6,409		
6169	Sedan	15,738		
61	Chassis	1		
Series 62	(V8-126″)		55,643	
6207	Coupe	7,515		
6237	Coupe de Ville	2,150		
6267X	Convertible Coupe	8,000		
6269	Sedan	37,617		
6269	Export Sedan, CKD	360		
62	Chassis	1		
Series 60 Special Fleetwood (V8-133″)			11,400	
6037X	Special Coupe de Ville	1		
6069X	Sedan	11,399		
Series 75 Fleetwood (V8-136″)			3,363	
7519X	Sedan, 5-pass.	220		

Model	Description	Model	Model (prod)	Calendar
7523L	Business Sedan, 9-pass.	35		
7523X	Sedan, 7-pass.	595		
7533L	Business Imperial, 9-pass.	25		
7533X	Imperial Sedan, 7-pass.	626		
75	Chassis	1		
86	Commercial Chassis, 163″	1,861		
			92,554	81,545

1950

Model	Description	Model	Model (prod)	Calendar
Series 61	(V8-122″)		26,772	
6137	Coupe	11,839		
6169	Sedan	14,619		
6169	Export Sedan, CKD	312		
61	Chassis	2		
Series 62	(V8-126″)		59,818	
6219	Sedan	41,890		
6237	Coupe	6,434		
6237DX	Coupe de Ville	4,507		
6267	Convertible Coupe	6,986		
62	Chassis	1		
Series 60 Special Fleetwood (V8-130″)				
	Sedan		13,755	
Series 75 Fleetwood (V8-146¾″)			3,512	
7523L	Business Sedan	1		
7523X	Sedan	716		
7533X	Imperial Sedan	743		
86	Commercial Chassis, 157″	2,052		
			103,857	110,535

1951

Model	Description	Model	Model (prod)	Calendar
Series 61	(V8-122″)		4,700	
6137	Coupe	2,400		
6169	Sedan	2,300		
Series 62	(V8-126″)		81,844	
6219	Sedan	54,596		
6219	Export Sedan, CKD	756		
6237	Coupe	10,132		
6237DX	Coupe de Ville	10,241		
6267	Convertible Coupe	6,117		
62-126	Chassis	2		
Series 60 Special Fleetwood (V8-130″)				
	Sedan		18,631	
Series 75 Fleetwood (V8-146¾″)			5,165	
7523L	Business Sedan	30		
7523X	Sedan	1,090		
7533X	Imperial Sedan	1,085		
86	Commercial Chassis, 157″	2,960		
			110,340	103,266

1952

Model Description		Model	Calendar
Series 62	(V8-126″)	70,255	
6219	Sedan	42,625	
6237	Coupe	10,065	
6237DX	Coupe de Ville	11,165	
6267X	Convertible Coupe	6,400	
Series 60 Special Fleetwood (V8-130″)			
	Sedan	16,110	
Series 75 Fleetwood (V8-146¾″) Sedan		1.400	
Series 75 Fleetwood (V8-146¾″) Imperial		800	
8680S	Commercial Chassis, 157″	1,694	
		90,259	96,850

1953

Model Description		Model	Calendar
Series 62	(V8-126″)	85,446	
6219	Sedan	47,316	
6219	Export Sedan, CKD	324	
6237	Coupe	14,353	
6237DX	Coupe de Ville	14,550	
6267X	Convertible Coupe	8,367	
6267SX	Eldorado Convertible	532	
62	Chassis	4	
Series 60 Special Fleetwood (V8-130″)			
	Sedan	20,000	
Series 75 Fleetwood (V8-146¾″) Sedan		1,435	
Series 75 Fleetwood (V8-146¾″) Imperial		765	
8680S	Commercial Chassis, 157″	2,005	
		109,651	103,538

1954

Model Description		Model	Calendar
Series 62	(V8-129″)	77,345	
6219	Sedan	33,845	
6219	Export Sedan, CKD	408	
6219SX	De Ville Sedan	1	
6237	Hardtop, 2-door	17,460	
6237DX	Coupe de Ville	17,170	
6267X	Convertible Coupe	6,310	
6267SX	Eldorado Convertible	2,150	
62	Chassis	1	
Series 60 Special Fleetwood (V8-133″)		16,200	
Series 75 Fleetwood (V8-149¾″)			
	Sedan	889	
Series 75 Fleetwood (V8-149¾″)			
	Imperial	611	
8680S	Commercial Chassis, 158″	1,635	
		96,680	123,746

1955

Model Description		Model	Calendar
Series 62	(V8-129″)	118,586	
6219	Sedan	44,904	
6219	Export Sedan, CKD	396	
6237	Hardtop, 2-door	27,879	
6237DX	Coupe de Ville	33,300	
6267X	Convertible Coupe	8,150	
6267SX	Eldorado Convertible	3,950	
62	Chassis	7	
Series 60 Special Fleetwood (V8-133″)			
	Sedan	18,300	
Series 75 Fleetwood (V8-149¾″)			
	Sedan	1,075	
Series 75 Fleetwood (V8-149¾″)			
	Imperial	841	
8680S	Commercial Chassis, 158″	1,975	
		140,777	153,334

1956

Model Description		Model	Calendar
Series 62	(V8-129″)	133,502	
6219	Sedan	26,222	
6219	Export Sedan, CKD	444	
6237	Hardtop, 2-door	26,649	
6237DX	Coupe de Ville	24,086	
6237SDX	Eldorado Seville Coupe	3,900	
6239DX	Sedan de Ville	41,732	
6267X	Convertible Coupe	8,300	
6267SX	Eldorado Biarritz conv.	2,150	
62	Chassis	19	
Series 60 Special Fleetwood (V8-133″)			
	Sedan	17,000	
Series 75 Fleetwood (V8-149¾″)			
	Sedan	1,095	
Series 75 Fleetwood (V8-149¾″)			
	Imperial	955	
8680S	Commercial Chassis, 158″	2,025	
		154,577	140,873

1957

Model Description		Model	Calendar
Series 62	(V8-129½″)	118,372	
6237	Hardtop, 2-door	25,120	
6237DX	Coupe de Ville	23,813	
6237SDX	Eldorado Coupe	2,100	
6239	Sedan	32,342	
6239DX	Sedan de Ville	23,808	
6239SX	Sedan Seville	4	
6267X	Convertible Coupe	9,000	
6267SX	Eldorado Biarritz conv.	1,800	

Model	Description		Model	Calendar
62	Export Sedan, CKD	384		
62	Chassis	1		
Series 60 Special Fleetwood (V8-133″)			24,000	
Series 75 Fleetwood (V8-149.8″) Sedan			1,010	
Series 75 Fleetwood (V8-149.8″) Imperial			890	
Series 70 Eldorado Brougham (V8-126″)			400	
8680S	Commercial Chassis, 156″		2,169	
			146,841	153,236

1958

Model	Description		Model	Calendar
Series 62 (V8-129.5″)			105,127	
6237	Hardtop, 2-door	18,736		
6237DX	Coupe de Ville	18,414		
6237SDX	Eldorado Seville Coupe	855		
6239	Sedan, standard deck	13,335		
6239E	Sedan, extended deck	20,952		
6239EDX	Sedan de Ville	23,989		
6267X	Convertible Coupe	7,825		
6267SX	Eldorado Biarritz conv.	815		
6267SSX	Special Eldorado Coupe	1		
62	Export Sedan, CKD	204		
62	Chassis	1		
Series 60 Special Fleetwood (V8-133″)			12,900	
Series 75 Fleetwood (V8-149.8″) Sedan			802	
Series 75 Fleetwood (V8-149.8″) Imperial			730	
Series 70 Eldorado Brougham (V8-126″)			304	
8680S	Commercial Chassis		1,915	
			121,778	125,501

1959

Model	Description		Model	Calendar
Series 62-63-64 (V8-130″)			126,421	
6229	Sedan, 6-window	23,461		
6237	Hardtop, 2-door	21,947		
6239	Sedan, 4-window	14,138		
6267	Convertible Coupe	11,130		
62	Export Sedan, CKD	60		
6329	Sedan de Ville, 6-window	19,158		
6337	Coupe de Ville	21,924		
6339	Sedan de Ville, 4-window	12,308		
6437	Eldorado Seville Coupe	975		
6467	Eldorado Biarritz conv.	1,320		
Series 60 Special Fleetwood (V8-130″)			12,250	
Series 67 Fleetwood (V8-149.8″) Sedan			710	
Series 67 Fleetwood (V8-149.8″) Limousine			690	
Series 69 Eldorado Brougham (V8-130″)			99	
6890	Commercial Chassis, 156″		2,102	
			142,272	138,527

1960

Model	Description		Model	Calendar
Series 62-63-64 (V8-130″)			126,573	
6229	Sedan, 6-window	26,824		
6237	Hardtop, 2-door	19,978		
6239	Sedan, 4-window	9,984		
6267	Convertible Coupe	14,000		
62	Export Sedan, CKD	36		
62	Chassis	2		
6329	Sedan de Ville, 6-window	22,579		
6337	Coupe de Ville	21,585		
6339	Sedan de Ville, 4-window	9,225		
6437	Eldorado Seville Coupe	1,075		
6467	Eldorado Biarritz conv.	1,285		
Series 60 Special Fleetwood (V8-130″)			11,800	
Series 67 Fleetwood 75 (V8-149.8″) Sedan			718	
Series 67 Fleetwood 75 (V8-149.8″) Limousine			832	
Series 69 Eldorado Brougham (V8-130″)			101	
6890	Commercial Chassis, 156″		2,160	
			142,184	158,941

1961

Model	Description		Model	Calendar
Series 62-63 (V8-129.5″)			119,050	
6229	Sedan, 6-window	26,216		
6237	Hardtop, 2-door	16,005		
6239	Sedan, 4-window	4,700		
6267	Convertible Coupe	15,500		
62	Chassis	5		
6329	Sedan de Ville, 6-window	26,415		
6337	Coupe de Ville	20,156		
6339	Sedan de Ville, 4-window	4,847		
6367	Eldorado Biarritz conv.	1,450		
6399	Town Sedan, 6-window	3,756		
Series 60 Special Fleetwood (V8-129.5″)			15,500	
Series 67 Fleetwood 75 (V8-149.8″) Sedan			699	
Series 67 Fleetwood 75 (V8-149.8″) Limousine			926	
6890	Commercial Chassis, 156″		2,204	
			138,379	148,298

1962

Model	Description		Model	Calendar
Series 62-63 (V8-129.5″)			143,610	
6229	Sedan, 6-window	16,730		
6239	Sedan, 4-window	17,314		
6247	Hardtop, 2-door	16,833		
6267	Convertible Coupe	16,800		
6289	Town Sedan	2,600		
6329	Sedan de Ville, 4-window	16,230		

6339	Sedan de Ville, 6-window	27,378		
6347	Coupe de Ville	25,675		
6367	Eldorado Biarritz conv.	1,450		
6389	Park Avenue Sedan	2,600		
Series 60 Special Fleetwood (V8-129.5″)			13,350	
Series 67 Fleetwood 75 (V8-149.8″) Sedan			696	
Series 67 Fleetwood 75 (V8-149.8″)				
	Limousine		904	
6890	Commercial Chassis, 156″		2,280	
			160,840	158,528

1963

Series 62-63 (V8-129.5″)			145,172	
6229	Sedan, 6-window	12,929		
6239	Sedan, 4-window	16,980		
6257	Hardtop, 2-door	16,786		
6267	Convertible Coupe	17,600		
62-3	Chassis	3		
6329	Sedan de Ville, 6-window	15,146		
6339	Sedan de Ville, 4-window	30,579		
6357	Coupe de Ville	31,749		
6367	Eldorado Biarritz conv.	1,825		
6389	Park Avenue Sedan	1,575		
Series 60 Special Fleetwood (V8-129.5″)			14,000	
Series 67 Fleetwood 75 (V8-149.8″) Sedan			680	
Series 67 Fleetwood 75 (V8-149.8″)				
	Limousine		795	
6890	Commercial Chassis, 156″		2,527	
			163,174	164,735

1964

Series 62-63 (V8-129.5″)			147,345	
6229	Sedan, 6-window	9,243		
6239	Sedan, 4-window	13,670		
6257	Hardtop, 2-door	12,166		
6267	Convertible Coupe	17,900		
6329	Sedan de Ville, 6-window	14,627		
6339	Sedan de Ville, 4-window	39,674		
6357	Coupe de Ville	38,195		
6367	Eldorado Biarritz conv.	1,870		
Series 60 Special Fleetwood (V8-129.5″)			14,550	
Series 67 Fleetwood 75 (V8-149.8″) Sedan			617	
Series 67 Fleetwood 75 (V8-149.8″)				
	Limousine		808	
6890	Commercial Chassis, 156″		2,639	
			165,959	154,603

1965

Calais Series (V8-129.5″)			34,211	
68239	Hardtop Sedan	13,975		
68257	Hardtop Coupe	12,515		
68269	Sedan	7,721		
De Ville Series (V8-129.5″)			123,080	
68339	Hardtop Sedan	45,535		
68357	Hardtop Coupe	43,345		
68367	Convertible	19,200		
68369	Sedan	15,000		
Fleetwood Series (V8-129.5/133/149.8″)			24,144	
68069	Sixty Special Sedan	18,100		
68467	Eldorado Convertible	2,125		
69723	Seventy-Five Sedan	455		
69733	Seventy-Five Limousine	795		
69890	Commercial Chassis, 156″	2,669		
			181,435	196,595

1966

Calais Series (V8-129.5″)			28,680	
68239	Hardtop Sedan	13,025		
68257	Hardtop Coupe	11,080		
68269	Sedan	4,575		
De Ville Series (V8-129.5″)			142,190	
68339	Hardtop Sedan	60,550		
68357	Hardtop Coupe	50,580		
68367	Convertible	19,200		
68369	Sedan	11,860		
Fleetwood Series (V8-129.5/133/149.8″)			25,805	
68069	Sixty Special Sedan	5,445		
68169	Sixty Special Brougham	13,630		
68467	Eldorado Convertible	2,250		
69723	Seventy-five Sedan	980		
69733	Seventy-five Limousine	1,037		
69890	Commercial Chassis, 156″	2,463		
			196,675	205,001

1967

Calais Series (V8-129.5″)			21,830	
68247	Hardtop Coupe	9,085		
68249	Hardtop Sedan	9,880		
68269	Sedan	2,865		
De Ville Series (V8-129.5″)			139.807	
68347	Hardtop Coupe	52,905		
68349	Hardtop Sedan	59,902		
68367	Convertible	18,200		
68369	Sedan	8,800		

Model	Name (cylinders-wheelbase)		Model	Calendar
	Fleetwood Series (V8-120/133/149.8″)		38,363	
68069	Sixty Special Sedan	3,550		
68169	Sixty Special Brougham	12,750		
69347	Eldorado Coupe	17,930		
69723	Seventy-Five Sedan	835		
69733	Seventy-Five Limousine	965		
69890	Commercial Chassis, 156″	2,333		
			200,000	213,161

1968

Model	Name (cylinders-wheelbase)		Model	Calendar
	Calais Series (V8-129.5″)		18,190	
68247	Hardtop Coupe	8,165		
68249	Hardtop Sedan	10,025		
	De Ville Series (V8-129.5″)		164,472	
68347	Hardtop Coupe	63,935		
68349	Hardtop Sedan	72,662		
68367	Convertible	18,025		
68369	Sedan	9,850		
	Fleetwood Series (V8-120/133/149.8″)		47,341	
68069	Sixty Special Sedan	3,300		
68169	Sixty Special Brougham	15,300		
69347	Eldorado Coupe	24,528		
69723	Seventy-Five Sedan	805		
69733	Seventy-Five Limousine	995		
69890	Commercial Chassis, 156″	2,413		
			230,003	210,904

1969

Model	Name (cylinders-wheelbase)		Model	Calendar
	Calais Series (V8-129.5″)		12,425	
68247	Hardtop Coupe	5,600		
68249	Hardtop Sedan	6,825		
	De Ville Series (V8-129.5″)		163,048	
68347	Hardtop Coupe	65,755		
68349	Hardtop Sedan	72,958		
68367	Convertible	16,445		
68369	Sedan	7,890		
	Fleetwood Series (V8 120/133/149.8″)		47,764	
68069	Sixty Special Sedan	2,545		
68169	Sixty Special Brougham	17,300		
69347	Eldorado Coupe	23,333		
69723	Seventy-Five Sedan	880		
69733	Seventy-Five Limousine	1,156		
69890	Commercial Chassis, 156″	2,550		
			223,237	266,798

1970

Model	Name (cylinders-wheelbase)		Model	Calendar
	Calais Series (V8-129.5″)		9,911	

Model	Name (cylinders-wheelbase)		Model	Calendar
68247	Hardtop Coupe	4,724		
68249	Hardtop Sedan	5,187		
	De Ville Series (V8-129.5″)		181,719	
68347	Hardtop Coupe	76,043		
68349	Hardtop Sedan	83,274		
68367	Convertible	15,172		
68369	Sedan	7,230		
	Fleetwood Series (V8-120/133/149.8″)		47,115	
68069	Sixty Special Sedan	1,738		
68169	Sixty Special Brougham	16,913		
69347	Eldorado Coupe	23,842		
69723	Seventy-Five Sedan	876		
69733	Seventy-Five Limousine	1,240		
69890	Commercial Chassis, 156″	2,506		
			238,745	152,859

1971

Model	Name (cylinders-wheelbase)		Model	Calendar
	Calais Series (V8-130″)		6,929	
68247	Hardtop Coupe	3,360		
68249	Hardtop Sedan	3,569		
	De Ville Series (V8-130″)		135,426	
68347	Hardtop Coupe	66,081		
68349	Hardtop Sedan	69,345		
	Fleetwood Series (V8-126.3/133/151.5″)		46,182	
68169	Sixty Special Brougham	15,200		
69347	Eldorado Coupe	20,568		
69367	Eldorado Convertible	6,800		
69723	Seventy-Five Sedan	752		
69733	Seventy-Five Limousine	848		
69890	Commercial Chassis, 157½″	2,014		
			188,537	276,560

1972

Model	Name (cylinders-wheelbase)		Model	Calendar
	Calais Series (V8-130″)		7,775	
68247	Hardtop Coupe	3,900		
68249	Hardtop Sedan	3,875		
	De Ville Series (V8-130″)		194,811	
68347	Hardtop Coupe	95,280		
68349	Hardtop Sedan	99,531		
	Fleetwood Series (V8-126.3/133/151.5″)		65,201	
68169	Sixty Special Brougham	20,750		
69347	Eldorado Coupe	32,099		
69367	Eldorado Convertible	7,975		
69723	Seventy-Five Sedan	955		
69733	Seventy-Five Limousine	960		
69890	Commercial Chassis, 157½″	2,462		
			267,787	277,251

MODEL DESCRIPTION Name (cylinders-wheelbase)	PRODUCTION BY YEAR		
		Model	Calendar

1973

Calais Series (V8-130")			8,073
68247	Hardtop Coupe	4,275	
68249	Hardtop Sedan	3,798	
De Ville Series (V8-130")			216,243
68347	Hardtop Coupe	112,849	
68349	Hardtop Sedan	103,394	
Fleetwood Series (V8-126.3/133/151.5")			80,523
68169	Sixty Special Brougham	24,800	
69347	Eldorado Coupe	42,136	
69367	Eldorado Convertible	9,315	
69723	Seventy-five Sedan	1,043	
69733	Seventy-five Limousine	1,017	
69890	Commercial chassis, 157½"	2,212	
		304,839	**307,698**

1974

Calais Series (V8-130")			6,883
68247	Hardtop Coupe	4,559	
68249	Hardtop Sedan	2,324	
De Ville Series (V8-130")			172,620
68347	Hardtop Coupe	112,201	
68349	Hardtop Sedan	60,419	
Fleetwood Series (V8-126.3/133/151.5")			62,827
68169	Sixty Special Brougham	18,250	
69347	Eldorado Coupe	32,812	
69367	Eldorado Convertible	7,600	
69723	Seventy-five Sedan	895	
69733	Seventy-five Limousine	1,005	
69890	Commercial chassis, 157½"	2,265	
		242,330	**230,649**

1975

Calais Series (V8-130")			8,300
68247	Hardtop Coupe	5,800	
68249	Hardtop Sedan	2,500	
De Ville Series (V8-130")			173,570
68347	Hardtop Coupe	110,218	
68349	Hardtop Sedan	63,352	
Fleetwood Series (V8-126.3/133/151.5")			66,506
68169	Sixty Special Brougham	18,755	
69347	Eldorado Coupe	35,802	
69367	Eldorado Convertible	8,950	
69723	Seventy-five Sedan	876	
69733	Seventy-five Limousine	795	
69890	Commercial chassis, 157½"	1,328	
Seville (V8-114.3")			16,355
		264,731	**270,197**

MODEL DESCRIPTION Name (cylinders-wheelbase)	PRODUCTION BY YEAR		
		Model	Calendar

1976

Calais Series (V8-130")			6,200
68247	Hardtop Coupe	4,500	
68249	Hardtop Sedan	1,700	
De Ville Series (V8-130")			182,159
68347	Hardtop Coupe	114,482	
68349	Hardtop Sedan	67,677	
Fleetwood Series (V8-126.3/133/151.5")			77,008
68169	Sixty Special Brougham	24,500	
69347	Eldorado Coupe	35,184	
69367	Eldorado Convertible	14,000	
69723	Seventy-five Sedan	981	
69733	Seventy-five Limousine	834	
69890	Commercial chassis, 157½"	1,509	
Seville (V8-114.3")			43,772
		309,139	**304,485**

1977

De Ville Series (V8-130")			234,171
68347	Hardtop Coupe	138,750	
68349	Hardtop Sedan	95,421	
Fleetwood Series (V8-126.3/133/151.5")			79,256
68169	Sixty Special Brougham	28,000	
69347	Eldorado Coupe	47,344	
69723	Seventy-five Sedan	1,582	
69773	Seventy-five Limousine	1,032	
69890	Commercial chassis, 157½"	1,299	
Seville (V8-114.3")			45,060
		358,487	**335,785**

1978

De Ville Series (V8-130")			206,701
68347	Hardtop Coupe	117,750	
68349	Hardtop Sedan	88,951	
Fleetwood Series (V8-126.3/133/151.1")			85,998
68169	Sixty Special Brougham	36,800	
69347	Eldorado Coupe	46,816	
69723	Seventy-five Sedan	848	
69773	Seventy-five Limousine	682	
69890	Commercial chassis, 157½"	852	
Seville (V8-114.3")			56,985
		349,684	**350,813**

The Seville total included 2,822 diesels built in 1978; 1,100 Sevilles were assembled in Iran during 1978. Cadillac plant exports for 1978 were approximately 3,000 cars, most Sevilles. Cadillac diesel production for 1979 was planned at 35,000 over the three series.

NOTES ON THE CHAPTERS

These notes have been prompted by letters from interested readers in various countries commenting upon earlier editions of this book. The following, from David K. Birt, of Surrey, England, is typical:

"After obtaining and reading your fine publication, I feel I should write you, to register my protest over one point. It is the opinion of my friends as well who have purchased this fine book, that it does not do justice to the famous 1959 rocket-fin Cadillac. There is . . . very little mention in the text. I am pleased to see that they are acknowledged as being 'undeniably excellent.' I have owned two 1959 'Caddys' and along with a host of other features, '59 was the first to get away from the front bumper rubber cones. And the body line and style still do not look dated over in England even today."

We would like to assure Mr. Birt, and all like him who have written in about their favorite model or topic, that it was not the intention of the author, the editors, or the publisher, to slight any Cadillac model. We appreciate the interest of enthusiasts whatever the model or period. And it is their specialized knowledge which continues to assist in making each successive edition of this book better than the last. Thus, such comments are always welcomed and valued. From them, and from further research, we present the following addenda which we think will be of interest to Cadillac enthusiasts.

1922 MODELS: In 1922, *The Motor* in England published a road test of a 1922 seven-passenger touring car, and the performance figures and comments are revealing. The car was found to be "imposing in appearance. . .extraordinarily complete in equipment. . .nicely finished. . .smooth in operation and particularly responsive to the controls. Ample power. . .here is a roomy car that is as light and responsive at speeds up to 65 mph as the most lively 1½ litre road racer. Through its whole range of speeds it is as smooth as a clockspring . . . it has particularly good pickup in traffic, while on the open road the car glides at deceptive speeds up hill and down dale as the shadow of a wind-borne cloud flits tirelessly across the landscape.

"It is a notable top gear performer. It takes 5 secs to accelerate from 5 mph to 15 mph, another 5 secs from 15 to 25 mph, and precisely the same time between 25-35 mph and 35-40 mph. The accelerator and speedometer needle might almost be interconnected, for the car is one of the most responsive we have ever driven. The way the power unit performs seems to dissociate from one's mind the idea that combustion in any form is connected with the engine. Its speed is very deceptive on the road, for it is very quiet, and the engine gives no indication of the pace at which it is turning over.

"It surges up ordinary main road hills at 40-45 mph in a way that quickly establishes that its average cross country gait is high. The foot brake pulls up the car in a very short space without skidding—which makes for both safety and comfort. Up to 55 mph the suspension is excellent . . . and at ordinary speeds on the open road there is no question that the Cadillac is very well sprung, and moreover, devoid of any roll that might produce mental discomfort on corners. The car climbed the Brooklands test hill (maximum 1 in 4) in second gear and either the hand or the foot brake held it stationary on the 1 in 4 portion. The fuel consumption was 14 miles to the gallon."

"From the early days of automobilism," continued *The Motor*, "the Cadillac has been one of the most respected American cars sold in this country. It probably has done more than most to rid English motorists of the idea that all transatlantic productions are built down to a price. . . . [The Cadillac] must be classed as distinct from the common rut of cars. . .and to be looked upon in much the same way as all the highest class British cars are regarded in this country.

"The price of the Cadillac is £1,140 complete, at which figure there should be little doubt about its giving ample satisfaction to any motorist who likes a big car that is smooth in operation, particularly responsive to the controls, and obviously made for fast touring."

1928 MANUFACTURING STANDARDS: A series of articles in *Automotive Industries* by K.W. Stillman emphasized the unusual methods and tolerances at Cadillac, in contrast with general industry practice. For example, connecting rods were diamond bored for both crank and wristpin ends, thus ensuring the greatest possible accuracy. Both these operations were performed simultaneously in a two-spindle machine designed by Cadillac engineers. Tolerances were held to 0.00025 inch for crank pin and 0.00015 inch for wristpin holes.

Bolt bases were form-milled on a duplex milling machine, four rods at once. Bolt holes were drilled and reamed in multiple spindle drills, eight rods at once. Four specially designed six-spindle machines were used for gun drilling oil holes in rod shanks.

Rods were parkerized to stop babbitt adhering to outside surfaces, and after preparation, babbitting was pressure applied in a special machine. Rods were weighed on precision scales for both "end" and "overall" weight limits, and held to tolerances of 1/16 ounce. These limits made rod selection unnecessary in assembling engine sets, despite a production rate of sixty rods per hour.

Manufacture of cylinder blocks was cited as another example of Cadillac thoroughness, there being "a number of interesting operations employing tools and fixtures not generally used for this work." Rough blocks were mounted, eight at a time, in a drum-type milling machine where top and bottom surfaces were rough and finish milled. Grinding, drilling, boring and reaming operations followed. A large drum-type milling machine holding fourteen blocks milled the manifold faces. Initial valve hole boring was done four at a time to allow room for large boring bar collars and ensure rigidity and accuracy. An eight-spindle drill press was used for flush boring all valve holes per block at once.

A single reamer machined all four bores in each cylinder block, thus ensuring uniform bores. Honing was done on a multiple spindle machine, with out-of-round and taper held to a limit of 0.0005 inch.

Stillman noted similar standards in the transmission department, and remarked: "Typical examples of the best current practice in gear production are found in the plant of Cadillac Motor Car Co. Cadillac transmission gears are held to fine tolerances. . .two ten-thousandths of an inch are not at all uncommon." From Brinell testing of the blanks, through heat-treating and electric tempering, hardness testing, grinding, burnishing and final inspection, methods were "exacting."

1930 MADAM X: "This is the most mis-identified, talked-about, rumor-storied Cadillac ever built," wrote Norm Uhlir. "One feature distinguished the Madam X, and that was the 18-degree sloping one-piece windshield as compared to seven degrees and sixteen degrees on other closed models. The 21-degree and 22-degree sloping windshields were used only on open models. (Madam X's were, however, also built with V-windshields.)"

The Cadillac Motor Car Division Parts List shows the following to be the Madam X styles:

1930-1931 Model 452 & 452A V-16

4130	Five-Passenger Imperial
4130 S	Five-Passenger Sedan
4155	Five-Passenger Cabriolet
4155 C	Five-Passenger Imperial Cabriolet
4155 S	Five-Passenger Sedan Cabriolet
4161	Five-Passenger Close-Coupled Sedan
4161 C	Five-Passenger Close-Coupled Sedan
4161 S	Five-Passenger Town Sedan
4175	Seven-Passenger Imperial
4175 C	Seven-Passenger Imperial Sedan
4175 S	Seven-Passenger Sedan
4476	Two-Passenger Coupe (Madam X windshield)

1933 Model 370C V-12

5455	Five-Passenger Imperial Cabriolet

1933 Model 452C V-16

5555	Five-Passenger Imperial Cabriolet
5565	Seven-Passenger Imperial Sedan

It appears that unless the factory actually built (to order) one of the catalogued Madam X styles, it was not included in the parts list. Thus Madam X style catalogue drawings exist for which there are no equivalents in the Parts Book. It is unlikely that such cars were ever made. Madam X prices, according to the July 14, 1930 Parts List, ran about a thousand dollars above equivalent models in the regular line. However, the highest priced Madam X, Style 4175 at $7,525, was still lower than Town Cabriolets, Limousines, or Broughams which went to $9,700 or even more.

The jump from seven degrees to eighteen degrees on the windshield of sedan styles makes the Madam X stand out like a diamond under a spotlight, and resulted in more rake than the roadster windshield. Harley Earl was doing everything possible to break away from past convention. The front windshield post on the sedan styles, with dead vertical windshield and box-square roof line, found itself in for a real going-over. Was it possible to reproduce the graceful narrow side appearance of the open models? Without sacrificing structural strength? With the approval of cigar-smoking Fleetwood president Ernest

The LaSalle was bestowed with a wide-winged badge, left above at top of page, based naturally enough on the coat of arms of LaSalle, and different versions of this appeared with regular Cadillac crests in advertising of the late twenties, such as that shown at left immediately above. In 1930, Cadillac V-8's adopted a circular badge, right above: the usual crest with crown attached, on a black background. This was modified in late 1931 to the style shown at left below, with a smaller

black disc behind the crest, itself encircled with a white band. The V-8 emblem contrasted with that of the new V-12, which used an identical pattern and size crest but changed the black background to one of light blue, center below. These devices would persist through 1932, while the character of the engines behind would usually be symbolized by auxiliary badges mounted on a bar between the headlamps, or on triangular badges bolted directly to the radiator grille itself. The Cadillac V-16, during 1930 and for much of 1931, used a radiator badge of the same size and shape as that of the V-8 and V-12 models, but in this case the shield radiated numerous beams to the full 360 degrees of the circle, across a disc that was colored red, right below. This did not, however, last, and a new V-16 badge came in 1931.

The new radiator badge for the V-16, which succeeded the first version in late 1931, retained the red background with 360 degree rays, but made it smaller to allow a black circle separated by gold, as shown at left above. Many Cadillac dealers found that customers often preferred special badges, and sometimes they could even get away with emblems listing the location of large agencies, such as shown at center above. This unique device was done in a myriad of colors in jeweler's cloissoné, and does revert in many ways to the original trademark, with its floweret wreath (dropped after 1924 on standard badges), seven-point crown, and long-necked merlettes or swans. At right above is another dealer-installed design, this using the image of Cadillac for its pattern. Both of these special emblems are from the Swigart Museum, Huntingdon, Pennsylvania.

For the 1932 model year, the same devices adopted in 1931 for the V-8, V-12, and V-16 were given wings, as at top left below, for a newly designed radiator. The wings were fairly short and mildly curved, but the pattern lasted only for the one year. In 1933, as shown at bottom left below, to better match the more streamlined styling of the new Cadillacs, the wings were wider and thinner and the circular backing disc was gone. This new design remained unchanged on all radiators through the 1935 models, though in 1934 the crest became detachable. In 1936 the radiator grilles of the V-8 models bore the shield shown at right below, using a black background with a red stripe running down from right top to bottom, which interchanged with a "V8" pattern. The unique international symbol at center below is from a 1933 ad.

The standard emblem for 1938 used very squared-off, stubby wings while retaining the detachable Cadillac crest, angled in the center to fit the shape of the radiators, as shown above. On the Cadillac 60 Special, which was supposed to present a new trend in design, stylists decided to apply the more streamlined emblem immediately below, with wider, thinner

wings stretching out to the left and right fully half again as far as the standard badge. The central crests, during this period, were always done in jeweler's cloissoné, in an extensive, many-stepped process as painstaking as might be expected from a builder of super-luxury cars. When the 1939 models appeared, with their more barrel-shaped grilles, they were found to display yet another variation of the winged design to fit the contour, as illustrated below.

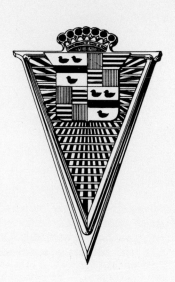

The 1939 Cadillacs used a very intricate design for the trunk lid, above, composed of a crown with seven points and prominent pearls at the top of a deep "V" emblem with many rays originating at the crest and pointing out in about 240 degrees, crossing horizontal bars in the lower portion. The 1939 LaSalle, as shown below, used the same idea but employed more geometric designs, with the usual LaSalle crest mounted at the top.

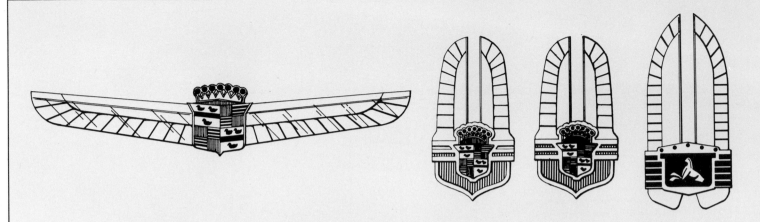

For 1940 the Cadillac radiator badge grew feathers in addition to the horizontally marked wing lines, as shown immediately above. The crest itself remained in the familiar pattern, and was made of cloissoné as in the past. For the 1941 models, the designs at right above were used. The first of these is from the 1941 Cadillac, and the second from a 1942 model. It is questionable whether there was any difference, though some 1942 badges have been found to have used painted horizontal bars flanking the crest as shown. The third badge in this row, based on the Cadillac design, is the proposed emblem for the ill-fated 1941 LaSalle, which reached prototype form but was never built. Perhaps more than any previous set of badges, these demonstrate the growing identity of LaSalle with Cadillac, hence the decreased importance of the former in the marketplace.

At left below is an interesting abstract of the Cadillac and LaSalle interlocking badges, from an advertisement of the 1940-1941 period. While never utilized on an automobile, it is shown here as an example of the flexibility of the two badges and one of the ways the artists took advantage of this fact. No matter what the style of the designs, they remained representative of all that the marque had stood for, by then for four decades. Of course a great many firms tried to capitalize on the "Cadillac image" in their advertising, as witness the two designs at center and right below. Neither of these are, of course, Cadillac in origin, and both replace the swans or ducks with other devices and shift the quarters of the arms; one even dropped the crown points to five. But the intent is unmistakable.

With the postwar cars came new emblem designs which evolved in a few years to the basic "V" and crest design we know so well.
At left above is the first postwar badge, marking the appearance of the "V" device for the first time with the crest (it had been used in the past in "V8" emblems). In 1947, as shown at center above, the space between crest and "V" was filled by a horizontally banded design, a remnant of the prewar style artwork. The wings returned, briefly, on the trunk lids of the 1947 models, as at right above, but this lasted only for one year and was superseded by the gold "V" and crest in 1948, left below, beginning the long continuance of this basic shape through the recent models.

It is rather surprising that an automobile manufacturer with such a long history of V-8 power took as long as Cadillac did to adopt a "V" device in its symbols, but except for an occasional "V8" emblem in the early years, this was the case for Cadillac. The 1949 design at left below lasted unchanged until the 1952 models appeared, when the "V" was slightly lowered and the angle it formed grew, as at center below. The crest was also made a bit shorter and wider in proportion. Then, for 1953-1954, it began drifting back to the earlier shape again, as shown in the device at right below. Still, in view of the many shifts in its badges before the war, Cadillac was being relatively consistent.

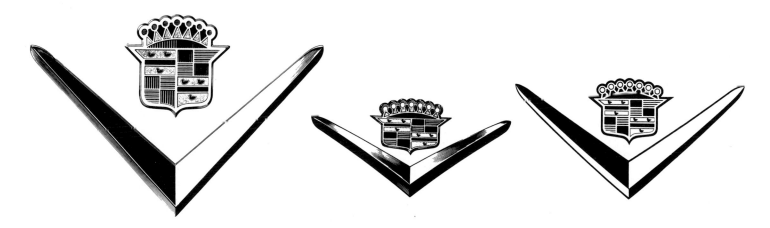

Here is the Cadillac badge for 1955, in nearly all ways
unaltered from 1954. Gold was now used in
many ways to decorate the cars, and this would
increase for a few years when tinsel was regaled in Detroit.

With the 1956 models the Cadillac badge began a second
trend to the long, low, and wide shape,
probably to emphasize the pattern of advertising
in this period, which lauded these attributes extensively.

The Cadillac crest for 1957. The widening and lowering
continues, but has not yet reached its
peak, though the swans are hardly more than
blurs by this time and the crown has become still flatter.

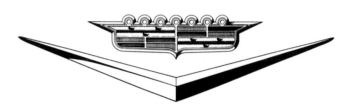

In 1958 the angle formed by the "V" was not increased
over that of 1957, and the Cadillac arms
remained of approximately the same dimensions.
The crown, on the other hand, had become perfectly level now.

Still the trend continued in 1959, though silver
(chrome) had replaced gold by now. The "V" angle
was retained, but the arms again were stretched
out and this time the crown at the top almost vanished.

For the 1960 model year the widening reached its final
limits at last. The "V" angle was at its
maximum and the height of the arms the minimum.
The arms were Vee'd as well, to match the "V" underneath.

The vaunted long, low, wide period, for both advertising and
Cadillac heraldry, came generally to an end in the
sixties, and though the coat of arms hardly increased in
height, the "V" angle returned to approximate
that of the 1958 and 1959 model years. The arms were
again flat, and though they were angled in future years to
meet hood contour, they were not Vee'd again as in 1959 models.

Here is the Cadillac emblem for the 1963-1966 period, one which is
probably most familiar to the typical motorist. The "V"
has regained an angle midway between the postwar extremes, and
the crest is again easily distinguishable. Below is
the famous wreathed emblem which graced Eldorados from 1963 on.

The 1970-1971 Cadillac badges were carried without
the traditional "V"—the Division
temporarily deciding that it was no longer
necessary to emphasize the obvious.
Below is the 1971 model's fender medallion, a
definite throwback to that of 1941-1942.

The first hood ornaments, it is virtually certain, originated with stylish adaptations of the moto-meter, first introduced by Boyce in 1912. This fascinating little device for keeping the driver constantly informed about the temperature of his coolant—which was admittedly likely to boil at any time in the pioneering days of the motorcar—became a universal accessory in just five years; by 1917, there were eighteen million moto-meters in use on vehicles in the United States. Cadillac, of course, had its famous script and heraldry applied to the moto-meter almost from the first, and like many another automobile, its radiator regalia developed from increasingly elaborate applications of the accessory until the meter disappeared with the coming of dashboard-mounted temperature gauges. From this point Cadillac (and LaSalle) vacillated somewhat in settling on a tradition for its hood ornamentry. Figures of Le Sieur Antoine, of course, were among the first considered, but somehow they never seemed to gain popularity. There were literally hundreds of others, few of them Cadillac in origin, supplied for the cars, ranging from brazen warriors out of mythology to curious lump-like mud puppies, but Cadillac itself refrained from prescribing an "approved" design until 1930. Then they settled on a heron, and a goddess. The former was a graceful, elegant mascot, but probably resembled the stork of Hispano-Suiza too closely to satisfy the sales department, and gradually the goddess became the sole Cadillac device. Once established, it was never replaced.

The Cadillac goddess did not, however, remain in the same exact shape year after year, as did that of Rolls-Royce, and this is probably the reason that the English car's legendary lady is rather better known in and out of automotive circles. Even Packard's cormorant or pelican, though experiencing almost as many changes, is better remembered, perhaps because you can only do so much to alter a pelican. Herewith a portfolio tracing the history of Cadillac's and LaSalle's mascotry from the moto-meter to the shaved hood of the present. Hopefully the now-retired goddess and her courtiers would approve of the tribute.

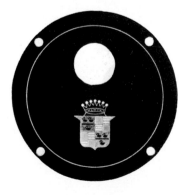

Moto-meters supplied the raw material for
the first "hood ornaments." At left,
examples from 1913, above, and 1920, below.
A very lovely late edition from
1927, complete with a wreathed coat of arms
which unknowingly predicted the
emblem of the Eldorado. At right, a LaSalle
accessory house ornament, 1928.

At left above is one of the first known Cadillac mascots, Canadian, circa 1929: a herald dressed in Cadillac livery, presumably trumpeting the praises of the marque. At center above is another 1929 ornament, from a LaSalle. Both these were accessory house products. At right above is the Cadillac heron, which with the first goddess, at left below, was available interchangeably on both makes through 1933. It was dropped in 1934 in favor of the goddess only on V-8's and V-12's, while the V-16's used the restyled goddess ornament shown at right below, less flowing and with more pronounced wings. LaSalle changed to a stylized device.

 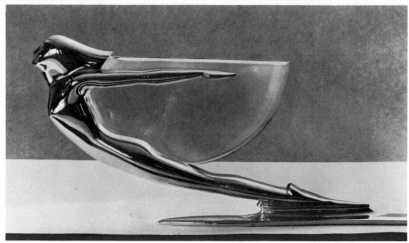

The new LaSalle ornament for 1934, at left above, was similar in shape to the corresponding Cadillac goddess, but completely abstract in design. It was continued for several years without change, and LaSalle never did go back to animate hood mascots. The goddess of the senior line, however, became more streamlined and received transparent wings for 1936, right above, and 1937, left below. The 1937 photograph also shows the placement of the grille badge described and illustrated earlier. Corresponding with the decreased height and more flowing contours of the 1938 LaSalle, its mascot, right below, was also streamlined.

Cadillac ornaments also followed the general streamlining of the cars themselves. By 1940, the V-8 goddess had evolved to the form at left above—very long and low, still retaining the transparent wings, though 1940 was the last year for these. The V-16 model always used the more upright, chunkier goddess, which was mildly redesigned from its earlier form on the preceding page to the shape at right above, for 1938 through 1940, its last year. The final years for the LaSalle witnessed a larger, rather clumsy looking "bomb" or "rocket" hood ornament, left below, although a more graceful variation was planned for the 1941's. Cadillac's new all-metal 1941 goddess is at right below.

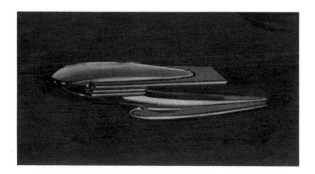

The prototype 1941 LaSalle carried a low and streamlined ornament, left above, along the lines of the 1938 model. The stretched and lengthened 1942 Cadillac ornament, right above, actually served a functional purpose, along with the 1941 version: they were the handles for the hood latching mechanism. Note the break about two-thirds back. After the war, Cadillac switched to the highly stylized sculpture below, which continued through 1956, giving way to twin fins on the Eldorado of that year and a shaved hood the following year. Still the Division continued to offer bolt-on copies of the first goddess (page 367), and later made available the spring-loaded Eldorado crest-and-wreath (page 365) as an accessory hood ornament on all Cadillac models.

THE MEN OF CADILLAC

Presidents and General Managers

Henry M. Leland	December 27, 1904—June 1, 1917
Richard H. Collins	June 26, 1917—May 12, 1921
Herbert H. Rice	May 13, 1921—April 30, 1925
Lawrence P. Fisher	May 1, 1925—May 31, 1934
Nicholas Dreystadt	June 1, 1934—June 1, 1946
John F. Gordon	June 5, 1946—July 10, 1950
Don E. Ahrens	July 10, 1950—December 31, 1956
James M. Roche	January 1, 1957—May 31, 1960
Harold G. Warner	June 1, 1960—March 31, 1966
Kenneth N. Scott	April 1, 1966—September 1, 1966
Calvin J. Werner	September 1, 1966—June 30, 1969
George R. Elges	July 1, 1969—December 31, 1972
Robert D. Lund	January 1, 1973—November 4, 1974
Edward C. Kennard	November 4, 1974—Present

Note: From Henry M. Leland to Lawrence P. Fisher, the heads of Cadillac were called "president and general manager." From Nicholas Dreystadt to date the title has been simply "general manager."

Chief Engineers

Frank Johnson	1902-1914
D. McCall White	1914—May 19, 1917
Benjamin H. Anibal	May, 1917—June, 1921
Ernest W. Seaholm	April 16, 1923—May 31, 1943
John F. Gordon	June 1, 1943—June 5, 1946
Edward N. Cole	June 5, 1946—August 31, 1950

Charles F. Arnold	September 1, 1950—February 28, 1965
Carl A. Rasmussen	March 1, 1965—December 31, 1972
Robert J. Templin	January 1, 1973—Present

Note: Ernest E. Sweet was de facto director of engineering from the founding of Cadillac through 1917, the top engineer after H. M. Leland himself. Frank Johnson's title was "chief design engineer." The appointment date for Ernest W. Seaholm is the official one, though the press reported his appointment as "chief engineer" in July, 1921. This was a time of some confusion at Cadillac, and it is possible that Seaholm was considered "on trial" for his first years, per his descriptions to the author.

Chief Designers (Cadillac Studio)

William Mitchell	Fall, 1936—October 16, 1949
Joseph Schemansky	May 1, 1949—June 1, 1951
Edward Glowacke	June 1, 1951—August 1, 1957
Charles Jordan	October 1, 1957—August 1, 1962
Stanley Parker	August 1, 1962—April 1, 1968
Stanley Wilen	April 1, 1968—September 1, 1974
Wayne Kady	September 1, 1974—Present

Note: Previous to the development of the 1938 automobiles, the Styling Section under Harley Earl was not organized in studio groups. And, between 1942 and December 21, 1945, William Mitchell was in the U.S. Navy; during this time the Styling Section was closed except for a very small group working on U.S. Army Camouflage and War Services.

General Sales Managers

Earl C. Howard	May 1912—1919
Lynn McNaughton	1919—December, 1925
H. M. Stephens	December, 1925—September, 1930
J. C. Chick	September, 1930—November 30, 1935
Don E. Ahrens	December 1, 1935—June 9, 1950
James M. Roche	July 10, 1950—December 31, 1956
Fred H. Murray	January 1, 1957—August 31, 1962
L. N. Mays	September 1, 1962—December 31, 1966
F. T. Hopkins	January 1, 1967—February 28, 1978
L. B. Pryor	March 1, 1978—Present

Note: No records exist at Cadillac Motor Division for this position prior to 1930. The earliest Cadillac sales manager was probably William E. Metzger, 1902-1908 approximately, who left to found E.M.F. From 1908 to Howard's taking of the position remains a mystery, although it is known that Howard joined Cadillac in 1906 and became assistant sales manager in 1909.

SPECIFICATIONS OF CADILLAC MOTORCARS: 1902–1979

Cadillac engineering history can be divided into three major eras: Leland, Seaholm, and modern. Consistency in general design and high standards of workmanship and reliability have characterized Cadillac from the start. In the early days — the single- and four-cylinder periods — these qualities were the exception rather than the general rule in the industry.

In the entire Leland era there were only three basic designs — singles, fours, and eights. These ran for six, ten, and fourteen years respectively. Although Leland left in 1917, his influence lingered for years afterwards. McCall White, Anibal and Seaholm, who followed as chief engineers, were from the Leland design group, as was Frank Johnson, who was chief designer from 1922 to 1926. But the 314 of 1925, with its many changes, shows that Seaholm was beginning to take off on his own. It was an "interim" design, but the changeover was complete by 1927 when the new 341 series and the LaSalle appeared. By now Owen Nacker, a non-Leland man, was chief designer, and the Seaholm era had begun.

The Cadillac engineering reputation made it a mecca for talent, attracting numbers of the finest automobile engineers in the world: Kettering; White of Napier; Strickland of Peerless; Nacker; Maurice Olley of Rolls-Royce; Davis of Pierce-Arrow. This has continued in the "modern era" of 1949 onward — a period dominated by men trained under Seaholm, such as Gordon, Cole, Barr, Arnold, and Rasmussen.

Cadillac's design can likewise be divided into eras, but in this case only two: Leland and Earl/Mitchell. Leland's, based on the strict dominance of Engineering, persisted until the coming of Harley Earl and his 1927 LaSalle, followed by his first Cadillacs in 1928. The rapid change in styling which occurred under Earl brought that phase of manufacturing abreast of engineering, and

created for Cadillac many flamboyant and advanced, yet tasteful and distinctive designs. The late fifties advent at GM Styling of Earl protégé William Mitchell in no way interrupted Cadillac's persistent seeking out of unique approaches to design; indeed Mitchell contributed to Cadillac for twenty years, beginning with his magnificent 60 Special of 1938. However, his personality was clearly expressed in Cadillacs that followed his promotion.

Performance of Cadillac models has usually been adequate to outstanding. The single-cylinders had excellent performance for their type. The four-cylinders were sufficient but not remarkable. The first V-8's performance was so good that little improvement was required for most of its life span. Despite the substantial increase in displacement, the 341-353 series engines were, like the fours, adequate rather than outstanding.

The V-12 and V-16, on introduction, were adequate and outstanding respectively. They were, however, overtaken by later developments. The first LaSalle V-8's performed on an acceptable level; the straight-eights were average. The new Cadillac V-8 for 1936 was exceptional, as was the 1949 ohv engine.

A handy, if rough, yardstick to Cadillac model speeds is the ratio sequence 1,2,3,4,5. If the single's top speed is conservatively taken as on the order of 25 mph and used as the "unit," we get 50 mph for the fours, 75 mph for the V-8's up to the early thirties, 100 mph for the V-16's and the V-8's which replaced them, and 125 mph for the recent Cadillac models. These are, of course, approximate orders only, too low in some cases, too high in others, but they are a useful and easily remembered guide.

These characteristics are represented in the following tables, which set forth the specifications of every complete Cadillac car ever built. (Commercial chassis were also manufactured; for number produced, see production tables, Appendix VI.)

MODEL A
INTRODUCED LATE 1902 • CURRENT 1903-04
ENGINE SERIAL NOS. — 1903, 1-2500
1904, 2500-5000 (INCLUDES MODEL B)

ENGINE. Single cylinder (5x5, 98.2 cubic inches). *Horsepower*: rated at 10, brake hp 9.7 to 10.25 at 900 rpm; maximum engine speed 1200 rpm. Valves opposed across the cylinder bore in ante-chamber in cylinder head. Both valves mechanically operated by slide rod (inlet valve) and pushrod (exhaust valve), with rockers. Variable lift inlet valve for controlling engine speed. Valves, double spark plug and ignition chamber in detachable cast iron housing screwed into cylinder head. Gasketless construction. Cast iron cylinder bolted to separate split cast iron crankcase. Engine horizontal in frame under seat, cylinder to the rear. *Ignition*: high tension coil and spark plug, current by dry cell. *Carburetor*: updraft mixer with feed valve and gauze vaporizer. *Lubrication*: mechanical lubricator; cam and rod operated from flywheel shaft; four sight feeds, one each to piston, con rod, crankshaft and main bearings. *Cooling*: separate water tank; tubular copper radiator with copper radiating discs; centrifugal water pump.

TRANSMISSION. Planetary, two-speed forward and reverse. Steel pinions and bronze ring gear. Two brake bands, one for low, one for reverse. Transmission in unit with engine. Drive by sprocket and chain to differential and live rear axle. Brown Lipe differential.

CHASSIS. *Frame*: angle steel, straight rails. *Axles*: front, tubular with longitudinal semi-elliptic springs; rack and pinion steering; drag link and tie rod. Rear, live axle; longitudinal semi-elliptic springs. Two adjustable stay rods between axle and frame take driving thrust and locate rear axle. *Brakes*: rear axle, band type; inboard brake drums; foot pedal, with hand lever for parking. *Wheels*: hickory spoke, mounted on ball bearings. *Tires*: 30x3½ clincher. *Wheelbase*: 70 inches. *Tread*: 53 inches. *Weight*: 1350 pounds.

BODIES. Two- or four-seater available. Car quickly convertible by owner to two- or four-seater by removal or addition of the detachable tonneau.

PRICE. Two-seater $750.

PERFORMANCE. Maximum speed 30-35 mph. Note: cases are on record of cars reaching 40 mph, and engines 1600 rpm. Gradient on high, 8½ percent; on low, any hill on which the wheels would grip. Gas mileage 25-30 mpg.

MODELS B, C, E, F, K, M, S and T
CURRENT 1904 (B ONLY); 1905 (B, C, E AND F)
1906-07 (K); 1908 (S AND T); (1906-09 (M)
ENGINE SERIAL NOS. — 1905: MODELS B AND C, 5000-8350
MODEL F, 13,728-14,206; MODEL E, 13,401-13,706.
1906: MODEL K, 8351-10,000
1907: MODEL M, 20,001-22,150
MODELS K AND M, 22,151-24,350
1908: MODELS M, S AND T, 24,351-26,382

ENGINE. (Including auxiliaries), same as for Model A.
TRANSMISSION. Same as for Model A.
CHASSIS. *Frame*: pressed steel, channel section. *Axles*: front, redesigned, arch-tubular with truss, single, transverse semi-elliptic spring shackled and pinned to frame; central rocker joint for axle; axle located by two tubular links, ball jointed. Note: at least some Model B cars had a special tapered I-beam axle with a window in central (deepest) section. *Wheels*: hickory spoke, ball bearing front, Hyatt roller rear. *Tires*: 28x3 on runabouts, 30x3½ on touring cars and commercial vehicles. *Wheelbase*: runabout, 74 inches; touring, 76 inches; commercial, 76 inches. Note: wheelbase increased to 82 inches on all models for 1908. *Tread*: all models, 56 inches; optional, 61 inches. *Weight*: runabout, 1100 pounds; touring car, 1350 pounds.

BODIES. Pressed steel dash and dummy hood, with door and storage compartment. Light runabout two-seater with or without leather or rubber top, light touring car (four-seater) with or without cape cart top, delivery van bodies available.

PRICES. Model K light runabout $750; with rubber top, sides and apron $780; with leather top, sides and apron $800. Model M touring car $950; with cape cart top $1025.

PERFORMANCE (AND GEAR RATIOS). Model K light runabout: 10-34 (3.4 to 1) fast, for smooth level roads; 10-38 (3.8 to 1) medium, for average roads and hills; 10-41 (4.1 to 1) slow, for steep hills. Speed range 30-40 mph according to gear ratio. Model M touring car: 10-38 (3.8 to 1) fast; 10-41 (4.1 to 1) medium; 10-45 (4.5 to 1) slow. Speed range 25-30 mph.

MODEL D
CURRENT 1905
ENGINE SERIAL NOS. 10,001-10,156

ENGINE. Four-cylinder L-head (4x5, 300.7 cubic inches). *Horsepower*: rated at 30.6, brake hp 30 at 1000 rpm. Cylinder construction similar to single cylinder. Drop forged steel crankshaft, machined all over; five white metal main bearings, bronze backed. Gear-driven camshaft, roller tappets. *Ignition*: Lacoste-type commutator, high tension coil and spark plugs, dry cell batteries. *Carburetor*: float feed, single jet, butterfly-throttle type with auxiliary air valve. Centrifugal ring governor acting on throttle with auxiliary air valve. *Lubrication*: feed pump operated by lever connected to one valve lifter: sight feed regulator on dash, tubular dippers on each big end; separate oil chambers for each crank. *Cooling*: fan and pump cooling, water pump gear driven at front of engine. Honeycomb radiator.

TRANSMISSION. Multi-disc plate clutch in flywheel; three-speed planetary transmission, lever controlled. Internal ratios: 3, 1.66 and 1 to 1. Neutral between reverse and low gear. Engine and transmission mounted on two large-diameter longitudinal steel tubes, carried by stamped steel brackets on frame side members and front cross member. Open shaft driven to rear axle.

CHASSIS. *Axles*: front, tubular, semi-elliptic springs, worm and nut steering gear. Rear, aluminum differential housing, steel tubes, tubular torque arm. *Brakes*: footbrake on transmission, handbrake on rear wheels, band type. *Wheels*: artillery type, selected second growth hickory; Hess-Bright wheel bearings. *Tires*: 34x4½. *Wheelbase*: 100 inches. *Tread*: 56½ inches. *Weight*: 2600 pounds.

BODIES. Five-passenger touring, wood construction standard; aluminum paneled $250 extra. Standard finish Brewster green with primrose running gear.

PRICE. $2800, top extra.

PERFORMANCE. Maximum speed 50 mph.

MODEL H
Current 1906-08
Engine Serial Nos. — 1906-07, 10,201-10,709
For 1908 serial numbers in same bracket as Model G

Similar to the Model D, with the following exceptions:

CHASSIS. *Tires*: 32x4. *Wheelbase*: 1907, 100 inches; 1908, 102 inches. *Tread*: 61 inches, optional. *Weight*: runabout, 2400 pounds; touring car and coupé, 2500 pounds.

BODIES AND PRICES. Two-passenger runabout $2400, $2450 with top; two-passenger coupé $3000; five-passenger touring $2500, $2625 with top. Standard finish Purple lake, dark carmine running gear.

MODEL L
Current 1906
Engine Serial Nos. — Bracketed with 1906 Model H
(10,201-10,709)

General design similar to other four-cylinder models, except:

ENGINE. Four cylinder L-head (5x5, 392.7 cubic inches). *Horsepower*: rated at and developed 40.

CHASSIS. Rear suspension two semi-elliptic and one transverse springs, Dennet or platform type. *Tires*: 36x4 front, 36x4½ rear. *Wheelbase*: 110 inches. *Weight*: touring car, 2850 pounds; limousine, 3600 pounds.

BODIES AND PRICES. All wood bodies. All prices without lamps. Five/seven-passenger touring car $3750, $3900 with top; seven-passenger limousine $5000. Limousine upholstered in morocco leather with satin headlining; plus interior electric light, signal bell and speaking tube.

MODEL G
Current 1907-08
Engine Serial Nos. 30,003-30,500

General design similar to other four-cylinder models, except:

ENGINE. Four-cylinder L-head (4x4½, 226 cubic inches). *Horsepower*: rated at 25.6, brake hp 26-27. *Cooling*: fin and tube radiator.

TRANSMISSION. Three-speed selective sliding gear. Aluminum transmission case.

CHASSIS. Full elliptic rear suspension; worm and sector steering. *Tires*: 32x3½. *Wheelbase*: 100 inches. *Tread*: 56 inches.

BODIES AND PRICES. Five-passenger touring car $2000, $2120 with top; two-passenger runabout $2000; limousine $3600. Lamps extra.

MODEL THIRTY
Introduced December 1908 • Current 1909
Engine Serial Nos. 32,002-37,904

ENGINE. Four-cylinder (4x4½, 226 cubic inches). *Horsepower*: rated at 25.6, developed on dynamometer test 30. Cylinders cast singly. Five bearing crankshaft. Similar to 1908 Model G. *Ignition*: induction coil and jump spark current with storage battery and dry cells. Magneto optional equipment, extra charge. *Carburetor*: float feed type, own make. *Lubrication*: automatic splash system; oil uniformly distributed; supply maintained by mechanical force feed lubricator with positive sight feed

on dash. *Cooling*: copper jacketed cylinders, gear driven water pump; fin and tube radiator; fan attached to motor, running on two point ball bearings; center distances of fan pulleys adjustable to take up stretch in belt.

TRANSMISSION. Sliding gear selective type, three speeds forward and reverse. Chrome nickel steel gears and shafts (on touring car and demi-tonneau 3½ to 1; on roadster 3 to 1; options 3, 3½ or 4 to 1); five annular ball bearings. Cone-type clutch, leather faced with special spring ring in flywheel. Drive by direct shaft in housing to bevel gears; universal joint enclosed in housing and running in oil bath.

CHASSIS. *Frame*: dropped, pressed steel, channel section. Width, 30 inches in front; 33 inches in rear. *Axles*: rear, special alloy steel live axle shafts running on special roller and ball bearings. Front, tubular with drop forged yokes, spring perches, tie rod ends and steering spindles, the latter having ball thrust bearings. Front wheels fitted with two-point ball bearings. *Suspension*: front, semi-elliptical springs 36 inches long by 2 inches wide. Rear, three-quarter platform; sides, 42 inches long by 2 inches wide; rear 38 inches long by 2 inches wide. *Steering*: own worm and sector type, adjustable, with ball thrust bearings. Spark and throttle levers at steering wheel. Steering wheel 16 inches in diameter. *Brakes*: service brake (external) operated by foot lever; emergency brake (internal) operated by hand lever. *Wheels*: artillery type, well seasoned second growth hickory with steel hubs, fitted with quick detachable rims; special large hub flanges and special strength wide spokes. *Tires*: 32x3½, optional 33x4 at extra cost. *Wheelbase*: 106 inches. *Tread*: 56 inches; optional 61 inches. *Weight*: touring car, 2520 pounds.

BODIES. All exclusive Cadillac patterns. Body frames ash; doors of touring car and demi-tonneau aluminized sheet steel. Wide-door touring model with seating for five passengers; demi-tonneau with seating capacity for two in the tonneau. Tonneau detachable so that plain deck or rumble seat could be substituted. Rumble seat on roadster detachable. Fenders special Cadillac pattern, made in Cadillac sheet metal department; finished in several coats of black enamel, each coat baked on at high temperature and rubbed down before succeeding coat applied. Upholstery black leather over genuine curled hair and deep coil steel springs. All finishing done in Cadillac shops; standard finish on all styles Royal Blue, including body, hood, frame, axles and wheels — with light blue striping. Fenders and radiator baked black enamel. Dash highly finished mahogany with brass edge. Door trimming strip and hood sills mahogany finish. Standard equipment: one pair side oil lamps and taillamp; one horn and set of tools, including pump and repair kit for tires.

PRICES. Touring car, demi-tonneau, roadster: $1400.

PERFORMANCE. On high gear, 5 to 50 mph. Gas mileage approximately 13 mpg.

MODEL THIRTY
Current 1910
Engine Serial Nos. 40,001-48,008

Similar to the 1909 model, with the following exceptions:

ENGINE. Four-cylinder (4¼x4½, 255.3 cubic inches). *Horsepower*: rated at 28.9, brake hp 33. *Ignition*: jump spark; two complete and independent systems, two plugs per cylinder. Low tension magneto. Delco four-unit coil with controlling relay. Dry cell current.

CHASSIS. *Tires*: 34x4. *Wheelbase*: 110 inches.

BODIES. Touring car, demi-tonneau, gentleman's roadster (rumble seat), limousine. Standard equipment: one pair gas lamps and generator; one pair side oil lamps and taillamp; one horn; set of tools, pump and tire repair kit; robe rail and tire holders.

PRICES. Limousine $3000; all other body styles $1600.

MODEL "THIRTY"
CURRENT 1911
ENGINE SERIAL NOS. 50,000-60,018

Same as 1910 model, with the following exceptions:

ENGINE. Four-cylinder (4½x4½, 286.3 cubic inches). *Horsepower*: rated at 32.4, brake hp 40.

CHASSIS. Wheelbase: 116 inches.

PRICE. Base price $1700.

MODEL "THIRTY"
CURRENT 1912
ENGINE SERIAL NOS. 61,006-75,000

"Thirty" designation dropped and following changes occurred:

ENGINE. Addition of Delco system of starting, ignition and lighting.

CHASSIS. *Tires*: 36x4.

BODIES AND PRICES. Five-passenger touring car $1800, $1890 with mohair cape top; four-passenger phaeton $1800, $1865 with mohair cape top; four-passenger torpedo $1900, $1950 with mohair cape top; two-passenger roadster $1800, $1860 with mohair cape top; four-passenger coupé $2250; seven-passenger limousine $3250.

MODEL "THIRTY"
CURRENT 1913
ENGINE SERIAL NOS. 75,001-90,018

ENGINE. Four-cylinder (4½x5¾, 365.8 cubic inches). *Horsepower*: 48.7. Valves enclosed. Camshaft and generator shaft driven by silent chains from crankshaft. Five-bearing crankshaft, two inches in diameter. Bearings bronze with Babbitt lining. *Ignition*: two complete and independent systems. Delco Dynamo ignition, electric cranking device and electric lights. Automatic spark control. Reverse distributor system with dry cell current. *Carburetor*: Cadillac water-jacketed single adjustment, auxiliary air adjustment on steering column. *Lubrication*: automatic splash system, oil uniformly distributed. Supply maintained by mechanical pump force-feed lubricator with single sight feed on dash. *Cooling*: copper jacketed cylinders, copper inlet and outlet water manifolds; cooling pump; radiator, tubular and plate type. Fan attached to motor on two point ball bearings; center distance of fan pulleys adjustable.

TRANSMISSION. Sliding gear, selective type, three speeds forward and reverse. Chrome nickel steel gears (on roadster 3.05 to 1, optional 3.43 to 1; on limousine 3.66 to 1, optional 3.92 to 1; on other models 3.49 to 1, optional 4 and 3.92 to 1.) Chrome nickel steel transmission shaft and clutch shaft running on five annular ball bearings. Cone-type clutch; large, leather-faced with special spring ring in flywheel. Drive by direct shaft to bevel gears, special cut teeth. Drive shaft on Timken bearings. Two universal joints, the forward telescopic, each enclosed in

housing running in oil bath.

CHASSIS. *Frame*: double dropped (2½-inch drop) pressed steel, channel section. *Axles*: rear, Timken full floating type; special alloy steel live axle shaft; Timken roller bearings, double torsion tubes arranged in triangular form. Front axle forged I-beam section with drop forged yokes, spring perches, tie rod ends and steering arms. Upper ends of spindles fitted with Timken bearings. *Suspension*: front, semi-elliptic springs 36 inches long by 2 inches wide; rear, three-quarter platform; rear cross 59½ inches long by 2 inches wide. *Steering*: own patented worm and worm gear sector type, adjustable, with ball bearings, 1¾-inch steering post, 18-inch steering wheel with corrugated walnut rim, aluminum spider. *Brakes*: one internal and one external brake direct on wheels, 17x2½ drums; both equipped with equalizers. *Wheels*: wood artillery type, fitted with demountable rims, special large hub flanges, heavy spokes. Rear wheel spokes bolted to brake drums. *Tires*: 36x4½. *Wheelbase*: 120 inches. *Tread*: 56 inches, optional 61 inches.

BODIES. Limousine and coupé aluminum; all other models steel. All bodies with fore doors. Upholstery hand buffed black leather over genuine curled hair and deep coil steel springs. Running boards linoleum covered, with metal binding. Finish, Cadillac blue body and chassis, striped; torpedo option, steel gray with black mohair hood and fenders. Standard color for limousine and coupé blue lower panels and doors, with black upper panels and moldings, chassis and wheels Cadillac blue. All trimmings nickel plated. Standard equipment: Cadillac mohair top; windshield; Gray & Davis lamps (especially designed for Cadillac); black enamel and nickel trimmings; two headlights with adjustable globes to regulate light rays; two side and taillights; Hans gasoline gauge on dash; horn; foot rail in tonneau of open cars; robe rail; set of tools including pump and tire repair kit; cocoa mat in all tonneau models; Warner speedometer with electric light. (No allowance was made for any part of standard equipment if requested omitted.)

PRICES. Five-passenger touring, four-passenger phaeton, two-passenger roadster $1975; seven-passenger touring $2075; three-passenger landaulet coupé $2500; five-passenger inside drive limousine $2800; seven-passenger standard limousine $3250.

MODEL "THIRTY"
CURRENT 1914
ENGINE SERIAL NOS. 91,005-99,999 AND A-1-A-5008

Same as 1913 model, with the following exceptions:

ENGINE. Pressure feed to carburetor by camshaft driven air pump. Electric heater-vaporizer on carburetor. *Ignition*: dual (one plug per cylinder) replacing the "double" (two plugs).

TRANSMISSION. Two-speed axle. Spiral bevel ring gear and pinion.

TYPE 51 V-8
INTRODUCED SEPTEMBER 1914 ● CURRENT 1915
ENGINE SERIAL NOS. A-6000 - A-19,001

ENGINE. Eight-cylinder 90° V-type (3⅛x5⅛, 314 cubic inches). *Horsepower*: rated at 31.25, brake hp 70 at 2400 rpm. *Torque*: 180 lb/ft at 1800-2200 rpm. *Compression ratio*: 4.25 to 1. Engine and transmission built in unit, three-point suspension. Cylinders cast in two blocks of four cylinders each, with internally machined combustion

chambers; integral heads, removable valve caps. Aluminum crankcase. Tungsten steel valves. Valve mechanism enclosed. Three-bearing crankshaft 1⅞ inches in diameter of chrome nickel alloy steel, heat treated. Main and connecting rod bearings of Cadillac special bearing metal, with bronze reinforcement. Single camshaft, five bearings. Camshaft and generator shaft driven by silent chains from crankshaft. *Ignition*: Cadillac Delco, improved system. Current supplied by generator and storage battery of Exide manufacture, designed especially for Cadillac. Automatic spark control. *Carburetor*: Cadillac-designed especially for this engine; auxiliary air control to facilitate starting; integral leaning device; intake pipe, hot water jacketed. *Lubrication*: automatic pressure feed by gear pump; oil forced to crankshaft and connecting rod bearings. *Cooling*: water, forced circulation. Jackets cast integral with cylinders. Two centrifugal pumps, one for each block of cylinders. Radiator Cadillac tubular and plate type. Fan attached to generator shaft, driven by silent chain. Water temperature regulated by Sylphon thermostats. Radiator condenser, conserving alcohol in anti-freezing solution.
TRANSMISSION. Multiple disc clutch, dry plate type; fifteen high carbon steel plates 7¾ inches in diameter, plates driven by flywheel faced with wire. Aluminum transmission case. Selective type sliding gear, three speeds forward and reverse. Chrome nickel steel gears and shafts. Spiral-type bevel driving gears, ratios 4.45 and 5.08. Drive by tubular shaft; two universal joints, with telescopic connection at forward joint, each joint enclosed in housing and running in lubricant.
CHASSIS. *Frame*: channel section, carbon steel, 6 inches deep in center portion; width 30 inches in front, 33 inches in rear; three cross members, one of them tubular. *Axles*: rear, full floating type; special alloy steel live axle shafts. Front, drop forged, special alloy steel, I-beam section with integral yokes and spring perches; drop forged tie rod ends and steering spindles, the latter fitted with special bearings at upper ends. *Suspension*: front, semi-elliptic springs 42 inches long by 2 inches wide; rear, three-quarter platform; sides 54 inches long by 2 inches wide; rear cross 39½ inches long by 2 inches wide. *Steering*: Cadillac patented worm and worm gear sector type, adjustable, with ball thrust bearings; 18-inch steering wheel with corrugated walnut rim, aluminum spider; steering wheel hinged to swing downward facilitating entrance to front seats. *Brakes*: one internal and one external brake direct on wheels, 17x2½ drums, both equipped with equalizers. *Wheels*: wood artillery type, running on taper roller bearings, fitted with demountable rims for straight side tires. Special large hub flanges and substantial spokes. *Tires*: 36x4½. *Wheelbase*: 122 inches. *Tread*: 56 inches.
BODIES. Open cars finished in Cadillac blue, black trimmings (cream wheels on two-passenger model); upholstery in English long grain hand buffed black leather, laid in plaits. Closed cars finished in Calumet green with black trimmings, upholstery in high quality selected cloth fabrics. Running boards linoleum covered, with metal binding.
PRICES. Body styles available and prices same as 1914.

TYPE 53 V-8
CURRENT 1916
ENGINE SERIAL NOS. A-20,000 - A-38,003
Same as the Type 51, with the following exceptions:

ENGINE. *Horsepower*: 77 bhp at 2600 rpm. Enlarged intake manifold. Distributor moved from rear to front of engine. Tire pump moved from motor to transmission.
TRANSMISSION. Sixteen-plate clutch. Higher numerical second gear.
BODIES. Hood and body line slightly higher. Tonneau light, Waltham clock and inspection lamp added.
PRICES. Two-passenger roadster, five-passenger salon, seven-passenger touring $2080; three-passenger victoria with leather top $2400; five-passenger brougham $2950; seven-passenger limousine $3450; seven-passenger berlin $3600.
PERFORMANCE. Maximum speed 55-65 mph, according to body and axle ratio.

TYPE 55
CURRENT 1917
ENGINE SERIAL NOS. 55-A1 - 55-S2
Same as for Type 53, with the following exceptions:
ENGINE. Redesigned pistons, lighter in weight.
CHASSIS. *Frame*: increased to 8 inches in depth, with three tubular cross members. *Wheelbase*: 125 and 132 inches.
BODIES. Crowned fenders, molding around top of body, new headlamps.
PRICES. On the 125-inch wheelbase: two/four-passenger roadster, four-passenger club roadster and phaeton, seven-passenger touring $2080; four-passenger victoria $2550; seven-passenger convertible $2675; four-passenger coupé $2800; five-passenger brougham $2950. On the 132-inch wheelbase: seven-passenger limousine $3600; seven-passenger landaulet and Imperial $3750.

TYPE 57
CURRENT 1918-19
ENGINE SERIAL NOS. 57A1 - 57 TT 146
Same as for Type 55, with the following exceptions:
ENGINE. Detachable cylinder heads.
TRANSMISSION. Seventeen-plate clutch, improved transmission.
CHASSIS. *Tires*: 35x5 on all models except two-passenger roadster which retained the 34x4½. Metric tire size (895 x 135 mm) available at extra cost. Kellogg tire pump.
BODIES. Radiator and hood higher and longer. New cowl. Tilt beam headlights, lever on steering column. Addition of two body styles: town car and town landaulet. Town car similar to limousine, but with roofless driving compartment and narrower body. Town landaulet similar, with landaulet rear.
PRICES. On the 125-inch wheelbase: two-passenger roadster, four-passenger phaeton and seven-passenger touring $2805; four-passenger convertible victoria $3205; five-passenger brougham $3650. On the 132-inch wheelbase: seven-passenger limousine $4145; seven-passenger town limousine $4160; seven-passenger landaulet $4295; seven-passenger town landaulet $4310; seven-passenger Imperial $4345.

TYPE 59
CURRENT 1920-21
ENGINE SERIAL NOS. 59-A-1 - 59-BB-12

Same as for Type 57, with the following exceptions:
ENGINE. *Horsepower*: 79 bhp.
BODIES AND PRICES. The price tag for a Cadillac exceeded the
$5000 mark for the first time in 1920, the line including the four-pas-
senger phaeton and two-passenger roadster at $3590; the seven-pas-
senger touring at $3740; the victoria at $4340; the sedan at $4750; the
suburban at $4990; the coupé, the limousine and town brougham at
$5090; the Imperial at $5190. For 1921 the prices remained the same,
but the coupé and town brougham were dropped from the line.

TYPE 61
INTRODUCED SEPTEMBER 1921 • CURRENT 1922-23
ENGINE SERIAL NOS. 61A - 61Z 18,006
Same as Type 59, with the following exceptions:
ENGINE. New carburetor with thermostatic control of auxiliary air
valve by bi-metallic strips. Thermostatically controlled throttle pump.
Two-inch carburetor intake. Camshaft drilled for lubrication in place of
separate piping. Eccentric adjustment for timing chain. Two pole
generator instead of four.
TRANSMISSION. Redesigned rear axle and torque tube. Axle ratios
4.15, 4.5 and 4.9.
CHASSIS. Hi-pressure grease cups for chassis lubrication. *Tires*: 33x5.
Wheelbase: 132 inches. *Tread*: 56 inches.
BODIES. Higher, fuller radiator and hood. Six vertical aluminum strips
at body rear on phaeton and five-passenger sedan. Bausch & Lomb
headlamp lenses. Addition of two body styles: two-passenger and four-
passenger coupé.
PRICES. Upon introduction in September 1921: touring $3940;
phaeton and roadster $3790; two-passenger coupé and victoria $4540;
five-passenger coupé $4690; sedan $4950; limousine $5290; Imperial
limousine $5390. After January 1, 1922: touring and phaeton $3150;
roadster $3100; two-passenger coupé and victoria $3875; five-passenger
coupé $3925; sedan $4100; limousine $4550; Imperial limousine $4600.

TYPE V-63
INTRODUCED SEPTEMBER 1923 • CURRENT 1924-25
ENGINE SERIAL NOS. 63A-1 - 63M-2572
1925 STARTS AT 63E-1
Redesigned from previous model as follows:
ENGINE. *Horsepower*: 83 bhp at 3000 rpm. Redesigned with inherently
balanced two-plane 90° crankshaft. Crankshaft dimensions, in inches, as
follows:

	V-63	61
Main bearing journals diameter	2 3/8	2
Length - front	2 7/8	3 1/4
center	2 3/8	2 1/2
rear	4 1/16	4 1/16
Crank journals diameter	2 3/8	1 7/8
length	2 7/8	2 3/4

Flywheel weight reduced on V-63 because of flywheel effect of heavier
shaft and counterweights. Firing order changed to: 1L, 4R, 4L, 2L, 3R,
3L, 2R, 1R. Redesigned cam drive with single sprockets, non-adjustable.
Sixteen cam lobes instead of eight. Redesigned rocker assembly.
CHASSIS. *Frame*: two additional frame cross members. *Axles*: new
front axle design; reverse Elliott; rear-mounted track rod with ball and
socket ends. *Brakes*: four-wheel brakes; Perrot system on front wheels.
Internal expanding bands with toggle operation. Separate sets of brakes
on rear drums for hand and foot operation. Brake linkage and design
arranged so that rear wheels lock first, with the outer front wheel in
turn free to rotate and maintain steering effect. Brakes equalized front
and rear. Hand brake linkage fully independent.
BODIES. Eleven body styles, all new, with increased room. Two-piece
V-V (ventilation and vision) windshield. Higher radiator with nickel
plating standard. Scrolled radiator on 1925 models (custom only until
January 1925). Longer hood, deeper fender crowns. Range of bodies extended to fourteen by June 1924; in October five more "custom-built"
closed models announced, as follows: two-passenger coupé (132-inch
wheelbase) $3975; and on a special 138-inch wheelbase, the following:
five-passenger coupé $4350; five-passenger sedan $4550; seven-
passenger suburban $4650; seven-passenger Imperial $4950. In January
1925 a Fisher-built coach (two-door, five-passenger closed car) was added, priced at $3185.
PRICES. Base price in 1924 was $2985; in 1925, $3195. Custom built
models as noted above.

SERIES 314
INTRODUCED JULY 1925 • CURRENT 1926-27
ENGINE SERIAL NOS. 100,001 - 130,000
ENGINE. Eight-cylinder 90° V-type (3⅛x5⅛, 314 cubic inches).
Horsepower: rated at 31.25, brake hp 85.5 at 3000 rpm. *Compression
ratio*: 4.7 to 1. Engine and transmission built in unit, three-point
suspension. Cylinders cast in two blocks of four, detachable heads.
Although using the same bore and stroke, this model — with a few ex-
ceptions — was an entirely fresh design. Cadilite alloy crankcase.
Crankshaft shortened slightly. Rod length reduced from 12½ to 11 inches (c-c) allowing a narrower engine. This, together with other
modifications, reduced engine weight by 130 pounds, to 714 pounds.
Direct acting roller tappets, no rockers. Valves angled to bore axis.
Silichrome valves, smaller exhaust. Six-bearing camshaft instead of five.
Spring-loaded idler sprocket for Morse timing chain. Pressed steel timing
cover instead of light alloy. One timing chain only. Generator and 21-inch
fan V-belt driven. No friction clutch. Distributor at rear skew driven off
camshaft. Two four-lobe cams and dual breaker arms. Electric gasoline
gauge (Nagel). *Ignition*: two-unit electrical system, 6 volt; generator
atop timing case; vertical starter mounted atop flywheel housing and
driven by crown wheel and pinion. *Carburetor*: lower in valve alley since
generator drive shaft omitted, with redesigned intake and exhaust manifolding giving smoother gas flow. Dual exhausting continued. *Lubrication*:
oil pump on other end for greater capacity; crankcase ventilation via
drilled pistons and cylinder walls (sealed breather and oil filler) and
vented valve chamber. Purolator filter, by-pass type from oil regulator.
Cooling: single water pump, skew gear and shaft, water pump capacity

exceeding previous two pumps combined. Single hose from radiator to pump. Divided delivery to cylinder blocks via copper pump cast in crankcase. One outlet per head to radiator. Thermostatically controlled radiator shutters. Entire engine designed for maximum accessibility. All accessory units of the car individually removable—camshaft and crankshaft removable as well—with engine in place in the automobile, for ease of service.

TRANSMISSION. Multiplate clutch retained, but flywheel retention changed. Pedal engagement and switch operation, with overrunning clutch. Minor transmission and drive shaft changes. Torque arm shifted from right to left. Thermoid pad replaced ball and spring thrust assembly, quieter and eliminating lubrication. Rear axle modified, but gears and pinion bearings identical.

CHASSIS. *Frame*: design similar, but thickness reduced to 5/32 inch, saving 30 pounds in weight. Entire chassis 250 pounds lighter. *Suspension*: all new at the rear, two longitudinal semi-elliptic springs replacing the platform type. Springs fixed to rear axle instead of free pivoting as formerly. Rear springs 60x2¼; front 42x2. Combined ball and pin shackle attachment. *Brakes*: basically unchanged, except for drum design to accommodate new tires. *Tires*: changed from 33x5 high pressure to 33x5.75 balloon.

BODIES. Improved Fisher bodies in Standard and Custom lines listed, with prices lowered as much as $500. Closed bodies all featured Fisher one-piece ventilating windshield, adjustable rear-view mirror and automatic windshield wiper. A variety of accessories — robe rails, smoking and leather-covered vanity sets — included. Standard line cars had mohair double tufted velvet upholstery with Marshall springs. Custom cars were trimmed to the buyers' orders. Windows in Standard cars were operated by segment and pinion mechanism; in the Custom line, by cable lifts. The two-door brougham had specially wide doors (37 inches). To prevent drumming, all closed car tops had two-inch wide wooden slats covered with padding and leather fabric. Custom cars had bumpers at the front, bumperettes at the rear, spring gaiters and motometer. Duco finish in three color schemes — blue, Waverly gray and Arizona gray — used on the Standard line. The Custom line had six standard Duco color schemes in regular production, and any color scheme to the buyer's order on sixty-days notice. Drum lamps and dual filament bulbs replaced tilt-beam headlamps.

PRICES. The Standard line, on a 132-inch wheelbase: five-passenger brougham $2995; two-passenger coupé $3045; four-passenger victoria $3095; five-passenger sedan $3195; seven-passenger sedan $3295; seven-passenger Imperial $3435. The Custom line: two-passenger roadster (132-inch wheelbase) $3250; and on the 138-inch wheelbase, the following: touring car and phaeton $3250; five-passenger coupé $4000; five-passenger sedan $4150; seven-passenger suburban $4285; seven-passenger Imperial $4485.

PERFORMANCE. With its lighter weight and increased power, the 314 was livelier than its immediate predecessors. The redesigned cylinder head, with turbulent combustion chamber and compression ratio increased to 4.7, gave a bmep of 89 lb/sq. in. and about 86 hp at 3000 rpm. The standard five-passenger sedan would do 65-70 mph, with acceleration from 10 to 25 in high in 7.1 seconds, 10 to 35 in high in 12.1 seconds. Open models, such as phaetons and roadsters, would reach 70-75 mph or more, and with slightly better acceleration. Gas mileage

(five-passenger sedan): 13-14½ mpg at 20-40 mph, dropping to 12 at 45-50 mph, which was considered fast cruising in the mid-twenties.

SERIES 314-A
INTRODUCED AUGUST 1926 ● CURRENT 1927
ENGINE SERIAL NOS. 130,001 - 150,000

Fifty body styles and 500 color combinations were advertised. These were made up as follows: five new Fisher bodies added to the thirteen of the previous year, making eighteen total Fisher bodies in Standard and Custom production; thirty-two bodies by outside custom builders, known as the "special custom line," comprising eighteen bodies by Fleetwood (five of them new), four new bodies by Brunn and ten by various other coachbuilders. All 500 color combinations were available on the three groups. The five new Fisher models were: a five-passenger sport landau sedan and custom two-passenger convertible coupé (both on a 132-inch wheelbase), the Imperial sedan seven-passenger on a 138-inch wheelbase, a sport phaeton with tonneau windshield and a five-passenger victoria coupé. Few changes in body line were made, although generally the appearance was improved. One-piece stamped front fenders (instead of three-piece), the elimination of the separate battery and tool boxes and relocations behind the side dust shields above the running boards, a sharp point to the radiator with a new filler and medallion, and the larger custom lamps adopted on the standard models all contributed to the more striking exterior. Chassis and interior changes were minor: an AC oil filter replaced the Purolator. There was a Klaxon horn. A new dashboard with walnut veneer embossed with a German silver inlay by a patented process, and push/pull switches appeared in the interior. The latter had no lock, and a transmission lock was provided.

PRICES. Typical models and prices for 1927 were, for the Standard line: five-passenger brougham $2995; five-passenger victoria $3195; two-passenger coupé $3100; five-passenger sedan $3250; seven-passenger sedan $3350; seven-passenger Imperial $3535; two-passenger sport coupé $3500; sport sedan $3650. And, for the Custom line: roadster $3350; touring and phaeton $3450; five-passenger coupé $3855; five-passenger sedan $3955; seven-passenger suburban $4125; seven-passenger Imperial $4350; sport phaeton $3975; convertible coupé $3450.

SERIES 341
INTRODUCED SEPTEMBER 1927 ● CURRENT 1928
ENGINE SERIAL NOS. 300,001 - 320,001

ENGINE. Eight-cylinder 90° V-type L-head (3 5/16x4 15/16, 341 cubic inches). *Horsepower*: rated at 35.1, brake hp 90 at 3000 rpm. *Torque*: 208 lb/ft (net). Engine and transmission in unit, three-point suspension with rubber-lined supports at rear. Cylinders cast in two blocks of four cylinders each, with detachable heads. Pistons gray cast iron, special formula, annealed; three rings, two above wrist pin and one below; lower ring special oil regulating type. Connecting rods drop-forged special formula steel; side by side, two on each crank pin; bearings 2⅜x1⅜; Babbitt in rod lower ends. Valves, intake 1½-inch tungsten steel; exhaust 1½-inch silichrome steel, 23/64-inch lift. Mechanism enclosed. Valve stems automatically lubricated. Copper-aluminum alloy crankcase. Crankshaft diameter 2⅜ inches; length 23 25/32 inches. Three main bearings. Crank throws 90° apart, provided with compensators. Single, hollow camshaft with sixteen cams, four bearings; driven from crankshaft by silent chain. *Ignition*: Cadillac-Delco high-tension system, two breaker arms, four-lobed cam. Two-pole Cadillac-Delco type generator; drive by chain from crankshaft; thermostatic control of charging current. Cadillac-Delco separate six-pole starting motor, special design, unusual stalling torque. Cadillac-Exide 130 ampere hour, 6-volt, 3 cell battery, in molded box in right-hand dust shield. *Carburetor*: Cadillac design and manufacture; automatic thermostatic mixture control; intake header exhaust heated. *Lubrication*: pressure system, gear pump. Oil under pressure to all main bearings, connecting rod bearings and camshaft bearings. Automatic pressure regulator; oil level indicator. AC oil filter. *Cooling*: copper radiator with cellular core; polished nickeled casing; capacity six gallons. Circulation by pump driven by silent chain from crankshaft. Cylinder blocks interconnected by brass tube cast in crankcase. Thermostatically controlled radiator shutters with vertical balanced shutter blades. Fan diameter 20¼ inches; six blades; belt driven by pulley mounted on end of camshaft. Fan bearing positively lubricated. Vacuum feed gasoline system, vacuum in intake manifold assisted by vacuum created by special vacuum pump. Positive feed under all conditions.

TRANSMISSION. New design disc dry plate clutch. Two driven discs 9½ inches in diameter, both sides faced with compressed asbestos fabric, driven by flywheel to which were attached all springs, levers and other parts of clutch with the exception of the clutch thrust bearing carried on a sleeve bolted to the transmission case. Transmission three speeds forward, one reverse. Chrome-nickel steel gears and shafts. Faces of gear teeth ground on special grinding machines for silent operation. Cast iron case. Hollow steel drive shaft 2½ inches in diameter in center, tapering 2 1/6 inches at each end; torque tube completely sealed assembly. Rear end of drive shaft rigidly connected to rear axle by splined sleeve, front end to transmission shaft through universal joint. Torque tube bolted to differential carrier at the rear, front end pivoted in ball and socket joint at rear of transmission, for transmission of drive of rear wheels to chassis and absorption of torque reactions due to acceleration and braking.

CHASSIS. *Frame*: channel section with wide top flange, carbon steel, maximum depth 7½ inches; width 30 inches in front, 35 inches in rear; four channel cross members and three tubular cross members. Front ends of side members reinforced by plates riveted to side members. *Axles*: rear, Cadillac make, full floating with special alloy steel axle shafts, gears and housing tubes. Spiral bevel gears mounted on large bearings. Front, reversed Elliott type, drop forged chrome-nickel steel, I-beam section drop forged steering spindles and arms; steering spindles with adjustable tapered roller bearings at upper ends. Parallel track rod with spring compensated ball and socket connections at end. *Suspension*: semi-elliptic springs. Rear underslung; rear shackle of rear spring tension-type with universal ball and socket connection to frame. Front springs 42x2¼; rear 60x2½. Shock absorbers of hydraulic type front and rear. *Steering*: Cadillac design worm and

sector, completely adjustable. Nineteen-inch steering wheel, rubber composition, narrow rim with black finish aluminum die cast hub and spokes. *Brakes*: mechanically operated service brakes, internal expanding on front wheels, external contracting on rear. Division of pedal pull automatically proportioned between front and rear systems. Front brakes equalized when straight ahead, outer brake released on turn; 16-inch brake drums on all wheels. Hand brakes internal expanding on rear wheels. No adjustment during life of brake lining required. *Wheels*: artillery type, twelve hickory spokes with steel felloes. Adjustable roller bearings, demountable split type rim with six lugs. Large steel hub flange with twelve bolts. Disc wheels and wire wheels obtainable at additional cost. *Tires*: straight side 32x6.75 cord balloon. *Wheelbase*: 140 inches.

BODIES. First Harley Earl designed Cadillac. New design instrument board; instruments arranged in individual assembly, not grouped; windshield wiper control; carburetor heat control; spark control; oil pressure gauge; button control for carburetor enriching device; switch for instrument board lighting, independent of switch on steering column; speedometer; ammeter; electrically operated gasoline gauge; eight-day clock; ignition lock; motor temperature indicator; combination inspection lamp and cigar lighter. Lighting equipment included two headlamps (beams controlled from steering wheel switch), fluted lenses, 21 C.P. double-filament bulbs and side lamps with 3 C.P. bulbs. Two rear lights: right-side stop light, left-side rear light. Step lights in dust shield operating automatically with opening of doors.

PRICES. Typical models and prices for 1928 were: two-passenger coupé $3295; roadster $3350; five-passenger touring $3395; touring and phaeton $3450; convertible coupé and five-passenger coupé $3495; five-passenger sedan $3595; seven-passenger sedan $3695; five-passenger Imperial $3745; seven-passenger Imperial $3895.

SERIES 341B (V-8)
INTRODUCED AUGUST 1928 ● CURRENT 1929
ENGINE SERIAL NOS. 320,001 - 499,999

Same as 1928 car, with the following exceptions:
ENGINE. Pressure feed to piston pins (drilled rods).
TRANSMISSION. Syncro-Mesh.
CHASSIS. Frame strengthened. Double acting Delco shock absorbers. New braking system, all internal with two independent systems at rear (three shoes per drum).
BODIES. Safety glass. Adjustable front seats (except Imperials). Minor styling changes.

SERIES 353 (V-8)
INTRODUCED SEPTEMBER 1929 ● CURRENT 1930
ENGINE SERIAL NOS. 500,001 - 511,005

Same as 1929 car, with the following exceptions:
ENGINE. Bore increased to 3 3/8 inches. Displacement 353 cubic inches. *Horsepower*: rated at 36.45, brake hp 95 at 3000 rpm. Spark plug covers on cylinder heads.

CHASSIS. Third shoe on rear brakes eliminated. *Tires*: 7.00x19.
BODIES. Eleven models. Minor styling changes. Radio aerial.

SERIES 355 (V-8)
INTRODUCED SEPTEMBER 1930 • CURRENT 1931
ENGINE SERIAL Nos. 800,001 - 810,717

Same as 1930 car, with the following exceptions:
TRANSMISSION. Second gear ratio altered.
CHASSIS. New frame. *Tires*: 6.50x19 and 7.00x18.
BODIES. New bodies, similar to V-12. Chrome radiator screen; twin horns; hood ventilating doors.
PRICES. Eleven body styles $2695 - $3795.

SERIES 355B (V-8)
INTRODUCED JANUARY 1932 • CURRENT 1932
ENGINE SERIAL Nos. 1,200,001 - 1,202,700

Same as 1931 car, with the following exceptions:
ENGINE. *Horsepower*: 115 bhp at 3000 rpm.
TRANSMISSION. Triple-Silent Syncro-Mesh (all three speeds helical).
CHASSIS. Ride regulator. Controllable free-wheel. *Tires*: 7.00x17 (smaller). *Wheelbase*: 134 and 140 inches.
BODIES. Restyling, with gradual transition to streamlining —"clam shell" fenders, curved running boards, more bullet-shaped headlights. Instruments now in front of driver.

SERIES 355C (V-8)
INTRODUCED JANUARY 1933 • CURRENT 1933
ENGINE SERIAL Nos. 3,000,001 - 3,100,000

Same as 1932 car, with the following exceptions:
CHASSIS. *Brakes*: vacuum booster, cast moly drums.
BODIES. Pivotal year between pure classic and streamlined styling, with skirted fenders, V-radiator with concealed cap, first full wheel covers, hood doors two over two. No draft ventilation via quarter windows.
PRICES. Sixteen body styles, $2695 - $4145.
PERFORMANCE. For the seven-passenger sedan with 4.6 axle; maximum speed 76 mph; minimum speed (high) 2 mph; acceleration 10 to 60 in high, 28 seconds. Gas mileage 12.5 mpg at 30 mph; 9.5 mpg at 50 mph.

SERIES 355D (V-8)
INTRODUCED JANUARY 1934 • CURRENT 1934
ENGINE SERIAL Nos. 3,100,001-3,104,877

Same as 1933 car, with the following exceptions:
ENGINE. *Horsepower*: 130 bhp at 3400 rpm. Aluminum pistons.

Detroit Lubricator carburetor, downdraft.
CHASSIS. Dual X frame, open drive shaft. Ride stabilizer. Handbrake on dash. Knee action front suspension. *Wheelbase*: 128, 136 and 146 inches.
BODIES. Restyled, with "biplane" bumpers.
PRICES. Thirty-one body styles $2545 - $5795
PERFORMANCE. For the seven-passenger sedan with 4.6 axle: maximum speed 85 mph; minimum speed (high) 2 mph; acceleration 10 to 60 on high, 19.9 seconds. Gas mileage 12.8 mpg at 35 mph; 10.5 mpg at 60 mph.

SERIES 10 (V-8)
INTRODUCED JANUARY 1935 • CURRENT 1935
ENGINE SERIAL Nos. 3,105,101 - 3,108,336

Mechanical specifications almost identical to the 1934 Series 355D, being the last year of the basic engine design of 1927. Exterior changes comprised an all-steel turret top body and conventional bumpers. Prices ranged from $2345 -$5595.

SERIES 452/452A (V-16)
INTRODUCED JANUARY 1930 • CURRENT 1930-31
ENGINE SERIAL Nos. 700,001 - 703-251
(1930 ENDS AT 701,827)

ENGINE. Sixteen-cylinder 45° V-type (3x4, 452 cubic inches). *Horsepower*: rated at 57.6, brake hp 165 at 3400 rpm. *Torque*: 320 lb/ft at 1200-1500 rpm. Pushrod ohv with hydraulic dashpot valve silencers. Cast iron blocks and heads, offset blocks with plain rods. Separate aluminum crankcase, five main bearings. Two separate eight-cylinder-inline-type intake manifolds, each with updraft Cadillac carburetor. Full dual exhausting from each bank. Vacuum brake booster. Oil filter. Dual coil ignition.
TRANSMISSION. Unit transmission and clutch similar to V-8. Rear axle ratios: 3.47 (dropped after June 1, 1930), 4.07, 4.39 and 4.75.
CHASSIS. Same general design characteristics as the V-8. *Wheelbase*: 148 inches. *Tires*: 7.50x19.
BODIES AND PRICES. Fifteen body styles offered in base prices ranging from $5350 to $9200.
PERFORMANCE. Maximum speed 84-100 mph, depending upon axle ratio and body style.

SERIES 370/370A (V-12)
INTRODUCED SEPTEMBER 1930 • CURRENT 1930-31
ENGINE SERIAL Nos. 1,000,001 - 1,005,733

ENGINE. Twelve-cylinder version of the V-16 (except bore of 3⅛ inches and displacement of 368 cubic inches). *Horsepower*: rated at 46.9, brake hp 135 at 3400 rpm.
CHASSIS. Similar to V-16. *Tires*: 7.00x19 and 7.50x18. *Wheelbase*: 140 and 143 inches.

BODIES AND PRICES. Eleven body styles offered in base prices ranging from $3795 to $4895.

SERIES 452B (V-16)
INTRODUCED JANUARY 1932 • CURRENT 1932
ENGINE SERIAL Nos. 1,400,001 - 1,400,300
Similar to 1931 car, with the following exceptions:
ENGINE. Air cooled generator. Mechanical fuel pump.
TRANSMISSION AND CHASSIS. Triple-silent synchromesh. Ride control. Controlled free wheeling and vacuum clutch. Frame modifications.
Wheelbase: 143 and 149 inches.
BODIES. Restyled with sloping windshield. Inside sunvisor and new instrument panel with watch crystal dials.
PRICES. Lowest priced model (two-passenger coupé) reduced to $4495.

SERIES 370B (V-12)
INTRODUCED JANUARY 1932 • CURRENT 1932
ENGINE SERIAL Nos. 1,300,001 - 1,302,000
Same as 1931 car, with the following exceptions:
The changes wrought in the V-8 and V-16 for this year. And a wheelbase revision to 134 and 140 inches.

SERIES 370C (V-12) AND SERIES 452C (V-16)
INTRODUCED JANUARY 1933 • CURRENT 1933
ENGINE SERIAL Nos. 4,000,001 - 4,000,953 (V-12)
ENGINE SERIAL Nos. 5,000,001 - 5,000,126 (V-16)
These cars were mechanically similar to the 1932 models. Axle ratio changes were as follows: 4.31 and 4.64 for the V-16; and 4.60 and 4.80 for the V-12. The restyling of these models was along similar lines to the 1933 V-8. Price range for the V-12, $3395 - $4345; for the V-16, $6250 - $8000.

SERIES 370D (V-12) AND SERIES 452D (V-16)
INTRODUCED JANUARY 1934 • CURRENT 1934
ENGINE SERIAL Nos. 4,100,001 - 4,100,662 (V-12)
ENGINE SERIAL Nos. 5,100,001 - 5,100,060 (V-16)
The following changes were made to the 1933 design:
ENGINE. *Horsepower*: for the V-12, 150 bhp at 3600 rpm; for the V-16, 185 bhp at 3800 rpm.
CHASSIS. The cars shared the V-8's chassis improvements, all sporting the new front suspension, redesigned frame and Hotchkiss drive. *Wheelbase*: for the V-12, 146 inches; for the V-16, 154 inches.
BODIES. Restyled, with new front end treatment similar to the V-8.
PRICES. For the V-12, $4195 - $6495; for the V-16, $6950 - $9250.

SERIES 40 370D (V-12) AND SERIES 60 452D (V-16)
INTRODUCED JANUARY 1935 • CURRENT 1935
ENGINE SERIAL Nos. 4,100,701 - 4,101,150 (V-12)
ENGINE SERIAL Nos. 5,100,101 - 5,100,200 (V-16)
Specifications generally similar to 1934; changes shared with V-8, except turret top.

SERIES 80 AND 85 (V-12) AND SERIES 90 (V-16)
CURRENT 1936
ENGINE SERIAL Nos. 4,110,001 - 4,110,901 (V-12)
ENGINE SERIAL Nos. 5,110,001 - 5,110,252 (V-16)
Similar to 1935 cars, with the following exceptions:
CHASSIS. Hydraulic brakes on the V-12. *Wheelbase*: 131 inches for the Series 80; 138 inches for the Series 85, the long wheelbase V-12 being for town cars and seven-passenger sedans.
BODIES. Changes included addition of the turret top and V-windshields.
PRICES. For the V-12, $3145 - $5145; for the V-16, $7250 - $8850.

SERIES 85 (V-12) AND SERIES 90 (V-16)
CURRENT 1937
ENGINE SERIAL Nos. 4,130,001 - 4,130,478 (V-12)
ENGINE SERIAL Nos. 5,130,001 - 5,130,350 (V-16)
This was the last year for the V-12 and ohv V-16 cars. Hydraulic brakes introduced on the V-16. The V-12's wheelbase revised to 138 inches. Base price for the V-12, $3445; for the V-16, $7450.

SERIES 90 (V-16)
CURRENT 1938-39-40
ENGINE SERIAL Nos. 5,270,001 - 5,270,315 (1938)
ENGINE SERIAL Nos. 5,290,001 - 5,290,135 (1939)
ENGINE SERIAL Nos 5,320,001 - 5,320,061 (1940)
ENGINE. Sixteen-cylinder 135° V-type L-head (3¼x3¼, 431 cubic inches). *Horsepower*: rated at 67.6, brake hp 185 at 3600 rpm. *Compression ratio*: 6.75. Blocks and crankcase unit cast iron. Nine main bearings. Hydraulic tappets. *Carburetor*: dual downdraft Carter carburetors with separate straight-eight-type manifolding for each bank. *Cooling*: twin water pumps, twin distributors.
TRANSMISSION. Single plate clutch. All helical three-speed synchromesh transmission. Hotchkiss drive to hypoid rear axle. Standard ratio 4.31.
CHASSIS. *Tires*: 7.50x16. *Wheelbase*: 141 inches. *Weight*: 5105 pounds. Except for engine, car generally similar to long wheelbase (141 inches) V-8 of 1938. Car remained current through 1939 and 1940 with very little change.

BODIES. Twelve body styles available. Wide die-cast radiator grille. Smaller Cadillac crest. New long and streamlined headlamps. Higher and wider doors.
PRICE: Base $5140.
PERFORMANCE. Maximum speed 100 mph. Acceleration, high gear, 10–25 mph in 4.8 seconds, 10–60 mph in 16 seconds. The highest performance factors of any American cars of the period. Fuel consumption 10 mpg at 60 mph.

SERIES 60, 70, 75 (V-8)
CURRENT 1936
ENGINE SERIAL NOS. 6,010,001 - 6,016,713 (60)
ENGINE SERIAL NOS. 3,110,001 - 3,115,249 (70 AND 75)

ENGINE. Eight-cylinder 90° V-type L-head. Two versions. For the 60: 3⅜x4½, 322 cubic inches, 125 bhp. For the 70 and 75: 3½x4½, 346 cubic inches, 135 bhp. Unit block and crankcase in cast iron. Three main bearings and counterweights. Dual downdraft carburetion. The all-new all-iron engine was basically the same in the two displacements.
TRANSMISSION. Single-plate clutch. Three speed helical gears. Hotchkiss drive. Hypoid axle. Standard ratio 4.10.
CHASSIS. Bendix hydraulic brakes. *Weight*: 4171 pounds for the 60.
BODIES. The 60 shared the new GM "B" body shell with Buick; the 70 and 75, the larger Buick body shell but with furnishings and fittings by Fleetwood.
PRICE: Base for the 60, $1645.

SERIES 60, 65, 70, 75 (V-8)
CURRENT 1937
ENGINE SERIAL NOS. 6,030,001 - 6,037,003 (60)
ENGINE SERIAL NOS. 7,030,001 - 7,032,401 (65)
ENGINE SERIAL NOS. 3,130,001 - 3,139,232 (70 AND 75)

ENGINE. All cars shared the 346-cubic-inch engine. *Horsepower*: 135 bhp at 3400 rpm. *Torque*: 250 lb/ft at 1700 rpm.
TRANSMISSION. New closer ratio transmission.
CHASSIS. *Wheelbase*: 124 inches for the 60; 131 inches for the 65 and 70; 138 inches for the 75. *Weight*: 4385 pounds for the 65; 4745 pounds for the 75.
BODIES. New die cast, egg crate type grille and revised bumpers. Altered side molding and more integrated running board.
PRICES. Base for the 65 and 70, $2090; for the 75, $2185.

SERIES 61, 60S, 65, 75 (V-8)
CURRENT 1938
ENGINE SERIAL NOS. 8,270,001 - 8,272,052 (61)
ENGINE SERIAL NOS. 6,270,001 - 6,273,704 (60S)
ENGINE SERIAL NOS. 7,270,001 - 7,271,476 (65)
ENGINE SERIAL NOS. 3,270,001 - 3,271,911 (75)

ENGINE. All cars shared the 346-cubic-inch 135 hp engine, although the 75 was rated at 140 hp.
CHASSIS. *Wheelbase*: 124 inches for the 61; 127 inches for the 60S; 132 inches for the 65; 141 inches for the 75. *Weight*: 4540 pounds for the 65; 4865 pounds for the 75. The 60 Special had a new frame and distinctive (and exclusive) styling. All cars had column gearshift. Optional winking signals.
BODIES. The 60 Special was all new, notch-backed with convertible-style window styling, smaller than recent V-8 predecessors.
PRICES. Base for the 65, $2290; for the 75, $3080.

SERIES 61, 60S, 75 (V-8)
CURRENT 1939
ENGINE SERIAL NOS. 8,290,001 - 8,295,904 (61)
ENGINE SERIAL NOS. 6,290,001 - 6,295,506 (60S)
ENGINE SERIAL NOS. 3,290,001 - 3,292,066 (75)

ENGINE. Same as for 1938.
CHASSIS AND BODIES. *Wheelbase*: 126 inches for the 61; 127 inches for the 60S; 141 inches for the 75. *Weight*: 4110 pounds for the 60S; 4785 pounds for the 75. New sharp-nosed front-end styling for the 75; "B-O-P" style body for 61 and to a lesser extent on 60S.
PRICES. Base for the 60S, $2090; for the 75, $2995.

SERIES 62, 60S, 72, 75 (V-8)
CURRENT 1940
ENGINE SERIAL NOS. 8,320,001 - 8,325,903 (62)
ENGINE SERIAL NOS. 6,320,001 - 6,324,600 (60S)
ENGINE SERIAL NOS. 7,320,001 - 7,321,525 (72)
ENGINE SERIAL NOS. 3,320,001 - 3,320,956 (75)

Same as 1939, with the following exceptions:
CHASSIS AND BODIES. *Wheelbase*: 129 inches for the 62; 127 inches for the 60S; 138 inches for the 72; 141 inches for the 75. *Weight*: 4032 pounds for the 60S; 4620 pounds for the 72; 4785 pounds for the 75. Sealed beam headlamps. Restyle on most bodies, with bolder grille, more chrome, greater Cadillac identity.
PRICES. Base for the 62, $1745; for the 60S, $2090; for the 72, $2670; for the 75, $2995.

SERIES 61, 62, 63, 60S, 67, 75 (V-8)
CURRENT 1941
ENGINE SERIAL NOS. 5,340,001 - 5,369,258 (61)
ENGINE SERIAL NOS. 8,340,001 - 8,364,734 (62)
ENGINE SERIAL NOS. 7,340,001 - 7,345,050 (63)
ENGINE SERIAL NOS. 6,340,001 - 6,344,101 (60S)
ENGINE SERIAL NOS. 9,340,001 - 9,340,922 (67)
ENGINE SERIAL NOS. 3,340,001 - 3,342,104 (75)

Schebera, and the help of Vince Kaptur, head of Engineering-Styling Studio, and Steve McDaniels, head of Design Blackboard Room, these problems were elegantly solved.

"At some point during this development," noted Mr. Uhlir, "Harley Earl attended a play at the old Fisher Theater in Detroit. One of the central characters in the plot was named Madam X. She was different, mysterious, exciting and, above all, the name in itself was intriguing. It captured his imagination and, in turn, he felt certain that this name would have a similar effect on others. Thus, he adopted the pseudonym Madam X for the new style.

"With the new Cadillac V-16 under test and development it was appropriate that the Madam X styles would be an exclusive for this superlative chassis."

Among the first recipients of a Madam X were Fred Fisher and his brother Larry, who was president of Cadillac Motor Car Company. At least several of the early Madam X Cadillac V-16's had stainless steel moldings in place of paint stripes. These were painstakingly sweat-soldered in position. If you could find one of these cars today, you wouldn't need to have it restriped. Some of the cars also had gold-faced instruments, and it is said that the first stainless steel spoked wire wheels were incorporated, utilizing snap-on stainless steel caps. (Steve McDaniels, head of Design Blackboard Room, is reported to have later designed those fabulous 1933-1934 Hollywood Hubcaps for the V-16.)

The play, *Madam X*, was later made into a movie, and a V-16 "co-starred." Later re-makes also featured Cadillacs. Thus the story of "the mysterious Madam X and the fabulous V-16."

1933-1937 AERODYNAMIC COUPES: "The original World's Fair Aerodynamic Coupe design . . . will be recorded as a major styling advancement in the evolution of the automobile," wrote Robert T. DeMars, one of the owners of the six Aerodynamic Coupes known to exist today. Twenty of these cars were built to special order during the years 1933-1937. They were designed to be "something so different and entirely new in concept that the Country Club set will just have to come look, feel and anticipate the excitement of sitting behind the wheel, and burst with pride at the thought of owning this new concept of automobile. Something that will generate sales for all General Motors autos. It is time to make a break with the past."

Up to this time most automobiles were basically shoeboxes, which Harley Earl's young designers considered "very dull and ordinary." An automobile should cut the wind and flow in an aerodynamic line from front to rear, they decided, it should revolutionize cars to come, be streamlined—and a new word was coined: fastback.

The first Aerodynamic Coupe design differed slightly from the car displayed. It had full skirted fenders at the rear, suspended type running boards, chrome fender base trim, and two hood louvers only. The V-16 chassis was used and the car was finished in gleaming black.

The World's Fair car was exhibited at the entrance hall of the GM Pavilion, one of the most beautiful rooms of the entire fair. It was 118 feet long, 57 feet wide, the ceiling was 50 feet high, and its walls were of marble and inlaid woods. Central, and next to the Aerodynamic V-16, there stood a sixteen-foot statue of an American auto mechanic, on a base nine-feet high. Holding a rod and piston in his hands, this "American Automobile Workman" was the creation of the noted Swedish sculptor, Carl Milles. The General Motors Exhibit was the largest structure erected by a private exhibitor, having over 120,000 square feet of floor space. The building was designed by Albert Kahn, decorations were by the Wittbold Studios of Chicago, and the builders were Lundorff-Bicknell of Cleveland.

On both sides of the entrance hall were luxurious display rooms with all GM cars. Beyond was an assembly room where visitors could watch the building of 1933 Chevrolet cars. Below was a truck display and an air-conditioned theater.

It is believed that after the close of the 1933 World's Fair, the show car was delivered to William Knudsen, then executive vice-president of General Motors. He probably used it until the 1934 models were introduced, when he took delivery of his specially built V-16, the 1934 Aerodynamic Coupe, Body No. 1.

"This fabulous car," wrote Bob DeMars, "featured many custom, luxurious interior appointments. Mr. Knudsen was chauffeured, in his Aerodynamic Coupe, throughout the Detroit-Flint areas of Michigan and was frequently seen racing about, performing his daily executive vice-presidential chores. Knudsen finally sold the car in the New York City area, and from there it disappeared. It had about 50,000 miles on the odometer. Persistent rumors indicate this car, or the show car of the World's Fair, may still exist."

Cadillac offered the Aerodynamic Coupe as a custom Fleetwood in its 1934-1937 catalogues. The V-8 was priced at around five thousand dollars, the V-12 (although it used the same 146-inch chassis) was substantially higher in price, and the 154-inch V-16 topped the eight grand mark. Only twenty of these cars were built through the four years: eight V-16's, seven V-12's and five V-8's. The line was finally discontinued with the introduction of the all-new Cadillac bodies for 1938. A production fastback Cadillac did not reappear until the 1941 Series 61.

The original 1933 show car was called by Cadillac the "Aerodynamic Coupe," but it passed into folklore as "The World's Fair Cadillac." Mused Bob DeMars: "Perhaps somewhere, on a lonesome highway, the ghost of William Knudsen is blasting along in his Phantom Fastback, with his chauffeur, Blaine Evenson, proudly behind the wheel."

1938-1941 SUNROOF: This idea came from the British motor industry, and it appeared commonly in England even on lower-priced cars. The sunroof was offered on both Cadillac and LaSalle cars from the 1938 through 1941 model years. Patents covering the GM sunroof were assigned to the Ternstedt Manufacturing Company, the General Motors division producing body trim hardware.

Sunroof cars were built only on special order, and of the 1,509 total cars delivered, about half were 1939 models. The 1941 catalogue noted: "On special order you may have another unique feature—the Sunshine Turret-Top Roof. This desirable extra feature adds surprisingly little to cost of the car." Despite this enthusiasm, demand was low—and there were leakage problems, so the idea was abandoned, and did not appear on the postwar models. Today's "Moon Roof" and "Astro Roof" are greatly improved variations, but trace their origins to the "Sunshine" roof.

DEATH OF THE LASALLE: It has been pointed out by Dave Cummings of Blairsville, Pennsylvania, that the customary reasons given for dropping the LaSalle nameplate are inaccurate. It was certainly not price overlap between Cadillac and LaSalle. "The 50 Series LaSalle four-door sedan had an advertised delivered price of $1,320. The ADP of the cheapest Cadillac four-door sedan—62 series—was $1,745. This was a difference of $425—very considerable in 1940 when the ADP of the 1940 Chevrolet was only $740."

"The reason for dropping LaSalle was much more deeply rooted than price overlap," he continued. "In 1939 LaSalle *out-registered* Cadillac. Cadillac only sold 13,000 autos in 1939. LaSalle sold over 22,000 autos in 1939—outselling their parent by over 9,000 units. Actually, success was killing the car. Cadillac Division was deeply concerned. They felt the public realized that Cadillac quality was available in a medium-priced car and they would have nothing to gain by purchasing the Series 62 Cadillac. . . . But there was also additional pressure from within General Motors. The Buick 91 Limited four-door sedan had an ADP of $1,942. The more expensive models of Oldsmobile were not far from the LaSalle price either."

"In addition the Packard story was fresh in their minds," Mr. Cummings concluded. "They felt that Mr. Average Citizen driving a 'cheap' Cadillac could easily destroy their image of America's finest automobile."

DIRECTIONAL SIGNALS: Blinking directional signals were not factory-fitted in 1938, as might be understood from page 244 in the text. Some batches were installed in late 1939 production, followed by full production for 1940.

Augustus N. Drake III of Devon, Pennsylvania, wrote: "You say (on page 236) that Cadillac had directional blinkers in 1938 and 1939, self-cancelling, no less. You imply that was factory-installed optional equipment. Now, this interests me, because in 1966 I met a man in Norwood, Pennsylvania, James Legg by name, who owned a 1939 Cadillac Series 61 convertible coupe with heater, running boards, and six-wheel equipment, all as originally supplied by the factory. The odd thing about it was that it had 1940 Cadillac parking lights on the front fender crowns, 1940 Cadillac/LaSalle (non-cancelling) directional switch on the steering column, and 1940 LaSalle Series 50 tail/stop lights, which look externally like 1939 Cadillac/LaSalle Series 50 and 61, except that the 1940 units have two bulbs and two 'bulls-eyes' in each lens, as the 1939 lights have but one bulb and one 'bulls-eye' in the lens. I asked Jim *when* he had installed the 1940 equipment on his 1939 car, and he told me unequivocally that *he* had *not* put it there; the factory had put it there when the car was built. He was right, too. When I examined the wiring harnesses under the dash and under the car, and the binding post strips on the inner front fender panels, I became convinced that this was no private owner's or Cadillac dealer's modification. The car actually had been built that way originally.

"Jim Legg told me that he worked as a mechanic for a Cadillac dealer from late in 1937 to late in 1940, and first encountered turn-signals on factory-delivered cars during the summer of 1939, late in the 1939 model run, before the 1940's came out. As well as he could remember, he worked on at least five or six cars so equipped, and all had the same directional equipment as his car. None were the expensive Series 60's, 75, or 90 cars, (which would have looked mighty funny with round taillights), and none of the work he did involved the directionals on any of the cars; he just remembered seeing them. So the car Jim had was not a one-off 'freak'; the factory did build a number of them."

SERIES 72: This rare model—produced only for 1940 and of which only 1,526 were built—was, according to Cadillac, "an extraordinary paradox. It has every attribute of the most luxurious cars ever built—unusual room, rich appointments and true distinction, yet is priced at an unusually moderate figure." After examining and riding in examples on either side of the Pacific, the author is inclined to agree with the above ad copy. The car is Fleetwood-built, with the workmanship and detail refinement associated with the name. Its styling, as Roy Schneider remarked in *Cadillacs of the Forties*, would "last a decade," and was highlighted by a pair of unique, high-mounted, taillights exclusive to this model. Eight body styles, from formal limousine to sedan, were offered on the same 138-inch wheelbase. Base price was $2,670.

A continuing cry from readers and reviewers has been for more data on the postwar Cadillacs. This, of course, becomes a more important period as each year goes by, as the cars become rarer and more valuable, and as various clubs admit the cars to their ranks. These cars are important in their own right, too, and the following notes have been selected to add to the general background of the period and the particular attributes of the cars themselves.

1946 CADILLACS: The 61 Series "fastbacks" used the higher 1941 GM body, and gave greater head and leg room over the lower styled 62 series. But the 62's were big sellers. All these models for '47 had the 1942 body. The club coupe was a fastback design and provided a second two-door style with lower, more modern lines. The 62 series four-door had a trunk back, and was typically featured in advertising. The 1942 deluxe and non-deluxe distinction was dropped. 60 Specials closely followed the 1942 concept, but the vertical chrome trim was eliminated from front fenders.

Series 75 Fleetwoods continued through 1949 with their original 1941 style. (Thus was ignored, to the joy of traditionalists, the 1942 and 1948 major restylings.) Prewar fender spears and hood side grilles were eliminated. Early postwar years saw a sharp decline in private touring use of "limousine-type" cars and the number of 75 models was reduced from eight to five, including the elegant blind-quarter formal models.

One problem with these cars, ranging through to 1953 models, was the Hydro-Lectric windows, seats, and convertible tops. For 1954 this system was replaced with the more satisfactory all-electric operation. "Nevertheless," commented Currell Pattie, "the 1946 Cadillac line has earned a reputation for high mechanical reliability and quality workmanship. Two non-profit consumer testing periodicals recommended Cadillac over all other cars in its price range in 1946. The 1946 (and virtually identical 1947) models grow increasingly desirable with

each year."

1947 CADILLACS: "Cadillac scarcely suffered from its prewar styling; dealers effortlessly sold every car that rolled off the assembly line," commented Currell Pattie. "Cadillac's position vis-à-vis the other luxury domestic cars was favorable. Packard, the traditional rival, had been caught without a truly 'senior' body style distinctive from the medium-priced Clipper line, and was forced to make across-the-board use of this basic shell in 1946-47. Even the limousine for the period revealed strong Clipper influence, and a plebian touch was doubtless déclassé for the flagship of the Packard series. The absence of a convertible body additionally dismayed devotees. Continental continued to excite, but the V-12 found in the entire Lincoln line had earned low marks for durability and performance, and would remain a disappointment. Chrysler was simply content to compete with Buick. One might conclude that Cadillac's luxury-level dominance was almost by default, although the premier GM division would have proved a formidable competitor had its rivals entered a serious contender. . . . Most observations appropriate for the 1947 Cadillac line apply equally to the 1946 models. In terms of innovation, 1947 stands as an uneventful year for Cadillac. Indeed, little was necessary. It was busy cementing its reputation as the dominant luxury car made in the United States."

1948 CADILLACS: "These new bodies," remarked Burton Weaver, "represented another in the series of aggressive tactics by General Motors. . .tactics aimed directly at further domination of the American luxury market. By 1948 Cadillac had removed any earlier feeling that someone else led the way. The new '48 Cadillacs did more than their share in establishing senior GM leadership. The totally new body made significant advances in that intangible factor of prestige. The fishtail rear fenders gave the typical American something he could remember, readily identify, and even poke fun at. . . . Often overlooked are two other significant features of the new body. That year's new instrument panel. . .and the actual design of the taillamp itself. The driver-center hooded dash design began for Cadillac in 1948. And even twenty-five years later, we still saw that thin, vertical taillamp lens."

While most interior dimensions were increased and the cars looked longer, the 61 and 62 Series cars were actually shorter than their predecessors. Exterior width was *reduced* two inches, while interior width was *increased* that same amount. Windshields were now curved, and on sedans, coupes, and convertible they all differed to meet the varying heights of these models. Including the 75 Series, there were four different windshields for 1948! The driver of a new '48 immediately noted the huge increase in glass area and "fishbowl" visibility. He noted, too, that changed front end geometry had given him such easier steering that it made the '47 feel "like an old car."

Performance was adequate:

Top speed	93.3 mph
0-60	16.3 sec
14 mpg @ 60 mph	
(All Hydra-Matic figures)	

The '48's were introduced late in the model year (March, 1948) and considering production lasted less than nine months and prices had been lifted sixteen to twenty-one percent, it is interesting to see that sales (52,706 units) came close to the 1941 record of 66,130 cars. Evidently management thought it could pass the costs of the new body onto the buyer (even in a period of inflation), and he would gladly pay.

"They were right," noted Burt Weaver. "Cadillac was on its way up . . . in both sales and prestige. The '48's were very important cars in their time, and remain highly interesting today."

1949 CADILLACS: The Coupe de Ville was a new style for 1949. This was the industry's first hardtop, and only 2,150 were built, making them very rare, and carrying steep or ridiculous prices today. This pillarless coupe style has remained popular in the Cadillac range ever since.

GM president Charles E. Wilson used the very first Coupe de Ville for a number of years, then presented it to his secretary in 1957.

"Of all the friendly family arguments among Cadillac owners," wrote Currell Pattie, "perhaps the most fascinating is the L-head versus overhead valve debate. Of course the ohv is more efficient; it is hard to dismiss increased power *and* economy. The confluence of a number of factors and events made the eventual industry-wide switch to overhead valves inevitable. Better highways, larger bodywork, availability of high octane fuel at reasonable cost (sweet memories), a generally affluent postwar economy, and heightened public desire for greater horsepower, acceleration and high cruising speeds. I learned to drive on a 1949 Series 62 sedan with Hydro-Lectric windows. The durability was amazing. . .it provided my family faithful service for well over 150,000 miles."

1951 CADILLACS: The principal styling changes are described in Chapter Eleven. Following are samples of interior treatment: 60 Specials were upholstered in green, tan, blue or gray fabrics; seats and seat backs were pleated in rich broadcloth or whipcord; door panels were highlighted in contrasting tones; headlining was in lighter tones, with wool pile carpeting to match the general color scheme; hydraulic front seat adjustment was provided. The 61 Coupe de Villes were available in combinations of dark, rich broadcloth upholsteries with harmonizing leather trim in three color combinations, blue and gray, tan and buff, and two-tone green; wool pile carpeting matched the upholstery color; headlining color matched the leather trim. The 61 sedans had bolstered seat cushions and backs, in two-tone combinations of either gray or tan; materials were plain broadcloth and a figured pattern or striped cord; door panels were also two-tone, the upper quarter trimmed with broadcloth risers, the lower in figured or striped cord material. The 62 sedans had two tones of gray or tan, either patterned or plain cloth with six-inch pleats in seat backs and seats; door panels had successive dark and light shades. The 62 convertible was trimmed in leather; three single colors were available, as well as two-tone combinations in green or blue; top, windows and seat adjustment were hydraulic.

1952 CADILLACS: The 60 Specials offered eight interior two-tone combinations; leather was combined with cloth in new arrangements on seats and doors. The Series 62 sedans and coupes had deep-tufted cushions and seat backs. Coupe de Villes featured leather combinations of light matching tones. Rear compartments of Imperial and eight-passenger sedans were trimmed alike. Rear-seat cushions and seat backs were tufted, with wide plain bolsters and harmonizing leather welts. There was a choice of either Bedford cord or broadcloth in shades of light tan or light gray. Hydraulically-operated division glass was featured.

1954 CADILLACS: Coupe and sedan interiors were available in six different interior combinations of gray, blue or green. Seat and back inserts were tailored in plain all-wool gabardine or pattern nylon of light hues, while bolsters were in darker gabardine to harmonize. Coupe de Ville interiors were in light nylon and darker leather, in green, blue or gray, along with a new combination of white leather and metallic silver gray floral pattern tapestry. Convertible all-leather interiors were completely restyled, and offered in two-tone green or blue, green or blue with white, and solid red, black or tan. The stately 75 limousine continued its traditional Bedford cord or broadcloth, but offered new patterns in gray, tan or blue in either fabric. Eldorado interiors were "entirely new" and in eight different all-leather combinations of red, yellow, black or blue, with white. All cars had a new instrument panel with Elascofab covered top. Eldorados had special body colors: Aztec Red, Azure Blue, Alpine White, and Apollo Gold.

1957 CADILLACS: The new frame and rear-axle design was of note. The traditional Cadillac rear axle remained more than adequate operationally, but was obsolete from a manufacturing standpoint. The trend was to a central casting with pressed-in housings and almost complete automation. Cadillac's new axle had increased offset (by 0.5 inch) for a lowered driveline, reduced deflection by mounting the pinion gear in one straight and two taper roller bearings, and easier servicing that enabled cone distance, backlash and preloads to be adjusted without removing the axle from the car. (This was not the case previously.)

The new X-frame stemmed from tests on experimental designs from 1950 onwards, arising from studies of a 1948 Hudson unit body design. The idea was to accomplish a similar result with a more economical, separate frame construction having more flexibility in design. Development work by A.O. Smith produced a long X arrangement with the X junction at the front of the rear compartment and the elimination of the usual parallel side members. The X member was designed to perform their function.

Co-ordinated design of frame and body was essential. Head room could not be reduced, cushion thickness had to be maintained, so a more efficient floor pan cross-section had to be developed. The tubular design center section allowed a narrow tunnel in the rear even in the eight-passenger models where the rear seat was 28½ inches further back than in a coupe. This floor pan provided a better rear seat chair height than the 1956 four-door sedan, without impairing head room. Entrance heights (seat cushion to door opening windcord, and floor pan to windcord) were also kept the same as 1956. Yet overall height was lowered three inches.

On the Eldorado Brougham, with lower floor pan, the tunnel had to clear the exhaust pipe, and so was wider. But because the rear seat of this car was two-passenger only, with a center armrest, this did not matter. Since there was no side bar to clear at the body rocker sill, the ledge was only six inches wide and easily stepped over when entering or leaving the car. The same applied to front seat exit and entrance.

Structurally, said Cadillac engineer Lester Milliken, "this new frame is considerably more rigid than the 1956 Cadillac frame—which already had the highest structural efficiency of any car frame in terms of stiffness per pound of weight adjusted for wheelbase. For example, the bending rigidity of the frame of the 1957 model 62 four-door hardtop sedan exceeds that of the frame of the equivalent 1956 model by forty-one percent; its torsional rigidity by seven-and-a-half percent.

"Cadillac's normal complement of models involves wheelbases of 129½, 133, 150 and 156 inches. Since some of these models were produced in limited numbers it would have been impractical to provide special tooling for each wheelbase. But if the mid-sections could be lengthened for wheelbase, the same basic tooling would suffice for all models. Extending the central section would not greatly harm stiffness and could be easily compensated by modest changes in gauge. The tools for the higher volume models could be inserted to allow for the gauge changes without any substantial cost penalty. The final design for the 1957 model 75 frame for the 150-inch-wheelbase eight-passenger car is lighter and considerably more rigid than its 1956 counterpart."

With all these advantages, why did Cadillac abandon the X frame only eight years later? One reason (there may have been others in design and production) was put to the author by La Rue Thomas, Los Angeles dealer. It was that the frame was actually too stiff! On concrete strip roads, with regular joints, the X frame gave an annoying and repetitious "thump-thump." This was eliminated, or much reduced, with the more flexible perimeter frame from 1965 onward.

The styling of the all-new 1957's was covered in some detail in Chapter Eleven. The entire styling studio at that time consisted of Ed Glowacke, chief designer; Bob Schelk, assistant; and Ned Walters, Dave Holls, and Ron Hill, staff. Hill was given the Eldorado Biarritz project. At the time he was only twenty-three, having come to GM in October, 1954, direct from Art Center School. Hill recalled that "the Eldorado was meant as a blue sky version of the Standard Series 62. The front end was exactly the same. But Dave Holls and I were responsible for styling the standard line as well, so there was no problem integrating the Biarritz design. We just worked on all the cars together. The Eldorado actually occupied only a small portion of the total time we spent that year. I derived that rather rotund shape of the rear deck by cutting away at the standard rear quarters. There was no prototype program or anything that fancy, and unlike the standard car it wasn't inspired by anything else. We just needed something that looked different, and I came up with it."

Hill, and the rest of Styling Division, were taken with the new X frame. "The 57 program," he said, "was particularly exciting, because it required an all-new body to go with that fancy frame. We were very free in what we could do, although the standard cars had to have a solid dose of marque continuity in the styling. We couldn't stray too far there. But the tenor of the time at Cadillac was for management to let us explore some pretty far-out things, particularly on the Eldorado. We managed to take full advantage of that."

1959 CADILLACS: Controversial because of their "Zap" fins, these nevertheless remain among the most impressive models of the postwar Cadillacs. The author recalls a wealthy New Zealand businessman who owned two Cadillacs—a '49 and a '59—a Mark VIII Jaguar, a Rolls-Royce Silver Cloud, and a Chevrolet. He was an ardent advocate of the 1959 Cadillac, stating that none of the other cars compared with it and that whether judged on driving for driving's sake (including handling qualities) or for sheer comfort alone, the '59 Cadillac was "outstanding." Even on turning circles and maneuverability in traffic, he won bets from skeptical observers and critics. An Aucklander, he kept his older Cadillac and the other cars for driving in the North Island only, using the '59 throughout the country.

Australian road-tester Peter Hall of *Wheels* magazine, a European and sports car fan and admitted cynic where Cadillacs were concerned, wrote that an actual test-drive of a 1959 Cadillac had turned him into an "ex-critic."

"I have sneered with the best of them," he remarked, "but at the end I was forced to withdraw my sneering attitude. There is gold behind the glitter. . . . I was forced to admire the great quality of the finish . . . there was not a blemish on the duco, not a panel a fraction out of place. The interior was luxuriously appointed in a glamorous but not over-showy way. . . . All the best American effort-saving devices were there in profusion. The driving position was utterly comfortable. . .vision was magnificent. Speedometer was most accurate I have tested.

"On test the car handled remarkably well. . .rock-steady on all surfaces. . .with a solid, level ride. . . . I took it over a bad disused railway crossing at more than 100 mph . . . apart from a barely perceptible nosedown the car gave no sign at all. Part of its handling secret was its superb power steering, as direct as anyone could want, with the feel that makes a driver's car.

"The automatic transmission was one of the best ever . . . 'Top' came in about 90 mph . . . it was quite an uncanny feeling to sense the gears shifting automatically beneath the floor at that speed. The performance was sensational . . . delivered in utter silence, with such luxurious smoothness. The brakes equal the car's performance.

"Hard to beat on the scores of performance, comfort, driving ease and sheer impressiveness. . .the Cadillac is undoubtedly a great car. . .one of the finest automobiles built in the world today."

The test figures from *Wheels* were as follows:

Top speed:	115.4 mph
Standing quarter-mile:	18.2 seconds
0 - 60 mph:	10.6 seconds
0 - 80 mph:	18 seconds
Gas mileage:	12.1 mpg (driven hard)
Price in Australia:	£7,000

The 1959 390 engine was tailored to favor "stop-and-go" driving and be economical in traffic. Overall economy was improved by about ten percent. However, these engines did show performance gains at both the low speed and high speed ends of the curve.

Cadillac salesmen were well-briefed on the features of their car. They were well-briefed on the competition also. "Today's market" said the factory, "dictates that a salesman must not only have a thorough knowledge of his own product, but in addition be fully aware of the competitive products in the field. Knowledge, particularly of Chrysler and Lincoln, is all-important to Cadillac salesmen." One factory folder listed "29 ways to sell Cadillac over Imperial" and "24 ways to sell Cadillac over Lincoln." Topics ranged from styling through mechanical to convenience features, and from quality of finish to resale value. Cadillac's superior power steering, automatic transmission (and control), air-conditioning, and three-speed electric wipers typified its engineering advantages over its rivals, while its acrylic finish and forty-eight choices of interior decor did the same in comparison with Lincoln and Imperial's enamel paint and limited decor.

A typical sales briefing at Cadillac began with films and slides. After detailed comparisons, Cadillac dealers were then divided into groups and taken on road demonstrations with Cadillacs, Lincolns and Imperials. All dealers were given the opportunity to both drive and examine all three cars on the same demonstration. Afterward, there was a further group discussion, and each was given a Comparison Kit with film and literature for use by the dealership.

SHORT DECK SEDANS: A "bobtail" model was often featured in the Cadillac lineup (cf. page 332). The 1950 range, for example, listed two such cars: the Series 61 (all body types) at 212 inches, and the Series 62 sedan at 216 inches. The contemporary Series 62 coupe was 221 inches, and the Series 60S sedan 225 inches. Turning radius for the 61 was a foot less than the 60S. Nineteen fifty-one saw a similar lineup, but the 61 was dropped at the end of that year. The 62 continued, and in 1954 was lengthened slightly to 216-7/16 inches. It was later dropped, and remained out of line until 1960. In 1961 it reappeared again as the "Short-Deck Sixty Two Sedan." It was described as "this new body style, a virtual twin of the Sixty Two Sedan. Differing only in shorter overall body length, it features the same trim lines and generously proportioned interior. . . ."

The following year, the short decks were designated the "Town Sedan" and the "Park Avenue Sedan," with overall lengths of 215 inches. Said Cadillac, "the Town Sedan is reduced in overall length" and "the new Park Avenue Sedan is specially designed with a shorter rear deck for easier parking and garaging." In 1963 there was only one short deck, the Park Avenue at 215 inches—and by 1964, there were none. A glance at the sales figures in the production table (Appendix VIII) will show why.

1961 CADILLACS: Performance figures available for the Coupe de Ville show a top speed of 115 mph, with acceleration of 0-60 in 9.5 seconds, 0-80 in 17.8 seconds and the standing quarter mile in 17.1 seconds. Normal range of gas mileage was twelve to fourteen.

1964 CADILLACS: Performance figures quoted earlier in the text have taken only the most conservative acceleration times. Other reliable tests show 0-60 times of 8.5 seconds, 0-80 in 14.1 seconds, and 0-100 in 23.5 seconds. Standing quarter mile times ranged from 16.4 to 16.8 seconds. Gas mileage ran from nine to twelve.

1965 CADILLACS: A Japanese road test has become available on the 1965 Fleetwood Sixty Special. The only translatable items were:

Top speed:	121 mph
0 - 60 mph:	8.5 seconds
0 - 100 mph:	23.5 seconds
Standing quarter mile:	16.4 seconds
plus the comments:	"Big Enough," "Strong Enough" and "Gorgeous Enough"

Nineteen sixty-five comparisons were also made around the world by a number of journals. Following is a compilation of their findings:

	Cadillac Fleetwood	Lincoln Continental	Chrysler Imperial	Mercedes 600	Jaguar Mk X	Rolls-Royce Silver Cloud
Price:	$8,360	$7,473	$5,600	$20,500	$6,990	$17,320
Engine:	V-8 ohv	V-8 ohv	V-8 ohv	V-8 ohc	6-cyl-ohc	V-8 ohv
C.I.D.	429	430	413	386	255	380
Weight	4600	5280	5035	5380	4000	4500
Max. Speed	122	121	117	124	118	114
0-60, sec.	9.2	11.3	12	9.4	10.3	12.4
0-80, sec.	15.5	19.4	22	16.5	18	21.4
Gas Mileage	10.5	13.3	15.1	10.9	15.3	14.5

CADILLAC'S COMPETITION, DOMESTIC AND IMPORTED

The most successful top-flight American marques, it seems, since the beginning have gone in threes. First the "Three P's"—Packard, Peerless and Pierce-Arrow. Then Cadillac, Packard and Lincoln. When Packard ceased to be in this company by 1955, to the enduring regret of many, the trinity became Cadillac, Lincoln and Imperial. The latter highlighted its improved status by becoming a separate make, listed simply as "Imperial," rather than "Chrysler Imperial." Doubtless this reflected thinking similar to Packard's earlier decision to deemphasize the Packard and Clipper designations, and give a "lift" to the senior marque-image. The move made no immediate difference to Imperial fortunes, and sales hovered around 11,000 to 12,000 for the first two years, but this improved substantially during 1957 to 1960, including a high of 18,500 in 1959. A drop below 12,000 in 1961 was followed by a recovery to 21,000 units by 1964. Another decline, 17,000 in 1965 and 14,000 in 1966, saw another recovery to 15,700 in 1967, 17,500 in 1968 and 18,600 in 1969. Despite the emphasis implied in its changed marque-name, the Imperial during its first nine years was treated by Chrysler stylists in the family image of the other corporate makes, particularly the Chryslers, and this "diluted the Imperial effect." In 1964, however, the car was given a separate distinctive style and was, as noted, well received. By this time the Imperial was the only car in the Chrysler line with a separate frame and body, and the size and weight of the car considerably exceeded both Cadillac and Lincoln. As it had the smallest displacement engine of the three, its performance fell short of the Lincoln and well short of the Cadillac. But it was the quietest of the three, had the most usable trunk space, its own distinctive look and features (torsion bar suspension, pushbutton transmission), all the "extras" as standard equipment, and a general level of quality beyond serious criticism. It was, however, offered in only three models, the four-door sedan, and two-door coupe and convertible—and this, plus its inevitable lingering association with the Chrysler line, kept sales from ever going regularly into the 20,000 range, topping that mark only occasionally.

It was Lincoln which stepped into Packard's place as the most serious competition. As mentioned, the ohv V-8 introduced for the 1952 model year was an outstanding car, and probably the best high-speed road car built in America in the early 1950's, a position emphasized by its record in the Mexican Road Race. Its sales were much higher than the Imperial's, ranging between 29,000 and 43,000 units annually from 1952 to 1956. The jump to 43,000 may have resulted from public interest in the new Continental and a restyling of the standard line onto a longer car, the Premiere. This line continued through 1957, and a new car appeared. This was the oversized and so-called Continental Mark III (which wasn't). While these cars had some striking style features, more than adequate performance and were all well-made, they were just too big to be popular, and Lincoln sales nosedived to 21,000 by 1960. For the following year, Lincoln returned to a more compact concept, the justly acclaimed all-new Continental for the sixties. Sales at once jumped by fifty percent, increased further in 1964-1965 and reached almost 50,000 in 1966. A fall to 35,000 in 1967 was immediately recouped the following year, when the new Continental Mark III (the second) sold over 18,000 units, and the regular model over 45,000, putting Lincoln's total at over 64,000 in one year. This increased to more than 65,000 in 1969. Throughout the sixties, the Lincoln record was extremely impressive, reflecting the superb standards of the car itself. On a straight comparison, car to car, there can be no doubt the Lincoln was fully the equal of the Cadillac, in design, construction, manufacture, refinement, equipment, and behavior. The Cadillac sales lead stemmed from its longer period of dominance, its more consistent policy, its greater dealer strength (between forty and fifty percent more outlets), and its much wider model range. But of course, as we will see later, these advantages did not just happen.

During the sixties, the traditional top three were joined by a number of other makes. Cadillac ran its usual sharp eye over the field for a reappraisal in 1962 and, in addition to its usual brace of rivals, noted eight newcomers whom, it was felt, were "chipping away at [Cadillac] sales." Several of these cars, ironically, were built by other GM divisions. Prior to 1962 Cadillac had considered its only competition to be Lincoln, Imperial, and the Buick Electra 225. The new survey started with any car priced over $4,700, if fully equipped to a level comparable with a Cadillac.

They ranked as follows:

Make and Model	Sales	Market Percentage
Cadillac	151,528	31.9
Ford Thunderbird	73,975	15.5
Olds 98	64,389	13.5
Buick Electra 225	57,904	12.2
Olds Starfire	39,224	8.3
Lincoln Continental	31,533	6.6
Chrysler New Yorker	19,258	4.1
Chevrolet Corvette	15,239	3.2
Chrysler Imperial	13,558	2.9
Buick Riviera	8,108	1.7
Studebaker Avanti	441	0.1

The biggest change in these placings came the following year, when the Riviera sold 36,318 units and 7.2 percent of the market. (The Avanti made an even greater percentage increase, but from a negligible base to an overall market percentage of 0.6 only.) Others made gains, and several suffered losses, but Cadillac remained dominant at around thirty-two percent.

This survey was interesting, and accepted within the industry as realistic. But several points should be noted. Most makes did not qualify "as of right," but only "when equipped and priced" in the Cadillac class. Recession times would doubtless change Cadillac, Lincoln and Imperial the least, but might well eliminate almost all the others. (The Olds Starfire was already one casualty from the above list, by 1966. And the pigeons really came home to roost in 1973-1974.)

Along with Cadillac, Lincoln suffered a sales drop in 1970. About ten percent, it reflected in production figures of 59,000 cars. In 1971, the Continental Mark III was retired after a four-year run which saw more than 79,000 cars built, and the Mark IV began to improve on what was already an impressive record for a car priced at around $10,000. The regular Lincoln line continued to sell at a rate of 35,000 to 40,000 units annually, although the Ford Motor Company hope was for at least a ten percent increase back to its level of the mid-sixties. Maybe the decision to drop the four-door convertible (the only one in America) in 1968 was a mistake, but overall the Lincoln picture remained very satisfactory, and the Mark III at times outsold the Eldorado. The reputation of the car was never higher, both domestically and overseas. Exports were a trickle, but recently one of the pillars of the Bentley Drivers Club in England told readers of *Motor* that non-Lincoln owners "did not know what they are missing."

But with a range of only three body styles (two-door coupe, four-door sedan, and two-door Mark IV coupe), it was impossible for Lincoln to seriously overtake Cadillac sales and they remained no more than a comfortable second at a fraction of Cadillac volume. For 1971 also, Eldorado went ahead with a production of 40,000 plus, and total Cadillac volume was 276,000—the highest in its history.

Imperial continued in its by-now traditional (for fifteen years) third place, at a volume of around 15,000 units, and a changeover to unitized body with new styling was made during the second half of the 1960's. In 1970, for the first time anywhere, Imperial offered an electronic four-wheel anti-skid control. In its luxury equipment it continued to match Cadillac and Lincoln, and even surpass them in some areas, while general opinion was that it was a better road car than the standard Cadillac line although inferior, of course, to the Eldorado. Performance, however, continued to be less than that of both Cadillac and Lincoln.

A static (or, in comparison with Cadillac, a declining) sales position led to persistent rumors that the car was below breakeven point and was receiving lower and lower priority at Chrysler. Observers saw it quietly being downgraded within the corporation, losing its identity and gradually merging with the big Chryslers as it had a decade earlier. Ultimately, it was predicted, complete integration would come and separate body designs and dies would cease. The Imperial would be merely a Chrysler with its own grille and taillamps.

But for 1972 the Imperial came out with completely new sheet metal and styling and a number of improvements throughout. There was little or no commonality with the New Yorker styling, but much with the Newport.

Considering the overall sales picture, not even Lincoln, Imperial and all Mercedes imports taken together—let alone singly—constituted a real threat to Cadillac. Their *combined* 1972 total was on the order of 90,000 to 100,000 units. For 1972, Cadillac had at first scheduled a production of 250,000, the highest in its history, an unprecedented figure for a car of this class, and comparable to the total production of American Motors Corporation for the same year! Actual production resulted in 268,000 units for 1972—higher even than planned—and in 1973, the 300,000 mark was reached.

The only imported rivals to Cadillac initially after World War II—German industry was still prostrate—were Jaguar and Rolls-Royce. Their market impact can be gauged by the fact that even by 1959—more than a decade later—General Motors spokesmen regarded them complacently. One said: "Jag, Rolls, have their devoted following, but they are not in the large growth area. They appeal to the 'button shoe' buyer, who will continue to exist but is of minor significance to the volume manufacturer."

The Jaguar image was normally "sports car," and it was seldom regarded as a luxury sedan in the Cadillac class. The cachet value of the Rolls as a piece of exclusive, high quality, imported merchandise was undoubtedly important to a certain group. But the fact that GM made no objection when certain Buick and Chevrolet dealers agreed to represent Rolls-Royce interests indicates the negligible importance GM attached to the matter. Moreover, due to its faithful following of Detroit technical leadership, Rolls-Royce had become known even in its homeland as "the most American of our cars" (L.J.K. Setright). Much earlier the English-born Bob Hope had referred to the Rolls as "the Cadillac that's been to Oxford."

Of all Cadillac's foreign competition, the most impressive in the last twenty years has been Mercedes. In 1958 Daimler-Benz made arrangements with Studebaker-Packard to act as its American sales outlet. This was a shrewd move, characteristic of the company's thoroughness, and its determination to become established in the United States. By cooperating with Studebaker-Packard, the aid of a widely-spread, long-experienced American distributorship was enlisted without the expense (and mistake-making possibilities) of Daimler-Benz building itself up to that position. Steady progress since that time has been made and Mercedes soon displaced Jaguar as the most successful high-class import. By 1962, nearly 53,000 Mercedes of all models and years were registered in the United States, compared with 23,000 Jaguars. In 1963, 9,970 Mercedes new models were registered; in 1964, 13,374; in 1965, 14,462; 1966, 18,796; 1967, 17,614. Sales continued to grow—19,761 in 1967; 23,724 in 1968; 24,693 in 1969; the 1970's saw 30,000 topped. These figures, incidentally, form approximately the same percentage of total imports as Cadillac's for total domestic, i.e. between two and three percent. In contrast, Jaguar, with as many as 14,000 cars in operation in the United States as early as 1954, failed to keep pace. Its 1963 sales total was less than half that of Mercedes, and by 1967 this had dropped to nearly a quarter. In fact, while Mercedes was consistently running seventh among the imported car makes (a remarkable feat for a price range spanning $3,000 to $13,000), Jaguar was not even in the first ten, and was relegated to "All Others." This was highlighted by the unit sales-per-dealer comparison. Although the total number of dealers was similar for both makes (approximately 250-260 in the late 1960's), Mercedes dealers sold between three and four cars to every one sold by a Jaguar dealer. Annual Jaguar sales in the late 1960's were around 5,000, the bulk (4,500) made up of E-Type coupes and open two-seaters. In other words, Jaguar sedans were a negligible factor in the American luxury market, selling only slightly more units than the Rolls-Royce of three times the price. (In fact, the larger Jaguar sedan models were not even very successful in their own home market.) In 1968 the 420 saloon was phased out in preparation for the XJ-6, announced in September that year. But by April 1969, when the International Automobile Show in New

York was opened, XJ-6 deliveries had still not begun, and as late as 1972 Americans continued to refer to the "phantom" Jag. The V-12 certainly proved a very impressive performer, but this car has not generated any great upsurge in sales. The blunt fact is that the Jaguar sedan has not been an effective competitor in the Cadillac class.

Mercedes has always held an enviable reputation. However, despite this, the initiative in the North American market in the first postwar decade, lay more with Jaguar than Mercedes. Until 1951, the former's Mark V and Mark VII sedans were certainly more impressive than anything the latter had to offer. In the early 1950's the Mercedes image was "good little cars, but expensive and hard to find parts."

By 1957, however, German industry (heavily aided by U.S. money, aid, and technical advice) was well on the road to recovery and prosperity. That year, Mercedes introduced its fine Type 300. It lacked torque, its styling can be charitably called "teutonic traditional" and it also had that failing usually attributed to American cars—inadequate brakes. But it was an all-new design well fitted to represent Germany in the high-class sedan field.

The 300 ran for a decade, but its total sales were only 11,000 units. Since this represented only 1,100 cars annually, no U.S. import figures are needed to prove that it made no real sales impact on the American market. But its prestige factor, offsetting Rolls-Royce, could well have been considerable—and Mercedes, profiting from the experience, began to develop a line of impressively engineered sedans in the following years. The all-new 220 arrived in 1955, with more modern body styling and construction, and further enhanced the Mercedes postwar reputation. By 1960, when all but a quartet of imported sedans suffered a heavy sales drop in the United States, Mercedes was one of the four that actually managed an increase. And in 1961, when the company introduced yet another new series, it was announced that U.S. sales had trebled over the preceding three years. Most of this was due to the 220 series which was the big seller. Whether it should be compared with the Cadillac is open to some question, since the 300 (in the new body style also) was certainly the senior and most expensive of the line. However, some mention of 220 characteristics can be made here, since it shared most of them with the 300. While the quality and engineering standards were very high, the handling outstanding, and the ride on rough roads among the best in the world, in some other important areas the Mercedes showed up less happily. One comment was that—particularly for the American buyer—the car required the most careful analysis and understanding by a prospect "lest he later be dissatisfied with the car's features and behavior."

Because of German taxation policy, which hit hard at large-displacement engines, Mercedes volume models (until relatively recently) have been excessively large and heavy in relation to their piston displacement. To overcome this, overhead camshaft, high output engines, often with fuel injection, were used. These were very well designed, very refined and very efficient. But no amount of German magic could make them as effortless and silent as the best American V-8's, and while Mercedes spared no effort to make them as durable as possible, repairs when they *did* come were costly, and so was maintenance. Another drawback was the frequent shifting necessary with the weight-displacement ratio, not helped by stiff, vague column lever action and high clutch pedal pressures. And although Mercedes offered a "Hydrak" with fluid coupling, this unit was not automatic and far below the standard of the Hydramatic. Later, Mercedes adopted a much better transmission directly patterned on Hydramatic itself, but this was still hampered by unsuitable engine characteristics and noisy, rough shifting was still noticeable. (Rolls had earlier experienced similar troubles in somewhat lesser degree.)

Likewise the Mercedes swing axle independent rear suspension, while giving an excellent ride over rough roads, was not beyond criticism. Tire scrub was always an objection, and under some conditions the suspension behavior was less predictable than the live axles of American contemporaries.

Nevertheless, these criticisms have to be read in the light of the steadily progressing Mercedes sales position in the U.S. and a high reputation well and truly earned. The only qualification is that the sales figures are actually less impressive than they appear. Over half of the cars are diesels, and the other small Mercedes models likewise are not really comparable with Cadillac.

The 600 Grosser model was announced in 1964-1965 with a great fanfare, and an avalanche of awed adulation from all and sundry, but it was obvious from the beginning that it could not effectively compete against the Cadillac and was certainly not a commercial proposition. In 1973 it was quietly retired from the American market.

Following the 600, Mercedes produced the ponderously-designated 300 SEL 6.3, a 300 with the big V-8 engine and a shattering performance. However, its market slot at well over $10,000 was insignificant, and it suffered the further embarrassment of actually starting to steal sales from the 600 which could not afford to lose them. It too was retired for 1973.

By far the most significant V-8's Mercedes has built came in 1969-1971 with the 3.5- and 4.5-liter models, which had much of the engineering excellence of the bigger V-8's, but were intended to reach a much wider market. As a viable product they represented far better propositions, and in practical engineering details they have been acclaimed as substantial improvements over their bigger brothers, while their V-8 engines have removed, at long last, the main drawback of the volume Mercedes models.

GENERAL INDEX

INDEX OF ILLUSTRATIONS

NOTE: Page numbers in boldface refer to illustrations in color.

ILLUSTRATION CREDITS